SALAMANDERS

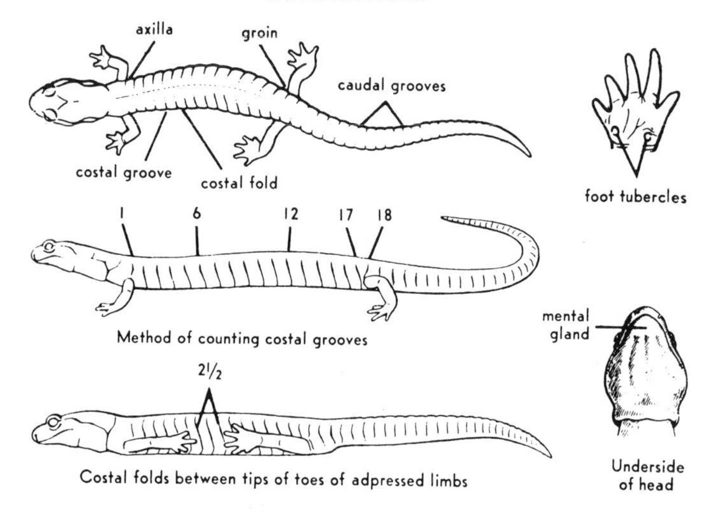

FROGS AND TOADS

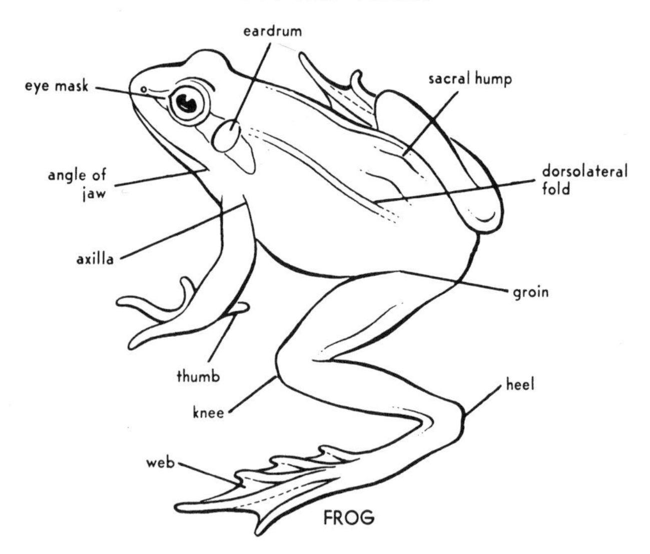

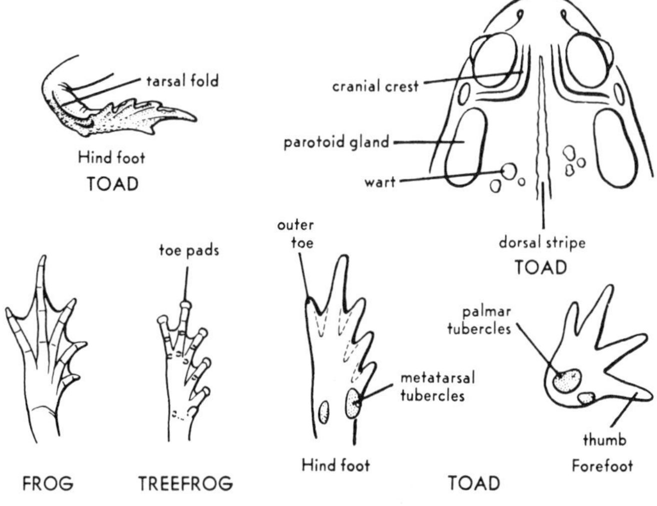

TURTLES

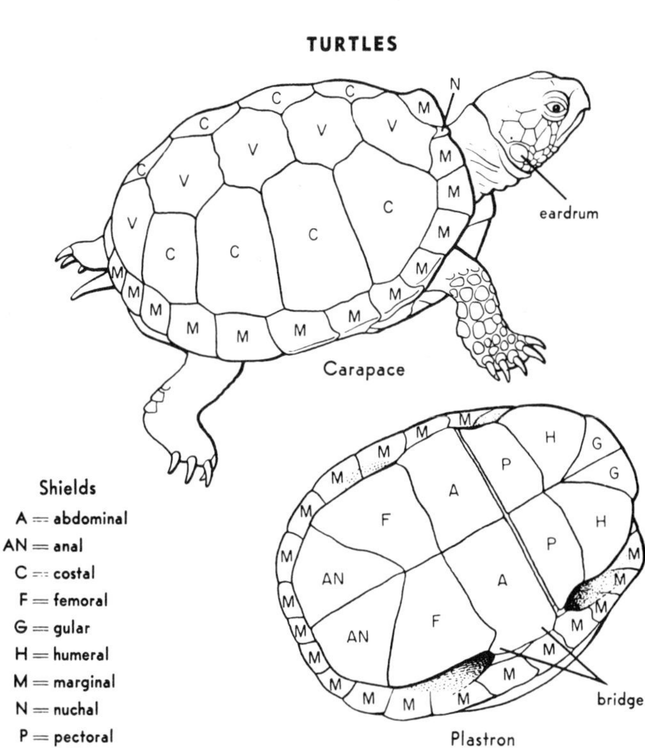

Shields
A = abdominal
AN = anal
C = costal
F = femoral
G = gular
H = humeral
M = marginal
N = nuchal
P = pectoral
V = vertebral

THE PETERSON FIELD GUIDE SERIES®
Edited by Roger Tory Peterson

1. Birds (eastern) — *R.T. Peterson*
1A. Bird Songs (eastern) — *Cornell Laboratory of Ornithology*
2. Western Birds — *R.T. Peterson*
2A. Western Bird Songs — *Cornell Laboratory of Ornithology*
3. Shells of the Atlantic and Gulf Coasts, W. Indies — *Abbott & Morris*
4. Butterflies (eastern) — *Opler & Malikul*
5. Mammals — *Burt & Grossenheider*
6. Pacific Coast Shells (including Hawaii) — *Morris*
7. Rocks and Minerals — *Pough*
8. Birds of Britain and Europe — *Peterson, Mountfort, & Hollom*
9. Animal Tracks — *Murie*
10. Ferns (ne. and cen. N. America) — *Cobb*
11. Eastern Trees — *Petrides*
11A. Trees and Shrubs — *Petrides*
12. Reptiles and Amphibians (e. and cen. N. America) — *Conant & Collins*
13. Birds of Texas and Adjacent States — *R.T. Peterson*
14. Rocky Mt. Wildflowers — *Craighead, Craighead, & Davis*
15. Stars and Planets — *Pasachoff & Menzel*
16. Western Reptiles and Amphibians — *Stebbins*
17. Wildflowers (ne. and n.-cen. N. America) — *R.T. Peterson & McKenney*
18. Birds of the West Indies — *Bond*
19. Insects (America north of Mexico) — *Borror & White*
20. Mexican Birds — *R.T. Peterson & Chalif*
21. Birds' Nests (east of Mississippi River) — *Harrison*
22. Pacific States Wildflowers — *Niehaus & Ripper*
23. Edible Wild Plants (e. and cen. N. America) — *L. Peterson*
24. Atlantic Seashore — *Gosner*
25. Western Birds' Nests — *Harrison*
26. Atmosphere — *Schaefer & Day*
27. Coral Reefs (Caribbean and Florida) — *Kaplan*
28. Pacific Coast Fishes — *Eschmeyer, Herald, & Hammann*
29. Beetles — *White*
30. Moths — *Covell*
31. Southwestern and Texas Wildflowers — *Niehaus, Ripper, & Savage*
32. Atlantic Coast Fishes — *Robins, Ray, & Douglass*
33. Western Butterflies — *Tilden & Smith*
34. Mushrooms — *McKnight & McKnight*
35. Hawks — *Clark & Wheeler*
36. Southeastern and Caribbean Seashores — *Kaplan*
37. Ecology of Eastern Forests — *Kricher & Morrison*
38. Birding by Ear: Eastern and Central — *Walton & Lawson*
39. Advanced Birding — *Kaufman*
40. Medicinal Plants — *Foster & Duke*
41. Birding by Ear: Western — *Walton & Lawson*
42. Freshwater Fishes (N. America north of Mexico) — *Page & Burr*
43. Backyard Bird Song — *Walton & Lawson*
44. Western Trees — *Petrides*
46. Venomous Animals and Poisonous Plants — *Foster & Caras*
47. More Birding by Ear: Eastern and Central — *Walton & Lawson*
48. Geology — *Roberts & Hodsdon*
49. Warblers — *Dunn & Garrett*
50. California and Pacific Northwest Forests — *Kricher & Morrison*
51. Rocky Mountain and Southwest Forests — *Kricher & Morrison*

THE PETERSON FIELD GUIDE SERIES®

A Field Guide to Western Reptiles and Amphibians

Field marks of all species in western North America, including Baja California

Text and Illustrations by

Robert C. Stebbins

Professor Emeritus of Zoology and Curator Emeritus of Herpetology, Museum of Vertebrate Zoology, University of California, Berkeley

· SECOND EDITION ·

Sponsored by the National Audubon Society and National Wildlife Federation

HOUGHTON MIFFLIN COMPANY BOSTON NEW YORK

Library of Congress Cataloging in Publication Data

Stebbins, Robert C. (Robert Cyril), 1915–
A field guide to western reptiles and amphibians.

(The Peterson field guide series; 16)
Bibliography: p. 278
Includes index.
1. Reptiles – North America – Identification.
2. Reptiles – West (U.S.) – Identification. 3. Amphibians – North America – Identification. 4. Amphibians – West (U.S.) – Identification. I. National Audubon Society.
II. National Wildlife Federation. III. Title.
IV. Series.
QL651.S783 1985 597.6′0978 84-25125
ISBN 0-395-38254-8
ISBN 0-395-93611-X (pbk.)

Printed in the United States of America

VB 19 18 17 16 15 14

Editor's Note

Robert Stebbins' classic *Field Guide to Western Reptiles and Amphibians,* first published in 1966, has been hailed as one of the most beautiful as well as one of the most scholarly books in the Field Guide Series. As I pointed out in my Editor's Note in that earlier edition, the bottleneck in the preparation of most Field Guides is the problem of illustration. There are competent field specialists to write such guides and a lesser number of competent illustrators, but to find an author who is equally skilled both as a biologist and as a biological illustrator is extremely rare. Such a man is Robert Stebbins. The reproductions in this book, though excellent examples of the engraver's art, cannot fully record the delicacy of detail and loving care that went into the originals.

During the last two decades a great deal of new information about western reptiles and amphibians has accumulated and the science of herpetology is becoming increasingly sophisticated. Dr. Stebbins shares this new knowledge and his expertise in this 1985 edition. There are now 48 plates (35 in color); a dozen of these are new. In the 1966 edition there were 39 plates (24 in color). A total of 244 species are now described, 239 of which are illustrated. In addition, 260 subspecies are described and 31 of the most distinctive are illustrated. There are several additional line drawings in the text. The book includes a total of 601 separate illustrations, 245 in color. In addition there are 200 distribution maps.

Among the other important new features: All species of amphibians and reptiles found on mainland Baja California are now covered. Information on reproduction in reptiles is now included — clutch (or litter) size, as well as frequency and time of laying.

During the International Galapagos Expedition of 1964 I was privileged to share quarters with Dr. Stebbins at Academy Bay in the Galapagos Archipelago. It was there that I first realized what a perfectionist he is, a demon for work. He had chosen as one of his projects the function of the parietal, or third, eye in the Lava Lizard, *Tropidurus.* A thorough man, he spent five weeks patrolling the coral-strewn paths in the immediate vicinity of the station between the dormitories and the landing. While the rest of us were enjoying high adventure on the more remote islands and sea-girt rocks, he patiently snared 200 frisky lizards with a noose of thread suspended from a rod. He took their cloacal temperatures, marked them with dye, and then dosed them with radioactive iodine, which enabled him to locate the elusive reptiles later with a Geiger counter. From dawn to dark he charted their activities, saw them wake in the morning, followed their daily routine, and by means of the clicking Geiger counter, discovered where they spent the night.

He performed simple surgery on one group of lizards, deftly removing the minute "third eye," a fleck of tissue on the forehead, to observe the effect on their daily activities. Whenever a lizard with a purple leg darted across our path, we knew we were seeing one of Dr. Stebbins' subjects.

It was with the same devotion to detail and relentless singleness of purpose that Dr. Stebbins tackled the long and exacting task of preparing the text, range maps, and illustrations for this manual — No. 16 in the Field Guide Series — and its revision.

Recognition is step number one in any branch of natural science. That is why the Field Guide Series was launched — as a shortcut to recognizing and naming the multitude of living things which populate North America, a *Who's Who* of the outdoors. The first volume to appear, *A Field Guide to the Birds,* met with instant success. This was followed by guides to other groups of animals and plants, including Roger Conant's splendid *Field Guide to Reptiles and Amphibians of Eastern and Central North America.*

This *Field Guide* supplements Roger Conant's book, which stops at the 100th meridian (except in west Texas). Between the eastern borders of New Mexico, Colorado, Wyoming, Montana, and Saskatchewan north (the eastern limits of the present book, or, roughly, the 103rd meridian), there is a blend zone — a "twilight zone" — where eastern and western influences intermingle. Here the student should carry both *Field Guides.*

The West may not be as rich as the East in salamanders and turtles, but it makes up for this deficiency in its wealth of lizards and snakes, particularly in the diversified terrain of the arid Southwest. Some species are local and rare; all are exciting to the field naturalist.

When you travel, take this handbook with you in your jacket pocket, backpack, briefcase, or in your car. Do not leave it home on the library shelf; it is a Field Guide, intended to be used.

Roger Tory Peterson

Acknowledgments

It is with deep gratitude that I acknowledge the contribution of many persons to the preparation of this 2nd edition of this *Field Guide.* I am especially grateful to Charles H. Lowe and John W. Wright, who reviewed all the accounts of species and the distribution maps, offering many corrections and helpful suggestions. Professor Lowe gave generously of his unpublished information on southwestern herpetology, and the book has been greatly improved by his important contributions. He also procured live reptiles for use in the preparation of new color plates. In addition to his general assistance on the text and distribution maps, John W. Wright provided special help on the accounts and distribution of the whiptail lizards and supplied live animals for the color plates of these lizards. Theodore J. Papenfuss and Robert L. Seib encouraged me to expand the coverage of Baja California; their extensive knowledge of that region was invaluable in the preparation of the maps and species accounts. I would not have attempted to cover Baja California without their help. I have also been given excellent assistance on Baja California herpetology by Richard B. Loomis, Robert W. Murphy, Norman C. Roberts, and Hartwell H. Welsh, Jr. I am grateful to the Mexican government for allowing me to collect amphibians and reptiles in Mexico.

Many people have helped in the preparation of the distribution maps, reviewed sections of manuscript, or contributed in other ways. Geographic areas or taxonomic groups to which some of them have given special attention appear in parentheses. They are: John S. Applegarth (sw. U.S. and New Mexico); Stevan J. Arnold; Andrew H. Barnum (Utah); Harold E. Basey; George T. Baxter (Wyoming); Kristin H. Berry; Jeffrey H. Black (nw. U.S.), Charles M. Bogert (patch-nosed snakes); Jeff J. Boundy (cen. California); Bayard H. Brattstrom; John M. Brode; Ted L. Brown (New Mexico); R. Bruce Bury; Stephen D. Busack; R. Wayne Campbell (Canada); James P. Collins; Charles J. Cole; Joseph F. Copp (sand snakes); Francis R. Cook; James W. Cornett; Blair Csuti (California); William G. Degenhardt (New Mexico); Dorothy M. DeLisle; Benjamin E. Dial; Philip C. Dumas (nw. U.S.); Jim W. Grace (Guadalupe Mts.); Denzel E. Ferguson; Henry S. Fitch; Darrel Frost (sw. U.S.); John S. Frost (leopard frogs); David Good (alligator lizards); David Green (Canada); Frederick R. Gehlbach (New Mexico); Geoffrey A. Hammerson (Colorado); Robert W. Hansen (cen. California); John R. Hendrickson; David M. Hillis (leopard frogs); Robert P. Hodge (Alaska); Mark R. Jennings; Ernest L. Karlstrom; Fenton R. Kay; Enid A. Larson (e. California); Michael C. Long (s. California); James F. Lynch (salamanders); Ronald W. Marlow; T. Paul Maslin (Colorado); John S. Mecham (leopard frogs); Richard R. Montanucci; Ronald A. Nussbaum (salamander reproduction); James E. Platz (leopard frogs); Gregory Pregill; Andrew H. Price (sw. U.S.); Douglas A. Rossman (garter snakes); Richard D. Sage (leopard frogs); Paul W. Sattler (spadefoot toads); Jay M. Savage; Frederick W. Schueler (Canada); James R. Slater (Washington); James A. St. Amant (African Clawed Frog); Alan D. St. John (Oregon); Glenn R. Stewart; James R. Stewart (alligator lizards); Hobart M. Smith; Robert M. Storm (Oregon); Sam S. Sweet (s. California); Wilmer W. Tanner (Utah); John H. Tashjian (rattlesnakes); Kristine Tollestrup (leopard lizards); Richard G. Zweifel; Kay P. Yanev (slender salamanders).

Among the people listed above, I wish to especially thank Robert W. Hansen, David M. Hillis, Ronald A. Nussbaum, Bayard H. Brattstrom, Ted L. Brown, John S. Frost, Geoffrey A. Hammerson, and Sam S. Sweet for their particularly extensive help and generosity with information pertaining to the distribution maps and manuscript of my revision of *Amphibians and Reptiles of Western North America* (McGraw-Hill, 1954). Some of the information they provided for that book has found its way into this *Field Guide* as well.

Roger and Isabelle Conant, creators of the eastern *Field Guide to Reptiles and Amphibians,* kindly allowed me to use their original map format in the preparation of western distributions.

The McGraw-Hill Book Company and the University of California Press generously allowed me to use illustrations from *Amphibians and Reptiles of Western North America* (McGraw-Hill, 1954), *Amphibians of Western North America* (University of California Press, 1951), and *Reptiles and Amphibians of the San Francisco Bay Region* (University of California Press, 1959). These illustrations are identified on p. xiv. Charles J. Cole provided drawings of the hemipenes of Black-headed Snakes (Fig. 30). Most of the drawings of frog eggs are based on "A Synoptic Key to the Salientian Eggs of the United States" by Robert L. Livezey and Albert H. Wright (Amer. Mid. Nat. 37 (1): 179–222). The map of natural vegetation of the western United States (pp. 282–283), is adapted from H. L. Shantz and R. Zon, 1924, U.S. Dept. Agric., Atlas Amer. Agric., Sect. E. and that for Baja California (p. 284), from D.I. Axelrod, 1979, Occas. Papers Calif. Acad. Sci. 132. Full color prints of paintings by the author of some of the amphibians and reptiles described in this book, shown in their natural habitats, are available from *Wildlife Impressions,* P.O. Box 11440, Eugene, OR 97440. Information sent on request.

David Wake, director of the Museum of Vertebrate Zoology and fellow herpetologist, reviewed the section on amphibians and has been a source of encouragement, advice, and information throughout the preparation of this revision. Harry Greene, Associate Curator in Herpetology, Museum of Vertebrate Zoology, offered many valuable suggestions for the section on reptiles. Nathan W. Cohen, dear friend and companion on many field trips and photographer par excellence, helped in many ways to bring this new version to completion.

I am indebted to Harry Foster and Barbara Stratton, Field Guide editors of Houghton Mifflin Company, for their counseling throughout the preparation of this book.

Special thanks go to my children — John, Melinda, and Mary — whose interest in animals helped motivate me, and to my wife, Anna-rose, who typed the manuscript, helped with the artwork on the distribution maps, and who for many years graciously coped with frogs in her refrigerator, snakes in the living room, and tortoises on the sundeck.

Robert C. Stebbins

To the late
Raymond B. Cowles,
mentor and friend

Credits for Use of Illustrations

The numbers in parentheses indicate the positions of drawings in plates and figures. Count from the top downward or from left to right when there are two or more columns of illustrations. The three books listed below are by Robert C. Stebbins.

Amphibians of Western North America
(University of California Press, 1951)

Plates
7 (7–9), 12 (1–7), 13 (all)
Figures
1, 2, 4, 5, 8–13, 15, 30–39
Endpapers
Salamanders (except 3 and 5), frogs, and toads

Reptiles and Amphibians of the San Francisco Bay Region
(University of California Press, 1959)

Plates
1 (1, 2, 4), 2 (1, 2), 6 (1–7), 10 (3), 11 (1), 14 (1–4, 7), 16 (5, 6), 26 (3–6), 28 (4–6), 29 (5, 6), 31 (1), 34 (4), 36 (2, 4–6, 9), 37 (2, 4, 6–8), 39 (1–3, 7), 43 (1–4), 44 (1)

Amphibians and Reptiles of Western North America
(McGraw-Hill, 1954)

Plates
7 (1–6), 17 (all), 18 (all), 19 (1, 2, 4), 20 (all), 21 (all), 25 (all), 30 (all), 40 (1–10, 13, 14), 41 (1–5, 7–9)
Figures
6, 7, 16–18, 20, 21 (1–4), 22–26, 28, 29
Endpapers
Lizards, turtles, snakes

A Field Guide to Western Reptiles and Amphibians

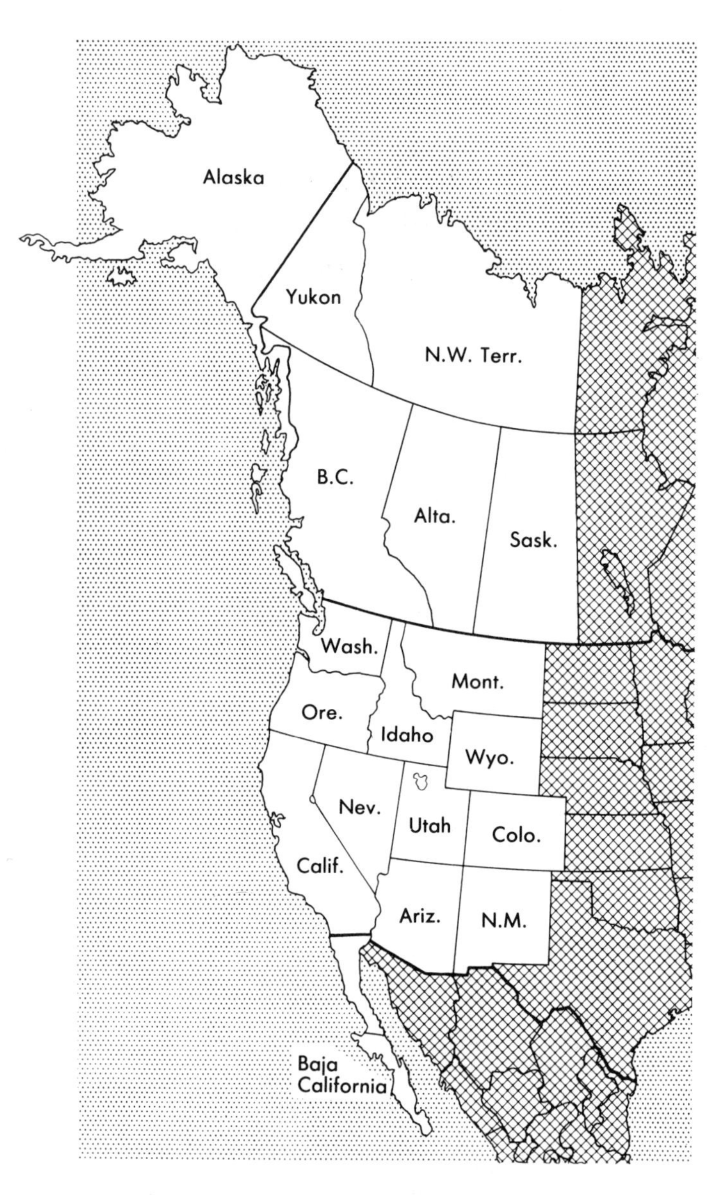

MAP OF AREA COVERED

Range maps showing the distribution of species and subspecies within this area begin on p. 285.

1

Introduction

Many people are discovering the pleasures of observing amphibians and reptiles, and biologists are turning increasingly to these animals as subjects for scientific research. Such growing interest has greatly expanded the information available on the habits, distribution, and taxonomic relationships of our western herpetofauna since this Field Guide was first published in 1966. The present book attempts to bring things up-to-date. Allowances, however, must be made for the lag time between the author's efforts (ending in March 1984) and publication, along with some probable oversights. I have included Baja California, an area rich in reptiles, already partly covered by the previous edition, because of the growing interest of herpetologists and outdoor recreationists in that area. This new edition includes 31 species of salamanders, 44 species of frogs and toads, 16 species of turtles, 76 species of lizards, 1 mole lizard (amphisbaenid), and 76 species of snakes — a total of 244 species, 37 more than in my previous book.

The primary function of the book is identification. In this connection I have included information on methods of capture, for in contrast to birds, reptiles and amphibians must usually be in hand to be identified. Captivity should be only temporary, however, and after examination the animals should be released where they were found. An attitude of "leave it alone," watch, and study should be developed. The undisturbed animal in its natural setting can provide much valuable information. Some collecting may be necessary for scientific studies and can be arranged for by state and federal permits.

When traveling through natural terrain, stop occasionally to explore the roadsides. Armed with a lizard noose, easily improvised (see p. 12); a jar for specimens; and the information supplied in this book; you may find much of interest. The desert, a forbidding place at first, will seem more hospitable after you meet some of its inhabitants. Discovery of a Long-tailed Brush Lizard, hiding camouflaged on the branch of a creosote bush, will leave a pleasant memory. The desert will never look the same again.

Area Covered. This book covers western North America including Baja California, from a line formed by the eastern boundaries of New Mexico, Colorado, Wyoming, Montana, and Saskatchewan north to the Arctic Circle. The area is referred to in the text as "the West" or "our area." The remaining portion of North America is referred to as "the East."

How to Use This Book. To identify most reptiles and amphibians, scales must be examined, costal grooves counted, and details of pattern studied (see endpapers). Fortunately, nearly all species can be caught easily and nearly all western forms are harmless. Only the rattlesnakes, Western Coral Snake, and Gila Monster are dangerous, and they are easily recognized. A few harmless species may bite hard enough to break the skin, but such injury can usually be avoided by proper handling (see p. 12).

In making identifications, you should have no difficulty in finding the appropriate major sections of this book. Turtles, snakes, and frogs are all easily recognized as to group. Salamanders, although resembling lizards in form, lack claws and scales and have a soft, moist skin. Our only snakelike lizards (two) have movable eyelids and lack the straplike belly scutes of snakes. Those familiar with reptiles and amphibians can go directly to the proper plates; the inexperienced should consult the keys (pp. 24–32). When an identification is made, check the appropriate distribution map at the back of the book to see if the species is expected in the area. If not, a mistake has probably been made. Most reptiles and amphibians do not have great mobility; natural vagrants are rare. However, escaped or released captives of many species are now being found in increasing numbers.

When range and illustration have been checked, turn to the species accounts for verification. The accounts give a more detailed description, and information on behavior, habitat, and similar species; important characteristics are highlighted in italics. The **Identification** section in each account mentions key features of color and structure of adult animals and is sometimes followed by a brief section describing the young when they differ notably from adults. So far as possible, familiar terminology has been used. However, a few technical terms are unavoidable. A brief time spent learning them will speed use of the book. The anatomical terms are explained in the figures on the endpapers inside the covers, and in the text; other terms can be found in the Glossary at the back of the book.

Although most of the characteristics mentioned in the descriptions can be seen easily, it has been necessary to refer to a few internal ones — tooth arrangements in salamanders, gill rakers in larvae, and cranial-boss structure in spadefoot toads. As regards teeth, with the exception of the Pacific Giant and Arboreal Salamanders, the mouths of salamanders can be opened without danger of being bitten. In studying the teeth of preserved specimens, you will usually have to sever the jaw on one side to free it enough to expose the teeth, unless the specimen has been preserved with mouth open.

Illustrations. Most of the drawings and paintings have been made from living animals. The area designation of the specimen illustrated is usually indicated in parentheses on the legend page opposite the plate. The live animal is a far cry from the often contorted specimen in the museum jar. A toad's eyes may be jewel-like and the geometry of reptilian scales is a harmony of line and shape. Life colors of some species rival the brilliance of brightly colored birds. Each species has its characteristic facial "expression."

I have tried to record what I have seen in the living animals. Many of the illustrations are generalizations based not only on the subject in hand but upon long personal acquaintanceship with the species. In some cases, however, my artistic sense has prevailed and I have illustrated a particularly colorful individual. My bias in such instances will be remedied by the species description. To attempt to render a scientifically accurate drawing is time-consuming. This is especially true in illustrating reptiles with scales too large to suggest. It becomes necessary to draw them all, faithfully recording size, number, shape, and arrangement to obtain a satisfactory result.

To show details in structure, young animals and some of the smaller species have been enlarged relative to the other illustrations. The treefrogs, ground snakes, and black-headed snakes are examples. Refer to the size scale on the legend pages opposite the plates.

Size. Range in adult size is given in inches and centimeters at the beginning of the descriptions and applies to each species throughout its geographic range. Measurements are of snout-to-vent (SV) length in salamanders, frogs, and lizards; shell length in turtles; and total length in snakes.

Color. Colors may vary with locality, age, sex, and color phase. In some species color may change within a few minutes. A dark frog or lizard may become pale while being handled. The brief color descriptions presented here will often be lacking, and one can expect to find individuals that fit neither description nor illustration. In such instances, special attention must be given to structure. Counts of middorsal blotches or crossbands in snakes do not include those on the tail, unless so indicated.

Young. Proportions usually differ from those of adults. Head, limbs, and eyes may be relatively larger. Young turtles usually have a more rounded shell with a median ridge, and a relatively long tail. At hatching, many young turtles, including the hatchlings of some of the large marine turtles, are only an inch or so in length. The colors of young animals may also differ. In identifying young, rely heavily on structural characteristics — scale counts and arrangement, coastal-groove counts, and other traits that do not change with age. Amphibian larvae are described on pp. 259–272.

Sex Differences. The species accounts give details pertaining to species. General remarks are set forth here.

1. Salamanders. Breeding males usually have a swollen vent, the lining of which is roughened by tubercles (villi) of the cloacal glands (Fig. 1). In contrast, the vent of females is not enlarged and lacks tubercles; the lips and walls are usually smooth or pleated. Hold the salamander in a damp cloth or paper towel and spread the vent with forceps. View with hand lens or dissecting microscope. In addition to vent differences, males generally have a longer tail and, in the aquatic stage, broader tail fins.

2. Frogs and Toads. Males usually have a voice and a well-developed vocal sac (Fig. 2); voice in females is weak or absent. When the vocal sac is deflated the skin of the throat is often dark and loose. When breeding, males develop dark nuptial pads of minutely roughened (sandpaperlike) skin on one or more of the inner fingers (Fig. 2). In frogs the base of the innermost finger (or "thumb") may become enlarged. The forelimbs often become stout and muscular and webbing of the hind feet increases. Males are generally smaller than females. Amplexus may be pectoral or pelvic, the male embracing the female from behind. In pectoral amplexus the male holds the female about her chest; in pelvic amplexus he holds her about her waist.

3. Turtles. Males typically have a concave plastron and longer tail than females. When the tail is extended full length the vent lies at or beyond the shell margin. Females have a flat or convex plastron and the vent is situated inside the shell margin.

4. Lizards. In breeding males, the base of the tail usually appears swollen. The enlargement results from the hemipenes (copulatory organs), which are imbedded there. These organs can often be everted in most species by gentle squeezing with thumb and forefinger, applying pressure toward the vent opening from a point at or just behind the swollen tail base. In individuals in which eversion does not occur, hold the lizard by its head and gently probe the rear edge and sides of the vent with a toothpick, straightened paper clip, or bobby pin, thrusting the probe backward. If the

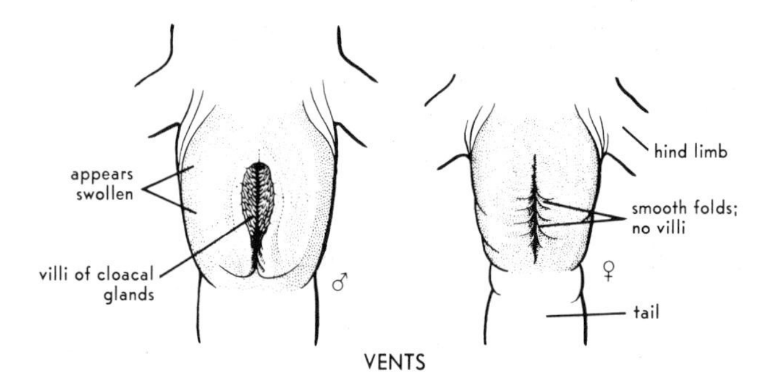

Fig. 1. Sexual characteristics of salamanders

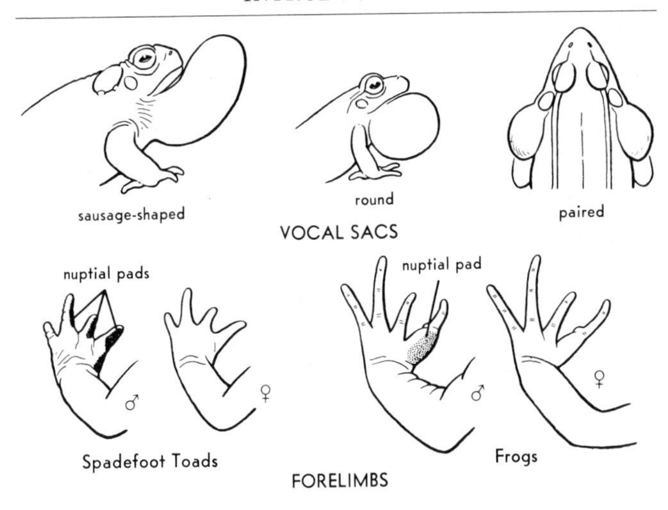

Fig. 2. Sexual characteristics of frogs

animal is a male, the probe should pass into the opening of the inverted hemipenis.

5. *Snakes.* Males usually have longer tails than females and a broader tail base. Their hemipenes can seldom be everted, and the probing technique will have to be used.

Voice. With the exception of the Tailed Frog — an apparently mute species — males of most western frogs and toads have well-developed voices, which can be helpful in identification. The calls described in the accounts are the mating or "advertisement" calls; other vocalizations are usually not included. Pitch, cadence, and duration of calls are usually given, but these characteristics may vary with locality, size of the individual, and temperature. In particular, individuals from the extremes of the range of some of the more widely-ranging species may differ in vocal characteristics. Young adults, as a consequence of their small size, may have higher-pitched voices than older adults. A cold frog may produce slower and lower-pitched calls than a warm one. In hybrid areas unusual combinations may occur. When an unfamiliar call is heard, locate the frog by triangulation (see p. 14). Attempt to imitate the animal and write a description of both its voice and the method you used to imitate it. Try whistles, vocal sounds, tongue clicks, or combinations thereof. Some calls can best be imitated mechanically. I have stimulated the Northern Cricket Frog to call by striking pebbles together, one held in each hand and struck with a sliding motion. A Striped Chorus Frog may respond to stroking the teeth of a pocket comb. Knowledge of animal sounds can greatly increase enjoyment of the outdoors, but many of us have become accustomed to ignoring sounds in our noisy civilized environment. An awareness of animal sounds usually must be cultivated.

Knowledge of amphibian voices makes it possible to determine the species present in mixed choruses, and, during the height of the breeding season, their vocalizations can be used to help locate the boundaries of ranges. I observed the western border of the range of the Striped Chorus Frog one spring as I traveled at night from Wyoming into Utah. The sounds of this frog, which I had heard for several hundred miles throughout southern Wyoming, suddenly stopped at the western base of the Central Plateau, at the edge of the Great Basin. For a start in recognizing the voices of amphibians, listen to *Sounds of North American Frogs* by Charles M. Bogert (Folkways Records, FX 6166).

Time of Activity and Breeding. Many amphibians and reptiles have limited periods of yearly activity. In the second paragraph of the main descriptions, the span of months over which various species may be found or heard has been given. Calling and other activity often reaches its peak during the breeding season. Some amphibians may gather in large numbers then, but are seldom seen at other times. The duration of the breeding period is included when information is available and reliable. Clutch size, given as a range in number of eggs laid during a single laying period, is based on counts of eggs actually laid and/or the presence of mature eggs (ova) in the oviducts or ovaries. For most reptiles the minimum size is a single egg, but published ranges may not go that low. Abdominal eggs have also been used in estimating the duration of the egg-laying period. In species that lay 2 or more clutches per season, total egg counts for the season are sometimes given. Unfortunately, information on clutch size, total egg complement per season per female, and other aspects of reproduction is often fragmentary. Statements in the accounts are general and apply to the species over its entire range. Information on egg-laying and birth dates in captives have seldom been used. In a wide-ranging form, activity usually begins sooner and lasts longer in the south and in the lowlands than in the north and at higher elevations. However, local climatic effects and, with amphibians, fluctuations in pond and stream water levels, may influence the timing of breeding activity.

Prolonged retreat from the surface may occur in winter (hibernation), summer (estivation), or both. The former is an escape from cold; the latter an escape from heat and dryness. Hibernation occurs in many species even in some lowlands and southern desert areas. Only the smaller species there escape its grip during brief warm spells. It is universal and prolonged at high altitude and in the far north. Even the cold-tolerant salamanders of the humid coastal district may disappear for short periods during cold snaps. However, the depth of torpor in hibernating amphibians and reptiles is usually not as great as in mammals, and most can be easily aroused by warming. Estivation occurs in most species in the arid and semiarid warmer areas and in most of our northwestern salamanders. In dry summers the soil and duff of even the shady forests may dry out. Exceptions are certain frogs and toads which breed during the period of summer rains.

Conditions of temperature and rainfall will usually be the best guide for successful field observation. Select warm days in spring and fall for reptiles and cool (but not freezing) wet weather for salamanders. Go to the mountains in summer, when spring reaches the higher elevations, or to the lowlands of the Southwest during the period of summer rainfall for reptiles and frogs. Weather, however, is not the entire story. Some seasonal activity patterns appear to be inborn and partly independent of climatic and seasonal effects. Possibly in response to internal timing mechanisms, some species disappear from the surface when conditions of temperature and humidity seem favorable. Be guided by information in the accounts.

Knowledge of the pattern of daily activity is also important. Most species are diurnal (active during the day), and unless otherwise noted diurnality may be assumed. In many species activity is greatest in mid-morning and in mid- or late afternoon. Many amphibians, the geckos, and some snakes are nocturnal. Some species change their daily pattern with season, being diurnal when days are short and cool and nocturnal during warm summer months. Crepuscular species prowl at twilight.

Habits. Manner of locomotion, defense postures, and other aspects of behavior may aid identification. The defense pose of the salamander Ensatina (p. 48) and the tail-coiling habit of the Ringneck Snake (p. 174) are as useful in identifying these animals as their color. Habits and behavior that may be helpful in identification have been pointed out in the species accounts.

Food. Amphibians will eat almost any creature that moves and can be swallowed; therefore food items have not been listed. Reptiles, on the other hand, are usually more particular in their tastes, so their food habits are described in some detail. I have emphasized foods eaten in nature, and have tried to avoid listing items taken in captivity. Information on diet may be of interest to persons who wish to keep reptiles and amphibians for enjoyment and study.

Subspecies. The characteristics of many species differ in various parts of their ranges. Color may change with the prevailing color of the soil, scale counts and arrangements may differ with latitude, and less easily detected but important changes may occur in physiology and behavior. Many such variants have been described as subspecies, and the variable species of which they are a part is referred to as "polytypic." However, professional herpetologists differ in their opinions as to the magnitude and nature of differences justifying application of subspecies names. Many people using this book may be little interested in subspecies. Nevertheless, some of the geographic variants are well marked and in certain respects display greater differences than exist among some species. The subspecies of the salamander Ensatina (illustrated on Plates 3 and 4) are an example. It would be unfortunate to disregard such distinct forms.

I have been selective in recognizing subspecies. Certain ones have been ignored, pending intensive study of total species variation; others because the differences described are not easily detected. One or more subspecies described for the following species have been omitted from this book: Rough-skinned Newt; Arboreal and Black Salamanders; Tailed Frog; Pacific Treefrog; Wood and Spotted Frogs; Yellow Mud Turtle; Desert Iguana; Colorado Desert Fringe-toed, Zebra-tailed, Lesser Earless, Leopard, Western Fence, Crevice Spiny, Clark Spiny, Side-blotched, Tree, Short-horned, Coast Horned, and Desert Night Lizards; Orange-throated and Little Striped Whiptails; Western and Texas Blind Snakes; Sonoran Mountain Kingsnake; Checkered Garter Snake and Night Snake; and Baja California Rattlesnake.

A word of caution: the printed word sometimes carries more weight in shaping thought than is desirable. The scientific enterprise is constantly in a state of flux, and science advances by a continual re-evaluation of currently accepted "truths." The nomenclature, or classification scheme, presented in this book should be viewed in this light. Probably no two authors would have made precisely the same taxonomic decisions. This applies with special force to subspecies. Subspecies, along with higher categories in the hierarchy of classification are, of course, a construction of the human mind and sometimes may only crudely represent the real world of animal and plant evolutionary relationships in nature. Unfortunately, the subspecies category has all too frequently been applied in the absence of adequate information and with considerable subjectivity.

Biochemical Taxonomy. Many taxonomic problems are being investigated using electrophoresis, a biochemical technique that probes the actual degree of genetic difference among groups of organisms. Often the findings support taxonomy based on morphological, physiological, and behavioral criteria, but sometimes they do not. The biochemical approach has shown that some populations that closely resemble one another, or even appear to be identical, are actually full species. Electrophoresis has become a routine procedure, along with more traditional techniques employed in field and laboratory, aimed at clarifying the evolutionary relationships of organisms. In time it may help solve some of the remaining taxonomic problems identified in this book.

Distribution Maps. The range of each species is shown in pattern (dots, cross-hatching, etc.) on the 200 maps at the back of the book. Usually only one species is included on each map. Distributions for subspecies that occur entirely outside our area are outlined in a lightly speckled grayish pattern. Specific and subspecific names on the maps can be distinguished by type size: species names are larger and are followed by the scientific name; scientific names of subspecies are given in the text. Question marks on the maps signify doubt as to the accuracy of range boundaries or whether or not the species occurs in the area — the situation which applies can be determined by referring to the text.

Subspecies distributions usually fit together like the pieces of a jigsaw puzzle. At points of contact, characteristics of one subspecies usually change gradually into those of another. Such zones of change are known as areas of "intergradation." Patterns representing some subspecies are separated by areas of fine stippling (Map 5) or solid black (Map 10). Both arrangements represent broad areas of intergradation. Black is used when the scale is small, or the area of intergradation complicated. Few areas of intergradation have been studied in sufficient detail to make such precise representation possible on all maps. Overlapping of species or subspecies patterns indicates areas of coexistence or sympatry (see Glossary).

Ranges are never as continuous as shown. In the West, with its varied topography and climate, spotty or "disjunct" distributions are the rule. Agriculture and other human impacts have also eliminated large segments of the range of some species. Supplement map information with knowledge of habitat. Fringe-toed lizards, for example, will usually not be found on rocky hillsides without sand, nor Chuckwallas on sand dunes. Many miles of uninhabited territory may separate populations of such species.

Isolated populations are represented on the maps by patches of appropriate pattern or black dots. Many of these isolated populations are also mentioned in the accounts. Often in mainland areas they are remnants of populations that formerly lived over a much larger area. Examples are salamanders and frogs on mountaintops in the desert. Some isolates, however, are the result of introductions, such as the Bullfrog west of the Rocky Mts.

If a reptile or amphibian is found outside its known range, one of the following explanations may apply: (1) A new locality of occurrence may have been discovered. Many areas in the West remain little explored. Even distinctive new species still turn up: the Inyo Mountains Salamander was found in 1973, in the Inyo Mts. of California, and the Barefoot Gecko in Baja Calif. in 1974. Other species probably await discovery. (2) An unusual individual may have been found — a hybrid or oddly marked specimen that does not fit the brief descriptions in this book. Such individuals are especially likely to occur in areas of intergradation or where two species have come into contact and hybridize. Consult the species accounts for remarks concerning areas of hybridization. (3) A waif may have been found — a species or subspecies transported out of its normal range by natural or human means. Tiger Salamanders appear in cotton fields in the desert in Arizona, having metamorphosed from escaped larvae used as fish bait. Increasing commercial and private traffic in amphibians and reptiles is a growing source of such introductions. I have included in the species accounts only those introduced species that appear to have established breeding colonies.

Maps showing the distribution of natural vegetation (pp. 282–284) are included to help explain the boundaries of the species and subspecies ranges, and to aid in the search for new localities. Because of the small size of the maps, the distribution of vegetation can only be roughly indicated. The Sonoran Desert, for example, shown as occupying most of Baja California (map, p. 284) actually consists of an extensive patchwork of different plant communities. Vegetation belts reflect conditions of climate and terrain that greatly influence distribution, but there is seldom a close relationship between the distribution of amphibians and reptiles and that of particular plant species. Note how the ranges of the Chuckwalla and Desert Iguana stop at the northern limit of the creosote bush plant community in southern Nevada. With the construction of new roads and the increase in the number of people entering remote areas, much new information on distribution will be forthcoming. Keep the maps up to date by adding localities from the literature and personal study. Use them as a life list by checking off species as they are encountered.

Use of Names. I have tried to follow common names set forth in official lists and in use in other field guides, to minimize confusion and multiplicity of names. However, in a few instances I have felt that current names are so misleading or inappropriate that I have changed them. For example, the "Colorado River Toad" has been changed to "Sonoran Desert Toad" to reflect more precisely its distribution, habits, and tolerance of arid conditions, and "Chuckwalla" has been changed to "Common Chuckwalla" in recognition of other species on islands off Baja California in the Gulf of California. Where I have changed an established common name, or deviated from a name set forth in the standard herpetological lists, I usually have placed the previous name in parentheses. In cases where, in the past, a subspecies common name has been the same as the species name, I have changed one or the other (usually the subspecies name) to avoid such confusing duplication. When the previous species name (common or scientific) contained the name of a person, I have tried to retain this honorary patronym by applying it to the subspecies (if any exists) that bears the patronymic scientific name.

I dislike using the possessive in common names (Woodhouse's Toad, for example) and have therefore dropped the possessive throughout this book.

In accord with the recent decision by the International Commission on Zoological Nomenclature, I have used the double *i* where called for in scientific names, breaking with the treatment in the first edition of this book.

Metric System. Metric equivalents follow all measurements in inches and feet throughout the book. Elevation measurements have been rounded off to the nearest 10 meters.

2

Making Captures

Many reptiles and amphibians can simply be picked up. No special methods are needed to capture them. However, it is dangerous to handle venomous species — the Gila Monster, Western Coral Snake, and rattlesnakes. Sooner or later, as when playing with a loaded gun, disaster may strike. Other species can be taken in hand but should be handled with care to avoid injuring or overheating them. Hold large individuals behind the head to avoid being bitten. Individuals that have taken refuge under logs, rocks, and boards may be sluggish or momentarily light-struck. Active ones abroad on the surface can sometimes be overtaken before they escape into a burrow or other retreat. A fast snake may be pinioned lightly underfoot while a neck hold is secured, but be very careful not to apply too much pressure. Gloves will help reduce wear and tear but must not be counted on as protection against venomous species. Success in making captures will be greatly increased if a few standard techniques are used.

Making and Using a Snake Stick. The traditional forked stick is unsatisfactory for catching snakes. Instead, attach an angle iron to the end of a broom handle or a 4-foot (120 cm) length of ¾-in. (20 mm) doweling, placing the surface of the iron flush with the end of the dowel. Bevel the free edge so that it will slip easily beneath a snake when the animal is on a hard surface such as pavement. The bar can be used either as a hook to pull a snake from brush or rocks or to pin it down while a neck hold is secured. Although the bite of even our largest nonvenomous species will usually only superficially lacerate the skin, most people prefer to avoid being bitten. Therefore, use gloves in capturing large snakes, or maneuver the snake stick to the head region so that the animal can be grasped just behind the head. Thumb and index finger should be against the rear of the jaws; if there is slack the snake may turn and bite.

Noosing. When warm, most lizards and some snakes are too fast to catch by hand. A slip noose of thread, fishline, or copper wire can be used to snare them. Use No. 50 thread for lizards up to about 4–5 in. (10–12 cm) long from snout to vent, and No. 8 thread or fishline for larger species. The noose should be tied to the notched end of a slender stick or through the last rung of a telescopic fishing rod to prevent its pulling off. The shank should be short, usually no more than 6 in. (15 cm) long when the noose is open. If excessively long, it may become tangled in vegetation or be blown about so that it is hard to control. A wire noose avoids this difficulty and can be bent to thrust into small openings. Make a small loop of ¼-inch (6-mm) diameter at the end of a thread. Tie the loop with a square knot so that it will not close. Pass the shank through the loop and attach it to the pole. Should the noose tend to close when in use, open to the desired diameter and moisten with saliva both loop and shank where they come into contact, or apply a small pinch of wax.

To make a copper wire noose, cut a 10- or 12-in. (25–30 cm) length from an electric light cord. "Zipcord," obtainable in most hardware stores, can be used. Remove the insulation and separate out a single strand of wire. Twist the ends of the remaining strands in opposite directions so that they will not separate. Coil the bundle for convenience in carrying. Since copper wire nooses must be replaced frequently, a reserve supply will be needed. Twist a small loop of ⅛- to ¼-in. (3–6 mm) diameter at the end of the strand. Pass the shank through and orient the loop so that the shank moves freely; compress the sides of the loop slightly to make it somewhat elongate; then curve the loop to conform to the lizard's neck. In attaching the noose, take several turns around the end of the pole and twist the free end of the wire and shank together. Twist the wires up close to the pole to make sure the attachment is firm. Then wind the free end of the wire along the shank to strengthen its base. It is here that most breakage occurs. After noosing a lizard, reduce the diameter of the noose to ½ in. (12 mm) or less and carefully untwist all kinks. Pass the shank between thumb and index finger to straighten it. Re-form the noose to the desired diameter and reshape the "neck" curve in the loop.

In noosing a lizard, avoid quick movements. When the noose is within 5 or 6 in. (12–15 cm) of the head, move it slowly or pause for a moment, allowing the animal to become accustomed to the presence of a strange object nearby; then move the remaining distance gradually. When the noose has passed over the lizard's head and has reached the neck region, jerk upward and slightly backward. Remove the animal quickly, before it has a chance to wriggle free. Wary species can sometimes be noosed by creating a diversion. Gently shake a handkerchief at arm's length to one side or wriggle your fingers to attract attention away from the noose.

Although noosing may appear cruel, it rarely does harm. Only a heavy-bodied lizard with a slender neck may be injured if it thrashes violently when suspended. Support part of the weight of such animals by resting their hindquarters on the ground.

Night Driving. Certain snakes, geckos, toads, and salamanders can be found on highways at night. Reptiles may be attracted to the warmth of the pavement and amphibians to roadside ditches. Night driving to observe animals on roadways must be done with great care. It can be done safely on little-traveled roads, but requires constant vigilance in watching for approaching cars. Drive slowly (15 to 20 miles per hour) and watch both pavement and shoulders. Select roads that pass through suitable habitat. An ideal road is dark-colored, little-traveled, and without curbs or broad, bare shoulders. Roads with bordering wild-plant growth are especially favorable. Small species can easily be overlooked. On dark pavement the yellow spots of a Tiger Salamander may resemble pale-colored pebbles, a blind snake can be mistaken for a twig, and a toad for a rock. Check all suspicious-looking objects, even if it means stopping for fan belts, banana peels, and other artifacts.

Success in night collecting will depend in large part on weather conditions, particularly temperature, and not just the weather at the time but that which prevailed several days or a week before. When looking for reptiles avoid cool evenings. Air temperatures below 60° to 65° F (15–18°C) will usually be too low. However, if the pavement remains warm some individuals may be found. Bright moonlight and winds seem to depress activity. Warmth is less important to amphibians. Some salamanders may be abroad at a few degrees above freezing.

Wet weather is the time for amphibians. After rains in arid portions of the Southwest, the response of frogs and toads, long ensconced below dry sunbaked earth, may be dramatic. Within an hour an area powder-dry for many months may reverberate with their cries and the ground may swarm with hopping forms. Watch for thunderstorms. In open terrain where there are good roads and broad vistas, one can sometimes spot a storm and drive to it in time to arrive just after dark during or shortly after a rain.

Triangulation. Locating a small, calling animal hidden in a large expanse of rough terrain would appear to be almost impossible. However, it usually can be accomplished easily by means of triangulation. The technique is particularly helpful in finding creatures whose voices are ventriloquial and thus give a deceptive impression of location. Triangulation is best done by two people. When a calling frog, for example, has been singled out of a chorus, and its approximate position determined, move 15 to 30 ft. (5–10 m) apart and listen quietly. After a few moments of listening each person, without discussion with the other, should decide on the location of the sound. Then, at a signal, each should point with arm extended and sight on a distant object that will serve as a reference point. Finally, both should walk forward toward the reference point and seek the animal where pathways cross. If alone, you can listen at one position for a time, decide on direction, then move to one side and listen again. Triangulation is often easier to do at night than in the daytime if flashlights or headlamps with distinct beams are used; the point of intersection of the beams can be determined precisely. The lights should not be turned on, however, until direction has been determined. Sudden illumination may alarm wary species and they may not call again for some time. First trials may not bring success, and it may be necessary to withdraw and repeat the procedure several times.

Eyeshines. Fortunately for the night-time observer, many animals reflect light from their eyes. One of the pleasures in the field is to walk quietly through wild country at night in search of eyeshines, pausing occasionally to illuminate the surroundings with a headlamp or flashlight. Dewdrops and the eyes of spiders glint silver and green, those of moths and toads yellow or red; a murky stream becomes a cascade of light. To obtain an eyeshine, the light source must be held near your eyes. Hold a flashlight at the side of your head, or with the base resting on your forehead; a headlamp works well and frees the hands. The eyeshine method works best on toads, frogs, and turtles. Eyeshines of snakes and salamanders are too faint to be seen well, and our lizards are chiefly active in the daytime.

Tracking. Seek areas of fine loose soil, sand, or mud — sandy flats, dunes, dusty roads, trails, fresh mud of washes, or the banks of ponds and streams. Go out when the sun is low and highlights and shadows are strong. Start early, before there is a maze of tracks, or later in the day after a wind has erased old tracks and new ones are appearing. Follow a fresh track. Direction of travel can be determined by ridges formed by the backward pressure of toes, feet, or coils of a snake. Tracking demands attention to details and use of clues. From meager evidence an interesting story may unfold. I once tracked a lizard across the barren rippled surface of a sand dune. The track indicated that at first the animal had moved slowly. Marks of all four feet showed, the stride was short, the tail dragged. Then the track of a roadrunner appeared, a lizard-eating bird. The lizard's stride suddenly lengthened and marks of only two feet could be seen; the tail mark disappeared. The lizard was running now, on its hind legs with tail lifted. An occasional small dent indicated that at high speed it occasionally touched down with its front feet to maintain balance. Just over the crest of the dune, the track suddenly stopped. To one side was a faint V-shaped mark. The roadrunner track continued at full clip over the hill, then slowed and wandered. The bird seemed confused. I grabbed at the V-shaped mark and something wriggled beneath it. In my hand I held a beautiful fringe-toed lizard.

Containers for specimens. Cloth bags are standard for transporting reptiles. Use flour sacks, inexpensive pillowcases, or bags made for the purpose. Useful sizes are 24 × 10 in. (60 × 25 cm) and 40 × 20 in. (100 × 50 cm). They may be made from unbleached muslin. Sew with French seams and hem the top. Attach a drawstring 2–4 in. (5–10 cm) below the hem by sewing a 12-in. (30-cm) length of heavy twine, at its midpoint, to the side of the bag. The bags are long and the top can be wound around your belt to prevent the bag from working loose. The length also enables you to double back the top when you tie it closed — some snakes have remarkable ability to work their way out of sacks. Inspect the sacks occasionally to detect holes or loose threads that might snarl specimens. Even small holes may give trouble, because they may be enlarged by the probing efforts of captives. Do not carry venomous species in sacks next to your body.

Quart or gallon glass or plastic jars with screw caps are better than bags for carrying amphibians. Place damp moss, leaves, or moist paper towels in the bottom to provide moisture. Avoid dirt and rocks. Punch a few holes in the lid for air, poking the holes outward so that sharp edges will not damage specimens, and file the edges to avoid personal injury in handling (or make the holes with an electric drill). In perforating lids, make only four or five ⅛-in. (3-mm) openings. Numerous holes may result in excessive drying of specimens. A knapsack or canvas shoulder bag is convenient for carrying sacks and other collecting gear.

3

Caring for Captives

Temporary Quarters. For temporary housing, use widemouth gallon jars with perforated lids. Place sand or pea gravel in the bottom for reptiles or moist earth for amphibians. A small, flat block of wood, propped up off the substratum, can serve as cover and a twig can be put in for species that climb.

Cages. A permanent cage can be made of wood or glass. A container measuring approximately 15 × 30 × 18 in. (37 × 75 × 45 cm) will be adequate for most species. If the cage is made of wood, one of the long sides should be of glass and the top should be screened. If screening is kept at the top, there is less chance that snakes will rub their noses raw in attempts to get out.

To make a glass cage, have a glazier cut panels for the sides, ends, and bottom. Assemble these by taping them together with masking tape. Tape the outside of the joints only: if tape is placed in the corners lizards may climb out. The surface must be slippery. Tape the rim of the cage to cover sharp edges. Cover with ¼-in. (6-mm) hardware cloth, bent to fit as a lid.

Substratum. The type of substratum will depend on the animals to be confined. Clean pea gravel can be used for amphibians that enter water — frogs, toads, newts, and ambystomatid salamanders. It need not be wet if a water dish is always kept filled so that the animals can immerse themselves and a moist shelter is available. Some lizards and snakes can also be kept on such a surface. Sand should be provided for species that habitually bury themselves. Examples are the horned, spiny, earless, Zebra-tailed, and fringe-toed lizards, and the Rubber Boa, hognose, ground, and sand snakes. From time to time remove the soiled surface layer and replace with fresh material. Lungless salamanders should be given damp earth strewn with dead leaves. Sprinkle the surface occasionally to keep it moist. A spray bottle is excellent for this purpose. Terrariums should always offer hiding places for the confined animals. Construct crevices or tunnels by propping up boards or rocks and anchoring them so that they will not collapse. Sink a water dish in the substratum; but keep the rim aboveground to keep the water from draining away by capillary action. Lizards and snakes can be provided water from a birdcage drinking tube. Fill the trough with gravel to prevent their getting into the vertical reservoir chamber and drowning. Tape a small bar magnet at the top and bottom of the tube and a metal plate to the side of the cage. The drinking container will then be held firmly in an upright position and can be refilled and replaced with ease.

Temperature. The cages of most reptiles must be heated. Place a 75- to 100-watt light at one end with the bulb 8–10 in. (20–25 cm) above the substratum. The heat source should be at the opposite end from the shelter. Check temperature. The cool end should not go above 75–80°F (24–27°C). If it goes higher, reduce the wattage. Lower temperatures should be no cause for concern. If the light has a reflector, as in a desk lamp, it will help concentrate the heat and reduce the glare.

Feeding. Most amphibians, lizards, and some of the smaller snakes will eat live mealworms, which can be purchased in pet shops. If you plan to keep captives for long periods, establish a mealworm colony. Cut out the side of a clean 5-gallon can, leaving enough border so the edges can be turned under to form a smooth-edged overhang. Cover with window screening to keep out moths and spiders. Place 1½ to 2 in. (4–5 cm) of wheat bran in the bottom and introduce the worms. Expand the colony to other cans as needed. Occasionally place half a potato or a piece of cabbage (including the stalk) in the container to provide moisture and variety in the diet. Replace the bran as necessary. When feces accumulate, sift to extract the worms and discard. Since animals on a diet of mealworms fed only bran may languish, place the worms in a container with a shallow layer of egg-layer mash or other vitamin- and mineral-enriched meal the day before they are to be used in feeding. Enriched meal can be obtained from poultry suppliers or at some pet shops. Your captive animals will then get not only the worms but the enriched mash contained in their digestive tracts.

Termites obtained from rotting logs can also be reared. Keep them in plastic trays about 8 × 11 × 4 in. (20 × 25 × 10 cm) with tightly fitting lids. Bore one or two small holes in the tops and feed them paper towels. Place 1 in. (2.5 cm) of coarse sand in the bottom of the tray and a 2 in. (5 cm) stack of towels on top. The towels should be separated and restacked or their edges cut so they are no longer interleaved. Moisten both sand and towels. Introduce several hundred termites. The termites will make tunnels in the towels and, by separating layers of the towels, you can remove them as needed. If winged sexual forms have been included and demands are not great, the colony will maintain itself indefinitely.

Colonies of mealworms and termites are subject to attack by ants. It may be necessary to put containers in trays of water or keep them on stands, the legs of which are placed in water, thereby providing moats that ants cannot cross.

Rearing Amphibian Larvae. In rearing larvae, the essentials are well-oxygenated, uncontaminated water; avoidance of crowding and high temperatures; and adequate food. You can maintain suitable oxygen levels by rearing only 3 or 4 tadpoles per gallon of water, using a tray instead of a jar to increase the amount of water surface exposed to the air, and changing the water once every few days. Use a tea strainer to handle larvae. Most species will do well at room temperature, but Olympic Salamander larvae and tadpoles of the Tailed Frog should be kept at lower temperatures and their aquarium water should be thoroughly oxygenated by air flow from an aerator.

Herbivorous tadpoles can be fed algae (green pond scum), spinach, or lettuce (boiled to help soften the tissues and reduce rate of decay), and/or egg-layer mash. Mash can be sprinkled on the surface. Bits of hard-boiled egg yolk or luncheon meat may be offered to provide protein. Carnivorous larvae (spadefoot tadpoles and all salamander larvae) can be fed live brine shrimp (purchased in pet shops), bits of fresh liver, luncheon meat, earthworms, and small animals shaken from the roots and leaves of pond plants. Roots of the floating water hyacinth are often rich in small organisms relished by amphibian larvae. Watch for overfeeding and contamination of the water by uneaten decayed food.

As the time for transformation approaches, prepare a rocky shore for emergence on land. Imminent transformation is indicated in salamander larvae by shrinking of the gills and reduction in size of the tail fins, and in tadpoles by appearance of the forelimbs and atrophy of the tail. In general, it is best to release amphibians after transformation because of the difficulty in providing them with small live animal food. If a few transformed individuals are kept, supply food by means of a Berlese funnel. Tape a large opaque plastic funnel to the bottom of a metal cylinder (gallon can with both ends removed). Turn the cylinder upright and fill with dead leaf litter scraped from beneath trees. Before selecting the litter, remove the surface layer and look closely to be sure there are plenty of small insects and other invertebrates present. To make certain that the contained animals can move freely, avoid compacting the litter when it is placed in the funnel. Gradually heat and dry out the upper layers with light from a desk lamp, removing the dried material as the animals move downward. By repeated drying and removal of leaves, lowering the lamp each time, the animals can be driven into a collecting tube at the spout of the funnel. A small piece of moist paper toweling should be placed in this tube and its connection with the funnel should be sealed with cotton to prevent the animals from escaping.

Rearing Reptile Eggs. Sooner or later the guardian of captive reptiles will be confronted with a batch of eggs. At one time, the fate of such eggs was almost always assured — they would spoil. Now, however, there is an excellent technique for rearing them that results in a high rate of survival. Since the eggs and young of many reptiles are little known, here is an opportunity for obtaining new information. Keep records on the length of incubation, the process of hatching, and size and coloration of the young. Be sure to record the temperature under which the eggs developed.

Place a layer of damp earth, peat moss, or sand in the bottom of a plastic bag. Pat the surface smooth and make a dent with your index finger to hold each egg. Dents should be far enough apart so that the eggs do not touch; then if one spoils it will not contaminate the rest. Vermiculite (moistened with water) also makes a good substratum for eggs. It may also be placed in a plastic bag or in the bottom of a gallon jar closed with a lid from which the liner has been removed. Billow out the sides of the bag and draw the top together, sealing it with a rubber band. Keep the bag at room temperature or higher (around 70–80°F., or 20–25°C) in lighted surroundings to inhibit the growth of mold. Watch moisture droplets on the inside of the bag or jar. If they disappear and the substratum seems dry, add water with a teaspoon or sprayer. Avoid flooding the eggs.

Choice of Captives. In selecting reptiles and amphibians for laboratory or home study, consider problems of feeding and care. Some species can be kept more easily than others. If a captive does not feed well, release it where you found it and get another. There may be great individual differences in feeding. Keep the number of captive animals small, to facilitate observation and care.

4

Field Study and Protection

Field Study. There is much to be learned about the distribution, habits, and behavior of western reptiles and amphibians. The many question marks on the range maps should be a challenge to fill in gaps in our knowledge of distribution. We have not even found the eggs or young of some species, and much remains to be learned about time of breeding, courtship behavior, enemies, and other matters.

A field notebook is essential. Write notes in nonfading waterproof black ink to make a permanent record. Higgins Eternal Ink has proved to be long-lasting. Use a hard-back ($17\frac{1}{2} \times 10$ in. — 18×25 cm) looseleaf notebook. Enter your name in the upper left-hand corner (Fig. 3) and head each page with the species name, entering below your observations by locality, date, and time of day. Group together pages pertaining to each species. In addition to the species account, keep a journal. Describe the route traveled and general features of terrain, vegetation, and weather. When an animal is found, watch it for a time from a distance if possible. Field glasses will help. Describe the ground surface (sand, hardpan, rock), vegetation (grassland, chaparral, or forest — listing species of plants if possible), temperature, and moisture conditions. Note other animals present. Try to interpret what you see.

If you can visit the locality frequently, you can carry out an extended study of the species that live there. Individuals of a species can be marked, measured, sexed, and released at points of capture. Map the area, using as reference points rock outcrops, trees, and other natural features, or numbered stakes set out in a grid. Movements of individuals, their interrelationships, activity patterns, growth rate, and other facts can be ascertained.

Procedures for marking individuals under study must be undertaken with care so as not to reduce the chances of survival of the marked animals. Consult an experienced professional herpetologist before embarking on such studies. Each marked animal should be given a number in the field notebook and the date and place of captures, sex, and size (snout-vent length) recorded. Locations of captures should be plotted on the map of the study area. Such field studies are recommended rather than the amassing of large numbers of hapless captives. The animals remain little disturbed in their natural setting. Since they are recognizable as individuals and under study, they appeal in much the same way as one's pets, yet do not demand care. Information obtained is more likely to be reliable than that procured under artificial conditions, and there is always the excitement of the hunt and the anticipation of meeting an old friend.

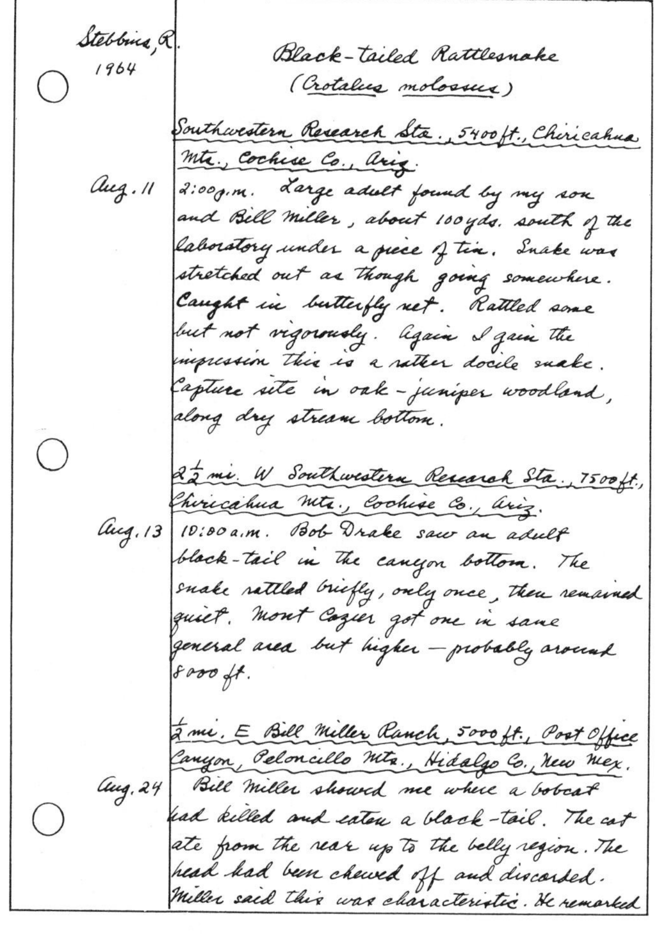

Stebbins, R.
1964

Black-tailed Rattlesnake
(Crotalus molossus)

Southwestern Research Sta., 5400 ft., Chiricahua Mts., Cochise Co., Ariz.

Aug. 11 2:00 p.m. Large adult found by my son and Bill Miller, about 100 yds. south of the laboratory under a piece of tin. Snake was stretched out as though going somewhere. Caught in butterfly net. Rattled some but not vigorously. Again I gain the impression this is a rather docile snake. Capture site in oak-juniper woodland, along dry stream bottom.

2½ mi. W Southwestern Research Sta., 7500 ft., Chiricahua Mts., Cochise Co., Ariz.

Aug. 13 10:00 a.m. Bob Drake saw an adult black-tail in the canyon bottom. The snake rattled briefly, only once, then remained quiet. Mont Cazier got one in same general area but higher—probably around 8000 ft.

½ mi. E Bill Miller Ranch, 5000 ft., Post Office Canyon, Peloncillo Mts., Hidalgo Co., New Mex.

Aug. 24 Bill Miller showed me where a bobcat had killed and eaten a black-tail. The cat ate from the rear up to the belly region. The head had been chewed off and discarded. Miller said this was characteristic. He remarked

Fig. 3. Sample page from field notebook

Protection: Reptiles and amphibians are important to us in many ways. They play a part in the balance of nature; they are a storehouse of unexplored scientific information that can benefit us; they have contributed enormously to the advance of vertebrate physiology and embryology, and they enhance the outdoor experiences of a growing number of people who gain pleasure from observing them. Yet at a time of growing awareness of their value, their numbers are declining. The greatest destructive force is habitat disturbance. Most species of wild animals are adapted to a specific and complex set of conditions which must be met if they are to survive. Growth of the human population brings great and rapid changes. Marshes are drained, streams are placed in concrete troughs, canyons are dammed and inundated, the ground is cleared for subdivisions and highways, agriculture spreads into marginal lands and, spurred on by water developments, reaches out even into deserts, the stronghold of reptiles. Air, water, and soil are contaminated. Although a few species may be temporarily benefited by some of these changes, most are not and the list of creatures rendered extinct in historic times can be expected to grow. The trend is toward an ordered, domesticated world, reduced in organic variety and crowded with people and their possessions. Interest in wildlife preservation and the well-being of humanity cannot be separated from concern with efforts to limit human population growth and prevent careless exploitation of remaining natural areas. Our western amphibians and reptiles that are listed as "Threatened" or "Endangered" by the Federal Government are identified as such in the species accounts. These species must not be collected without special permits.

Throughout this book I have given particular attention to methods of collecting, because it is often necessary to have the animals in hand for identification. This information can be misused. Some populations of reptiles and amphibians have been severely damaged by overcollecting and by disruption of habitat. Commercial traffic in reptiles and amphibians has sometimes been damaging and increases the probability of the establishment of exotics, to the detriment of native species. Amateur trading of live specimens has a similar effect. This practice and the development of private collections should, in general, be discouraged. Establishment of study collections is better left to educational and scientific institutions. The number of animals kept as pets should be small, and when they are released they should be returned to their area of origin or given to a scientific institution. In obtaining specimens, treat the habitat with special care. Replace rocks, logs, and other objects turned over in the search, to minimize disturbance to the microenvironment and in consideration of people who will follow. Some populations are so small that they should not be collected at all. Many of the isolated populations represented on the maps by a black dot are examples.

5

Identification Keys

The four keys in this chapter are designed to help you locate the plates illustrating the species. All major groups of reptiles and amphibians are included except the turtles — they are easily recognized and there are few western species (see Plates 17, 18, and 19). Baja California "endemics" (see p. 235) are also excluded. They can readily be identified by consulting Plates 46, 47, and 48.

To aid recognition, species have been grouped by means of easily observed characteristics, sometimes without regard for taxonomic relationships. For example, the kingsnakes, Long-nosed Snake, and coral snakes are grouped because they are banded; the Brown Vine, hook-nosed, leaf-nosed, and Western Hognose Snakes because they have modified snouts. Those interested in taxonomic relationships will find such information in the text.

At each step in a key a choice must be made between two alternatives. To illustrate: in the salamander key below, decide first whether or not the animal has a nasolabial groove (furrow between the nostril and edge of lip), alternatives 1A and 1B. Examine also its teeth and skin. If 1A is selected, go to alternatives 3A and 3B, where again a choice must be made. If 1B is chosen, go to 2A or 2B, thence to the plates.

Drawings illustrating key characteristics accompany each key. Numbers in parentheses in the keys refer to the numbered parts of each drawing; the right-hand column leads to the next step in the key or else to the identification plate(s). Consult also the illustrations on the endpapers of the book for types and locations of scales and other structural characteristics.

SALAMANDERS

Salamanders are lizardlike but lack scales and claws and have a moist, soft skin. See Fig. 4 for numbers in parentheses.

1A.	Nasolabial groove present (1); clusters of teeth at back of roof of mouth (2); skin always smooth **Lungless Salamanders**	see 3
1B.	Nasolabial groove and tooth clusters absent; skin smooth or rough	see 2

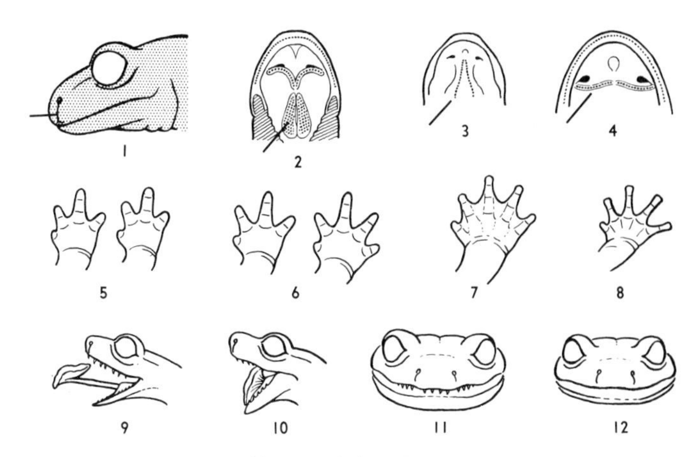

Fig. 4. Characteristics of salamanders

2A.	Teeth in roof of mouth in 2 diverging lengthwise rows (3); skin rough, except in breeding males	**Newts**	**Pl. 1**
2B.	Teeth in roof of mouth in transverse row (4); skin smooth	**Mole, Giant, and Olympic Salamanders**	**Pls. 1, 2**
3A.	Tail constricted at base	**Ensatina**	**Pls. 3, 4**
3B.	Tail not constricted at base		see 4
4A.	Four toes on both front and hind feet (5); often wormlike	**Slender Salamanders**	**Pls. 6–9**
4B.	Four toes on front feet, 5 on hind feet (6); never wormlike		see 5
5A.	Toes short and webbed (7); tongue unattached in front, edges free all around (9)	**Web-toed Salamanders**	**Pl. 6**
5B.	Toes relatively longer than in 5A, with little or no web (6); tongue attached in front (10)		see 6
6A.	Adults often with protruding upper jaw teeth — felt by stroking tip of salamander's snout from below, while holding its mouth closed (11); toes often with squarish tips (8); no stripe on back	**Climbing Salamanders**	**Pls. 6, 7**
6B.	Teeth rarely protrude (12); toe tips round (6); back stripe usually present	**Woodland Salamanders**	**Pl. 5**

FROGS AND TOADS

See Fig. 5 for numbers in parentheses.

1A. Eyes without lids; black claws on hind toes **African Clawed Frog Fig. 14 (opp. Pl. 14)**
1B. Eyes with lids; no claws on toes see 2

2A. 5th toe of hind foot broader than other toes (1) **Tailed Frog Pl. 16**
2B. 5th toe not broadened (2) see 3

3A. Fold of skin across head behind eyes (8) see 4
3B. No skin fold on head see 6

4A. Small brown or gray toad, adult body length under $1\frac{1}{2}$ in.; small black eyes; extreme s. Ariz.
Great Plains Narrow-mouthed Toad Pl. 16
4B. Adults larger than in 4A, eyes not small and black see 5

5A. Eardrum conspicuous, partly transparent; many tubercles on underside of toes (4); back blotched **Barking Frog Pl. 12**
5B. Eardrum not transparent; toes without tubercles; back has large spots with definite borders **Northern Casque-headed Frog Pl. 16**

6A. Parotoid glands present (9) **True Toads Pls. 10–12**
6B. Parotoid glands absent see 7

7A. Single sharp-edged black "spade" on underside of hind foot (5); eye with vertical pupil — except when pupil is greatly dilated (11) **Spadefoot Toads Pl. 10**
7B. No sharp-edged black "spade" on hind foot; rounded pale or brownish tubercle(s) sometimes present on hind foot; pupil not vertical (12) see 8

8A. Extra joint at tips of toes (6); toe pads often present (3); no dorsolateral folds
Treefrogs and Allies Pl. 16
8B. No extra joint at tip of toes (7); no toe pads; dorsolateral folds often present (10)
True Frogs Pls. 13–15

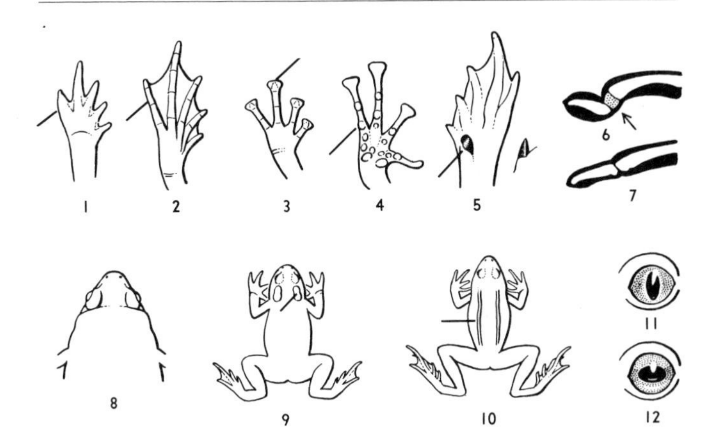

Fig. 5. Characteristics of frogs and toads

LIZARDS

All have scales and (with the exception of the snakelike legless lizards) clawed toes; movable eyelids distinguish the latter from the snakes. See Fig. 6 for numbers in parentheses.

1A.	Eye with a fixed transparent covering; no movable eyelids		see 2
1B.	Movable eyelids present		see 3
2A.	Tips of toes very broad, with pair of large flat scales (1)	**Leaf-toed Geckos**	**Pls. 35, 47**
2B.	Toe tips not broadened	**Night Lizards**	**Pl. 30**
3A.	Large, pale yellow catlike eyes with vertical pupil	**Banded and Barefoot Geckos**	**Pl. 35**
3B.	Eyes not unusually large and pupil round or not easily seen (eyes dark)		see 4
4A.	Snakelike, legless, but tiny eyes with movable lids	**Legless Lizards**	**Pls. 34, 47**
4B.	Limbs present		see 5

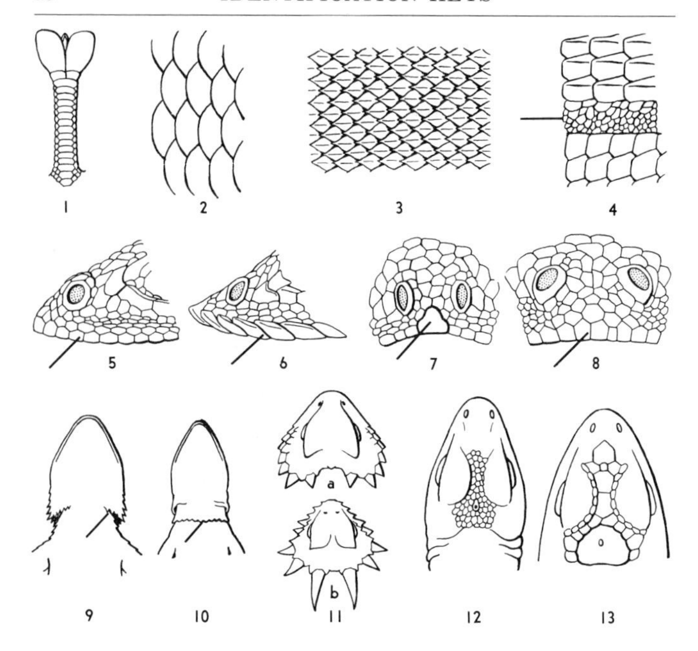

Fig. 6. Characteristics of lizards

5A. Scales cycloid, very smooth and shiny all over body (2) **Skinks** **Pl. 28**
5B. Scales not cycloid all over body see 6

6A. Horns at back of head (11a, 11b); usually 1 or 2 rows of enlarged fringe scales at sides of body **Horned Lizards** **Pl. 21**
6B. No horns or fringe scales see 7

7A. A fold on side of body, separating large squarish scales on back and belly (4) **Alligator Lizards** **Pl. 29**
7B. No fold on side of body separating squarish back and belly scales see 8

8A. Fourth and 5th toes about same length; tail stout, much shorter than body, often sausage-shaped **Gila Monster** **Pl. 20**

8B. Fourth toe much longer than 5th; tail as long or longer than body, not swollen see 9

9A. Great difference between back and belly scales — those on back fine and granular, those on belly many times larger and arranged in straight transverse and lengthwise rows **Whiptails** **Pls. 31-34, 46**

9B. Black and belly scales not greatly different in size — those on belly usually overlap like shingles see 10

10A. A single enlarged row of scales down middle of back, extended as spines on neck in Spiny-tailed Iguana **Desert and Spiny-tailed Iguanas** **Pls. 24, 47**

10B. No enlarged row of scales down middle of back see 11

11A. Rostral absent (8) **Chuckwalla** **Pl. 20**

11B. Rostral present (7) see 12

12A. All scales on back keeled and pointed (3); an incomplete gular fold (9) **Spiny Lizards** **Pls. 26, 27, 46**

12B. Some or all scales on back granular, if keeled often not pointed; complete gular fold (10) see 13

13A. Labials separated by diagonal furrows (6); usually with distinct black crossbars or spots on underside of tail **Zebra-tailed, Earless, and Fringe-toed Lizards** **Pls. 22, 23**

13B. Labials separated by vertical furrows (5); underside of tail without black crossbars see 14

14A. Scales on top of head between and behind eyes small (12) **Leopard and Collared Lizards** **Pl. 24**

14B. Scales on top of head between and behind eyes variously enlarged (13) **Side-blotched, Tree, Brush, and Rock Lizards** **Pls. 25, 46, 47**

SNAKES

All are legless and lack eyelids; our legless lizards have movable eyelids and small ventral scales. See Fig. 7 for numbers in parentheses.

1A. Cycloid scales completely encircling body (1); no large ventrals (belly scales); eyes pigmented spots under head scales **Blind Snakes** **Pl. 36**

1B. Belly scales (2) more than twice as broad as those on back and sides; eyes well developed see 2

2A. Tail with rattle (3) **Rattlesnakes** **Pls. 44, 45, 48**

2B. Tail without rattle see 3

3A. Only small scales on underside of lower jaw between labials (4) **Boas** **Pl. 36**

3B. Large scales on underside of lower jaw between labials (5) see 4

4A. Rostral modified — much enlarged, turned up, and pointed (6a), or flat and attached patchlike to tip of snout (6b, 6c) **Hognose, Hook-nosed, Patch-nosed, and Leaf-nosed Snakes** **Pl. 40**

4B. Rostral normal, not greatly enlarged or shaped as in 4A see 5

5A. Dorsal (back) scales smooth see 9

5B. Some or all dorsal scales keeled see 6

6A. Scales weakly keeled along middle of back only, becoming smooth on sides **Rat Snakes** **Pls. 38, 48**

6B. All dorsal scales keeled see 7

7A. Usually 4 prefrontals (8) **Gopher Snake** **Pl. 39**

7B. 2 prefrontals (6b) see 8

8A. Anal single; no scale pits **Garter and Lined Snakes** **Pls. 41–43, 48**

8B. Anal divided; scale pits present; in our area found only in e. Colorado, se. New Mexico, and Baja Calif. **Water Snakes** **Pls. 43, 48**

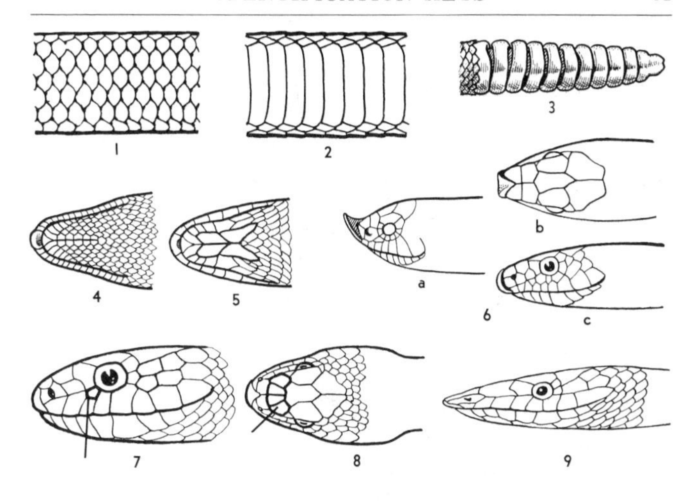

Fig. 7. Characteristics of snakes

9A.	Plain green above (gray in preservative) and plain white or pale yellow below		see 10
9B.	Not colored as in 9A		see 11
10A.	Lower preocular wedged between upper labials (7)	**Racer**	**Pl. 36**
10B.	Lower preocular not wedged between upper labials	**Smooth Green Snake**	**Pl. 39**
11A.	Lower preocular wedged between upper labials (7)	**Racers and Whipsnakes**	**Pls. 36, 48**
11B.	Lower preocular not wedged between upper labials		see 12
12A.	Extremely slender, vinelike; head and snout very long (9)	**Brown Vine Snake**	**Pl. 40**
12B.	Not vinelike; head not extremely long		see 13
13A.	All ventral scales marked with regular narrow black crossbands, a band at base of each scale; tail with sharp point	**Sharp-tailed Snake**	**Pl. 39**

13B. All ventrals not uniformly marked with black crossbands; markings, when present, more widely spaced, confined to sides, or in less regular arrangement; tail with or without sharp point — see 14

14A. Plain-colored, without pattern on dorsum (back). Uniformly colored head cap, often darker than body and sometimes set off from body color by whitish, yellow, or orange collar
Ringneck and Black-headed Snakes **Pls. 37, 41**

14B. Body with dorsal pattern of spots, blotches, crossbands, or stripes — see 15

15A. Belly pale and plain-colored or with dusky bars, scattered dots or fine speckling, usually confined to sides — see 16

15B. Belly marked with bold crossbands or bars or sometimes plain black with pale spots
Coral, Long-nosed, and Kingsnakes **Pl. 37**
Ground, Shovel-nosed, and Sand Snakes **Pl. 38**

16A. Dorsal scales in 17 or fewer rows at mid-body — see 17

16B. Dorsal scales in more than 17 rows — see 18

17A. Dorsal pattern of spots; vertical pupils
Night Snake **Pl. 39**

17B. Dorsal surface plain or with pattern of crossbands or a broad lengthwise stripe; pupils round or not visible
Ground, Shovel-nosed, and Sand Snakes **Pls. 38, 48**

18A. Head much broader than neck, usually with lyre-shaped marking; pupils vertical
Lyre Snake **Pl. 39**

18B. Head only slightly broader than neck, no lyre-shaped marking; pupils not distinctly vertical
Glossy Snake **Pl. 39**

6

Salamanders

Mole Salamanders and Relatives: Families Ambystomatidae and Dicamptodontidae

Mole salamanders (ambystomatids) vary greatly in size, proportions, and coloration but can be distinguished from all other western species by their teeth, which form a continuous or broken row across the roof of the mouth (Fig. 4, No. 4, p. 25). Typically they have a broad head, small eyes, prominent costal grooves, and a tail that is flattened from side to side. Males usually have a bulbous vent and a longer tail than females. Mole salamanders are usually seldom seen except during their brief breeding season. Then they crawl over land to ponds, lakes, and streams and sometimes stumble into cellars or light wells. Migrations usually occur at night, during or after rains.

Most species breed in winter or spring but, depending on locality, the wide-ranging Tiger Salamander may be found breeding throughout most of the year. Breeding may start early, soon after ice melts from lakes and ponds, but at high altitudes and in the north it may be delayed until summer. Throughout the rest of the year, except occasionally during rains, these salamanders stay inside rotten logs and animal burrows, or in other moist places underground.

Larvae may be found all year. At high elevations and in the north, where temperatures are low and the growing season short, they may not transform until their second or third season. Some larvae (neotenics) may fail to transform and may breed in the larval condition.

To find ambystomatids, go out at night, during or shortly after the first hard rain at the start of the breeding season, and drive slowly or walk through favorable habitats. Carry a lantern or some other kind of light that will illuminate a large area. Seine the water of breeding ponds with a dip net, or look under objects in moist places on land.

The ambystomatids are a New World family ranging from se. Alaska and s. Labrador to the southern part of the Mexican Plateau. Around 30 species — 3 in the West, and the rest in the East and Mexico.

The dicamptodontids (3 species) include our largest and smallest highly aquatic salamanders, the Pacific and Cope Giant Salamanders and the Olympic Salamander (see Pl. 1). They inhabit cold streams, lay their unpigmented eggs in concealed aquatic sites, and are found in or near water throughout the year.

Mole Salamanders: Family Ambystomatidae

TIGER SALAMANDER *Ambystoma tigrinum* **Pl. 2**
Identification: 3–6½ in. (7.5–16.2 cm). A large, stocky salamander with *small eyes;* a broad, rounded snout; and *tubercles on the underside of the front and hind feet* (one on each side of rear undersurface). No parotoid glands. Color varies greatly, depending upon locality. Over much of its range (Calif., e. and s. U.S., and Mexico) markings consist of spots and bars of white, cream, or yellow on a black background. Elsewhere the black ground color may be reduced to dusky spots or a more or less broken network of "tiger" markings. In the north-central part of its range, the dorsal ground color may be plain olive or yellowish (Fig. 10, opp. Pl. 2).

Frequents quiet water of ponds, reservoirs, lakes, temporary rain pools, and streams, from arid sagebrush plains and rolling grassland to mountain meadows and forests. Found in subtropical environments in se. U.S. and Mexico. Adults found under objects near water or crawling at night to and from breeding sites. Migrations generally occur during or shortly after rains, in cold areas soon after the ice begins to melt from ponds. Adults spend much time underground, in the burrows of ground squirrels, gophers, and badgers, and usually emerge only for brief periods to breed. Breeds spring to fall on the eastern plains and in parts of the Rocky Mts., spring and summer in the arid Southwest during periods of rainfall, fall through spring during mild winters in N.M., and chiefly from Dec. to Feb. in cen. Calif. In cold areas larvae may overwinter and are sometimes neotenic. Neotenics, known as **axolotls** (a Mexican Indian name), reach a total length of 7–15 in. (17.5–37 cm).
Similar species: (1) Northwestern Salamander (p. 36) has parotoid glands, a glandular ridge on the tail, and lacks foot tubercles. (2) Black Salamander (p. 50) has a more rounded tail and projecting upper-jaw teeth, felt by stroking tip of snout.
Range: Eastern to western coasts of N. America; s. Canada to Puebla, Mexico. Absent from most of Great Basin, most of Pacific Coast, Mojave and Colorado Deserts, Appalachian region, and s. Fla. Old records along Columbia R. in Klickitat Co., Wash. and Wasco Co., Ore. need verification. Near sea level to around 12,000 ft. (3660 m) in Rocky Mts. **Map 5**
Subspecies: BLOTCHED TIGER SALAMANDER, *A. t. mela-*

nostictum (Fig. 10). Irregular whitish, yellow to dark olive spots, bars, or network on dark dorsum (upper body); pattern more contrasting on sides and markings lighter and smaller in young adults. Markings often have indefinite borders. Some individuals nearly patternless, having only a few black spots. Colorado animals have black spots, separate or variously joined on ground color of dark olive, dark gray, to dark cream; spots are often surrounded by bronze flecking, producing lichenlike markings. In Mont., barred individuals occur on the plains, mottled to green ones in the mountains. An isolated occurrence in Moon Reservoir area, Harney Co., Ore., where it may have been introduced. Neoteny frequent. GRAY TIGER SALAMANDER, *A. t. diaboli* (Fig. 10). Above with small, circular dark brown to black spots on a gold, light olive, olive green, to dark brown ground color; 26–178 spots (avg. 71) between fore- and hind limbs. Spots may tend to unite, forming short reticulations. Neoteny frequent; axolotls reach total length of 15 in. (37 cm). BARRED TIGER SALAMANDER, *A. t. mavortium* (Pl. 2). Black above, with bright yellow to olive vertical bars or large spots, 6–36 (avg. 17) between fore- and hind limbs. Ground color often suffused with pale green or olive in recently transformed individuals. Neoteny occasional; axolotls to around 12 in. (30 cm) in total length. Cannibalistic larvae at some localities. CALIFORNIA TIGER SALAMANDER, *A. t. californiense* (Pl. 2). Black above, with large, pale yellow spots that are often scarce or absent along middle of back. Individuals from s. coastal Calif. may have few spots and a prominent cream band on lower sides. Breeds in temporary rain pools and permanent waters of grassland and open woodland of low hills and valleys. Agriculture and urban developments have eliminated this salamander from much of its former range in the Central Valley of Calif. Extends south in coastal Calif. to Santa Rita Hills. ARIZONA TIGER SALAMANDER, *A. t. nebulosum* (Fig. 10). Above with yellow to dark olive spots and blotches that often have irregular edges, 11–50 (avg. 32) between fore- and hind limbs. Individuals from nw. N.M. may be dull olive with yellow mottling or spots. Those from Colo. may be uniformly dark gray or dark brown above, or may have a network of black spots or intermingling of shades of brown on a dark background. They tend to be larger and stouter-bodied than the members of other subspecies in Colo. Some individuals have *diaboli*-like coloration — gold or olive with round black spots — and coexist with individuals of *A. t. nebulosum* at higher elevations; others, with *mavortium*-like pattern, occur at Fraser, Grand Co. The subspecies *nebulosum* was based on populations on the central Colorado Plateau. Other subspecies, or zones of intergradation, may exist in adjacent areas. For example, the subspecies *A. t. utahensis,* not recognized in this book, was described north of the Plateau in Utah. More specimens are needed from this complex part of the range.

Remarks: Descriptions and distributions of Tiger Salamander subspecies are uncertain because of lack of adequate numbers of living transformed adults available for study. Old adults of all subspecies tend to darken and develop a less distinct pattern, making subspecies recognition difficult.

Extensive use of live Tiger Salamander larvae as fish bait and expanding irrigation in arid lands has resulted in introductions of this species outside its natural range and in mixing of natural populations. Tiger Salamanders in southern Ariz., including all populations south of the Salt and Gila Rivers, appear to have been introduced. These populations, and others, include the Barred and Arizona Tiger Salamanders. Larvae have been found in many reservoirs in Calif., along the Colorado R., in the vicinity of Las Vegas, Nev., and elsewhere in the Southwest. It is unknown whether the populations at Worden, Klamath Co., Ore. and near Boise and Caldwell in sw. Idaho are natural or introduced.

An isolated, evidently natural, population occurs at Grass Lake, Siskiyou Co., Calif. Perhaps populations in the Huachuca Mts. (Parker and Scotia Canyons) and Patagonia Mts., Ariz. are also natural. One of them in the Huachuca Mts. has been called the subspecies *stebbinsi.*

NORTHWESTERN SALAMANDER **Pl. 2**

Ambystoma gracile

Identification: 3–4½ in. (7.5–11.2 cm). A brown, gray, or black salamander with a broad head and relatively small eyes, *parotoid glands,* and a *glandular thickening* along the upper border of the tail. The glandular areas are pitted with openings of poison glands and the skin there is rougher than elsewhere. No tubercles on underside of feet. In northern part of range, back flecked with cream or yellow.

Inhabits open grassland, woodland, or forest where it is found by day under rocks, boards, and logs near water. Look under driftwood on streambanks after storms, when water is receding. Spawns in ponds, lakes, and streams Jan.–Aug., later in the season in the north and at high elevations. In cold areas larvae may overwinter and some may be neotenic. When molested, adults close their eyes, assume a butting pose, elevate the tail, and secrete a sticky white poison from the glands on the head, back, and tail. This secretion may cause skin irritation in some people.

Similar species: See Tiger Salamander (above).

Range: Humid coast from extreme se. Alaska, chiefly west of crest of Cascade Mts. to mouth of Gualala R., Calif. Sea level to around 10,200 ft. (3110 m). **Map 2**

Subspecies: BROWN SALAMANDER, *A. g. gracile.* Plain brown above, often with touches of rust on head and tail. 2 joints in 4th toe of hind foot. BRITISH COLUMBIA SALAMANDER, *A. g. decorticatum.* Light flecks on dorsal surfaces. 3 joints in 4th toe.

LONG-TOED SALAMANDER **Pl. 2**
Ambystoma macrodactylum
Identification: $2\frac{1}{8}$–$3\frac{1}{4}$ in. (5–8.1 cm). A dusky or black salamander usually with a *dorsal stripe* of tan, yellow, or olive-green. Stripe often with irregular borders and in some subspecies more or less broken into a series of spots. Usually a sprinkling of fine white flecks on the sides. Belly dark brown or sooty. Foot tubercles as in the Tiger Salamander (p. 34), but they are sometimes weakly developed.

Frequents a great variety of habitats, from the semiarid sagebrush and cheatgrass plains east of the Cascade Mts. to alpine meadows and the barren rocky shores of high mountain lakes. Found in piles of rotten wood, under bark, rotting logs, rocks, and other objects near quiet water of ponds, lakes, or streams. When in the water, adults seem to prefer shallows near shore.

Breeds early, sometimes entering ponds not yet free of ice. The time depends on elevation and latitude. In the lowlands to the south breeding occurs in late Jan. or Feb. and in the mountains, or in the far north, from April to July. In cold areas larvae may overwinter, transforming the following summer or fall. In warmer areas, as in the lowlands of the Willamette Valley, Ore., adults migrate to breeding ponds in late Oct. and early Nov. with the onset of fall rains and, except for cold spells, remain active all winter.

Similar species: Striped woodland salamanders have nasolabial grooves (Fig. 4, No. 1, p. 25), a different tooth pattern, and no foot tubercles.

Range: Se. Alaska and Telegraph Creek, B.C. to Spicer Reservoir, Tuolumne Co., Calif., east to Rocky Mts., south to cen. Idaho and w. Mont. Isolated populations near Aptos, Santa Cruz Co., Calif. Near sea level to about 10,000 ft. (3000 m) in Sierra Nevada, Calif. **Map 3**

Subspecies: WESTERN LONG-TOED SALAMANDER, *A. m. macrodactylum* (Pl. 2). Gray above, with a greenish to yellowish dorsal stripe that has indefinite edges; stripe diffuse on head. Sides heavily sprinkled with small white flecks, sometimes appearing whitewashed. CENTRAL LONG-TOED SALAMANDER, *A. m. columbianum.* Dorsal stripe bright yellow to tan, usually unbroken on body, even-edged or irregularly indented, its width exceeding distance between nostrils. Stripe broken into spots on head. SOUTHERN LONG-TOED SALAMANDER, *A. m. sigillatum* (Pl. 2). Dorsal stripe bright yellow, with irregular borders and often broken into smooth-edged spots; its greatest width less than distance between nostrils. Small, distinct yellow spots on head. SANTA CRUZ LONG-TOED SALAMANDER, *A. m. croceum* (Pl. 2). **Endangered.** Similar to Southern Long-toed Salamander, but stripe yellow-orange and ground color of back darker, usually black. Valencia Lagoon near Aptos, Ellicott Pond area near Watsonville (a State Wildlife Reserve), Santa Cruz Co., and north of Elkhorn Slough, Monterey Co., Calif. EASTERN LONG-TOED SALAMANDER, *A. m. krausei* (Pl. 2). Dorsal stripe narrow, its edges nearly parallel; stripe yellow and unbroken, continuing onto snout and widest behind eyes. A large patch of stripe color on each eyelid.

Dicamptodontids: Family Dicamptodontidae

PACIFIC GIANT SALAMANDER — Pl. 1

Dicamptodon ensatus

Identification: 2½–6⅘ in. (6.2–17 cm). A large, formidable-looking salamander with a massive head and often marbled coloration. Skin smooth and costal grooves inconspicuous. 2 joints in 4th toe of hind foot. No foot tubercles. Dark brown to almost black above, with a *network of irregular spots* or marbling of tan, copper, gray, or purplish. Ground color darkens in northern populations, and marbling becomes especially fine-grained in Rocky Mts. of Idaho. Rocky Mt. populations are considered by some taxonomists to be a distinct species, *D. aterrimus*.

Frequents damp forests in or near clear, cold streams or seepages and the rocky shores of mountain lakes. Found under logs, bark, rocks, and other objects near streams, or crawling exposed in damp woods, even in daytime. Occasionally climbs, and has been recorded in trees and shrubs to a height of 8 ft. (2.4 m). In spring, adults may be found near springs in the headwaters of streams, where they lay their eggs. Breeding occurs in both spring and fall. Handle large individuals with care — their bite can lacerate the skin. Larvae frequent clear cold rivers, creeks, and lakes, and can be found by carefully turning over stones in shallow water or searching the bottom and plant debris, especially along the downstream border of shallow pools. In the south larvae hatch in winter, but may not transform until their second or third summer. Neotenic individuals may reach a total length of 14 in. (35 cm).

Voice: May emit a low-pitched, rattling sound when molested.

Similar species: (1) Mole salamanders (*Ambystoma* species, p. 33) lack pattern of tan or gray to purplish marbling on dark brown ground color. (2) See also Cope Giant Salamander (below).

Range: Extreme sw. B.C. to Santa Cruz Co., Calif. Inland in n. Calif. to headwaters of Sacramento R. Rocky Mts. of extreme w. Mont. and Idaho, where it is found in headwater streams from the Salmon R. to the Coeur d'Alene drainage. Reliable sight record for Little Sur R., Monterey Co., Calif. Near sea level to around 7000 ft. (2160 m). **Map 1**

COPE GIANT SALAMANDER — not shown

Dicamptodon copei

Identification: 2½–4¾ in. (6.2–11.9 cm). A "larval" species that apparently rarely transforms. The larval form resembles the larva of the Pacific Giant Salamander (p. 38) but is slimmer and does not reach such a large size. Head smaller and narrower. *0–2½ costal folds between toes of adpressed limbs.* Tail fins lower and shorter, the dorsal fin usually not reaching area above vent. Fins with less dark mottling, eyestripe faint or missing, and belly darker (at sizes greater than 2 in. — 5 cm). A transformed individual found at Spirit Lake, Wash., was sooty with no pattern above and dark gray below, with faint mottling on lower sides.

Found in cold streams, seepages, and sometimes in mountain lakes and ponds, usually in moist coniferous forests. This salamander coexists with larval Pacific Giant Salamanders and was long considered a variant of that species. Where the two species share habitat, they can usually be distinguished by the size of the breeding larvae (females with enlarging ova) at sexual maturity: a breeding female Pacific Giant Salamander usually measures at least 4⅗ in. (11.5 cm) from snout to vent (SV); a female Cope Giant Salamander, 2⅘–4⅕ in. (7–10.5 cm) SV. The Cope Giant Salamander apparently lays its eggs throughout spring, summer and fall; females guard their eggs.

Similar species: The toes of adpressed limbs of large Pacific Giant Salamander larvae usually overlap by as much as 4 costal folds.

Range: Olympic Peninsula, Wash., south through the southern Cascades and Willapa Hills to streams that drain into the Columbia R. Gorge in nw. Ore. Near sea level to around 4500 ft. (1370 m). **Map 1**

Remarks: The eruption of Mt. St. Helens in 1980 eliminated some habitat and buried the lower portion of Maratta Creek, the type locality for this species.

OLYMPIC SALAMANDER *Rhyacotriton olympicus* **Pl. 1**

Identification: 1⅔–2½ in. (4.1–6.2 cm). *Small size and large eyes* are distinctive among our aquatic and semiaquatic salamanders. The diameter of the eye opening roughly equals the distance between the front corner of the eye and the tip of the snout. In other salamanders except the slender salamanders (*Batrachoseps* species, p. 52), eye diameter is only ½–⅓ this distance. Head small, body long, limbs and tail short. Plain brown above, or olive mottled with dusky. Orange or yellow below. ***Male:*** Prominent, *squarish vent lobes.*

Inhabits cold streams, springs, and seepages in the Douglas fir-redwood belt of the humid coast. When on land, usually found under stones within the splash zone, and in moss-covered talus where water trickles among the rocks. Streams frequented are usually well shaded, the banks often grown to moss and ferns. In coastal Ore., most breeding occurs in spring and early summer with a lesser peak in fall and winter. Larvae have short gills and adult

proportions and live in clear shallow water, in the muck of seepages, and in accumulations of dead leaves in creeks. They are slow to metamorphose, perhaps requiring over 3 years to do so.
Range: Coastal areas from Olympic Peninsula, Wash. to vicinity of Point Arena, Mendocino Co., Calif. Inland populations west of Cascade crest from vicinity of Kosmos, Lewis Co., Wash. to upper Umpqua R. drainage, Douglas Co., Ore. **Map 4**
Subspecies: NORTHERN OLYMPIC SALAMANDER, *R. o. olympicus* (Pl. 1). Plain brown above, speckled on sides with white. Yellow-orange below, sparsely flecked with black. SOUTHERN OLYMPIC SALAMANDER, *R. o. variegatus* (Pl. 1). Olive above, mottled with dusky. Yellowish green below, heavily spotted with black.

Newts: Family Salamandridae

In North America this family is represented by the Pacific and eastern newts, with 3 species in each genus. Pacific newts range from Alaska to s. Calif.; eastern newts are found chiefly east of the Great Plains. The family is also represented in Europe, North Africa, and Asia, where they are the dominant salamanders. About 45 species.

Pacific newts are plain brown or black above, and yellow, orange, or red below. During much of the year they are terrestrial and rough-skinned, but they must enter ponds and streams to breed. Breeding males develop a smooth skin and flattened tail. Eastern newts are more aquatic and change directly from the larval stage into water-dwelling adults or into rough-skinned, round-tailed red efts that live on land for a while and then return to water.

Pacific Newts: Genus *Taricha*

Readily distinguished from all other western salamanders by their distinctive tooth pattern (Fig. 8, opposite), lack of costal grooves, and rough skin (except in breeding males). The latter have a smooth skin, flattened tail, swollen vent, and dark patches of roughened skin (nuptial pads) on the underside of the feet (Fig. 8).

Newts are familiar salamanders on the Pacific Coast. They are less disturbed by light than other species and are often seen crawling over land in the daytime or moving about fully exposed on the bottom of ponds, lakes, and streams. Their potent skin secretion repels most predators.

The poisonous properties of newts are not confined to their skin secretions but are widespread throughout the body and can cause death in most vertebrates, including man, if newt tissue is eaten in sufficient quantity. Newts can be handled without danger, but

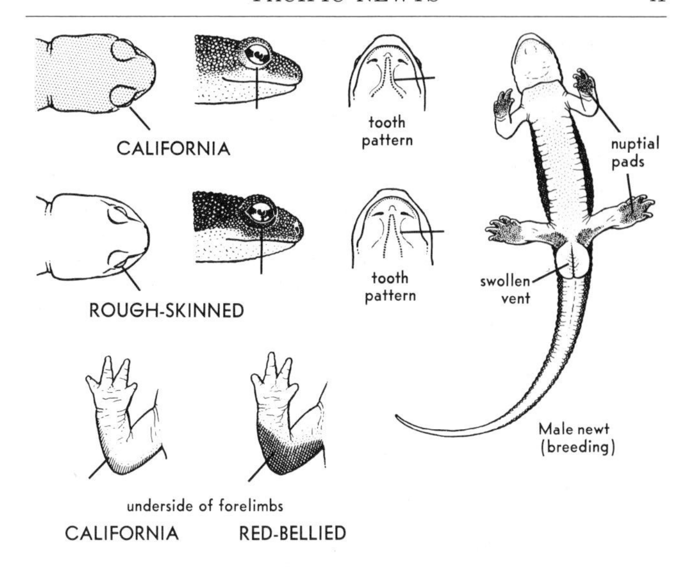

Fig. 8. Characteristics of newts

wash your hands after doing so. When a newt is slapped on the back or seized, it assumes a characteristic sway-backed defense pose with the eyes closed, head and tail bent upward, limbs extended, and toes flexed. This brings the bright color of the ventral surface into view and probably serves as a warning to potential predators.

During or after rains in fall, winter, and spring (except during cold weather), newts are often seen moving in large numbers to their aquatic breeding sites. Larvae transform at the end of their first or second summer. Terrestrial newts spend the summer under bark, inside decayed logs, in rock crevices, and in the burrows of other animals.

ROUGH-SKINNED NEWT **Fig. 8**

Taricha granulosa

Identification: $2\frac{1}{4}$–$3\frac{1}{2}$ in. (5.6–8.7 cm). Note the *dark lower eyelids.* Black to dark brown above, sometimes tan. Yellow to reddish orange below. Dark color of the back stops abruptly on the sides or blends into the belly color. Eyes relatively small, usually not extending to outline of head when viewed from above. Teeth in roof of mouth in V-shaped arrangement. ***Breeding male:*** Brown to olive above, with a broad dusky patch on each side, smooth skin, bulbous vent, flattened tail, and dark skin on underside of feet.

Individuals at some localities have dark blotches on ventral surfaces. At Crater Lake, Ore., some are nearly all black below (basis for subspecies name Mazama Newt, *T. g. mazamae,* not recognized in this guide). Some individuals in the Siskiyou Mts., Calif., have dark blotches on both dorsal and ventral surfaces and some at Fay Lake, Linn Co., Ore., have dorsal blotches.

Frequents grassland, woodland, and forest. Breeds chiefly from late Dec. to July, in ponds, lakes, reservoirs, or slowly flowing streams. Our most aquatic newt. When on land, it may be found crawling in the open or hiding under rocks, logs, bark, and in rotten wood. The Rough-skinned Newt differs from other western newts in laying its eggs singly and, in some parts of its range, in curling the tip of its tail when in the extreme defense pose (see p. 41). Our most poisonous newt.

Similar species: (1) The California Newt (below) usually has light-colored lower eyelids, larger eyes, and teeth in a Y-shaped arrangement. However, in some areas some individuals defy identification even by experts. (2) Red-bellied Newt (p. 43) has dark eyes.

Range: Humid coast from se. Alaska to s. Santa Cruz Co., Calif., chiefly west of crest of Cascade Mts.; south in foothills of Sierra Nevada to Magalia, Butte Co., Calif. Populations near Moscow, Latah Co., Idaho may have been introduced. Sea level to around 9200 ft. (2800 m). **Map 6**

CALIFORNIA NEWT *Taricha torosa* **Pl. 1**

Identification: $2\frac{3}{4}$–$3\frac{1}{2}$ in. (6.9–8.7 cm). Similar to Rough-skinned Newt, but usually lighter brown above, with less contrast between the dorsal and ventral color on the sides. *Light-colored lower eyelids* (Fig. 8, p. 41); larger eyes, the corneal surfaces extending to or beyond outline of head when viewed from above; and teeth in roof of mouth usually in a Y-shaped arrangement. ***Breeding male:*** Smooth skin, bulbous vent, flattened tail, dark skin on underside of feet.

Habitat similar to Rough-skinned Newt's but generally less humid. Breeds in ponds, reservoirs, and slowly flowing streams. In the Sierra Nevada and in the mountains of s. Calif., it enters the larger rivers and streams where it may frequent fast water. Goes to water during the first fall rains, breeding Dec. to May, with a peak from Feb. to April. In the Sierra, migrations start in Jan. or Feb. and breeding lasts until the end of April.

Similar species: (1) Red-bellied Newt (below) has dark eyes. (2) See also Rough-skinned Newt (above).

Range: Coast Ranges of Calif. from Mendocino Co. to western slope of Peninsular Ranges in San Diego Co. (Boulder Creek) and western slope of Sierra Nevada south to Breckenridge Mt. and Mill Creek, Kern Co. Isolated population at Squaw Creek, Shasta Co., Calif. Near sea level to about 6500 ft. (2000 m). **Map 8**

Subspecies: COAST RANGE NEWT, *T. t. torosa.* As described above. Grotesquely warty individuals, known as the "Warty Newt," occur in the southern part of the range; wartiness reaches its most extreme form at Boulder Creek. The warts are apparently caused by disease. Coexists with the Rough-skinned Newt from Santa Cruz to Mendocino Cos. SIERRA NEWT, *T. t. sierrae.* More orange above and below than Coast Range Newt; eyes paler yellow.

RED-BELLIED NEWT *Taricha rivularis* **Pl. 1**
Identification: $2\frac{3}{4}$–$3\frac{1}{4}$ in. (5.9–8.1 cm). *A dark-eyed newt.* Eyes larger, head narrower, and snout longer than in other western species. Brown to nearly black above, tomato-red below. Dark color conspicuous on underside of limbs. *A prominent dark band across the vent,* especially broad in males. Less sex difference in skin texture than in other species.

A stream- or river-dwelling newt of coastal woodlands, entering water as early as the 1st week in Feb. and breeding from late Feb. to May in flowing water of rivers and creeks.
Similar species: (1) California and (2) Rough-skinned Newts (above) have yellow eyes and less dark color on the underside of the limbs (Fig. 8, p. 41).
Range: Coastal region of Calif. from Russian R. area, Sonoma Co., and Lower Lake and Kelsey Creek, Lake Co., north to Honeydew, Humboldt Co. Coexists with the Rough-skinned Newt but generally breeds in flowing water. **Map 9**

Lungless Salamanders: Family Plethodontidae

The largest family of salamanders, with around 225 species. Confined to the New World — s. Canada to n. Bolivia and e. Brazil — except for the web-toes (*Hydromantes* species), which are represented by 2 species in Europe and 3 in Calif. Most are terrestrial, living under rocks, bark, logs, in rotten wood and animal burrows, but in eastern N. America many species live in and near streams. Terrestrial forms rarely, if ever, enter water, and lay their eggs in moist places on land. These salamanders have no free-living larva; the young emerge fully formed. All western species are terrestrial.

All plethodontids are lungless. They breathe through their thin, moist skin, which is smooth and slippery. All have a nasolabial groove (Fig. 4, No. 1, p. 25) — a hairline furrow that extends from the nostril to the edge of the upper lip and sometimes out onto a lobe (or palp). Most have well-defined costal grooves and folds, which are sometimes useful in distinguishing species. When counting grooves, include the groove at the rear of the front limb (in the axilla), even if not well developed, and both parts of a pair of grooves that may join in the groin (see front endpapers). Tooth pattern is distinctive (Fig. 4, No. 2). The family name means "many teeth."

In North America, mating occurs in fall, winter, and spring. Eggs are usually deposited in spring and summer (some species of slender salamanders may lay their eggs in winter).

Woodland Salamanders: Genus *Plethodon*

Slim-bodied, short-legged salamanders, usually with a dorsal stripe of reddish, tan, or yellow. Some 25 species in the U.S. and Canada; 5 in the Pacific Northwest, 1 in northern N.M., and the rest in the East.

There are 4 toes on the front and 5 on the hind feet, the edges of the tongue are free except in front, the tail is round or oval with no constriction at the base, and the upper jaw teeth extend to the angle of the mouth. Males typically have a broader head, a more pointed lower jaw, and a longer tail than females. Costal-groove counts are useful in distinguishing species (see above).

These salamanders usually frequent damp woods, where they are found by day under bark, logs, moss, in moist leaf litter, rotten wood, rock outcrops, and talus. They are active on the surface at night, usually during or shortly after rains. Eggs are laid in moist concealed places on land.

DUNN SALAMANDER *Plethodon dunni* **Pl. 5**

Identification: 2–3 in. (5–7.5 cm). *Dorsal stripe tan, yellow, or greenish yellow,* brightening on the tail but *not reaching its tip.* Stripe flecked with dusky, the flecks sometimes nearly concealing it. Occasional melanistic individuals that are dark-colored and unstriped (Mary's Peak Salamander — see Remarks) coexist at some localities with striped individuals. Sides dark brown or black, spotted with yellowish or tan and speckled with white. Upper surface of base of limbs yellow, flecked with dusky, like the dorsal stripe. Slaty below, with small spots of yellowish or orange. Tail slightly flattened from side to side. 15 costal grooves (rarely 16). $2\frac{1}{2}$–4 costal folds between tips of toes of adpressed limbs. ***Male:*** A small lobe on each side of rear edge of vent.

Lives in moss-covered rock rubble or seepages and under rocks and logs on shady streambanks, preferring wetter locations than other western plethodons except the Van Dyke Salamander (p. 45). Sometimes found beneath stones in water trickles. Presumably lays its eggs mainly in spring.

Similar species: Western Red-backed Salamander (below) usually has 16 costal grooves, a network of light and dark markings on the belly (Fig. 11A, opp. Pl. 5), and the stripe color extends to tip of tail. In yellow-striped individuals, the stripe lacks the greenish yellow tone of the Dunn Salamander.

Range: From near South Bend, Pacific Co., Wash., west of Cascade crest, to the Smith R. area, Del Norte, Co., Calif. Sea level to around 3200 ft. (1000 m). **Map 12**

Remarks: Mary's Peak Salamander *(P. gordoni)* — unstriped when adult and sympatric with striped individuals in Benton, Lincoln, and Lane Cos., Ore. — is regarded in this guide as an unstriped morph (form) of the Dunn Salamander.

WESTERN RED-BACKED SALAMANDER Pl. 5

Plethodon vehiculum

Identification: $1\frac{1}{2}$–$2\frac{1}{2}$ in. (3.7–6.2 cm). Dorsal stripe usually well defined — tan, reddish brown, orange, yellow, or dusky edged with black. *Stripe with even edges, extending to tip of tail.* Tan or reddish brown colors are most common, but sometimes all stripe colors are present at the same locality. Sides of body dusky, sprinkled with white. Occasionally all dark color is subdued and the stripe color suffuses the entire body. Such plain-colored individuals may be orange or pale yellow. Occasionally melanistic (dark) individuals are found, especially in coastal areas. Blue-gray below, with varying amounts of yellowish or orange flecking, which sometimes reduces the dark ventral color to a network or to scattered spots and blotches (Fig. 11A, opp. Pl. 5). *Usually 16 costal grooves,* occasionally 14 to 18. $2\frac{1}{2}$–$5\frac{1}{2}$ costal folds between toes of adpressed limbs.

Found under rocks, logs, bark, and boards in damp locations in humid forests, but generally in drier locations than Dunn Salamander, which shares its range in Ore. In Ore., mates chiefly from Nov. through early March. Eggs are laid in spring and are brooded by the female.

Similar species: See (1) Dunn Salamander (above) and (2) Larch Mountain Salamander (p. 46).

Range: Chiefly west of Cascade crest from sw. B.C., including Vancouver I., to vicinity of Powers, Coos Co., and Rogue R., Curry Co., Ore. Near sea level to about 4100 ft. (1250 m). **Map 11**

VAN DYKE SALAMANDER *Plethodon vandykei* Pl. 5

Identification: $1\frac{3}{4}$–$2\frac{1}{2}$ in. (4.4–6.2 cm). Dorsal stripe yellowish, greenish, tan, or reddish, with even or scalloped edges, bordered with black or dark brown. *Throat pale yellow* (Fig. 11B, opp. Pl. 5), contrasting in some individuals with dark belly color, which is black or dusky flecked with white. Large adults from Wash. may be nearly plain dull yellow, tan, or pinkish rose (especially in Willapa Hills), and the dark color of the sides and belly faint or absent. *14 costal grooves,* rarely 15. $\frac{1}{2}$–3 costal folds between toes of adpressed limbs. Parotoid glands often evident in large adults. ***Young:*** A conspicuous yellow dorsal stripe, black sides, black belly, and large *yellow throat patch.* ***Male:*** Nasolabial groove ends in a tubercle on upper lip.

Found under rocks, logs, and bark near lakes, rivers, and streams, often in seepages where the soil is thoroughly wet. Occurs in both wooded and open areas from the lowlands well up into the mountains. In Idaho, known to breed in spring and fall; eggs are presumably laid chiefly in spring.

Similar species: (1) Dunn and (2) Western Red-backed Salamanders (above) lack the pale throat. (3) The Larch Mountain Salamander (following species) is reddish below. (4) Lack of a constriction at base of tail distinguishes unstriped individuals from plain-colored Ensatina (p. 48).

Range: W. Wash., n. Idaho, and nw. Mont. Near sea level to around 5000 ft. (1550 m). Sometimes sympatric with Dunn and Western Red-backed Salamanders. **Map 16**

Subspecies: WASHINGTON SALAMANDER, *P. v. vandykei* (Pl. 5). Broad, usually even-edged dorsal stripe yellow or tan; some adults plain-colored. Stripe color on upper surface of base of limbs. Willapa Hills, Olympic, and Cascade Mts., Wash. Coexists with Dunn Salamander southeast of South Bend, Pacific Co., Wash. COEUR D'ALENE SALAMANDER, *P. v. idahoensis* (Pl. 5). Dorsal stripe narrower and usually with scalloped borders, contrasting sharply with black of upper sides. Upper surface of base of limbs dark-colored. Sooty below; yellow throat conspicuous. Southern shore of Wolf Bay, Coeur d'Alene Lake, Kootenai Co.; south of Emida, Benewah Co.; and Lochsa R. east of Lowell, Idaho Co., Idaho; Big Hoodoo Mt., Lincoln Co., and Cascade Creek, south of Paradise, Mineral Co., Mont. Biochemical evidence suggests that this form perhaps should be considered a full species, *P. idahoensis.*

LARCH MOUNTAIN SALAMANDER **Pl. 5**

Plethodon larselli

Identification: 1½–2⅛ in. (3.7–5.3 cm). Dorsal stripe reddish, tan, or yellowish, tending to become obscure on head. Stripe edged with black or dark brown, and often speckled or heavily mottled with small dark flecks that may be concentrated along midline. Sides black or dark brown sprinkled with white. *Red to reddish orange or salmon-pink below,* brightest on tail, lightly and irregularly speckled with black. Underside of feet usually reddish. Throat cream or dull yellow. Toes partly webbed as in Van Dyke Salamander and only 1 segment in 5th toe. Usually 18 or 19 costal grooves. ***Young:*** Dorsal stripe well defined. Less reddish below, with more dark color than adult.

Inhabits lava talus slopes of the Columbia R. gorge, chiefly in dense stands of Douglas fir, where there is considerable moss and humus. Found in rotten wood and under rocks and bark. Breeds in spring and fall.

Similar species: Differs from all other woodland salamanders in having reddish color on belly and underside of feet and tail. (1) Dorsal stripe heavily mottled with small dark flecks, darker than in Van Dyke Salamander (p. 45), which typically has 2 segments (not 1) in the 5th toe. (2) Edges of dorsal stripe more irregular and belly pattern less variegated than in Western Red-backed Salamander (p. 45).
Range: Lower Columbia R. gorge between Troutdale and Hood R., Ore.; Archer Falls and about 13 mi. (21 km) east of Stevenson, Skamania Co., to 4.8 mi. (7.9 km) west of Lyle, Klickitat Co., Wash. Some other Ore. localities are northern slope of Larch Mt., 3 mi. (5 km) from summit on Multnomah Falls Trail, Multnomah Co., and Starvation Falls between Wyeth and Hood River, Hood River Co. To around 3900 ft. (1190 m). **Map 14**

JEMEZ MOUNTAINS SALAMANDER **Pl. 5**
Plethodon neomexicanus

Identification: $1\frac{7}{8}$–$2\frac{5}{8}$ in. (4.7–6.5 cm). Our slimmest plethodon, approaching the slender salamanders in proportions. Usually 18–19 costal grooves. Legs short, in adults 6–$8\frac{1}{2}$ costal folds between tips of toes of adpressed limbs. *Fifth toe absent, or with only 1 segment.* Brown above, with fine brassy-colored stippling. Sooty to pale gray below, lighter on throat and tail. ***Young:*** A faint gray or brassy dorsal stripe.

Found in moss-covered rockslides, especially on north-facing slopes and under bark and beneath logs in and near mixed forests of fir, spruce, aspen, and maple above 7000 ft. (2130 m) in the Jemez Mts., N.M. A subterranean salamander that spends little time on the surface except during the period of summer rains — June–Aug. Eggs laid between mid-Aug. and spring. May be locally abundant.
Similar species: Del Norte Salamander (below) has 2 segments in the 5th toe and usually 18 costal grooves.
Range: Jemez Mts., Sandoval, and Los Alamos Cos., N.M.
Map 15

DEL NORTE SALAMANDER *Plethodon elongatus* **Pl. 5**

Identification: $2\frac{3}{8}$–3 in. (6–7.5 cm). A long-bodied, dark brown or black plethodon with *18* (occasionally 17–20) *costal grooves* and short limbs. *Toes short and slightly webbed.* 3–$8\frac{1}{2}$ costal folds between toes of adpressed limbs. 2 segments in 5th toe. An even-edged dorsal stripe of brown, reddish brown, or olive tan, often lacking in specimens from outer coastal areas, where adults are dark brown or solid black. The Siskiyou Mountains subspecies *(P.e. stormi)* is chocolate to purplish brown with pale speckling above. Sides sprinkled with fine white flecks in all color phases. Belly black, slaty, or lavender, usually flecked with light gray. Pale orange-yellow flecks on underside of head. ***Young:*** Sooty to nearly black above, or with a reddish brown or tan dorsal stripe that usually fades with age. ***Male:*** Mental gland present, absent in female.

Often found in rock rubble of old riverbeds, road fills, and outcrops, and in moss-covered talus. It generally occurs in drier locations than Dunn Salamander. The Siskiyou Mountains subspecies *(P.e. stormi)* presumably mates in spring and fall. Females remain with their eggs in well-hidden nest sites until fall, when the eggs hatch.

Similar species: (1) Dark-colored Dunn Salamander (p. 44) has 15 (rarely 16) costal grooves, less webbing between toes, and 2½–4 costal folds between adpressed limbs. (2) See also Jemez Mountains Salamander (p. 47).

Range: Humid coastal forest from the vicinity of Port Orford, Curry Co., and Powers, Coos Co., Ore. to near Orick, Humboldt Co., Calif. and inland to near Salyer, Trinity Co., and Seiad Valley, Siskiyou Co., Calif. Coexists with Dunn Salamander at some localities in s. Ore. Sea level to around 3900 ft. (1200 m).

Map 13

Subspecies: STRIPED DEL NORTE SALAMANDER, *P. e. elongatus* (Pl. 5). Usually 6½–7½ costal folds between adpressed limbs. Usually 18 costal grooves. Brown or black above, unstriped or with a brown stripe (inland areas). SISKIYOU MOUNTAINS SALAMANDER, *P. e. stormi* (Pl. 5). Usually 4–5½ costal folds between adpressed limbs. Usually 17 costal grooves. Chocolate or light purplish brown above, profusely speckled with whitish or yellowish. No dorsal stripe. Chiefly in Applegate R. drainage, Ore. and upper Klamath R. drainage, Calif.

Ensatina: Genus *Ensatina*

ENSATINA *Ensatina eschscholtzii* **Pls. 3, 4**

Identification: 1½–3 in. (6.2–7.5 cm). A smooth-skinned salamander with 12–13 costal grooves and a *"swollen" tail, constricted at its base.* The defense posture is characteristic: when tapped on the back, an ensatina may stand stiff-legged and sway-backed, with its tail arched. Color varies greatly (see plates), but nearly all ensatinas have yellow or orange limb bases. ***Male:*** Enlarged upper lip. Tail slimmer and longer than in female.

Found in both deciduous and evergreen forests under rotting logs, bark, and rocks. To the south, frequents forests and well-shaded canyons, as well as oak woodland and old chaparral. Permanent water may or may not be present. In the north this salamander may be found in clearings as well as wooded areas. During cold or dry weather, ensatinas retreat to the interior of rotten logs and woodrat nests, or enter rotted-out root channels and the burrows of gophers and meadow mice. Breeds chiefly in spring and fall. At higher altitudes and to the north, activity may extend into early summer and may occur during summer rains in the mountains. Females brood their eggs underground, or under the bark of or within rotting logs in summer.

Similar species: See Van Dyke Salamander (p. 45).

Range: Sw. B.C. (north to South Bentinck Arm) to extreme nw. Baja Calif., chiefly west of Cascade-Sierran crest. Absent from Great Valley of Calif. Sea level to around 8000 ft. (2440 m).

Map 10

Subspecies: MONTEREY SALAMANDER, *E. e. eschscholtzii* (Pl. 4). Reddish brown above; whitish below. Eyes black. Ranges inland in s. Calif. to Kitchner Peak above Cabazon and to Sawmill Canyon, headwaters of San Gorgonio R. above Banning, where it hybridizes with individuals that are intergrades between the Yellow-blotched and Large-blotched Salamanders (below). YELLOW-EYED SALAMANDER, *E. e. xanthoptica* (Pl. 4). Orange-brown above; orange below. Yellow patch in eye. Hybridizes with the Sierra Nevada Salamander in the Sierran foothills. Arrow on Map 10 shows presumed dispersal route across Central Valley of Calif. OREGON SALAMANDER, *E. e. oregonensis* (Pl. 4). Brown to nearly black above; whitish to pale yellow below, with very fine black speckling. PAINTED SALAMANDER, *E. e. picta* (Pl. 4). Small form — ⅔ size of ensatinas to south. Brown above, blotched with black, yellow, or orange. Tail often mottled with black and yellow. Young Oregon Salamanders often similarly blotched. SIERRA NEVADA SALAMANDER, *E. e. platensis* (Pl. 3). Gray to brown above, with prominent orange spots. YELLOW-BLOTCHED SALAMANDER, *E. e. croceater* (Pl. 3). Blackish above, with large greenish yellow, yellow, or cream blotches. Tehachapi Mts., Mt. Pinos, and vicinity of Fort Tejon, Calif. LARGE-BLOTCHED SALAMANDER, *E. e. klauberi* (Pl. 3). Blackish above, with large orange or pale salmon blotches. In San Jacinto Mts. blotches are cream-colored in adults, greenish yellow in young. Coexists with the Monterey Salamander (above) at some localities in the Peninsular Ranges and hybridizes with it on Mt. Palomar and elsewhere in s. Calif. Arrow on Map 10 shows presumed dispersal route, or former connection, between blotched forms in Transverse Mt. system in s. Calif.

Remarks: The only species in the genus.

Climbing Salamanders: Genus *Aneides*

There are 4 western species in this genus. Most, but not all, climb; the Black Salamander spends most of its time on the ground. A fifth climbing species, the rock-dwelling Green Salamander, occurs in the Applachian Mts.

These salamanders have distinct costal grooves and prominent jaw muscles (especially well developed in males), which give the head a triangular shape. In males the front teeth in the upper jaw project beyond the lip when the mouth is closed, and can be felt by stroking the tip of the snout; there are no teeth at the back of the upper jaw. Males have an oval or heart-shaped mental gland (see front endpapers) and a broader head than females. Adaptations for climbing are the well-developed limbs; the long, often somewhat truncate (squared-off) toes; and a rounded, somewhat prehensile tail. Eggs develop during summer and are brooded by the female.

SACRAMENTO MOUNTAIN SALAMANDER **Pl. 7**
Aneides hardii

Identification: 1¾–2⅜ in. (3.7–5.9 cm). A slim-bodied, short-legged climbing salamander, with 14 or 15 costal grooves. 2–4½ costal folds between tips of toes of adpressed limbs. *Toe tips rounded.* Light to dark brown above, with varying amounts of greenish gray to bronze mottling. Belly light brown, throat cream-colored, and underside of tail slate. ***Young:*** Throat whitish. Dorsal stripe brown or bronze.

Found during period of summer rains under bark and inside rotting logs, in old rockslides, and beneath logs, bark, and boards in forests of Douglas fir, white fir, and spruce. Usually most abundant on north- and east-facing slopes. Emerges late June and July. Brooding females with eggs have been found in hollows in Douglas fir logs in summer.

Range: Isolated in the Sacramento and Capitan Mts. of southern N.M. Some localities are Cloudcroft, Agua Chiquite, Wofford Lookout, southwest of Monjeau Lookout (Sacramento Mts.); north of Summit Spring, and southeast of Koprian Springs (Capitan Mts.). From around 8500 to 11,700 ft. (2600–3600 m).

Map 21

BLACK SALAMANDER *Aneides flavipunctatus* **Pls. 6, 7**

Identification: 2–3¾ in. (5–9.4 cm). Dorsal coloration varies greatly depending upon locality — uniformly black, or black with very small white flecks (extreme southern part of range); black with large white spots (interior Coast Range from Alder Springs, Glenn Co., and Lucerne, Lake Co., Calif. south); black with pale yellow or whitish spots (outer Coast Range from Sonoma Co. to middle Mendocino Co.); black frosted with gray, olive, or green but few or no light spots (redwood country of Mendocino Co. and Humboldt Co.); and black with many small white spots (Klamath Mts. east to near Mt. Shasta). *Black or slaty below.* Projecting upper-jaw teeth (felt by stroking the salamander's snout when its mouth is closed) and the triangular head will distinguish it as a climbing salamander. 14–16 costal grooves. Limbs short, 3–5 costal folds between adpressed limbs. *Toe tips rounded.* ***Young:*** Black above, often suffused with olive or green — brilliant green (in light phase) in redwood country of the Northwest coast. Limb bases yellow. ***Male:*** Heart-shaped mental gland. Small gray glands on belly.

Frequents mixed deciduous woodland, coniferous forests, and

coastal grasslands. Chiefly ground-dwelling. Found under rocks along streams, in talus of road cuts, under logs, bark, boards, and other objects, and occasionally beneath bark and in cracks in logs. Some populations are more tolerant of wet soil than other climbing salamanders, often occurring under rocks in seepages but rarely completely immersed. Females have been found brooding their eggs in summer.

Similar species: (1) Tiger Salamander (p. 34) has a flattened tail, widely set small eyes, and lacks projecting teeth. (2) Arboreal Salamander (p. 52) and (3) Clouded Salamander (below) have less than 2 costal folds between adpressed limbs, and squarish toe tips. Arboreal Salamander has a whitish belly and Clouded Salamander a brown or gray belly.

Range: Coastal areas from sw. Ore. to cen. Santa Cruz Co. and w. Santa Clara Co., Calif. Interiorly, in northern part of range, to near southern base of Mt. Shasta, Calif. Headwaters of Applegate R., Jackson Co., Ore. Sea level to over 5500 ft. (1700 m).

Map 22

CLOUDED SALAMANDER *Aneides ferreus* Pl. 7

Identification: 1⅘–3 in. (4.5–7.5 cm). Slim, long-legged, and agile; an excellent climber. *Tips of toes of adpressed limbs separated by no more than 1½ costal folds and sometimes overlapping by as much as 1½ folds.* Usually 16 costal grooves. The toes have slightly broadened and squarish tips. Brown above, clouded with ash, greenish gray, pale gold, or reddish; dusky below. In the dark phase these salamanders may be nearly plain dark brown above. In the light phase, pale gray color may predominate and the brown color may be reduced to a network. Some adults in Ore. and extreme nw. Calif. are almost uniformly dark brown above with a few cream-colored spots. ***Young:*** Hatchlings have a copper or brassy dorsal stripe that soon becomes reduced to patches on the snout, shoulders, and tail. Stripe color on upper surface of base of limbs. ***Male:*** Heart-shaped mental gland, absent in female.

Occurs in forests of Douglas fir, cedar, alder and redwood, often at the borders of clearings. Found under the bark of standing or fallen dead trees, in rotten logs, under loose bark on the ground, under rocks, and in crevices in cliffs. May climb to heights above 20 ft. (6 m) in trees. Seems to prefer logs with a firm interior and bark that is separated ¼ in. (6 mm) or so from the heartwood. Search piles of leaf litter on top of sawed stumps and peel bark from logs, especially Douglas fir. In summer, colonies sometimes occur deep inside decayed logs. Eggs laid in spring and probably early summer. Both sexes have been found together at nest sites.

Similar species: See (1) Arboreal Salamander (p. 52) and (2) Black Salamander (above).

Range: Coast Ranges of Calif. and Ore., from nw. Sonoma Co. to Columbia R.; lower western slope of Cascade Mts., Ore.; Vancou-

ver I., where it may be introduced. Sea level to around 5400 ft. (1650 m). **Map 19**

ARBOREAL SALAMANDER *Aneides lugubris* **Pls. 6, 7**
Identification: 2¼–4 in. (6.2–10 cm). A plain brown salamander, usually spotted with yellow. Spotting conspicuous in San Benito Co. and Monterey Co., and on South Farallon I. off San Francisco Bay; weak or absent in Sierra Nevada. *Whitish below, unmarked.* Enlarged jaw muscles give head a triangular shape. Toes have slightly enlarged, squarish tips. *Adpressed limbs overlap, or separated by as much as 1 costal fold.* Usually 15 costal grooves. The tail is prehensile and usually coiled when the salamander is at rest. ***Young:*** Dark above, clouded with light gray or brassy color and a rust or brassy mark on snout, on each side above forelimbs, on upper surface of bases of limbs, and along upper surface of tail. ***Male:*** Chunky, broad head with powerful jaw muscles. Heart-shaped mental gland, absent in female.

Occurs chiefly in coastal live-oak woodland, but ranges into forests of yellow pine and black oak, especially in the Sierra Nevada. Found both on the ground and in trees. In summer during dry weather it enters damp caves and mine shafts; large numbers may aggregate in tree hollows. Found under logs, boards, and rocks and under the bark of standing or fallen dead trees. Examine tree trunks, rock surfaces, and crevices of rock walls at night with a flashlight. (A slender wire with a "shepherd's" hook can be used to remove salamanders from cracks.) This salamander sometimes squeaks when first caught. Large adults can bite severely but usually are not prone to do so. Eggs are brooded in hollows in trees, logs, and the ground in summer.
Similar species: (1) Clouded Salamander (p. 51) usually has 16 costal grooves, mottled dorsal coloration, and a dark belly that is finely speckled with white. See also (2) Black Salamander (p. 50) and (3) Limestone Salamander (p. 62).
Range: Coastal mountains and valleys of Calif., from Humboldt Co. to nw. Baja Calif. Foothills of Sierra Nevada, from El Dorado Co. to Madera Co., Calif. South Farallon, Catalina, and Los Coronados Is. off coast of Calif. and Baja Calif. Sea level to around 5000 ft. (1520 m). **Map 20**

Slender Salamanders: Genus *Batrachoseps*

Slender salamanders are confined to the Pacific Coast. All but one of the 8 species occur in Calif. They are sometimes called "worm salamanders" because many of them have a slim form, and all have conspicuous costal and caudal grooves that give them a segmented appearance; most have small limbs. They have 4 toes on both front and hind feet; all other western salamanders typically have 4 toes on the front feet and 5 toes on the hind feet. Most of them have a dorsal stripe of reddish, tan, or buff. Young individuals have relatively long limbs, a large head, and short tail. Males have a blunt snout and their premaxillary teeth perforate the upper lip.

Found in a variety of habitats — desert springs, grassland, chaparral, woodland, and moist forests. Slender salamanders occur in damp locations under logs, bark, and rocks, in leaf litter, in termite galleries, and in crevices of rocks, logs, and stumps. When first exposed, the more elongate species may remain motionless, sometimes coiled like a watchspring. Occasionally, when first picked up they may slip away and bounce randomly over the ground. The tail may break when seized, but is soon regenerated.

In the first edition of this book, only 2 species of slender salamanders were recognized in Calif. — the California and Pacific Slender Salamanders. Since then, 5 more slender salamanders have been described in Calif., several of them within the range formerly considered to be occupied only by the California Slender Salamander. Furthermore, the range of the Pacific Slender Salamander has been extended to include populations considered to be members of the California Slender Salamander group. Some of these confusingly similar ("cryptic") species have been revealed through biochemical studies, and field recognition is difficult or impossible in some cases. Rely heavily on distributional information. There is probably much more to be learned about species and subspecies relationships in this diverse group of salamanders.

OREGON SLENDER SALAMANDER **Pls. 7, 8**

Batrachoseps wrighti

Identification: $1\frac{1}{2}$–$2\frac{2}{5}$ in. (3.7–5.6 cm). A long-legged, slender salamander with a *black belly* that is marked with *large white blotches*. 16 or 17 costal grooves, counting one each in axilla and groin. $4\frac{1}{2}$–$7\frac{1}{2}$ costal folds between adpressed limbs. Dark brown above, often with a reddish or yellowish brown or occasionally greenish gold stripe. In some, back color contrasts with brick-red tail.

Frequents moist woods of Douglas fir, maple, hemlock, and red cedar. Found under boards, rocks, wood, or bark and wood chips at the base of stumps, under the bark and moss of logs, and inside logs in crevices or termite burrows. Generally scarce, occurring in scattered and often widely separated colonies, but sometimes locally common. Becomes active on the surface of the ground in April or May. Probably lays its eggs underground or in rotting logs in spring or early summer.

Similar species: Differs from all other slender salamanders in having conspicuous white blotches on the belly.

Range: Northern base of Mt. Hood, along Columbia R. from Starvation Falls, Hood River Co., to near Crown Point, Multnomah Co.; south on western slope of Cascade Mts. to northeast of Westfir and Erma Bell Lake area, Lane Co., Ore. Some additional localities: near mouths of Moose and Trout Creeks, tributaries of Quartzville Creek, Middle Santiam R., Linn Co.; and 2 mi. (3.2 km) south of McKenzie Bridge, Lane Co. Near sea level to around 4700 ft. (1430 m). **Map 18**

Remarks: The Oregon and Inyo Mountains Slender Salamanders (below) are considered to be closest to the ancestral stock that gave rise to the genus *Batrachoseps.*

INYO MOUNTAINS SALAMANDER Pl. 8

Batrachoseps campi

Identification: 1½–2⅜ in. (3.7–5.9 cm). The stockiest of the slender salamanders, with nearly the proportions of a web-toed salamander. *Tail short,* averaging only about ¾ of the snout-vent length. 16–18 costal grooves. 2–5 costal folds between adpressed limbs. Brown above with gray blotches, which may be very sparse to numerous depending on the locality. Populations on the east side and toward the north in Inyo Mts. may have a continuous pale gray tinge (often with a faint greenish cast) on the back. Some individuals may have a gray dorsolateral stripe on each side. ***Young:*** Dark, usually without an extensive gray tinge.

Found in isolated spring and stream areas chiefly below the piñon-juniper belt. Willows and wild rose grow along the water courses. Found under stones and in crevices in damp places near water. Surrounding slopes are arid, grown to sagebrush, buckwheat, rabbitbrush, and cactus.

Similar species: (1) Differs from other slender salamanders in having gray lichenlike blotches or suffusion on a dark brown ground color. (2) Web-toed salamanders (*Hydromantes* species, p. 60) have 5 toes on the hind feet.

Range: Inyo Mts., Inyo Co., Calif. From around 1800–8600 ft. (550–2620 m). **Map 17**

Remarks: Slender salamanders that resemble the Inyo Mountains Salamander in proportions but differ in coloration occur in open coniferous forests on the Kern Plateau of the southern Sierra Nevada, Calif. Their taxonomic status has not yet been determined.

TEHACHAPI SLENDER SALAMANDER Pl. 8

Batrachoseps stebbinsi

Identification: 2–2⅜ in. (5–5.9 cm). A broad-headed, long-limbed slender salamander with broad toes and feet. Toes seem to be more fully webbed than in other slender salamanders, with only 1 segment of each toe free of the web. 18–19 costal grooves; 6–7 costal folds between toes of adpressed limbs. Above light to dark brown, reddish, or with light beige patches. Dorsal stripe, when present, is often diffuse with uneven borders. Few or no light specks along central part of belly.

Occurs chiefly in moist canyons and ravines in oak or mixed

pine-oak woodland. Found under rocks often in or near talus slopes and beneath rotting logs, especially in areas where there is considerable leaf litter.

Similar species: Black-bellied Slender Salamander (below), with which it coexists at several localities in the Tehachapi Mts., is slimmer, has a narrower head, shorter legs, and it seems to be more subterranean and more tolerant of lower, drier conditions.

Range: Scattered localities in the Caliente Creek drainage. Piute Mts., at the southern end of the Sierra Nevada, Kern Co., Calif. Populations scattered through the Tehachapi Mts. to Fort Tejon, Kern Co., have been tentatively assigned to this species on a biochemical basis. From around 2000–4600 ft. (610–1400 m).

Map 17

BLACK-BELLIED SLENDER SALAMANDER **Pl. 9**

Batrachoseps nigriventris

Identification: 1¼–1⅞ in. (3.1–4.7 cm). Head narrow, little wider than neck. Shares with the California Slender Salamander the shortest limbs among all slender salamanders. Tail to around 2 times snout-vent length, but may be about body length on Santa Cruz I. 18–21 costal grooves. *9–15 costal folds* between toes of adpressed limbs. Usually has a dorsal stripe of tan, brown, reddish, or beige. Dark below, with a sprinkling of fine white specks, usually *over all ventral surfaces.*

Chiefly an oak-woodland salamander but it also ranges into mixed oak-pine forests, streamside habitats, and arid treeless grassland. Found under rocks and logs, under bark, and in termite channels in damp locations. Often occurs in scattered colonies. In s. Calif. eggs are laid in winter and hatch in winter and early spring. In Sierra Nevada individuals were found laying in foothills near town of White River, Tulare Co., at around 1400 ft. (430 m) in early Dec. and in uplands at Sugarpine, 4300 ft. (1310 m), Madera Co., in May. The Sugarpine animals are tentatively regarded as of this species.

Similar species: The Black-bellied Salamander coexists with 4 subspecies of the Pacific Slender Salamander (p. 56): (1) Relictual Slender Salamander has a broader head, longer limbs, and shorter tail. (2) Channel Islands and (3) Garden Slender Salamanders have broader heads, longer limbs, and usually paler coloration. (4) Gabilan Slender Salamander is biochemically distinct but is indistinguishable in appearance in areas where it coexists with the Black-bellied Slender Salamander.

Range: Found in 3 distinct geographic areas of Calif.: (1) Southern coastal mts., chiefly south of Calif. State Highway 198 and San Simeon, Monterey Co., through the Transverse Mt. Ranges to Cajon Pass, San Bernardino Co., thence south into the uplands of the Peninsular Ranges and coastally to the Palos Verdes Hills and Santa Ana Mts. (2) Western slope of the cen. and s. Sierra Nevada from Merced River drainage south through the Techachapi Mts. to Mount Pinos and the Pine Mts., Ventura Co. (3) Santa Cruz I. Overlaps the ranges of the Tehachapi and Pacific Slender Salamanders (see p. 54 and below). Sea level to around 7400 ft. (2260 m). **Map 17**

KERN CANYON SLENDER SALAMANDER **Pl. 9**

Batrachoseps simatus

Identification: 1⅝–2⅛ in. (4–5.4 cm). A narrow-headed slender salamander with relatively long limbs and long body and tail (to about 1½ times snout-vent length). *Head and body somewhat flattened,* suggesting crevice-dwelling habits. 20–21 costal grooves. 7–9 costal folds between toes of adpressed limbs. A vague dorsal stripe may be present. Sides and undersurfaces dark, speckled with small light flecks.

Occurs in isolated colonies along stream courses and on ridges and hillsides. North-facing slopes and shaded narrow tributary canyons seem to be favored. Found in talus slopes and under logs and other surface objects, especially after rains. Frequents streamside vegetation of willows and cottonwoods, and slopes grown to interior live oak, canyon oak, and pine. Slender salamanders, presumably of this species, were found laying eggs in mid-June at Squirrel Meadow, 6300 ft. (1920 m) on Breckenridge Mt., Kern Co.

Similar species: (1) Pacific (Relictual) Slender Salamander (p. 58) has broader head, usually a lower costal-groove count (16–20, not 20–21), and generally prefers wetter locations. See also (2) Tehachapi Slender Salamander (p. 54).

Range: Known only from the Kern R. drainage in the southern Sierra Nevada, Calif., from near the canyon mouth to above Fairview. From 1400 to 6300 ft. (430–1920 m). **Map 17**

Remarks: Animals from Breckenridge Mt. and Fairview are somewhat different from those in Kern River Canyon and are therefore tentatively included in this species.

PACIFIC SLENDER SALAMANDER **Pls. 7,9**

Batrachoseps pacificus

Identification: 1¼–2¾ in. (3.2–6.9 cm). A highly variable species or group of semispecies ("almost species"), varying greatly in size, proportions, and coloration (see subspecies accounts below). There is no known overall structural or color characteristic or group of characteristics that will distinguish this species from other slender salamanders; however, some of its subspecies are distinctive and can be recognized in areas where they coexist with other species of slender salamanders (see below). 16–21 costal grooves. 5½–13 costal folds between toes of adpressed limbs. Tail from slightly less than, to around 2 times snout-vent length. The slimmer, shorter-legged populations are often found in the drier habitats where these animals, unable to burrow effectively, must retreat to earthworm burrows, crevices, and other small underground locations to avoid desiccation.

Frequents a great variety of habitats over its wide range — oak woodland, coniferous and mixed deciduous and evergreen forests, chaparral, and grassland. It has also been found along washes, in salt marshes, and under beach driftwood. Usually found on damp soil or in moist leaf litter but in some areas — southern Sierra Nevada and Santa Lucia Mts., Calif. — individuals have been found in water of seepages. Egg-laying in the southern Calif. lowlands occurs in fall and winter. Breeding habits elsewhere are unknown.

Similar species: Considered here are only those species which the Pacific Slender Salamander overlaps or approaches in range (see Map 17). (1) Black-bellied Slender Salamander differs from subspecies of the Pacific Slender Salamander as follows: (a) from Relictual Slender Salamander (in s. Sierra Nevada) in having a narrower head, short limbs, and usually a longer tail; (b) from Channel Islands Slender Salamander in being generally smaller, darker, and slimmer, with a narrower head, and in usually having white specks across underside of tail; (c) from Garden Slender Salamander (in areas of overlap in Los Angeles and Orange Cos.) in being generally smaller, slimmer, and shorter-limbed, with a narrower head and darker coloration; a dorsal stripe is usually present. No reliable field characteristics are available for distinguishing the Black-bellied Slender Salamander from the (d) Gabilan and (e) Santa Lucia Slender Salamanders. These salamanders differ biochemically. (2) Kern Canyon Slender Salamander is usually larger, has a narrower head, shorter limbs, a longer and flatter body, paler coloration, and is less prone to enter seepages. (3) Where the ranges of Pacific Slender Salamander and California Slender Salamander approach or contact one another (see Map 17), no useful field differences have been found that will distinguish them.

Range: Fragmented. Southern Sierra Nevada, central Coast Ranges from Monterey region to n. San Luis Obispo Co.; s. Calif. from base of San Gabriel and San Bernardino Mts. to near El Rosario in nw. Baja Calif. Islands off coast of s. Calif. and n. Baja Calif. Sea level to around 8000 ft. (2440 m). **Map 17**

Subspecies: CHANNEL ISLANDS SLENDER SALAMANDER, *B. p. pacificus.* Large size. Broad head, long legs. Brownish to pinkish above, with a broad dorsal stripe that usually has indefinite borders. Pale on sides and below, with a weak network or speckling of melanophores. 18–20 costal grooves. 6–8 costal folds between toes of adpressed limbs. Tail to about $1\frac{1}{4}$ snout-vent length. San Miguel, Santa Rosa, Santa Cruz, and Anacapa Is. off coast of Santa Barbara, Calif. GARDEN SLENDER SALAMANDER, *B. p. major.* Size similar to previous subspecies but more elongate, with relatively shorter limbs, usually a longer tail, and a narrower head. Usually pale above — brownish, light tan, pink, or

grayish, frequently with rust on tail, snout, and shoulders, but some populations are dark in uplands of Peninsular Ranges and San Pedro Mártir Mts. and on Todos Santos I., and those from near El Rosario, Baja Calif. are very pale. Stripe often has diffuse borders or is obscure. Belly light gray with a weak network or speckling of melanophores. Belly sooty, with a dense melanic network in dark populations. 17–21 costal grooves. 9–12 costal folds between toes of adpressed limbs. Tail to about 2 times snout-vent length. Southern Calif. from base of San Gabriel and San Bernardino Mts. south to vicinity of El Rosario and in San Pedro Mártir Mts., Baja Calif. On Catalina, Los Coronados, and Todos Santos Is. RELICTUAL SLENDER SALAMANDER, *B. p. relictus.* A broad-headed, long-legged subspecies with proportions resembling those of the Channel Islands Slender Salamander, but smaller and generally darker above and below. Dorsal stripe of reddish, yellowish brown, or dark brown; obscure in dark individuals. 16–20 costal grooves. 7–9 costal folds between toes of adpressed limbs. Tail to around 1¾ times snout-vent length. At northern end of range, limbs are proportionally shorter than at southern end and animals often occur in less moist surroundings. Spotty distribution on western slope of southern Sierra Nevada from Kings R. drainage to Kern River Canyon. In mixed coniferous forest usually at higher elevations than Black-bellied Slender Salamander that parallels its range (see Map 17). GABILAN SLENDER SALAMANDER. Closely resembles California Slender Salamander (p. 59) in size, proportions, and coloration. Slim, short-legged; usually long-tailed and often has a well-defined dorsal stripe. 20–21 costal grooves. 10–12 costal folds between toes of adpressed limbs. Chiefly in oak-woodland habitats of east slope of Santa Lucia Mts. and Gabilan and southern Diablo Ranges from vicinity of Soquel and San Benito R. to Polonia Pass area, San Luis Obispo Co. SAN LUCIA SLENDER SALAMANDER. Hind limbs larger, feet wider, and generally darker above and below than previous subspecies. Dorsal stripe obscure in dark individuals. 19 costal grooves. 8–9 costal folds between toes of adpressed limbs. Tail to around 1¾ times snout-vent length. Generally occurs in wetter locations than Gabilan Slender Salamander, in deep leaf litter of moist canyons, in redwood and mixed evergreen forests. Western slope of Santa Lucia Mts. from Monterey area to n. San Luis Obispo Co., Calif.
Remarks: Because of the complexity of Map 17, subspecies ranges have not been shown. The Pacific Slender Salamander coexists with the Black-bellied Slender Salamander on Santa Cruz I., in Los Angeles and Orange Cos., and in n. San Luis Obispo Co. and s. Monterey Co., Calif., at the southern end of the Santa Lucia Mts. where it tends to be restricted to the crests and north-facing slopes of the mountains. The Black-bellied Slender Salamander, on the other hand, is widespread in the surrounding lowlands, occasionally entering upland areas. The latter also coexists with the Pacific

Slender Salamander on Mustang Ridge of the southern Diablo Range and near the mouth of the South Fork of the Kaweah River in the Sierra Nevada. The Pacific Slender Salamander coexists with the Kern River Canyon Slender Salamander in Kern River Canyon, Calif. and with the California Slender Salamander; their ranges meet at the southern end of the Santa Cruz Mts., at the juncture of oak woodland and redwood forest. Determination of the taxonomic relationships of slender salamanders in the central Sierra Nevada (see Map 17) awaits further study (see p. 60).

The Gabilan and Santa Lucia forms have been described and named in a dissertation by Kay Yanev, but their formal scientific recognition awaits publication, hence no scientific names are given.

DESERT SLENDER SALAMANDER — Pl. 8

Batrachoseps aridus Endangered

Identification: 1¼–2 in. (3.1–5 cm). A relatively long-legged, broad-headed slender salamander. Tail short. 16–19 costal grooves (usually 18). 3½–6½ costal folds between adpressed limbs. *Dorsal surfaces suffused with silvery to brassy flecks,* giving adults a pale gray, whitish, or pinkish coloration. Underside of tail flesh-colored, contrasting with the dark belly. ***Young:*** Black to dark brown above, often with little or no frosty to brassy tinge.

This salamander is isolated in a palm oasis at the head of a canyon on the east slope of the Santa Rosa Mts. in s. Calif. California fan palms, willows, mesquite, and sugar bush grow at the site, but the surrounding slopes are arid and contain creosote bush, juniper, manzanita, buckwheat and cactus. The salamanders occur beneath limestone slabs and talus in the canyon bottom and in rock crevices and holes in moist soil on the canyon walls.

Similar species: The broad head, long limbs, and usually silvery to grayish tinge on the dorsal surfaces distinguish this slender salamander from others, except the Inyo Mountains Salamander (p. 54). It is more slender than that species.

Range: Isolated in Hidden Palm Canyon, at around 2800 ft. (850 m), a tributary of Deep Canyon southwest of Palm Desert, Riverside Co., Calif. A population of slender salamanders in nearby Guadalupe Canyon, Riverside Co., may also be of this species. The Hidden Palm Canyon site is a State Ecological Reserve and can be entered only by permit. **Map 17**

CALIFORNIA SLENDER SALAMANDER — Pls. 6, 7, 9

Batrachoseps attenuatus

Identification: 1¼–1⅞ in. (3.1–4.7 cm). Head narrow, body and tail long (overall length to over 1½–2 times snout-vent length). Limbs very short. *Belly black or dusky, the dark color usually arranged in a fine unbroken network.* Underside of tail often lighter than the belly and tinged with yellow. Ventral surfaces, including midline of tail, *finely speckled with white.* Dorsal stripe often present — brick-red, brown, tan, buff, or yellow, the frequency of the colors varying with locality. Red to reddish brown predominates in the redwood belt in the Northwest. Individuals with a variety of stripe colors can be found in the vicinity of San Francisco Bay. The remaining dorsal ground color is sooty to black. 18–21 costal grooves. 10–12 costal folds between adpressed limbs. ***Male:*** Lower jaw more pointed and snout broader and more squared-off than in female. Premaxillary teeth project slightly beyond edge of closed mouth.

Frequents grassland (usually where there are scattered trees), chaparral, woodland, forest, and yards and vacant lots in some suburban areas. Found under logs, boards, bark, in damp leaf litter and rotting logs, from the time of the first fall rains to the beginning of the dry period in late spring or summer. Eggs are laid in late fall and winter, often in communal nests, and the young emerge in winter and spring.

Similar species: Differs from all other slender salamanders except the Black-bellied Slender Salamander (p. 55) and some populations of the Pacific Slender Salamander (p. 56) in having the shortest legs and slimmest body.

Range: Coastal area from extreme sw. Ore. (near mouth of Rogue R.) to vicinity of San Benito R., and in Sierran foothills from Big Chico Creek to the American R. drainage. Scattered populations in the Sacramento Valley, including Sutter Buttes. Isolated populations at Clipkapudi and Little Cow Creeks, Shasta Co., Calif. Sea level to about 4000 ft. (1220 m). **Map 17**

Remarks: The taxonomic status of slender salamander populations in the area between the southern known limit of the California Slender Salamander's range (American R. drainage) and the northernmost localities for the Sierran Pacific Slender Salamander (Kings R. drainage) and the Black-bellied Slender Salamander (Merced R. drainage) has not been determined. Within this area, all 3 species are very similar in appearance; thus biochemical studies are underway.

Web-toed Salamanders: Genus *Hydromantes*

Webbed toes, a mushroomlike tongue with free edges (unattached at front), and a flattened body are distinctive. Tongue very long; can be extended ⅓ the length of the body (excluding tail) to capture prey. Males have projecting upper-jaw teeth and an oval mental gland.

Web-toes are excellent climbers, moving with ease over smooth rock surfaces. When on a steep slope, the California species use the tail as an aid in locomotion, curling the tip forward and placing it against the ground as the hind foot is lifted, a habit that distinguishes them from our other western salamanders.

These salamanders live in rocky habitats, hiding by day under stones and in crevices and caves. They frequent cliff faces, vertical walls of caverns, and occasionally level ground.

There are 5 species, 2 in Europe and 3 in Calif.

MOUNT LYELL SALAMANDER Pl. 6

Hydromantes platycephalus

Identification: $1\frac{3}{4}$–$2\frac{3}{4}$ in. (4.4–9.4 cm). Easily recognized by its flattened head and body, *granite-matching coloration,* blunt webbed toes, and short tail. Dusky below, flecked with white. Usually $\frac{1}{2}$–$1\frac{1}{2}$ costal folds between adpressed limbs. ***Young:*** Black ground color above overlain with a greenish tinge (under magnification seen to consist of pale gold flecks).

Found chiefly among granite exposures of the Sierra Nevada of Calif. Typical habitat includes rock fissures, seepages from streams or melting snow, shade, and low-growing plants. Look under rocks near cliffs, cave openings, melting snow banks, and in the spray zone of waterfalls. Seems to favor north-facing slopes. Active from late spring to fall, depending upon the elevation and local moisture conditions.

Similar species: (1) The adult Shasta Salamander (below) is often tan to reddish above, without or with less definite granitelike markings; usually has white blotches on chest, and toes of adpressed limbs overlap by $\frac{1}{2}$–$1\frac{1}{2}$ costal folds. (2) Limestone Salamander (p. 62) is uniformly brown above and whitish or yellowish below. Young pale green or yellowish.

Range: Sierra Nevada from Sierra Buttes, Sierra Co. to Franklin Pass area, Tulare Co., Twin Lakes, Silliman Gap, Sequoia National Park, and Mt. Williamson, Calif. Low-altitude records are from the upper edge of the talus slope on the south side of Yosemite Valley (Staircase Falls, base of Cathedral Rocks, and base of Bridal Veil Falls). 4000–12,000 ft. (1220–3660 m). **Map 7**

SHASTA SALAMANDER Pl. 6

Hydromantes shastae

Identification: $1\frac{3}{4}$–$2\frac{1}{2}$ in. (4.4–8.7 cm). Primarily a cave dweller, less specialized for crevice dwelling than the Mount Lyell Salamander (above). Body not so flat, toes less webbed, and limbs longer. Adpressed limbs overlap by $\frac{1}{2}$–$1\frac{1}{2}$ costal folds. Gray-green, beige, tan, or reddish above, *usually with yellow on tail.* White blotches on chest and abdomen. ***Young:*** Gray-green, olive, tan, or reddish on upper body, yellowish above on tail.

Found in moist limestone fissures and caves, and in wet weather under rocks in the open, in mixed forest of Douglas fir, Digger pine, black and canyon oak. Enters moist caves in summer, where it lays and broods its eggs.

Similar species: See (1) Mount Lyell Salamander (above) and (2) Limestone Salamander (p. 62).

Range: Known only from limestone country in n. Calif. south of Mt. Shasta in headwaters of Shasta Reservoir — Backbone Ridge,

Mammoth Butte, Hirz Mt., Potter and Low Pass Creeks, McCloud R., Brock Mt., Samwell Cave, and near Ingot. 1000–3000 ft. (300–910 m).
Map 7

LIMESTONE SALAMANDER *Hydromantes brunus* **Pl. 6**
Identification: 2–3 in. (5–7.5 cm). *Uniformly brown above and pale below.* Underside of tail yellowish. Eyes larger, and limbs, toes, and tail longer than in the Mount Lyell Salamander (above). Toe tips of adpressed limbs overlap by 1½ costal folds. ***Young:*** Pale yellowish green above, changing with age through pale yellow and beige to brown.

Frequents limestone in the Digger pine, oak, buckeye, and chaparral belt of the lower Merced Canyon, Calif., living in crevices of cliffs and ledges and in talus, especially where the rocks are overgrown with moss. Active during period of fall, winter, and early spring rains, except during cold spells. Often coils its body when molested.
Similar species: (1) See Mount Lyell Salamander (p. 61). (2) Shasta Salamander (p. 61) usually is tan or reddish above, with a dusky belly. (3) Arboreal Salamander (p. 52) has a triangular head, tongue attached in front, and unwebbed toes with broadened, squarish tips.
Range: Vicinity of Briceburg, Mariposa Co., Calif., at confluence of Bear Creek and Merced R., along tributaries of Bear Creek, on North Fork of Merced R., and at Hell Hollow. The Briceburg locality is a State Ecological Reserve. 1200–2500 ft. (370–760 m).
Map 7

7

Frogs and Toads

Tailed Frogs: Family Ascaphidae

The family as treated in this guide contains only 1 species, the Tailed Frog, *Ascaphus truei,* of the Pacific Northwest. Some herpetologists place the Tailed Frog in the same family (Leiopelmatidae) with 3 species of New Zealand frogs of the genus *Leiopelma* because of some shared characteristics that are presumed to be primitive; I followed that taxonomic arrangement in the first edition of this book, but placed them in the family Ascaphidae. Recent studies now seem to support separate family status for these frogs, which are widely separated geographically. The Tailed Frog is named for its tail-like copulatory organ. Fertilization is internal by copulation, a method of breeding unique among frogs. The Tailed Frog inhabits cold streams, where its tadpole lives in torrents or quiet water and clings to rocks with its large suckerlike mouth. It may not breed until 7–8 yrs. old. Amplexus is pelvic.

TAILED FROG *Ascaphus truei* **Pl. 16**
Identification: 1–2 in. (2.5–5 cm). Olive, brown, gray or reddish above, usually with a pale yellow or greenish triangle on the snout and a dark eyestripe. Colors match rock colors in and near streams. Flat-bodied and toadlike. Skin rather rough. Eye with a vertical pupil. *Outermost hind toe broadest.* ***Male:*** Tail-like copulatory organ with vent opening at tip. Palmar and forearm tubercles (see endpapers) darken in fall and small, horny, black pads develop on each side of the chest. No "tail" or pads in female.

Frequents clear, cold, rocky streams in humid forests of Douglas fir, pine, spruce, redwood, maple, alder, and bay. Grassland, chaparral, or shrub growth may be interspersed. Trees sometimes absent. In dry weather, found on moist streambanks or under stones on the bottom of streams. Look for eyeshine near water's edge at night. Usually stays close to water but may venture into damp woods after rains. Adults abroad from April to Oct., but time varies with locality. Breeds May–Oct., but mostly in fall. Eggs laid in summer (July), hatching in Aug. and Sept. (n. Idaho and se. Wash.). Eggs unpigmented; laid in rosary-like strings under stones.
Voice: Apparently none.
Similar species: (1) In the Foothill Yellow-legged Frog (p. 86),

which may share the habitat in Ore. and Calif., the eye has a horizontal pupil; 5th toe not enlarged. (2) Pacific Treefrog (p. 80) has toe pads.
Range: Chiefly west of crest of Cascade Mts., from B.C. to near Anchor Bay, Mendocino Co., Calif. Rocky Mts. of extreme se. B.C., Idaho, and Mont.; extreme se. Wash. and ne. Ore. in the Blue and Wallowa Mts. Many isolated populations, including one at Kitimat near coast and several in Crowfoot Mts. (Shuswap Lake area), B.C. Sea level to over 6500 ft. (1980 m). **Map 27**

Leptodactylid Frogs: Family Leptodactylidae

A large family of New World frogs (over 500 species), well represented in the American tropics. Land-dwelling, aquatic, and arboreal. Most lay their eggs in water, and the tadpoles develop in the usual fashion, but some lay eggs in foamlike masses in pockets in the ground and rains wash the tadpoles into nearby pools. Others, such as members of the genus *Eleutherodactylus,* are completely terrestrial, lay their eggs on land and guard them; young emerge fully formed. A Puerto Rican species is ovoviviparous.

Proportions frog- or toadlike. The underside of the toes usually has prominent tubercles at the joints, teeth are present in the upper jaw, and the eardrums generally are smooth and semitransparent. Some species have a circular fold of skin on the belly.

Six species in the U.S., 1 introduced.

BARKING FROG *Hylactophryne augusti* **Pl. 12**
Identification: 2–3¾ in. (5–9.5 cm). Toadlike, but toes slender and unwebbed, with prominent tubercles beneath the joints. Walks in stilted fashion with its hindquarters and heels well off the ground. *Fold of skin across back of head and circular fold on belly. Eardrum smooth and semitransparent.* Greenish to light brown above, marked with dark blotches that often have light borders. Conspicuous dark brown eyes. ***Male:*** Much smaller than female. ***Young:*** Light-colored band across back that rapidly fades with age.

A secretive, terrestrial, often rock-dwelling species that is frequently found in limestone areas. Hides by day under rocks and in mines, wells, caves, and fissures. Ranges from treeless, dry, yucca-covered hills or brushy woodland into open pine forests. In Tex., found in juniper-live oak woodland; in Sonora in large, low, dense clumps of cactus. Eggs large-yolked and unpigmented; laid on land in caves, fissures, or under rocks, during periods of rainfall.
Voice: Resembles the bark of a small dog — a series of rapid yapping notes, at intervals of 2–3 secs.
Range: Extreme s. Ariz. (Santa Rita and Pajarito Mts.), se. N.M.

(lower Pecos R. drainage), and cen. Tex. (escarpment of Edwards Plateau) south to Isthmus of Tehauntepec. Distribution spotty. Near sea level to 8900 ft. (2710 m) in Mexico. **Map 28**
Subspecies: EASTERN BARKING FROG, *H. a. latrans.* Adult males usually over $2\frac{3}{4}$ in. (7 cm). Usually yellow-brown to tan above. Dark bars on dorsal surface of femur, relatively weak and poorly defined. Near Roswell, Chaves Co., and Carlsbad, Eddy Co., N.M.; cen. Tex. WESTERN BARKING FROG, *H. a. cactorum.* Adult males usually less than $2\frac{3}{4}$ in. (7 cm). Yellowish gray to gray-green above. Leg bars darker than in Eastern Barking Frog. Pajarito and Santa Rita Mts. in se. Ariz.; Mexico.

Spadefoot Toads and Relatives: Family Pelobatidae

Our species, members of the genus *Scaphiopus,* are found only in the New World. They are distinguished from the true toads (genus *Bufo*) by their catlike eyes, the single black, sharp-edged "spade" on each hind foot, teeth in the upper jaw, and the rather smooth skin; parotoid glands are absent or indistinct. Pupils vertical in bright light, round at night. Males may have a dusky throat and dark nuptial pads on the innermost front toes. Amplexus is pelvic. True toads typically have horizontal pupils, 2 rounded brown tubercles on each foot, no teeth, a warty skin, large parotoid glands, and amplexus is pectoral.

Spadefoot toads breed in pools that form after heavy rains or in slow streams, reservoirs, or irrigation ditches. Their voices are audible for a great distance and are important in bringing the sexes together for breeding in arid country where the number, location, and suitability of breeding sites is uncertain. A parched region may reverberate with their cries soon after rain begins.

Dry periods are spent in self-made burrows, or those of gophers, squirrels, or kangaroo rats. Spadefoots are active chiefly at night during spring and summer rains. When burrowing, they back into the ground by pushing dirt with their spades while rotating the body. The hind feet move alternately in a circular fashion, like the motion used to stamp out a cigarette.

The genus *Scaphiopus* ranges from Canada to s. Mexico and from coast to coast. 6 species, 5 in our area. Other members of the family occur in Europe, extreme nw. Africa, Asia, and the East Indies. Over 60 species in the family.

COUCH SPADEFOOT *Scaphiopus couchii* **Pl. 10**
Identification: $2\frac{1}{4}$–$3\frac{1}{2}$ in. (5.6–8.7 cm). A large greenish, greenish yellow, or brownish yellow spadefoot with an irregular network, blotches, or flecks of black, brown, or dark green. Whitish below. Eyes widely separated — width of eyelids about the same as or less

than the distance between them. No boss between the eyes, and no pug-dog profile. *Spade* on hind foot black, *sickle-shaped* (Fig. 12, opp. Pl. 10). ***Male:*** Often more greenish than female. Dark markings above usually subdued or absent. Throat pale.

Frequents shortgrass plains, mesquite savannah, creosote bush desert, thornforest and tropical deciduous forest (w. Mexico), and other areas of low rainfall.

Voice: A plaintive cry or groan, declining in pitch, like the anxious bleat of a sheep; a drawn-out *yee-ow,* lasting ½–1¼ secs. In our area, breeds chiefly from May–Sept., during period of rainfall.

Similar species: Other spadefoots have a wedge-shaped spade, eyes set closer together, and a pug-dog profile. Plains and Great Basin Spadefoots (p. 67) have a cranial boss between the eyes.

Range: From sw. Okla., cen. N.M., and s.-cen. Ariz. to tip of Baja Calif., Nayarit, and s. San Luis Potosí; se. Calif. to cen. Tex. Isolated populations in vicinity of Petrified Forest National Monument and southeast of La Junta, Otero Co., Colo. Scattered populations in Calif. between Amos and Ogilby on eastern side of Algodones Dunes; Purgatory and Buzzard's Peak Washes, Imperial Co.; and 15 mi. (24 km) north of Vidal Junction, San Bernardino Co. Near sea level to around 5600 ft. (1710 m). **Map 26**

WESTERN SPADEFOOT *Scaphiopus hammondii* **Pl. 10**

Identification: 1½–2½ in. (3.7–6.2 cm). *No cranial boss between the eyes.* Dusky green or gray above, often with 4 irregular, light-colored stripes on the back; the central pair sometimes set off a dark, hourglass-shaped area. Skin tubercles tipped with orange or reddish. Eye (iris) usually pale gold. Whitish below, without markings. A wedge-shaped, glossy black spade on each hind foot. Distance between eyes usually less than width of eyelid.

Primarily a species of the lowlands, frequenting washes, floodplains of rivers, alluvial fans, playas, and alkali flats, but also ranges into the foothills and mountains. Prefers areas of open vegetation and short grasses, where the soil is sandy or gravelly. Found in valley and foothill grasslands, open chaparral, and pine-oak woodlands. Breeds in winter and spring (Jan.–May) in quiet streams and temporary pools. When handled, this toad may smell like roasted peanuts. Its skin secretion may cause sneezing.

Voice: Hoarse, snore-like; lasting about ½ to 1 sec. May call from a floating position. A distant chorus suggests the sound of someone cutting wood with a handsaw.

Similar species: (1) Plains and (2) Great Basin Spadefoots (p. 67) have a boss between the eyes. (3) Southern Spadefoot (below) has a more elongate spade, is brownish above, and has a copper-colored iris. (4) Couch Spadefoot (p. 65) has an elongate, sickle-shaped spade and widely spaced eyes.

Range: Great Valley, bordering foothills, and Coast Ranges south of San Francisco Bay, Calif., into nw. Baja Calif. (to Mesa de San

Carlos). Mostly below 3000 ft. (910 m). Now extinct throughout much of lowland s. Calif. **Map 25**

SOUTHERN SPADEFOOT **not shown**
Scaphiopus multiplicatus
Identification: $1\frac{1}{2}$-$2\frac{1}{2}$ in. (3.7–6.4 cm). Closely resembles the Western Spadefoot (Pl. 10) and formerly considered of that species. Differs in having a more elongate spade, usually more brown on the back, and a copper-colored iris.

Frequents desert grassland, shortgrass plains, creosote bush and sagebrush desert, mixed grassland and chaparral, piñon-juniper and pine-oak woodlands, and open pine forests. Soil is often sandy or gravelly. Breeds during period of summer rains.
Voice: Similar to Western Spadefoot, but call tends to be a longer, slower trill, lasting about 1 sec.
Similar species: See Western Spadefoot (above).
Range: Sw. Utah and s. Colo. to Guerrero and Oaxaca; w. Ariz. to w. Okla. and w. Tex. Near sea level to around 8100 ft. (2470 m). **Map 25**

GREAT BASIN SPADEFOOT **Pl. 10**
Scaphiopus intermontanus
Identification: $1\frac{1}{2}$–$2\frac{1}{2}$ in. (3.7–6.4 cm). Resembles the Western Spadefoot (p. 66) in structure and color. Ash-gray streaks usually set off a well-defined hourglass marking of gray or olive on the back. A dark brown spot is usually present on each upper eyelid. Spade on hind foot wedge-shaped. *Glandular boss between eyes,* which may help protect head when the spadefoot pushes its way to the surface after a period of burial underground.

Found in the Great Basin, in habitats ranging from sagebrush flats, semi-desert shrublands, and piñon-juniper woodland to high elevations in the spruce-fir belt (Cedar Breaks, Utah). Breeds May–July in permanent and temporary water, often (but not necessarily) after spring and summer rains.
Voice: A hoarse *wa-wa-wa;* a series of short rapid calls, each lasting about $\frac{1}{5}$–1 sec. Rounded, slightly bilobed vocal sac.
Similar species: (1) Western (p. 66) and (2) Couch Spadefoot Toads (p. 65) lack the boss between the eyes. (3) In the Plains Spadefoot (below), the boss is hard and supported by thickened bone.
Range: From extreme s. B.C. (north to 70 Mile House) through the Great Basin to extreme nw. Ariz. and from eastern base of Cascade-Sierran mountain system to Rockies. In Wyo., it ranges east to near Alcova, Natrona Co. To around 9200 ft. (2800 m). **Map 23**

PLAINS SPADEFOOT *Scaphiopus bombifrons* **Pl. 10**
Identification: $1\frac{1}{2}$–$2\frac{1}{2}$ in. (3.7–6.2 cm). A spadefoot with a *prominent boss* (often supported by thickened bone) between the eyes

and a pug-dog profile. Usually with 4 light stripes of irregular outline, the middle pair often setting off an hourglass shape in the middle of the back. Above generally dusky, purplish brown, dark brown, or greenish, flecked with orange to yellow-tipped tubercles; white below. A single glossy, black, wedge-shaped spade on each hind foot. Width of eyelids usually greater than the distance between them.

The prairie spadefoot — inhabits plains, hills, and river bottoms in mixed-grass prairie, sagebrush habitats, desert grassland, and farmland chiefly east of the Rocky Mts., in regions of low rainfall. Prefers loose, sandy or gravelly soil that is suitable for burrowing. Frequents both permanent and temporary water. Usually breeds in flooded areas and temporary pools. In the southern part of its range, it breeds in July during the period of summer rains, in Colo. from May to Aug., and in the north (Alberta) as early as the latter part of May. Tadpoles often cannibalistic.

Voice: A short, distinct, ducklike note usually lasting about $\frac{1}{3}$–$\frac{3}{4}$ sec., but in some fast-trill populations as brief as $\frac{1}{6}$ sec. Call is shorter and more rapidly trilled than the Southern Spadefoot's.

Similar species: (1) Western (p. 66), (2) Southern (p. 67), and Couch Spadefoots (p. 65) have no boss between the eyes. The Couch Spadefoot has a sickle-shaped spade and widely spaced eyes. (4) In the Great Basin Spadefoot (p. 67) the boss tends to be more glandular (fleshy), and the spade is longer and narrower. (5) The Great Plains Toad (p. 74) has 2 brown tubercles on each foot.

Range: Eastern and southern outwash plains of Rocky Mts. from s. Alberta, Saskatchewan, and Manitoba to nw. Tex. and Chihuahua, east to Mo. and e. Okla. Skirts Rockies to south and enters e. Ariz. Isolated populations in s. Tex. and Mexico. An old record from Dauphin, Manitoba. To about 8000 ft. (2440 m). Occasionally hybridizes with the Southern Spadefoot (p. 67) in the southern part of its range. **Map 24**

True Toads: Family Bufonidae

Worldwide, but absent from extremely cold or dry areas and remote oceanic islands. Some 300 species. The only true toad in Australia, the Marine Toad, *Bufo marinus,* has been introduced. Many toads can live under adverse conditions. They range from below sea level in Death Valley, Calif., to above 16,000 ft. (4880 m) in the Andes of S. America and from the tropics nearly to the Arctic Circle. 13 species are found in the West.

Our species (genus *Bufo*) are chunky, short-legged, and warty. Parotoid glands distinguish them from all our other tailess amphibians (see spadefoot toads, p. 65). The parotoids and warts secrete a sticky white poison, which in some species can paralyze or kill dogs and other predators. Many animals, however, eat toads with no ill effect. The skin secretion may irritate the eyes or mouth, and if swallowed in quantity can cause illness. However, ordinary handling poses no danger, and handling toads does not cause warts.

Western U.S. species differ in color, size, shape of the parotoid glands, prominence and arrangement of the cranial crests (ridges that frame the innerside of the upper eyelids), wartiness, and appearance of the foot tubercles. Color may change from light to dark in response to temperature.

Breeding usually occurs in spring and summer, often after rains. Adult males of most species have a dark throat; exceptions are the Western, Black, Yosemite, Southwestern, and Sonoran Desert Toads. All male toads develop brown nuptial pads on the thumb and inner fingers that help them cling to the slippery body of the female during amplexus, which is pectoral in true toads.

SONORAN DESERT TOAD (Colorado River Toad)
Bufo alvarius **Pl. 11**

Identification: 4–7½ in. (10–19 cm). Our largest western toad. Dark brown, olive, or gray above, with smooth skin; long, kidney-shaped parotoids; and prominent cranial crests. *Several large warts on the hind legs stand out conspicuously against the smooth skin.* An enlarged whitish wart near angle of the jaw. Cream below. ***Young:*** Light-colored warts, set in dark spots. ***Male:*** Throat pale, as in female.

Ranges from arid mesquite-creosote bush lowlands and arid grasslands into the oak-sycamore-walnut groves (plant community) in mountain canyons. Enters tropical thorn forest in Mexico. Often found near permanent water of springs, reservoirs, canals, and streams, but also frequents temporary pools and has been reported several miles from water. Widespread throughout the desert. Nocturnal. Activity stimulated by rainfall, but not dependent on rainfall for breeding. Most active May–July. Like most toads, it assumes a butting pose when molested, with its parotoid glands directed toward the intruder. A dog may be temporarily paralyzed (or rarely, killed) if it mouths one of these toads.

Voice: Weak, low-pitched, resembling a ferryboat whistle. Hoots last ½ to about 1 sec. Vocal sac absent or vestigial.

Range: From the Bill Williams R. and lower Colorado R. drainages across s. Ariz. to extreme sw. N.M., south to nw. Sinaloa; extreme se. Calif., where it is now near extinction. Sea level to 5300 ft. (1610 m). **Map 38**

WESTERN TOAD *Bufo boreas* **Pl. 11**

Identification: 2½–5 in. (6.2–12.5 cm). The *white or cream-colored dorsal stripe and lack of cranial crests* will usually identify this toad. The parotoid glands are oval, well separated, and slightly larger than the upper eyelids. Well-developed tarsal fold. Dusky, gray, or greenish above, with warts set in dark blotches and often tinged with rust. ***Young:*** When recently transformed, around $\frac{1}{4}$ in. (6 mm). Dorsal stripe weak or absent. Larger young have prominent spotting, with undersides of feet yellow. ***Male:*** Usually less blotched and with smoother skin than female. Throat pale, as in female.

Frequents a great variety of habitats: desert streams and springs, grassland, woodland, and mountain meadows. In and near ponds, lakes, reservoirs, rivers, and streams. Active at night in warm, low-lying areas; diurnal at high elevations and in the north. Buries itself in loose soil or seeks shelter in the borrows of gophers, ground squirrels, and other animals. Tends to walk rather than hop. Active Jan.–Oct., breeding late Jan.–July, depending on latitude, elevation, and local conditions.

Voice: A mellow chirruping, suggesting the peeping of a chick. No vocal sac.

Similar species: (1) Woodhouse Toad (p. 72) has conspicuous cranial crests or a cranial boss and the male has a dark throat. (2) Black Toad (p. 71) is heavily mottled above and below with black. (3) See also Yosemite Toad (p. 71).

Range: S. Alaska to n. Baja Calif.; Rocky Mts. to Pacific Coast. Absent from most of arid Southwest, but isolated populations at Owen's Valley, Westgard Pass, Darwin Falls, and Grapevine Canyon, Inyo Co., and introduced at California City, Kern Co., Calif. Hybridizes with the Red-spotted Toad (p. 73) at Darwin Falls, and occasionally with Canadian Toad (p. 75) in cen. Alberta. Sea level to over 11,800 ft. (3600 m). **Map 30**

Subspecies: BOREAL TOAD, *B. b. boreas.* Considerable dark blotching both above and below. Sometimes almost all dark above, and individuals from eastern side of Hot Creek Range, Nye Co., Nev., are dark-bellied. CALIFORNIA TOAD, *B. b. halophilus.* Generally less dark blotching than in Boreal Toad. Head wider, eyes larger (less distance between upper eyelids), and feet smaller.

AMARGOSA TOAD *Bufo nelsoni* **not shown**

Identification: 2–3 in. (5–7.5 cm). Resembles Western Toad but head narrow, snout long, and limbs short — elbow and knee do not touch when placed along sides with body held straight. Dorsal ground color may be brownish.

Usually found near water. Diurnal in spring, becoming nocturnal in summer. Breeds mid-March to early April.

Similar species: (1) Western Toad (p. 69) has broader head, blunter snout, longer limbs, larger feet with more webbing, and tends to have rougher skin. (2) Black Toad (below) is much darker in color.

Range: Amargosa R. Valley (Oasis Valley) in vicinity of Springdale and Beatty, including Crystal and Indian Springs, Nye Co., Nev. **Map 30**

BLACK TOAD *Bufo exsul* **not shown**

Identification: 1¾–2⅞ in. (4.4–7.1 cm). A *small, dark-colored* relative of the Western Toad (p. 69). Often nearly solid black above, with scattered whitish flecks and lines. A narrow white or cream middorsal stripe. White or cream below, heavily spotted and blotched with black. Skin relatively smooth. ***Young:*** Olive-colored above. Foot tubercles yellow-orange, becoming whitish or cream in older individuals. ***Male:*** Throat pale, unmarked or lightly spotted, like female's.

Found only in marshes of grass, sedge, dwarf bulrush and watercress, formed by water flow from springs in Deep Springs Valley. Surrounding areas are dry. Highly aquatic, but has been seen on dry soil over 40 ft. (12 m) from nearest water. Blends with surroundings when on damp soil along canal banks, among bushes, and in dark-colored water courses, but is conspicuous on pale, dried-out soil. Diurnal, but in warmer weather active at night. Active late Mar. to mid-Sept. Breeds chiefly from late Mar. to May, perhaps as late as June.

Voice: Resembles the Western Toad's, but higher pitched.

Range: Deep Springs (Buckhorn Springs) at around 5000 ft (1520 m), Deep Springs Valley, between the Inyo and White Mts., Inyo Co., Calif. A population (evidently introduced) at Antelope Springs (5600 ft. — 1710 m) about 5 mi. (8 km) north of Buckhorn appears to have died out. **Map 30**

YOSEMITE TOAD *Bufo canorus* **Pl. 11**

Identification: 1¾–2¾ in. (3.1–6.9 cm). The toad of the high Sierra Nevada, a close relative of the Western Toad. Differs in having smoother skin; *large, flat parotoids that are less than the width of a gland apart;* and closely set eyes — distance between them less than the width of the upper eyelid (as viewed from above). Sexes differ greatly in color. ***Female and young:*** Many blotches on a pale background, parotoids usually tan-colored, and the dorsal stripe is usually narrow or absent. ***Male:*** Pale yellow-green or dark olive above, with dark blotches virtually absent or reduced to small scattered flecks. Throat pale like female's.

Frequents high mountain meadows and forest borders, emerging soon after the snow melts. Active April–Oct., breeding in shallow pools and lake margins, or in the quiet water of streams, May–July and perhaps Aug. Chiefly diurnal and usually active only in sunlit areas. On cool days may not be active until afternoon. Seeks shelter in burrows of gophers and meadow mice and in clumps of grass, sedges, or willows near water.

Voice: A mellow, sustained musical trill of 10–20 or more notes, usually uttered rapidly and at frequent intervals.

Similar species: Immature Yosemite Toads are colored like the Western Toad (p. 69), but parotoids of the latter are farther apart (separated by about twice the width of a gland). The Western

Toad is present at high altitudes in the s. Sierra Nevada south of Kaiser Pass, Fresno Co., where the habitat resembles that occupied by the Yosemite Toad farther north.
Range: High Sierra of Calif. from vicinity of Grass Lake, Eldorado Co., to south of Kaiser Pass and Evolution Lake, Fresno Co. From 4800–12,000 ft. (1460–3630 m), mostly above 9000 ft. (2740 m). Hybridizes with the Western Toad in Blue Lakes region and elsewhere in the northern part of its range. **Map 31**

WOODHOUSE TOAD *Bufo woodhousei* **Pl. 12**
Identification: 1¾–5 in. (4.5–12.5 cm). The *whitish dorsal stripe, prominent cranial crests,* and elongate, divergent parotoids should distinguish this toad. A boss is sometimes present between the cranial crests. Gray, yellowish brown, olive, or blackish above, usually with dark blotches. Yellow and black network on rear of thighs. Cream to beige below, with or without dark flecks. ***Male:*** Throat sooty, setting off pale yellow border of lower jaw.

Frequents a great variety of habitats — grassland, sagebrush flats, woods, desert streams, valleys, floodplains, farms, and even city backyards. It seems to prefer sandy areas, breeding in quiet water of streams, marshes, lakes, freshwater pools and irrigation ditches, usually during or soon after rains. Breeds Mar.–July, sometimes as late as early Sept.
Voice: Has been compared to a snore, an infant's cry, and the bawling of a calf — a nasal *w-a-a-a-ah.* An explosive, wheezy sound usually lasting about 1–2½ sec., often suddenly dropping in pitch at the end. Vocal sac round.
Similar species: (1) Southwestern Toad (below) lacks the dorsal stripe, has weak cranial crests (if any), more rounded parotoids, and males have a pale throat. (2) Canadian Toad (p. 75) has a narrow, parallel-sided boss, is heavily spotted below, and has a softer, more musical call. (3) See also Western Toad (p. 69) and Red-spotted Toad (p. 73).
Range: N. Mont. to Durango; Atlantic Coast to se. Wash., w. Utah, and se. Calif. Big Sandy R. near Wikieup, Mohave Co., Ariz. (see dot on map). To 8500 ft. (2590 m). Hybridizes with Southwestern Toad (below) and with Texas Toad (p. 74). **Map 33**
Subspecies: WESTERN WOODHOUSE TOAD, *B. w. woodhousei.* Cranial crests blend with rather smooth, elevated area on forehead. Dorsal stripe complete. SOUTHWESTERN WOODHOUSE TOAD, *B. w. australis.* Distinct narrow crests, separated by a trough toward the front. Tends to lack stripe on snout and to have well-developed black markings on each side of chest. S. Ariz., s. N.M., sw. Tex., into n. Mexico.

SOUTHWESTERN TOAD *Bufo microscaphus* **Pl. 12**
Identification: 2–3¼ in. (5–8.1 cm). A rather uniformly warty, stocky toad with a light-colored stripe across the head, including

the eyelids. Parotoid glands oval-shaped and widely separated, *pale toward front.* Above greenish gray, buff, brown, or salmon, the color harmonizing with the general color of soil and rocks. *Usually a light area on each sacral hump* (see front endpapers) *and in middle of back.* Buff below, often unspotted. Cranial crests weak or absent. ***Young:*** Ash-white, light olive, or salmon above, with or without prominent black spots; red-tipped tubercles on back. Underside of feet yellow. ***Male:*** Throat pale, like female's.

A toad of washes, streams, and arroyos in semiarid parts of the Southwest. Breeds in brooks or streams; does not depend directly on rainfall. In Calif., frequents sandy banks grown to willows, cottonwoods, or sycamores, and in Ariz. and N.M. rocky streams in the pine-oak belt. Adults nocturnal except during the breeding season. Hops more often than walks. Breeds Mar.–July but may be abroad until Sept. Height of breeding season in June in sw. Utah, but at higher elevations breeding may occur until July and perhaps Aug.

Voice: A melodious trill, usually lasting 8–10 secs.; often rising in pitch at first and usually ending abruptly. Vocal sac round.

Similar species: See (1) Woodhouse Toad (above) and (2) Texas Toad (p. 74).

Range: S. Nev. to s. Durango; coastal s. Calif. to nw. Baja Calif. east to sw. N.M. Many isolated populations. From near sea level to around 6000 ft. (1830 m) in U.S. and 8500 ft. (2590 m) in Mexico. **Map 32**

Subspecies: ARIZONA TOAD, *B. m. microscaphus* (Pl. 12). Usually little or no dark spotting on back. Skin relatively smooth. Found at scattered localities in headwaters of tributaries of Colorado R. in sw. Utah, s. Nev., cen. Ariz., and w. N.M.; Sierra Madre Occidental. Hybridizes with Woodhouse Toad along Virgin R. and in cen. Ariz. ARROYO TOAD, *B. m. californicus* (Pl. 12). Dark-spotted above. Skin rough. S. Calif., chiefly west of desert from near Santa Margarita, San Luis Obispo Co., to nw. Baja Calif. Desert population along Mojave R., San Bernardino Co., Calif.

RED-SPOTTED TOAD *Bufo punctatus* **Pl. 12**

Identification: $1\frac{1}{2}$–3 in. (3.7–7.5 cm). A small toad with a *flattened head and body and round parotoids,* each about same size as an eye. Snout pointed. Cranial crests weak or absent. Light gray, olive, or reddish brown above, with reddish or orange warts. Whitish to buff below, with or without spotting. ***Young:*** Numerous red- or orange-tipped warts. Dark-spotted below. Underside of feet yellow. ***Male:*** Throat dusky.

A toad of desert streams and oases, open grassland and scrubland, oak woodland, rocky canyons and arroyos. Although sometimes found on the floodplains of rivers, it is more often found on or among rocks, where it finds shelter in the crevices. Climbs rocks with ease. Breeds Mar.–Sept. during or after rains in springs,

rain pools, reservoirs, and temporary pools of intermittent streams. Chiefly nocturnal, but may be diurnal when breeding.
Voice: A prolonged, clear musical trill, less rapid and clearer than the Green Toad's (p. 76), lasting about 6–10 secs. Pitch high, often nearly constant but occasionally dropping toward the end. Vocal sac round.
Similar species: Young Woodhouse Toads (above), which may have reddish-tipped warts, usually have elongate parotoids and a middorsal stripe.
Range: S. Nev. and sw. Kans. to Hidalgo and tip of Baja Calif. Cen. Tex. to se. Calif. From below sea level (Death Valley, Calif.) to around 6500 ft. (1980 m). Hybridizes with Western Toad at Darwin Canyon, Inyo Co., Calif. and perhaps with Woodhouse Toad near Grand Junction, Mesa Co., Colo. **Map 39**

GREAT PLAINS TOAD *Bufo cognatus* **Pl. 11**
Identification: 1⅘–4½ in. (4.5–11.2 cm). A toad with large, well-defined, *pale-bordered dark blotches, in symmetrical pairs on its back*. Cranial crests diverge widely toward the rear and are more or less united on the snout to form a boss. Inner tubercle on each hind foot usually sharp-edged. Generally light brown, olive, or gray above, with dusky, olive, or green blotches. Sometimes a narrow middorsal stripe. Whitish below, usually unspotted. ***Young:*** Numerous small, brick-red tubercles. Crests form a V. ***Male:*** Dark loose skin of deflated vocal sac often partly concealed by pale skin flap.

Inhabits prairies or deserts, often breeding after heavy rains in summer in shallow temporary pools or quiet water of streams, marshes, irrigation ditches, and flooded fields, where it may gather in large numbers. Primarily a grassland species but frequents creosote bush desert, mesquite woodland, and sagebrush plains in the West. Nocturnal. A proficient burrower. Breeds Mar.–Sept.
Voice: A harsh explosive clatter, lasting 5–50 or more secs., almost deafening when large numbers are heard at close range. When inflated, vocal sac sausage-shaped, ⅓ size of body.
Similar species: (1) Texas Toad (below) may have pairs of spots on its back, but they are smaller and less well defined. Cranial crests and boss on snout are less prominent. Voice a series of short trills rather than a prolonged clatter. (2) See also Plains Spadefoot (p. 67).
Range: Great Plains from extreme s. Canada to San Luis Potosí, Mexico; w. Tex. to extreme se. Calif. and s. Nev. Highly spotty distribution in desert part of range. Near sea level to around 8000 ft. (2440 m). Hybridizes with the Texas Toad and apparently rarely with the Canadian Toad. **Map 35**

TEXAS TOAD *Bufo speciosus* **Pl. 12**
Identification: 2–3½ in. (5–8.7 cm). A close relative of the Great

Plains Toad (above). A rather *plain-colored, uniformly warty* species with *no dorsal stripe. Cranial crests weak or absent.* Tubercles on hind foot usually blackish and sharp-edged, the inner one sickle-shaped. Parotoid glands oval and widely separated. Greenish gray to brown above, sometimes with dark blotches on the back that are arranged in symmetrical pairs. White to cream below, unmarked or with dark spots. ***Young:*** Gray-brown above, blotched with green and flecked with black. Warts tipped with red. ***Male:*** Olive-colored skin of deflated vocal sac covered by pale skin fold.

A nocturnal, burrowing species of mesquite woodland, prairie, and farmland. Breeds after rains, April–Sept., in quiet water of rain pools, reservoirs, and cattle tanks.

Voice: A continuous series of explosive, shrill trills, each lasting about ½–1 sec., often given at intervals of about 1 sec. After some minutes of calling there may be a distinct drop in pitch followed by a return to the original pitch. Vocal sac sausage-shaped.

Similar species: (1) Southwestern Toad (p. 72) has a light-colored band across the head and a light-colored patch at the front end of each parotoid gland and on each sacral hump. Hind foot tubercles brown, not sharp-edged. (2) See also Great Plains Toad (p. 74).

Range: Extreme sw. Kans., s. N.M., and Tex. into ne. Mexico. Near sea level to about 4000 ft. (1220 m). Hybridizes with the Woodhouse Toad (p. 72) and Great Plains Toad (p. 74). **Map 36**

CANADIAN TOAD *Bufo hemiophrys* **Pl. 12**

Identification: 1½–3 in. (3.7–7.5 cm). Generally brownish, greenish, to light gray above, with reddish tubercles that are located in dark spots. Spots usually lack light-colored borders. Some individuals may be rust-red to reddish brown, and some may be tinged with greenish. Whitish stripe on back. A *parallel-sided boss on the head;* boss may be slightly convex or flat, and sometimes has a furrow down the middle. Whitish below, spotted with dusky and becoming yellowish on sides. ***Young:*** Cranial crests appear with age and eventually unite to form a boss. ***Male:*** Throat dark-colored.

A toad of the prairies and aspen parklands, usually found in or near water. Frequents lakes, ponds, streams, marshes, potholes, and roadside ditches, where it usually breeds in the shallows. May swim well out from shore when frightened. Chiefly diurnal during the breeding season, retiring to sandy or loamy areas to bury itself at night. May be active on warm nights. Active from late Mar. to Sept.; breeds May–July, depending on locality.

Voice: A clear, soft trill uttered about twice per minute and lasting about 1⅓–5 secs. Vocal sac round.

Similar species: See Woodhouse Toad (p. 72).

Range: Fort Smith area, Canada, to ne. S.D.; cen. Alberta to e.

Manitoba. Isolated populations in se. Wyo. along Big and Little Laramie Rivers to about 15 mi. (24 km) north and 15 mi. (24 km) west of Laramie, Albany Co. These populations, classed as Endangered, are now in sharp decline and perhaps on the verge of extinction. From around 1000–7000 ft. (300–2130 m). Interbreeds with the American Toad *(B. americanus)* outside our area, in eastern part of its range. Coexists with Western Toad in cen. Alberta (north of Edmonton). **Map 34**

GREEN TOAD *Bufo debilis* **Pl. 10**

Identification: 1⅛–2 in. (2.8–5 cm). A small, flat, *green or yellow-green* toad with small black spots and bars on its back. The black markings may be more or less united to form a network. Large, elongate, widely separated parotoids. Cranial crests weak or absent. White below. ***Male:*** Throat dark; yellow or cream in female.

A species of arid and semiarid plains, valleys, and foothills — treeless or with scattered shrubs and trees and grass around the pools usually sought as spawning sites. Frequents grasslands, mesquite savannah, and creosote bush flats. Ordinarily not found on steep slopes or in barren rocky areas. A secretive, burrowing, nocturnal toad, generally abroad for only a brief period during and after rains. Breeds April–Aug. in temporary streams and pools that form during the summer rainy season; occasionally in irrigation ditches and reservoirs. When trilling, Green Toads often hide under clumps of grass or other growth near water, and are difficult to see. Use triangulation to find them (see p. 14).

Voice: A wheezy buzz lasting about 2–10 secs., usually at intervals of 5 secs. or more. Vocal sac round.

Similar species: See Sonoran Green Toad (below).

Range: Se. Colo. and sw. Kans. to Zacatecas; se. Ariz. to e. Tex. To above 6000 ft. (1830 m), but mostly to around 4000 ft. (1220 m). **Map 37**

Subspecies: The WESTERN GREEN TOAD, *B. d. insidior,* occurs in our area.

SONORAN GREEN TOAD *Bufo retiformis* **Pl. 10**

Identification: 1⅛–2¼ (2.8–5.6 cm). Similar to the Green Toad (Pl. 10) but *vividly marked above with a network of black* or brownish that sets off oval areas of greenish yellow ground color. These oval areas are about twice the size of those on a Green Toad of similar size. ***Male:*** Throat dark.

A secretive nocturnal species of mesquite grassland and creosote bush desert. Breeds July–Aug. in rainwater sumps and wash bottoms bordered by fresh grass and scattered shrubs. Males begin to call at nightfall after summer rains, usually from among grass within a foot or so of the water's edge, but occasionally from more distant sites.

Voice: A combined buzz and whistle, a wheezy call lasting $1\text{–}3\frac{1}{5}$ secs., gradually lowering in pitch or remaining constant and ending abruptly. May be highly ventriloquial, sounding as if 20 ft. (6 m) away when within 5 ft. (1.5 m). Voice resembles the Great Plains Narrow-mouthed Toad's. Vocal sac round.
Similar species: The Green Toad (above) has a more broken black network dorsally, often represented by scattered spots and bars that enclose areas of light ground color which are usually only half the size of those of the Sonoran Green Toad.
Range: S.-cen. Ariz. south to w.-cen. Sonora. In s. Ariz. from Santa Rosa Wash, Pinal Co. and Organ Pipe Cactus National Monument to the vicinity of the San Xavier Mission, Pima Co. From about 500–2400 ft. (150–730 m). **Map 37**

Treefrogs and Their Allies: Family Hylidae

A large family (about 600 species) of usually slim-waisted, long-legged frogs, mostly of small size. Many hylids are arboreal (tree-dwelling) and have well-developed toe pads that are set off from the rest of the toe by a small, extra segment (Fig. 5, No. 6, p. 27). These frogs are found on all continents except Antarctica, but are most abundant and varied in the New World tropics. Treefrogs *(Pternohyla* and *Hyla),* a cricket frog *(Acris),* and a chorus frog *(Pseudacris)* occur in our area. Amplexus is pectoral.

NORTHERN CRICKET FROG *Acris crepitans* **Pl. 16**
Identification: $\frac{5}{8}\text{–}1\frac{1}{2}$ in. (1.5–3.7 cm). A small, slim-waisted frog with slender webbed toes and a triangular mark on the head (occasionally absent). No toe pads. Above gray, light brown, green, reddish, or reddish green, usually with a middorsal stripe of similar color. The gray form is common in the western and northern parts of range. Dark markings on back and dark bands on legs. *White bar* extends from eye to base of foreleg. *A dark stripe on the rear of the thigh.* ***Male:*** Throat dusky, suffused with yellow. More spotting below than in female.

Ranges widely over eastern and central U.S., entering the shortgrass plains of e. Colo. and N.M. along streams and rivers. Basks on sunny banks of shallow pools. Often found in groups; individuals scatter when frightened, leaping high and fast or skittering over the surface of water. Active all year except midwinter in the north. Breeds Feb.–Aug.
Voice: A metallic *gick, gick, gick* — resembling the sound made by striking two stones together; about 1 call per second, the rate gradually increasing. Vocal sac round.
Similar species: Young frogs (*Rana* species, p. 82) may be mistaken for a Cricket Frog. Look for the thigh stripe, triangular mark on the head, and white facial bar of Cricket Frog.

Range: Mich. to ne. Mexico; L.I., N.Y. to e. Colo. and se. N.M. Near sea level to around 4000 ft. (1220 m). **Map 42**
Subspecies: BLANCHARD CRICKET FROG, *A. c. blanchardi,* occurs in our area.

STRIPED CHORUS FROG *Pseudacris triseriata* **Pl. 16**
Identification: ¾–1½ in. (1.9–4 cm). A small, slim frog *without toe pads* and little webbing. Proportions stockier, the tibia shortened in nw. part of range. Dorsal coloration highly variable — gray, brown, reddish, olive, or green. Several different color types may occur at the same locality. A dark stripe extends from snout through eye to groin, contrasting with a white stripe on the upper jaw. Usually 3 dark stripes on the back, sometimes broken or replaced by spots. Often a triangular spot on the head. Whitish, yellowish, or pale olive below; unmarked or with a few dark spots on throat and chest. ***Male:*** Throat greenish yellow to dark olive, with lengthwise folds of loose skin.

A frog of grassy pools, lakes, and marshes of prairies and mountains. Frequents grassland, woodland, and forest. Usually breeds Nov.–July in shallow, temporary pools in the open, but also uses deep, more permanent water in dense woods. Breeds earliest in the south. Has adapted well to human habitation, occurring on farms and in cities except in areas where pesticides are used heavily.
Voice: A vibrant *prreep, prreep* with rising inflection, lasting about ½–1½ secs.; some 30–90 calls per minute. To imitate the call, stroke the teeth of a pocket comb. Choruses occur night and day during the height of the breeding season, and calling may continue to as late as Aug. Vocal sac round.
Similar species: (1) Pacific Treefrog (p. 80) and (2) Mountain Treefrog (p. 81) have toe pads. In the Pacific Treefrog, the eyestripe stops at the shoulder.
Range: Great Bear Lake in nw. Canada to Gulf of Mexico; N.J. to cen. Ariz. and eastern border of Great Basin. Near sea level to above 12,000 ft. (3670 m) in Uintah Mts., Utah. **Map 40**
Subspecies: MIDLAND CHORUS FROG, *P. t. triseriata* (Pl. 16). Proportions relatively slender. Tibia not notably shortened. BOREAL CHORUS FROG, *P. t. maculata* (Pl. 16). Proportions stockier. Tibia shortened — so much so that this frog is a less efficient jumper than the Midland Chorus Frog.

NORTHERN CASQUE-HEADED FROG **Pl. 16**
(Lowland Burrowing Treefrog) *Pternohyla fodiens*
Identification: 1½–2½ in. (3.7–6.2 cm). A *casque-headed* frog — the upper surface of the head is very hard and the skin is firmly attached. Prominent ridge between eye and nostril, and *fold of skin at back of head.* Toe pads small but distinct. A *single large whitish tubercle on each hind foot.* Brown or pale yellow above, with large, dark brown spots edged with black. Plain white below. ***Male:*** Dark patch on each side of throat.

A terrestrial, burrowing, nocturnal frog of open grassy terrain and tropical scrub forests. Occurs in mesquite grassland in extreme s. Ariz., where it breeds June–Sept. during period of summer rains. After the first hard rain in July, choruses quickly form around temporary pools.

Voice: A loud, low-pitched *walk, walk, walk;* 2–3 calls per sec., each lasting $\frac{1}{5}$–$\frac{1}{2}$ sec. and given on one pitch. Resembles the call of the Pacific Treefrog, but the sounds are lower-pitched, hoarser, shorter, faster, and with no rising inflection. Large vocal sac that looks slightly bilobed from the front.

Range: San Simon Valley between Sells and Ajo, Ariz., north to near Hickiwan, Pima Co., Ariz., south in w. Mexico from Sonora to Michoacán. Near sea level to about 4900 ft. (1490 m). **Map 41**

Treefrogs: Genus *Hyla*

Found on all continents except Antarctica and Australia, but in Africa only north of the Sahara. Most diverse and abundant in the American tropics. Probably over 400 species; 13 in the U.S. — most in the Southeast, 4 in the West.

Typically, these frogs have a rather large head, a rounded snout, large eyes, a slim waist, and prominent toe pads. Most are jumpers and climbers and can cling to twigs or climb a vertical surface with their adhesive toe pads. The genus includes both tree-dwelling and ground-dwelling species. Most can change color rapidly.

CANYON TREEFROG *Hyla arenicolor* **Pl. 16**

Identification: $1\frac{1}{4}$–$2\frac{1}{4}$ in. (3.1–5.6 cm). A brown, cream, or olive-gray treefrog that *usually has no eyestripe;* blotched or spotted with dark brown or olive, but sometimes with little or no pattern (sw. Utah). Cream below, grading to yellow on hind legs. Large toe pads. Webbing of hind foot moderately well developed (Fig. 15, opp. Pl. 16). Skin rather rough. ***Male:*** Throat dusky.

A small, well-camouflaged frog that often huddles in niches on the sides of boulders or streambanks, within easy jumping distance of water. Favors intermittent or permanent streams with quiet pools that have a hard, rocky bottom. Frequents arroyos in semi-arid grassland, streams in piñon-juniper and pine-oak woodlands, and tropical scrub forest (Mexico). Chiefly a ground-dwelling frog but occasionally climbs trees. Breeds April–July, perhaps through Aug., often in rock-bound pools in canyon bottoms.

Voice: An explosive, single-pitched whirring that sounds like a rivet gun and lasts $\frac{1}{2}$–3 secs. Vocal sac looks weakly bilobed from above.

Similar species: See California Treefrog (p. 80).

Range: W. Colo. and s. Utah to n. Oaxaca; w. Tex. to Colorado R. in nw. Ariz. Isolated populations in Mogollon highlands of Ariz., on the Canadian R. and upper Pecos R., in the Big Florida Mts.

and Cookes Peak area, N.M., and in the Davis and Chisos Mts. in w. Tex. Old record (1886) for Mesa de Maya, Las Animas Co., Colo. From near sea level to around 9800 ft. (2990 m). **Map 45**

CALIFORNIA TREEFROG *Hyla cadaverina* **Pl. 16**
Identification: 1–2 in. (2.5–5 cm). Typically a *gray or brown treefrog with dark blotches; usually no eyestripe.* Blends in well with background — frogs on granite tend to be dark-blotched, those on sandstone are usually plain. Whitish below with yellow on underside of hind legs, in groin, and on lower abdomen. Toes with well-developed webbing and conspicuous pads. ***Male:*** Throat dusky.

Found near canyon streams and washes where there are rocks, quiet pools, and shade. Ranges from the desert and coastal stream courses to the pine belt in the mountains. Sometimes occurs along stretches of rather rapidly flowing water. Breeds Feb.–early Oct.
Voice: A ducklike quack — short, low-pitched, ending abruptly and given repeatedly, lacking the whirring quality of the Canyon Treefrog's. Calls usually last about $\frac{1}{5}$–$\frac{1}{2}$ sec., have little or no inflection, and seldom have two parts. Usually heard day and night at the peak of the breeding season. Vocal sac round.
Similar species: (1) Canyon Treefrog (p. 79) tends to be more brown than pale gray, and has reduced webbing on the hind foot and larger toe pads and ear drums; the voice is quite different. (2) See also Pacific Treefrog (below).
Range: Distribution very spotty. Mountains of s. Calif., including western fringe of desert along streams and at oases (desert slope of Peninsular Ranges, Forty-nine Palms, Indian Cove), south into n. Baja Calif. to area near Bahia de los Angeles. From near sea level to around 7500 ft. (2290 m). **Map 45**
Remarks: Although the range of this treefrog overlaps that of the Pacific Treefrog in s. Calif. and n. Baja Calif., the two species are seldom found together at the same locality.

PACIFIC TREEFROG *Hyla regilla* **Pl. 16**
Identification: $\frac{3}{4}$–2 in. (1.9–5 cm). A small frog with toe pads and *black or dark brown eyestripe.* The stripe is almost always present but is difficult to see in dark individuals. Dorsal coloration highly variable — green, tan, reddish, gray, brown, or black, but usually green or shades of brown. An individual may change from dark to light phase in a few minutes, but its basic hue does not change. Often a triangular dark spot on the head. Dark spots on back and legs vary in distinctness depending on color phase. Cream below, yellowish on hindquarters. ***Male:*** Throat dusky, wrinkled.

Frequents a variety of habitats from sea level high into mountains — grassland, chaparral, woodland, forest, desert oases, and farmland. Breeds Nov.–July in marshes, lakes, ponds, roadside ditches, reservoirs, and slow streams. Chiefly a ground-dweller, found among low plant growth near water.

Voice: The most commonly heard frog on the Pacific Coast. Calls often uttered in sequence, about 1 per second; a loud, two-parted *kreck-ek,* the last syllable with rising inflection. Call resembles California Treefrog's but is longer, higher-pitched, inflected, more musical, and more often has two parts. Vocal sac round.
Similar species: (1) California Treefrog (above) usually has no eyestripe, has larger toe pads and more fully webbed hind toes (Fig. 15), and is rarely green. (2) In the Mountain Treefrog (below), the eyestripe extends well beyond the shoulder. Webbing is reduced (Fig. 15). (3) See Tailed Frog (p. 63).
Range: From Mt. Scriven and McBride areas, B.C. to tip of Baja Calif., east to w. Mont. and e. Nev. The only native frog presently known from islands off the coast of s. Calif. Introduced at Eutsuk Lake, B.C. Desert populations in s. Calif. at California City and Soda Springs, probably also introduced. Pushwalla Palms population appears to be native. Sea level to around 11,600 ft. (3540 m). **Map 43**

MOUNTAIN TREEFROG *Hyla eximia* **Pl. 16**
Identification: $^3/_4$–$2^1/_4$ in. (1.9–5.6 cm). Resembles the Pacific Treefrog (above). Green to brownish above, with a *dark eyestripe that extends beyond the shoulder,* sometimes to the groin; toward the rear the stripe may break up into spots. Note the thin white line separating the dark stripe from the back color. Spotting on head and upper back usually scarce or absent. Some individuals have a spot on each upper eyelid and dark lengthwise bars or spots on the lower back and some completely lack such markings. Toe pads distinct but small. Webbing reduced. ***Male:*** Throat dusky.

Frequents meadows in oak-pine or pine-fir forests in the U.S., generally at elevations above 5000 ft. (1520 m). In Mexico in mesquite grassland, scrub, and pine-oak forests. Found both on the ground and in shrubs and trees, usually near grassy shallow pools and along the slower parts of streams. Breeds June–Aug., during and after rains.
Voice: A series of short, low-pitched notes, sometimes distinct and separate or given as a trill. Individual notes are brief, metallic clacks, each lasting about $^1/_4$–$^1/_2$ sec., uttered 40 to over 150 times per minute. (Individual frogs vary greatly in call rate.) Lacks the two-parted quality of the Pacific Treefrog's voice. Vocal sac round.
Similar species: See Pacific Treefrog (above).
Range: Mountains of cen. Ariz. and w. N.M., south in Sierra Madre Occidental to Guerrero (Mexico). Isolated population in Huachuca Mts., Cochise Co., Ariz. An old record from Nutria, McKinley Co. (?), N.M. From around 3000–9500 ft. (910–2900 m). **Map 44**

True Frogs: Family Ranidae

Typically slim-waisted, long-legged, smooth-skinned jumpers with webbed hind feet, and often with a pair of dorsolateral folds (glandular ridges) that extend from behind the eyes to the lower back (see front endpapers). Any western tail-less amphibian with *distinct dorsolateral folds* is a true frog. Family best represented in Africa, but species are found on all continents except Antarctica. Over 600 species. Only the large, widespread genus *Rana* (with some 250 species) occurs in the New World. 21 species in N. America north of Mexico; 7 in the East, 14 in our area. There are a dozen or so more in the New World tropics. Two of our species, the Bullfrog and the Green Frog, have been introduced. Two native species, the Northern Leopard Frog and the Wood Frog, range across N. America. Some of our western frogs are difficult to identify — rely heavily on the range maps.

In males during the breeding season, the forelimbs and thumb bases become enlarged and webbing increases; a dark nuptial pad appears on each thumb. Amplexus is pectoral. Vocal sac paired or single, often inconspicuous.

RED-LEGGED FROG *Rana aurora* **Pls. 13, 14**
Identification: 1¾–5¼ in. (4.4–13.1 cm). Red on lower abdomen and underside of hind legs, often overlying yellow ground color. Usually has a *dark mask bordered by a whitish jaw stripe* (Fig. 13, opp. Pl 13). Back often has many small black flecks and larger, irregular dark blotches with indistinct outlines on brown, gray, olive, or reddish ground color. In some individuals, the flecks join to form a more or less continuous network of black lines. Dark bands on legs. *Usually with coarse black (or gray), red, and yellow mottling in groin.* Relatively long legs; heel of adpressed hind limb extends to or beyond nostril. Eyes turned outward, well covered by lids as viewed from above. Prominent dorsolateral folds. ***Young:*** May have yellow instead of red on underside of legs and in groin. ***Male:*** Enlarged forelimbs, thumb base, and webbing.

Chiefly a pond frog that inhabits humid forests, woodlands, grasslands, and streamsides, especially where cattails or other plants provide good cover. Most common in the lowlands and foothills. Frequents marshes, streams, lakes, reservoirs, ponds, and other, usually permanent, sources of water. Generally found in or near water, but disperses after rains and may appear in damp woods and meadows far from water. Breeding period short, often lasting only 1–2 weeks; usually Jan.–April, depending on locality. When not breeding, may be found in damp woods.
Voice: A stuttering, accelerating series of guttural notes on one pitch — *uh-uh-uh-uh-uh-rowr;* the last note, sometimes omitted, resembles a growl. Calls last about 1–3 secs. but are weak and

easily missed. Occasionally only 2–4 chuckles are given. When the frogs are in chorus a continual low clucking is heard. Calls sometimes given under water. When frog calls, throat enlarges at center and sides.

Similar species: (1) In the Spotted Frog (p. 84) the light jaw stripe usually extends to the shoulder, the groin is usually unmottled, and the eyes are slightly upturned and are less completely covered by the lids (Fig. 13). (2) The Cascades Frog (p. 85), a mountain species, usually has distinct black spots on its back; yellowish color on lower abdomen and underside of legs; a yellowish, lightly mottled groin; and generally rougher skin. (3) See also Foothill Yellow-legged Frog (p. 86).

Range: Chiefly west of Cascade-Sierran crest from sw. B.C. (Sullivan Bay) to nw. Baja Calif. (Arroyo Santo Domingo). At one time its range included parts of the Great Valley of Calif., but it is now apparently absent there. In Nye Co., Nev., introduced at Millett and elsewhere in Big Smoky Valley and at Duckwater. The Red-legged Frog may now be extinct in the southern Sierra Nevada, Calif., because of habitat disturbances and the introduction of the Bullfrog. It was heavily marketed in cen. Calif. and elsewhere as a source of frog legs in the late 1800s and early 1900s. An old record (1919) from Santa Cruz I. (near Pelican Bay), Calif. From near sea level to about 8000 ft. (2440 m). **Map 48**

Subspecies: NORTHERN RED-LEGGED FROG, *R. a. aurora.* Dorsal spots often lack light centers. To 3 in. (7.5 cm). CALIFORNIA RED-LEGGED FROG, *R. a. draytonii.* Dorsal spots more numerous, usually with light centers. Skin rougher, limbs shorter, and eyes smaller than in the Northern Red-legged Frog. To 5¼ in. (13.1 cm).

WOOD FROG *Rana sylvatica* **Pl. 14**

Identification: 1¼–3¼ in. (3.1–8.1 cm). A black or *dark brown mask* ends abruptly just behind the eardrum and is bordered below by a *white jaw stripe.* Brown, pink, gray, or greenish above, often with 2 broad, light-colored stripes down back, separated by a dark stripe. Dark middorsal stripe sometimes bisected by a whitish line. Dark spot on each side of chest, near base of foreleg. Prominent dorsolateral folds. Individuals in the northwestern part of the range are short-limbed and toadlike in proportions. The white-striped form, rare in the East, occurs with increasing frequency to the northwest. ***Male:*** Swollen and darkened thumb base.

In the East this species is truly a wood frog, inhabiting damp shady woods and forests near clear streams and leafy pools. It favors shade, but when breeding it may move out of the forests. In the Northwest, in the colder parts of its range, it is chiefly diurnal and less of a forest dweller. There it may be found in open grassy areas bordered by thickets of willow and aspen, and in tundra ponds. Spruce or other trees are often present nearby. The coloration of this frog blends well with fallen leaves and the mottled light and shade of the forest floor. Breeds Jan.–July. Breeding usually starts soon after the ice begins to melt from ponds — in the southern part of its range (s. Appalachians and the Ozarks) in Jan. and Feb., at the coldest time of the year and in the far Northwest from April to June. Breeding lasts 1–2 weeks, after which the frogs usually disperse.

Voice: Resembles the Northern Leopard Frog's (p. 88) but shorter, higher-pitched, and weaker. A series of rather high grating notes lasting 1 sec. or less, like the clucking of a domestic duck. Paired vocal sacs, one over each forelimb.

Similar species: (1) Spotted Frog (below) has a less distinct mask, no stripes except on jaw, and is red, orange, or yellow below. (2) Red-legged Frog (p. 82) has a less well-defined mask and reddish color on underside of hind legs.

Range: North of Brooks Range, Alaska, to Labrador, southward in e. U.S. to southern Appalachian Mts. The distribution of this frog follows closely the distribution of spruce. Ranges farther north than any other N. American amphibian. Isolated populations in Ozark Mts., n. Colo. (vicinity of Rand, Jackson Co., 5 mi. (8 km) northwest of Grand Lake, Grand Co., and Chambers' Lake, Larimer Co.), and adjacent s. Wyo. (Medicine Bow Mts.), and in n. Wyo. (Big Horn Mts.). Sea level to about 10,000 ft. (3050 m).

Map 46

SPOTTED FROG *Rana pretiosa* **Pl. 13**

Identification: 1¾–4 in. (4.4–10 cm). Light brown, dark brown, or sometimes grayish above, with varying numbers of spots often having rather indistinct borders and generally light centers. Mask present, sometimes faint. Light-colored *jaw stripe* (Fig. 13, opp. Pl. 13). Red, salmon, or yellow below, depending on locality and age. In contrast to the Red-legged Frog, the color appears to be more superficial, almost painted on. Throat, and sometimes entire ventral surface, spotted and mottled with dusky. Legs relatively short, heel of adpressed hind limb seldom reaching nostril. *Eyes turned slightly upward.* Dorsolateral folds usually present. ***Young:*** Yellow or orange ventral color faint or absent. ***Male:*** Swollen and darkened thumb base.

Populations in Nev., Utah, Idaho south of Salmon R., and se. Ore. (but not Blitzen R. system) are usually yellowish below; elsewhere red or salmon predominates.

A highly aquatic species found near cool, usually permanent, water — streams, rivers, marshes, springs, pools, and small lakes, but may move considerable distance from water after breeding. Chiefly a pond or quiet-water frog that frequents mixed coniferous and subalpine forests, grassland, and brushland of sage and rabbitbush. Rather sluggish. Breeds from late Feb. to early July, beginning as early as the winter thaw will permit.

Voice: A series of faint, rapid, low-pitched clicks, increasing in intensity, some 4–50 clicks per call. The call has also been described as a series of 6–9 short bass notes. Calls last about 1–10 secs. and may be given above or occasionally under water. Imitate by clicking your tongue against the roof of your mouth.
Similar species: Distinguished from (1) Cascades Frog (below) and (2) Red-legged Frog (p. 82) by usual lack of mottling on sides, shorter legs, greater webbing, and rougher skin. (3) See also Wood Frog (p. 83).
Range: Extreme se. Alaska (Sergrief I.) to w. Alberta, n. Wyo., n. Utah, cen. Nev. west to Pacific Coast in Ore. and Wash. Isolated populations in Big Horn Mts., Wyo., and in southern part of range at Deer Creek near Ibapah, Tooele Co., Utah; Humboldt drainage and headwaters of Reese R., Nev. Sea level to about 10,000 ft. (3050 m). **Map 50**
Remarks: The Spotted Frog is losing ground to the Northern Leopard Frog and the Bullfrog in some areas. The Bullfrog appears to have been a factor in its decline in w. Ore. and Wash., where it now appears to be nearly extinct.

CASCADES FROG *Rana cascadae* **Pl. 13**
Identification: $1\frac{3}{4}$–3 in. (4.4–7.5 cm). Brown to olive-brown above, with *inky black spots on back* (usually *sharply defined*) and dark spotting on legs. Black flecks between spots scarce or absent. *Yellow, orange-yellow, or yellowish tan on lower abdomen and underside of hind legs.* Groin usually bright yellow with dark mottling; lower sides yellowish or cream. Dorsolateral folds present. ***Male:*** Swollen and darkened thumb base.

A mountain frog, usually found near water. Frequents small streams, potholes in meadows, ponds, and lakes usually in open coniferous forests. Found in the water or among grass, ferns, and other low herbaceous growth nearby. Ranges to near timberline. A rather sluggish frog, often allowing close approach. When frightened it usually attempts to escape by swimming rather than seeking refuge on the bottom. It may swim to the opposite bank or return to the same bank downstream. Diurnal. Breeds Mar. to mid-Aug., soon after pond ice begins to melt.
Voice: A low-pitched grating, chuckling sound, resembling the Red-legged Frog's. 4–5 notes per sec. A series of rapid clucks or double clucks, each lasting about $\frac{1}{2}$ sec. May call from above or under water.
Similar species: (1) Range overlaps slightly with that of Spotted Frog (above), which has a more conspicuous light-colored upper jaw stripe, no mask, and nostrils that are set closer together and higher on the snout; eyes turned upward. (2) See also Red-legged Frog (p. 82).
Range: Cascade Mts. from n. Wash. to vicinity of Lassen Peak, Calif. Isolated populations in Olympic Mts., Wash.; Mt. Shasta

and Lassen Peak area, and Trinity Mts., Calif. Coexists with Red-legged Frog at intermediate elevations in w. Ore. and Wash. From about 2600–9000 ft. (800–2740 m). **Map 51**

FOOTHILL YELLOW-LEGGED FROG **Pl. 14**

Rana boylii

Identification: 1½–2⅞ in. (3.7–7.1 cm). Gray, brown, reddish or olive above; sometimes plain-colored but more often spotted and mottled with dusky. Colors usually harmonize with the prevailing color of rocks and soil. Truly *yellow-legged;* the yellow extending from the underside of the hind legs onto the lower abdomen. *Snout with a triangular, usually buff-colored patch* from its tip to a line connecting the eyelids. No mask. Throat and chest often dark-spotted. Skin, including the eardrums, granular. Indistinct dorsolateral folds. ***Young:*** Yellow on hind legs faint or absent. ***Male:*** Swollen and darkened thumb base.

A stream or river frog of woodland, chaparral, and forest. Usually found near water, especially near riffles where there are rocks and sunny banks. When frightened, it dives to the bottom and takes refuge among stones, silt, or vegetation. Breeds mid-Mar. to early June, after high water of streams subsides.

Voice: Seldom heard. A guttural, grating sound on one pitch or with rising inflection, a single croak lasting ½–¾ sec. Four or 5 croaks may be given in rapid series followed by a rattling sound, the entire sequence lasting about 2½ secs. Inconspicuous vocal sac on each side of throat, in front of the forelimbs.

Similar species: (1) Red-legged Frog (p. 82) has red on underside of hind legs, usually a dark mask, well-defined dorsolateral folds, and smooth eardrums. (2) Mountain Yellow-legged Frog (below) has a smoother skin, generally heavier spotting and mottling dorsally, usually lacks the snout patch, and often has dark toe tips. (3) See also Tarahumara Frog (p. 87) and Tailed Frog (p. 63).

Range: West of crest of Cascade Mts., Ore., south in coastal mts. of Calif. to San Gabriel R., Los Angeles Co.; Sierra Nevada foothills to about 6000 ft. (1830 m) (near McKessick Peak, Plumas Co.); San Pedro Mártir (lower end of La Grulla meadow, 6700 ft. — 2040 m), Baja Calif. Isolated populations in Elizabeth Lake Canyon and San Gabriel R. drainage (near Camp Rincon), Los Angeles Co.; Sutter Buttes, Butte Co., Calif. The Camp Rincon population is perhaps now extinct. A single record 5 mi. (8 km) north of Lodi, San Joaquin Co., Calif., perhaps a stray from the Sierran foothills. Coexists with the Mountain Yellow-legged Frog (below) along the North Fork of San Gabriel R. Sea level to around 7000 ft. (2130 m). **Map 49**

MOUNTAIN YELLOW-LEGGED FROG **Pls. 13, 14**

Rana muscosa

Identification: 2–3⅛ in. (5–7.8 cm). The only frog of the Sierran highlands in Calif., a relative of the Foothill Yellow-legged Frog (above). Yellowish or reddish brown above, with black or brown spots or lichenlike markings. *Toe tips usually dusky.* Underside of hind legs and sometimes entire belly yellow or orange, usually more opaque than in Foothill Yellow-legged Frog. Yellow often extends forward to level of forelimbs. Dorsolateral folds present but frequently indistinct. When handled, these frogs smell like garlic. ***Male:*** Swollen, darkened thumb base.

A frog of sunny riverbanks, meadow streams, isolated pools, and lake borders in the high Sierra Nevada and rocky stream courses in the mountains of s. Calif. Seems to prefer sloping banks with rocks or vegetation to the water's edge. Seldom found more than 2 or 3 jumps from water. Chiefly diurnal. At high altitudes, breeds May–Aug., beginning as soon as meadows and lakes are free of snow and ice. At lower elevations and in s. Calif., breeds Mar.–June, when high water in streams subsides. Tadpoles may overwinter.

Voice: A faint clicking sound. Apparently lacks vocal sacs.

Similar species: See (1) Foothill Yellow-legged Frog (above) and (2) Tarahumara Frog (below).

Range: Sierra Nevada, Calif., from around 4500 ft. to over 12,000 ft. (1370–3650 m), with an isolated population in Butte Co., north of Feather R. Mountains of s. Calif. from Pacoima R. south at 1200–7500 ft. (370–2290 m), with southernmost population isolated on Mt. Palomar. A population on Mt. Rose, Nev., formerly probably around the whole of Lake Tahoe. Populations in s. Calif. appear to be dying out. **Map 52**

TARAHUMARA FROG *Rana tarahumarae* **Pl. 13**

Identification: 2½–4½ in. (6.2–10.6 cm). Appears to be the Mexican counterpart of the Mountain Yellow-legged Frog (above). Rust, olive, or dark brown above, with dark spots that often have light centers. Prominent dark banding on hind legs. Whitish to cream below, *often clouded with dusky. No mask or light jaw stripe.* Dorsolateral folds and eardrums indistinct; eardrum frequently granular. ***Male:*** Swollen and darkened thumb base.

A species of the Sierra Madre Occidental, barely entering the U.S. in the mountains of extreme s. Ariz. Ranges from oak woodland into pine forest, along rocky, gravelly stream courses. A "plunge pool" frog, usually found within a jump or two of water, on the banks of pools, under stones, in niches in cliffs, or sitting in riffles. Although these frogs apparently prefer moving water, individuals gather at quiet pools and springs in dry weather. In Ariz., breeds July–Aug., during the period of summer rains.

Voice: Silent except for an occasional series of grunts, given by both sexes.

Similar species: The Foothill and Mountain Yellow-legged Frogs (above) are smaller and usually have a spotted throat.

Range: In Ariz. in the Pajarito, Tumacacori, and Santa Rita Mts. (Alamo Spring and Sycamore, Tinaja, Big Casa Blanca, Adobe, and Gardener Canyons); south in Sierra Madre Occidental to Sinaloa. 1500 to over 6100 ft. (460–1860 m). **Map 53**
Remarks: Now apparently replaced by the Bullfrog in Peña Blanca area and extremely rare or absent throughout its former range in Ariz.

NORTHERN LEOPARD FROG *Rana pipiens* **Pl. 15**
Identification: 2–$4\frac{3}{8}$ in. (5–11.1 cm). A slim green or brownish frog with well-defined, *pale-bordered, oval or round dark spots* on its back. White to cream below. White stripe on upper jaw. Well-defined, pale dorsolateral folds that are *continuous and not angled inward.* ***Young:*** Spotting may be reduced or absent. ***Male:*** Swollen, darkened thumb base and loose skin between the jaw and shoulder during the breeding season.

Found in a variety of habitats — grassland, brushland, woodland, and forest, ranging high into the mountains. The most cold-adapted of all the leopard frogs. Frequents springs, slowly flowing streams, marshes, bogs, ponds, canals, and reservoirs, usually where there is permanent water and growth of cattails or other aquatic vegetation. May forage far from water in damp meadows. When frightened on land, it often seeks water in a series of zigzag jumps. Most easily found at night by its eyeshine (see p. 15). Breeds mid-Mar. to early June.
Voice: A low "motorboat" or snorelike sound interspersed with grunting and chuckling, lasting about 1–5 secs. Choruses are a medley of moaning, grunting, and chuckling that suggests the sounds made by rubbing a well-inflated rubber balloon. Individuals may squawk when they jump into the water and may scream when caught. Paired vocal sacs expand over the forelimbs.
Similar species: (1) Plains Leopard Frog (p. 90) is paler, with spots that are less set off by pale borders; usually has a well-defined light eardrum spot. Dorsolateral folds not continuous (broken toward rear), and folds curve slightly inward toward rear. (2) Chiricahua Leopard Frog (below) has "salt-and-pepper" pattern of small tubercles on back of thighs, and stockier proportions. (3) Lowland Leopard Frog (*Rana* species, p. 91) is stockier and paler. (4) Relict Leopard Frog (p. 90) is smaller, with shorter legs; spotting toward head often reduced; underside of hind limbs yellow to yellow-orange.
Range: Great Slave Lake and Hudson Bay, Canada, south to n. Va., Neb., N.M., and cen. Ariz.; ne. Atlantic coast to s. B.C. and e. Wash., Ore., and Calif. Introduced on Vancouver I., B.C. and in Calif. at Red Bluff, near Mineral, at Yettem, Malibu Creek, Santa Ana R., and other localities. Sea level to around 11,000 ft. (3350 m). **Map 54**
Remarks: The distribution of this frog in Nev. and elsewhere in

arid parts of the West is spotty. Frogs at Mescalero, Otero Co., and in the Rio Grande Valley, N.M., have been reported as this species. These Rio Grande frogs and those from w. Tex. may represent an undescribed form of the Rio Grande Leopard Frog (p. 92). In our area, the Northern Leopard Frog coexists and occasionally hybridizes with the Plains Leopard Frog (*Rana blairi*, p. 90) in se. Colo. It also hybridizes with the Chiricahua Leopard Frog (below), in areas of cen. Ariz. and w. N.M. where their ranges overlap.

CHIRICAHUA LEOPARD FROG Pl. 15

Rana chiricahuensis

Identification: 2–5⅖ in. (5–13.5 cm). Similar to the Northern Leopard Frog (above) but stockier, with a more rounded head, shorter limbs, and slightly upturned eyes. *Dorsolateral folds usually broken into short segments toward rear and angled inward.* Skin rougher, with more tubercles; dorsal spots generally smaller and more numerous than in other leopard frogs. Ground color above greenish or brown. Upper lip stripe diffuse or absent in front of eye. Face usually green. *Rear of thigh speckled with "salt-and-pepper" markings — small light dots, each with a tubercle,* scattered over a dark ground color. Dull whitish or yellowish below, usually with gray mottling on throat and sometimes on chest. Yellow in groin and on lower abdomen. Many separate populations in restricted aquatic sites, differing in color and pattern. ***Male:*** Swollen and darkened thumb base.

A highly aquatic frog, found chiefly in oak and mixed oak and pine woodlands and pine forests where it frequents rocky streams with deep rock-bound pools. This leopard frog also ranges into areas of chaparral, grassland, and even desert, and, in addition to streams, is also attracted to river overflow pools, oxbows, permanent springs, ponds, and earthen stock tanks. In upland areas, it breeds late May–Aug. and in lower, warmer localities from mid-Mar. to June and sporadically through the fall.

Voice: Long and snorelike; a single note lasting 1–2 secs., dropping in pitch slightly at the end, and repeated intermittently. The pulses that make up the call are given more rapidly (usually over 30 per sec.) than in our other leopard frogs, with the possible exception of the Northern Leopard Frog.

Similar species: See (1) Northern Leopard Frog (above). (2) Plains Leopard Frog (p. 90). (3) Lowland Leopard Frog (p. 91).

Range: Mountain regions of cen. and sw. Ariz., sw. N.M., and the Sierra Madre Occidental, to s. Durango in Mexico. There appears to be a gap in the range along the lower Gila R. basin. Isolated populations at Alamosa Draw Warm Spring, Socorro Co., and perhaps at Ash Canyon, north of Radium Springs, Dona Ana Co., N.M., but species identity of Ash Canyon population uncertain and viability questionable because of habitat disturbances. See descriptions of Northern, Plains, and Lowland Leopard Frogs for interactions of the Chiricahua Leopard Frog with those species. From around 3500–7900 ft. (1070–2410 m). **Map 55**

PLAINS LEOPARD FROG *Rana blairi* **Pl. 15**

Identification: 2–4$\frac{3}{8}$ in. (5–11.1 cm). A generally pale-colored leopard frog. Light buffy brown to dull green above with brown to olive-green dorsal spots that lack or have very narrow pale borders. Whitish stripe on upper lip. *Usually a well-defined pale spot in center of eardrum.* White below, sometimes with some fine dark stippling or mottling on throat. Some yellow may be present in groin, on lower abdomen, and at base of thighs. *Dorsolateral folds usually not continuous* (segmented on lower back) and angled inward toward rear. ***Young:*** Whitish upper lip stripe often well defined. ***Male:*** Deflated vocal sacs (below jaw angle) tend to have lengthwise folds (skin usually less folded in Northern Leopard Frog, p. 88).

Found chiefly on the central and southern Great Plains, in prairie and desert grassland, but this frog also enters oak and oak-pine woodland and farmland. It frequents prairie pools, ponds, and streams (including temporary water sources) where the water at times is muddy and shallow. More drought-resistant than the Northern Leopard Frog. Breeds Mar.–Oct.

Voice: Usually 1–4 guttural, chucklelike notes, each call usually lasting less than 1 sec. — shorter and slower-pulsed than Northern Leopard Frog's.

Similar species: (1) Chiricahua Leopard Frog (above) has smaller and more numerous spots, "salt-and-pepper" markings on back of thighs, green on face, lacks whitish eardrum spot, and has upturned eyes. (2) Rio Grande Leopard Frog (p. 92) has large eyes and faint upper lip stripe, fading or absent in front of the eye. (3) Lowland Leopard Frog (p. 91) usually lacks whitish eardrum spot. See also (4) Northern Leopard Frog (p. 88).

Range: Se. S.D. and w. Iowa to e. N.M. and cen. Tex.; e. Colo. to cen. Ind. and cen. Okla. Extends west in N.M. along the Rio Bonito, Rio Hondo, and upper Rio Penasco to around 7000 ft. (2130 m) near Sierra Blanca, Lincoln Co., south along the Pecos R. to near Carlsbad, Eddy Co. Isolated on western side of Chiricahua Mts. (Turkey Creek, etc.) and adjoining Sulphur Springs Valley in se. Ariz. From around 350–8500 ft. (110–2590 m). **Map 54**

Remarks: Coexists with the Chiricahua Leopard Frog (above) at Turkey Creek and elsewhere; range overlaps with that of the Rio Grande Leopard Frog (p. 92) in se. N.M. Hybridizes with the latter in cen. Tex.

RELICT LEOPARD FROG *Rana onca* **not shown**

Identification: 1$\frac{3}{4}$–3$\frac{1}{2}$ in. (4.4–8.7 cm). Resembles the Northern Leopard Frog (Pl. 15) but usually smaller, with shorter legs (heel of leg extended along side of body usually does not reach tip of snout). *Indistinct dorsolateral folds end well before groin.* Brown, gray, or greenish above, with greenish brown spots that are often reduced or obscure on front of body. Whitish below, sometimes with gray or brown mottling, especially on throat. Undersides of hind limbs yellow or yellow-orange. ***Male:*** Swollen, darkened thumb base and usually less spotting than in female.

Frequents lowland streamsides and springs in areas surrounded by desert. Usually found in or near water. Probably breeds Mar.–May.

Voice: Resembles the Northern Leopard Frog's but not as long or loud.

Similar species: See (1) Northern Leopard Frog (p. 88) and (2) Lowland Leopard Frog (below).

Range: Vegas Valley, Nev. and Virgin R. drainage of extreme sw. Utah, nw. Ariz., and se. Nev. From 1200–2500 ft. (370–760 m).

Map 55

Remarks: The Vegas Valley Leopard Frog, originally described as a distinct species, *Rana fisheri,* and now considered extinct, is tentatively treated in this guide as a subspecies of the Relict Leopard Frog. The Vegas Valley frogs occurred in an artesian spring area northwest of Las Vegas and at Tule Springs, Clark Co., Nev. They suffered from loss of habitat to human developments in the desert, and perhaps also from the introduction of the Bullfrog. The Virgin River frogs may experience the same fate unless steps are taken to protect them. The taxonomic relationship of the Vegas Valley-Virgin River frogs and their relationship to other leopard frogs is uncertain.

LOWLAND LEOPARD FROG — Pls. 14, 15

Rana yavapaiensis

Identification: Similar to the Chiricahua Leopard Frog (Pl. 15), but biochemically distinct. Tan, gray-brown, or light gray-green to green above; yellow below. Dorsolateral folds, tuberculate skin, and usually vague upper lip stripe as in Chiricahua Leopard Frog. Chin mottled in older individuals. *Dark network on rear of thighs.* Yellow groin color often extends onto rear of belly and underside of legs. ***Male:*** Swollen and darkened thumb base.

Frequents desert, grassland, oak and oak-pine woodland, entering the permanent pools of foothill streams, overflow ponds and side channels of major rivers, permanent springs, and, in drier areas, more or less permanent stock tanks. Usually stays close to water. Breeds Feb.–April, sometimes in fall.

Voice: Similar to Plains Leopard Frog's (p. 90). Pulse number almost as low but repetition rate somewhat faster — 10–16 pulses per sec. rather than 4–7. Calls often last a little over ½ sec., the first note held longer than the 6–15 accelerating notes that follow.

Similar species: (1) The Chiricahua Leopard Frog (p. 89) has more prominent vocal sacs and dark thighs with a scattering of light dots rather than a dark network. See also (2) Northern Leopard Frog (p. 88).

Range: Colorado R. drainage from the Virgin R. in extreme nw. Ariz. and the Hoover Dam area to Yuma and Somerton; w. and cen. Ariz. below around 4800 ft. (1460 m) south of Mogollon Rim; sw. N.M. (Gila R. near Red Rock and Rio San Francisco); n. Sonora and nw. Chihuahua. Isolated desert population at San Felipe Creek, southwest of Salton Sea, Imperial Co., Calif. Range boundaries are uncertain. Range of this frog overlaps that of the Chiricahua Leopard Frog on Rio San Francisco and in cen. and s. Ariz.; the two frogs hybridize at California Gulch and in Casa Blanca Canyon, Santa Rita Mts., Ariz. Near sea level to around 4800 ft. (1460 m). **Map 54**

Remarks: The Lowland Leopard Frog closely resembles the Chiricahua Leopard Frog and hybridizes with it in areas where their ranges overlap in Ariz. (see above). However, researchers have found biochemical and other differences between the two frogs that indicate that the Lowland Leopard Frog is a distinct species. However, its scientific description appeared too late for full coverage in this *Field Guide.*

RIO GRANDE LEOPARD FROG **Pl. 15**
Rana berlandieri

Identification: $2\frac{1}{4}$–$4\frac{1}{2}$ in. (5.6–11.2 cm). Resembles the Northern Leopard Frog but generally much paler above, varying from grayish brown, brownish olive, to green or even blue-green (Rio Grande Valley); dorsal spots lighter and less clearly edged with light color. *Dorsolateral folds segmented in front of groin and deflected inward. Eyes large.* A wide, light-colored jaw stripe fades or is absent in front of the eye. Often dusky below, especially on chest and throat where the dark pigment is mottled. Groin and underside of hind limbs often yellow. ***Male:*** Swollen and darkened thumb base.

Frequents grassland and woodland, where it enters streams, rivers and their side pools, springs, pools along arroyos, and stock tanks. Over much of its range, it appears to dwell chiefly in streams. Waters may be permanent or temporary. In the more arid parts of its range, as in our area, it breeds opportunistically after rainfall, at almost any time of year. A nervous, excitable species.

Voice: A short, guttural trill lasting about $\frac{2}{3}$ sec., given singly or in rapidly repeated sequences of 2–3 trills.

Similar species: See Plains Leopard Frog (p. 90).

Range: Extreme s. N.M. (Pecos R. drainage), cen. and w. Tex. into Mexico. The w. Tex. frogs may be an undescribed form (see Northern Leopard Frog, p. 88). Coexists with the Plains Leopard Frog at Delaware Creek southeast of the Guadalupe Mts. near the N.M.-Tex. border and in n.-cen. Tex. where some hybridization occurs. Near sea level to around 5000 ft. (1520 m). **Map 54**

BULLFROG *Rana catesbeiana* **Pl. 14**

Identification: $3\frac{1}{2}$–8 in. (8.7–20 cm). Our largest frog. Olive, green, or brown above, often grading to light green on the head; sometimes light green only on upper jaw. Legs banded and blotched with dusky, and usually some spotting on the back. Whitish mottled with gray below, a yellowish tinge on the chin and hindquarters. A fold of skin extends from the eye around the eardrum. No dorsolateral folds. Eardrums conspicuous. ***Male:*** Yellow throat. Eardrum larger than eye (about same size as eye in female). Swollen and darkened thumb base.

Highly aquatic, remaining in or near permanent water, its activities largely independent of rainfall. Frequents prairie, woodland, chaparral, forests, desert oases, and farmland. Enters marshes, ponds, lakes, reservoirs, and streams — usually quiet water where there is thick growth of cattails or other aquatic vegetation. Wary by day but readily found at night by its eyeshine. Often easily caught when dazzled by light. When first seized, it may "play possum," hanging limp and motionless; be alert for sudden recovery! In the East, where this frog is native, it breeds Feb.–Aug. (earliest in the South); in the West, it breeds Feb.–July. Tadpoles may overwinter.

Voice: A deep-pitched bellow suggesting *jug-o-rum* or *br-wum.* Frightened individuals may give a squawk or catlike *miaow* when they leap into the water. Vocal sac single and internal.

Similar species: The Green Frog (below) has dorsolateral folds.

Range: Atlantic Coast to e. Colo. and e. N.M.; s. Canada to ne. Mexico. Near sea level to around 9000 ft. (2740 m), at Hot Springs Creek, Gunnison Co., Colo. **Map 47**

Remarks: The Bullfrog is not native west of the Rockies (see Map 47), but has been successfully introduced at many localities in the West. In some areas it has adversely affected populations of native frogs. Also introduced in Hawaiian Is., Mexico, Cuba, Jamaica, Japan, and Italy.

GREEN FROG *Rana clamitans* **not shown**

Identification: $2\frac{1}{8}$–$4\frac{1}{5}$ in. (5.3–10.5 cm). A green, brown, or bronze frog with a plain or dark-spotted back and often with green or bronze on sides of head (especially in southern part of range). White below with irregular dusky lines or blotches. *Prominent dorsolateral folds* that do not reach groin. Eardrum conspicuous. ***Young:*** Usually profusely dark-spotted above. ***Male:*** Eardrum twice as large as eye (eye-sized in female). Throat usually yellow or yellow-orange, and thumb base swollen and darkened.

A "shoreline" frog — usually found in or near water of marshes, ponds, lakes, streams, and springs. Introduced in the West. In the East, where this frog is native, it breeds Mar.–Sept. Tadpoles may overwinter.

Similar species: See Bullfrog (above).

Voice: An explosive *bung* or *c'tung,* a low-pitched note resembling the sound made by plucking the lowest string of a banjo, often repeated several times in succession. Calls sometimes two-parted. When startled this frog emits a high-pitched squawk as it leaps. Vocal sacs paired and internal; throat forms a flattened pouch when inflated.

Range: Maritime Provinces to n.-cen. Fla., west to Minn. and e. Tex. In the West, introduced in the lower Fraser Valley, and at Victoria, Duncan, Coombs, and on Texada I., B.C.; at Toad Lake, Whatcom Co., Wash., and along lower Weber R., Ogden, Utah. Reportedly introduced at Glacier National Park, Mont., but whether established is unknown. **Map 49**

Narrow-mouthed Toads: Family Microhylidae

A large, diverse family of frogs, with representatives in the Americas, Africa, Madagascar, Asia, and the Indo-Australian Archipelago. Habitat and habits vary: some burrow, others are terrestrial, and still others are arboreal. Arboreal species often have adhesive toe pads. Some microhylids lay their eggs on land and the young hatch fully formed.

Two closely related genera, *Gastrophryne* (narrow-mouthed toads) and *Hypopachus* (sheep frogs), are primarily tropical, with most species in Cen. America. They are the only genera that reach the U.S. Only 1 species, the Western Narrow-mouthed Toad *(Gastrophryne olivacea),* occurs in our area. Another species, the Eastern Narrow-mouthed Toad *(G. carolinensis),* occurs in the se. U.S., and the Sheep Frog *(H. variolosus)* reaches extreme s. Tex. In the New World these toads are small, stout amphibians with a small, pointed head; tiny eyes; a fold of skin across the back of the head; short legs; and a smooth, tough skin, which probably helps protect them against ants, upon which they feed.

GREAT PLAINS NARROW-MOUTHED TOAD Pl. 16

Gastrophryne olivacea

Identification: $\frac{4}{5}$–$1\frac{5}{8}$ in. (2–4 cm). A tiny brown or gray, smooth-skinned, toadlike amphibian with a *small, pointed head* and broad waist. Hind legs short and stout. Fingers and toes lack webbing. A fold of skin often present across the back of the head. ***Young:*** A dark, leaf-shaped pattern may cover up to half the width of the back. Color becomes paler and leaf pattern disappears with growth. ***Male:*** Dark throat. Small tubercles on lower jaw and chest.

A secretive toad, hiding by day in damp burrows, crevices, and under rocks, bark, and boards, in the vicinity of streams, springs, and rain pools. Look under the bark and in the interior of rotten termite-infested stumps and under flat rocks near or covering ant nests. In Ariz. this toad ranges from mesquite grassland in San

Simon Valley, Pima Co., to oak woodland in the Pajarito and Patagonia Mts. Narrow-mouths are difficult to find because of their small size and habit of calling from sites hidden in grass. Use triangulation (see p. 14). Breeds from mid-Mar. to Sept., during the period of summer rains. Breeding stimulated by rainfall.
Voice: A short *whit* followed by a low nasal buzz lasting 1–3½ secs. and declining in pitch. At a distance a chorus sounds like a band of sheep; nearby it resembles a swarm of bees. Vocal sac round, about the size of a pea.
Range: In the West, occurs in extreme s. Ariz. from vicinity of Patagonia, Santa Cruz Co., and just south of San Xavier Mission and near Robles, Pima Co. to San Simon Valley between Quij[illegible] and Ajo; ranges north to 24 mi. (38 km) south of Casa Grande; Peña Blanca Springs area and Sycamore Canyon, Pajarito Mts., thence south, west of crest of Sierra Madre Occidental, to n. Nayarit (Mexico). East of the Continental Divide, it ranges from se. Neb. to s. Coahuila and from Chihuahua to e. Tex. Near sea level to around 4100 ft. (1250 m). **Map 29**
Subspecies: PLAINS NARROW-MOUTHED TOAD, *G. o. olivacea.* Completely unmarked below or with scattered melanophores. Light-colored above, usually tan; not blotched, rarely with dark spots. A faint bar sometimes present on femur and tibia. SINALOAN NARROW-MOUTHED TOAD, *G. o. mazatlanensis.* Scattered melanophores below. Light tan or grayish above, with at least some dark spots. A distinct bar on femur and tibia. In s. Ariz., Sonora, and Sinaloa, there are upland populations of this subspecies that resemble in color the Eastern Narrow-mouthed Toad, *G. carolinensis* (e. Tex. to Atlantic Coast), with populations graded in color at intermediate elevations. These upland animals have vague, often somewhat irregular to fairly distinct dorsolateral stripes and are strongly mottled below.

Tongueless Frogs: Family Pipidae

Somewhat flattened, rather smooth-skinned, tongueless frogs that are almost completely aquatic. The head is small and the eyes generally lack movable lids. Fingers are slender and the hind feet are large and fully webbed. Adults of some species reach about 10 in. (25 cm).

These frogs (some 20 species) occur in Africa, south of the Sahara, and in Panama and northern South America. One species, the African Clawed Frog, *Xenopus laevis,* has become established in the West, a result of the release of aquarium and laboratory animals.

The family includes the Surinam Toad *(Pipa pipa)* and other aquatic species in which the young develop in capped pits in soft skin on the mother's back and emerge as tiny froglets.

AFRICAN CLAWED FROG **Fig. 14, opp. Pl. 14**
Xenopus laevis

Identification: 2–5⅝ in. (5–12.5 cm). Head and body rather flat; head small, snout blunt, and skin smooth — except where ridges of the lateral line system give it a "stitched" appearance. Eyes small, without lids, and turned upward. No tongue or teeth. Fingers slender, unwebbed. Hind feet large, fully webbed and with *sharp black claws on inner toes.* Olive to brown above, with dark spots, blotches, or mottling. Whitish below, with or without dark spots. ***Male:*** Lacks cloacal claspers found in female and has small dark tubercles on fingers and forelimbs during breeding season.

A highly aquatic frog that seldom leaves the water. In its native habitat in Africa, it frequents veldt ponds, lakes, and reservoirs in arid and semiarid regions. Its tadpole is translucent, has soft mouth parts, a tentacle on each side of the mouth, and a slender tail that ends in a filament. The tadpole hangs suspended with its head downward and the tail filament vibrating as it filters protozoa, bacteria, and other small food particles from the water; adults feed on smaller amphibians and fish (see Remarks). In Calif. this frog breeds Nov.–June. Amplexus is pelvic.

Voice: A faint, two-parted trill, lasting about ½–¾ sec., sometimes uttered over 100 times a minute. Calls are given under water.

Range: Established in Calif. as follows: San Diego Co. (lower Sweetwater R. drainage, west Mt. Helix area), Orange Co. (many localities in western part), Riverside Co. (Arroyo Seco Creek and Vail Lake), Los Angeles Co. (Munz Lake, Vasquez Rocks County Park, Upper Rio Hondo, and Compton Creek area), and Imperial Co. (irrigation canals). Introduced into golf course ponds in the Tucson area, Ariz. Possibly more than one species of *Xenopus* has been involved in these introductions. **Map 56**

Remarks: This frog was brought to the U.S. in the 1940s for human pregnancy tests and later, in increasing numbers, was used for experimental studies and kept as an aquarium pet. It has become established in slow streams and ponds in Calif. and elsewhere where it threatens certain native amphibians and fish. The importation and/or possession of this species is now prohibited by the states of Calif., Ariz., Nev., and Utah, but black market sales as an aquarium pet continue.

8

Turtles

Snapping Turtles: Family Chelydridae

Large freshwater turtles with a long tail, powerful hooked jaws, and a small plastron, less than half the width of the carapace. Two species: the large Alligator Snapping Turtle of the se. U.S., and the Snapping Turtle.

SNAPPING TURTLE *Chelydra serpentina* **Pl. 17**
Identification: 8–18½ in. (20–47 cm). A turtle that seems too large for its shell. Chunky head with powerful hooked jaws, *long tail with a sawtoothed crest, and a small, narrow plastron.* Tail usually longer than half the length of the carapace. Carapace black, brown, olive, or horn-colored. ***Young:*** 3 prominent, lengthwise sawtoothed ridges on the carapace, becoming less prominent with age. Tail as long as or longer than shell. Generally dusky. Carapace margin and plastron with white spots.

Inhabits marshes, ponds, lakes, rivers, and slow streams, especially where aquatic plants are abundant. Usually found in or near water. Well camouflaged when resting on the bottom among plants, its concealment sometimes enhanced by the growth of algae on its shell. Individuals sometimes bask in shallow water or float at the water's surface. Often ill-tempered and prone to bite. Emerges from hibernation Mar.–May. Clutch of 15–60 (up to 83) eggs, laid May–Oct., mostly in June and July. Eats crayfish, snails, insects, fish, frogs, salamanders, reptiles, birds, mammals, and aquatic plants.
Similar species: The small plastron (Fig. 17, opp. Pl. 17) distinguishes this turtle from all other western species.
Range: Extreme s. Canada to Ecuador; western base of Rocky Mts. to Atlantic Coast. Apparently established at Andreé Clark Bird Refuge and elsewhere in Santa Barbara, Calif. Individuals have been found at other localities in Calif.; west of Fallon, Nev.; at St. George, Utah; Phoenix, Ariz.; and along the lower Colorado R. Whether populations are established in all these areas is unknown. Sea level to around 6700 ft. (2040 m). **Map 57**
Remarks: Importation into Calif. is now prohibited.
Subspecies: The COMMON SNAPPING TURTLE, *C. s. serpentina,* occurs in our area.

Musk and Mud Turtles: Family Kinosternidae

In the U.S. represented by 2 genera, musk turtles *(Sternotherus)* and mud turtles *(Kinosternon)*. 23 species in the family. Other members occur in Cen. and S. America. These turtles give off a musky odor when handled, hence they are sometimes called "stinkpots" or "stinking-jims." The odor glands are located on each side of the body where the skin meets the underside of the carapace. Note the barbels (nipple-like projections) on the chin and neck, the short tail (prehensile in males), and the number of marginal shields, including the nuchal (these turtles usually have 23; most others have 25).

Two species of mud turtles *(Kinosternon)* occur in our area.

YELLOW MUD TURTLE **Fig. 16, opp. Pl. 17**
Kinosternon flavescens

Identification: $3\frac{1}{4}$–$6\frac{5}{8}$ in. (8–17 cm). *Head and neck brown or olive above, contrasting with plain yellow or cream below.* Barbels present on throat. Carapace elongate and high, flat or slightly concave on top with a single keel down the middle and without flaring edges; olive or brown, sometimes with black borders along the seams between the scutes. *Supraorbital ridge above each eye. 9th and 10th marginal shields,* counting from front of shell, *usually distinctly higher than 8th.* Bridge with distinct lengthwise groove. Tail short, without sawtoothed edge above and ending in a nail. Musky odor when handled. ***Young:*** Carapace nearly round, with a weak middorsal ridge. Shell edge yellow in hatchlings, with a dark speck at rear border of each marginal scute. 9th and 10th marginals not enlarged. ***Male:*** Two patches of horny scales on inner surface of each hind leg. Tail with horny, hooked tip.

A highly aquatic turtle of semiarid grasslands and open woodland, frequenting both permanent and intermittent waters. Primarily a pond turtle; found in ponds, marshes, lakes, streams, rivers, canals, and reservoirs. Seems to prefer mud or sandy bottoms. Often only its snout is seen when it rises to the surface for air. Clutch of 1–6 eggs, laid May–June. Eats insects, spiders, crustaceans, worms, mollusks, amphibians, carrion, and aquatic plants.

Similar species: Distinguished from all western turtles except the Sonoran Mud Turtle (below) by its single gular shield and the 5 pairs of plastral shields. The Sonoran Mud Turtle lacks supraorbital ridges, usually has 3 lengthwise keels on the carapace, the 9th marginal shield is not enlarged, and the head and neck are mottled (Fig. 16, opp. Pl. 17).

Range: Neb. and Ill. to Durango and Tamaulipas (Mex.); e.-cen. Tex. to s. Ariz. In Ariz., occurs in Swisshelm Mt. area, Cochise Co., west to a few miles east of Sells, Pima Co., and Tempe-Mesa area,

Maricopa Co. Near sea level to around 5200 ft. (1600 m).
Map 62

Remarks: Because of the great similarity between the Yellow and Sonoran Mud Turtles, there is uncertainty as to the distribution of the two species in the western part of their ranges.

SONORAN MUD TURTLE **Pl. 17**
Kinosternon sonoriense

Identification: 3⅛–6½ in. (8–16 cm). Resembles the Yellow Mud Turtle (above), but lacks supraorbital ridges. Carapace has 3 lengthwise keels (except in very old individuals); 9th marginal shield not enlarged; bridge of plastron (see front endpapers) lacks lengthwise groove. *Head and neck heavily mottled with contrasting light and dark markings.* ***Male:*** As in Yellow Mud Turtle.

Chiefly a stream-dwelling turtle that frequents springs, creeks, ponds, and the water holes of intermittent streams. Inhabits woodlands of oaks and piñon-juniper, or forests of ponderosa pine and Douglas fir. Also occasionally inhabits foothill grasslands and desert. Less often found in the lowlands than the Yellow Mud Turtle. Usually stays in or near water. Clutch of 2–9 eggs, laid May–Sept. Eats insects, crustaceans, snails, fish, frogs, and some plant materials.

Similar species: See Yellow Mud Turtle (above).

Range: Cen. Ariz. to Durango; w. Tex. to se. Calif. In Ariz., in Gila R. drainage of cen. and se. part (to slightly over 5000 ft — 1520 m), at Quitobaquito Spring, Pima Co., near Laguna Dam, Yuma Co., and in Big Sandy-Burro R. drainages. Habitat along the lower Gila R. was destroyed by dam construction. In N.M., in the Animas and Peloncillo Mts. and headwaters of Gila R. east to Taylor Creek, Catron Co., at 6700 ft. (2040 m). Old records for Palo Verde and Yuma Indian Reservation, Imperial Co., Calif., along the Lower Colorado R. Sighting of a mud turtle at Pyramid Canyon, Clark Co., Nev. may have been of this species. Near sea level to around 6700 ft. (2040 m). **Map 61**

Box and Water Turtles: Family Emydidae

The largest family of turtles (some 80 species), with representatives nearly worldwide; absent from high latitudes and the Australian continent, Madagascar, and Africa south of the Sahara. Many species are aquatic and have webbed toes, but the box turtles are mainly terrestrial. Well represented in eastern N. America; 5 species in the West.

WESTERN POND TURTLE *Clemmys marmorata* **Pl. 17**

Identification: 3½–7½ in. (9–19 cm). Carapace low; olive, dark brown, or blackish, occasionally without pattern but usually with a *network of spots, lines, or dashes of brown or black that often* *radiate from the growth centers of the shields.* Plastron with 6 pairs of shields — yellowish, blotched with blackish or dark brown, occasionally unmarked. Limbs with prominent scales, flecked and lined with black. Head with spots or network of black. Crushing surface of upper jaw usually smooth or rippled. ***Young:*** Tail nearly as long as shell. Carapace uniformly brown or olive above with yellow markings at edge of marginals; shields with numerous small tubercles. Plastron yellowish, with large irregular central black figure. Head, limbs, and tail marked with dusky and pale yellow. ***Male:*** Throat lighter, and shell usually flatter and less heavily marked than in female.

A thoroughly aquatic turtle of ponds, marshes, rivers, streams, and irrigation ditches that typically have a rocky or muddy bottom and are grown to watercress, cattails, water lilies, or other aquatic vegetation. Found in woodland, grassland, and open forest. May be seen basking on logs, cattail mats, and mudbanks. Found from Feb. to mid-Nov. in the north; all year in the south. Clutch of 3–11 eggs, laid April–Aug.; the time varying with the locality. Eats plants, insects, worms, fish, and carrion.

Similar species: (1) Painted Turtle (below) has yellow lines on head and limbs. (2) See also the Slider (p. 101).

Range: Western Wash. south to nw. Baja Calif., chiefly west of the Cascade-Sierran crest. Outlying areas are Mojave R., Calif., and Truckee and Carson Rivers, Nev. Old record (1894) for Eagles Nest near Shoshone Falls, Jerome Co., Idaho. Introduced in Canyon Creek area, Grant Co., Ore. Formerly at Burnaby Lake, east of Vancouver, B.C., but now appears to be extinct. Sea level to around 6000 ft. (1830 m). **Map 59**

Subspecies: NORTHWESTERN POND TURTLE, *C. m. marmorata.* A pair of triangular inguinal plates (in groin region). Neck markings dull. SOUTHWESTERN POND TURTLE, *C. m. pallida.* Inguinal plates usually small or absent. Neck markings contrast with light ground color.

PAINTED TURTLE *Chrysemys picta* Pl. 18

Identification: 2½–10 in. (6–25 cm). Carapace low, smooth, unkeeled; generally black, brown, or olive, *with olive, yellowish, or red borders along front edge of shields.* Shell sometimes has an open network of lines, and a red or yellow middorsal stripe (e. U.S.). *Yellow lines on head and limbs* and a red blotch or bar behind the eye. In our area the plastron is usually marked with red and with a large, dark central figure that has branches extending along the furrows between the scutes. Crushing surface of upper jaw often with a ridge or row of tubercles parallel to the jaw margin. Rear of carapace with smooth border. ***Young:*** Plastron red or orange, the central dark figure well developed. ***Male:*** Much smaller than female. Very long nails on front feet.

An aquatic turtle that frequents ponds, marshes, small lakes, ditches, and streams where the water is quiet or sluggish and the bottom sandy or muddy, grown to aquatic plants. Often seen sunning on mudbanks, logs, or rocks near water, sometimes in groups of a dozen or more. May not emerge from hibernation until Mar. or April in the north. Clutches of 1–20 eggs, laid May–Aug.; 1–2 clutches in the north, 2–4 in the south. Eats aquatic plants, insects, spiders, earthworms, mollusks, crayfish, fish, frogs, and tadpoles. Sometimes scavenges.

Similar species: See (1) Western Pond Turtle (p. 99) and (2) Slider (below).

Range: S. Canada to the Gulf of Mexico and n. Chihuahua (Río Santa Maria); Atlantic Coast to the Pacific Northwest. Isolated populations in San Juan R. drainage of sw. Colo. and nw. N.M.; depleted and threatened populations in Rio Grande and Pecos R., N.M. Reported from Labyrinth Canyon, Kane Co., Utah. Evidently introduced and established at Kaiser Meadow, Siskiyou Co., and at Twitchell Reservoir on the Cuyama R., Calif. Probably introduced on Vancouver I., B.C.; far northern record at Vanderhoof, B.C. may be based on an escaped pet. Old record (1875) for Rock Creek Canyon, Navajo Co., Ariz. Sea level to around 7300 ft. (2220 m). **Map 63**

Subspecies: The WESTERN PAINTED TURTLE, *C. p. belli,* occurs in our area.

SLIDER *Pseudemys scripta* **Pl. 18**

Identification: 3½–14½ in. (9–36 cm). Carapace usually has lengthwise wrinkles and streaks and bars of yellow on an olive or dusky background. Yellow markings sometimes more or less hidden by black pigment; some individuals are almost completely black. Streaking on 2nd and 3rd costal shields tends to parallel the long axis of the shields. Head and limbs striped with yellow. Usually a *broad red or orange stripe,* or a *yellow or orange spot behind the eye.* Underside of carapace and plastron yellow with dusky blotches, or "eyespots," usually in symmetrical arrangement. Lower jaw appears rounded when viewed from front. Rear of carapace with sawtoothed margin. ***Young:*** Carapace green, streaked with yellow. Usually a red or yellow stripe behind the eye. Plastron with many dark eyelike spots. ***Male:*** More often dark-colored than female. Usually long nails on front feet.

A thoroughly aquatic turtle that seldom ventures far on land. Often seen basking singly or in groups on logs or other objects in the water. Prefers quiet water with abundant aquatic vegetation. 1–3 clutches of 2–25 eggs, laid April–July. Young have been widely sold as pets. Eats aquatic plants, crayfish, snails, tadpoles, fish, and insects, which are especially preferred by young Sliders.

Similar species: (1) The carapace of the Painted Turtle (above) is usually marked with red and lacks lengthwise wrinkles and sawtoothed rear margin. (2) River Cooter (below) usually has a

maze of light and dark lines on the 2nd and 3rd costal shields rather than vertical streaking, and a lower jaw that looks flattened when viewed from the front. (3) Western Pond Turtle (p. 99) has spotted head and limbs.
Range: Mich. to n. Argentina; Atlantic Coast to s. N.M., southern half of Baja Calif. north to San Ignacio. The population in the Cape region of Baja Calif. may now be extinct. Introduced at Andreé Clark Bird Refuge and elsewhere in Santa Barbara, Calif., in the San Diego R. and associated reservoirs, in several ponds near Long Beach, and may be reproducing in the Sacramento-San Joaquin drainage area. Introductions for human food may have occurred in Baja Calif. Established at Papago Park, Phoenix (Red-eared Slider, subspecies *elegans*), and introduced along the Gila R. southwest of Buckeye, Ariz. Sea level to around 4600 ft. (1400 m).
Map 64
Subspecies: RED-EARED SLIDER, *P. s. elegans.* Broad reddish stripe (occasionally yellowish) usually present behind the eye. No network of lines on carapace. BIG BEND SLIDER, *P. s. gaigae.* Oval, black-bordered, red to orange spot(s) behind eye. Carapace with network of lines. In our area occurs at Elephant Butte Lake and Bosque del Apache National Wildlife Refuge, Rio Grande drainage, N.M.

RIVER COOTER *Pseudemys concinna* **not shown**
Identification: $5\frac{3}{4}$–$16\frac{3}{8}$ in. (15–42 cm). Resembles the Slider (Pl. 18). Generally brown to olive above, carapace of adults with lengthwise furrows and *whorls and circles of brown or black on a lighter ground color.* Yellow streaks on head. The Texas River Cooter, the subspecies found in our area, has intricate whorls and the head markings are highly variable, consisting of broad stripes, spots, or vertical bars variously joined together or separated by dark pigment. Underside of shell with eyelike markings on marginals and narrow dark lines along plastral sutures. Plastral markings fade with age. Notch in front of upper jaw, flanked by a cusp on each side. ***Young:*** Pattern vivid; in our subspecies carapace marked with tight whorls, head and neck striped. ***Male:*** Forelimbs with elongate toenails. Shell flatter than in female. Old males may become uniformly mottled on shell, head, and limbs; ridges may extend downward from the nostrils, ending in the jaw cusps.

Chiefly a river turtle, but also enters ditches, cattle tanks, and salt water near the mouths of rivers. Fond of basking and usually slides into the water at the first sign of danger. Up to 19 eggs, laid May–July. Eats aquatic plants, snails, crayfish, tadpoles, fish, insects, and carrion.
Similar species: See the Slider (above).
Range: Va. and s. Ill. to Gulf Coast and nw. Fla. Atlantic Coast to w. Tex., se. N.M., and Nuevo León. In N.M., reported at Bitter

Lakes National Wildlife Refuge and in Carlsbad area (Blue Springs, Pecos R.). Sea level to around 4000 ft. (1220 m).

Map 65

Subspecies: The TEXAS RIVER COOTER, *P. c. texana,* occurs in our area.

Remarks: This turtle appears to be on the verge of extinction in N.M.

WESTERN BOX TURTLE *Terrapene ornata* **Pl. 17**

Identification: 4–5¾ in. (10–15 cm). A land turtle that can completely enclose itself in its shell. *The front of the plastron is hinged* and can be drawn up tightly against the carapace. Shell high, rounded, and typically marked with radiating lines or a series of dots of black or dark brown on a yellow background. Similar markings may be found on plastron. Occasional individuals have a plain yellow or horn-colored shell. ***Male:*** First nail on each hind foot turns inward. Iris and spots on forelegs reddish (yellowish in female) and head sometimes greenish.

Primarily a prairie turtle. Over much of its range it inhabits treeless plains and gently rolling country grown to grass or scattered low bushes where the soil is sandy. Also occurs in open woodland. In some areas tortoise "sign" consists of disturbed piles of cow dung into which they have dug in search of beetles and other insects. They also eat berries, melons, tender shoots, and leaves. Seeks shelter under boards, rocks, and other objects or in self-made burrows. Active Mar.–Nov. Breeds both spring and autumn. Clutch of 2–8 eggs, laid May–July. Activity stimulated by rainfall.

Range: Southwestern S.D., s. Mich., and Ind. south to Gulf Coast and extreme n. Mexico; e. Tex. across s. N.M. to se. Ariz. (to as far west as eastern base of the Baboquivari Mts.) and Sonora. Near sea level to around 6600 ft. (2010 m). **Map 60**

Subspecies: DESERT BOX TURTLE, *T. o. luteola.* Pale radiating lines on shell more numerous than in the Ornate Box Turtle, 11–14 on 2nd costal shield. Markings become less distinct with advancing age and eventually are lost; shells of most old individuals are uniform straw color or pale greenish brown. ORNATE BOX TURTLE, *T. o. ornata.* Fewer pale radiating lines (5–10) on 2nd costal shield than in Desert Box Turtle. Usually no obvious fading of shell with advancing age.

Land Tortoises: Family Testudinidae

Land-dwelling chelonians with a domed shell and elephantlike limbs, ranging into some of the most arid parts of the world. About 40 species. The majority are herbivorous, feeding on leaves, soft stems, and fruits, but some occasionally eat animal matter. Occur on all continents except Australia and Antarctica. Includes the giant tortoises of the Galápagos Islands and islands in the Indian Ocean. 39 species, 10 genera. Only the gopher tortoises (genus *Gopherus*) occur in N. America. In addition to our species, the Desert Tortoise (below), the gopher tortoises include its close relative the Texas Tortoise of s. Tex. and ne. Mexico, the Gopher Tortoise of se. U.S., and the large Bolson Tortoise of n.-cen. Mexico. As a result of recent research, the generic name of the Desert and Texas Tortoises may become *Xerobates*.

DESERT TORTOISE *Gopherus agassizii* **Pl. 18**

Identification: 8–15 in. (20–36 cm). *A high-domed shell, usually with prominent growth lines on shields* of both carapace and plastron. Carapace brown or horn-colored, usually without definite pattern. Plastron yellowish, without a hinge. Forelimbs covered with large conical scales; when drawn in, limbs close opening of shell. Limbs stocky. Tail short. ***Young:*** Flexible shell. Nails longer and sharper than in adult. Carapace dull yellow to light brown; shields usually with dark borders. ***Male:*** Gular shields longer than in female, and lump (chin gland) on each side of lower jaw larger.

A completely terrestrial desert species, requiring firm, but not hard, ground for construction of burrows (in banks of washes or compacted sand); adequate ground moisture for survival of eggs and young; and herbs, grass, or cacti for food. Frequents desert oases, riverbanks, washes, dunes, and occasionally rocky slopes. Creosote bush is often present in its habitat; in Mexico this tortoise occurs in thornscrub. Tortoise tracks consist of parallel rows of rounded dents, the direction of travel indicated by sand heaped up at the rear of each mark. Burrows, often found at the base of bushes, have halfmoon-shaped openings and may be 3–30 ft. (1–9 m) long; each may be occupied by one to many individuals. Short tunnels afford temporary shelter; longer ones, called dens, are used for estivation and hibernation. Clutch of 1–15 eggs, laid May–July, with 2 or rarely 3 clutches in favorable years. Nests sometimes constructed inside tortoise burrows. Captives usually do well on dry alfalfa hay and on lawn and other grasses. Avoid regular feeding of fruits.

Range: S. Nev. and extreme sw. Utah to n. Sinaloa (Mex.); sw. Ariz. (Rincon Mts., Pima Co.) west to Mojave Desert and eastern side of Salton Basin, Calif.; absent from Coachella Valley, Calif., although habitat seems suitable. Recent remains found at Lehman Caves National Monument, Nev. Sea level to around 4000 ft. (1220 m). Populations on Beaver Dam Slope, Utah, are classed as Threatened. **Map 58**

Remarks: Fully protected by state laws in the U.S.

Sea Turtles: Families Cheloniidae and Dermochelyidae

Large marine turtles, primarily of tropical and subtropical seas. Low, streamlined shell and powerful flippers. The cold Alaskan current usually keeps most of them south of s. Calif., but occasional individuals range far north. Six species in the family Cheloniidae, including 4 in our area, and 1 species in the family Dermochelyidae.

Sea Turtles: Family Cheloniidae

GREEN TURTLE *Chelonia mydas* Threatened **Pl. 19**
Identification: 30–60+ in. (70–150 cm); usually 120–200 lbs., but some reach over 600 lbs. Carapace smooth, with *4 costal shields* on each side, the 1st not touching the nuchal; carapace greenish to olive, or brown, gray, or black. *A pair of large scales (prefrontals) between the upper eyelids.* Plastron without pattern, usually pale yellow or whitish. Head plates olive, edged with yellowish. ***Young:*** Carapace scutes overlap slightly and flippers are relatively larger than adult's. Generally brown to blackish, the shell and flippers edged with cream. Pale below. ***Male:*** Longer, narrower carapace then female's. Very long, prehensile tail, tipped with a horny nail. Enlarged curved claw on front flipper.

A thoroughly aquatic turtle of lagoons and bays that seldom comes on land. It basks and sleeps on remote rocky or sandy shores and lays its eggs on gently sloping sandy beaches, usually of islands, at habitually used communal nesting sites. May be seen near mangroves, beds of eelgrass, or seaweed, where it comes to graze. When migrating, may occur far out at sea. Clutches of 3 to over 200 eggs, laid 1–8 times per season, often for a total of some 500–1000 eggs. Commercially valuable — its flesh highly esteemed. The common name of this turtle comes from the color of its fat.
Similar species: See Loggerhead (below).
Range: Worldwide in warm seas. On Pacific Coast, common as far north as San Quintín Bay, Baja Calif.; ranges south to Peru. Occasional in San Diego Bay and elsewhere along coast of s. Calif. Records for Ucluelet Inlet, B.C. and Eliza Harbor, Admiralty I., Alaska. A small population occurs Nov.–April in the warm-water effluent channel of the San Diego Gas and Electric Co. power plant in San Diego Bay.
Supspecies: The PACIFIC GREEN TURTLE, *C. m. agassizii,* occurs in our area.

LOGGERHEAD *Caretta caretta* Threatened **Pl. 19**
Identification: 28–84 in. (70–210 cm), most under 60 in. (150 cm). Large individuals 300–400 lbs.; some to over 900 lbs. Shell high in

front. *Five or more costal shields on each side,* not overlapping, the first touching the nuchal. Broad head with 2 pairs of prefrontals. Carapace usually reddish brown, the shields often edged with yellow. Head shields yellowish brown to olive-brown, grading to yellowish at their edges. Cream below, more or less clouded with dusky. ***Young:*** Carapace yellowish buff, brown, or grayish black, with 3 lengthwise ridges and a tendency toward slight overlapping of shields. Plastron creamy white to grayish black mottled with white.

A wide-ranging turtle of the open ocean. Enters bays, lagoons, estuaries, salt marshes, and river mouths to forage and breed. Nests on gently sloping sandy beaches, singly or in groups. Clutch of 50–300+ eggs, laid 1–4 times a season. Eats crabs, mollusks, sponges, jellyfish, fish, eelgrass, and seaweed.

Similar species: (1) Green Turtle (p. 105) has 4 costal shields and 1 pair of prefrontals. (2) Hawksbill (p. 107) has 4 costal shields and hawklike mandibles. (3) See also Pacific Ridley (below).

Range: Warmer parts of Pacific, Indian, and Atlantic Oceans and the Mediterranean Sea. Pacific coast from s. Calif. (vicinity of Santa Cruz I.) and upper end of Gulf of California to Chile. Sporadically farther north. Reported at mouth of Columbia R. (Fort Canby State Park, Ilwaco, Wash.).

Subspecies: The PACIFIC LOGGERHEAD, *C. c. gigas,* occurs in our area.

PACIFIC RIDLEY *Lepidochelys olivacea* Threatened **Pl. 19**

Identification: 24–36 in. (60–90 cm); 80–100+ lbs. A relatively small sea turtle with a uniformly olive-colored, heart-shaped carapace that looks nearly round from above and rather flat-topped from the side. *Usually* 6–8 (occasionally 5–9) *costal shields on each side,* the 1st pair in contact with the nuchal. Head large, with *2 pairs of prefrontals. Four enlarged inframarginals* (scales below marginals) *on each side on the bridge,* each usually perforated by a pore. Plastron light greenish yellow or greenish white. ***Young:*** Nearly uniform grayish black, except for lighter shade on ventral keels, which are strong and sharp from the humeral to anal shields. Carapace with lengthwise keels.

Evidently more of a bottom dweller than other marine turtles. Frequents protected and relatively shallow water of bays and lagoons, but also ranges well out to sea. Nests on beaches. Clutch of around 30–170 eggs. Eats seaweed, mollusks, crustaceans, jellyfish, sea urchins, and fish.

Similar species: The 2 pairs of prefrontals and high costal-shield count will distinguish this turtle from other marine turtles.

Range: Warmer parts of the Pacific and Indian Oceans. In the Atlantic off the west coast of Africa and the Surinam and Guiana coasts of S. America; sporadically in Caribbean Sea to Puerto Rico and northern coast of Cuba. Off west coast of Calif. and Baja

Calif. south to Chile. Records for La Jolla, Monterey Bay, and beaches of Mendocino Co. and Humboldt Co. (Table Bluff area), Calif.

HAWKSBILL **not shown**
Eretmochelys imbricata Endangered
Identification: 18–36 in. (45–90 cm); 30–280 lbs., most under 250 lbs. Carapace shield-shaped, with a central keel and sawtoothed rear margin; note *strongly overlapping, shinglelike shields* (except in young and old specimens) that are dark greenish brown with a radiating or marbled pattern. *4 costal shields on each side,* the 1st not touching nuchal. 4 inframarginals at outer edge of bridge. *2 pairs of prefrontals. Hawklike mandibles.* ***Young:*** Midkeel on carapace and carapace shields black or dark brown. Plastron with 2 lengthwise ridges and some dark blotching, especially toward the front. Lighter brown color on shell edges and ridges, and on neck and flippers. ***Male:*** Tail longer and thicker then in female; a curved nail on each front flipper.

A pugnacious turtle that defends itself spiritedly with its sharp, hawklike beak. Lays clutches of 50–200+ eggs Aug.–Nov. Eats mollusks, sponges, coelenterates (including corals), sea urchins, crustaceans, fish, seaweed, and mangroves. A source of "tortoiseshell" and human food.
Similar species: See Loggerhead (p. 105).
Range: Warmer parts of the Pacific, Indian, and Atlantic Oceans. S. Calif. to Peru; Gulf of California.
Subspecies: The PACIFIC HAWKSBILL, *E. i. bissa,* reaches our area.

Leatherbacks: Family Dermochelyidae

LEATHERBACK *Dermochelys coriacea* **Pl. 19**
Identification: 48–96 in. (120–240 cm); 600–1600 lbs., possibly reaching a ton. The largest living turtle. *Carapace and plastron with smooth leathery skin (no horny shields) and prominent tuberculate lengthwise ridges.* Carapace dark brown, slaty, or black, unmarked or blotched with whitish or pale yellow, in profile often having a toothed outline from the tubercles on the median (central) ridge. ***Young:*** Hatchlings covered with small scales. Tail rudderlike, with a thin, high dorsal keel. Scales and keeling soon shed. Dark-colored above, with pale-edged flippers and light-colored ridges on shell.

A wide-ranging species that may be seen far out to sea. Females ascend gently sloping sandy beaches of tropical and subtropical shores to lay their eggs, in clutches of 50–170. Eats jellyfish, sea urchins, mollusks, crustaceans, tunicates, fish, and seaweed, sometimes gathering in schools to feed on jellyfish. Floating plastic bags (which resemble jellyfish) are also consumed, probably with detri-

mental effects. Nests throughout the year, but individual females probably nest only every 2 or 3 years.
Range: Worldwide, chiefly in warm seas, but occasionally enters cold water. On Pacific coast recorded north to Alaska (vicinity of Cordova).
Subspecies: The PACIFIC LEATHERBACK, *D. c. schlegelii,* occurs in our area.

Softshell Turtles: Family Trionychidae

These are the "pancake" turtles, named for their round, flat, flexible shell. The neck is long and the nostrils open at the end of a proboscis-like snout. Feet broadly webbed and paddle-like. Although thoroughly aquatic, they venture onto land to bask and nest. Softshells actively seek prey (insects, crayfish, worms) or ambush it as they lie with shell buried in mud or sand. When in the shallows the long neck and snout can be extended to the surface from time to time for air while the turtle remains concealed. Handle with care — they are quick and can inflict a painful bite.

About 25 species; 3 in the U.S., others in Mexico, s. Asia, East Indies, and Africa.

SPINY SOFTSHELL *Trionyx spiniferus* **Pl. 18**
Identification: 5–18 in. (12–45 cm). An extremely flat turtle with a *flexible, pancakelike shell that is covered with leathery skin* rather than horny shields. Front edge of shell often covered with tubercles or "warts" (occasionally smooth in Texas Softshell subspecies). Limbs flat and toes broadly webbed. A flexible proboscis (snout). Note *whitish ridge in each nostril,* on either side of median septum. Lips fleshy, concealing sharp-edged jaws. Olive-brown, brown, or grayish above, variously flecked with black, sometimes with dark eyelike spots on shell. Carapace with cream-colored border. Cream or yellowish below, unmarked. Markings tend to fade with age. ***Young:*** Carapace border conspicuous. Shell often spotted with black, sometimes profusely so. Prominent dark markings on head and limbs. ***Male:*** Averages smaller than female and has a more contrasting pattern, retaining juvenile markings. Carapace with sandpaperlike texture. Tail thick and fleshy, extending beyond edge of shell. ***Female:*** Tends to become blotched and mottled with age. Carapace smoother than in male and with well-developed warts along front edge.

In the West, primarily a river turtle attracted to quiet water with bottom of mud, sand, or gravel. It also enters ponds, canals, and irrigation ditches, but generally avoids temporary water. Agile both in water and on land. Can retract head out of sight beneath its shell, among folds of neck skin. Active April–Sept. in the north, all year in the south. One, perhaps 2, clutches of 4–33 eggs, laid

May–Aug. on sandy banks. Eats earthworms, snails, crayfish, insects, fish, frogs, tadpoles, and occasionally aquatic plants. Sometimes scavenges.

Similar species: The Smooth Softshell (below) has less contrasting marks on limbs, usually lacks tubercles on carapace, and has no ridge on each side of the septum between the nostrils.

Range: Widespread throughout Mississippi R. basin and se. U.S. In West, in western tributaries of Mississippi R.; Rio Grande and Pecos R., N.M.; Gila and lower Colorado Rivers. Sea level to around 5200 ft. (1580 m). Probably introduced into Colorado R. system from N.M. around 1900. Has extended its range through the Imperial Valley, Calif. to the Salton Sea. Introduced in Lower Otay Reservoir and San Diego R., and individuals have been taken in San Pablo Reservoir and San Gabriel R., Calif. **Map 66**

Subspecies: WESTERN SPINY SOFTSHELL, *T. s. hartwegi.* Retains juvenile pattern of small ocelli, or solid black dots, on carapace. Only 1 dark marginal line separates pale border of carapace from dorsal ground color; pale border not conspicuously widened toward the rear. Bold pattern of dark and light markings on head and limbs. TEXAS SPINY SOFTSHELL, *T. s. emoryi.* Juvenile pattern of white dots confined to rear third of carapace. Pale border conspicuously widened, 4–5 times wider at rear than at sides. Pattern on head and limbs reduced.

SMOOTH SOFTSHELL *Trionyx muticus* **not shown**

Identification: $4\frac{1}{2}$–$14\frac{1}{2}$ in. (11–36 cm). Resembles the Spiny Softshell (Pl. 18). *Nostrils round, with no median ridges;* front end of carapace smooth. Juvenile pattern of large dusky spots (sometimes eyelike) or small dark dots and bars persists in males. A pale, usually unbroken stripe behind the eye; side of head otherwise unpatterned. Usually lacks contrasting marks on dorsal surface of limbs. ***Young:*** Carapace brown or olive-gray, marked with dots and dashes that are only a little darker than the ground color. ***Male:*** Tends to be colored like young. ***Female:*** Mottled with various shades of gray, brown, or olive.

Chiefly a river turtle, apparently more restricted to running water than the Spiny Softshell. Frequents large rivers and streams but also lakes and impoundments, the latter principally in the southern part of its range. 1–3 clutches of 4–33 eggs, laid May–July on small islands or gently sloping muddy or sandy shores. Eats invertebrates, frogs, and fish.

Similar species: See Spiny Softshell (above).

Range: Chiefly in Mississippi R. drainage from extreme w. Pa., s. Minn., and S.D. to Gulf Coast; from western end of Fla. Panhandle to cen. Tex. In our area, known only from above Conchas Dam and downstream from Ute Reservoir on the Canadian R. in ne. N.M. Sea level to around 4500 ft. (1370 m). **Map 67**

Subspecies: The MIDLAND SMOOTH SOFTSHELL, *T. m. muticus,* occurs in our area.

9

Lizards

Geckos: Family Gekkonidae

A large family of tropical and subtropical lizards (about 750 species), found on all continents except Antarctica and widespread on oceanic islands. Most species are nocturnal and are therefore limited in distribution by low nighttime temperatures. Geckos communicate by chirping and squeaking; the name "gecko" is based on the sound made by an oriental species. Most geckos are excellent climbers. Many species crawl with ease on walls and ceilings and are often found in houses and public buildings in the tropics.

Typically, geckos have soft skin with fine granular scales, large eyes with vertical pupils and immovable eyelids, a fragile tail that is easily lost but readily regenerated, and toes with broad flat tips and well-developed claws. In most species, the undersides of the toes are covered with broad plates that bear numerous villi (microscopic hairlike structures with spatula-shaped tips). The villi, which cling to surfaces by friction, and the sharp claws, which anchor in surface irregularities, give these lizards their remarkable climbing ability.

Six native species in the U.S. and Baja Calif., 5 of which enter our area. The banded geckos *(Coleonyx)* differ from most geckos in having movable eyelids and slender toes that lack villi. In addition, several species have been introduced in the U.S., in Fla. and along the Gulf Coast. One species, the Mediterranean Gecko, has become established in our area.

WESTERN BANDED GECKO **Pl. 35**
Coleonyx variegatus
Identification: 2–3 in. (5–7.5 cm). *The soft, pliable skin; vertical pupils; and movable eyelids* distinguish this lizard from all others except its close relatives, the Texas Banded Gecko and Barefoot Gecko. Scalation finely granular, *toes slender,* and tail constricted at base. Brown bands on both body and tail, on a pink to pale yellow background. The bands tend to break up with age or in certain localities into a blotched, spotted, or mottled pattern. Plain whitish below. May squeak when caught. ***Young:*** Brown bands above usually well defined and unbroken. ***Male:*** Prominent spur on each side at base of tail. Spurs weak or absent in female. Usu-

ally 6–10 preanal pores, in contact at ventral midline. Corresponding scales in female usually enlarged and sometimes pitted.

Athough it appears delicate, this lizard can live in extremely dry parts of the desert because of its nocturnal and subterranean habits. It ranges from creosote bush flats and sagebrush desert to the piñon-juniper belt, and from catclaw-cedar-grama grass plant community in the eastern part of the range to chaparral areas in the West. Often associated with rocks, and may seek shelter under them or in crevices. In some parts of its range, it occurs on barren dunes. To find these lizards, drive slowly along blacktop roads and watch for a small, pale, twiglike form. In the daytime turn over rocks, boards, and other objects, especially in spring before ground surfaces heat up. 1–3 clutches, usually of 2 eggs, laid May–Sept. Eats insects and spiders.

Similar species: See Texas Banded Gecko (below) and Barefoot Gecko (p. 112).

Range: S. Nev. to tip of Baja Calif. and s. Sinaloa; coastal s. Calif. to sw. N.M. Ranges from desert across southern Sierra Nevada via Kern R. Canyon to Granite Station area and Caliente Creek drainage, Kern Co., on eastern side of San Joaquin Valley, Calif. On islands in the Gulf and off western coast of Baja Calif. Below sea level in desert sinks to around 5000 ft. (1520 m). **Map 69**

Subspecies: DESERT BANDED GECKO, *C. v. variegatus.* Usually 7 or fewer preanal pores in males. Dark body bands same width as or narrower than interspaces between them; bands with light centers, or replaced by spots. Light collar mark indistinct or absent. Head spotted. TUCSON BANDED GECKO, *C. v. bogerti.* Pattern similar to Desert Banded Gecko, but usually 8 or more preanal pores in males. SAN DIEGO BANDED GECKO, *C. v. abbotti.* Dark body bands uniform in color, same width as or narrower than interspaces. Distinct narrow, light-colored collar mark. Head unspotted in adults. UTAH BANDED GECKO, *C. v. utahensis.* Dark body bands in adult wider than interspaces; edges of bands highly irregular, often merged with dark spots in the interspaces. SAN LUCAN BANDED GECKO, *C. v. peninsularis.* Differs from other subspecies in having even-edged, dark dorsal bands that are wider than interspaces; reduced head spotting; and prominent light lines on the snout.

TEXAS BANDED GECKO *Coleonyx brevis* **not shown**

Identification: 1¾–2¼ in. (4.4–5.6 cm). Closely resembles the Western Banded Gecko (Pl. 35), but usually has *fewer preanal pores (3–6, seldom more than 4),* which are interrupted by 1 or more small scales at the ventral midline. Dark body bands in adult wider than the interspaces, often fading with age and often replaced by dark spotting. ***Male:*** As in Western Banded Gecko (above).

Frequents desert grassland, creosote bush scrub, and open arid

brushland and woodland. Like its western relative, it is often associated with rocks. It may be found in crevices and under rocks, on arid flats, hillsides, and in canyons. Nocturnal; found on roadways at night. 1, perhaps 2, clutches of 1–4 (usually 2) eggs, laid April–June. Eats insects, spiders, centipedes, millipedes, and isopods.
Similar species: See Western Banded Gecko (p. 110).
Range: Southern N.M. to s.-cen. Tex., south to ne. Durango and s. Coahuila (Mex.). In limestone areas of se. Eddy Co., N.M., but scarce or absent now in Rio Grande Valley, N.M. Near sea level to around 5000 ft. (1520 m). **Map 69**

BAREFOOT GECKO *Coleonyx switaki* **Pl. 35**
Identification: 2–3⅓ in. (5–8.4 cm). Resembles Western Banded Gecko but has *small sooty tubercles on scales on upper sides, back of neck, and upper base of tail.* Pale beige, yellowish, yellowish olive, to brown above, with numerous round to oval brown and often somewhat larger light spots; the light spots sometimes more or less unite to form pale crossbands. Individuals from areas with dark rocks may have dark ground color and contrasting light spots. Tail usually with conspicuous light and dark crossbands. ***Young:*** Pale crossbands on body and tail. ***Male:*** As in Western Banded Gecko (p. 110).

Frequents arid hillsides and canyons, usually where there are many large boulders and massive rock outcrops, in thornscrub desert. Its nocturnal habits and use of deep crevices make this gecko difficult to find. It squeaks when disturbed and walks with its tail elevated, curled, and waving.
Similar species: Western Banded Gecko (p. 110) has broader lamellae on underside of toes and lacks tubercles on back.
Range: S. Calif. from near Borrego Springs and Yaqui Pass, San Diego Co., southward in desert foothills of Peninsular Ranges into Baja Calif., to the vicinity of Bahia de los Angeles, San Ignacio, and Santa Rosalia. On San Marcos I. in the Gulf of Calif. Reported as far north as Pines to Palms Highway area, Riverside Co., Calif. Near sea level to around 2000 ft. (600 m). **Map 70**

LEAF-TOED GECKO *Phyllodactylus xanti* **Pl. 35**
Identification: 1–2½ in. (2.5–6.2 cm). A typical gecko with *enlarged toe pads* and large *eyes that have immovable eyelids.* Pupils vertical. 2 large flat scales at tip of each toe, with a claw between them. Scales on dorsal surfaces of body mostly granular, but *interspersed with enlarged keeled tubercles.* Pinkish, brown, or gray above, marked with dark brown. Pale below.

A rock dweller, inhabiting areas of desertscrub, thornscrub, and broken chaparral. Often found in canyons with massive boulders. Likely to occur in the vicinity of streams and springs, but also frequents areas with no permanent water. An excellent climber that seldom ventures far from rocks, hence seldom found on roadways at night. Often squeaks when caught. Tail readily lost. Sev-

eral clutches of 1–2 eggs, laid May–July. Eats insects and spiders.
Similar species: See (1) Granite Night Lizard (Pl. 30, p. 143) and (2) San Lucan Gecko (p. 236).
Range: Lower desert slope of mountains of s. Calif., from north of Palm Springs to tip of Baja Calif. On islands in the Gulf of Calif. and off west coast of Baja Calif. Sea level to around 2000 ft. (610 m). **Map 68**
Subspecies: CAPE LEAF-TOED GECKO, *P. x. xanti.* Usually smaller than the Peninsular Leaf-toed Gecko; has tubercles on thighs. PENINSULAR LEAF-TOED GECKO, *P. x. nocticolus.* Usually larger than above subspecies; no thigh tubercles. Other subspecies occur on islands in Gulf of Calif. and on Magdalena and Santa Margarita Is. off west coast of Baja Calif.

MEDITERRANEAN GECKO Pl. 35

Hemidactylus turcicus

Identification: $1\frac{3}{4}$–$2\frac{3}{8}$ in. (4.4–6 cm). Eyes large, without lids, pupils vertical. Broad toe pads of lobed transverse plates. Prominent, often keeled, knobby tubercles on dorsal surfaces. Undergoes marked color change: In pale phase, ground color light pink to very pale yellow or whitish; dorsum (upper body) spotted and blotched with brown or gray. In dark phase, ground color darkens to gray or brownish and blotches become less evident. ***Young:*** Tail often more banded than in adult. ***Female:*** When gravid, whitish eggs can be seen through translucent skin of abdomen.

Chiefly nocturnal. In the U.S. and elsewhere where it has been introduced it is usually an "urbanized" gecko that lives in or near human dwellings. It feeds on insects attracted by lights and may be seen on walls, ceilings, and window screens, stalking or awaiting its prey. It is also found in rock crevices, cracks in tree trunks, and occasionally under palm fronds and other objects on the ground. Clutches of 1–2 eggs, laid Apr.–Aug.
Voice: Advertisement call of male a series of clicks in succession. Utters a mouselike squeak when fighting or threatened by an adversary.
Similar species: (1) Leaf-toed Gecko (above) has 2 large flat scales at the tip of each toe. (2) Banded geckos (p. 110) and (3) Barefoot Gecko (p. 112) have movable eyelids and no toe pads.
Range: Introduced and well-established in the West in the Tucson-Phoenix area, Ariz. Elsewhere found in Tex., La., Ala., peninsular Fla., Mexico, Cuba, Puerto Rico, and Panama. Native to w. India, Somalia, the Middle East, the Mediterranean basin, and the Canary Is. **Map 70**
Remarks: A close relative of the Mediterranean Gecko, the Common House Gecko, *H. frenatus* (not shown in this guide), may be established at La Paz, in Baja Calif. It has similar proportions and foot structure, is grayish or purplish brown, has a dark stripe on each side of head, and light and dark crossbands on tail. Widespread in s. Asia and on Pacific Is.

Iguanids: Family Iguanidae

Includes most N. American lizards. Form and habits greatly varied — some are arboreal, others ground-dwelling, and one is marine (Marine Iguana of the Galapagos). Dorsal scales range from smooth and granular to spiny and keeled. Body rounded or broad and flat (horned lizards). Restricted to the New World except for a few species in the Madagascan region and 2 in the Tonga and Fiji Is. Ranges from s. Canada to the tip of S. America. Over 600 species.

Our species have 3–5 lengthwise keels on the underside of each toe. Males often have enlarged postanal scales and, when breeding, a swollen tail base, from which the copulatory organs (hemipenes) can usually be extruded by gentle squeezing with thumb and forefinger.

DESERT IGUANA *Dipsosaurus dorsalis* **Pl. 24**

Identification: 4–5$\frac{3}{4}$ in. (10–14.4 cm). A large, pale, round-bodied lizard with a long tail and a rather small, rounded head. Scales small, granular on sides, smooth and overlapping on belly. A *row of slightly enlarged, keeled scales down middle of back.* Pale gray above, with barring or network of brown on sides; variously spotted and blotched with light gray. Pale below, with pinkish to buff areas on sides of belly in both sexes during breeding season.

Typical habitat in the northern part of its range consists of creosote bush desert with hummocks of loose sand and patches of firm ground with scattered rocks. In the south it frequents subtropical scrub. Most common in sandy habitats but also occurs along rocky streambeds, on bajadas, silty floodplains, and on clay soils. May be seen basking on rocks or sand hummocks, near a burrow in which it may take refuge. Tolerant of high temperatures, remaining out on hot, sunny days when most other lizards seek shelter. Chiefly herbivorous; climbs among the branches of the creosote bush and other plants to obtain fresh leaves, buds, and flowers. It also eats insects, carrion, and its own fecal pellets. Breeds April–July. Clutch of 3–8 eggs, laid June–Aug.

Range: From s. Nev. to tip of Baja Calif. and n. Sinaloa. Desert side of mountains in s. Calif. to cen. Ariz. On islands off the Gulf coast of Baja Calif., and on Magdalena I. off the Pacific coast of Baja Calif. Below sea level in desert sinks to around 5000 ft. (1520 m). Its range in the U.S. coincides closely with that of the creosote bush, a staple food. **Map 74**

COMMON CHUCKWALLA *Sauromalus obesus* **Pl. 20**

Identification: 5$\frac{1}{2}$–8 in. (13.7–20 cm). A large, flat, dark-bodied lizard with *lose folds of skin on neck and sides.* Often seen sprawled on a rock in the sun. Skin on back covered with small granular scales. Tail with blunt tip and broad base. *Rostral scale absent.* ***Young:*** Crossbands on body and tail. Bands on tail conspicuous — black on an olive-gray or yellowish background. ***Male:*** Head, chest, and limbs usually black, sometimes spotted and flecked with pale gray. Rest of body usually red or light gray, depending on age and locality. Tail pale yellow. ***Female:*** Tends to retain juvenile crossbands. Adults of both sexes usually banded in sw. Utah.

A rock-dwelling, herbivorous lizard, widely distributed in the desert. The creosote bush occurs throughout most of its range. Nearly every lava flow, rocky hillside, and outcrop will have its Chuckwallas. Rocks provide shelter and basking sites. To find this lizard, drive on desert roads in late morning and afternoon to spot basking individuals among the rocks. Approach on foot and take note of the crevice the lizard enters, or listen for the sandpaperlike sound made as it slides into a crack. Look for droppings (elongate, cylindrical pellets containing plant fibers), which mark basking sites and favored retreats. Shine a flashlight into the crevice to see the "chuck" in its retreat. When disturbed, Chuckwallas gulp air, distend their body, and wedge themselves tightly in place. Clutch of 5–16 eggs, laid June to perhaps Aug. Eats a variety of desert annuals, some perennials, and occasionally insects.

Range: S. Nev., nw. Baja Calif. and Guaymas, Sonora; desert side of mountains in s. Calif. to cen. Ariz.; drainage of Colorado R. in s. Utah to the Henry Mts. Sea level to around 6000 ft. (1830 m). **Map 73**

Subspecies: WESTERN CHUCKWALLA, *S. o. obesus.* A single row of femoral pores. Dark crossbands on body usually uniformly colored. Adult males at some localities have considerable red color on the body. When present, 3–5 dark tail bands alternate with 2–4 light bands; end of tail usually light-colored. GLEN CANYON CHUCKWALLA, *S. o. multiforaminatus.* Most individuals have a secondary row of femoral pores. Both sexes usually have dark and light crossbands on body. 5–6 dark tail bands alternate with 4–5 light bands; end of tail usually dark. Young often brick-red speckled with cream, and with light and dark bands across back. Colorado R. from Glen Canyon Dam at Page, Ariz., to near Hite and the Henry Mts., Garfield Co., Utah. ARIZONA CHUCKWALLA, *S. o. tumidus.* Differs from other subspecies in having fewer than 50 scales encircling the middle of the forearm. Adult males suffused with a more or less brilliant reddish tinge on both dorsal and ventral surfaces.

The Peninsular Chuckwalla *(S. australis)* of cen. and s. Baja Calif. appears to intergrade with the Western Chuckwalla *(S. o. obesus)* and probably should be regarded as a subspecies of the Common Chuckwalla *(S. obesus).* However, it has not yet been formally recognized as such in the scientific literature. In contrast to the Western Chuckwalla, its body crossbands tend to have light centers and dark brown or black borders, giving a double-banded effect. Its size decreases to the south.

Remarks: The Common Chuckwalla occurs on Tiburon I. in the Gulf of Calif. Chuckwallas, currently recognized as other species, occur on other islands in the Gulf. The taxonomy of these island forms is uncertain and in need of study.

LESSER EARLESS LIZARD Pl. 22

Holbrookia maculata

Identification: 2–$2\frac{1}{2}$ in. (5–6.2 cm). A small, ground-dwelling lizard with *no ear openings. Smooth, granular scales above.* Upper labials overlap and are separated by diagonal furrows. A fold of skin across the throat. Tail short; *no black bars on underside.* Ground color brown, tan, gray, or whitish above, usually closely matching the soil color of the habitat. Back usually marked with scattered light spots and 4 lengthwise rows of dark blotches, each blotch pale-edged at rear. A pair of black marks on each side of belly. Light-bordered dark stripe on rear of thighs. ***Male:*** Enlarged postanal scales. Dark blotches on back often faint; usually light-edged when present. Belly markings more conspicuous than in female and set off by blue borders. ***Female:*** Often develops a vivid orange or yellow patch on the throat during the breeding season.

Primarily a plains lizard, most common where there are exposed patches of sand or gravel. Frequents washes, sandy streambanks, sand dunes (White Sands, N.M.) shortgrass prairie, mesquite and piñon-juniper woodland, sagebrush flats and farmland. Not a particularly fast runner; can sometimes be caught by hand. 1 or 2 clutches of 1–12 eggs, laid April–Sept. Eats insects, spiders, and small lizards.

Similar species: (1) The Side-blotched Lizard (p. 135) has ear openings and usually has a dark spot behind the axilla ("armpit"); upper labials do not overlap. (2) Greater Earless and (3) Zebra-tailed Lizards (below) have black bars on the underside of the tail, and the Zebra-tailed Lizard has ear openings.

Range: Great Plains and cen. Mexican plateau, from southern S.D. to Guanajuato, across southern part of Continental Divide in U.S. to se. Utah and n. and cen. Ariz. Sea level to about 7000 ft. (2130 m). **Map 75**

GREATER EARLESS LIZARD Pl. 22

Cophosaurus texanus

Identification: $1\frac{7}{8}$–3 in. (4.7–7.5 cm). A slim-legged lizard with a long, flat tail that has black crossbars on the underside (bars missing if tail regenerated). Ground color above tends to blend with the soil color of the habitat and may be gray, brown, or reddish, with numerous small light flecks. *Each side of belly marked with 2 black or sooty crescents, which extend up onto sides. Black markings behind midpoint of body. No ear openings.* Light-bordered dark stripe on rear of thigh. Dorsal scales granular. Diagonal furrows between upper labials. Gular fold present. ***Male:*** Enlarged postanal scales. Black crescents bordered by blue or greenish on belly and by yellowish on flanks. ***Female:*** Lacks blue color on belly. Dark crescent-shaped markings faint or absent. During the breeding season some females develop a pinkish wash, especially on flanks, and a vivid orange throat patch.

A lizard of middle elevations, avoiding extreme desert lowlands and the higher mountains. Look for this lizard in areas where cactus, mesquite, ocotillo, creosote bush, and paloverde grow. It seems to prefer the sandy, gravelly soil of flats, washes, and intermittent stream bottoms where plants are sparse and there are open areas for running. Occasionally found on rocky hillsides. Sometimes runs with its tail curled over the body, but not as consistently as the Zebra-tailed Lizard (below). Clutches of 2–12 eggs, laid Mar.–Aug., for a seasonal total of about 25. Eats insects.

Similar species: (1) Zebra-tailed Lizard (below) has ear openings, and the black belly bars are located at midbody. (2) See also Lesser Earless Lizard (above).

Range: W. Ariz., N.M. and n. Tex. south to Zacátecas and s. Tamaulipas (Mex.). Cen. Tex. west to eastern edge of Mojave Desert at Bill Williams R. and in Cerbat Mts., Mohave Co., Ariz. 100 to around 5600 ft. (30–1700 m). **Map 76**

Subspecies: SOUTHWESTERN EARLESS LIZARD, *C. t. scitulus.* Usuallly 28 or more femoral pores. Numerous small orange, red, or yellow flecks on back, and a series of large, prominent, paired, dark spots down middle of back. Some males very colorful — pinkish on upper back and yellowish or greenish on lower back and groin. TEXAS EARLESS LIZARD, *C. t. texanus.* Usually 27 or fewer femoral pores. Usually no orange or yellow spots on back; dark middorsal spots, when present, not prominent.

ZEBRA-TAILED LIZARD **Pl. 22**

Callisaurus draconoides

Identification: 2½–4 in. (6.2–10 cm). A slim-bodied lizard with a long, flat tail and extremely long, slender legs, well adapted for running at high speed. Fringe of pointed scales on rear of toes in lizards from Viscaiño Desert, Baja Calif. *Ear openings present. Black crossbars on white undersurface of tail* (the "zebra" markings). Dorsal scales granular. Upper labials separated by diagonal furrows. Gular fold present. A gray network on back and dusky crossbars on upper surface of tail. Sides usually lemon yellow. 2 or 3 black or gray bars (3 in Viscaiño Desert, Baja Calif.) on each side of belly, extending slightly up the sides. *Black belly markings at or in front of midpoint of body.* Light-bordered dark stripe on rear of thigh. Throat dusky, often with a pink or orange spot at center. ***Male:*** Enlarged postanal scales. Belly markings conspicuous and located in blue patches on each side of belly. ***Female:*** Belly markings faint or absent.

Frequents washes, desert "pavements" of small rocks, and hardpan, where plant growth is scant and there are open areas for running. Occasionally found in rocky arroyos (Baja Calif.) and on fine windblown sand, but usually not far from firm soil. When about to run, it curls and wags its tail; it runs at great speed, with the tail curled forward. The bold tail markings may divert the attack of hawks or other predators to the tail, which can be regenerated. 1 to perhaps 5 clutches (more in southern part of range) of 2–15 eggs, laid June–Aug. Eats insects, spiders, other lizards, and occasionally plants.

Similar species: See (1) Greater Earless Lizard (p. 116), (2) fringe-toed lizards (below), and (3) Lesser Earless Lizard (p. 116).

Range: Nw. Nev. south to s. Sinaloa and tip of Baja Calif.; extreme sw. N.M. to desert slope of mountains in s. Calif. and on coastal slope along Cajon and San Jacinto Washes (see black dots on map). On islands in the Gulf of Calif. Below sea level in desert sinks to around 5000 ft. (1520 m). **Map 77**

Subspecies: COMMON ZEBRA-TAILED LIZARD, *C. d. draconoides*. Usually only 2 dark bars on abdomen, most evident in male. No fringe of pointed scales on toes. VISCAIÑO ZEBRA-TAILED LIZARD, *C. d. crinitus*. Three dark bars on abdomen, most evident in male. Fringe of pointed scales along rear border of 2nd, 3rd, and 4th toes, probably an adaptation for running on sand. Toe fringe and spots on back and tail suggest those of the fringe-toed lizards (below). Apparently more likely to bury itself in sand than the Common Zebra-tailed Lizard. A sand-adapted lizard, found only in the Viscaiño Desert of Baja Calif.

COLORADO DESERT FRINGE-TOED LIZARD Pl. 23

Uma notata

Identification: $2\frac{3}{4}$–$4\frac{4}{5}$ in. (6.9–12.1 cm). A flattened, sand-dwelling lizard with velvety skin, *fringed toes* that have projecting pointed scales, a countersunk lower jaw, and well-developed earflaps — adaptations to life in sand. Well camouflaged — the dorsal ground color and pattern of black flecks and eyespots (ocelli) harmonize with background. Ocelli tend to form broken lengthwise lines that extend over the shoulders. White below, with dark *diagonal lines on throat,* black bars on underside of tail, and a *conspicuous black spot or bar on each side of belly.* Sides of belly with a permanent orange or pinkish stripe; these colors more vivid during breeding season. In Sonoran populations, a pinkish wash appears along sides, usually only during breeding season. ***Young:*** Orange or pink belly color faint or absent. ***Male:*** Enlarged postanal scales.

Restricted to fine, loose, windblown sand of dunes, flats, riverbanks, and washes in some of the most arid parts of the desert.

Vegetation is usually scant, consisting of creosote bush or other scrubby growth. When frightened, fringe-toes often dart suddenly to the opposite side of a sand hummock or bush, where they freeze, plunge into the sand, or disappear into a burrow. When running at high speed, they run primarily on their hind legs (are bipedal). Their tracks are distinctive, consisting of alternating large, round dents made by the hind feet and occasional smaller ones made by the front feet in maintaining balance. These lizards are usually so wary that you will probably need the help of a companion to catch them. Walk abreast, 25 or 30 ft. (7–9 m) apart, keeping sand hummocks and bushes between; this will let you see hiding places as the lizards dash to the opposite side of hummocks. Clutches of 1–5 eggs, laid every 4–6 weeks from May to Aug. Eats chiefly insects, but occasionally other lizards and buds, leaves, and flowers.
Similar species: (1) Mojave Fringe-toed Lizard (p. 120) has black crescents on the throat and the belly is usually tinged with greenish yellow. (2) In the Coachella Valley Fringe-toed Lizard (below) the black belly spots are absent or reduced to one or several small dots. (3) Zebra-tailed Lizard (p. 117) usually lacks fringed toes (the Viscaiño Desert subspecies has weakly developed fringes), is slimmer, and less often found in areas of fine windblown sand.
Range: Vicinity of Salton Sea and Imperial Sand Hills, Calif., south across Colorado R. delta, around head of Gulf of Calif. to Tepoca Bay, Sonora; ne. Baja Calif. Below sea level to around 300 ft. (90 m). **Map 78**

COACHELLA VALLEY FRINGE-TOED LIZARD Pl. 23

Uma inornata Threatened
Identification: $2\frac{3}{4}$–$4\frac{7}{8}$ in. (6.9–12.2 cm). Similar to Colorado Desert Fringe-toe but paler. *Black spots on each side of belly (if present) are reduced to a single small dot or cluster of dots;* streaks on throat are paler. Breeding coloration consists of a pinkish wash on the sides of the belly in males and bright orange in gravid females.

Habits and habitat similar to those of the Colorado Desert Fringe-toe (above). Clutches of 2–4 eggs, laid April–Sept. Eats insects, blossoms, and leaves.
Similar species: (1) Mojave Fringe-toed Lizard (p. 120) has black crescents on the throat. Ocelli on its back do not form broken lines that extend over the shoulders; belly tinged with yellow-green during breeding season. (2) See also Colorado Desert Fringe-toed Lizard (above).
Range: Sand deposits of the Coachella Valley, Riverside Co., Calif. Near sea level to around 1600 ft. (490 m). **Map 78**
Remarks: This lizard has lost 75% of its habitat to human activities. Land purchases are underway to save the lizard and sample portions of the Coachella Valley Desert.

MOJAVE FRINGE-TOED LIZARD Pl. 23

Uma scoparia

Identification: 2¾–4½ in. (6.9–11.2 cm). Resembles the Colorado Desert Fringe-toe (p. 118) but ocelli on back do not form broken lengthwise lines that extend over the shoulders and the *dark throat markings are crescent-shaped.* A conspicuous black spot on each side of belly. Breeding coloration consists of a yellow-green ventral wash that becomes pink on sides of body.

Habits and habitat resemble those of the Colorado Desert Fringe-toe. Clutches of 1–5 eggs, laid May–July. Eats insects, spiders, seeds and flowers.

Similar species: See (1) Colorado Desert and (2) Coachella Valley Fringe-toed Lizards (pp. 118–119).

Range: Sand deposits of the Mojave Desert, Calif., north to southern end of Death Valley National Monument. Enters Ariz. along Bouse Wash, south of Parker, Yuma Co. From about 300 to around 3000 ft. (90–910 m). **Map 78**

COMMON COLLARED LIZARD Pl. 24

Crotaphytus collaris

Identification: 3–4½ in. (7.5–11.2 cm). A robust lizard with a relatively large, broad head; a short snout; and a long, rounded tail. Scales mostly smooth, granular. *Two dark collars:* the first (anterior) one is of equal width throughout or narrows at sides and *does not encircle throat;* the second (posterior) one often reaches the forelimbs in males, less often in females. Numerous light spots and often a series of dark crossbands on body. Ground color above varies — may be greenish, bluish, olive, brown, or yellowish, depending on locality, sex, age, and color phase. Markings tend to fade with age, the collar least. Throat spotted. *Mouth and throat lining usually black. Some greenish reflections usually present on upper surfaces* over most of range. Dorsal surface of tail usually spotted and crossbanded. Belly whitish or cream. ***Young:*** Broad dark crossbands or transverse rows of dark spots on body and tail. Sometimes with red or orange markings like breeding female's (see below). ***Male:*** Usually considerable greenish color on dorsal surfaces, including sides and limbs. Throat dark-spotted — green, bluish, and in eastern part of range, orange or yellow. Enlarged postanal scales. ***Female:*** Lacks or has slight tinge of green above. Throat unmarked or lightly spotted with brown or gray. In breeding season, develops spots and bars of red or orange on sides of neck and body, which fade after the eggs are laid.

A rock-dwelling lizard that frequents canyons, rocky gullies, limestone ledges, mountain slopes, and boulder-strewn alluvial fans, usually where vegetation is sparse. Essentials appear to be boulders for basking and lookouts, open areas for running, and adequate warmth. Collared lizards jump nimbly from rock to rock and seize other lizards and insects with a rush, often running with

their forelimbs lifted off the ground and the tail raised. Most are easily caught in the morning when they bask at the top of boulders. To avoid being bitten, handle these lizards by the sides of the head. Do not cage them with smaller animals (potential prey). 1–2 clutches of 1–13 eggs, laid June–July. Eats insects, lizards, and occasionally berries, leaves, and flowers.
Similar species: (1) Desert Collared Lizard (below) lacks greenish color and dark mouth lining, and has large dark patches on flank and groin. See also (2) Long-nosed Leopard Lizard (p. 123), (3) Crevice Spiny Lizard (p. 127), and (4) Banded Rock Lizard (p. 137).
Range: E. Utah, w. and se. Colo., east to extreme sw. Ill., south through cen. Tex., N.M., and Ariz. to cen. Sonora and Zacatecas. On Tiburon I. in the Gulf of Calif. Near sea level to around 8000 ft. (2440 m). **Map 80**
Subspecies: EASTERN COLLARED LIZARD, *C. c. collaris.* First (anterior) collar has a wide gap above, sometimes bridged by several dark bars or spots; does not encircle throat. Second (posterior) black collar usually extends onto base of upper arm. 1–4 scales in region between the eyes (interorbital area) are fused. Usually 10 or fewer upper labials. Throat of male yellow to deep orange. SONORAN COLLARED LIZARD, *C. c. nebrius.* Resembles Eastern Collared Lizard (above) in collar markings, but interorbitals form 2 rows, usually without fusion of their scales. Usually 11 or more upper labials. Head cream-colored, with no yellow traces. Brown above, with large whitish spots along middle of back — each dorsal spot 1½–3 times larger than light spots on sides. Conspicuous dark spot behind forelimbs. Adult males have little or no green or blue coloring. WESTERN COLLARED LIZARD, *C. c. baileyi.* Resembles Eastern Collared Lizard (above) in collar markings and coloring of throat and groin (in male), and Sonoran Collared Lizard (above) in arrangement of interorbitals, upper labial count, and male throat markings. Greenish or bluish above, especially adult males. Head yellow or whitish; if yellow, color does not extend under chin or behind supraorbital semicircles. Throat of male west of Continental Divide often bluish. CHIHUAHUAN COLLARED LIZARD, *C. c. fuscus.* Brown above with no trace of green. Light to cream-colored head with no traces of yellow. YELLOW-HEADED COLLARED LIZARD, *C. c. auriceps.* Resembles the Western Collared Lizard (above), but head yellow, the color extending under chin and to or past second (posterior) collar. Yellow head contrasts strongly with green body in breeding adult males.

DESERT COLLARED LIZARD **not shown**

Crotaphytus insularis
Identification: 2¾–4½ in. (6.9–11.2 cm). Similar in general proportions and scalation to Common Collared Lizard (above, Pl. 24),

but head usually less broad, snout longer, and tail flattened from side to side, especially in adult male. *Usually no green highlights above. Two conspicuous black collar markings:* the anterior one wide laterally, usually incomplete at the dorsal midline (gap usually wide in individuals south of San Gorgonio Pass, Riverside Co., Calif.) and in males, connected across the throat; the posterior collar usually does not reach forelimbs. Often numerous light lines and spots above on tan to olive ground color. Pale yellow or orange crossbands on body. Upper midline of tail usually uniformly colored, especially in adult male. *Lining of throat and mouth pale.* ***Young:*** Crossbands usually conspicuous; the dark ones may consist of closely set large dark spots. No dark throat and groin blotches. ***Male:*** Blue-gray throat with black center and large dark blotches on flanks and in groin. Black pigment may extend to chest and base of hind limbs. Enlarged postanal scales. ***Female:*** When gravid, has vivid reddish orange spots and bars on sides.

Frequents rocky areas — arroyos, gullies, and hill slopes — in arid and semiarid regions. Found in creosote bush, saltbush, and Basin sagebrush deserts and thornscrub. Eats insects, lizards, berries and other plant materials. Clutch of 3–8 eggs in summer.

Similar species: See Common Collared Lizard (above).

Range: Sw. Idaho and se. Ore., south through Great Basin of Nev., w. and s. Utah through se. Calif. and sw. Ariz. to s. Sonora and s.-cen. Baja Calif. (to vicinity of Loreto). Records for e. Idaho are about 15 mi. (24 km) (air line) north-northeast of Atomic City, Butte Co. and Montpelier, Bear Lake Co. In Baja Calif., this lizard appears to be found only on the mountainous eastern side of the peninsula. On Angel de la Guardia I. in the Gulf of Calif.

Localities beyond the desert in Calif. are the North Fork of Lytle Creek and San Antonio Canyon, headwaters of the East Fork of the San Gabriel R.; San Jacinto Wash, near the point where the North Fork of the San Jacinto R. enters the main wash; an old record from Kernville in the southern Sierra Nevada. Hybridizes with the Common Collared Lizard (*C. collaris*) in the Cerbat Mts., Mohave Co., and west of Cameron, Coconino Co., Ariz. near the Little Colorado R., and perhaps elsewhere along drainages of the Colorado R. where the upland range of the Common Collared Lizard is penetrated by the Desert Collared Lizard, which is better adapted to arid conditions at lower elevations. Sea level to around 7500 ft. (2290 m). **Map 80**

Subspecies: GREAT BASIN COLLARED LIZARD, *C. i. bicinctores.* Two black collars, each separated at dorsal midline by 12 or fewer pale scales. Only faint traces (if any) of pale transverse lines between the broad, dark, often obscure bands on upper body in adults. Populations to the north and west tend to retain juvenile crossbanding even in adult males. Usually 6 or more internasals. BAJA CALIFORNIA COLLARED LIZARD, *C. i. vestigium.* Two black collars, each separated at dorsal midline by 13 or more pale scales. Distinct broad, dark bands on upper body (often with pale dots and dashes running lengthwise along center of each band) separated by broken or continuous pale transverse lines. Usually 5 or fewer internasals.

These two subspecies closely approach one another at the base of the San Bernardino and San Jacinto Mts., in the vicinity of San Gorgonio Pass. Differences in their appearance and behavior there, and lack of evidence of interbreeding, suggest that they actually may be distinct species.

LONG-NOSED LEOPARD LIZARD — Pl. 24

Gambelia wislizenii

Identification: 3¼–5¾ in. (8.1–14.4 cm). *A large lizard with many dark spots,* a rounded body, a long round tail, and a large head. Capable of marked color change: in the dark phase, the spots are nearly hidden and light crossbars are conspicuous on both body and tail; in the light phase the reverse is true. Ground color gray, pinkish, brown, or yellowish brown above. Throat streaked or spotted with gray. Scales on top of head small, including interparietal. ***Young:*** Markings, especially crossbars, usually more contrasting than in adults; upper back often rust-colored. ***Male:*** Usually smaller than female. ***Female:*** During breeding season, reddish orange color appears on underside of tail, and as spots and bars on sides of neck and body. The reddish color disappears after the breeding season.

Inhabits arid and semiarid plains grown to bunch grass, alkali bush, sagebrush, creosote bush, or other scattered low plants. The ground may be hardpan, gravel, or sand. Rocks may or may not be present. This lizard avoids dense grass and brush, which interfere with running. It often lies in wait for insect or lizard prey in the shade of a bush, where its spotted pattern blends in. Tap bushes with a stick to flush these lizards. They run with forelimbs raised when running fast. Will attempt to bite when caught. Do not cage with smaller animals. Clutch of 1–11 eggs, laid Mar.–July; a second clutch may be laid in the south. Eats insects (grasshoppers, crickets, beetles, termites), spiders, lizards, small rodents (pocket mice), and soft leaves, blossoms, and berries.

Similar species: (1) Collared lizards (*Crotaphytus* species, pp. 120–123) have collar markings; sides of tail flattened in the Desert Collared Lizard. (2) See also Blunt-nosed Leopard Lizard (p. 124).

Range: Great Basin south to Magdalena Plain, Baja Calif., Sonora, and n. Zacatecas; desert base of mountains in s. Calif. east to se. N.M. and w. Tex. Old records from Gavilan Peak area, Riverside, Calif. and Hat Rock, Umatilla Co., and The Dalles, Wasco Co., Ore. Near sea level to around 6000 ft. (1830 m). **Map 79**

Subspecies: LARGE-SPOTTED LEOPARD LIZARD, *G. w. wislizenii.* Spots large, crossbars usually conspicuous. Color pattern varies — wide pale crossbands and large dark spots (especially in e. Nev. and w. Utah); large dark spots sometimes reduce pale background to a network (in northern and western desert areas); or background often quite dark, with many pale dots among the dark spots (s. Calif., s. Ariz., and N.M., southward). SMALL-SPOTTED LEOPARD LIZARD, *G. w. punctatus.* Spots small and numerous, crossbars usually narrow and faint. Upper Colorado R. Basin, Utah, w. Colo., nw. N.M., and n. Ariz.

Remarks: Scattered populations in the upper Cuyama drainage (Cuyama Badlands, in nw. Ventura Co.), Calif. have characteristics that indicate former interbreeding (hybridization or intergradation) between the Long-nosed Leopard Lizard and the Blunt-nosed Leopard Lizard (below). At present, however, there is no known contact between them and it is unknown whether interbreeding could now occur. In behavior, structure, and color these populations appear to favor the Long-nosed parental type (*G. wislizenii*).

BLUNT-NOSED LEOPARD LIZARD **Pl. 24**

Gambelia silus Endangered

Identification: 3–5 in. (7.5–12.5 cm). Resembles the Long-nosed Leopard Lizard (above) in body proportions, but *snout blunt.* Grayish to yellowish above, with dark spots that tend to be arranged in rows on each side of dorsal midline. Pale crossbands on body usually distinct, except when in light phase or in older individuals. *Throat with pale gray to dusky spots,* sometimes merging to form a network or lengthwise streaks. ***Young:*** Red or rust-colored spots on body; yellow on thighs and underside of tail. Sides often blotched with yellow in young females. ***Male:*** Head broader than in female. During the breeding season males develop a pink, salmon, or rust wash on throat, chest, and sometimes over most of body except on top and sides of head. ***Female:*** When breeding, reddish orange spots and blotches appear on head and sides and reddish orange on underside of thighs and tail. The reddish color fades after the eggs are laid.

Frequents semiarid grasslands, alkali flats, and washes of the San Joaquin Valley, Calif., and nearby valleys and foothills. The soil may be sandy, gravelly, loamy, or occasionally hardpan. Vegetation often includes clump grasses, annual grasses, saltbush, and, in some areas, Mormon tea. These lizards frequently seek refuge in burrows of small mammals. Clutch of 1–6 eggs, laid June–July. Eats chiefly insects and occasionally lizards.

Similar species: The Long-nosed Leopard Lizard (p. 123) has a much longer snout, and more often has lengthwise stripes on throat.

Range: San Joaquin Valley and the surrounding foothills, the Carrizo Plains south over the Temblor and Caliente Ranges into the Middle Cuyama Valley, Calif. From about 100–2400 ft. (30–730 m). **Map 79**

Remarks: This lizard has hybridized with the Long-nosed Leopard Lizard (see above). It has been eliminated over large portions of its former range by agriculture and housing developments; encroachment continues. It is protected on the Pixley Wildlife Refuge and at several other localities in the San Joaquin Valley.

Spiny Lizards: Genus *Sceloporus*

These are the "blue-bellies." Males of most species have a blue patch on each side of the belly and on the throat, enlarged postanal scales and, when breeding, a broad tail base. Blue color reduced or absent in females. All have keeled, pointed, overlapping scales on the dorsal surfaces, which (along with the incomplete gular fold) will distinguish them from the utas (*Uta* and *Urosaurus*). Spiny lizards are usually gray or brown above with a pattern of crescents or stripes, are round-bodied or somewhat flattened, and the tail is longer than the body. Limbs are of moderate length.

Below sea level to above 13,500 ft. (4110 m). S. Canada to Panama. Some 64 species. Habitats vary from tropical forests to the sparse growth of timberline. Some are ground dwellers; others climb on rocks, stumps, tree trunks, and sides of buildings with ease. Confirmed baskers, they are frequently seen on top of rocks, fenceposts, stumps, or other objects in full sun. Some species are live-bearing.

BUNCH GRASS LIZARD *Sceloporus scalaris* **Pl. 26**
Identification: 1½–2½ in. (4–6.2 cm). A mountain form distinguished from all other spiny lizards by the arrangement of the femoral-pore rows, and the scales on the sides of the body. The femoral rows are separated at the midline by only 1 or 2 scales rather than 3 or more, and the *lateral scale rows parallel the dorsal rows.* In other spiny lizards, the lateral rows extend diagonally upward. Various shades of brown above, with a white or orange stripe on each upper side and brown blotches on the back; rear edge of each dorsal blotch black. Usually a black blotch at base of each front leg. ***Male:*** Usually has orange stripe on each upper side and blue patches on belly. Brown blotches on back faint or absent. ***Female:*** Blotched pattern. Blue markings on belly reduced or absent.

Found in our area chiefly in isolated mountains, mostly above 6000 ft. (1830 m), where it occupies sunny patches of bunch grass in open coniferous woods; also occurs as low as about 4000 ft. (1220 m), on grassy plains. Search for these lizards in late morning on warm, bright days. Walk softly through the grass. Individuals may be seen or heard scurrying into grass clumps or to hiding places under rocks, logs, or pieces of bark. Trap them

by hand in the grass tangles. Most active during period of summer rains. Clutch of 9–13 eggs, laid June–Aug. Eats insects and spiders.
Similar species: In the Striped Plateau Lizard (p. 133), with which the Bunch Grass Lizard coexists in some areas, the lateral scales are in diagonal (not lengthwise) rows; no blue markings on belly.
Range: Huachuca, Dragoon, Santa Rita, and Chiricahua Mts., Ariz.; Animas Mts., N.M.; Sierra Madre Occidental and Sierra del Nido to Puebla. To around 11,000 ft. (3350 m). Found at lower elevations in Empire Valley, 4300 ft. (1310 m), Santa Cruz Co., Ariz.; upper Animas Valley, east of Cloverdale, 5200 ft. (1580 m), N.M.; and on grassy plains between the desert and the Sierra Madre, Chihuahua, Mexico. **Map 89**

MOUNTAIN SPINY LIZARD **Pl. 26**

(Yarrow Spiny Lizard) *Sceloporus jarrovii*
Identification: 2¼–3⅞ in. (5.6–9.7 cm). *Black-edged scales* form a *meshlike* (*lace stocking*) *pattern above;* center of scales whitish with a pinkish or bluish green sheen. Head with sooty markings or nearly all black in adult males. Broad black collar edged with whitish along rear; collar often connected with dark markings on head. *Supraocular scales small, sometimes in more than 1 row.* Usually over 40 scales between interparietal and rear of thighs. ***Young:*** Usually a blue patch on rear part of throat, on each side of belly behind the axilla, and in front of the groin. ***Male:*** Sides of belly and throat patch blue. ***Female:*** Blue colors subdued, and back often spotted and flecked with gray.

A mountain species, attracted to rocky canyons and hillsides. Frequents open oak woodland, thornscrub, and mixed oak and pine forests, mostly above 5000 ft. (1520 m). On lower mountain slopes this lizard lives in the more humid areas near streams, canyon pools, or damp sand. Occasionally climbs trees, but more often seen perched on boulders or climbing nimbly over rocks. When these lizards first emerge from their retreats they are nearly black, and are conspicuous on light-colored rocks. Live-bearing. 2–13 young, born May–June. Eats insects and spiders.
Similar species: The Crevice Spiny Lizard (below) has larger scales (usually less than 40 between the interparietal and rear of thighs) and a black collar band with a conspicuous whitish anterior border.
Range: Chiricahua, Dos Cabezas, Dragoon, Graham, Huachuca, Santa Rita, Quinlan, and Baboquivari Mts. in Ariz.; Peloncillo, Pyramid, San Luis, Animas, and Hatchet Mts. in N.M.; Sierra Madre Occidental and Oriental to State of Mexico and s.-cen. Veracruz. From around 4500–11,000 ft. (1370–3350 m). **Map 90**
Subspecies: The YARROW SPINY LIZARD, *S. j. jarrovii,* occurs in our area.

CREVICE SPINY LIZARD **Pl. 27**

Sceloporus poinsettii

Identification: 3¾–4⅝ in. (9.9–11.6 cm). A large, flat-bodied, spiny rock dweller. The *conspicuously banded tail and broad black collar* can be seen from a great distance. Collar bordered in front and back with whitish. Ground color yellowish, olive, or reddish above. Beige to pale orange below, grading to pinkish orange on underside of tail. *Scales large, keeled, and pointed;* usually less than 40 between interparietal and rear of thighs. Outer row of supraoculars about same size as inner row. ***Young:*** Crossbands on body and tail often more conspicuous than in adult. Sometimes a narrow dark stripe down middle of back. ***Male:*** Sides of belly and throat blue. Belly markings bordered with black toward midline. Crossbands on back indistinct or absent. ***Female:*** Blue color weak or absent; crossbands usually retained.

A wary lizard that inhabits rocky canyons, gullies, hillsides, and outcrops of limestone, granite, or lava in mesquite grassland, creosote bush desert, and arid woodland. Usually retreats to the opposite side of a rock or into a crevice when approached. Use a mirror or flashlight to see the animal in its retreat. Live-bearing; 7–16 young, born June–July. Eats insects, spiders, and occasionally buds, blossoms, and leaves.

Similar species: (1) Collared lizards (*Crotaphytus* species, pp. 120–123) have a double black collar; no dark crossbands on tail; and small, smooth scales. (2) See also Mountain Spiny Lizard (above).

Range: Southern N.M. (San Mateo and Magdalena Mts.) south to Zacatecas; sw. N.M. to cen. Tex. From around 1000–8400 ft. (300–2560 m). **Map 83**

Subspecies: The NORTHERN CREVICE SPINY LIZARD, *S. p. poinsettii,* occurs in our area.

DESERT SPINY LIZARD *Sceloporus magister* **Pl. 27**

Identification: 3¼–5½ in. (8.1–13.7 cm). A stocky, usually light-colored lizard with large, pointed scales and a *black wedge-shaped mark on each side of the neck.* Rear edge of neck markings whitish or pale yellow. Straw-colored, yellow, yellowish brown, or brown above, with crossbands or spots of dusky that usually fade with age. Sides often tinged with rust. Head sometimes orange. 5–7 pointed ear scales. Supraorbital semicircles incomplete. ***Young:*** Usually with many small blotches arranged in 4 lengthwise rows. Crossbands often conspicuous. ***Male:*** Dorsal markings vary with subspecies (see below). Enlarged postanals and swollen tail base. Blue-green patch on throat and on each side of belly. Belly patches edged with black and sometimes joined at midline. ***Female:*** Blue markings weak or absent. Head orange or reddish when breeding.

Inhabits arid and semiarid regions on plains and lower slopes of mountains. Found in Joshua-tree, creosote-bush, and shad-scale deserts, mesquite-yucca grassland, juniper and mesquite woodland, subtropical thornscrub, and along rivers grown to willows and cottonwoods. A good climber of rocks and trees, but also found on the ground. Seeks shelter in crevices, under logs and other objects on the ground, in woodrat nests, and in rodent burrows. Often bites when captured. Clutch of 4–19 eggs, laid May–June; more than 1 clutch may be laid per season. Eats insects, lizards, and occasionally buds, flowers, berries, and leaves.

Similar species: (1) The Clark Spiny Lizard (p. 129) is gray, greenish, or bluish above, has dark crossbands on wrists and forearms, and usually 3 ear scales. (2) The Granite Spiny Lizard (p. 129) is darker, lacks conspicuous neck markings, and has more rounded, less spiny scales.

Range: Nw. Nev. and s. Utah to tip of Baja Calif., nw. Sinaloa, and sw. Coahuila; inner Coast Ranges and desert of s. Calif. to N.M. and w. Tex. In Coast Ranges north to Panoche Hills. Near sea level to around 5000 ft. (1520 m). **Map 81**

Subspecies: (Based on differences in adult males only.) SONORAN SPINY LIZARD, *S. m. magister*. Broad black or deep purple middorsal stripe bordered by a light stripe on each side. Dark shoulder patch usually extends upward to meet light stripe. TWIN-SPOTTED SPINY LIZARD, *S. m. bimaculosus*. 2 parallel lengthwise rows of dark blotches on back. Usually a well-defined dark stripe behind the eye. BARRED SPINY LIZARD, *S. m. transversus*. 6–7 dark crossbars on back (also sometimes in female). Dark shoulder patch often extends well up on neck, nearly forming a collar. Ground color usually yellow. YELLOW-BACKED SPINY LIZARD, *S. m. uniformis*. Usually uniformly light yellow or tan above, with no distinct markings; back color grades into darker brown on sides. Faint blotches usually present on back of adult females and occasionally in juveniles and adult males. ORANGE-HEADED SPINY LIZARD, *S. m. cephaloflavus*. Usually with 5–6 chevron-shaped bars on back, from shoulders to base of tail. Adults of both sexes have yellowish orange on head. RED-STRIPED SPINY LIZARD, *S. m. rufidorsum*. Pale middorsal stripe 1½–2½ scale rows wide, with a broader rusty red stripe on each side, extending from rear of head to tail. Lateral scale rows accented with continuous or somewhat broken, oblique dark lines. SOUTHERN SPINY LIZARD, *S. m. monserratensis*. Similar to Red-striped Spiny Lizard but lacks reddish stripes on back. SAN LUCAN SPINY LIZARD, *S. m. zosteromus*. Similar to Southern Spiny Lizard but light middorsal stripe is broader (6 scale rows wide) and lacks distinct borders of dark lines or spots.

Remarks: Biochemical differences between the Red-striped and Yellow-backed Spiny Lizards are great. Field studies should be conducted in ne. Baja Calif. to determine whether these lizards warrant full species status.

CLARK SPINY LIZARD *Sceloporus clarkii* **Pl. 27**
Identification: 2$\frac{7}{8}$–5 in. (7.1–12.5 cm). A large, often wary lizard, usually only glimpsed as it scrambles to the opposite side of a limb or tree trunk. *Gray, bluish green, or blue above, with dusky or black bands on wrists and forearms.* Black shoulder mark as in Desert Spiny Lizard. Irregularly crossbanded with dark and light markings, which may become faint or disappear, especially in old males. Projecting spine-tipped scales on body. Incomplete supraorbital semicircles. Usually 3 ear scales. ***Young:*** Crossbands on body and tail. ***Male:*** Enlarged postanals and swollen tail base. Throat patch and sides of belly blue. ***Female:*** Blue markings usually weak or absent.

Inhabits chiefly lower mountain slopes in oak-pine woodland, tropical deciduous forest, and subtropical thornforest. Prefers more humid environments, generally at higher elevations than the Desert Spiny Lizard. Chiefly a tree-dweller but also occurs on the ground among rocks. Often heard before it is seen. Two people are usually required to keep these lizards in sight because they tend to stay on the opposite side of rocks and tree trunks. To noose them usually requires careful stalking while a companion diverts their attention. Clutch of 4–24 eggs, laid May–Nov.; sometimes more than 1 clutch may be laid each season. Eats insects and occasionally leaves, buds, and flowers.
Similar species: See (1) Desert Spiny Lizard (p. 127) and (2) Granite Spiny Lizard (below).
Range: Cen. Ariz. and sw. N.M. to n. Jalisco. In Ariz. ranges west to Kitt Peak, Ajo and Puerto Blanco Mts., Pima Co., and north to Valentine, Mohave Co. Sea level to around 6000 ft. (1830 m).
Map 82

GRANITE SPINY LIZARD *Sceloporus orcutti* **Pl. 27**
Identification: 3$\frac{1}{4}$–4$\frac{5}{8}$ in. (8.1–11.6 cm). *A large, spiny, dark-colored rock dweller.* Dark wedge-shaped mark on each side of neck and crossbands on body and tail often hidden by general dark coloration. Scales with rounded rear margins, weakly keeled on the body, strongly keeled and pointed on the tail. Incomplete supraorbital semicircles. ***Young:*** Head rusty. Crossbands and neck markings evident. ***Male:*** When in the light phase, one of our most beautiful lizards. Dorsal scales marked with yellow-green and bluish, a broad purple strip down middle of the back, and blue or blue-green throat and belly patches; entire ventral surface sometimes vivid blue. ***Female:*** No gaudy blue and purple markings; crossbands more distinct than in male.

On the coastal side of the mountains in s. Calif. this lizard frequents granite outcrops in areas of oak and chaparral, ranging into the yellow pine belt below 5500 ft (1680 m). On the desert side it is found in rocky canyons and on the rocky upper portions of alluvial fans where there is sufficient moisture for growth of chaparral,

palms, or mesquite. In Baja Calif. it occurs in piñon-juniper woodland and subtropical thornforest. An excellent climber on rocks and vegetation. Conspicuous on light-colored rocks, but wariness makes up for lack of camouflage. Look for these lizards when they first emerge; once they warm up, they will seldom allow close approach. Clutch of 6–15 eggs, laid May–July. Eats insects, lizards, and occasionally buds and fleshy fruits.
Similar species: (1) Clark Spiny Lizard (p. 129) has a well-defined black neck patch, is paler, and has more pointed and prominently keeled scales. (2) See also Desert Spiny Lizard (p. 127) and (3) Hunsaker Spiny Lizard (p. 237).
Range: Lower slopes of the Peninsular Ranges of s. Calif. from northern side of San Gorgonio Pass south to tip of Baja Calif. Sea level to around 7000 ft. (2130 m). **Map 84**

WESTERN FENCE LIZARD **Pl. 26**

Sceloporus occidentalis

Identification: $2\frac{1}{4}$–$3\frac{1}{2}$ in. (5.6–8.7 cm). A black, gray, or brown lizard with blotched pattern. Dark-striped individuals are occasionally found in s. Calif. Sides of belly blue. Rear surfaces of limbs yellow or orange. Dorsal scales keeled and pointed, relatively smaller than in Desert, Clark, and Granite Spiny Lizards. *35–51 scales between interparietal and rear of thighs.* Complete supraorbital semicircles. Scales on back of thigh mostly keeled. ***Young:*** Little or no blue on throat. Blue belly markings faint or absent. No yellow or orange on limbs in hatchlings. ***Male:*** Enlarged postanals, swollen tail base. Blue patch on throat, sometimes partly or completely divided (occasionally absent). Blue belly patches edged with black. When in light phase, dorsal scales become blue or greenish. ***Female:*** No blue or green above. Dark crescents or bars on back. Blue markings below usually less vivid or absent.

One of the most common western lizards, popularly known as "swift" or "blue-belly," seen on fenceposts, rocks, logs, piles of lumber, and the sides of buildings. Occupies a great variety of habitats — grassland, broken chaparral, sagebrush, woodland, open coniferous forest, and farmland — but absent from severe parts of the desert, although it may descend close to the desert floor on mountain slopes. Although it occasionally climbs trees, it is more often found on or near the ground. One to perhaps 3 clutches of 3–17 eggs, laid April–July. Eats insects and spiders.
Similar species: (1) Both sexes of the Eastern Fence Lizard (below) have a small blue patch (often faint in female) on each side of the throat; patches usually edged in front with black in male. Western Fence Lizard (where the two species approach one another or coexist — see below) has a large, single or partly divided throat patch, usually weak or absent in female (see Fig. 9, p. 132). (2) Sagebrush Lizard (p. 133), with which the Western Fence Liz-

ard sometimes coexists, usually has rust on sides of neck and body, usually a black bar on each shoulder, usually lacks yellow color on the rear of the limbs, and has smaller dorsal scales. Blue throat patch of male flecked with white or pink. (3) Side-blotched Lizard (p. 135) has small, usually unpointed scales on the back, usually a black spot behind the axilla, and a complete gular fold.

Range: Wash. to nw. Baja Calif.; Pacific Coast to w. Utah. Absent from desert except in mountains. Desert outposts are Ord and Providence Mts., Midhills region, and Kingston Range, San Bernardino Co., Calif. Sea level to around 9000 ft. (2750 m). Overlaps range of Eastern Fence Lizard in Pine Valley Mts. west of Ashy, Washington Co., Utah. **Map 85**

Subspecies: NORTHWESTERN FENCE LIZARD, *S. o. occidentalis.* Males usually have 2 blue throat patches connected at the midline by a lighter blue band; rarely, throat patch single. Light-colored or with scattered dark flecks below, except in blue areas. GREAT BASIN FENCE LIZARD, *S. o. biseriatus.* Similar to the Northwestern Fence Lizard, but blue on throat of male usually in a single patch. Often gray or black below, excluding blue areas. SIERRA FENCE LIZARD, *S. o. taylori.* Large; males 3¼ in. (8.1 cm) or more. Many with entire venter blue (belly patches not separated by a pale area). Small males resemble the Northwestern Fence Lizard in ventral coloration. Sierra Nevada, mostly above 7000 ft. (1800 m). Tuolumne R. drainage to Sequoia National Park, Calif. ISLAND FENCE LIZARD, *S. o. becki.* Rear of throat black, with blue-black lines radiating forward to blue chin. Santa Cruz, Santa Rosa, and San Miguel Is. off coast of s. Calif.

EASTERN FENCE LIZARD **Fig. 9**

Sceloporus undulatus

Identification: 1⅝–3¼ in. (4–8.1 cm). Similar to the Western Fence Lizard (Pl. 26). Gray, brown, reddish, or nearly black above, with pattern of crossbars, crescents, or lengthwise stripes. Striped patterns are prevalent in the Great Plains area. *Blue on throat usually divided,* often into 2 widely separated patches, a characteristic that distinguishes this lizard from the Western Fence Lizard where the ranges of the 2 species come close together or overlap (Maps 85 and 86). ***Male:*** As in Western Fence Lizard, but usually has 2 widely separated blue patches on throat (Fig. 9, p. 132).

Like its western relative, this lizard lives in a great variety of habitats — forests, woodland, prairie, shrubby flatlands, sand dunes, rocky hillsides, and farmlands. It seeks shelter in bushes, trees, old buildings, woodpiles, rodent burrows, and under rocks, logs, or other objects on the ground. In forested parts of its range it climbs trees, and when frightened keeps to the opposite side of the trunk. Where trees are scarce this lizard is primarily a ground dweller. It is active throughout the year in the southern part of its

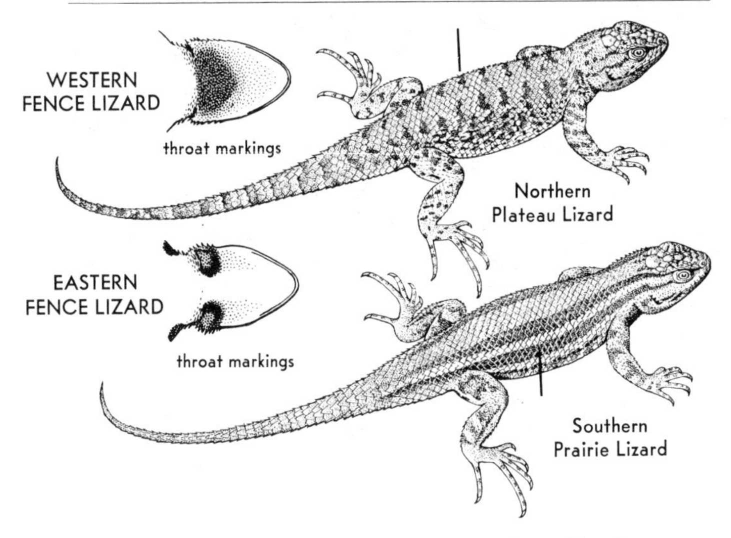

Fig. 9. Pattern variation in Eastern Fence Lizard

range. Clutches of 4–17 eggs, laid Mar.–Aug. Eats insects, spiders, ticks, millipedes, snails, and small lizards.

Similar species: See Western Fence Lizard (p. 130).

Range: Cen. S.D., s. Ill., and se. N.Y. to cen. Fla., Gulf Coast, and Zacatecas; sw. Utah and nw. Ariz. (including Hualapai Mts.) to Atlantic Coast. Sea level to around 10,000 ft. (3080 m).

Map 86

Subspecies: NORTHERN PLATEAU LIZARD, *S. u. elongatus* (Fig. 9). 45 or more scales between interparietal and rear of thighs. Most other subspecies have lower scale counts (44 or fewer). Narrow crossbars or wavy crosslines usually present on back in both sexes. Blue throat and belly patches. SOUTHERN PLATEAU LIZARD, *S. u. tristichus*. Light stripes usually present on back. Breeding male has intense blue patches on throat and sides of belly. Female often has pale blue patches on belly. Throat patches are separate or joined in male, separate in female. 45 or more scales between interparietal and rear of thighs. SOUTHERN PRAIRIE LIZARD, *S. u. consobrinus* (Fig. 9). Resembles Southern Plateau Lizard, but females usually lack blue belly patches. RED-LIPPED PLATEAU LIZARD, *S. u. erythrocheilus*. Light stripes on upper sides weakly developed, broken, or absent. Blue throat patches often connected at midline in both sexes. In breeding season lips, throat, and sometimes head turn red or orange, especially in males. A rock dweller, usually found below 7000 ft. (1800 m), rarely above 9000 ft. (2770 m). Not known to overlap the range of the Northern Prairie Lizard. NORTHERN PRAIRIE LIZARD, *S. u. garmani.* Light stripes on upper sides distinct in both sexes. Blue belly patches, but no blue on throat in males. A prairie species. Isolated populations in sand hill country in e. N.M., surrounded by *S. u. tristichus* in nonsandy areas and on rocky slopes. COWLES PRAIRIE LIZARD (White Sands Prairie Lizard), *S. u. cowlesi.* Pale gray to nearly white above, with an obscure dorsal pattern. White Sands, N.M.

STRIPED PLATEAU LIZARD **Pl. 26**
Sceloporus virgatus

Identification: 1¾–2¾ in. (4.4–6.9 cm). A brownish lizard, usually with a distinct striped pattern. *2 unbroken light stripes on each side (1 dorsolateral and 1 lateral), separated by a broad, dark brown band.* Each dorsolateral stripe is bordered above by a row of brown or brown and white spots; the rows of dark dorsal spots are separated along the dorsal midline by a broad, pale gray area. Usually some dark flecking on throat and chest. *Belly plain white or cream,* without blue markings. Small blue patch on each side of throat. ***Young:*** Stripes well defined. Blue patches on throat faint or absent. ***Male:*** Enlarged postanals; swollen tail base. Blue throat patches more prominent than in female, and dorsal dark spots usually absent or reduced. Each dorsolateral stripe may be bordered above by a brown stripe and the dorsal spots may be vague or absent. ***Female:*** When breeding, blue throat patches surrounded or replaced by orange.

A mountain form, most abundant in mixed pine and oak woods, but ranges upward into coniferous forest and downward in oak woodland along streams. Although this lizard has been found within a mile of the Eastern Fence Lizard, which occurs in the lowlands, it is not known to overlap the range of this species. Most abundant in the vicinity of rocky and sandy intermittent streams where there is shade and water or damp sand. Chiefly a ground dweller but readily climbs boulders, logs, and trees. Clutch of 5–15 eggs, laid June–July. Eats insects, centipedes, and other arthropods.

Similar species: Differs from (1) the Eastern Fence Lizard (p. 131) in lacking blue belly patches and usually having notches on the femoral-pore scales. (2) See also Bunch Grass Lizard (p. 125).

Range: Mts. of extreme se. Ariz. and sw. N.M., south in Sierra Madre Occidental at least to s. Chihuahua. In the U.S., in the Chiricahua, Peloncillo, Guadalupe, and Animas Mts. From 4900 to around 10,000 ft. (1490–3080 m). **Map 88**

SAGEBRUSH LIZARD *Sceloporus graciosus* **Pl. 26**

Identification: 1⅞–2⅝ in. (4.7–6.5 cm). Resembles the Western Fence Lizard but is smaller and has relatively few scales (42–68 between interparietal and rear of thighs). Gray or brown above, usually with blotches or crossbars and light stripes on upper sides. Often a *black bar on the shoulder. Usually rust in axilla and often on sides of neck and body.* Usually no yellow or orange on rear surfaces of limbs. Blue belly patches. *Scales on back of thigh mostly granular.* ***Young:*** Orange on neck, blue markings below subdued or absent. ***Male:*** Enlarged postanals; swollen tail base. Blue throat with white or pink flecks, but throat patch sometimes absent. Belly patches darker blue than throat, edged with black. In light phase, blue or blue-green flecks appear in the dorsal scales. ***Female:*** Little or no blue below, none above. When breeding, sometimes yellow below, and orange may become more vivid on neck and sides.

A sagebrush lizard over much of its range, but also occurs in manzanita and ceanothus brushland, piñon-juniper woodland, pine and fir forests, and along river bottoms in the coastal redwood forests. In shin oak-dune habitat in N.M. and Tex. West of the Great Basin it lives chiefly in the mountains, generally occurring at higher elevations than the Western Fence Lizard, but often overlapping it in range at intermediate altitudes. Requirements seem to be good light, open ground, and scattered low bushes. A ground dweller, usually found near bushes, brush heaps, logs, or rocks. When frightened it retreats to rocks, thick brush, or occasionally climbs trees. One or 2 clutches of 2–8 eggs, laid June–Aug. Eats insects, spiders, mites, ticks, and scorpions.

Similar species: See Western Fence Lizard (p. 130).

Range: Cen. Wash., s. Idaho, and s. Mont. to nw. N.M., n. Ariz., and n. Baja Calif.; w. Colo. to coast in n. Calif. and s. Ore., to eastern slope of Cascade Mts. farther north. Isolated populations in N.D. (North Unit, Theodore Roosevelt National Memorial Park), se. N.M., w. Tex., and in Calif. in mountains to south and at Sutter Buttes, Mt. Diablo, San Benito Mt., Telescope Peak, and elsewhere. Old records for Pullman and Almota, Whitman Co., Wash. From 500 to around 10,500 ft. (150–3200 m). **Map 87**

Subspecies: NORTHERN SAGEBRUSH LIZARD, *S. g. graciosus.* 42–53 (avg. 48) dorsal scales between interparietal and rear of thighs. Usually has distinct light and dark dorsolateral stripes on upper sides. WESTERN SAGEBRUSH LIZARD, *S. g. gracilis.* 50–68 (avg. 61) scales between interparietal and rear of thighs. Striping less distinct than in preceding subspecies. Blue throat and belly patches in male separated by whitish areas. Female whitish below. SOUTHERN SAGEBRUSH LIZARD, *S. g. vandenburgianus.* 48–66 (avg. 55) scales between interparietal and rear of thighs. Blue belly patches in male separated by narrow strip of dark or light color, or connected. Blue or black color on belly often joins blue throat patch. Ventral surface of both tail and thighs frequently blue. Female often dusky below. DUNES SAGEBRUSH LIZARD, *S. g. arenicolus.* Pale coloration. Striping often vague. No blue on throat in male. Found only in sandy areas in se. N.M. and nw. Tex.

SIDE-BLOTCHED LIZARD *Uta stansburiana* **Pl. 25**

Identification: 1½–2⅜ in. (3.7–5.9 cm). A small, often brownish lizard with a *bluish black blotch on each side of the chest, behind the forelimb;* side blotch occasionally faint or absent. Ground color above brown, gray, or yellowish to nearly black — blotched, speckled, or sometimes unpatterned. Populations with little or no dorsal pattern are widespread in upper Colorado R. drainage of w. Colo., e. Utah, and n. Ariz. Whitish to bluish gray below, sometimes with orange to reddish orange on throat and sides of belly. A gular fold. Scales on back small and smooth, without spines at end. Frontal divided. ***Male:*** Slightly enlarged postanals; swollen tail base. In light phase, speckled above with pale blue. No distinct blue belly patches. ***Female:*** Blotched with brown and whitish, occasionally striped. No blue speckling. Side blotch usually less well-defined than in male.

One of the most abundant lizards in the arid and semiarid regions of the West. The habitat varies — sand, rock, hardpan or loam with grass, shrubs, and scattered trees. Often found along sandy washes where there are scattered rocks and low-growing bushes. Chiefly a ground dweller, active all year in the south. Eggs laid Mar.–Aug. In the north, female lays 1–3 clutches of 1–5 eggs, and in the south 2–7 clutches, each of 1–8 eggs. Eats insects, scorpions, spiders, mites, ticks, and sowbugs.

Similar species: See (1) Lesser Earless Lizard (p. 116), (2) Western Fence Lizard (p. 130), and (3) Tree Lizard (p. 136).

Range: Cen. Wash. to tip of Baja Calif., n. Sinaloa, and n. Zacatecas (Mex.); Pacific Coast to w. Colo. and w. Tex. Below sea level (desert sinks) to around 9000 ft. (2750 m). **Map 93**

LONG-TAILED BRUSH LIZARD **Pl. 25**

Urosaurus graciosus

Identification: 1⅞–2¼ in. (4.7–5.6 cm). A well-camouflaged, shrub- or tree-dwelling lizard that often lies motionless, with its slim body aligned with a branch. *Tail long and slender — often twice as long as body.* Gray above, with dusky to black crossbars, but when captured may change color from dark gray to pale beige in less than 5 min. A pale lateral stripe usually extends from the upper jaw along each side of the neck and body. *A broad band of enlarged scales down middle of back* (Fig. 20, opp. Pl. 25). Well-developed gular fold. Frontal usually divided. ***Male:*** A pale blue or greenish patch flecked with white on each side of the belly, lacking in female. Both sexes may have a reddish, orange, or lemon yellow throat.

A desert species. Frequents areas of loose sand and scattered bushes and trees, creosote bush, burrobush, galleta grass, catclaw, mesquite, and paloverde. Creosote bushes with exposed roots seem

to be especially favored, perhaps because of the shelter afforded by the root tangle. Being more heat-tolerant than its relative the Tree Lizard, it can live in sparser growth. At night and on windy days it may seek shelter in the sand or in burrows of other animals. At Palm Springs, Calif., it lives in olive trees and Washington palms near houses. Since these lizards resemble bark and tend to remain motionless when approached, carefully examine branches of bushes and trees to find them. Search the lower bare branches of creosote bushes on the side facing early morning sun. Although this lizard is diurnal, after a hot day it may sleep aloft and can be found by searching the tips of branches at night. 1 or perhaps 2 clutches of 2–10 eggs, laid May–Aug. Eats insects, spiders, and occasionally parts of plants.
Similar species: See (1) Tree Lizard (below) and (2) Small-scaled Lizard (p. 137).
Range: S. Nev. to nw. Sonora and ne. Baja Calif.; desert slope of mountains of s. Calif. to cen. Ariz. Coexists with the Tree Lizard near Wickenburg in Hassayampa R. drainage and along Verde R. near Tempe, Ariz. Near sea level to around 3500 ft. (1070 m).
Map 92
Subspecies: WESTERN BRUSH LIZARD, *U. g. graciosus.* Pale coloration. Pattern greatly subdued — some individuals are nearly patternless. Frequents both small and large desert shrubs. ARIZONA BRUSH LIZARD, *U. g. shannoni.* Male with highly contrasting dorsal pattern of black and gray. 6–7 bold black crossbars on back, often connected with paired black blotches. 6–8 blackish oblique bars on each side, which may form chevrons. Bold black collar usually incomplete middorsally. Frequents chiefly the larger desert trees — mesquite, catclaw, and occasionally paloverde.

TREE LIZARD *Urosaurus ornatus* **Pl. 25**
Identification: $1\frac{1}{2}$–$2\frac{1}{4}$ in. (3.9–5.6 cm). A slim, dark brown, black (when in dark phase), tan, sooty, or gray lizard with small scales and a long slender tail. Often a rusty area at the base of the tail. A gular fold. *Band of enlarged scales down middle of back, separated into 2 or more parallel rows by center strip of small scales* (Fig. 20, opp. Pl. 25). Above usually blotched or crossbarred with dusky. A fold of skin on each side of body. ***Male:*** *Vivid blue or blue-green belly patches,* sometimes united and occasionally connected with blue throat patch. Throat sometimes yellow, greenish, or pale blue-green. ***Female:*** Throat whitish, orange, or yellow. No belly patches.

A climbing lizard that spends much of its time in trees and on rocks; sometimes seen clinging head downward. Its color often blends with the background. Frequents mesquite, oak, pine, juniper, alder, cottonwood, and non-native trees such as tamarisk and rough-bark eucalyptus, but also may occur in treeless areas. Appears to be especially attracted to river courses. Ranges from desert to the lower edge of the spruce-fir zone. When encountered on the ground, it may run to a rock or tree and climb upward, keeping out of sight. 1–6 (higher counts in the south) clutches, each of 2–13 eggs, laid Mar.–Aug. Eats insects and spiders.

Similar species: (1) Differs from the spiny lizards (*Sceloporus* species, pp. 125–134) in having a complete gular fold and enlarged scales down the middle of the back. (2) Side-blotched Lizard (p. 135) is a ground-dweller, has a dark blotch behind the axilla, back scales of uniform size, and lacks blue belly patches. (3) Long-tailed Brush Lizard (p. 135) has a broad band of enlarged scales down the back, unbroken by small scales. (4) See also Small-scaled Lizard (below).

Range: Sw. Wyo. to s. Sinaloa and n. Coahuila (Mex.); lower Colorado R. to cen. Tex. Sea level to around 9000 ft. (2770 m).

Map 91

SMALL-SCALED LIZARD **Pl. 25**

Urosaurus microscutatus

Identification: $1\frac{1}{2}$–2 in. (3.7–5 cm). Resembles the Tree Lizard (above). Brown, gray, or sooty above, often darkening on the tail, especially in males. 2 rows of dark blotches on the back. Dorsal scales granular, *usually enlarging gradually toward the midline.* Gular fold present. A skin fold on each side of the body. Frontal usually single. ***Young:*** Often with pale yellow-orange throat patch. ***Male:*** Throat often blue with center spot of yellow or orange; a blue patch on each side of the belly, sometimes uniting to form a solid blue area. Enlarged postanal scales. ***Female:*** Usually smaller and paler than male and lacks blue markings.

Frequents chiefly rocky habitats grown to oak, sycamore, desert willow, chaparral, and thornscrub. Clutch of 2–8 eggs, laid May–July. Eats insects and spiders.

Similar species: (1) Tree Lizard (above) has several rows of enlarged scales down middle of back, separated along the midline by small scales. (2) Long-tailed Brush Lizard (p. 135) has a much longer tail — usually over twice the length of the body, lacks blue on throat, and has a well-defined band of enlarged scales down middle of back. (3) Side-blotched Lizard (p. 135) has a dark blotch behind the axilla and lacks distinct blue belly patches. (4) See also Black-tailed Brush Lizard (p. 238).

Range: S. Calif. from Borrego Palm Canyon on desert side and Cottonwood and Deerhorn Flat on coastal side of mountains, south to the vicinity of El Medaño, Baja Calif. Sea level to around 7000 ft. (2130 m). **Map 94**

BANDED ROCK LIZARD *Petrosaurus mearnsi* **Pl. 25**

Identification: $2\frac{7}{8}$–$3\frac{1}{2}$ in. (7.1–8.7 cm). A *flat-bodied* lizard with a *single narrow black collar and banded tail;* restricted to rocks. Scales on dorsal surfaces granular, except on tail and limbs, where keeled and pointed. Olive, brown, or gray above, with many small white or bluish spots. Wavy crossbars on back, sometimes faint. Ventral surfaces bluish or dusky. Whitish or pinkish spots on throat. ***Male:*** Throat pattern and bluish color more pronounced than in female. In light phase, blue spots on back, tail, and hind limbs. ***Female:*** When gravid, orange on throat and above eye.

This lizard crawls over the sides and under surfaces of rocks with ease, limbs extended well out from its sides, body held low, and hindquarters swinging from side to side. Most abundant among massive rocks in the shady, narrower parts of canyons, on the desert slope of the mountains. Often wary. To catch rock lizards use a fine copper wire noose opened to diam. of 1½–2 in. (4–5 cm). When you are within a foot or so, sweep the noose over the lizard's head with a single quick stroke. Clutch of 2–6 eggs, laid June–Aug. Eats insects, spiders, blossoms, and buds.

Similar species: Collared lizards (*Crotaphytus* species, pp. 120–123) have 2 black collar marks; a non-spiny, unbanded tail; and a round body.

Range: S. Calif. from San Gorgonio Pass south through Peninsular Ranges and northern ⅔ of Baja Calif. Near sea level to around 3600 ft. (1100 m). **Map 95**

Horned Lizards: Genus *Phrynosoma*

These are the "horny toads." Most are armed with daggerlike head spines ("horns") and sharp, projecting scales on the dorsal surfaces of the body. The horns, the flattened oval form, and pointed fringe scales on the sides of the body are distinctive. As with many iguanids, males have enlarged postanal scales and, when breeding, a swollen tail base.

Horned lizards are often difficult to find. They are usually solitary, and when approached often crouch low and "sit tight." Their coloration and spiny skin blend with the ground. One may nearly step on them before they move.

To find them, walk outward in a spiral from ant nests, near which they lie in wait for food, or search for their tracks. Ants and fine loose soil for burial seem to be essential for most species. When picked up horned lizards may inflate themselves by gulping air and jab with their horns. Some species may even spurt blood from the eyes. The blood comes from a large sinus behind the eye and emerges from a pore in the eyelid, often spurting for several feet. It seems to have a repellent effect on foxes and other predators.

Although favored as pets, horned lizards ordinarily do not live long in captivity. They seem to need large numbers of live ants, which their captors can seldom supply in sufficient quantity. Because of their popularity as pets, escaped or released individuals may be found far beyond their natural ranges.

The 14 species range from extreme sw. Canada to Guatemala and from w. Ark. to the Pacific Coast.

TEXAS HORNED LIZARD *Phrynosoma cornutum* **Pl. 21**
Identification: 2½–5 in. (6.2–12.5 cm). *Dark stripes radiate from eye region* on each side of face. Mostly brown, yellowish, tan, reddish, or gray above; ground color varies with prevailing soil color. Beige or whitish middorsal stripe. Sooty or dark brown blotches on back and tail and a pair of large dark blotches on the neck. Rear edge or each blotch whitish or yellow. Skin of gular fold yellow. The 2 central horns are notably long and sharp. A row of enlarged scales on each side of the throat, surrounded by small scales. Two rows of pointed fringe scales on each side of the body. Eardrums distinct. Belly scales weakly keeled.

Inhabits arid and semiarid open country with sparse plant growth — bunch grass, cactus, juniper, acacia, and mesquite. The ground may be of sand, loam, hardpan, or rock. Some loose soil is usually present in which these lizards bury themselves. They also seek shelter under shrubs, in burrows of other animals, or among rocks. Clutch of 14–37 eggs (perhaps to around 50), laid May–July. Eats chiefly ants but also takes beetles and grasshoppers.
Similar species: (1) Regal Horned Lizard (p. 142) has 4 large horns with bases that touch at the back of the head. (2) Coast Horned Lizard (below) has 2–3 rows of enlarged pointed scales on each side of the throat. (3) Desert Horned Lizard (p. 140) has a single row rather than a double row of pointed fringe scales on each side of the body.
Range: Kans. to Durango and Tamaulipas, and Gulf Coast of Tex. Miss. R. to extreme se. Ariz. Isolated population on Dauphin I., Mobile Co., Ala. Sea level to around 6000 ft. (1830 m). In the West it often coexists with the Round-tailed Horned Lizard (p. 142). **Map 101**

COAST HORNED LIZARD *Phrynosoma coronatum* **Pl. 21**
Identification: 2½–4 in. (6.2–10 cm). Two horns at back of head, longer than the rest; bases separated, not touching. *Two rows of pointed fringe scales on each side of body. Two or 3 rows of enlarged pointed scales on each side of throat* (Fig. 18, opp. Pl. 21). General coloration yellowish, brown, reddish, or gray. Wavy dark blotches on back and a pair of large dark blotches on the neck. No dark stripes on face. Cream, beige, or yellow below, usually with spots of dusky.

Frequents a variety of habitats — scrubland, grassland, coniferous forests, and broadleaf woodland. Common in the lowlands along sandy washes where scattered low shrubs provide cover. Other requirements seem to be warmth (especially open areas for sunning), patches of fine loose soil where it can bury itself, and ants and other insect prey. Clutch of 6–21 eggs, laid April–June.

Similar species: The Desert Horned Lizard (below) has a blunter snout, shorter horns and body spines, only 1 row of well-developed fringe scales on each side of the body, and 1 row of enlarged scales on each side of the throat.

Range: Throughout most of Calif. west of desert and Cascade-Sierran highlands; absent from humid Northwest; thoughout Baja Calif., except extreme northeastern part. In southern Sierra ranges to Walker Basin and Chimney Peak area,. A single dubious record from Grasshopper (4500 ft., 1380 m) south of Medicine Lake, Siskiyou Co., Calif. Sea level to around 6500 ft. (2000m).

Map 97

DESERT HORNED LIZARD **Pl. 21**

Phrynosoma platyrhinos

Identification: $2\frac{5}{8}$–$3\frac{3}{4}$ in. (6.5–9.4 cm). The desert counterpart of the Coast Horned Lizard. Snout very blunt. Horns and body spines relatively short. *One row of well-developed fringe scales on each side of body, and 1 row of slightly enlarged scales on each side of the throat* (Fig. 18). General coloration resembles the soil color of the habitat — beige, tan, reddish, gray, or black, the latter in individuals found on black lava flows. Wavy dark blotches on back and a pair of large dark blotches on neck.

A lizard of arid lands, found on sandy flats, alluvial fans, along washes and at the edges of dunes. Although this lizard is sometimes found on hardpan or among rocks, patches of sand are generally present. Associated with creosote bush, saltbush, greasewood, cactus, and ocotillo in the desert, and with Basin sagebrush, saltbush, and greasewood in the Great Basin. To find these lizards, drive slowly along little-traveled roads in the morning or late afternoon. Watch for them on the pavement and on rocks or earth banks along the roadside where they bask. Usually easily caught by hand. 1–2 clutches of 2–16 eggs, laid May–July, perhaps to Aug. Eats ants, other insects, spiders, and some plant materials (berries, etc.).

Similar species: See Coast Horned Lizard (above).

Range: S. Idaho and se. Ore. south to ne. Baja Calif. and nw. Sonora; western base of central plateau of Utah to eastern base of Sierra Nevada and desert slope of mountains of s. Calif.; San Jacinto R. Wash, Riverside Co., Calif., on coastal side of mountains; Ouray-Jensen area, Uintah Co., Utah. Possibly in the Shannon-Cuyama Valley area, Calif. An old, dubious record from Walla Walla, Wash. Below sea level (in desert sinks) to around 6500 ft. (1980 m). Occasionally found in same habitat with the Flat-tailed Horned Lizard. Hybrids have been found near Ocotillo, south of Salton Sea, Calif. **Map 98**

Subspecies: NORTHERN DESERT HORNED LIZARD, *P. p. platyrhinos*. Two longest horns at back of head usually less than 45% of head length; space between their bases roughly equals width of horn at its base. SOUTHERN DESERT HORNED LIZARD, *P. p. calidiarum.* Two longest horns at back of head slightly longer but closer together than in above subspecies: length of horn usually 45% or more of head length; space between their bases ½ width of horn at its base; tail tip flatter.

SHORT-HORNED LIZARD Pl. 21

Phrynosoma douglassii

Identification: 1¾–4⁵⁄₁₆ in. (4.4–10.8 cm). The *short, stubby horns and single row of fringe scales* on each side of the body will distinguish this horned lizard from our other species. Throat scales all small (none notably enlarged). Beige, gray, brown, reddish, or tan above, blotched with dark brown and often speckled with whitish; the color pattern usually closely matches the background. A pair of large dark brown blotches on back of neck. Rear of throat and chest usually buff or orange-yellow.

Ranges from semiarid plains high into the mountains. Frequents a variety of habitats — shortgrass prairie, sagebrush, and open piñon-juniper, pine-spruce, and spruce-fir forests. The ground may be stony, sandy, or firm, but usually some fine loose soil is present. More cold-tolerant than other horned lizards. Live-bearing; 5–36 (3–15 in Pacific Northwest) young, born July–Sept. Eats insects, including ants, spiders, and snails.

Range: Extreme s. Canada to s. Durango; w. Ariz. and Cascade crest in Ore. and Wash. to the western Dakotas, e. Colo., and Tex. Panhandle. Isolated population at Wadsworth, Washoe Co., Nev. A single old record (1910) from Osoyoos, B.C. Chiefly a mountain dweller in the more arid and southern parts of its range. From around 900–11,300 ft. (170–3440 m). **Map 96**

Remarks: A population of small (dwarfed) individuals inhabits San Luis Valley, s. Colo.

FLAT-TAILED HORNED LIZARD Pl. 21

Phrynosoma mcallii

Identification: 2½–3¼ in. (6.2–8.1 cm). A pale gray, buff, or rusty brown lizard restricted to fine windblown sand. Closely matches the sand color. The only horned lizard with a *dark middorsal stripe. Tail* long, broad, and *very much flattened.* Long slender horns. Two rows of fringe scales on each side of the body. White below; unmarked.

Lives only in areas of fine sand, sharing the habitat with fringe-toed lizards. Often occupies extremely barren country, where vegetation is sparse or lacking. May be difficult to find. When approached, it flattens out against the ground and blends with the sand or quickly buries itself. Flat-tails run with great speed and when fleeing may be mistaken for fringe-toed lizards. In summer flat-tails may be abroad in the evening. They occasionally are found on blacktop roads, where, although conspicuous, they can easily be mistaken for a rock. 1 or 2 clutches of 7–10 eggs, laid May–June. Eats ants and other insects, but ants form the bulk of the diet.

Range: Dunes and sandy flats of low desert in s. Calif. from Coachella Valley to head of Gulf of California; extreme ne. Baja Calif. to se. Ariz. Below sea level (in Salton sink) to around 600 ft. (180 m). **Map 102**

ROUND-TAILED HORNED LIZARD **Pl. 21**

Phrynosoma modestum

Identification: 1½–2¾ in. (3.7–6.9 cm). A small horned lizard with relatively short, spikelike, well-separated horns of about equal length. *Tail slender and round,* broadening abruptly at its base. *No fringe scales on sides of body.* Dark blotch on each side of neck, above groin, and on side of tail base. Tail barred. Center of back usually unspotted. Mostly ash white, gray, light brown, or reddish above, generally matching the predominant soil color.

Lives on sandy or gravelly soil of plains, desert flats, washes, and hill slopes in arid and semiarid habitats. Rocks may or may not be present. Plants present may be cedar, ocotillo, oak, mesquite, creosote bush, sumac, piñon, juniper, and ponderosa pine. At rest this lizard resembles a small rock. Its back is humped and the dark side markings look like shadows. In hot weather, it is most often abroad in the early morning or on overcast days. Clutch of 9–18 eggs, laid June–July. Eats ants, beetles and other insects.

Range: Northern N.M. to San Luis Potosí; n. Tex. to se. Ariz.; Cimarron Co., Okla. From around 700–6000 ft. (210–1850 m). Often shares habitat with Texas Horned Lizard (p. 139).

Map 99

REGAL HORNED LIZARD *Phrynosoma solare* **Pl. 21**

Identification: 3–4⅝ in. (7.5–11.6 cm). Our largest horned lizard, easily identified by the *4 large horns at rear of head. Horn bases in contact.* Large light-colored area on back — light gray, beige, or reddish, bordered on each side by a broad dusky band. Sometimes a pale middorsal stripe. A single row of fringe scales on each side of body.

Frequents rocky and gravelly habitats of arid and semiarid plains, hills, and lower slopes of mountains. Much of its range is in succulent plant habitat of upland desert. Plants present may include cactus (saguaro, etc.), mesquite, and creosote bush. Seldom found on sandy flats. Search the ground near scrubby plant growth along washes, both in rocky canyons and on the plains. Usually not found in the same habitat with other species of horned lizards. Clutch of 7–28 eggs, laid July–Aug. Eats chiefly ants.

Range: Cen. Ariz. to n. Sinaloa, west to Harquahala and Plomosa Mts., Ariz. Sea level to around 4800 ft. (1460 m). **Map 100**

Night Lizards: Family Xantusiidae

A small family of New World lizards with representatives from sw. U.S. to Panama; a single species in Cuba. 18 species.

Small, secretive lizards with lidless eyes and vertical pupils. Skin soft and pliable, dorsal scales granular, ventral scales large and squarish. A gular fold and a fold of skin low on each side of the body. Live-bearing.

GRANITE NIGHT LIZARD *Xantusia henshawi* **Pl. 30**
Identification: 2–$2\frac{3}{4}$ in. (5–6.9 cm). *A flat-bodied lizard with soft, pliable skin. Back marked with large dark brown or black spots* on a pale background. The light color between the spots becomes reduced to a network of whitish or pale yellow when the lizard is in the dark phase. Color change may occur rapidly. Scales smooth and granular above, large and squarish on belly; ventral scales in 14 lengthwise rows. Eyes with fixed transparent covering and vertical pupils. Head broad and flat, with large symmetrically arranged plates. ***Male:*** Whitish, oval-shaped patch along front (leading) edge of femoral-pore row.

Inhabits rocky canyons and hillsides in arid and semiarid regions, where it seems to prefer massive outcrops in the shadier parts of canyons or near water. Avoids hot, south-facing slopes. Secretive and crevice-dwelling, seldom venturing from its hiding place among the rocks except at night. Live-bearing; 1–2 young per brood, born in the fall. Eats insects, spiders, ticks, scorpions, centipedes, and some plant materials.
Similar species: (1) Leaf-toed Gecko (p. 112), with which it coexists in some parts of its range, has broad, flat toe tips. (2) Desert Night Lizard (below) has much smaller spots and 12 lengthwise rows of ventral scales.
Range: From southern side of San Gorgonio Pass in s. Calif., southward in the Peninsular Ranges, including their desert and coastal slopes, into the Sierra Juárez and Sierra San Pedro Mártir of n. Baja Calif. Isolated population near Pedriceña, Durango, Mex. From about 400–7600 ft. (120–2320 m). **Map 72**
Subspecies: The HENSHAW NIGHT LIZARD, *X. h. henshawi,* occurs in our area.

DESERT NIGHT LIZARD *Xantusia vigilis* **Pl. 30**
Identification: $1\frac{1}{2}$–$2\frac{3}{4}$ in. (3.7–5.9 cm). A slim, velvet-skinned lizard; usually *olive, gray, or dark brown above, speckled with black.* Ground color occasionally yellowish or orange-buff (especially in ne. Utah). In some areas spots may tend to form a network (s. Sierra) or lengthwise rows (cen. Ariz.). Usually a beige stripe edged with black extends from eye to shoulder. A light stripe may be present on each side of upper body in animals from cen. and s. Baja

Calif. No eyelids; *pupils vertical.* A single row of well-developed supraoculars. Dorsal scales smooth and granular, generally in 30–50 lengthwise rows at midbody; ventral ones large and squarish, in 12 lengthwise rows at midbelly. Head and body somewhat flattened in individuals that habitually seek shelter in rock crevices (s. Sierra and cen. Ariz.). ***Male:*** Large femoral pores give thigh a more angular contour in cross-section than female's.

A secretive lizard of arid and semiarid lands that lives chiefly beneath fallen branches of Joshua-trees, dead clumps of various other species of yucca (Mojave yucca, Whipple yucca, etc.), nolina, agave, and cardons. Also found in rock crevices, beneath cow chips, soil-matted dead brush and other debris, and beneath logs and under the bark of Digger pines (inner Coast Ranges and s. Sierra Nevada, Calif.). Ranges into the piñon-juniper belt in the Panamint Mts. and into the chaparral-oak belt in cen. Ariz. Chiefly diurnal and crepuscular; may be nocturnal during warm summer months. Seldom found in the open away from cover. Because of its secretive habits, this lizard was at one time considered extremely rare, but it is now known to be one of the most abundant lizards. Live-bearing; 1–3 young per brood, born Aug.–Oct. Eats insects, spiders, and other arthropods.

Similar species: See Granite Night Lizard (p. 143).

Range: Mojave Desert and inner s. Coast Ranges of Calif., s. Nev., s. Utah and cen. Ariz., south to sw. Sonora and throughout most of Baja Calif. Isolated populations in Durango and Zacatecas, Mexico. Sea level to around 9300 ft. (2830 m, at Telescope Peak, Calif.).

In Calif., ranges northward in inner Coast Ranges to Panoche Hills, to s. Sierra (Kelso Valley, Kern R. Canyon, Greenhorn and Piute Mts., Granite Station, Mercy Hot Springs), and Tehachapi Mts., and east of the Sierra to Inyo Mts. To the south, found on coastal side of Transverse Mts. in headwaters of Big Tujunga Canyon. In Utah, from the Henry Mts. east to Natural Bridges National Monument south to San Juan R. In Ariz., on western slope of Central Plateau (Weaver, McCloud, and Superstition Mts., Tonto National Monument, and Valentine), in Haulapai, Harquahala, Kofa, and Castle Dome Mts. and at other scattered localities. Catalina I. specimens may have been introduced from the Calif. mainland. **Map 71**

Subspecies: COMMON NIGHT LIZARD, *X. v. vigilis.* When present, spots on upper surfaces cover 2–3 adjacent dorsal scales. A narrow, usually inconspicuous light stripe behind eye extends onto neck. 17–23 lamellae (avg. 21) on 4th toe. ARIZONA NIGHT LIZARD, *X. v. arizonae.* Dorsal spots often cover 5 or more scales, and sometimes tend to form lengthwise rows. High dorsal scale row count (at midbody), 38–49 (avg. 43). 21–29 lamellae (avg. 26) on 4th toe. Head and body somewhat flattened. SIERRA NIGHT LIZARD, *X. v. sierrae.* Spots on upper surfaces tend to be interconnected, forming a dark network. Light eyestripe broad and conspicuous. High dorsal scale row count, 40–44 (avg. 42). 22–25 lamellae (avg. 23) on 4th toe. Head and body often somewhat flattened. UTAH NIGHT LIZARD, *X. v. utahensis.* Orange-buff to yellowish above, with small dorsal spots. 23–25 lamellae (avg. 24) on 4th toe. BAJA CALIFORNIA NIGHT LIZARD, *X. v. gilberti.* Few spots on upper surfaces, tending to concentrate on upper sides. A light stripe often present on each side of upper body. 15–18 lamellae (avg. 17) on 4th toe. 7th upper labial as high as or higher than 6th (in all our other subspecies, 7th not as high as 6th). Eyes relatively small.

ISLAND NIGHT LIZARD **Pl. 30**
Xantusia riversiana Threatened
Identification: 2½–3¾ in. (6.2–9.4 cm). A large night lizard found only on islands off the coast of s. Calif. *Sixteen instead of 14 or 12 lengthwise rows of squarish scales at midbelly. Two rows of supraoculars* (1 row in other species). Soft granular scalation above. Folds of skin on neck and along side of body. Back mottled with pale ash gray or beige and yellowish brown, darkened in varying amounts with black. Some individuals are uniformly colored above (San Nicolas I.) and some have a pale gray stripe on each side of upper body, edged with brown and black; a brown middorsal stripe may be present. Pale gray below, sometimes with a bluish cast, suffused on belly and often on tail with yellow. Underside of feet may be yellowish. ***Male:*** Femoral pores slightly larger than in female.

Inhabits grassland, chaparral, and oak savannah, clumps of cactus, dry sandy or rocky streambeds, cliffs, and rocky beaches. Found under rocks, driftwood, and fallen branches. Less secretive than other night lizards; may be seen abroad in the daytime. Live-bearing; 2–7 young, born in Sept. Eats insects, spiders, centipedes, scorpions, marine isopods, and the stems, leaves, blossoms, and seeds of plants.
Range: San Clemente, Santa Barbara, and San Nicolas Is. off coast of s. Calif. **Map 71**
Remarks: Striped individuals occur on San Clemente and San Nicolas Is., and rarely on Santa Barbara I.

Skinks: Family Scincidae

A widely distributed family with representatives on every continent (except Antarctica) and on many oceanic islands. Abundant in the Old World tropics. Over 1200 species. The northern skinks *(Eumeces,* the only genus in the West, with about 46 species) occur in n. Africa, Asia, and from s. Canada to Costa Rica and Bermuda.

Skinks are usually alert, agile, slim-bodied lizards with *shiny, cycloid scales,* reinforced with bone. The scales of the dorsal and ventral surfaces are similar in size, but those on top of the head are enlarged, symmetrically arranged, and of varied shape. Limbs are small, and in some burrowing species are variously reduced or absent. The tongue is forked and frequently protruded. Some skinks have a window in the lower eyelid that allows them to see when the eyes are closed. All our species have limbs and lack the eyelid window.

These lizards often occur in habitats where there is some moisture nearby — damp soil or a spring or stream. As a group, skinks seem to be more dependent on moisture than most lizards, yet some live in deserts.

It is almost impossible to noose skinks because of their wariness, slick scales, small head, and thick neck. Look for them under stones, boards, logs, and other objects and catch them by hand. Don't grab the tail; it is easily shed.

Skinks lay eggs or are live-bearing. With one exception our species lay eggs.

GREAT PLAINS SKINK *Eumeces obsoletus* **Pl. 28**
Identification: 3½–5⅝ in. (8.7–14.1 cm). Our largest skink. Unique among skinks in our area in having *oblique* instead of horizontal *scale rows on the sides of the body.* Light gray, olive-brown, or tan above, *usually profusely spotted with black or dark brown,* the spots uniting here and there to form scattered lengthwise lines. Occasionally spotting is absent. Sides generally flecked with salmon. Ground color of tail and feet yellowish or pale orange. Pale yellow below, unmarked. ***Young:*** Black above, dark gray below. Tail blue. Orange and white spots on head. With growth the black pigment fades and becomes limited to the rear edge or sides of the scales.

Frequents both grassland and woodland from the plains into the mountains. In the eastern and central part of its range this skink is chiefly a prairie species, most abundant in open habitats with low vegetation. In the West it enters semiarid environments of canyons, mesas, and mountains, usually where there is grass and low shrubby growth. Rocky outcrops near thickets along permanent or intermittent streams are especially favored. Usually found on fine-grain loose soils, under rocks, logs, bark, and boards. A secretive, nervous species that usually attempts to bite when caught. Nests beneath sunken rocks and tends its eggs. Clutch of 7–21 eggs, laid May–July. Eats insects, spiders, mollusks, and lizards.
Range: Neb. to n. Tamaulipas and Durango; Mo. and e. Tex. to w.-cen. Ariz. (Hualapai Mts.). Near sea level to around 8700 ft. (2650 m). **Map 104**

MANY-LINED SKINK *Eumeces multivirgatus* **Pl. 28**
Identification: 2¼–3 in. (5.6–7.5 cm). A slim, *short-limbed,* long-bodied skink with a very long tail. Proportions alone set it off from

our other species. Dorsal coloration varies (Fig. 20, opp. Pl. 28): many dark and light lengthwise stripes; a single light stripe on each side, bordered below by a dark one; a broad pale stripe down middle of back; or plain brown or olive, with an indistinct dark streak on each side. Plain-colored individuals tend to be most common at lower latitudes and elevations. When light stripes are present, 1 on each side is *confined to the 3rd scale row* (counting from middle of back — see Fig. 20). Stripes vary in intensity and some dark ones may actually consist of rows of spots. ***Young:*** Darker stripes may be obscured by dark ground color or, as with adults, stripes may be absent. Tail blue, fading with age. ***Male:*** May develop bright orange or red lips during breeding season.

Lives in a variety of habitats, from sand hills and shortgrass prairie into the mountains. Also occurs near houses and other buildings, in vacant lots, city dumps, and backyards. Local environments vary from creosote bush desert and dense streamside growth to juniper, pine-oak, and fir forests, and from arid to moist conditions. The soil may be loamy, sandy, or rocky. Most abundant where there is water or moist subsoil. Look for this skink under rocks, logs, boards, and dried cow chips. Clutch of 3–7 eggs, laid May–June and tended by female. Eats mainly insects.

Similar species: The Mountain Skink (below) has a Y-shaped mark on its head and neck.

Range: S. Neb. to w. Tex. and perhaps Chihuahua, west to cen. Ariz. Distribution spotty in southern part of range. From 3000 to around 8600 ft. (910–2620 m). **Map 106**

Subspecies: NORTHERN MANY-LINED SKINK, *E. m. multivirgatus.* Little variation in color pattern. Body pale, with light stripes on upper body that are only slightly lighter than ground color, and 2 broad, dark, clearly defined, narrow dorsal stripes that have uninterrupted (not zigzag) margins; dark dorsal stripes located on adjacent parts of 1st and 2nd scale rows, counting from midline (Fig. 20, opp. Pl. 28). Plain-colored form rare. Sandhill and prairie habitats below 5500 ft. (1680 m). VARIABLE SKINK, *E. m. gaigeae.* Coloration highly variable; both striped and plain-colored forms occur. Striped individuals are darker than Northern Many-lined Skink and have strongly contrasting light lines on upper sides (Fig. 20), a contrasting light middorsal line in the young, and varied reduction of dark lines through invasion of ground color from the sides. Some individuals are dark and plain-colored, with no stripes; these unstriped individuals are particularly common at lower elevations in the southernmost, drier parts of the range. Habitats vary — high mountains, plateaus, and lowlands, in pine and spruce forests, mesquite grassland, and creosote bush desert.

MOUNTAIN SKINK *Eumeces callicephalus* **Pl. 28**

Identification: 2–2½ in. (5–6.2 cm). Olive or tan above, with a pale stripe on each upper side, extending from above the eye to the trunk, where it is *confined to the 4th scale row* (counting from dorsal midline). Below the pale stripe is a broad, dark brown band extending from the eye to the groin. Sometimes a whitish or pale orange Y-*shaped mark on the head* with its base located on the neck. Tail bluish. ***Young:*** Blue tail and striping more vivid than in adult. Y-shaped mark distinct.

In the U.S., it frequents oak and pine habitats in rocky areas in the mountains, but in Mexico it ranges to near sea level. Lays and broods its eggs, or gives birth to its young. Eats insects and spiders. **Similar species:** (1) In the Many-lined Skink (p. 146) the light stripes are on the 3rd scale row from dorsal midline (Fig. 20). Striped individuals of (2) Gilbert Skink (p. 149) and (3) Western Skink (below) have a broad light stripe on 2nd and 3rd scale rows. **Range:** Pajarito, Baboquivari, Santa Rita, and Huachuca Mts., Ariz.; Guadalupe Mts. (Guadalupe Canyon), N.M.; w. Mexico southeast to Querétaro. From coastal plain in Sinaloa and Nayarit well up into Sierra Madre Occidental. Near sea level to over 6500 ft. (1980 m). **Map 107**

WESTERN SKINK *Eumeces skiltonianus* **Pl. 28**
Identification: $2\frac{1}{8}$–$3\frac{1}{4}$ in. (5.3–8.1 cm). Aside from fading with age, color pattern varies little. There is a *broad brown stripe down the back, edged with black and bordered on each side by a conspicuous whitish to beige dorsolateral stripe* that begins on the nose and extends over the eye and back along the side of the body onto the tail. The pale dorsolateral stripes are on joined halves of 2nd and 3rd scale rows (counting from middle of the back — see Fig. 20, opp. Pl. 28). A second pale stripe, starting on the upper jaw, occurs low on each side and is separated from the first by a broad dark brown or black band originating on the side of the head and usually extending well out onto the tail. Tail dull blue or gray. In the breeding season reddish or orange color appears on side of head and chin and occasionally on sides, tip, and underside of tail. Usually 7 upper labials and 4 enlarged nuchals. ***Young:*** Striped pattern more vivid than in adult and tail bright blue. Dark lateral stripe *usually extends well out on side of tail.*

Frequents grassland, broken chaparral, piñon-juniper and juniper-sage woodland, and open pine-oak and pine forests. Seems to prefer rocky habitats near streams where there is abundant plant cover, but is also found on dry hillsides far from water. In forested areas, search the sunnier parts of clearings. Active in the daytime but usually keeps out of sight. Clutch of 2–6 eggs, laid June–July and tended by female. Eats insects, spiders, and sowbugs.
Similar species: The striped, blue-tailed subspecies of the Gilbert Skink (Greater Brown and Northern Brown Skinks, p. 150) closely resemble the Western Skink, but their dorsal scales within the light lines on the back are usually edged with brown or gray, and

the blue tail color disappears in adults. Fortunately, where Western and Gilbert Skinks coexist in s. Calif. they are easily distinguished (see Gilbert Skink, below).

Range: Southern B.C. to tip of Baja Calif. and throughout most of Great Basin to extreme n. Ariz.; cen. Utah to Pacific Coast. Apparently absent from floor of San Joaquin Valley, cen. Sierra Nevada, and deserts of Calif. In s. Baja Calif. it extends from San Ignacio south, probably through Sierra de la Giganta to Sierra de la Laguna. Occurrence spotty north of La Paz. On Santa Catalina, Los Coronados, and Todos Santos Is. off coast of Calif. and Baja Calif. Isolated populations in Bodie Hills, White Mts., on Kern Plateau, on east slope of Sierra Nevada west of Independence and Olancha, in Greenhorn and Piute Mts., Calif.; and in Silver Peak Range and other mountainous localities, Nev. A sight record at Comox on Vancouver I., B.C. Sea level to around 8300 ft. (2530 m). Coexists with Gilbert Skink at some localities in Calif. and n. Baja Calif. **Map 105**

Subspecies: SKILTON SKINK, *E. s. skiltonianus.* Pale dorsolateral stripe, usually including no more than half of the 2nd scale row; at midbody, width of dorsolateral stripe less than half that of the dark middorsal stripe. GREAT BASIN SKINK, *E. s. utahensis.* Dorsolateral stripe wider than in Skilton Skink, including more than half of the 2nd scale row, at midbody equal in width to half or more of the dark dorsal stripe. In rocky areas in habitats of scrub oak, sagebrush, juniper, and grassland, from around 4500–8300 ft. (1370–2530 m). Red-tailed individuals (presumably of this subspecies) occur at Oak Grove on the south slope of Pine Mt., Washington Co., Utah. CORONADO SKINK, *E. s. interparietalis.* Differs from Western and Great Basin Skinks in having the interparietal scale reduced in size and enclosed toward the rear by the parietals, and longer middorsal and lateral dark stripes that extend to or beyond the middle of the tail. SAN LUCAN SKINK, *E. s. lagunensis.* Differs from above subspecies in having the interparietal enclosed by the parietals. Tail orange to reddish, brightest in young. S. Baja Calif.

GILBERT SKINK *Eumeces gilberti* **Pl. 28**

Identification: $2\frac{1}{2}$–$4\frac{1}{2}$ in. (6.2–11.2 cm). Adults are plain olive or brown above or have varied amounts of dark spotting, which may form an intricate pattern. Light and dark striping is more or less distinct in adults of some populations and varies with age and locality. The tail becomes brick red or orange with age in both sexes and some individuals develop red on the head. At some localities this skink is difficult to distinguish from the Western Skink except when full-grown and striping has been lost. *Commonly 8 upper labials and often 2 or 3 enlarged nuchals.* ***Young:*** Pair of whitish stripes on each side, enclosing a broad black or dark brown stripe that narrows on the tail and *usually stops abruptly near* *base of tail.* Broad olive stripe down middle of back. Tail blue in the northern and eastern part of the range, salmon or pink in the south (see Subspecies). ***Male:*** Tends to lose striping sooner than female.

Lives in a variety of habitats — grassland, salt flats, high desert, open chaparral, piñon-juniper woodland, and open pine forest, often in rocky areas in the vicinity of intermittent or permanent streams and springs. Clutch of 3–9 eggs, laid in summer. Eats insects and spiders.

Similar species: In the Western Skink (p. 148) the broad lateral stripe on each side is often uniformly brown (it is absent or variegated in Gilbert Skink), blue or blue-gray tail color usually persists in adults, and young have blue tails. In areas where the two species are known to coexist (mountains of s. Calif.), young Gilbert Skinks have pink or salmon tails and the dark lateral stripe stops near the base of the tail. Young Western Skinks have blue tails and stripe extends well out on the tail.

Range: Foothills and middle elevations in Sierra Nevada from Yuba R. south; inner Coast Ranges opposite San Francisco Bay south into mountains of s. Calif. and to the San Pedro Mártir Mts., Baja Calif. Scattered localities in the San Joaquin Valley (subspecies relationships of some of these Valley skinks uncertain, thus the Valley floor is tentatively shown on Map 103 as an area of intergradation). Isolated populations in mountains of se. Calif., s. Nev., and w.-cen. Ariz., including Harquahala and Harcuvar Mts. From near sea level to around 7300 ft. (2220 m). **Map 103**

Subspecies: GREATER BROWN SKINK, *E. g. gilberti.* Young with blue tail. Female averages smaller than male (not true of other subspecies). Usually 2 pairs of nuchals. For dorsal pattern, see Fig. 20, opp. Pl. 28. NORTHERN BROWN SKINK. *E. g. placerensis.* Young with blue tail. Retains striping longer than Greater Brown Skink. Usually 1 pair of nuchals. VARIEGATED SKINK, *E. g. cancellosus.* Young have a pink tail tinged with blue above. Older young and adults have barring or latticework of dark markings above (Fig. 20). WESTERN RED-TAILED SKINK, *E. g. rubricaudatus.* Young have a pink tail (blue in Panamint Mts. and other desert mountains), with no bluish tinge (see above). Striping and barring lost earlier (especially in females) than in Variegated Skink. Many isolated populations. In Calif., at Covington Flat, Riverside Co., Deep Springs and Saline Valleys, Inyo Co., and in Panamint, Kingston, Clark, and Providence Mts.; in Nev. in Sheep and Charleston Mts. and at Grapevine Peak; in Baja Calif. in San Pedro Mártir Mts. and at San Antonio del Mar. ARIZONA SKINK, *E. g. arizonensis.* Adults tend to retain juvenile striping. Young have pinkish on underside of tail. Isolated populations in Arizona in piñon-juniper woodland and yellow-pine forest in vicinity of Prescott, Bradshaw Mts.; chaparral-oak woodland at Yarnell, Weaver Mts.; cottonwood, willow, and mesquite bottomlands of Hassayampa R. near Wickenburg, and at Burro Creek in the Santa Maria Mts.; in chaparral in the Harquahala and Harcuvar Mts.; and in conifer woodland in the Cerbat and Music Mts.

Whiptails and Their Allies: Family Teiidae

A large New World family with about 225 species, distributed throughout the Americas and the West Indies. S. America has greatest number and variety of species. Fourteen species of whiptails *(Cnemidophorus,* the only genus reaching the U.S.) occur in the West.

Most larger teiids, including the whiptails, are slim-bodied, long-tailed, alert, and active diurnal lizards. They move with a jerky gait, rapidly turning the head from side to side, and frequently protrude the slender forked tongue. They may move their front feet gingerly, as though walking on a hot surface. At the other extreme are the smaller, more secretive burrowers with the limbs and toes reduced, sometimes to mere stumps. They spend much time under stones, in leaf litter, or dense plant growth; none of these species occur in the U.S.

Whiptails have large, squarish belly scales (ventrals) in regular lengthwise and transverse rows (*8 lengthwise rows* in our species), and small scales on the back, called dorsal granules. The number of granules (counted across the back at midbody) is important in classifying whiptails; hence, although they are of little use in field identification, counts of these scales have been given. Head plates are large and symmetrical, and the snout is slender. Most species have a divided frontoparietal. There are several throat folds. The hindmost fold, the gular, is referred to in the accounts. Supraorbital semicircles (Fig. 21, opp. Pl. 31) may extend forward for only a short distance, failing to reach the frontal, a condition referred to in the accounts as "normal," or they may penetrate far forward, separating the supraoculars from the frontal (Fig. 21). The scales on the back of the foreleg (postantebrachials) vary in size. The tail, covered with keeled scales, is long (2 or more times the length of the body), slender, and whiplike, hence the common name. Some whiptails are striped, others are striped and spotted, or spotted with a marbled or checkered pattern. In many species, the color pattern changes considerably with growth. In striped species and the young of most species, the narrow pale stripes alternate with broader darker areas, referred to as "dark fields" (Fig. 21, opp. Pl. 31).

Whiptails are among the most difficult lizards to capture. Although they sometimes allow close approach, they usually manage to stay just out of reach and may suddenly dash to cover. When relentlessly pursued, they often seek shelter in rodent burrows. The broad neck, slender head, and great activity make them difficult to snare with a noose.

They are difficult to identify because of the subtle differences among some species in scale counts and coloration, and the color variations which occur with sex, age, and geographic location. Characteristic color patterns in many instances are well developed only in large individuals, and females in particular may mature before the "adult" pattern is attained. Rely on habitat differences and distribution to aid identification.

These lizards are of special interest because a number of whiptail species consist only of females. Such species, labeled "all-female" in the accounts, reproduce by parthenogenesis. Adults (females) of these species lay viable but unfertilized eggs, which hatch only into females. Color pattern classes have been recognized in some species (see Checkered Whiptail, p. 163). They are geographic populations, each believed to be the descendants of a single individual. In some areas within their ranges, some of these populations overlap. Differences in color pattern and scalation are often subtle, however, and thus are not described in this *Field Guide.*

Whiptails eat insects, spiders, scorpions, centipedes, and other small animals, including other lizards, some of which they evidently detect by odor and dig out of the ground. Termites are often a staple food.

ORANGE-THROATED WHIPTAIL — Pl. 34

Cnemidophorus hyperythrus

Identification: 2–2¾ in. (5–9.4 cm). A striped, unspotted whiptail with an orange throat. *Frontoparietal single.* Top of head yellow-brown to olive-gray. Paravertebral stripes usually united, except in southern part of range. *Usually 6 or fewer light stripes above.* Color of upper dark field between pale dorsolateral stripe at upper side and lateral stripe lower on side varies: may be gray, reddish brown, or dark brown to black. ***Young:*** Tail bluish. ***Male:*** Throat, chest, and (far to the south in range) entire ventral surface (including underside of tail) may be orange, more distinctly so during breeding season.

Inhabits washes and other sandy areas where there are rocks and patches of brush and rocky hillsides. Frequents coastal chaparral, thornscrub, and streamside growth. 1–2 clutches of 1–4 eggs, laid June–July in northern part of range. Eats insects (termites, beetles, etc.) and spiders.

Similar species: (1) Baja California Whiptail (Pl. 46, p. 240) always has at least 6 light dorsal stripes (usually 7 or 8); in areas where the Orange-throated Whiptail shares its range, the latter usually has fewer than 6 stripes. (2) Western Whiptail (p. 161) has only vague striping (if any), a spotted pattern, and a divided frontoparietal.

Range: Dana Point, Orange Co., and near Colton, San Bernardino Co., Calif., west of crest of Peninsular Ranges, south to tip of Baja Calif. Sea level to perhaps around 2000 ft. (610 m). **Map 111**
Subspecies: CAPE ORANGE-THROATED WHIPTAIL, *C. h. hyperythrus.* Usually a total of 7 or more light stripes at midbody. Usually no granules between 2nd supraocular and frontal. Throat, belly, and underside of tail reddish orange in brightly colored individuals, but often yellowish white, somewhat clouded with bluish on body. BELDING ORANGE-THROATED WHIPTAIL, *C. h. beldingi.* Usually 5 light stripes at midbody, but middorsal stripe usually forked at both ends. 2nd supraocular usually at least partly separated from frontal by granules. Yellowish white below, often with gray or bluish slate on belly, more or less washed with bright reddish orange in adults; throat and chest especially so in breeding males.

CANYON SPOTTED WHIPTAIL **Pl. 34**
(Giant Spotted Whiptail) *Cnemidophorus burti*
Identification: 3½–5½ in. (8.7–13.7 cm). A large, spotted whiptail with 6–7 light stripes; stripes faint or absent in *large* adult males. Vertebral (middorsal) stripe may be present or absent. More or less speckled with pale spots above. *Reddish color on head and neck, sometimes over entire back.* Supraorbital semicircles normal (Fig. 21, opp. Pl. 31), extending toward the snout, to or near the front end of the frontoparietal. Abruptly enlarged postantebrachials and scales on gular fold. 85–115 dorsal granules. ***Young:*** Striping distinct. Spots in dark fields. Orange tail.

Inhabits mountain canyons, arroyos, and mesas in arid and semi-arid regions, entering lowland desert along stream courses. Found in dense shrubby vegetation, often among rocks near permanent and intermittent streams. Clutches of 1–4 eggs, laid in summer. Eats insects and spiders.

Similar species: Chihuahuan Spotted Whiptail (p. 157), Sonoran Spotted Whiptail (p. 158), and Gila Spotted Whiptail (p. 160).
Range: Southern and se. Ariz., extreme sw. N.M., and Sonora. **Map 118**
Subspecies: RED-BACKED WHIPTAIL, *C. b. xanthonotus* (Pl. 34). Back reddish brown to reddish orange; red color stops abruptly along upper sides. Sides and upper surfaces of neck, legs, and feet dark grayish green to bluish. Striping and spotting on back more or less obscured by reddish dorsal ground color, less so in young. Juniper-oak, desert-edge habitats from the Ajo Mt. area, Pima Co., to the Sierra Estrella near Phoenix, Maricopa Co., Ariz. GIANT SPOTTED WHIPTAIL, *C. b. stictogrammus* (Pl. 34). Adults reach much larger size than Red-backed Whiptail. Red on upper surfaces less extensive — usually confined to head and neck. Young have a bright orange to reddish tail. The only whiptail in the West except the Texas Spotted Whiptail that has 100 or more

dorsal granules. Santa Catalina, Santa Rita, Baboquivari, and Pajarito Mts.; vicinity of Oracle, Pinal Co., and Mineral Hot Springs, Cochise Co., Ariz. Guadalupe Canyon in extreme sw. N.M.; Sonora. Near sea level to around 4500 ft. (1370 m).

NEW MEXICAN WHIPTAIL Pl. 32

Cnemidophorus neomexicanus

Identification: 2⅜–3⅜ in. (5.9–8.4 cm). A whiptail with 6–7 pale stripes, including a *wavy middorsal stripe that forks on the neck.* Supraorbital semicircles *penetrate deeply toward snout,* usually separating the 3rd and often the 2nd supraocular from the frontal. Small, diffuse light spots on the sides between light stripes. Often pale greenish to bluish below. Tail grayish at base, grading to greenish or greenish blue toward tip. Postantebrachials not enlarged. 71–85 dorsal granules. ***Young:*** Ground color of body black, stripes yellow, well-defined whitish spots in dark fields on sides. Greenish to greenish blue tail. All-female (parthenogenetic); males unknown.

Primarily lives in bottomlands, in areas of loose sand or packed sandy soil amid low grass, saltbush, desert tea, and scattered yucca and mesquite. Inhabits primarily plains grassland, flood plain habitats of sandy river basins, and the edges of desert playas. 1–2 clutches of 1–4 eggs, laid June–July. Eats insects and spiders.

Similar species: Distinguished from other striped whiptails by the combination of the forward extension of the supraorbital semicircles, the well-defined stripes with light spots in the dark fields on the sides, the wavy middorsal stripe, and the greenish tail.

Range: Rio Grande Valley from vicinity of Chamita, north of Santa Fe through N.M. into extreme w. Tex. and probably n. Chihuahua. To the west in N.M. to lower Mimbres R. drainage and northwest of Lordsburg. Introduced at Conchas Dam, San Miguel Co., N.M. From around 3300–6200 ft. (1010–1890 m).

Map 117

Remarks: This species originated by hybridization between the Western Whiptail (*C. tigris,* p. 161) and the Little Striped Whiptail (*C. inornatus,* below) and now reproduces by parthenogenesis.

LITTLE STRIPED WHIPTAIL Pl. 32

Cnemidophorus inornatus

Identification: 2–2¾ in. (5–6.9 cm). 6–8 (usually 7) pale yellowish to whitish stripes; middorsal stripe sometimes faint or absent. Dark field between stripes blackish, brown, or brownish green to gray, *without light spots;* dark field becomes lighter with age. *Tail blue to purplish blue toward tip.* Usually bluish white to blue below (in males). A pale form with faint stripes occurs at White Sands, N.M. *Postantebrachials* (Fig. 21, opp. Pl. 31) *and scales in front of gular fold only slightly enlarged or not at all.* Supraorbital semicircles normal. 52–72 dorsal granules. Usually 3 enlarged, rounded scales in front of vent. ***Young:*** Less blue below than adult. ***Male:*** Chin and belly more bluish than in female. Both sexes have more vivid blue on the underside of the tail than on remaining underparts.

Chiefly a prairie grassland species, but ranges into grassy areas of shrubby desert, chaparral, the piñon-juniper zone, and, in northwestern part of range, into open ponderosa pine forests. Frequents sandy or silty, sometimes gravelly, ground of elevated plains or lowlands. Seldom found in rocky or very barren areas or in mesquite habitats occupied by the Desert Grassland Whiptail (below). Clutch of 1–3 eggs, laid May–July, perhaps Aug. Eats insects, spiders, and centipedes.

Similar species: (1) Plateau Striped Whiptail (p. 156) is larger, has conspicuously enlarged scales on rear of forelimb and gular fold, and generally occurs at higher elevations. (2) Chihuahuan Spotted Whiptail (p. 157), (3) Sonoran Spotted Whiptail (p. 158), and (4) Gila Spotted Whiptail (p. 160) have enlarged postantebrachials and light spots in the dark fields. (5) Six-lined Racerunner (p. 156) often has a broad brownish stripe down middle of back and generally greenish foreparts. See also (6) Desert Grassland Whiptail (below), which overlaps in range with the Little Striped Whiptail in the grasslands of sw. N.M. and se. Ariz.

Range: San Juan R. drainage southward throughout most of lowlands of N.M. and thence on to w. Tex., Zacatecas, and San Luis Potosí. Scattered populations in nw. and cen. Ariz. and in vicinity of Wilcox Playa, Cochise Co., and elsewhere in se. Ariz. From around 1000–5500 ft. (300–1680 m); occasionally to 7000 ft. (2130 m). **Map 113**

DESERT GRASSLAND WHIPTAIL **Pl. 31**

Cnemidophorus uniparens

Identification: 2–3 in. (5–7.5 cm). A small whiptail with 6–7 dorsal stripes; dark fields black, dark brown, or reddish brown, without light spots. *Tail greenish olive to bluish green.* Postantebrachials and gular scales enlarged. Supraorbital semicircles normal. 59–78 dorsal granules. Usually 3 enlarged, rounded scales in front of vent. ***Young:*** Tail bright blue.

Chiefly a lowland species of desert and mesquite grassland, but follows drainages into the mountains, where it occurs in evergreen woodland, as at Oak Creek, Ariz. Generally found on plains and gentle foothill slopes, occasionally in areas with scant cover of grasses and herbs, but more commonly where mesquite and yucca are present and often where mesquite is dense. Clutch of 1–4 eggs, laid May–July. Eats insects.

Similar species: (1) Plateau Striped Whiptail (below) has a blue tail, enlarged postantebrachials and gular scales, and more than 3 enlarged, angular (not rounded) scales in front of vent. It generally occurs at higher elevations than the Desert Grassland Whiptail. (2) Little Striped Whiptail (above) has a blue tail; postantebrachials

and gular scales only slightly enlarged, if at all, and usually 3 enlarged, rounded scales in front of vent.
Range: Prescott-Cornville area in cen. Ariz. to vicinity of El Paso, Tex., up Rio Grande Valley to Rio Salado, and south into Chihuahua. From about 3500–5000 ft. (1070–1520 m). Occasionally hybridizes with the Little Striped Whiptail. **Map 112**

PLATEAU STRIPED WHIPTAIL Pl. 32

Cnemidophorus velox

Identification: 2½–3⅜ in. (6.2–8.4 cm). 6–7 dorsal stripes; when present, middorsal stripe less distinct than the others. Few spots, if any, in black to blackish brown dark fields in either young or adults. *Tail light blue.* Whitish below, unmarked or with a tinge of bluish, especially on the chin. Postantebrachials enlarged. Scales bordering the gular fold conspicuously enlarged and abruptly differentiated from the adjacent granular scales. Supraorbital semicircles normal. 63–85 dorsal granules. *More than 3 enlarged, angular scales in front of vent.* ***Young:*** Bright blue tail. All female; males unknown.

Found chiefly in the mountains in piñon-juniper grassland, open chaparral, oak woodland, and lower edges of ponderosa pine and fir forests. At lower elevations, this whiptail frequents broadleaf woodlands along permanent and semipermanent streams. Clutch of 3–5 eggs, laid June–July. Eats insects.

Similar species: (1) Chihuahuan Spotted Whiptail (p. 157), (2) Sonoran Spotted Whiptail (p. 158), and (3) Gila Spotted Whiptail (p. 160) lack blue tail color and have distinct light spots in dark fields. (4) Little Striped Whiptail (p. 154) usually averages fewer dorsal granules and has small (granular) postantebrachials and only slightly enlarged scales bordering the gular fold. (5) Desert Grassland Whiptail (p. 155) usually has 3 enlarged, rounded scales in front of vent, and greenish on tail.

Range: Colorado Plateau of cen. and n. Ariz. and n. N.M., s. Utah and w. Colo. In N.M. ranges east to upper Ute Creek area. Introduced and apparently established at Cove Palisades State Park, Jefferson Co., Ore. From around 4500 to 8000 ft. (1370–2440 m). **Map 115**

SIX-LINED RACERUNNER Pl. 31

Cnemidophorus sexlineatus

Identification: 2⅛–3⅜ in. (5.3–8.4 cm). A small, unspotted whiptail with 6–8 light stripes (usually 7 in our subspecies). Head and body greenish in the West. Stripes usually fade from yellowish to white toward the rear, or are sometimes pale gray or pale blue. A broad, brownish middorsal stripe, sometimes divided; when middorsal stripe is divided by a dark middorsal line, a total of 8 pale stripes. Dark fields brown to blackish. Whitish or pale blue below. Tail brownish. Postantebrachials not or slightly enlarged. Scales bordering the gular fold conspicuously enlarged and usually not grading gradually into the smaller scales of the fold. Supraorbital semicircles normal. 62–110 dorsal granules (62–91 in our subspecies). ***Young:*** Distinct stripes. Tail blue. ***Male:*** Throat and belly bluish. Striping sometimes vague.

Frequents open grassland, often with scattered shrubs, and woodland edges, usually where the soil is sandy or loamy, but also in areas with gravel and hardpan. Found in both the lowlands and hills, occurring on the floodplains and banks of rivers, in clearings and dune areas, and near rocky outcrops. 1–3 clutches of 1–6 eggs, laid May–Aug. Eats insects, spiders, and snails.

Similar species: (1) Little Striped Whiptail (p. 154) has blue tail and is bluish on head and sides of body. (2) Chihuahuan Spotted (below) and (3) Texas Spotted Whiptails (p. 160) have light spots in the dark fields and enlarged postantebrachials; Texas Spotted Whiptail lacks short, dark-bordered light stripe on side of tail. (4) Plateau Striped Whiptail (p. 156) has enlarged postantebrachials and a bluish tail. (5) See also Checkered Whiptail (p. 163).

Range: Southern S.D., se. Minn., and Md. south to s. Tex., the Gulf Coast, and the Fla. Keys; e. Colo. and N.M. to the Atlantic Coast. Sea level to around 7000 ft. (2130 m). **Map 109**

Subspecies: The PRAIRIE LINED RACERUNNER, *C. s. viridis,* occurs in our area.

CHIHUAHUAN SPOTTED WHIPTAIL Pl. 33

Cnemidophorus exsanguis

Identification: $1\frac{3}{4}$–4 in. (4.4–10 cm). A striped whiptail with light spots in the brown or reddish brown dark fields. Spots cream to pale yellow, *sometimes bright yellow on rump,* especially in older adults. Usually 6 light stripes, pale yellowish to gray on neck, grading to whitish or beige toward rear. Middorsal stripe variable — may be narrow and broken into a series of spots, or indistinct or absent. Tail greenish, brownish, or tan. Whitish, cream, or bluish below, without pattern. Enlarged postantebrachials (4 or more times size of nearby scales) and enlarged scales along the front edge of the gular fold. Supraorbital semicircles normal. 65–86 dorsal granules. All female. ***Young:*** Tail bluish or greenish. Light spots in dark fields present even in hatchlings.

Chiefly an upland lizard, ranging from desert and desert grasslands into the oak-pine and ponderosa pine forests in the mountains, where it occurs on rocky hillsides, along sandy washes, and in canyons. Typical habitat consists of canyon bottoms in the oak and oak-pine belts. Clutch of 1–6 eggs, laid June–Aug. Eats insects, spiders, and scorpions.

Similar species: (1) Canyon Spotted Whiptail (p. 153) is larger, with more dorsal granules (over 95, where ranges overlap) and stripes tend to disappear with age. (2) New Mexican Whiptail (p. 154) has a wavy vertebral (middorsal) stripe. (3) Plateau Striped Whiptail (p. 156), (4) Desert Grassland Whiptail (p. 155), (5) Little

Striped Whiptail (p. 154), and (6) Six-lined Racerunner (p. 156) lack pale spots on upper surfaces. See also (7) Checkered Whiptail (p. 163), (8) Sonoran Spotted Whiptail (below), and (9) Gila Spotted Whiptail (p. 160).
Range: N.-cen. N.M. to cen. Chihuahua; extreme se. Ariz. and e. Sonora to Trans-Pecos, Tex. From around 2500–8000 ft. (760–2440 m). **Map 111**
Remarks: The Chihuahuan Spotted Whiptail originated through hybridization involving 3 species — the Little Striped Whiptail and 2 Mexican species, *Cnemidophorus septemvittatus* and *C. costatus.*

SONORAN SPOTTED WHIPTAIL Pl. 33
Cnemidophorus sonorae

Identification: 2½–3½ in. (6.2–8.7 cm). A close relative of the Chihuahuan Spotted and Gila Spotted Whiptails, with which this species was formerly confused. 6 stripes; 5–8 dorsal granules between middorsal pair of stripes (paravertebrals). Sometimes a trace of middorsal stripe on neck and lower back. Dark fields blackish, brown, to reddish, with spots of white, pale tan, or dull yellowish. *Pale stripes lack light spots.* Tail usually dull orange-tan, often grading to olive toward tip. Whitish to cream below, unmarked. 74–80 dorsal granules. 32–39 total femoral pores. *Usually 3 preanals* (enlarged scales in front of vent). All female. ***Young:*** Hatchlings lack spots in dark fields.

Occurs primarily in upland habitats of oak-woodland and oak-grassland; also in streamside woodland, desert-grassland, desert-scrub of paloverde and saguaro, and thornscrub.
Similar species: (1) Chihuahuan Spotted Whiptail (p. 157) is larger and the light stripes fade on the neck. (2) Gila Spotted Whiptail (p. 160) has light spots touching or located within the light stripes, less mottling on upper surface of hind legs, an olive-green tail that often has a bluish cast, and usually *2 preanals* instead of 3. Four to 5 dorsal granules between middorsal pair of stripes.
Range: Se. Ariz. to ne. Sonora; Santa Catalina Mts., Ariz. to basins of the Rio Yaqui and Rio Sonora, Sonora, and from the Baboquivari Mts., Ariz. east to the Peloncillo and Guadalupe Mts., N.M. From around 700–7000 ft. (210–2130 m). Coexists with the Gila Spotted and Chihuahuan Spotted Whiptails wherever the edges of their ranges overlap. Hybridizes with the Western Whiptail (*C. tigris,* p. 161) in s. Ariz., but hybridization is rare. **Map 115**

(Text continues on p. 160.)

Plates

Plate 1

NEWTS *(Taricha)* × $^3/_4$

Skin rough in terrestrial stage, smooth in breeding male. Teeth in roof of mouth in diverging lengthwise rows (Fig. 8, p. 41). Costal grooves indistinct.

CALIFORNIA, *T. torosa* p. 42
Lower eyelids pale; eyes reach outline of head, viewed from above (Fig. 8). Teeth in Y-shaped pattern. (Contra Costa Co., Calif.) Map 8

ROUGH-SKINNED, *T. granulosa* p. 41
Lower eyelids dark; eyes usually fail to reach outline of head, viewed from above. Teeth in V-shaped pattern. See Fig. 8. Map 6

RED-BELLIED, *T. rivularis* p. 43
Eyes dark brown. (Sonoma Co., Calif.) Map 9

DICAMPTODONTIDS × $^3/_4$

Skin smooth; teeth in roof of mouth in transverse row (Fig. 4, No. 4, p. 25). Costal grooves distinct.

PACIFIC GIANT SALAMANDER, p. 38
Dicamptodon ensatus
Marbled pattern. To 6 in. (15 cm). (Mendocino Co., Calif.)
Map 1

OLYMPIC SALAMANDER, p. 39
Rhyacotriton olympicus
Large eyes; squarish vent lobes in male. Map 4

Southern, *R. o. variegatus.* Mottled above; many dark blotches on yellowish green venter. (Trinity Co., Calif.) Map 4 p. 40

Northern, *R. o. olympicus.* Mostly plain brown above; yellow-orange below, with scant blotching. (Mason Co., Wash.) Map 4 p. 40

OLYMPIC SALAMANDER

Plate 2

AMBYSTOMATIDS *(Ambystoma)* × $^3/_5$

Costal grooves distinct. Teeth in roof of mouth in transverse row (Fig. 4, No. 4, p. 25).

TIGER SALAMANDER, *A. tigrinum* p. 34
Pattern varies (Fig. 10), but over much of its range spotted and/or barred with yellow or cream on dark ground color. Map 5

California, *A. t. californiense.* Yellow or cream spots on black ground color. Found only in Calif. (Contra Costa Co.) Map 5 p. 35

Barred, *A. t. mavortium.* Large bars and blotches of yellow on dark ground color. (Socorro Co., N.M.) Map 5 p. 35

Arizona, *A. t. nebulosum.* Yellow to dark olive spots and blotches. Two variations shown in Fig. 10 (below) are from Ariz. (specimen at left) and Rocky Mountain National Park, Colo. Map 5 p. 35

NORTHWESTERN SALAMANDER, *A. gracile* p. 36
Conspicuous parotoid glands and glandular ridge on tail. (Humboldt Co., Calif.) Map 2

LONG-TOED SALAMANDER, *A. macrodactylum* p. 37
Long slender toes; dorsal stripe or series of blotches. Map 3

Southern, *A. m. sigillatum.* Yellow dorsal stripe variously broken into series of blotches. (Amador Co., Calif.) Map 3 p. 37

Santa Cruz, *A. m. croceum.* Yellow-orange blotches on back; ground color black. Found only near Aptos, Santa Cruz Co., Calif. Map 3 p. 37

Western, *A. m. macrodactylum.* Greenish to yellowish dorsal stripe; sides seem whitewashed. (Benton Co., Ore.) Map 3 p. 37

Eastern, *A. m. krausei.* Well-defined yellow stripe originating on head. (Latah Co., Idaho) Map 3 p. 38

Fig. 10. Dorsal pattern in Tiger Salamanders

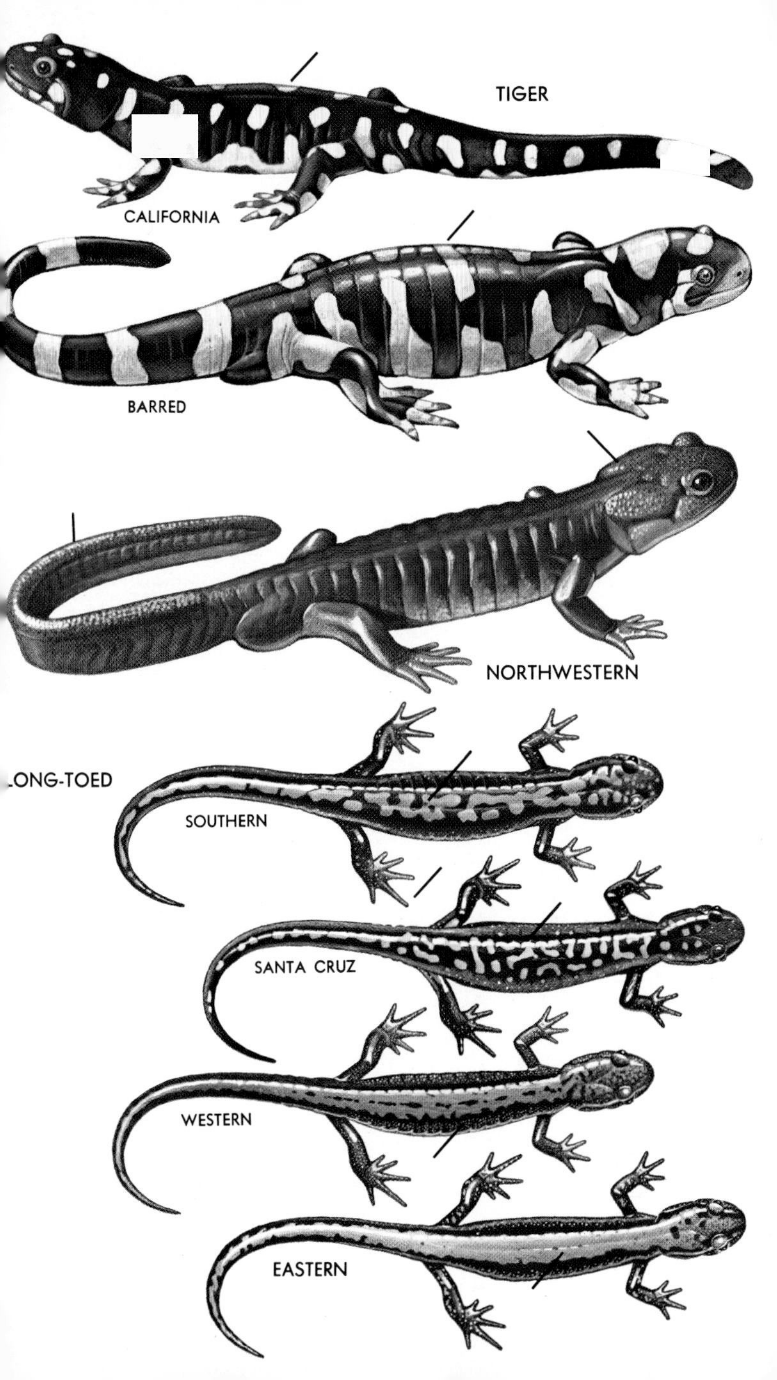
TIGER
CALIFORNIA
BARRED
NORTHWESTERN
LONG-TOED
SOUTHERN
SANTA CRUZ
WESTERN
EASTERN

Plate 3

ENSATINA *(Ensatina eschscholtzii)* × 3/5

Tail constricted at base; nasolabial grooves (Fig. 4, No. 1, p. 25).

Blotched Subspecies

Sierra Nevada Salamander, *E. e. platensis.* Orange spots on brownish ground color. (Kern Co., Calif.) p. 49
Map 10

Yellow-blotched Salamander, *E. e. croceater.* Greenish yellow to cream-colored blotches on blackish ground color. Young have greenish yellow blotches. (Kern Co., Calif.) p. 49
Map 10

Intergrade (between Yellow-blotched and Large-blotched Salamanders). Like Yellow-blotched, but markings less irregular in outline. Blotch color changes from greenish yellow to cream with age. (San Bernardino Co., Calif.)
Map 10

Large-blotched Salamander, *E. e. klauberi.* Orange or cream bars, bands, and blotches on blackish ground color. Young has bright orange marks. (San Diego, Calif.) p. 49
Map 10

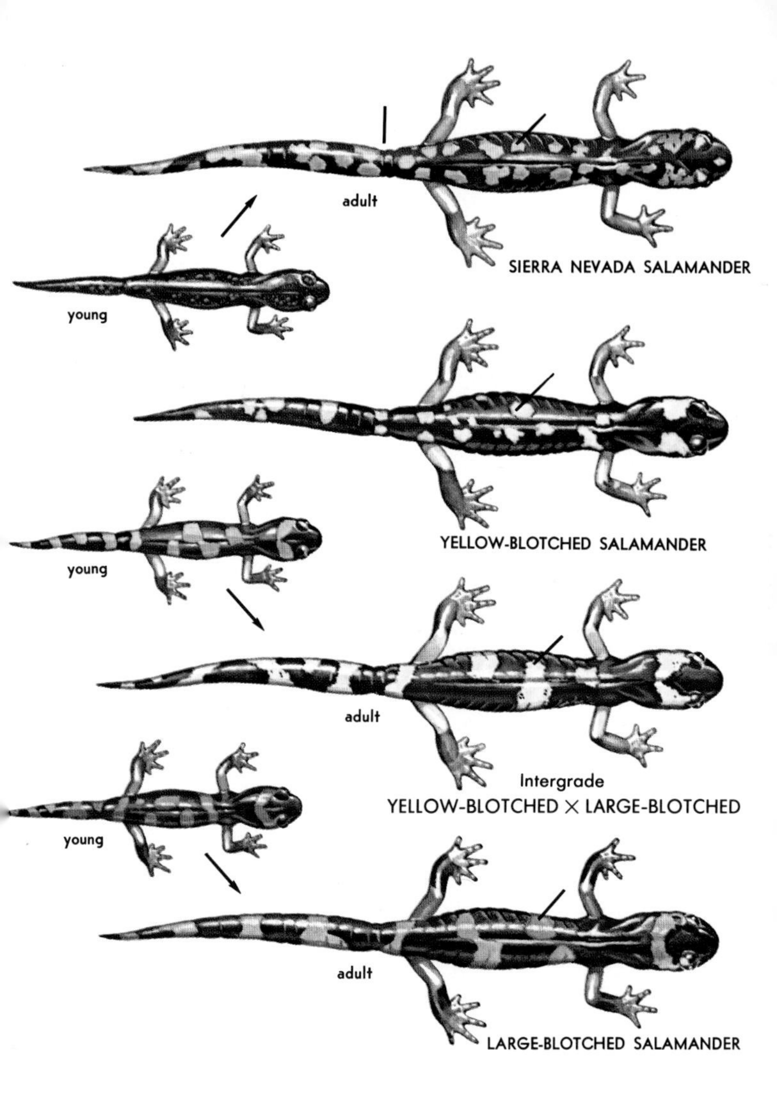
adult
young
SIERRA NEVADA SALAMANDER
young
YELLOW-BLOTCHED SALAMANDER
adult
Intergrade
YELLOW-BLOTCHED × LARGE-BLOTCHED
young
adult
LARGE-BLOTCHED SALAMANDER

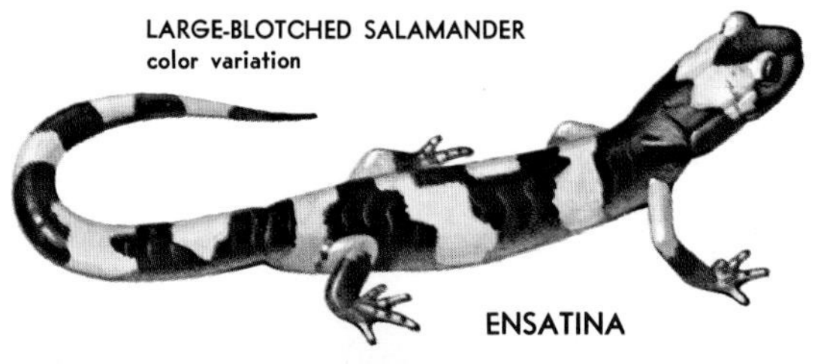
LARGE-BLOTCHED SALAMANDER
color variation

ENSATINA

Plate 4

ENSATINA *(Ensatina eschscholtzii)* × $^{3}/_{5}$

Tail constricted at base; nasolabial grooves (Fig. 4, No. 1, p. 25).

Blotched and Plain-colored Subspecies

Intergrade (between Oregon and Sierra Nevada subspecies). Diffuse orange spots on brownish ground color. Young black, with yellow limb bases. (Shasta Co., Calif.) Map 10

Painted Salamander, *E. e. picta* × 1. Mottled pattern of black and pale yellow or orange spots, especially on tail. (Del Norte Co., Calif.) Map 10 p. 49

Oregon Salamander, *E. e. oregonensis*. Plain brown or nearly black above; belly pale, with minute black specks. (King Co., Wash.) Young dark-blotched. (Multnomah Co., Ore.) Map 10 p. 49

Yellow-eyed Salamander, *E. e. xanthoptica*. Belly orange; conspicuous yellow eye patch. (Contra Costa Co., Calif.) Map 10 p. 49

Monterey Salamander, *E. e. eschscholtzii*. Belly whitish; eyes black. Map 10 p. 49

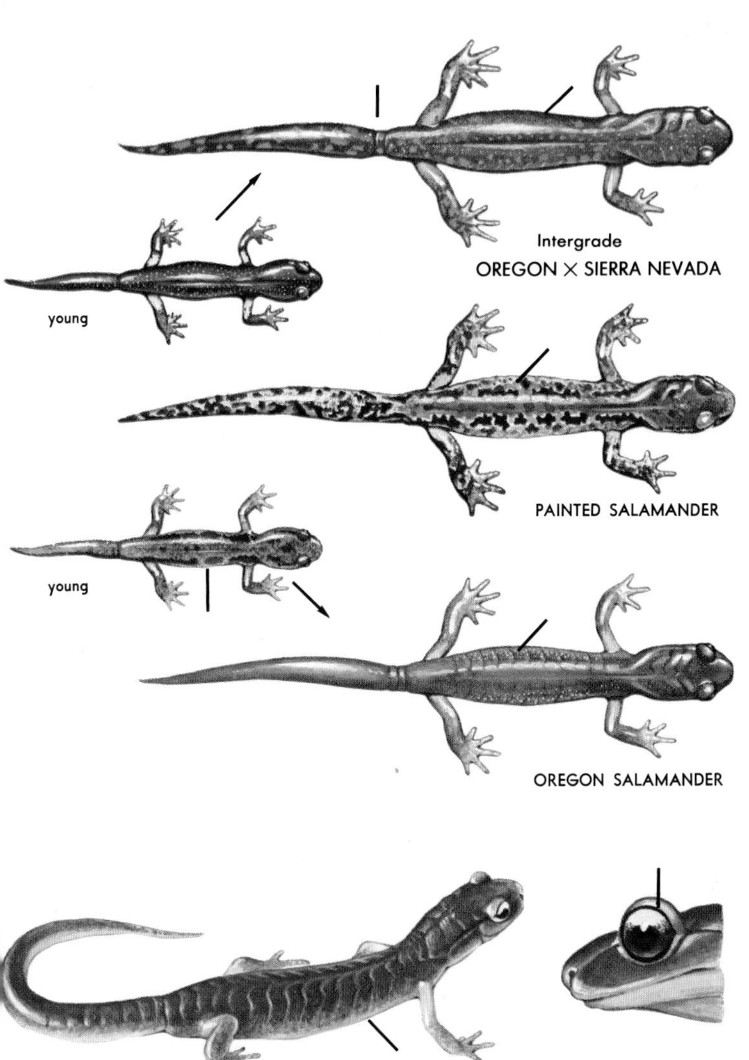
Intergrade
OREGON × SIERRA NEVADA
young
PAINTED SALAMANDER
young
OREGON SALAMANDER

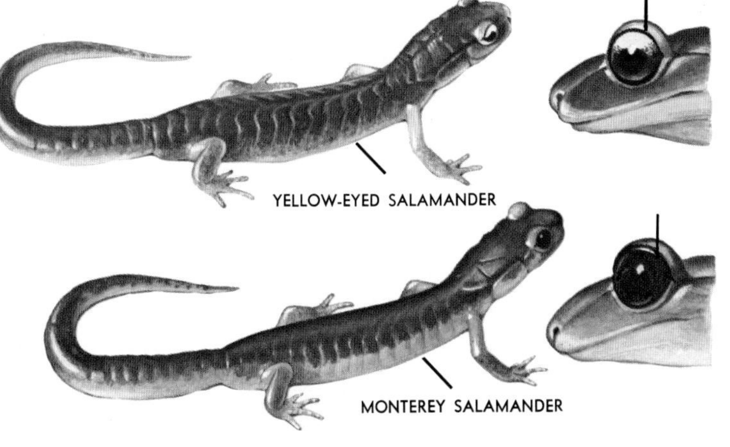
YELLOW-EYED SALAMANDER
MONTEREY SALAMANDER

ENSATINA

Plate 5

WOODLAND SALAMANDERS
(Plethodon) × $^2/_3$

Slim-bodied, short-legged; often with a dorsal stripe. Nasolabial grooves (Fig. 4, No. 1, p. 25).

DUNN SALAMANDER, *P. dunni* p. 44
Mottled tan to greenish yellow stripe does not reach tip of tail. Usually 15 costal grooves. (Benton Co., Ore.)
Map 12

WESTERN RED-BACKED SALAMANDER, *P. vehiculum* p. 45
Tan, reddish brown, orange, or yellow stripe, even-edged and extending to tip of tail; belly mottled (Fig. 11A). Usually 16 costal grooves. (Red phase, Benton Co., Ore.) Map 11

VAN DYKE SALAMANDER, *P. vandykei* p. 45
Stripe with even or scalloped edges; large pale throat patch (Fig. 11B). Usually 14 costal grooves. Map 16

Coeur d'Alene Salamander, *P. v. idahoensis*. Dark coloring generally more intense than in Washington Salamander. (Kootenai Co., Idaho) Map 16 p. 46

Washington Salamander, *P. v. vandykei*. Plain-color phase. (w. Wash.) Map 16 p. 46

LARCH MOUNTAIN SALAMANDER, *P. larselli* p. 46
Belly red to reddish orange or salmon-pink. Usually 15 costal grooves. (Multnomah Co., Ore.) Map 14

JEMEZ MOUNTAINS SALAMANDER, *P. neomexicanus* p. 47
5th toe absent or reduced. Usually 19 costal grooves. Known only from Jemez Mts., Sandoval Co., N.M. Map 15

DEL NORTE SALAMANDER, *P. elongatus* p. 47
Toes short and partly webbed. Usually 18 costal grooves.
Map 13

Striped Del Norte Salamander, *P. e. elongatus*. $6\frac{1}{2}$–$7\frac{1}{2}$ costal folds between toes of adpressed limbs. Brown or black above, with or without brown stripe. Map 13 p. 48

Siskiyou Mountains Salamander, *P. e. stormi*. 4–$5\frac{1}{2}$ costal folds between toes of adpressed limbs. Brown above, heavily speckled with small light flecks. (Jackson Co., Ore.) Map 13 p. 48

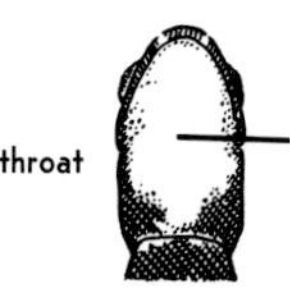

Fig. 11a (left). Venters of Western Red-backed Salamander
Fig. 11b (right). Van Dyke's Salamander

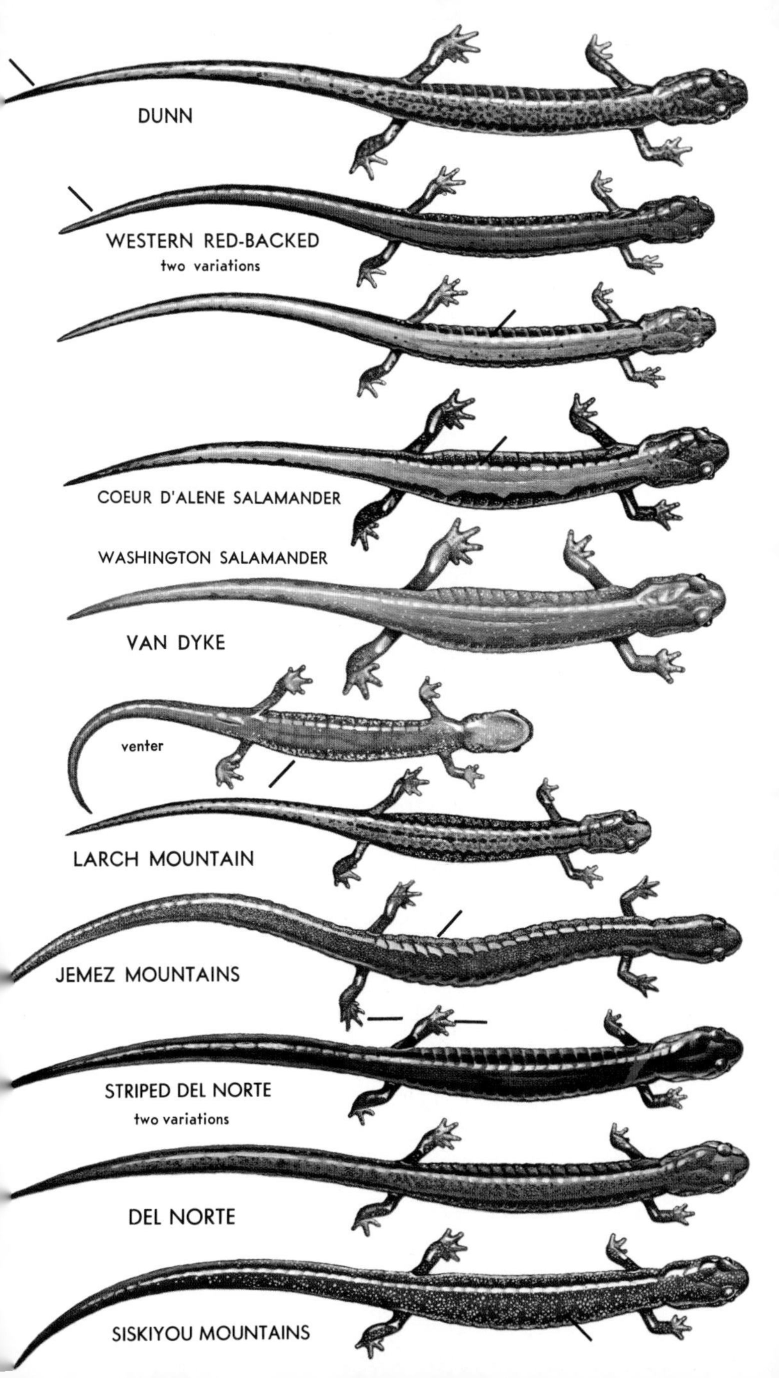

DUNN
WESTERN RED-BACKED
two variations
COEUR D'ALENE SALAMANDER
WASHINGTON SALAMANDER
VAN DYKE
venter
LARCH MOUNTAIN
JEMEZ MOUNTAINS
STRIPED DEL NORTE
two variations
DEL NORTE
SISKIYOU MOUNTAINS

Plate 6

CLIMBING SALAMANDERS *(Aneides)* × $^3/_5$

(See also Pl. 7.)

Triangular head; projecting upper jaw teeth (Fig. 4, No. 11, p. 25).

ARBOREAL SALAMANDER, *A. lugubris* p. 52
Adult usually brown with yellow spots; squarish toe tips. Young mottled; limb bases, tail, and shoulders yellowish. (Contra Costa Co., Calif.) Map 20

BLACK SALAMANDER, *A. flavipunctatus* p. 50
Slim-bodied; short toes and limbs; belly black, sometimes with ash gray markings. Dorsal coloration varies: solid black, black with white or cream spots, or suffused with ash gray to greenish. Map 22

SLENDER SALAMANDERS *(Batrachoseps)* × $^3/_5$

(See also Pl. 7.)

Slender body; short limbs; 4 toes on front and hind feet.

CALIFORNIA, *B. attenuatus* p. 59
Limbs very short; belly with fine black network. (Contra Costa Co., Calif.) Map 17

WEB-TOED SALAMANDERS *(Hydromantes)* × $^3/_5$

Toes short and webbed; tongue on a stalk (Fig. 4, No. 9, p. 25).

LIMESTONE SALAMANDER, *H. brunus* p. 62
Adult plain brown above. Young apple green to pale yellow. (Merced Co., Calif.) Map 7

MOUNT LYELL SALAMANDER, *H. platycephalus* p. 61
Adult with granite-matching pattern. Young greenish. (Tuolumne Co., Calif.) Map 7

SHASTA SALAMANDER, *H. shastae* p. 61
Adult gray-green to reddish, mottled; tail yellow to yellow-orange. Young resembles adult. (Shasta Co., Calif.) Map 7

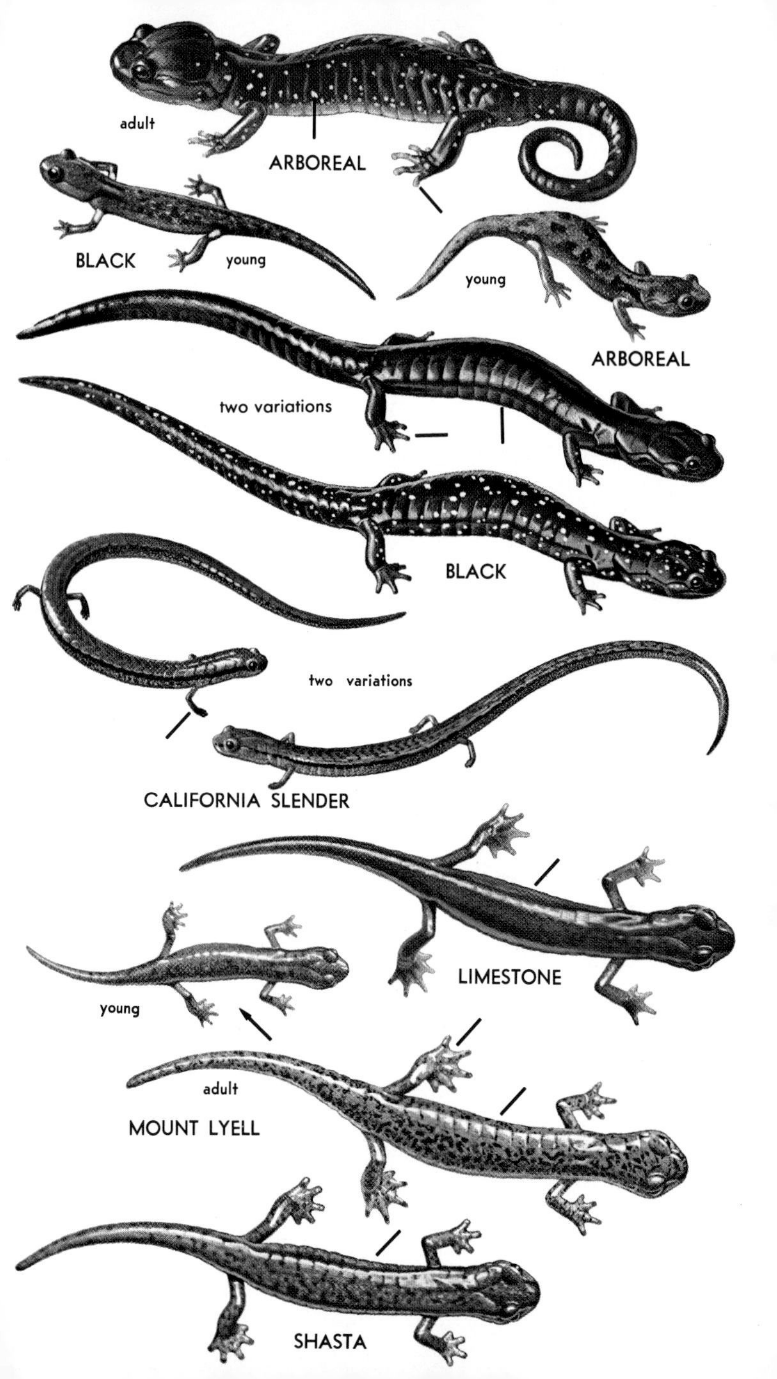
adult
ARBOREAL
BLACK
young
young
ARBOREAL
two variations
BLACK
two variations
CALIFORNIA SLENDER
LIMESTONE
young
adult
MOUNT LYELL
SHASTA

CLIMBING SALAMANDERS *(Aneides)* × 3/5

(See also Pl. 6.)

Triangular head; projecting upper jaw teeth (Fig. 4, No. 11, p. 25).

ARBOREAL SALAMANDER, *A. lugubris* p. 52
Adult brown above, often with yellow spots; toes square-tipped; curls tail. (Marin Co., Calif.) Young resembles young of Clouded Salamander, but proportions chunkier. Map 20

CLOUDED SALAMANDER, *A. ferreus* p. 51
Adult with mottled pattern of brown, ash gray, or brassy; long, square-tipped toes and long limbs. (Mendocino Co., Calif.) Young with yellowish to rust marks on snout, shoulders, limb bases, and tail. (Mendocino Co., Calif.) Map 19

BLACK SALAMANDER, *A. flavipunctatus* p. 50
Ground color of adult black, including belly; toes relatively short and tips rounded. (Mendocino Co., Calif.) Young speckled with whitish and variously suffused with green; bases of limbs yellow. (Humboldt Co., Calif.) Map 22

SACRAMENTO MOUNTAIN SALAMANDER, *A. hardii* p. 50
Limbs short; toe tips rounded; belly pale. Map 21

SLENDER SALAMANDERS *(Batrachoseps)* × 3/5

(See also Pl. 6.)

Slender body; short limbs; 4 toes on front and hind feet.

OREGON, *B. wrighti* p. 53
Large white spots on black belly. (Clackamas Co., Ore.) Map 18

PACIFIC, *B. pacificus* p. 56
Subspecies shown is **Channel Islands Slender Salamander,** *B. p. pacificus.* Belly pale gray, with speckling or a weak broken network of melanophores. Head broad; limbs and toes relatively long. (Santa Rosa I., Santa Barbara Co., Calif.) Map 17

CALIFORNIA, *B. attenuatus* p. 59
Belly dark, with fine network of black, speckled with minute white flecks. Head narrow; limbs and toes relatively short. (Contra Costa Co., Calif.) Map 17

CLIMBING SALAMANDERS
ARBOREAL
adult
CLOUDED
young
adult
BLACK
young
SACRAMENTO MOUNTAIN

SLENDER SALAMANDERS

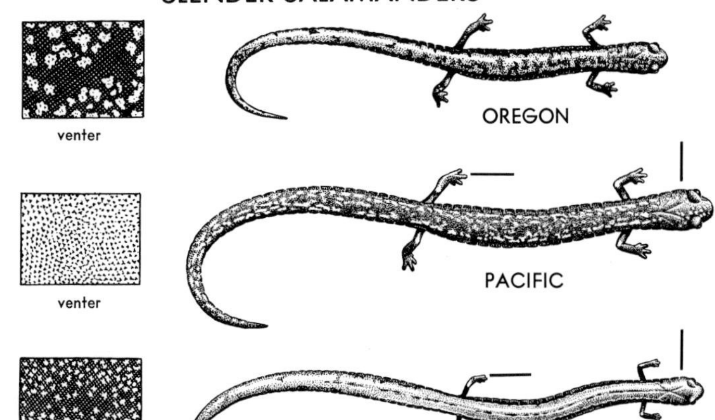
venter
OREGON
venter
PACIFIC
venter
CALIFORNIA

Plate 8

SLENDER SALAMANDERS
(Batrachoseps) × $^7/_8$

(See also Pls. 6 and 7.)

Slender body; short limbs; 4 toes on front and hind feet.

OREGON, *B. wrighti* p. 53
Large white spots on black belly. (Lane Co., Ore.)
Map 18

INYO MOUNTAINS, *B. campi* p. 54
Tail short. Brown above with gray blotches, or entirely suffused with pale gray. Map 17

KERN PLATEAU, *Batrachoseps* species p. 54
Dark spots above. An undescribed form from Kern Plateau, s. Sierra Nevada, Calif., related to Inyo Mountains Slender Salamander. (Kern Co., Calif.) Map 17

TEHACHAPI, *B. stebbinsi* p. 54
Head broader, limbs longer, and feet larger than in other species except Inyo Mountains Slender Salamander. No gray blotches or suffusion as in Inyo Mountains Slender Salamander. (Caliente Creek, Kern Co., Calif.)
Map 17

DESERT, *B. aridus* p. 59
Adults have extensive suffusion of silvery gray over upper surfaces. Broad-headed; long-legged. (Guadalupe Canyon, Riverside Co., Calif.) Map 17

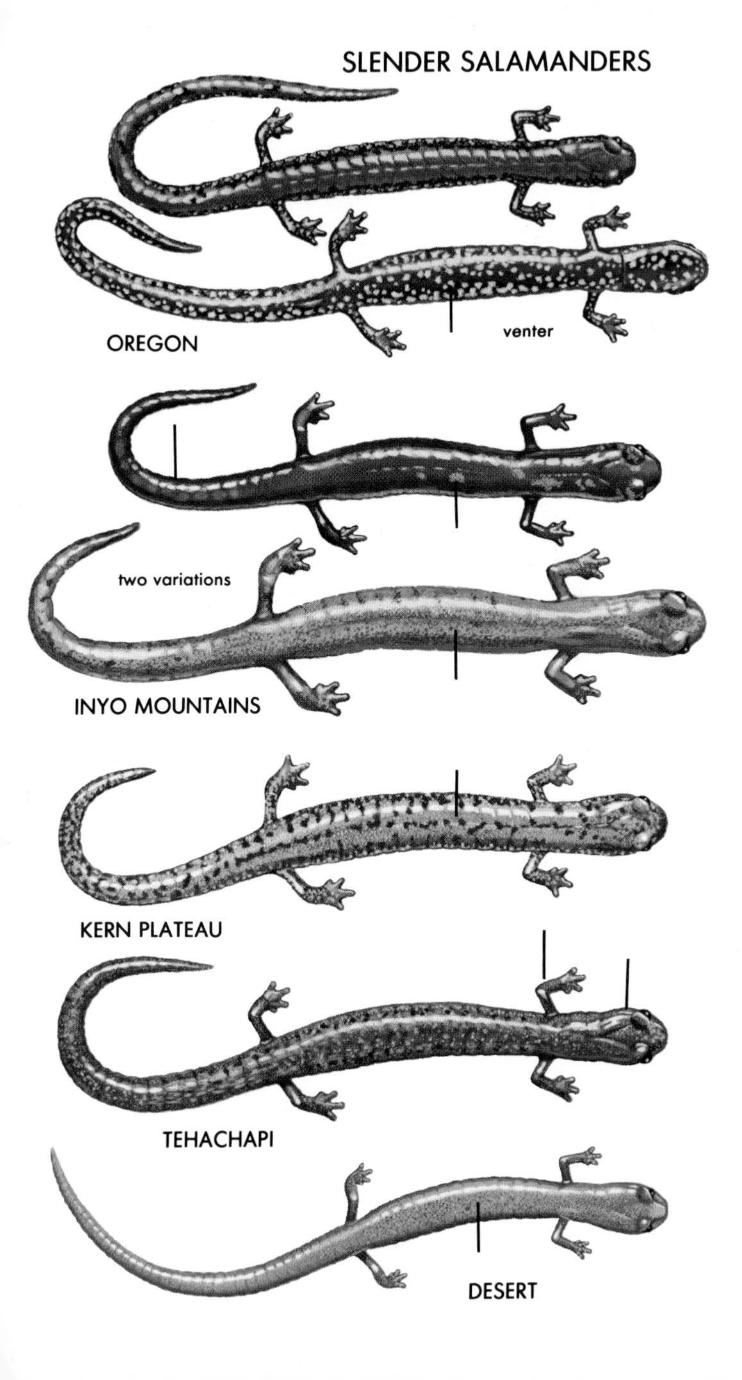
SLENDER SALAMANDERS
OREGON
venter
two variations
INYO MOUNTAINS
KERN PLATEAU
TEHACHAPI
DESERT

SLENDER SALAMANDERS
(Batrachoseps) × $^7/_8$

(See also Pls. 6, 7, and 8.)

Slender body; short limbs; 4 toes on front and hind feet.

KERN CANYON, *B. simatus* p. 56
Limbs and tail relatively long, but head narrow; head and body somewhat flattened. (Kern Canyon, Kern Co., Calif.) Map 17

PACIFIC, *B. pacificus* Map 17 p. 56

Garden Slender Salamander, *B. p. major.* Pale above, often with rust tinges, especially on tail. Light gray below, with small specks or a broken network of blackish melanophores. (Los Angeles Co., Calif.) Map 17 p. 57

Relictual Slender Salamander, *B. p. relictus.* Darker above than Garden Slender Salamander. Dark below, with melanophores forming a fine network. (Kern Co., Calif.) Map 17 p. 58

BLACK-BELLIED, *B. nigriventris* p. 55
Narrow head, short limbs, long tail. Usually a dorsal stripe. (Kern Co., Calif.) Map 17

CALIFORNIA, *B. attenuatus* p. 59
No suitable field characteristics separate this species from the Black-bellied Salamander, but it is biochemically distinct (see p. 60). Narrow head, small limbs. Usually a dorsal stripe. Map 17

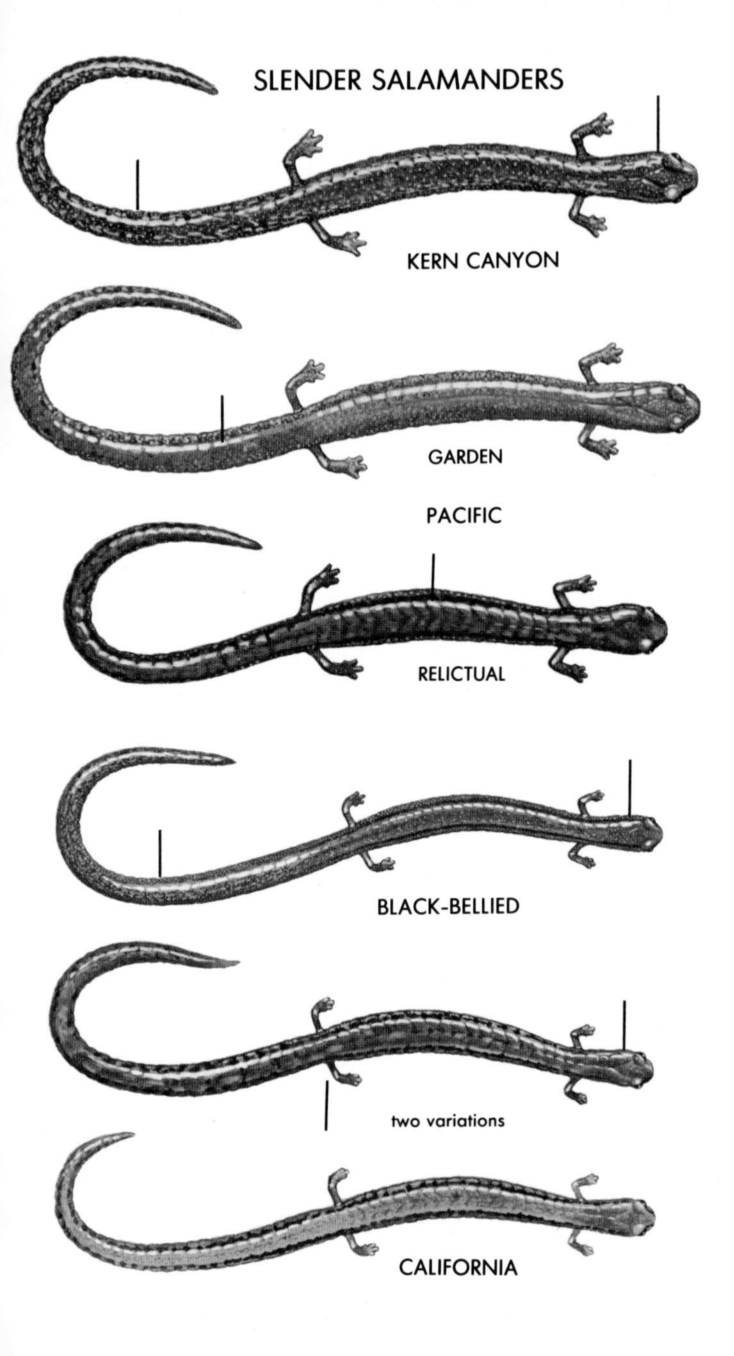
SLENDER SALAMANDERS
KERN CANYON
GARDEN
PACIFIC
RELICTUAL
BLACK-BELLIED
two variations
CALIFORNIA

Plate 10

TRUE TOADS *(Bufo)* × $^5/_6$

(See also Pls. 11 and 12.)

Stocky build; parotoid glands; warts.

SONORAN GREEN TOAD, *B. retiformis* p. 76
Large, divergent parotoids. Large, oval greenish to yellowish spots above, set off by black network. (Pima Co., Ariz.) Map 37

GREEN TOAD, *B. debilis* p. 76
Resembles Sonoran Green Toad, but usually smaller and with less complete black network. (Socorro Co., N.M.) Map 37

SPADEFOOT TOADS *(Scaphiopus)* × $^5/_6$

Single black "spade" on hind foot; pupils vertical.

WESTERN SPADEFOOT, *S. hammondii* p. 66
No boss between eyes. (Madera Co., Calif.) Map 25

GREAT BASIN SPADEFOOT, *S. intermontanus* p. 67
Glandular boss between eyes. (Salt Lake Co., Utah) Map 23

PLAINS SPADEFOOT, *S. bombifrons* p. 67
Bony boss between eyes. (Phillips Co., Colo.) Map 24

COUCH SPADEFOOT, *S. couchii* p. 65
No boss; eyes widely separated; sickle-shaped spade (Fig. 12). (Maricopa Co., Ariz.) Map 26

Fig. 12. "Spades" of spadefoot toads

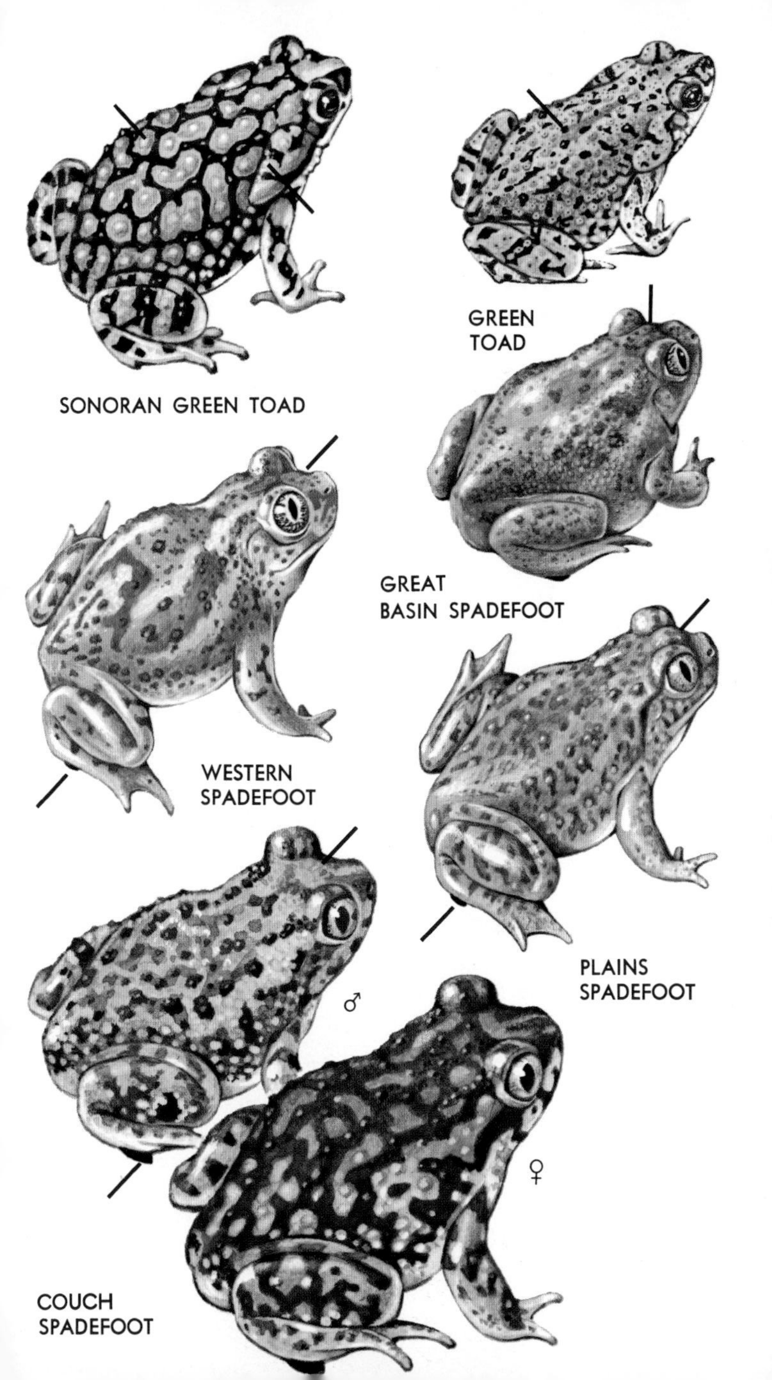

SONORAN GREEN TOAD
GREEN TOAD
GREAT BASIN SPADEFOOT
WESTERN SPADEFOOT
PLAINS SPADEFOOT
♂
♀
COUCH SPADEFOOT

Plate 11

TRUE TOADS *(Bufo)* × $^3/_5$

(See also Pls. 10 and 12.)

Stocky build; parotoid glands; warts.

WESTERN TOAD, *B. boreas* p. 69

Whitish dorsal stripe; weak cranial crests. (Contra Costa Co., Calif.) Map 30

YOSEMITE TOAD, *B. canorus* p. 71

Large, flat parotoids. Female with black blotches, absent or reduced in male. Found only in Sierra Nevada of Calif. Map 31

GREAT PLAINS TOAD, *B. cognatus* p. 74

Blotches on back often in pairs; prominent cranial crests. (Pima Co., Ariz.) Map 35

SONORAN DESERT (COLORADO RIVER) TOAD, *B. alvarius* p. 69

Skin relatively smooth; large warts on hind legs. To 6 in. (Dark phase, Santa Cruz Co., Ariz.) Map 38

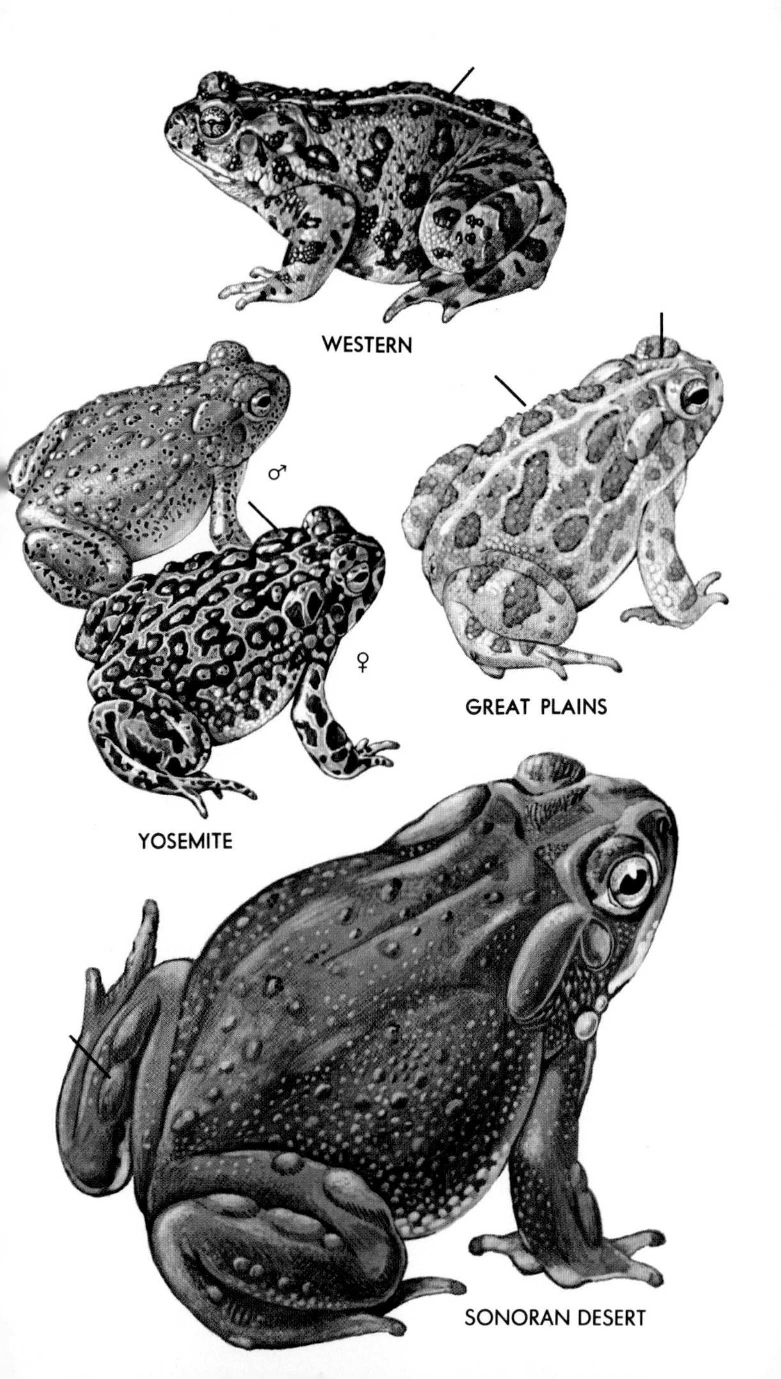
WESTERN
♂
♀
GREAT PLAINS
YOSEMITE
SONORAN DESERT

Plate 12

TRUE TOADS *(Bufo)* $\times \frac{2}{3}$

(See also Pls. 10 and 11.)

Stocky build; parotoid glands; warts.

WOODHOUSE TOAD, *B. woodhousei* — p. 72
Pale dorsal stripe. Prominent cranial crests. (Benton Co., Wash.) — Map 33

CANADIAN TOAD, *B. hemiophrys* — p. 75
Boss on top of head. (Saskatchewan, Can.) — Map 34

SOUTHWESTERN TOAD, *B. microscaphus* — p. 72
Front part of parotoids and eyelids usually pale-colored. — Map 32

- **Arroyo Toad,** *B. m. californicus.* Dark-spotted above. (San Bernardino Co., Calif.) — Map 32 — p. 73
- **Arizona Toad,** *B. m. microscaphus.* Dark spotting weak or absent. (Lincoln Co., Nev.) — Map 32 — p. 73

RED-SPOTTED TOAD, *B. punctatus* $\times \frac{5}{6}$ — p. 73
Small round parotoids. (Riverside Co., Calif.) — Map 39

TEXAS TOAD, *B. speciosus* — p. 74
No stripe. Cranial crests weak or absent. (Eddy Co., N.M.) — Map 36

LEPTODACTYLID FROGS $\times \frac{2}{3}$

BARKING FROG, *Hylactophryne augusti* — p. 64
Fold of skin at back of head; semitransparent eardrum. (Sonora, Mex.) Young with broad white body band. (Mex.) — Map 28

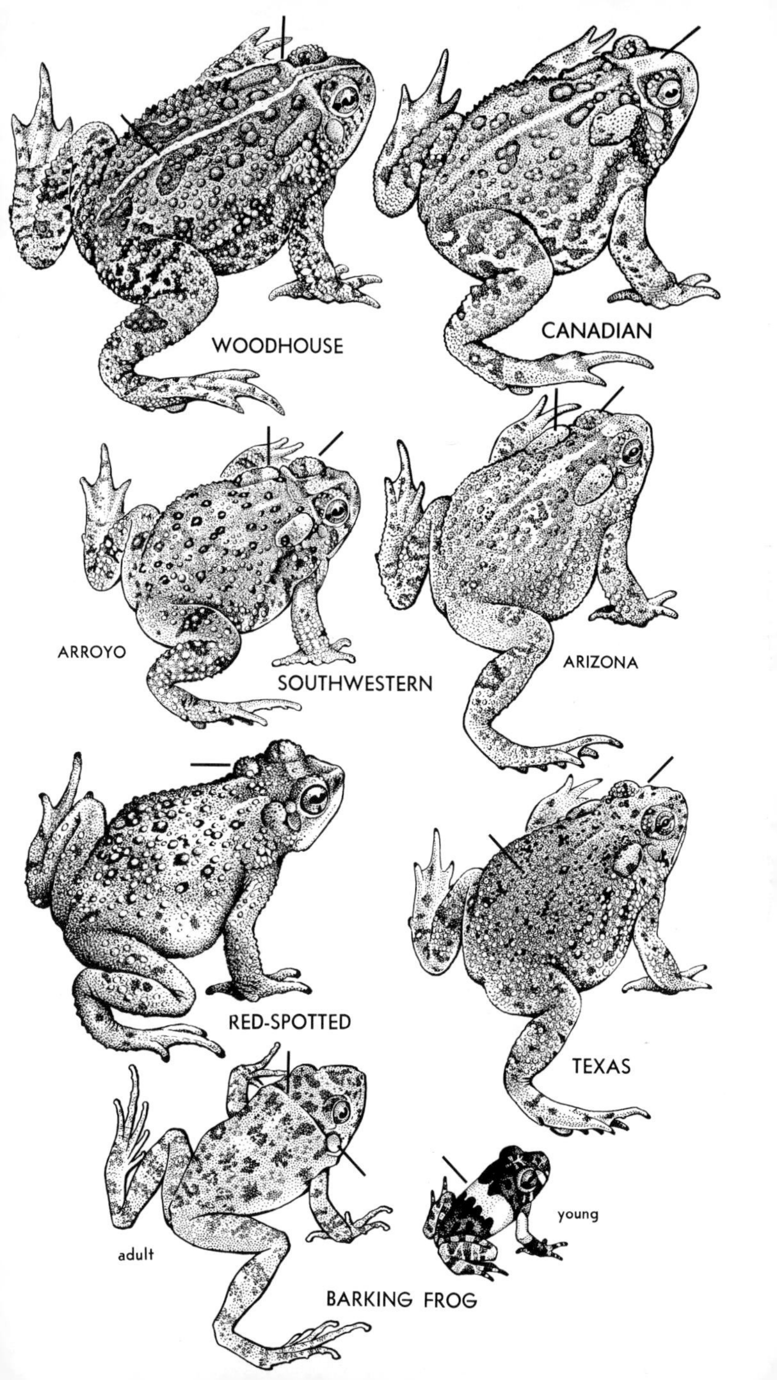
WOODHOUSE
CANADIAN
ARROYO
SOUTHWESTERN
ARIZONA
RED-SPOTTED
TEXAS
adult
young
BARKING FROG

Plate 13

TRUE FROGS *(Rana)* × $\frac{1}{2}$

(See also Pls. 14 and 15.)

Most have dorsolateral folds and long hind legs.

RED-LEGGED FROG, *R. aurora* p. 82
Light jaw stripe usually ends in front of shoulder (Fig. 13). Adults usually have red on underside of hind limbs. (Alameda Co., Calif.) Map 48

SPOTTED FROG, *R. pretiosa* p. 84
Light jaw stripe usually reaches shoulder. Adults red, orange, or yellow on underside of hind limbs. Eyes upturned (Fig. 13). (Benton Co., Ore.) Map 50

MOUNTAIN YELLOW-LEGGED FROG, *R. muscosa* p. 86
Vague dorsolateral folds. Toe tips usually dark. (Los Angeles Co., Calif.) Map 52

CASCADES FROG, *R. cascadae* p. 85
Ink-black spots on back, often with light centers. (Shasta Co., Calif.) Map 51

TARAHUMARA FROG, *R. tarahumarae* p. 87
No mask or light-colored jaw stripe; often dusky below, including throat. (Pima Co., Ariz.) Map 53

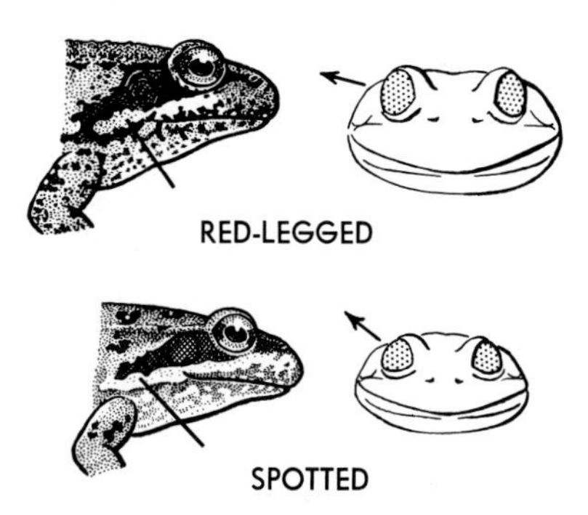

Fig. 13. Characteristics of frogs

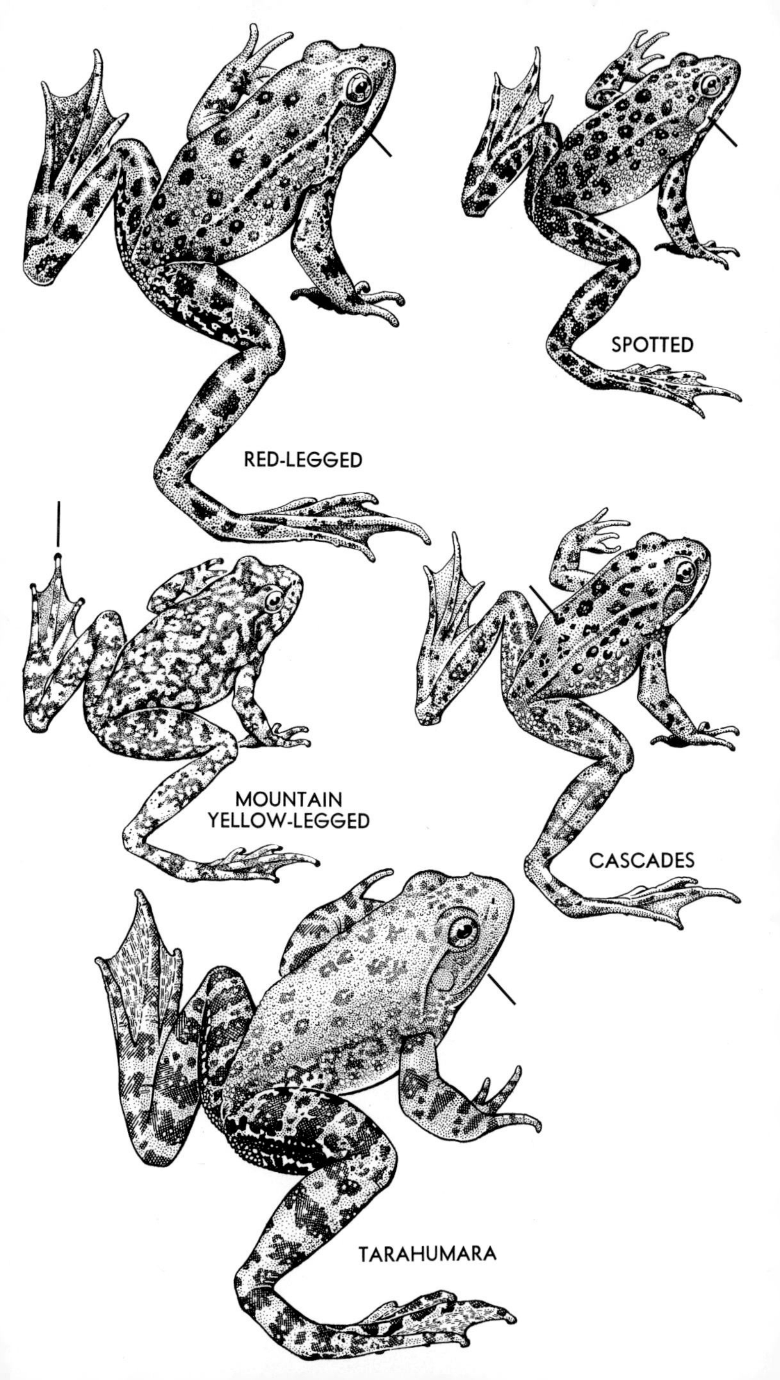
SPOTTED
RED-LEGGED
MOUNTAIN
YELLOW-LEGGED
CASCADES
TARAHUMARA

TRUE FROGS *(Rana)* × $^3/_4$

(See also Pls. 13 and 15.)

Most have dorsolateral folds and long hind limbs.

RED-LEGGED FROG, *R. aurora* p. 82
Usually with coarse, black, yellow, and/or red mottling in groin; red on underside of hind limbs. Well-developed dorsolateral folds. (Contra Costa Co., Calif.) Map 48

FOOTHILL YELLOW-LEGGED FROG, *R. boylii* p. 86
Pale triangle on snout. Dorsolateral folds vague. Underside of hind limbs yellow. (Contra Costa Co., Calif.) Map 49

LOWLAND LEOPARD FROG, *R. yavapaiensis* p. 91
Similar to Chiricahua Leopard Frog but has dark network on rear of thighs. (Maricopa Co., Ariz.) Map 54

MOUNTAIN YELLOW-LEGGED FROG, *R. muscosa* p. 86
Vague dorsolateral folds. Dusky toe tips; yellow or orange on belly and underside of hind legs. (Mariposa Co., Calif.) Map 52

BULLFROG, *R. catesbeiana* p. 92
Fold around conspicuous eardrum; no dorsolateral folds. Map 47

WOOD FROG, *R. sylvatica* p. 83
Conspicuous dark mask contrasts with whitish jaw stripe; dorsal stripe may be present or absent. Light phase. Map 46

CLAWED FROG

Fig. 14. African Clawed Frog, *Xenopus laevis,* × $^1/_2$. No eyelids or dorsolateral folds; claws on hind toes. Introduced.

venter
venter
RED-LEGGED
FOOTHILL YELLOW-LEGGED
LOWLAND LEOPARD
MOUNTAIN YELLOW-LEGGED
BULLFROG
WOOD

Plate 15

LEOPARD FROGS *(Rana)* × $^2/_3$

(See other true frogs on Pls. 13 and 14.)

Most have dorsolateral folds and long hind limbs. Note round or oval spots on back.

NORTHERN LEOPARD FROG, *R. pipiens* p. 88
Well-defined oval or round dark spots with pale borders. Dorsolateral folds continuous and not angled toward midline of body. Brown phase (Coconino Co., Ariz.); green phase (Colo.). Map 54

CHIRICAHUA LEOPARD FROG, *R. chiricahuensis* p. 89
Spots on back usually small and numerous. Dorsolateral folds broken toward rear and often angled toward midline. (New Tank, Coconino Co., Ariz.) Map 55

PLAINS LEOPARD FROG, *R. blairi* p. 90
Spots on back have very narrow pale borders (if any). Usually a well-defined pale spot in center of eardrum. Dorsolateral folds usually interrupted toward rear. (Douglas Co., Kans.) Map 54

LOWLAND LEOPARD FROG, *R. yavapaiensis* p. 91
Similar to Chiricahua Leopard Frog, but has dark network on rear of thighs. (Maricopa Co., Ariz.) Map 54

RIO GRANDE LEOPARD FROG, *R. berlandieri* p. 92
Eyes large. Dorsolateral folds interrupted toward rear and angled toward midline. (Nueces R., Dimmit Co., Tex.) Map 54

LEOPARD FROGS

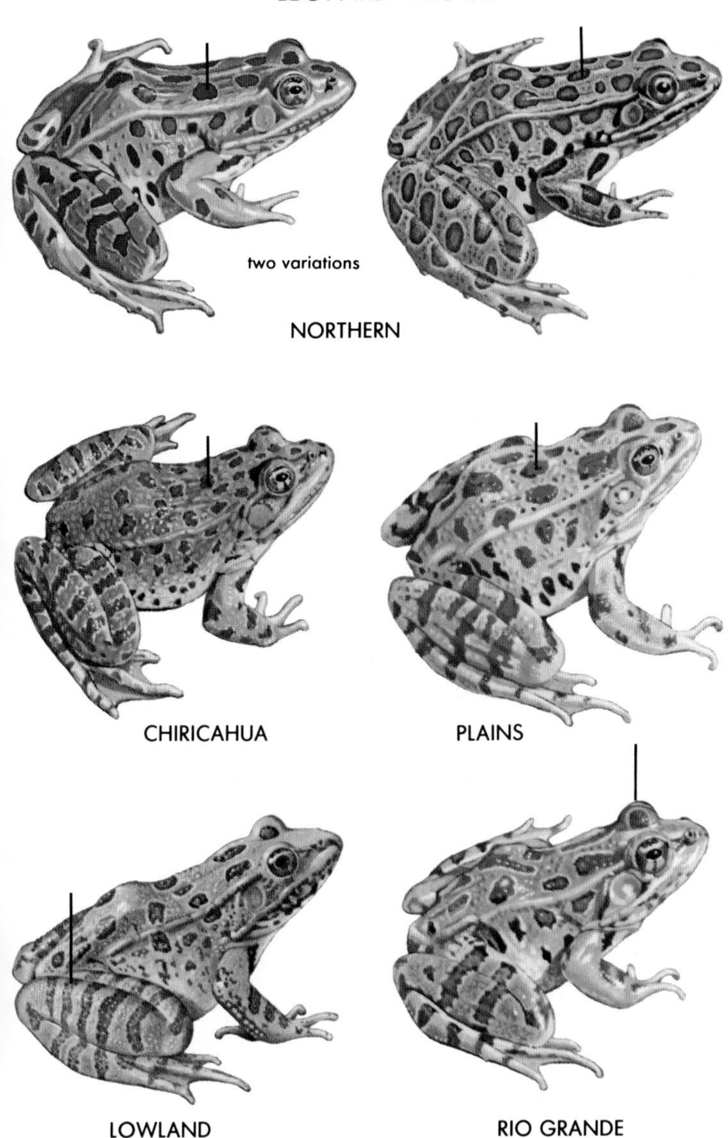

Plate 16

GREAT PLAINS NARROW-MOUTHED TOAD, TREEFROGS, AND TAILED FROG

(First two species life-size, the rest × $^5/_6$.)

GREAT PLAINS NARROW-MOUTHED TOAD *Gastrophryne olivacea* — p. 94
Fold of skin at back of head; narrow, pointed head. To $1^3/_8$ in. (3.4 cm). (Santa Cruz Co., Ariz.) Map 29

NORTHERN CRICKET FROG, *Acris crepitans* — p. 77
White bar on side of face; dark stripe on rear of thigh. To $1^3/_8$ in. (3.4 cm). Map 42

STRIPED CHORUS FROG, *Pseudacris triseriata* — p. 78
Back striped; stripe through eye, but no toe pads. Map 40

Boreal Chorus Frog, *P. t. maculata.* Short hind legs. Map 40 — p. 78

Midland Chorus Frog, *P. t. triseriata.* Hind legs not notably shortened. Map 40 — p. 78

PACIFIC TREEFROG, *Hyla regilla* — p. 80
Stripe through eye. Toe pads; webbing moderately developed (Fig. 15). (Contra Costa Co., Calif.) Map 43

MOUNTAIN TREEFROG, *Hyla eximia* — p. 81
Resembles Pacific Treefrog, but stripe extends well back along side of body. Webbing poorly developed (Fig. 15). (Cochise Co., Ariz.) Map 44

CANYON TREEFROG, *Hyla arenicolor* — p. 79
No eyestripe. Toe pads prominent; webbing well developed (Fig. 15). Voice a hoarse trill. (Washington Co., Utah) Map 45

CALIFORNIA TREEFROG, *Hyla cadaverina* — p. 80
Resembles Canyon Treefrog, but voice a quacking sound. Map 45

NORTHERN CASQUE-HEADED FROG, *Pternohyla fodiens* — p. 78
Fold of skin at back of head; 1 metatarsal tubercle (see front endpapers). (Pima Co., Ariz.) Map 41

TAILED FROG, *Ascaphus truei* — p. 63
Outer hind toe broadest; tail-like copulatory organ in male. (Shoshone Co., Idaho) Map 27

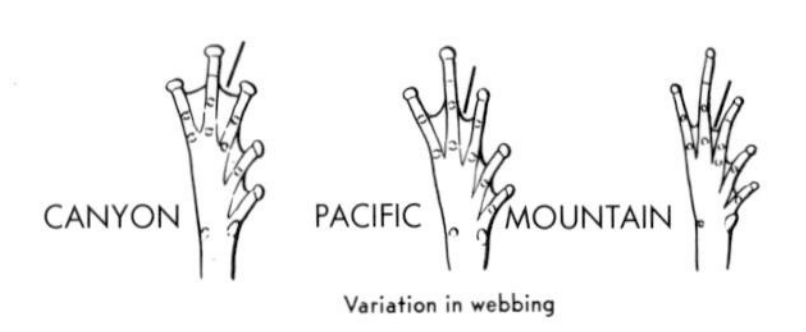

Fig. 15. Hind feet of treefrogs

GREAT PLAINS NARROW-MOUTHED TOAD
NORTHERN CRICKET FROG
BOREAL
STRIPED CHORUS FROG
MIDLAND
two variations
PACIFIC TREEFROG
MOUNTAIN TREEFROG
CANYON TREEFROG
two variations
CALIFORNIA TREEFROG
two variations
NORTHERN CASQUE-HEADED FROG
TAILED FROG

Plate 17

TURTLES × $^1/_2$

SONORAN MUD, *Kinosternon sonoriense* p. 99
Nipple-like projections on throat; head mottled (Fig. 16). 9th marginal shield not higher than it is wide. (Mexico) Map 61

YELLOW MUD, *Kinosternon flavescens* p. 98
Like Sonoran Mud Turtle but head not mottled (Fig. 16) and 9th marginal shield usually higher than it is wide. Map 62

SNAPPING, *Chelydra serpentina* p. 97
Prominent crest on tail; small plastron (Fig. 17). (Young individual, Kans.) Map 57

WESTERN POND, *Clemmys marmorata* p. 99
Dark flecks and lines radiating from center of shields. (Alameda Co., Calif.) Map 59

WESTERN BOX, *Terrapene ornata* p. 103
Shell with light and dark striping; plastron hinged in front. (Otero Co., N.M.) Map 60

Fig. 16. Head pattern in mud turtles

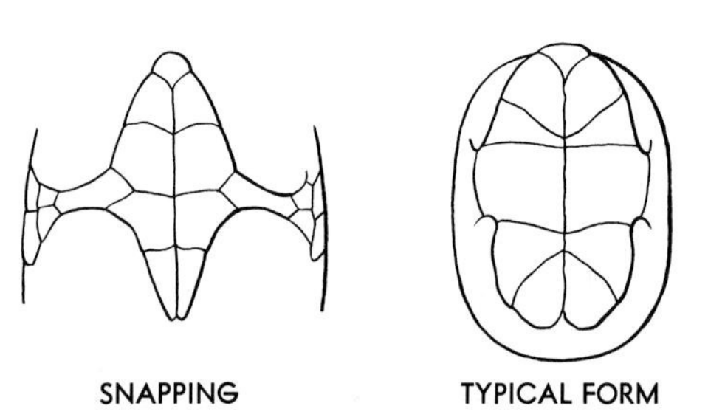

Fig. 17. Plastrons of turtles

SONORAN MUD
SNAPPING
WESTERN POND
WESTERN BOX

Plate 18

TURTLES × $^1/_3$

DESERT TORTOISE, *Gopherus agassizii* p. 104
High-domed shell with prominent growth lines; elephantlike limbs. (San Bernardino Co., Calif.)
Map 58

PAINTED TURTLE, *Chrysemys picta* p. 100
Front edge of shields bordered with yellow; rear of carapace smooth-edged. (Walla Walla Co., Wash.) Map 63

SLIDER, *Pseudemys scripta* p. 101
Rear edge of carapace sawtoothed; vertical streaking on costal shields. (Brazos Co., Tex.) Map 64

SPINY SOFTSHELL, *Trionyx spiniferus* p. 108
Flexible, pancakelike shell. Pointed snout; whitish ridge on each side of septum between nostrils. (Young individual, Kerr Co., Tex.) Map 66

DESERT TORTOISE
PAINTED TURTLE
SLIDER
SPINY SOFTSHELL

Plate 19

SEA TURTLES

Forelimbs modified as flippers; marine.

LEATHERBACK, *Dermochelys coriacea* p. 107
Carapace with lengthwise toothed ridges. To 8 ft. (2.4 m).

GREEN TURTLE, *Chelonia mydas* p. 105
1 pair of prefrontals. 4 costal shields on each side of carapace. To around 5 ft. (1.5 m).

PACIFIC RIDLEY, *Lepidochelys olivacea* p. 106
2 pairs of prefrontals. 5–9 costal shields on each side of carapace; bridge with 4 shields. To around 3 ft. (90 cm).

LOGGERHEAD, *Caretta caretta* p. 105
Shell high in front; 5 or more costal shields on each side of carapace, but bridge with 3 shields. To around 7 ft. (2.1 m).

LEATHERBACK
GREEN TURTLE
PACIFIC RIDLEY
LOGGERHEAD

Plate 20

CHUCKWALLA AND GILA MONSTER × ½

COMMON CHUCKWALLA, *Sauromalus obesus* p. 114
Loose folds of skin on sides of neck and body; no rostral. Tail banded with black and yellow in young. (Riverside Co., Calif.) Map 73

GILA MONSTER, *Heloderma suspectum* p. 169
Venomous. Beadlike scales and contrasting pattern of orange or yellow and black. (Pima Co., Ariz.) Map 120

young
COMMON CHUCKWALLA
GILA MONSTER

HORNED LIZARDS *(Phrynosoma)* × ½

Horns at back of head. Body flattened; tail short.

SHORT-HORNED, *P. douglassii* p. 141
Horns short. Often in mountains. Map 96

FLAT-TAILED, *P. mcallii* p. 141
Dark middorsal line; flat tail. (Riverside Co., Calif.) Map 102

REGAL, *P. solare* p. 142
Four horns at back of head with bases in contact. (Santa Cruz Co., Ariz.) Map 100

ROUND-TAILED, *P. modestum* p. 142
Slender rounded tail; no fringe scales on side of body. (Bernalillo Co., N.M.) Map 99

TEXAS, *P. cornutum* p. 139
Stripes radiate from eye. (Sutton Co., Tex.) Map 101

DESERT, *P. platyrhinos* p. 140
Lateral fringe scales and scales on throat small (Fig. 18). (Washoe Co., Nev.) Map 98

COAST, *P. coronatum* p. 139
Conspicuous lateral fringe scales; prominent pointed scales on throat (Fig. 18). (Riverside Co., Calif.) Map 97

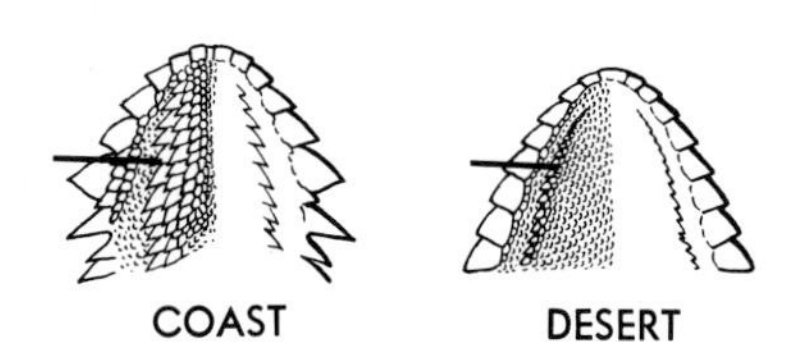

Fig. 18. Throat scales of horned lizards

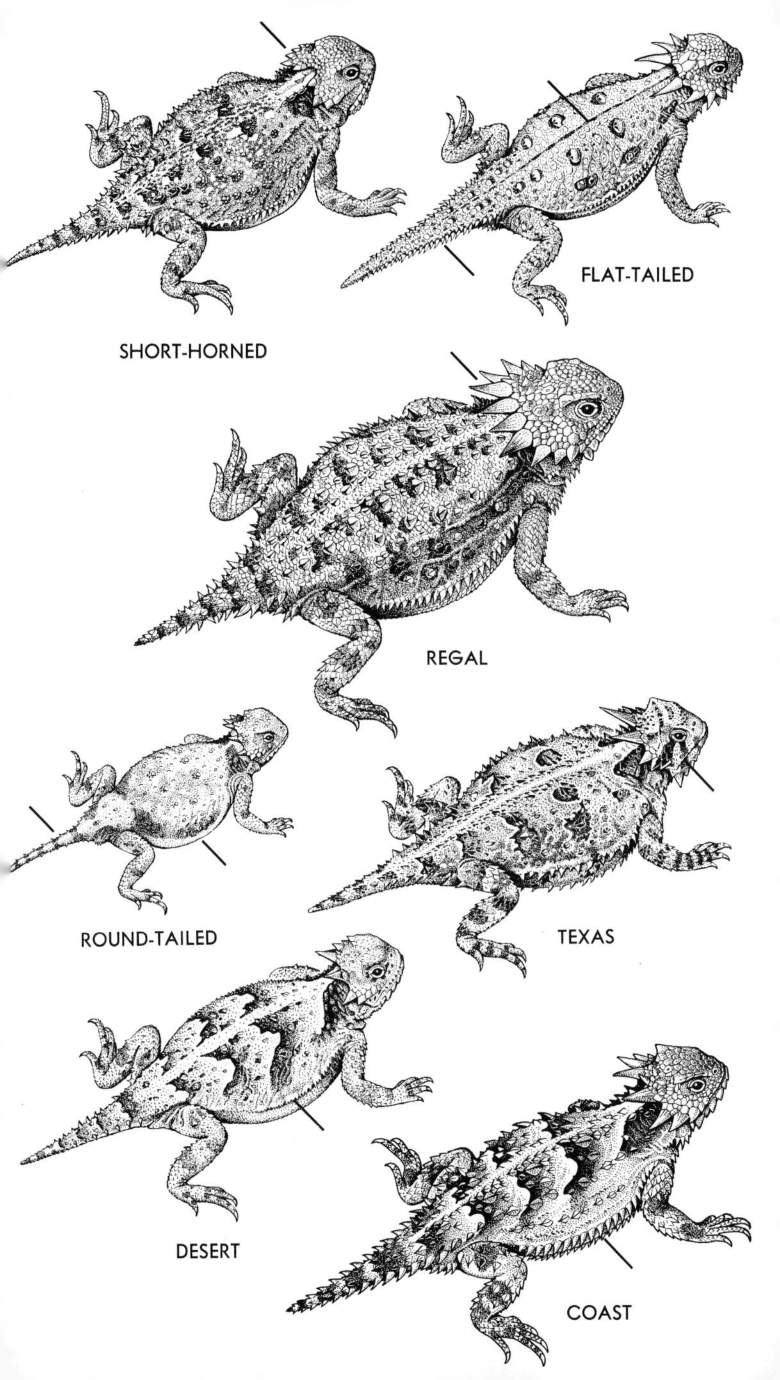
SHORT-HORNED
FLAT-TAILED
REGAL
ROUND-TAILED
TEXAS
DESERT
COAST

Plate 22

EARLESS AND ZEBRA-TAILED LIZARDS × 7/8

LESSER EARLESS, *Holbrookia maculata* p. 116
Ear openings absent. Underside of tail without markings. (Cochise Co., Ariz.) Map 75

GREATER EARLESS, *Cophosaurus texanus* p. 116
Ear openings absent. Underside of tail with black bars; belly markings behind midpoint of body. (Brewster Co., Tex.) Map 76

ZEBRA-TAILED, *Callisaurus draconoides* p. 117
Ear openings present. Underside of tail with black bars; belly markings at midpoint of body. (Kern Co., Calif.) Map 77

venter
♂
LESSER EARLESS
venter
♂
GREATER EARLESS
venter
♀
venter
♂
ZEBRA-TAILED

Plate 23

FRINGE-TOED LIZARDS *(Uma)* × $^7/_8$

Prominent fringe scales on hind toes.

MOJAVE, *U. scoparia* p. 120
Crescents on throat; black spots on sides of belly. (Pisgah area, San Bernardino Co., Calif.) Map 78

COACHELLA VALLEY, *U. inornata* p. 119
Streaks on throat; belly markings absent or reduced to small black dot(s) on each side. Map 78

COLORADO DESERT, *U. notata* p. 118
Streaks on throat; prominent black spots on sides of belly. (Algodones Dunes, Imperial Co., Calif.) Map 78

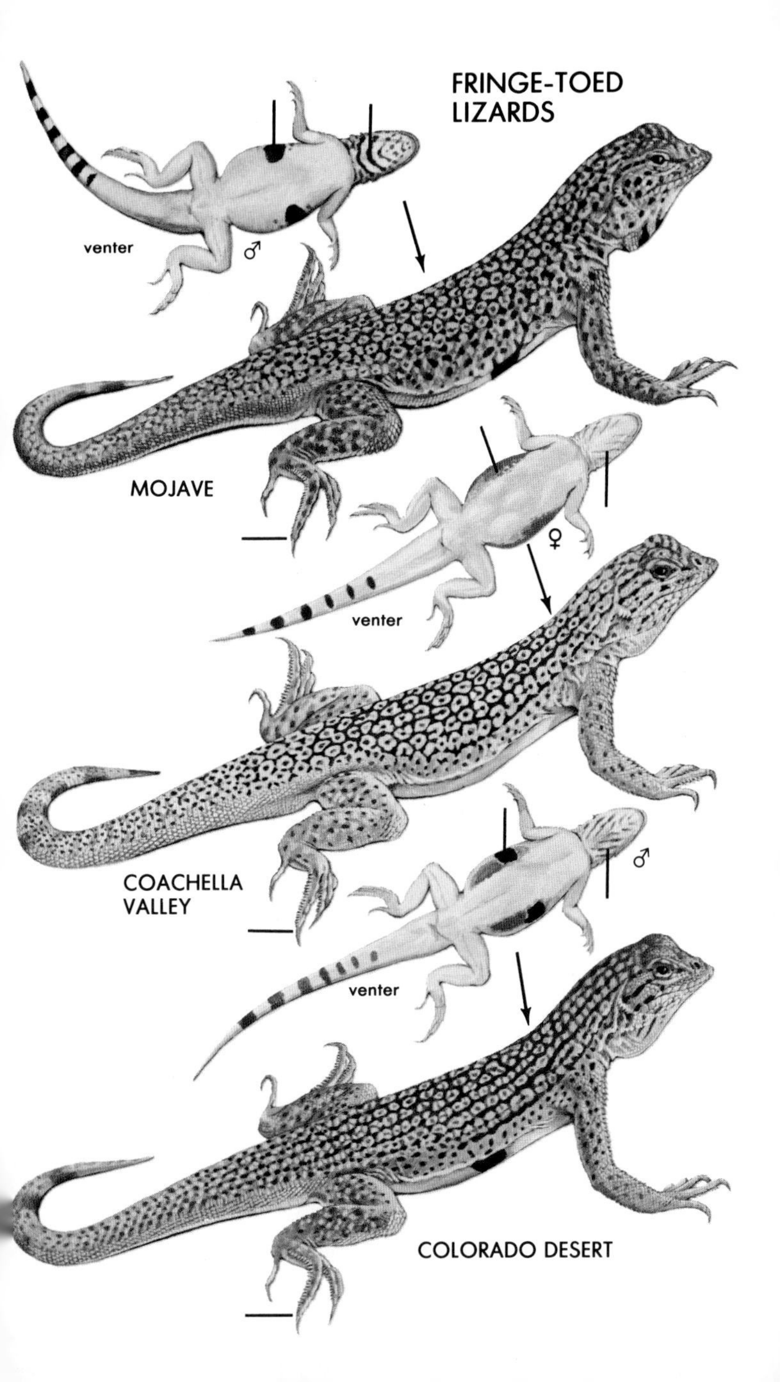
FRINGE-TOED
LIZARDS
venter
♂
MOJAVE
♀
venter
COACHELLA
VALLEY
♂
venter
COLORADO DESERT

Plate 24

LEOPARD AND COLLARED LIZARDS; DESERT IGUANA × $^{3}/_{4}$

LONG-NOSED LEOPARD LIZARD, p. 123
Gambelia wislizenii
Pattern of spots and pale crossbars; throat usually streaked with gray; long snout. Female shown in breeding color. (Kern Co., Calif.) Map 79

BLUNT-NOSED LEOPARD LIZARD, p. 124
Gambelia silus
Resembles Long-nosed Leopard Lizard, but throat usually spotted rather than streaked and snout blunt. Female shown in breeding color. (Pixley National Wildlife Refuge, Tulare Co., Calif.) Map 79

COMMON COLLARED LIZARD, p. 120
Crotaphytus collaris
Prominent collar markings. Most have some greenish color. Throat and mouth lining dark. (Aravaipa Canyon, Pinal Co., Ariz.) Map 80

DESERT IGUANA, *Dipsosaurus dorsalis* p. 114
Row of enlarged scales down middle of back. (Kern Co., Calif.) Map 74

breeding ♀
LONG-NOSED
LEOPARD LIZARD
♂
♀
BLUNT-NOSED LEOPARD LIZARD
COMMON
COLLARED LIZARD
DESERT IGUANA

Plate 25

SIDE-BLOTCHED, TREE, AND ROCK LIZARDS × $^2/_3$

Complete gular fold (Fig. 6, No. 10, p. 28); large scales on top of head between eyes (Fig. 6, No. 13).

SIDE-BLOTCHED, *Uta stansburiana* p. 135
Dark blotch on side. (Fresno Co., Calif.) Map 93

SMALL-SCALED, *Urosaurus microscutatus* p. 137
Resembles Tree Lizard. Dorsal scales gradually enlarge toward midline. (Baja Calif., Mex.) Map 94

TREE, *Urosaurus ornatus* p. 136
Large scales on back interrupted along midline by small scales (Fig. 19). (Cochise Co., Ariz.) Map 91

LONG-TAILED BRUSH, *Urosaurus graciosus* p. 135
Uninterrupted broad band of large scales down middle of back (Fig. 19); long tail. (San Bernardino Co., Calif.) Map 92

BANDED ROCK, *Petrosaurus mearnsi* p. 137
Single black collar; banded tail. A rock dweller. (Riverside Co., Calif.) Map 95

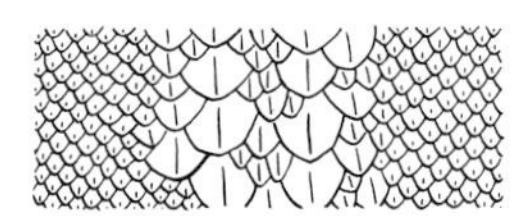

TREE

LONG-TAILED BRUSH

Fig. 19. Back scales in Tree and Long-tailed Brush Lizards

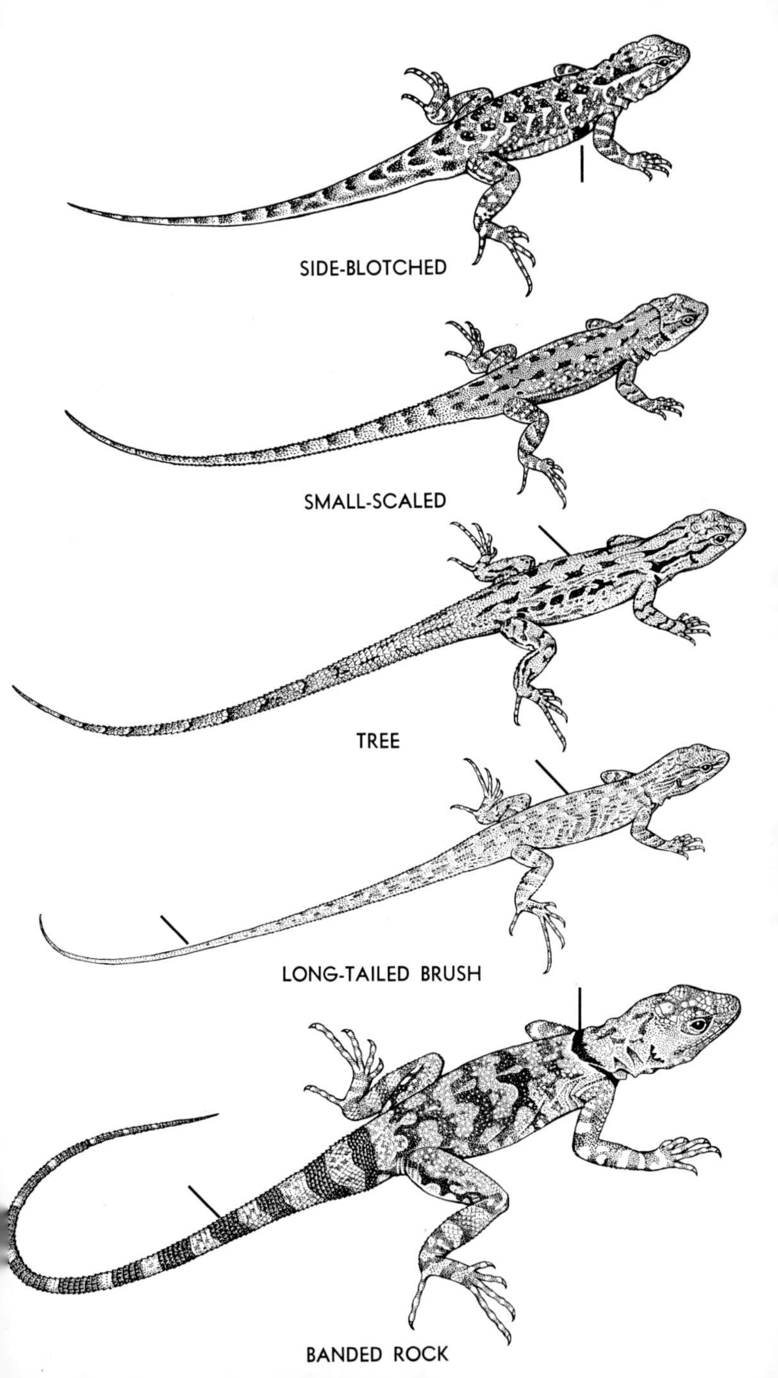
SIDE-BLOTCHED
SMALL-SCALED
TREE
LONG-TAILED BRUSH
BANDED ROCK

Plate 26

SPINY LIZARDS *(Sceloporus)* × $^2/_3$

Dorsal scales keeled and pointed; gular fold incomplete (Fig. 6, No. 9, p. 28).

BUNCH GRASS LIZARD, *S. scalaris* p. 125
Rows of scales on sides parallel rows on back. Males have blue belly patches. (Cochise Co., Ariz.) Map 89

SAGEBRUSH LIZARD, *S. graciosus* p. 133
Scales relatively small; no yellow on rear of limbs; axilla rust-colored. Males have blue throat and belly patches. (Contra Costa Co., Calif.) Map 87

WESTERN FENCE LIZARD, *S. occidentalis* p. 130
Scales coarser than in Sagebrush Lizard; yellow on rear of limbs. Males have blue on throat and sides of belly. (Contra Costa Co., Calif.) Map 85

STRIPED PLATEAU LIZARD, *S. virgatus* p. 133
Striped pattern; no blue patches on belly. Small blue spot on each side of throat in male. Mountains. Map 88

MOUNTAIN (YARROW) SPINY LIZARD, *S. jarrovii* p. 126
Black lace-stocking pattern; black collar edged with white. (Cochise Co., Ariz.) Map 90

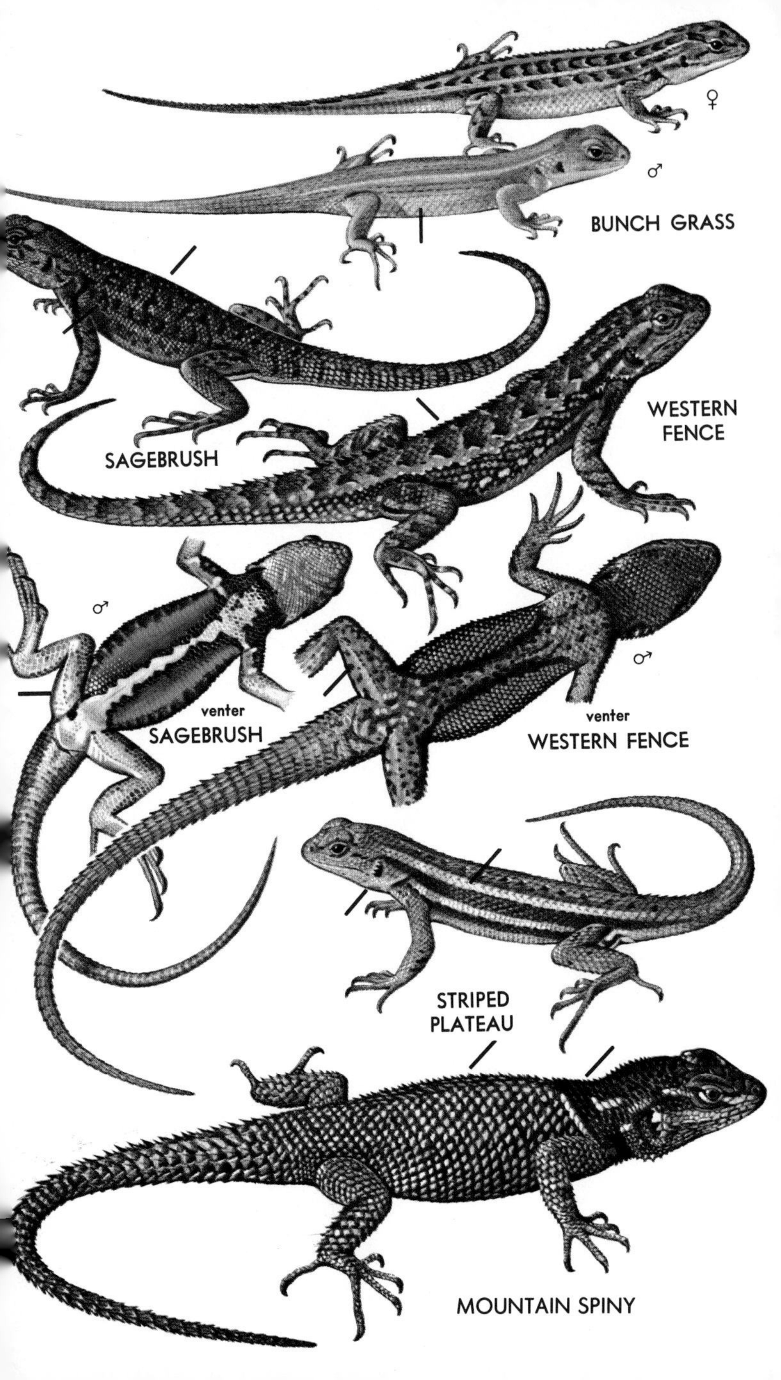
♀
♂
BUNCH GRASS
SAGEBRUSH
WESTERN
FENCE
♂
venter
SAGEBRUSH
♂
venter
WESTERN FENCE
STRIPED
PLATEAU
MOUNTAIN SPINY

Plate 27

SPINY LIZARDS *(Sceloporus)* × ½

Dorsal scales keeled and pointed; gular fold incomplete (Fig. 6, No. 9, p. 28).

GRANITE, *S. orcutti* p. 129
Dark coloration; males with blue belly and throat and purple stripe on back in light phase; black wedge on shoulder inconspicuous. (n. Baja Calif., Mex.)
Map 84

DESERT, *S. magister* p. 127
Paler than Granite Spiny Lizard; scales more pointed; conspicuous black wedge on shoulder. Males with blue belly patches and throat; sometimes a purple area on back. (Pima Co., Ariz.) Map 81

CLARK, *S. clarkii* p. 129
Black wedge on shoulder and black bars on forelimbs. Males with blue belly patches and throat. (Pima Co., Ariz.) Map 82

CREVICE, *S. poinsettii* p. 127
Conspicuous collar marking and banded tail. A rock dweller. (N.M.) Map 83

GRANITE
DESERT
CLARK
CREVICE

Plate 28

SKINKS *(Eumeces)* × $\frac{1}{2}$

Smooth cycloid scales (Fig. 6, No. 2, p. 28).

GREAT PLAINS, *E. obsoletus* p. 146
Network or heavy spotting of black or dark brown; scale rows on sides diagonal to rows on back. Young black, with white spots on labials. (Kans.) Map 104

GILBERT, *E. gilberti* p. 149
Adults plain olive or brown, with varied amounts of dark spotting (Fig. 20). Young with blue or red tail; dark side stripe stops at base of tail. Map 103

WESTERN, *E. skiltonianus* p. 148
Adult striped (Fig. 20). Young with blue tail; dark side stripe extends well out on tail. (Young, San Luis Obispo Co., Calif.; adult, Contra Costa Co., Calif.) Map 105

MOUNTAIN, *E. callicephalus* p. 147
Pale Y-shaped marking on head. (Santa Cruz Co., Ariz.) Map 107

MANY-LINED, *E. multivirgatus* p. 146
Short limbs; many dark and light lines on body (Fig. 20). Some individuals are dark-colored, without striping. (Adams Co., Colo.) Map 106

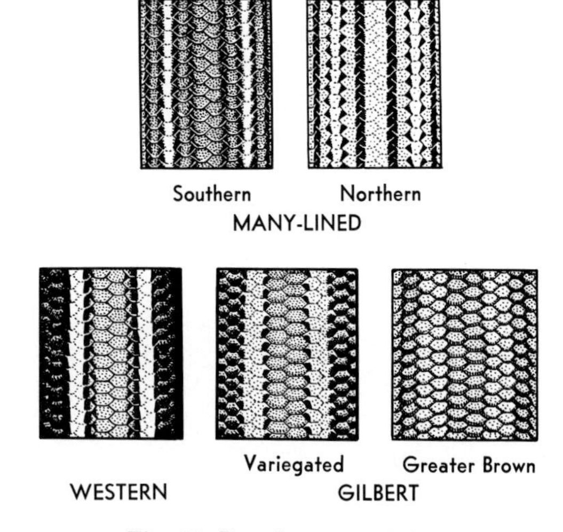

Fig. 20. Dorsal pattern of skinks

adult
young
GREAT PLAINS
young
adult
GILBERT
young
adult
WESTERN
MOUNTAIN
MANY-LINED

Plate 29

ALLIGATOR LIZARDS *(Gerrhonotus)* × $\frac{1}{2}$

Conspicuous fold on side of body; short limbs.

MADREAN (ARIZONA), *G. kingii* p. 166
Black and white spots on upper jaw; prominent crossbands on body and tail. Young banded. (Ariz.)
Map 119

PANAMINT, *G. panamintinus* p. 165
Paler than Madrean Alligator Lizard; lacks jaw markings. Young with contrasting dark and light crossbands. (Inyo Co., Calif.) Map 119

SOUTHERN, *G. multicarinatus* p. 164
Dusky lengthwise stripes or dashed lines down middle of scale rows on belly; crossbands usually distinct. Young with broad dorsal stripe. Map 119

NORTHERN, *G. coeruleus* p. 166
Dusky stripes between scale rows on belly; crossbands indistinct, often irregular. Young striped, as in Southern Alligator Lizard. Map 121

MADREAN
adult
young
PANAMINT
young
adult
SOUTHERN
NORTHERN

Plate 30

NIGHT LIZARDS × $^3/_5$

Vertical pupils; scales granular above, squarish below.

ISLAND, *Xantusia riversiana* p. 145
To $3^3/_4$ in. (9.4 cm). 2 rows of supraoculars. Found only on islands off s. Calif. (San Clemente I.) Map 71

DESERT, *Xantusia vigilis* p. 143
1 row of well-developed supraoculars. Olive, gray, or dark brown above, speckled with black. (San Benito Co., Calif.) Map 71

Arizona Night Lizard, *X. v. arizonae.* Coarse dark body spots; flattened head and body. (Yavapai Co., Ariz.) Map 71 p. 144

Common Night Lizard, *X. v. vigilis.* Small dark body spots; postorbital stripe on side of head and neck. (San Benito Co., Calif.) Map 71 p. 144

GRANITE, *Xantusia henshawi* p. 143
Large dark spots; head and body flat. A rock dweller. (San Diego Co., Calif.) Map 72

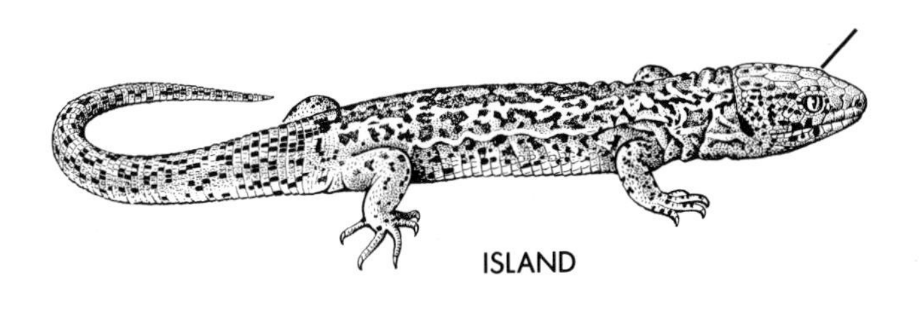

ISLAND

ARIZONA NIGHT

DESERT

COMMON NIGHT

GRANITE

Plate 31

WHIPTAILS *(Cnemidophorus)* × $^2/_3$

(See also Pls. 32, 33 and 34.)

Scales granular above, large and squarish below.

WESTERN WHIPTAIL, *C. tigris* p. 161
Back spotted with black or dusky; pale stripes usually present. Postantebrachials not enlarged as in Fig. 21.
Map 110

California Whiptail, *C. t. mundus.* Usually 8 stripes, but lateral ones often have irregular borders and are sometimes indistinct. (Alameda Co., Calif.) Map 110 p. 162

Marbled Whiptail, *C. t. marmoratus.* Marbled pattern on back. (Dona Ana Co., N.M.) Map 110 p. 162

DESERT GRASSLAND WHIPTAIL, *C. uniparens* p. 155
Tail greenish olive to bluish green. Dark fields (Fig. 21) unspotted. (Yavapai Co., Ariz.) Map 112

SIX-LINED RACERUNNER, *C. sexlineatus* p. 156
Foreparts greenish in adults. Dark fields unspotted.
Map 109

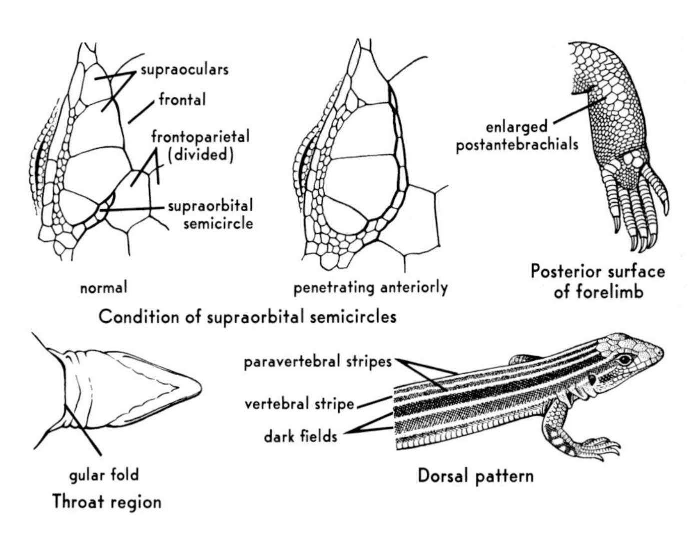

Fig. 21. Characteristics of whiptail lizards

CALIFORNIA WHIPTAIL
MARBLED WHIPTAIL
WESTERN WHIPTAIL
DESERT GRASSLAND WHIPTAIL
SIX-LINED RACERUNNER

Plate 32

WHIPTAILS *(Cnemidophorus)* × $^4/_5$

(See also Pls. 31, 33, and 34.)

Scales granular above, large and squarish below.

LITTLE STRIPED, *C. inornatus* p. 154
No spots in dark fields; tail bluish, especially toward tip. Bluish white to blue below. (Luna Co., N.M.)
Map 113

PLATEAU STRIPED, *C. velox* p. 156
Tail light blue. Whitish below, with a tinge of bluish green. (Soccoro Co., N.M.) Map 115

NEW MEXICAN, *C. neomexicanus* p. 154
Wavy middorsal (vertebral) stripe; supraorbital semicircles penetrate far forward (Fig. 21, opp. Pl. 31). Tail greenish or greenish blue toward tip. (Luna Co., N.M.)
Map 117

CHECKERED, *C. tesselatus* p. 163
Back with conspicuous black bars and spots; scales in front of gular fold abruptly and conspicuously enlarged. (Sierra Co., N.M.) Map 108

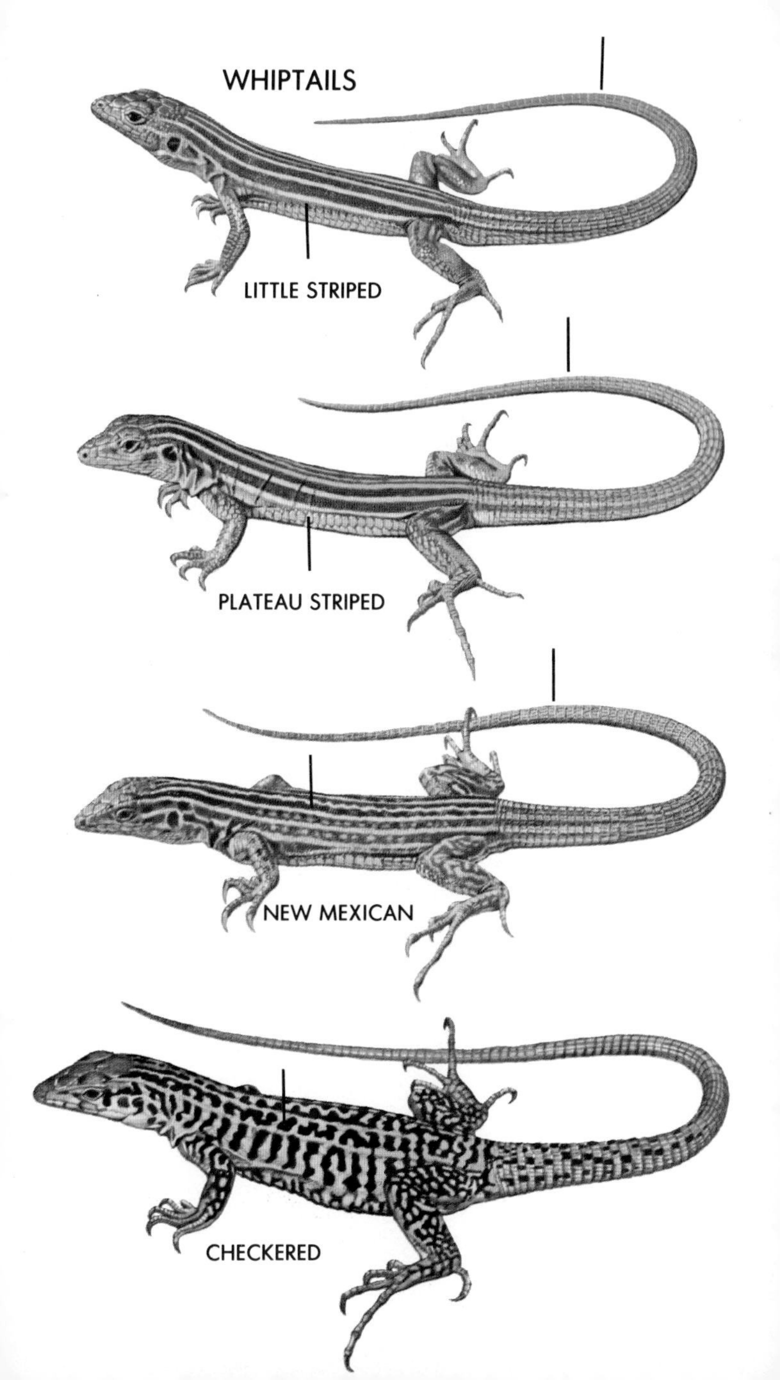
WHIPTAILS
LITTLE STRIPED
PLATEAU STRIPED
NEW MEXICAN
CHECKERED

Plate 33

WHIPTAILS *(Cnemidophorus)* × $^3/_5$

(See also Pls. 31, 32, and 34.)

Scales granular above, large and squarish below.

TEXAS SPOTTED, *C. gularis* p. 160
Whitish to yellow-brown spots in greenish to dark brown dark fields. Throat salmon-pink, and chest and belly purplish or bluish, often darkened with black in breeding male. (Terrant Co., Tex.) Map 116

CHIHUAHUAN SPOTTED, *C. exsanguis* p. 157
Cream to pale yellow spots in dark fields; some individuals have bright yellow spots on rump. Enlarged postantebrachials (Fig. 21, opp. Pl. 31). (Dona Ana Co., N.M.) Map 111

SONORAN SPOTTED, *C. sonorae* p. 158
Pale stripes lack light spots. Usually 3 preanals. (Santa Cruz Co., Ariz.) Map 115

GILA SPOTTED, *C. flagellicaudus* p. 160
Light spots on back in both the dark fields and on pale stripes. Usually 2 preanals. (Catron Co., N.M.) Map 114

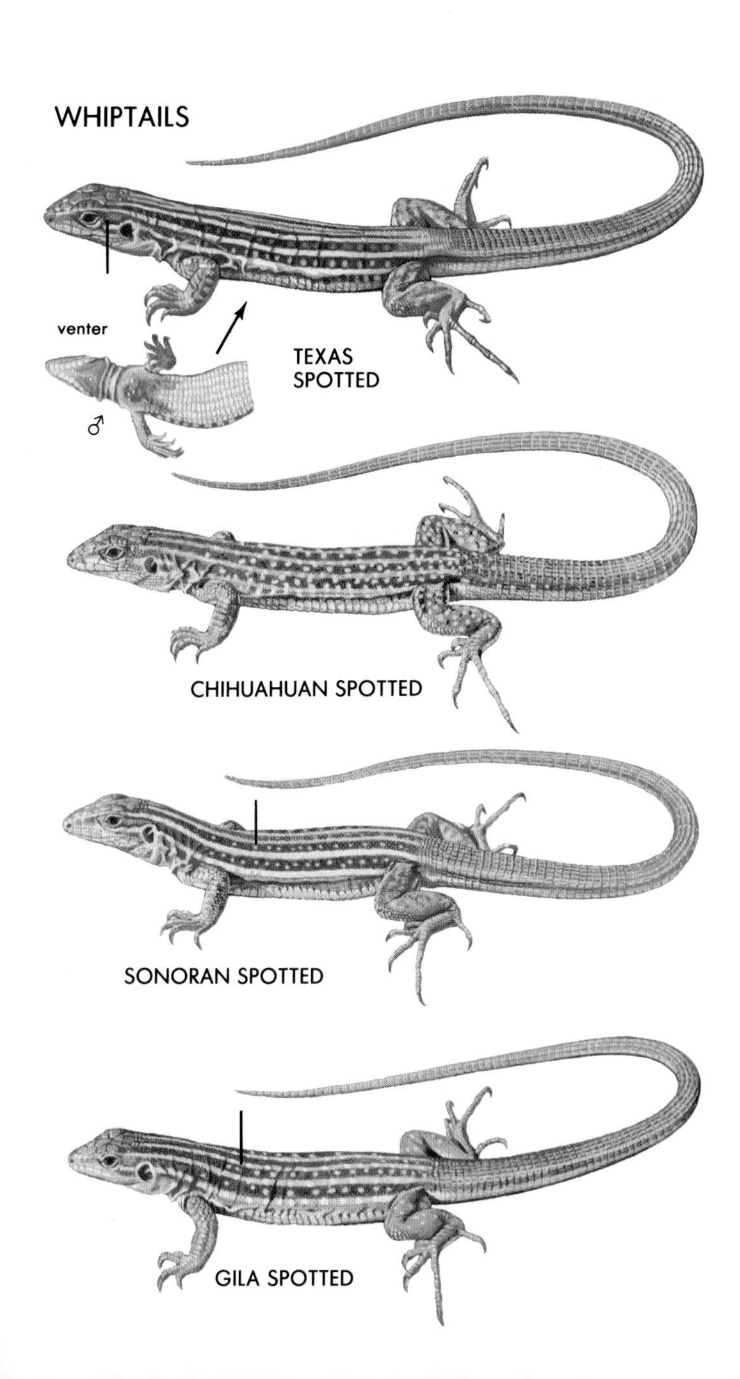
WHIPTAILS
venter
♂
TEXAS
SPOTTED
CHIHUAHUAN SPOTTED
SONORAN SPOTTED
GILA SPOTTED

Plate 34

WHIPTAILS *(Cnemidophorus)* × 3/5

(See also Pls. 31–33.)

Scales granular above, large and squarish below.

CANYON SPOTTED, *C. burti* p. 153
Reddish color on head and neck, sometimes over entire back. Map 118

Red-backed Whiptail, *C. b. xanthonotus.* Reddish color on back stops abruptly on sides. (Pima Co., Ariz.) Map 118 p. 153

Giant Spotted Whiptail, *C. b. stictogrammus.* Adults with large spots; striping faint or absent. Map 118 p. 153

ORANGE-THROATED, *C. hyperythrus* p. 152
Frontoparietal single (divided in other species, as shown in Fig. 21, opp. Pl. 31). Throat and sometimes chest and remaining underparts orange in breeding male. Map 111

LEGLESS LIZARDS *(Anniella)* × 2/3

CALIFORNIA, *A. pulchra* p. 168
Legless. Eyelids movable. Skin appears polished (unless shedding). Black form in coastal areas. Map 122

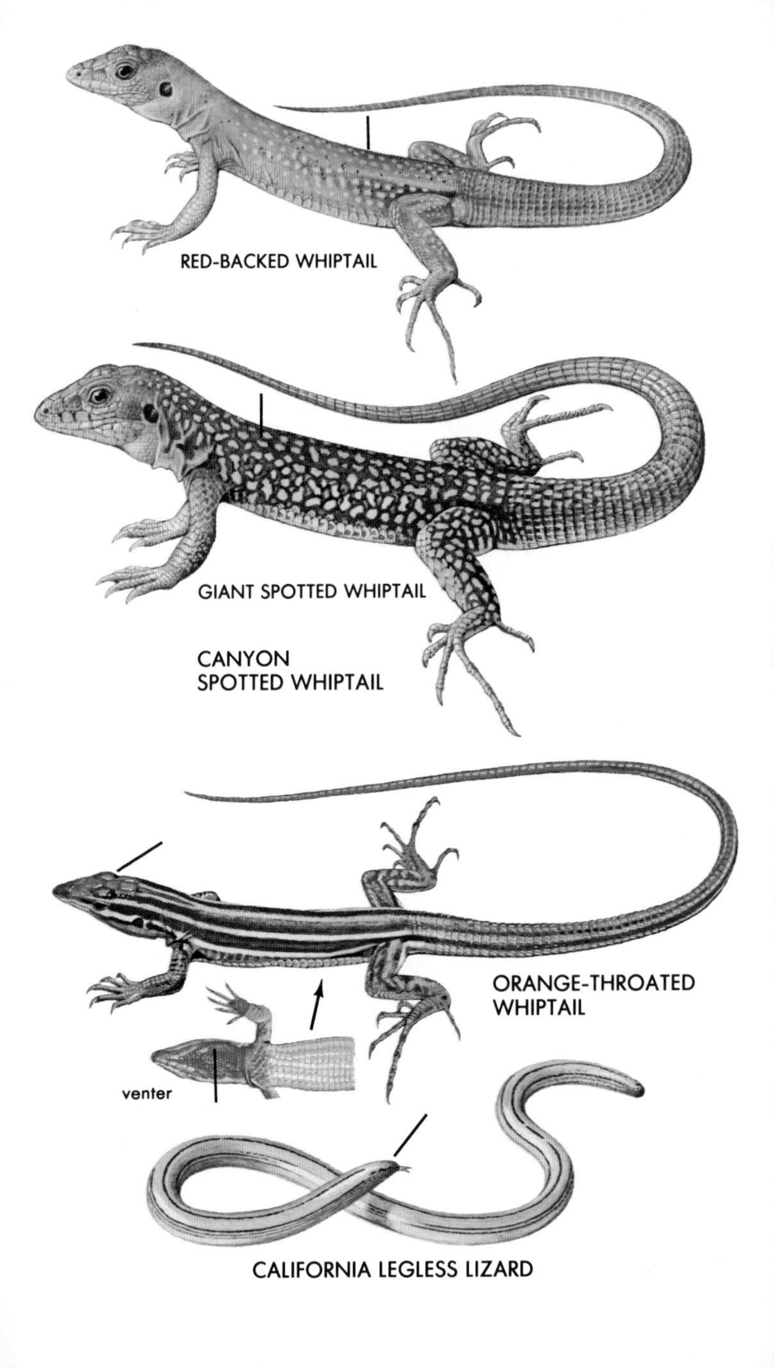
RED-BACKED WHIPTAIL
GIANT SPOTTED WHIPTAIL
CANYON
SPOTTED WHIPTAIL
ORANGE-THROATED
WHIPTAIL
venter
CALIFORNIA LEGLESS LIZARD

GECKOS

Pupils vertical (when contracted); scales mostly granular above.

BAREFOOT, *Coleonyx switaki* (× 1) p. 112
Eyes with lids. No toe pads. Small sooty spines on upper sides. Dark form (with regenerating tail) from region of dark rocks. (n. Baja Calif.) Map 70

WESTERN BANDED, *Coleonyx variegatus* (× 3/5) p. 110
Similar to Barefoot Gecko, but lacks spines on back; usually has 7 or more preanal pores which meet at ventral midline (see rear endpapers). (Upper individual is from Pisgah Crater area, San Bernardino Co., Calif.)
Map 69

LEAF-TOED, *Phyllodactylus xanti* (× 3/5) p. 112
No movable eyelids; a pair of large leaflike pads at the tip of each toe. Map 68

MEDITERRANEAN, *Hemidactylus turcicus* (× 1) p. 113
No movable eyelids; back with tubercles. Toe pads present, but different in structure from those of Leaf-toed Gecko. Introduced. (Chandler, Maricopa Co., Ariz.)
Map 70

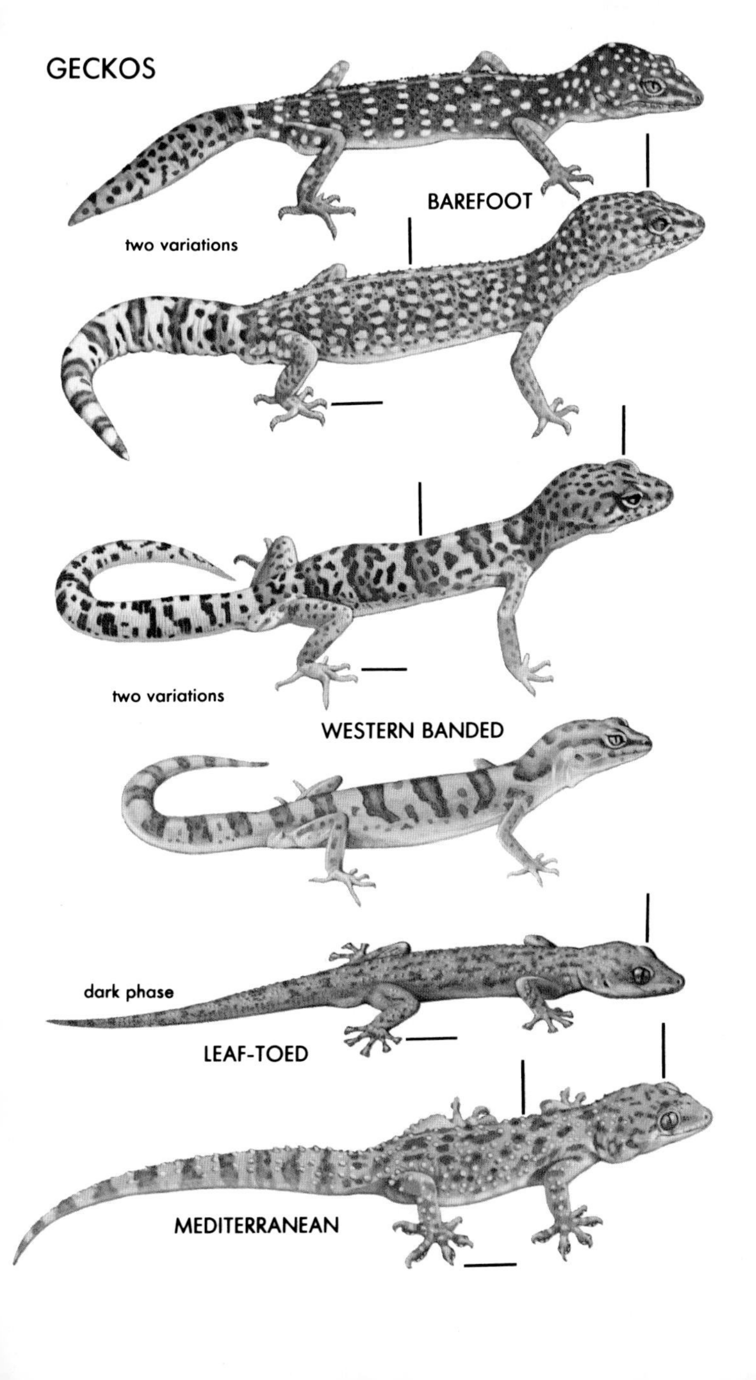
GECKOS
BAREFOOT
two variations
two variations
WESTERN BANDED
dark phase
LEAF-TOED
MEDITERRANEAN

BLIND SNAKES, BOAS, AND RACERS × $^3/_5$

Smooth scales.

WESTERN BLIND SNAKE, *Leptotyphlops humilis* p. 171
Vestigial eyes; body covered with cycloid scales; 1 scale between oculars (Fig. 22). (San Diego Co., Calif.) Map 123

TEXAS BLIND SNAKE, *Leptotyphlops dulcis* p. 172
Similar to Western Blind Snake, but usually 3 scales between oculars (Fig. 22). Map 125

RUBBER BOA, *Charina bottae* p. 173
Vertical pupils; large plates on top of head; plain olive to brown above. (Contra Costa Co., Calif.) Map 127

ROSY BOA, *Lichanura trivirgata* p. 173
Vertical pupils; broad lengthwise stripes or variegated pattern; small scales on top of head. (San Diego Co., Calif.) Map 126

RACER, *Coluber constrictor* p. 180
Plain olive or brown above. Young blotched. (Contra Costa Co., Calif.) Map 136

CALIFORNIA WHIPSNAKE, *Masticophis lateralis* p. 182
A single cream, yellow, or orange stripe on each side; underside of tail pink. (Contra Costa Co., Calif.) Map 132

SONORAN WHIPSNAKE, *Masticophis bilineatus* p. 183
Two or 3 light-colored stripes on each side; yellow on underside of tail. (Cochise Co., Ariz.) Map 135

STRIPED WHIPSNAKE, *Masticophis taeniatus* p. 183
Cream or white stripe on side bisected by a continuous or dashed black line. (Inyo Co., Calif.) Map 134

COACHWHIP, *Masticophis flagellum* p. 181
No stripes running length of body; general coloration often reddish, pink, or tan. Dorsal scales in 17 rows at midbody. (Santa Cruz Co., Calif.) Map 133

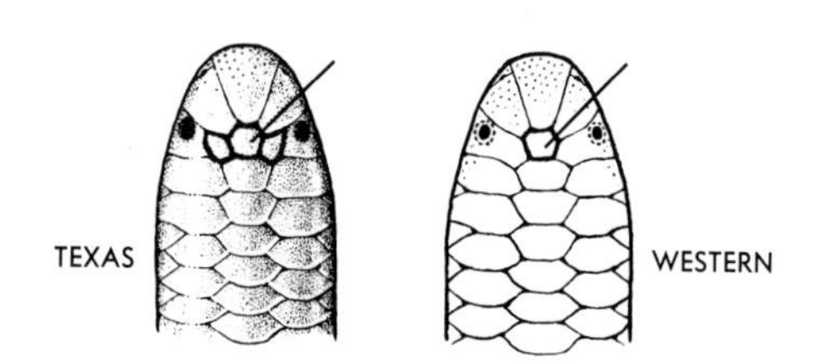

Fig. 22. Head scales of blind snakes

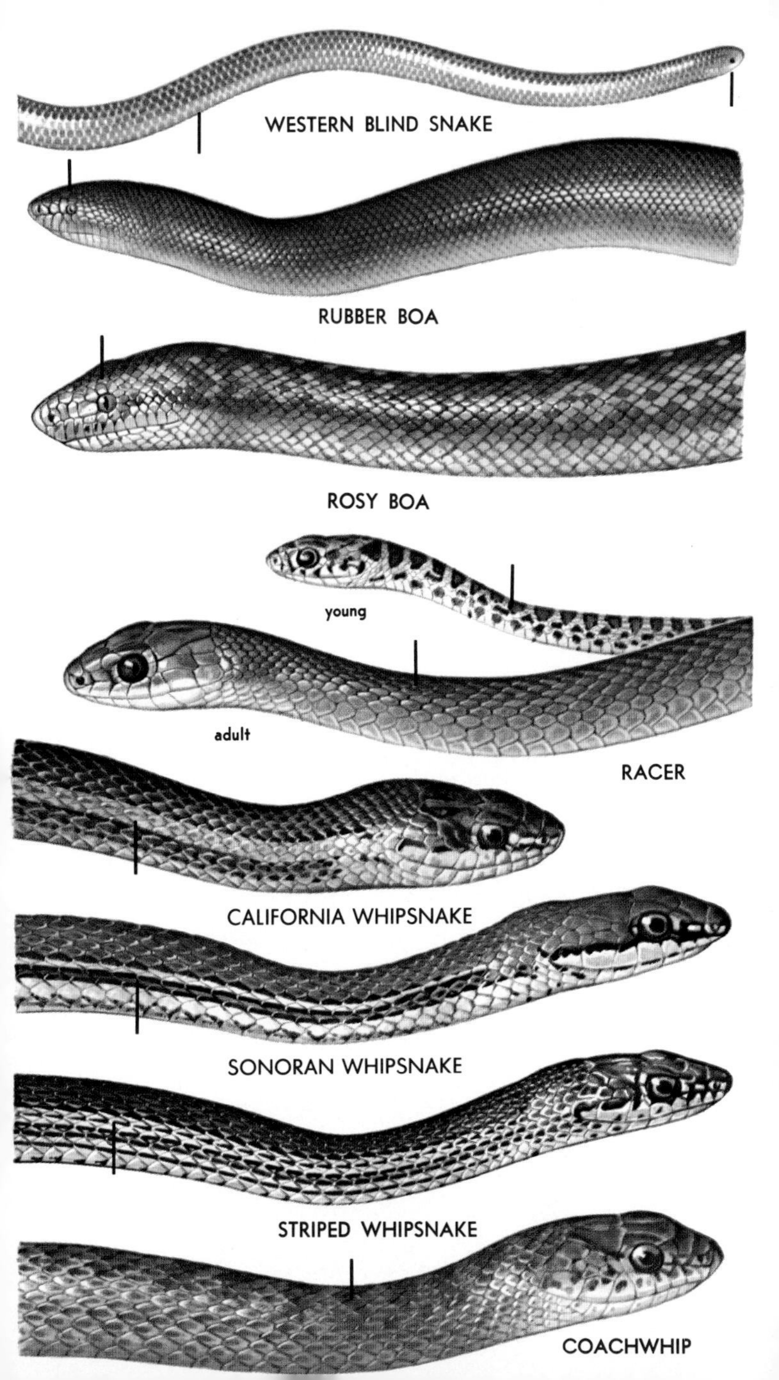
WESTERN BLIND SNAKE
RUBBER BOA
ROSY BOA
young
adult
RACER
CALIFORNIA WHIPSNAKE
SONORAN WHIPSNAKE
STRIPED WHIPSNAKE
COACHWHIP

CORAL AND LONG-NOSED SNAKES × 1/2

Smooth scales.

WESTERN CORAL SNAKE, *Micruroides euryxanthus* p. 222

Venomous. Red bands bordered by yellow or white (not by black, as in kingsnakes). (Santa Cruz Co., Ariz.) Map 176

LONG-NOSED SNAKE, *Rhinocheilus lecontei* p. 195

White spots on sides in black bands. (San Joaquin Co., Calif.) Map 150

KINGSNAKES *(Lampropeltis)* × 1/2

Smooth scales; usually a banded pattern.

SONORAN MOUNTAIN KINGSNAKE, *L. pyromelana* p. 193

Red bands bordered by black; white rings usually not widened below. Snout whitish or flecked with white. (Ariz.) Map 149

CALIFORNIA MOUNTAIN KINGSNAKE, *L. zonata* p. 192

Red bands and white rings as in Sonoran Mountain Kingsnake. Snout usually black, with or without red markings. (Santa Cruz Co., Calif.) Map 146

MILK SNAKE, *L. triangulum* p. 194

White bands widen below. Map 147

COMMON KINGSNAKE, *L. getulus* p. 191

Broad dark and light banding, or flecked with white or cream on a dark background (Fig. 23). (Contra Costa Co., Calif.) Map 148

BLACK-HEADED AND RINGNECK SNAKES × 1/2

CALIFORNIA BLACK-HEADED SNAKE, *Tantilla planiceps* p. 217

Blackish head; white neck ring; belly orange or reddish along midline. (Contra Costa Co., Calif.) Map 172

RINGNECK SNAKE, *Diadophis punctatus* p. 174

Entire belly yellow to orange red; orange neck ring, occasionally absent. Map 128

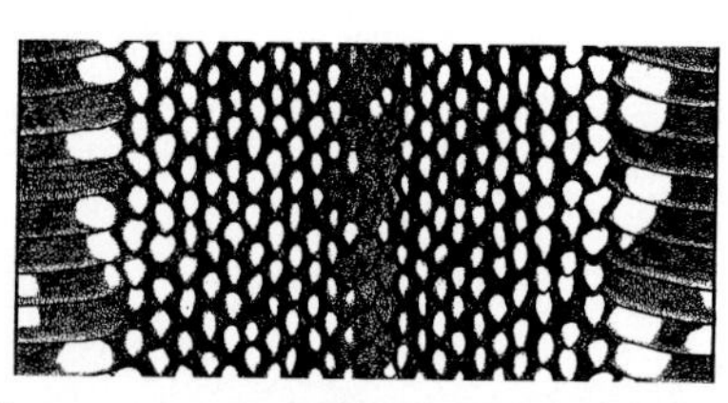

Fig. 23. Pattern of spotted subspecies of Common Kingsnake

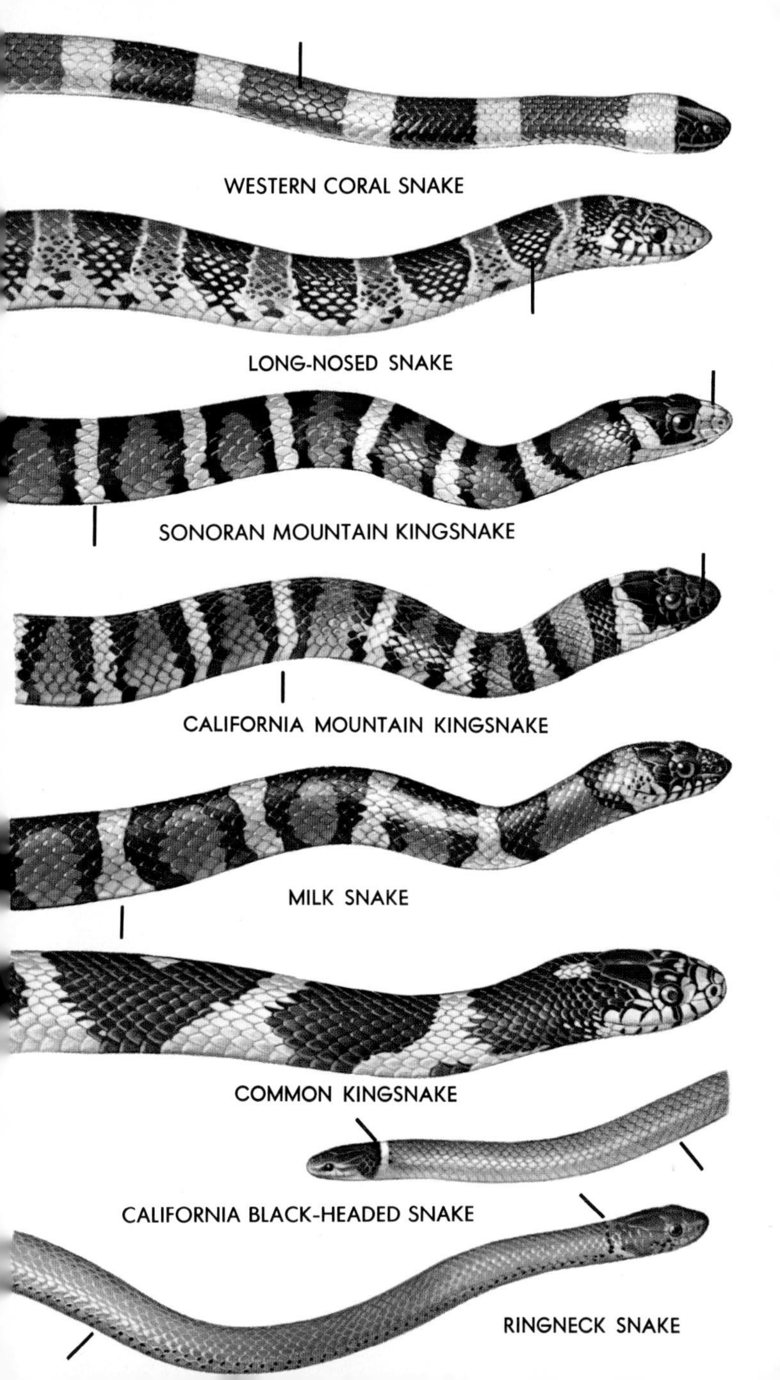
WESTERN CORAL SNAKE
LONG-NOSED SNAKE
SONORAN MOUNTAIN KINGSNAKE
CALIFORNIA MOUNTAIN KINGSNAKE
MILK SNAKE
COMMON KINGSNAKE
CALIFORNIA BLACK-HEADED SNAKE
RINGNECK SNAKE

Plate 38

SHOVEL-NOSED AND GROUND SNAKES × $1\frac{1}{4}$

Dorsal scales smooth; anal divided.

WESTERN SHOVEL-NOSED SNAKE, *Chionactis occipitalis* p. 213
Snout flat or only slightly convex; usually 21 or more black body bands. Map 167

SONORAN SHOVEL-NOSED SNAKE, *Chionactis palarostris* p. 214
Snout convex; usually fewer than 21 black body bands. Map 166

BANDED SAND SNAKE, *Chilomeniscus cinctus* p. 214
Rostral separates internasals. Map 168

GROUND SNAKE, *Sonora semiannulata* p. 212
Dark blotch at base of scales; back with stripe, dark crossbands, or plain. Map 165

RAT SNAKES *(Elaphe)* × $\frac{3}{5}$

Dorsal scales weakly keeled, in 25 or more rows; anal divided.

CORN SNAKE, *E. guttata* p. 186
Spear point between eyes. (Travis Co., Tex.) Map 143

TRANS-PECOS RAT SNAKE, *E. subocularis* p. 187
H-shaped markings on back; large eyes. (Young individual, Brewster Co., Tex.) Map 145

GREEN RAT SNAKE, *E. triaspis* p. 186
Plain green or olive above. (Cochise Co., Ariz.) Map 144

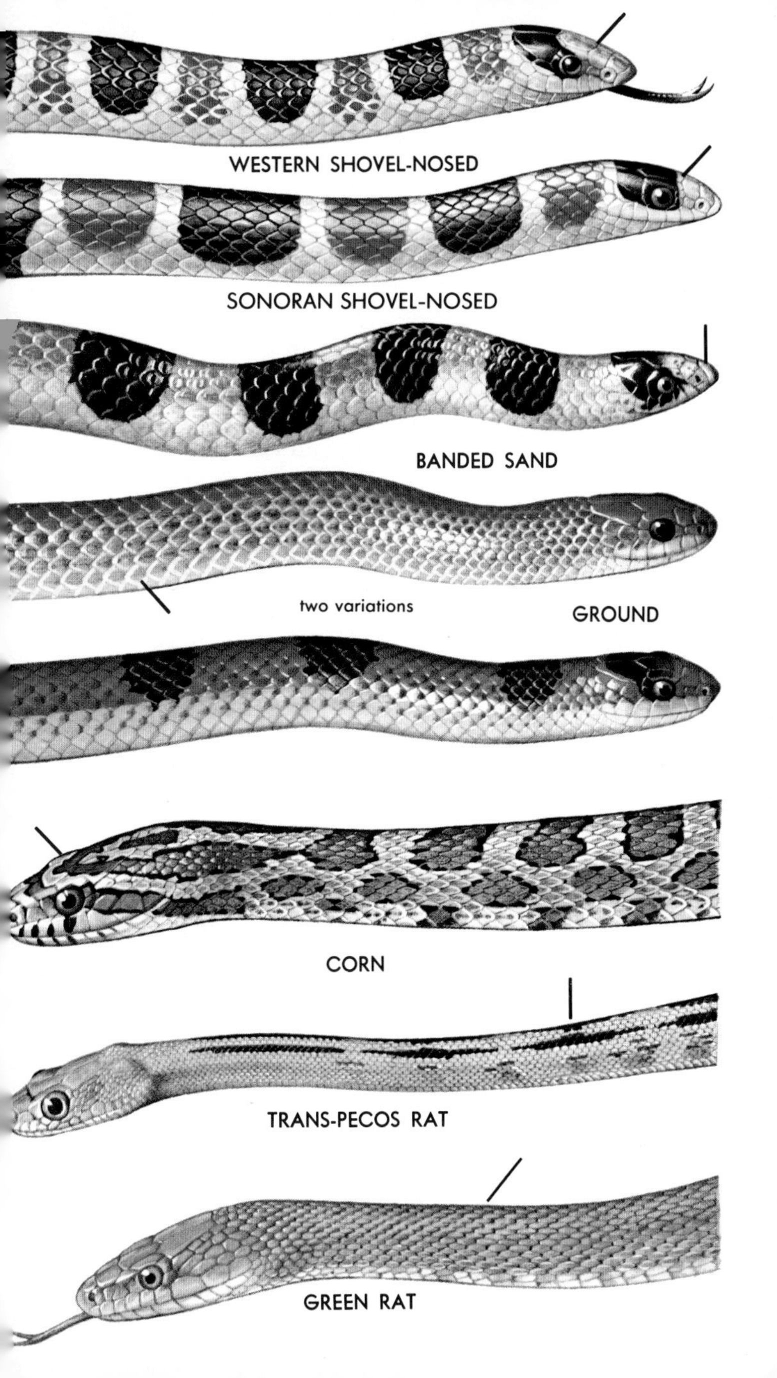
WESTERN SHOVEL-NOSED
SONORAN SHOVEL-NOSED
BANDED SAND
two variations
GROUND
CORN
TRANS-PECOS RAT
GREEN RAT

Plate 39

GOPHER, GLOSSY, SHARP-TAILED, GREEN, LYRE, AND NIGHT SNAKES × $^2/_3$

GOPHER SNAKE, *Pituophis melanoleucus* p. 189
Usually 4 prefrontals; dorsal scales keeled. (Contra Costa Co., Calif.) Map 141

GLOSSY SNAKE, *Arizona elegans* p. 187
Faded coloration; scales smooth and glossy. (San Joaquin Co., Calif.) Map 142

SHARP-TAILED SNAKE, *Contia tenuis* p. 176
Belly marked with regular black crossbars on pale gray ground color; tail ends in small sharp spine. (Contra Costa Co., Calif.) Map 129

SMOOTH GREEN SNAKE, *Opheodrys vernalis* p. 179
Plain green above; dorsal scales smooth. Map 137

ROUGH GREEN SNAKE, *Opheodrys aestivus*
Plain green above; dorsal scales keeled, in 17 or fewer rows. (Harris Co., Tex.) A single record for ne. N.M. now in doubt, but records for w. Tex. suggest it may eventually be found in N.M. Not described in text.

LYRE SNAKE, *Trimorphodon biscutatus* p. 221
Head broad and triangular, with a lyre-shaped marking (sometimes obscure or absent). Pupils vertical.
Map 177

NIGHT SNAKE, *Hypsiglena torquata* p. 221
Usually has large dark blotches on neck and spotted pattern on back. Pupils vertical. (Contra Costa Co., Calif.)
Map 175

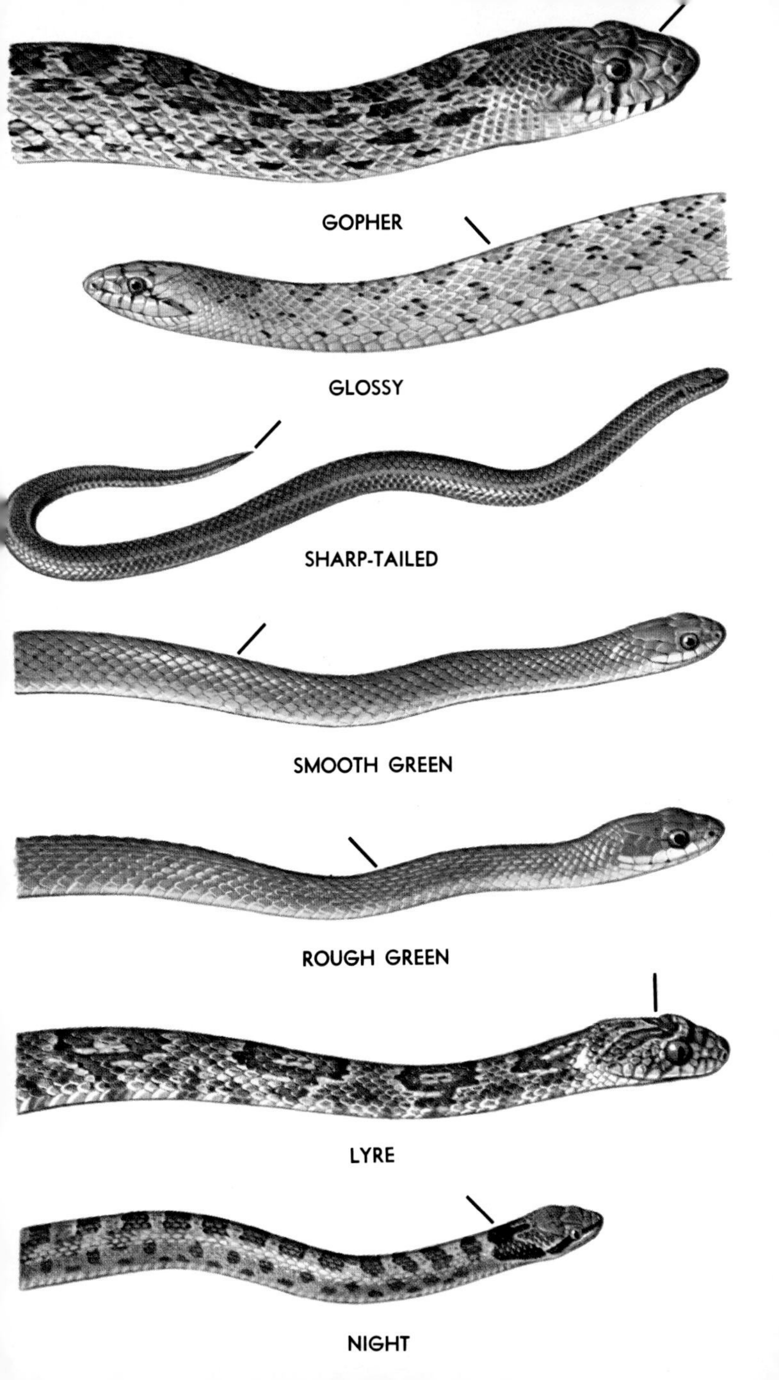

GOPHER
GLOSSY
SHARP-TAILED
SMOOTH GREEN
ROUGH GREEN
LYRE
NIGHT

HOGNOSE, LEAF-NOSED, PATCH-NOSED, HOOK-NOSED, AND VINE SNAKES × 1

All have modified rostrals.

WESTERN HOGNOSE SNAKE, *Heterodon nasicus* p. 176
Rostral keeled above and turned upward. Map 124

SPOTTED LEAF-NOSED SNAKE, p. 177
Phyllorhynchus decurtatus (× $1\frac{1}{3}$)
Rostral patchlike, completely separating internasals; spotted pattern; vertical pupils. Map 131

SADDLED LEAF-NOSED SNAKE, p. 178
Phyllorhynchus browni (× $1\frac{1}{3}$)
Rostral and pupils as in Spotted Leaf-nosed Snake, but pattern of large dark brown saddles. (Pima Co., Ariz.) Map 130

GRAHAM (MOUNTAIN) PATCH-NOSED SNAKE, p. 185
Salvadora grahamiae
Rostral patchlike but not completely separating internasals; broad, pale dorsal stripe bordered on each side by dark stripe (Fig. 24). Map 140

WESTERN PATCH-NOSED SNAKE, p. 184
Salvadora hexalepis
Similar to Graham Patch-nosed Snake, but dorsal stripe bordered on each side by several dark stripes (Fig. 24). Map 138

CHIHUAHUAN HOOK-NOSED SNAKE, p. 215
Gyalopion canum
Rostral upturned but flat or convex above and completely separating internasals; brown crossbands. (Grant Co., N.M.) Map 169

THORNSCRUB HOOK-NOSED SNAKE, p. 216
Gyalopion quadrangularis
Rostral as in Chihuahuan Hook-nosed Snake; pattern of black saddles setting off pale squarish areas on back. (Santa Cruz Co., Ariz.) Map 170

BROWN VINE SNAKE, *Oxybelis aeneus* p. 220
Extremely slender, vinelike; snout greatly elongated. Map 139

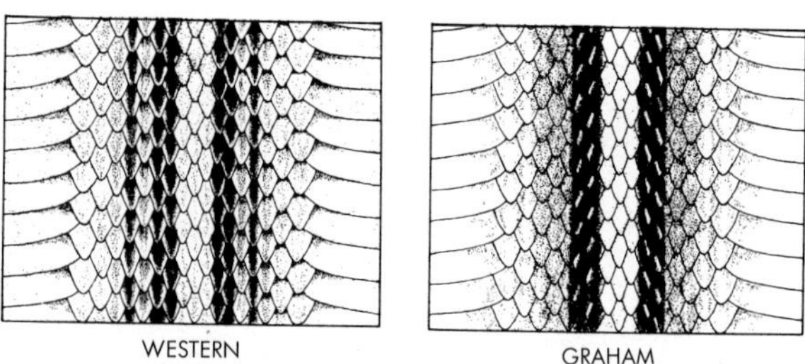

Fig. 24. Patterns of patch-nosed snakes

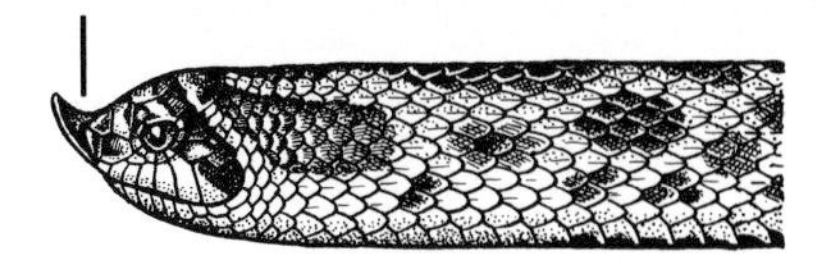

WESTERN HOGNOSE

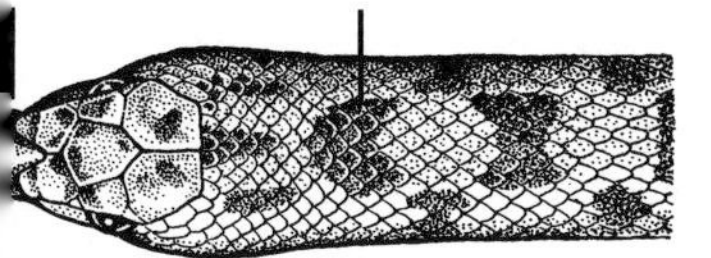
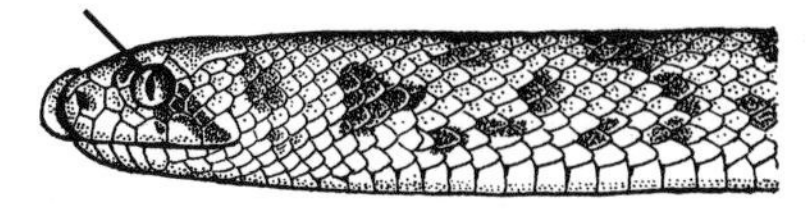

SPOTTED LEAF-NOSED

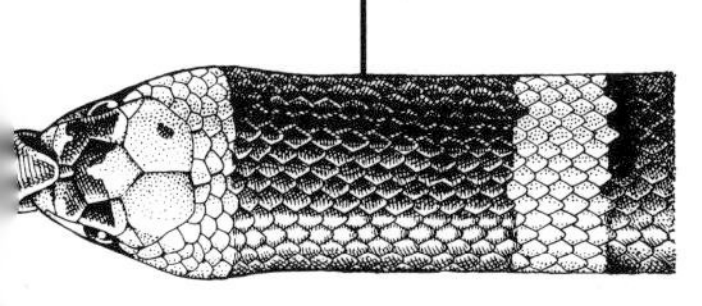
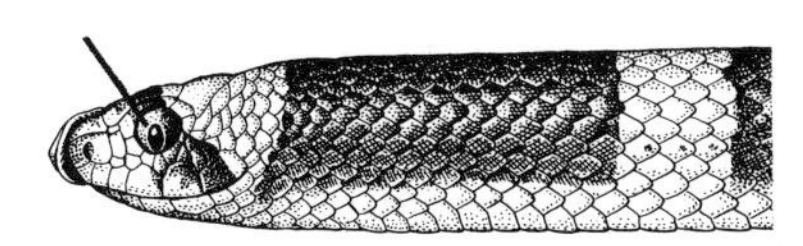

SADDLED LEAF-NOSED

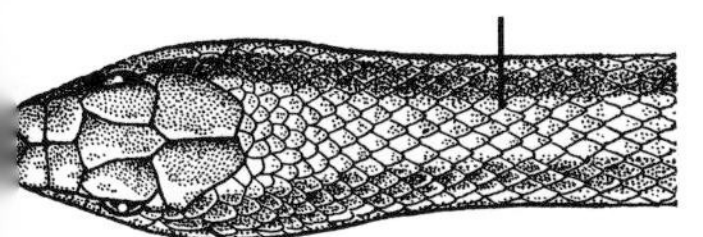
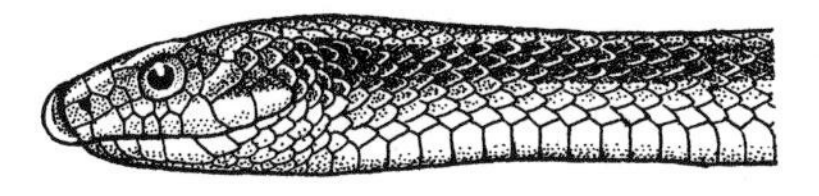

GRAHAM PATCH-NOSED

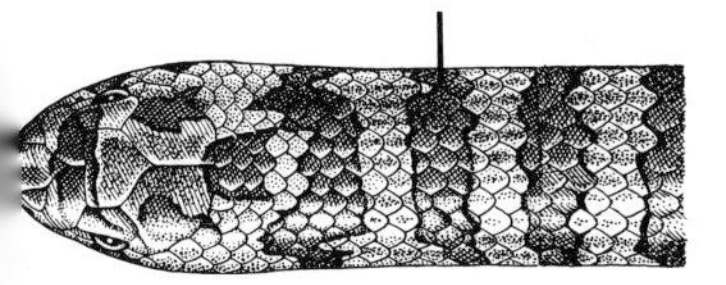
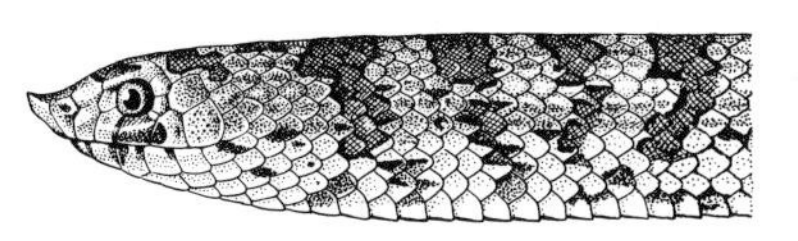

CHIHUAHUAN HOOK-NOSED

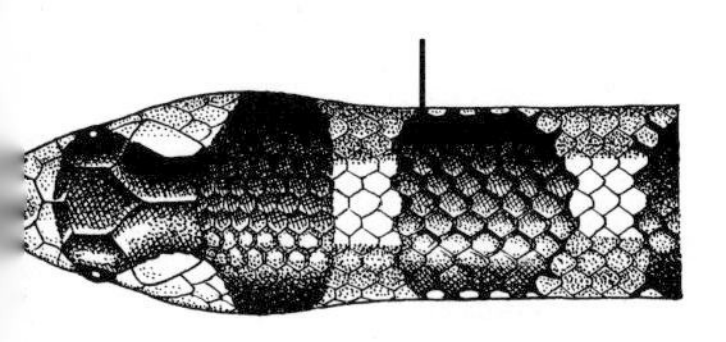
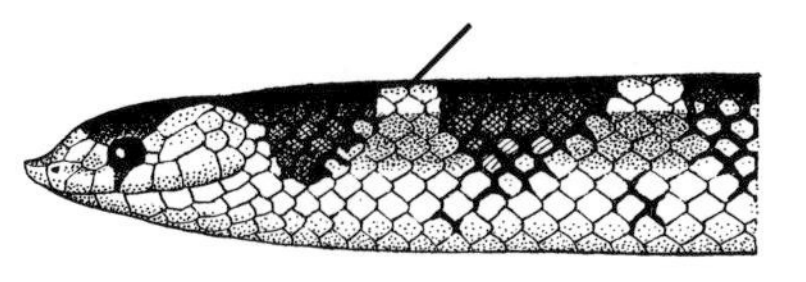

THORNSCRUB HOOK-NOSED

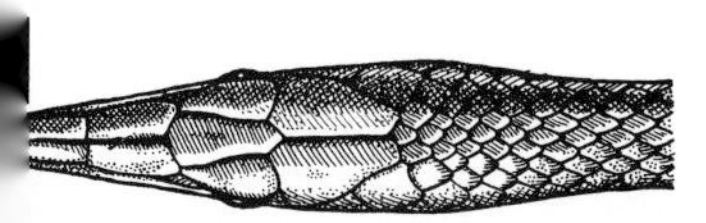
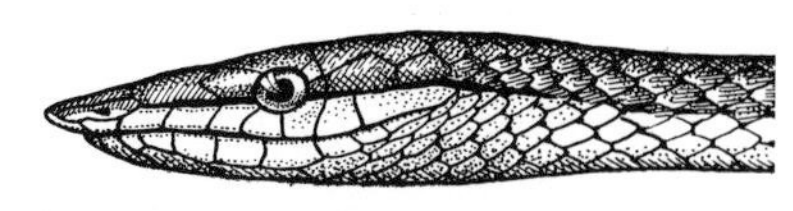

BROWN VINE

Plate 41

BLACK-HEADED SNAKES *(Tantilla)* × 2

Small snakes, usually under 16 in. (40 cm). Dark cap on head; back plain brown. Rely mainly on geographic distribution to identify them (see Fig. 30, p. 217, for species differences in hemipenes).

CALIFORNIA BLACK-HEADED SNAKE, *T. planiceps* p. 217
Black cap with a rounded or straight border at rear; cap usually extends 2–3 scale rows behind parietal and downward ½–2 scales below corner of mouth. A light collar marking; usually a faint dark middorsal line.
Map 172

SOUTHWESTERN BLACK-HEADED SNAKE, *T. hobartsmithi* p. 218
Resembles California Black-headed Snake, but black cap usually does not extend below corner of mouth.
Map 172

PLAINS BLACK-HEADED SNAKE, *T. nigriceps* p. 219
Cap often pointed at rear; usually extends 2–5 scale rows behind parietals. Usually no light collar marking.
Map 173

YAQUI BLACK-HEADED SNAKE, *T. yaquia* p. 220
Cream-colored spot on side of head; neck band usually prominent. Map 174

CHIHUAHUAN BLACK-HEADED SNAKE, *T. wilcoxi* p. 219
Broad, white neck band crosses tips of parietals; cap extends to or below corner of mouth (Cochise Co., Ariz.)
Map 171

LINED AND RED-BELLIED SNAKES × 1¼

LINED SNAKE, *Tropidoclonion lineatum* p. 212
Five or 6 upper labials; usually 2 rows of black spots on belly. Map 163

RED-BELLIED SNAKE, *Storeria occipitomaculata* p. 198
Blackish head; dorsal stripe; dorsal scales in 15 rows. In our area, found in Black Hills of ne. Wyo. Map 153

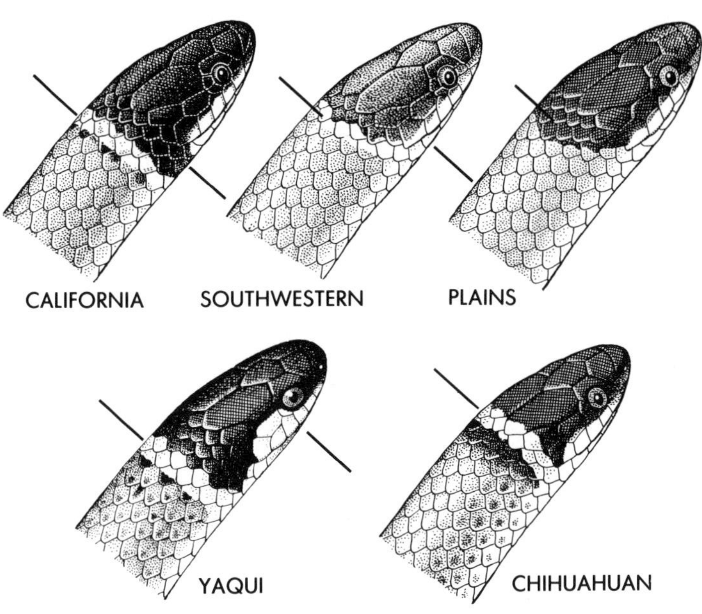

BLACK-HEADED SNAKES

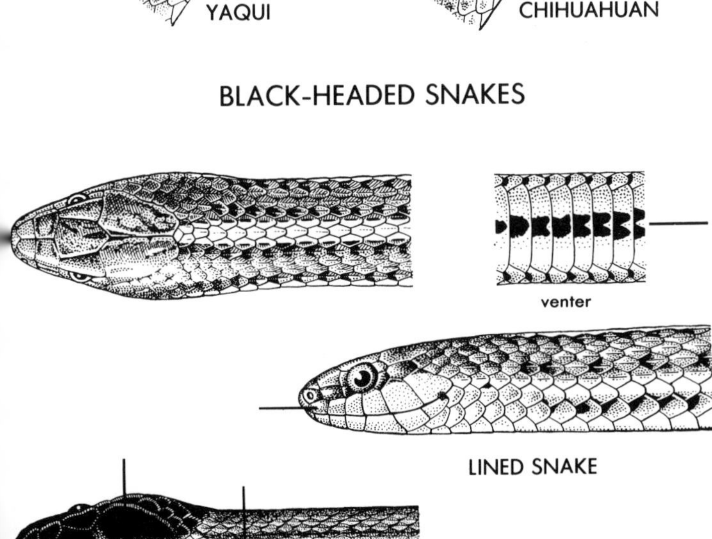

Plate 42

GARTER SNAKES *(Thamnophis)* × $^{2}/_{3}$

(See also Pl. 43).

Keeled scales with no apical pits (see rear endpapers); anal single.

MEXICAN GARTER SNAKE, *T. eques* p. 209
Paired black blotches on head; side stripe on 3rd and 4th scale rows at front of body. 8 or 9 upper labials. (Mexico) Map 155

BLACK-NECKED GARTER SNAKE, *T. cyrtopsis* p. 208
Paired black blotches on head; side stripe on 2nd and 3rd scale rows. (Pima Co., Ariz.) Map 156

CHECKERED GARTER SNAKE, *T. marcianus* p. 210
Checkered pattern; side stripe usually confined to 3rd scale row. (Santa Cruz Co., Ariz.) Map 154

PLAINS GARTER SNAKE, *T. radix* p. 210
Side stripe on 3rd and 4th scale rows at front of body. Usually fewer than 8 upper labials. (Boulder Co., Colo.) Map 160

NORTHWESTERN GARTER SNAKE, *T. ordinoides* p. 208
Belly often flecked or suffused with red; usually 7 upper and 8 or 9 lower labials. (Benton Co., Ore.) Map 164

WESTERN RIBBON SNAKE, *T. proximus* p. 211
Pale, unmarked upper labials contrast with dark head color. Map 159

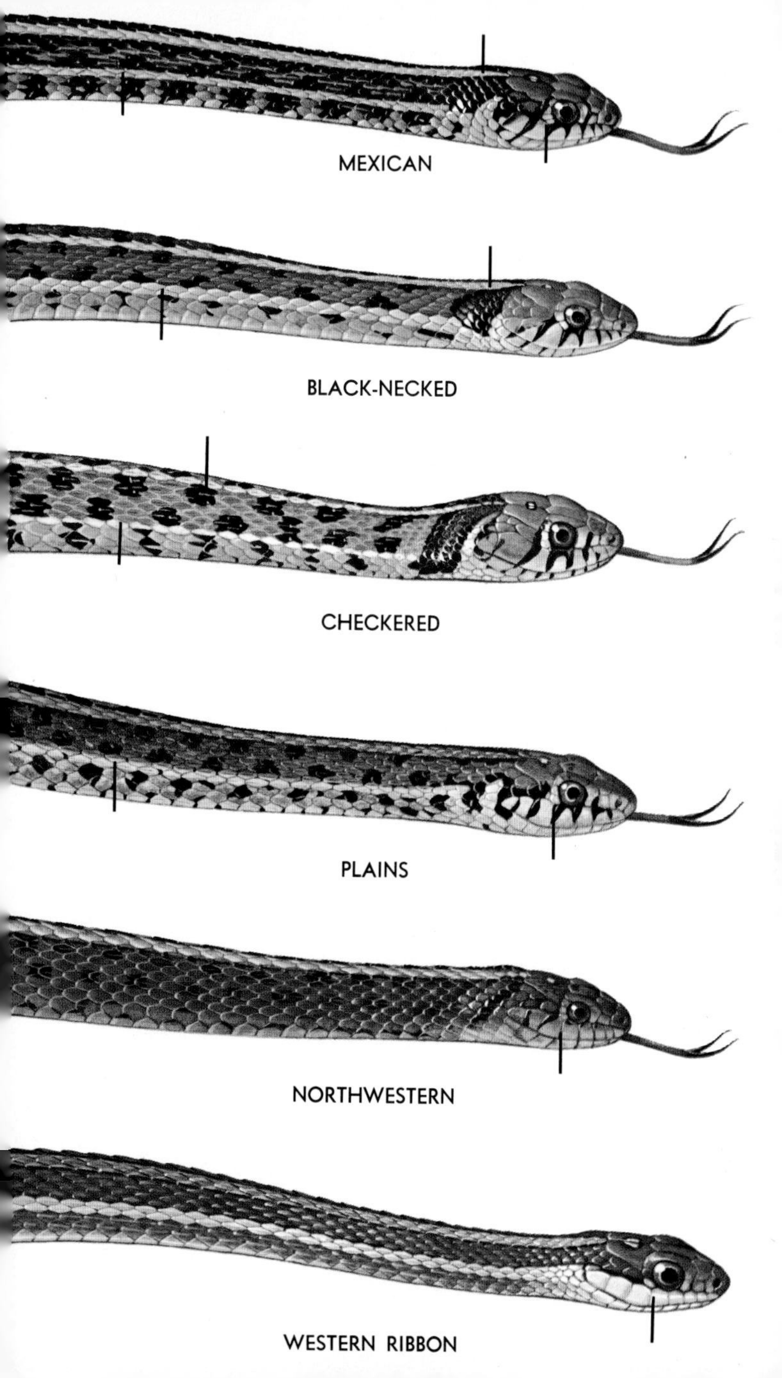
MEXICAN
BLACK-NECKED
CHECKERED
PLAINS
NORTHWESTERN
WESTERN RIBBON

Plate 43

GARTER SNAKES *(Thamnophis)* × ½

(See also Pl. 42.)

Keeled scales with no apical pits; anal single.

WESTERN AQUATIC, *T. couchii* p. 204
Usually 8 upper labials. Belly color varies but seldom bluish; great variation in dorsal pattern (Fig. 29, p. 205). Subspecies illustrated is **Santa Cruz Garter Snake,** *T. c. atratus.* Throat usually lemon yellow. (Santa Cruz Co., Calif.) Map 162

WESTERN TERRESTRIAL, *T. elegans* p. 201
Usually 8 upper labials. Belly color varies but seldom bluish; great variation in dorsal pattern (Fig. 28, p. 203). Subspecies illustrated is **Coast Garter Snake,** *T. e. terrestris.* Red flecks usually present on belly and sides, including lateral stripe. (Contra Costa Co., Calif.) Map 161

COMMON, *T. sirtalis* p. 199
Eyes relatively large. Usually 7 upper labials. Belly often bluish. Map 157

San Francisco Garter Snake, *T. s. tetrataenia.* Red on side usually forms continuous stripe; belly greenish blue. (San Mateo Co., Calif.) Map 157 p. 200

California Red-sided Garter Snake, *T. s. infernalis.* Red spots on sides; lateral stripe distinct. (San Francisco Bay area) Map 157 p. 201

NARROW-HEADED, *T. rufipunctatus* p. 199
Eyes set high on head. Olive or brown above, with spotted pattern. (Catron Co., N.M.) Map 158

WATER SNAKES *(Nerodia)* × ½

Keeled scales with apical pits (see rear endpapers); anal divided.

PLAIN-BELLIED, *N. erythrogaster* p. 196
Belly plain yellow, often tinged with orange and faintly spotted. (w. Tex.) Map 151

COMMON, *N. sipedon* p. 197
Crossbands on front part of body; black or reddish halfmoons on belly. (Kans.) Map 152

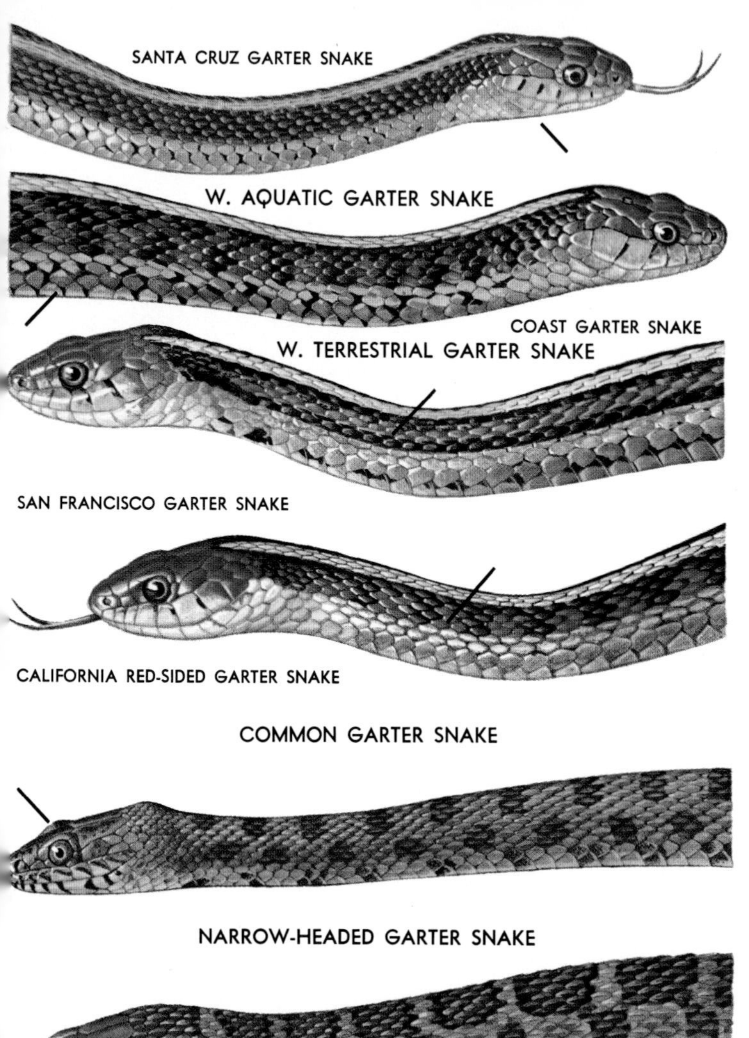
SANTA CRUZ GARTER SNAKE
W. AQUATIC GARTER SNAKE
COAST GARTER SNAKE
W. TERRESTRIAL GARTER SNAKE
SAN FRANCISCO GARTER SNAKE
CALIFORNIA RED-SIDED GARTER SNAKE
COMMON GARTER SNAKE
NARROW-HEADED GARTER SNAKE

PLAIN-BELLIED WATER SNAKE
COMMON WATER SNAKE

RATTLESNAKES *(Crotalus)* × 3/4

Venomous. Horny "button" or rattle on tail; keeled scales.

WESTERN RATTLESNAKE, *C. viridis* p. 231
Our only rattler with usually more than 2 internasals touching rostral (Fig. 25). (Contra Costa Co., Calif.) Size and shape of dorsal blotches vary. See Fig. 26 (below) for pattern of Prairie Rattlesnake, a subspecies. Map 184

MOJAVE RATTLESNAKE, *C. scutulatus* p. 232
Light scales of dorsal pattern usually unmarked; large scales on snout and between supraoculars (Fig. 25). (Santa Cruz Co., Ariz.) Map 189

WESTERN DIAMONDBACK RATTLESNAKE, *C. atrox* p. 226
Markings often indefinite and peppered with small dark spots; conspicuous black and white bands on tail. (Pima Co., Ariz.) Map 185

RED DIAMOND RATTLESNAKE, *C. ruber* p. 227
Often reddish or tan; tail as in Western Diamondback. 1st pair of lower labials usually divided transversely. (Riverside Co., Calif.) Map 187

SPECKLED RATTLESNAKE, *C. mitchellii* p. 228
Back often with salt-and-pepper speckling. Supraoculars pitted or creased (Panamint subspecies, Fig. 25), or prenasals separated from rostral by small scales (Southwestern subspecies, Fig. 25). (Riverside Co., Calif.) Map 188

SIDEWINDER, *C. cerastes* p. 229
Supraoculars hornlike. Crawls sideways. (Pima Co., Ariz.) Map 186

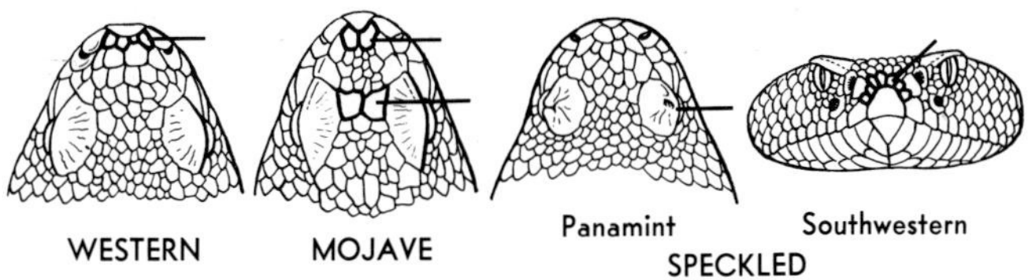

Fig. 25. Head scales of rattlesnakes

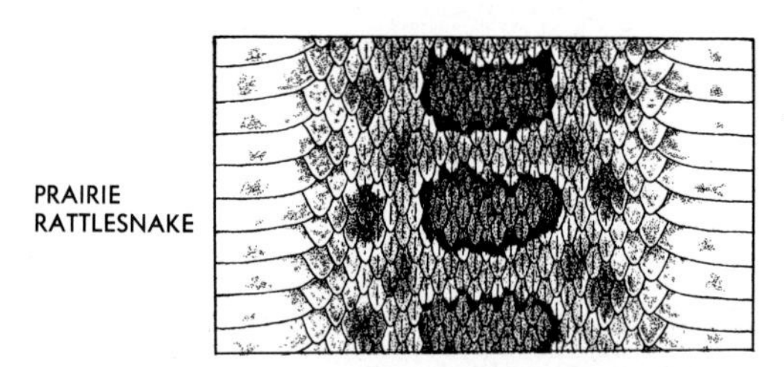

Fig. 26. Pattern of subspecies of Western Rattlesnake

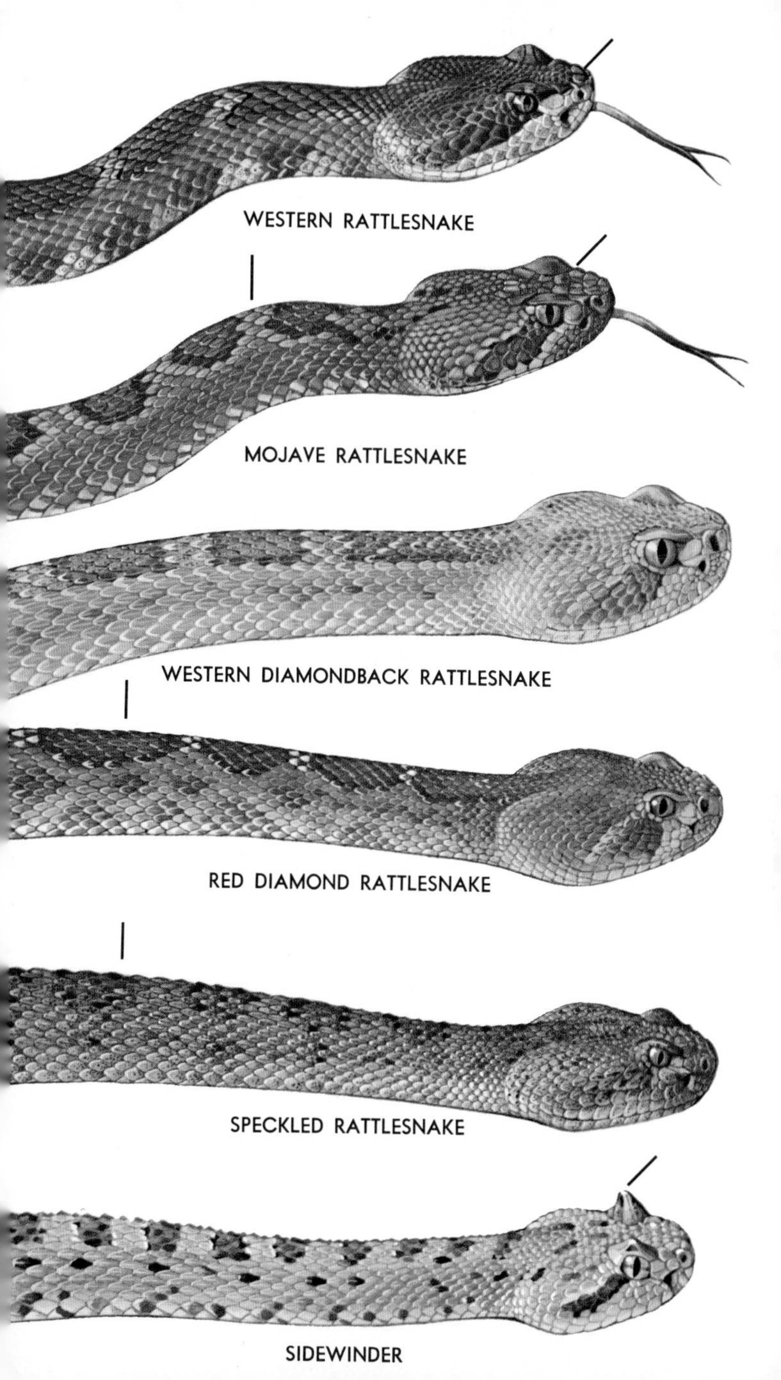
WESTERN RATTLESNAKE
MOJAVE RATTLESNAKE
WESTERN DIAMONDBACK RATTLESNAKE
RED DIAMOND RATTLESNAKE
SPECKLED RATTLESNAKE
SIDEWINDER

Plate 45

RATTLESNAKES *(Crotalus)* × $^2/_3$

Venomous. Horny "button" or rattle on tail; keeled scales.

TIGER RATTLESNAKE, *C. tigris* p. 230
Pattern of crossbands, often faint. Small head and relatively large rattle. (Pima Co., Ariz.) Map 181

ROCK RATTLESNAKE, *C. lepidus* p. 227
Pattern of distinct, widely spaced crossbands.
Map 182

BLACK-TAILED RATTLESNAKE, *C. molossus* p. 230
Tail, and often snout, black; light-colored scales interrupt dark markings on back. (Cochise Co., Ariz.)
Map 180

RIDGE-NOSED RATTLESNAKE, *C. willardi* p. 233
Ridge contours snout. Whitish crossbars on back edged with dusky. Map 183

TWIN-SPOTTED RATTLESNAKE, *C. pricei* p. 233
Two rows of brown spots on back. Map 179

MASSASAUGA, *Sistrurus catenatus* p. 225
Large plates on top of head; head markings extend onto neck. (Young individual, se. Colo.) Map 178

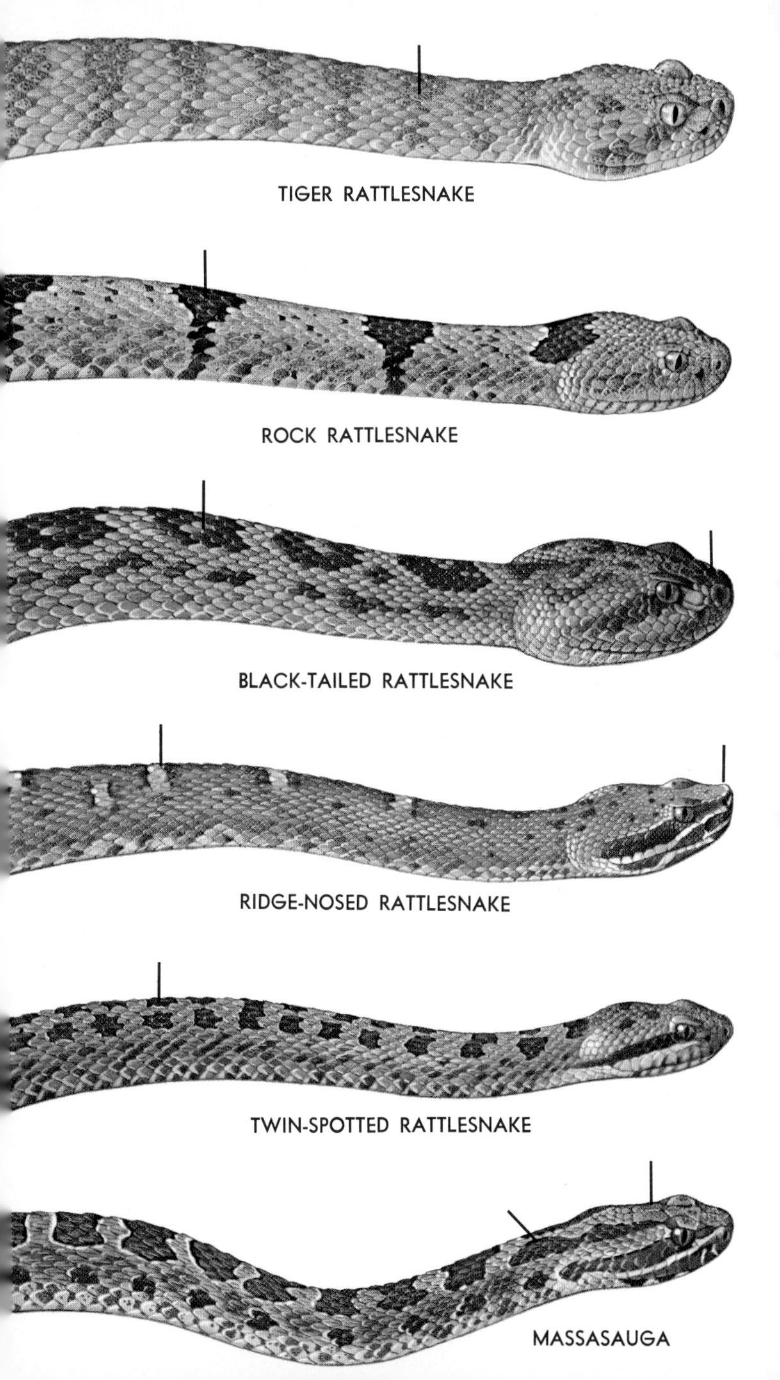
TIGER RATTLESNAKE
ROCK RATTLESNAKE
BLACK-TAILED RATTLESNAKE
RIDGE-NOSED RATTLESNAKE
TWIN-SPOTTED RATTLESNAKE
MASSASAUGA

Plate 46

BAJA CALIFORNIA "ENDEMICS"

BAJA CALIFORNIA ROCK LIZARD, *Petrosaurus thalassinus* (× 1/2) p. 239

Flattened body; collar marking and crossbands on body. Colorful in southern part of range. (San Bartolo) Map 192

HUNSAKER SPINY LIZARD, *Sceloporus hunsakeri* (× 2/3) p. 237

Dark coloration. Males with blue to blue-green belly and throat, and purple stripe evident on back in light phase. (San Bartolo) Map 84

CAPE SPINY LIZARD, *Sceloporus licki* (× 3/4) p. 237

Light stripe on upper side fades toward tail. Throat pale with diagonal gray streaks, the 2 at center usually parallel. (San Bartolo) Map 194

BAJA CALIFORNIA WHIPTAIL, *Cnemidophorus labialis* (× 1) p. 240

Dark fields on sides usually reddish brown to tan; 6–8 pale stripes. Middorsal stripe often forked at front, but single and usually squiggly toward rear. (Colonet) Map 194

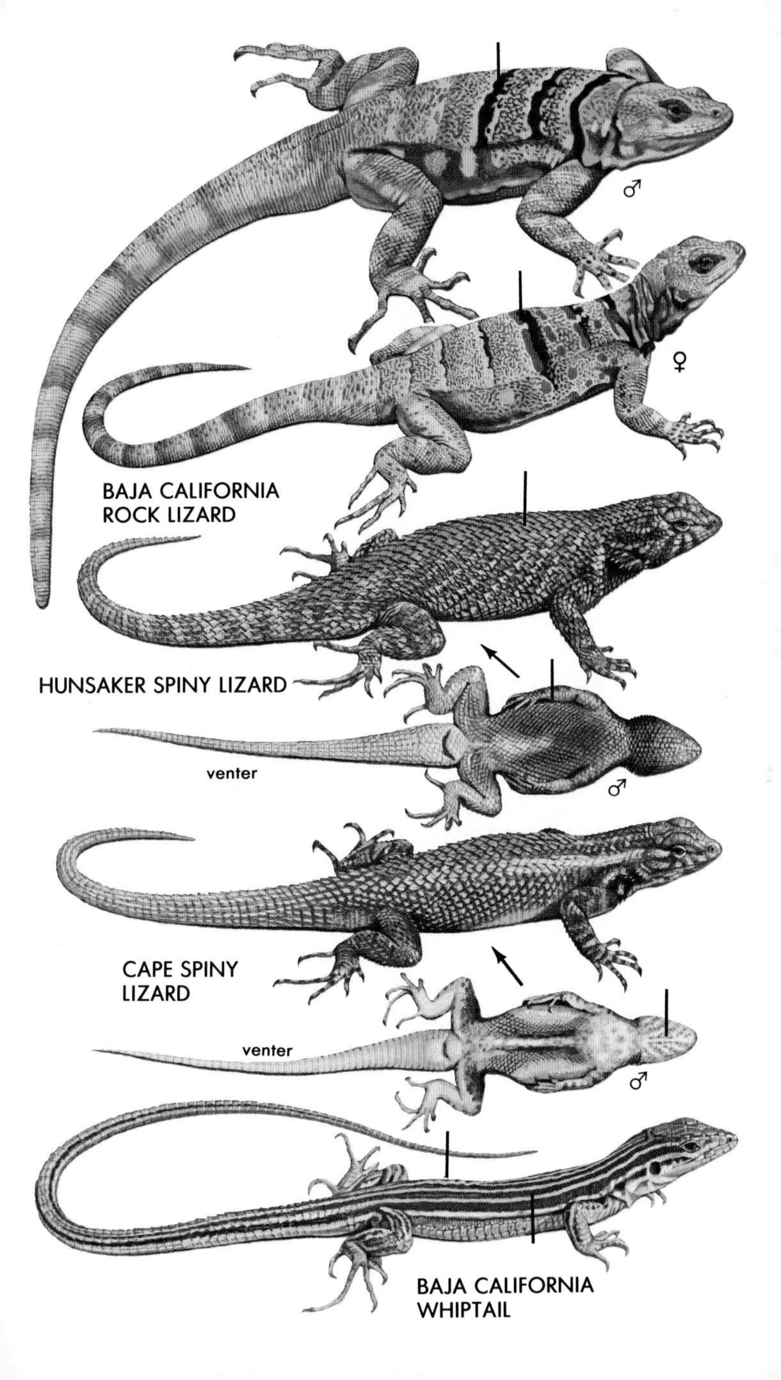
♂
♀
BAJA CALIFORNIA
ROCK LIZARD
HUNSAKER SPINY LIZARD
venter
♂
CAPE SPINY
LIZARD
venter
♂
BAJA CALIFORNIA
WHIPTAIL

Plate 47

BAJA CALIFORNIA "ENDEMICS"

SPINY-TAILED IGUANA, p. 236
Ctenosaura hemilopha (× ⅓)
Spiny tail. To over 10 in. (25 cm). (San Bartolo)
Map 191

BLACK-TAILED BRUSH LIZARD, p. 238
Urosaurus nigricaudus (× 1)
Sooty to blackish tail; broad area of enlarged keeled scales down center of back. (San Bartolo) Map 193

BAJA CALIFORNIA BRUSH LIZARD, p. 239
Urosaurus lahtelai (× 1)
Tail not darkened; strip of enlarged keeled scales down center of back; 1 frontal. (Catavina) Map 193

SAN LUCAN GECKO, p. 236
Phyllodactylus unctus (× 1)
Eyes without movable lids. A pair of leaflike scales at tip of each toe. Granular scales with intermixture of large tubercles. (Buena Vista) Map 190

BAJA CALIFORNIA LEGLESS LIZARD, p. 242
Anniella geronimensis (× 1)
Snakelike, with glossy, smooth scales, but eyelids movable. Black and whitish lines on sides. (Colonia Guerrero)
Map 195

MOLE LIZARD, *Bipes biporus* (× 1) p. 242
Molelike clawed forelimbs; no hind limbs. (La Paz)
Map 195

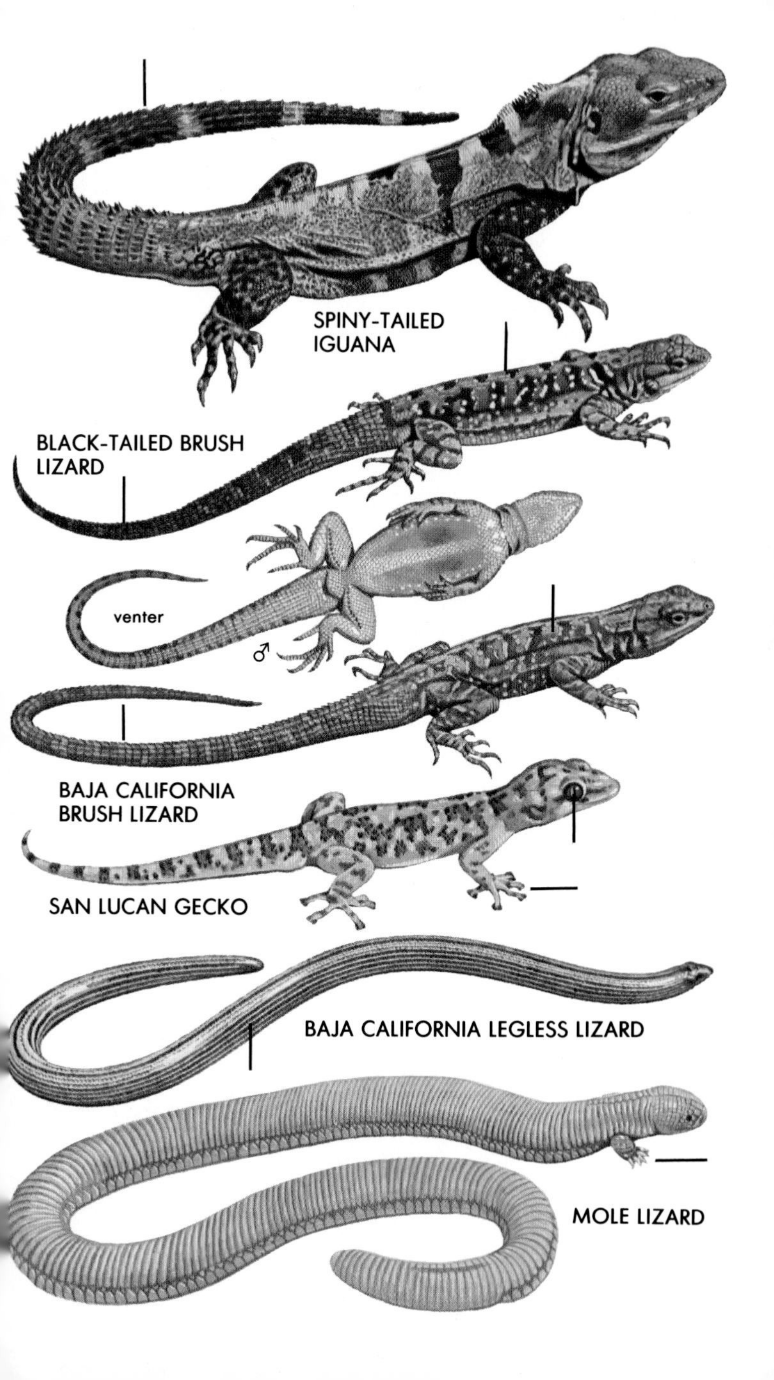
SPINY-TAILED
IGUANA
BLACK-TAILED BRUSH
LIZARD
venter
♂
BAJA CALIFORNIA
BRUSH LIZARD
SAN LUCAN GECKO
BAJA CALIFORNIA LEGLESS LIZARD
MOLE LIZARD

Plate 48

BAJA CALIFORNIA "ENDEMICS"

CAPE WHIPSNAKE, p. 243
Masticophis aurigulus (× 3/5)
Note series of dark dashes below light side stripe. Scales smooth. Map 132

BAJA CALIFORNIA RAT SNAKE, p. 244
Elaphe rosaliae (× 3/5)
Uniformly olive or reddish brown above, often with no dark markings. Scales smooth, in 33 or 34 rows. (Comondu) Map 198

PACIFIC WATER SNAKE, p. 244
Nerodia valida (× 3/5)
Eyes large, dark, set high on head. Scales keeled. Some individuals with stripes. (San Jose del Cabo) Map 199

TWO-STRIPED GARTER SNAKE, p. 207
Thamnophis hammondii (× 3/5)
Subspecies illustrated is Diguet Two-striped Garter Snake *(T. h. digueti),* which sometimes has vague stripes and is nearly uniform olive above. Scales keeled. (San Ignacio) Map 162

BANDLESS SAND SNAKE, p. 244
Chilomeniscus stramineus (× 1)
Lower jaw countersunk (inset). Brownish to yellowish above with dark brown spots near tips of dorsal scales. Scales smooth. (San Bartolo) Map 197

BAJA CALIFORNIA NIGHT SNAKE, p. 245
Eridiphas slevini (× 7/8)
Pupils vertical. Parietal scale touches lower preocular. Scales smooth. (near Mulege) Map 200

BAJA CALIFORNIA RATTLESNAKE, p. 246
Crotalus enyo (× 3/5)
Blotches on back often with black or dusky spot attached to lower border of blotch on each side, especially from midbody toward rear. No strongly contrasting light and dark rings on tail. (Guerrero Negro) Map 196

YELLOW-BELLIED SEA SNAKE, p. 224
Pelamis platurus (× 3/5)
Completely aquatic (marine). Eyes and nostrils set high on head.

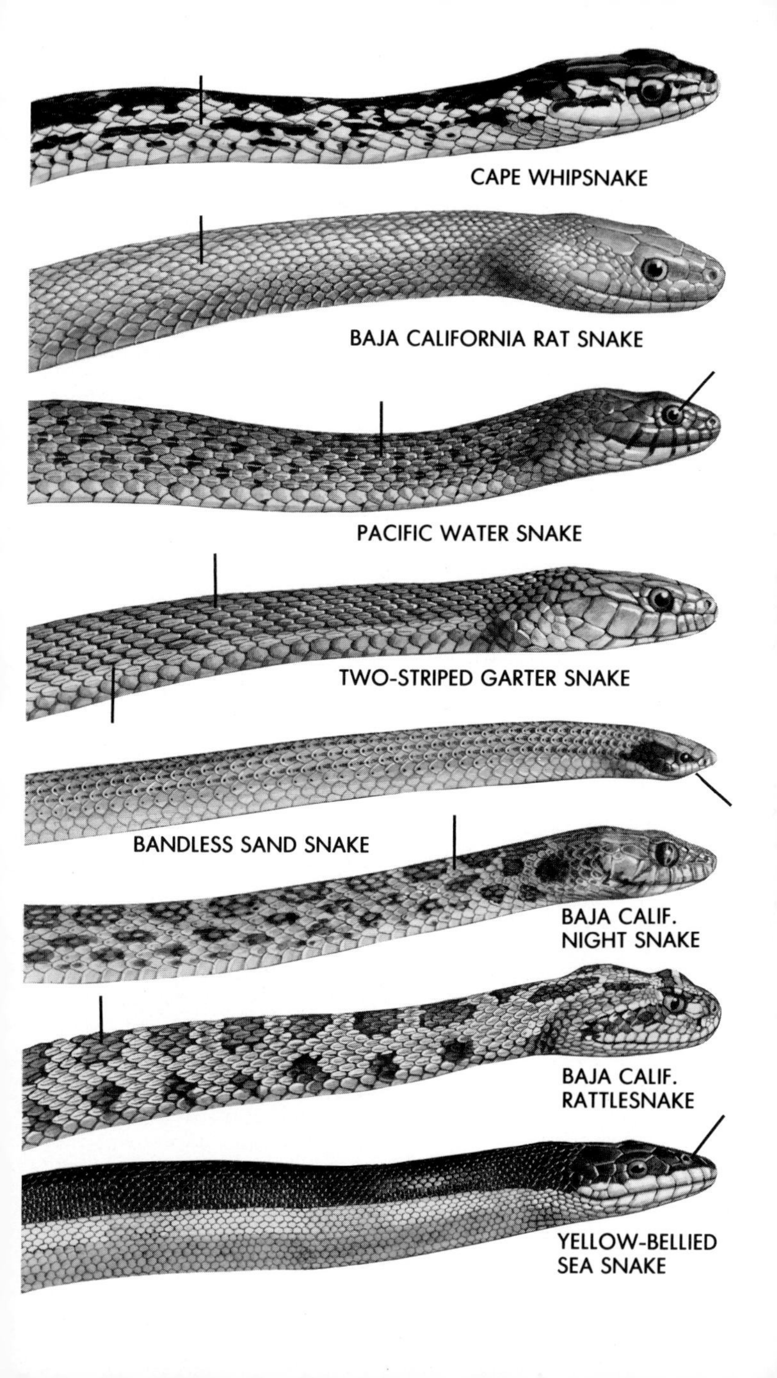

CAPE WHIPSNAKE
BAJA CALIFORNIA RAT SNAKE
PACIFIC WATER SNAKE
TWO-STRIPED GARTER SNAKE
BANDLESS SAND SNAKE
BAJA CALIF.
NIGHT SNAKE
BAJA CALIF.
RATTLESNAKE
YELLOW-BELLIED
SEA SNAKE

GILA SPOTTED WHIPTAIL Pl. 33

Cnemidophorus flagellicaudus

Identification: $2\frac{1}{2}$–$3\frac{3}{4}$ in. (6.2–9.9 cm). Similar to the Chihuahuan Spotted and Sonoran Spotted Whiptails, with which it was formerly confused. 6 stripes, upper ones tending to become gold or greenish yellow on neck. 3–6 dorsal granules between pair of middorsal stripes (paravertebrals). Traces of a middorsal stripe rarely present. Dark fields coffee brown to blackish, sometimes rust. *Yellowish to golden or light beige spots on back, present in both dark fields and touching or located within the pale stripes, especially the paravertebral stripes.* Tail light olive green, sometimes with bluish cast. Whitish to cream below, unmarked. 77–84 dorsal granules. 35–41 total femoral pores. *Usually 2 preanals,* the enlarged scales before vent (most whiptails have 3). All female. ***Young:*** Hatchlings lack spots.

Frequents piñon-juniper and oak woodlands, chaparral, streamside growth, and the upper edge of desert grassland.

Similar species: (1) Chihuahuan Spotted Whiptail (p. 157) lacks bright greenish yellow or gold color in stripes on neck; tail olive green, greenish brown, tan, or pinkish. May have bright yellow spots on rump. (2) See also Sonoran Spotted Whiptail (p. 158).

Range: From Cerbat and Hualapai Mts., Mohave Co., to Gila R. Basin on southern slope of Central Plateau of Ariz. and uplands of extreme sw. N.M. Isolated populations in the Catalina and Chiricahua Mts., Ariz. From 4000–6500 ft. (1220–1980 m). **Map 114**

TEXAS SPOTTED WHIPTAIL Pl. 33

Cnemidophorus gularis

Identification: $2\frac{1}{4}$–$3\frac{1}{2}$ in. (5.6–8.9 cm). *A striped and spotted whiptail.* Ground color above often greenish. 7–8 light stripes; middorsal stripe broader and less distinct than the others, often splitting in two to give a total count of 8. Whitish to yellow-brown spots, especially in the greenish to dark brown dark fields on the sides. Tail brown or reddish. Postantebrachials and scales on the front edge of the gular fold enlarged. Supraorbital semicircles normal. 76–96 dorsal granules, 10–21 (avg. 15) between the middorsal pair of stripes (paravertebrals). ***Young:*** Striped, but spotting faint or absent. With growth, the pair of wavy light lines down the back tends to fuse into the single broad light middorsal stripe of adults. Rump and tail reddish, fading with age. In our area, reddish cast to tail may persist even in some adults and can be seen at a considerable distance. ***Male:*** Throat and often underside of tail orange or pinkish salmon. Chest and belly purplish or bluish, often darkened with varying amounts of black. ***Female:*** Whitish to cream below, unmarked.

Frequents prairie grassland, rocky hillsides, washes, and river bottoms grown to mesquite, acacia, cactus, and shrubs. The soil is usually sandy or gravelly. More deliberate in its movements than the Six-lined Racerunner and generally less wary. 1–2 clutches (perhaps 3), each of 1–7 eggs; laid May–July, perhaps Aug. Eats insects and spiders.

Similar species: (1) Six-lined Racerunner (p. 156) has a short light stripe on each side of its tail, extending backward from each hind leg and bordered below by a dark line; no spotting in the dark fields. (2) In areas where their ranges overlap, the Chihuahuan Spotted Whiptail (p. 157) has 3–6 dorsal granules between the paravertebral stripes and prefers more rugged upland habitats. Its young lack the reddish tail and distinct middorsal stripe(s) of the juvenile Texas Spotted Whiptail. (3) See also Checkered Whiptail (p. 163).

Range: S. Okla. to n. Veracruz; e. Tex. to se. N.M. Coexists on lower mountain slopes with Chihuahuan Spotted Whiptail. Sea level to perhaps around 4000 ft. (1220 m). **Map 116**

WESTERN WHIPTAIL *Cnemidophorus tigris* **Pl. 31**

Identification: $2\frac{3}{8}$–$4\frac{1}{2}$ in. (5.9–11.2 cm). Back and sides with *spots, bars, or a network of dusky or black markings* on background of *gray, brown, yellowish, or tan.* Light stripes may be present but they often fade on the lower back and base of tail. Head, shoulders, and tail often gray-brown, yellowish brown, or olive, tail becoming dark brown, dusky, or bluish toward tip. Usually cream-colored or yellowish below, with *scattered spots of blackish, especially on chest and throat.* In extreme darkening, the throat, chest, underside of front legs, and belly are black; orange or pink on throat may be reduced to a few tan flecks. Rust-colored patches often present on sides of belly. Scales in front of gular fold only slightly enlarged and grading gradually into the small granules of the fold. Postantebrachials not enlarged. Supraorbital semicircles extend far forward. ***Young:*** Spotted, marbled, or striped with black above; black fields alternating with narrow orange-yellow ones. Tail bright blue.

An active lizard of deserts and semiarid habitats, usually where plants are sparse and there are open areas for running. Ranges from deserts to pine forests in the mountains. Also found in woodland, streamside growth, and in the warmer, drier parts of forests. Avoids dense grassland and thick growth of shrubs. The ground may be firm soil, sandy, or rocky. 1–2 (perhaps 3) clutches of 1–8 eggs, laid Apr.–Aug. Eats insects, spiders, scorpions, and lizards.

Similar species: The Checkered Whiptail (p. 163) has enlarged scales in front of the gular fold.

Range: N.-cen. Ore. and s. Idaho, south through the Great Basin and Calif. to Baja Calif. and s. Coahuila, east to w. Colo., N.M. and w. Tex. In Ore. in upper John Day Valley, in Alvord Basin and at Diamond Craters. Below sea level to around 7000 ft. (2130 m). A single record of hybridization with the Sonoran Spotted Whiptail (*C. sonorae,* p. 158) at Huerfano Butte, Pima Co., Ariz.

Map 110

Subspecies: GREAT BASIN WHIPTAIL, *C. t. tigris.* Four light stripes on back which tend to become obscure with age, particularly in southern part of range. Usually has vertical dark barring on sides. Hind limbs with black or dusky flecks or broken black network. Much variation in ventral color, from nearly plain unmarked throughout to heavily dark-spotted, particularly on chest. Both dorsal and ventral dark spotting tends to be reduced in southern part of range, but there is much variation. CALIFORNIA WHIPTAIL, *C. t. mundus* (Pl. 31). Typically 8 light stripes but lateral stripes often have irregular borders and are sometimes indistinct. Dorsal dark markings often large and vivid. Usually no distinct dark barring on sides. Throat pale, usually with distinct black spots. COASTAL WHIPTAIL, *C. t. multiscutatus.* Resembles the California Whiptail but stripes on sides usually less well defined. Perhaps a greater frequency of individuals with large dark spots on throat, but there is much variation. ARIZONA DESERT WHIPTAIL, *C. t. gracilis.* Large individuals tend to keep distinct even-edged brown stripes. Typically with 4 distinct stripes on back and an additional less distinct one on each side. Striping vague or absent in some adults. Hind limbs, sides, and dark fields commonly with rounded light spots, giving an overall spotted effect. Outstanding characteristic is a strong tendency toward darkening of throat, chest, and underside of forelimbs. In large adults throat and chest may be uniformly black. PAINTED DESERT WHIPTAIL, *C. t. septentrionalis.* Striped as in Southern Whiptail, but stripes yellow. Dark stripes usually stop short of hind legs. Throat with small black spots. MARBLED WHIPTAIL, *C. t. marmoratus* (Pl. 31). Adult often has a pronounced marbled pattern on dorsal surfaces but usually has alternating dark and light bars on sides and a hint of dorsal striping. Some individuals have a checkerboard pattern and some have pale spots in more or less lengthwise rows. Throat and chest pink or orange with some black spots. Throat sometimes plain white. Young spotted. REDDISH WHIPTAIL, *C. t. rubidus.* Brownish olive above, paler on sides, with narrow black crossbands. Rear bands may extend entirely across back, but others are broken into a series of black dorsal spots with corresponding bars on the sides. Reddish or deep pinkish color on throat, about ears and on underside of tail; sometimes an extensive pinkish to reddish tinge on upper surfaces. Young have 4–6 light lengthwise lines with short, irregular black spots between them. GIANT WHIPTAIL, *C. t. maximus.* Gray or brownish above, fading to olive gray on sides, with 3 lengthwise dark chestnut bands on each side. Each band is twice as wide as the interspace between bands, and is often so invaded by spots of the ground color that it resembles a series of merged brown spots. Tail tawny olive, tinged and spotted with dark chestnut. Young have 5–6 bluish white lengthwise lines on a black ground color, more or less broken by spots of the same color as the lines. Tail and hind limbs suffused with bright pinkish color. To over 5 in. (12.5 cm).

CHECKERED WHIPTAIL *Cnemidophorus tesselatus* **Pl. 32**
Identification: $2\frac{1}{2}$–$4\frac{3}{16}$ in. (6.2–10.6 cm). Resembles the Western Whiptail (above). Yellowish to cream above, with dark blotches in a checkered pattern or lengthwise rows. At least 6 pale stripes. Single or paired middorsal stripe may bring number of stripes to 7 or 8, respectively; another pair of stripes on lower sides may bring total to 10 stripes. Dark fields with light spots or bars that often merge with the light stripes. Whitish below, unmarked or with a few black spots on throat, chest, and belly. Tail brown to yellowish. *Scales in front of gular fold are abruptly and conspicuously enlarged. Postantebrachials not enlarged.* **Young:** Striped, with small pale spots in dark fields. Spotted or barred on sides. All-female.

Ranges from creosote bush plains to the piñon-juniper zone in the mountains. Frequents flatlands, canyon slopes, bluffs, and gullies. Although soil conditions may vary from hardpan to sand, this lizard seems to prefer rocky habitats with scant vegetation and open areas for running. One (perhaps 2) clutch(es) of 1–8 eggs, laid June–July. Eats insects, spiders, and centipedes.
Similar species: (1) In Chihuahuan Spotted Whiptail (p. 157) and (2) Texas Spotted Whiptail (p. 160), postantebrachials are more enlarged. (3) Six-lined Racerunner (p. 156), (4) Little Striped Whiptail (p. 154), (5) Desert Grassland Whiptail (p. 155), and (6) Plateau Striped Whiptail (p. 156) typically are smaller and have a striped pattern without light spots or other marks in the dark fields. (7) See also Western Whiptail (p. 161).
Range: Se. Colo. to e. Chihuahua; w. Tex. to extreme se. Ariz., and sw. N.M. (Antelope Pass and near Animas, Hidalgo Co.). Tends to occur in isolated pockets, especially where bisexual whiptails are abundant. Six localized color-pattern classes have been described, but have not been designated as subspecies (see Remarks, below). From around 900–6900 ft. (270–2100 m). **Map 108**
Remarks: Most pattern classes of the Checkered Whiptail arose by hybridization between the Western Whiptail (Marbled Whiptail subspecies) and a Mexican whiptail, *C. septemvittatus*. Pattern classes in s.-cen. Colo. have resulted from further hybridization with another species, the Six-lined Racerunner. The Checkered Whiptail reproduces by parthenogenesis. The Gray Checkered Whiptail *(C. dixoni)* of Hidalgo Co., N.M., and Presidio Co., Tex., is here considered as a geographical color-pattern class of the Checkered Whiptail *(C. tesselatus).*

Alligator Lizards and Their Allies: Family Anguidae

A small but widely distributed family (about 67 species) with representatives in the Americas, West Indies, Europe, North Africa, Asia, Sumatra, and Borneo. Only the alligator lizards *(Gerrhonotus)* reach our area, ranging from sw. Canada to Panama. They have short limbs, a slim body, long tail, and a *distinctive fold* on each side of the body, *formed in a strip of granular scales that separates large squarish scales* on the back and belly. Since the dorsal and ventral scales are reinforced with bone and form a firm exterior, the fold may enable the body to expand for breathing and accommodation of food, eggs, or developing young (some species are live-bearing). Lizards in this family tend to have a long body and short limbs (as in our species), or the limbs may be dwarfed, number of toes reduced, or limbs may be completely lacking, as in the "slow-worm" *(Anguis fragilis)* of Europe and the snakelike glass lizards *(Ophisaurus)* of the Old and New Worlds.

Alligator lizards generally frequent moist environments in foothills and mountains, but they may range into arid lowlands in the vicinity of springs and streams. They are secretive and generally seek cover among dense vegetation. Look for them by turning logs, rocks, boards, and other objects in sunny glades where there is an abundance of plant or rock cover. When caught they often attempt to bite and may writhe about, smearing their captor with feces. Males may extrude the hemipenes. Avoid grabbing the tail — it is easily lost.

SOUTHERN ALLIGATOR LIZARD **Pl. 29**

Gerrhonotus multicarinatus

Identification: 2⅞–7 in. (7.1–17.5 cm). Dark lengthwise stripes or dashed lines on belly, *down the middle of the scale rows,* but belly sometimes unmarked. *Dorsal scales in 14 rows at midbody.* Scales often strongly keeled on back, neck, and limbs. *Usually well-defined, regular dark crossbands* on back and tail; usually 9–13 bands (often 10–11) between back of head and rear of thighs. Black or dusky bars on sides, spotted with white. Mostly brown, gray, reddish, or yellowish above. *Eyes pale yellow.* Tail long; when not regenerated, length is over twice the length of body. Tail somewhat prehensile, sometimes wrapped around branches in climbing. ***Young:*** Back often with broad stripe of tan, reddish, beige, or gray, brightening on tail. Sides barred as in adult. ***Male:*** Head broader (more triangular) than female's.

Frequents grassland, chaparral, oak woodland, and open pine forest. In the drier parts of its range it is most likely to be found

near streams or in moist canyon bottoms where there is abundant plant cover. Occasionally enters water to escape an enemy. Around houses, it may live in old woodpiles and trash heaps. Partly nocturnal during warmer parts of year. 1–3 clutches, each of 5–20 eggs, laid May–July. Eats slugs, insects, centipedes, scorpions, and spiders, including the highly venomous black widow; also lizards and small mammals. May climb bushes and trees in search of insects and occasionally feeds on the eggs and young of birds.
Similar species: (1) Northern Alligator Lizard (p. 166) has lengthwise stripes *between* the scale rows on the belly, usually 16 dorsal scale rows, irregular markings on back, a shorter tail, and darker eyes. (2) See also Panamint Alligator Lizard (below).
Range: Chiefly west of Cascade-Sierran crest, from s. Wash. (Umtanum Creek Canyon, Kittitas Co.) to cen. Baja Calif. Islands off coast of s. Calif. (San Miguel, Santa Rosa, Santa Cruz, Anacapa, San Nicolas, and Catalina) and Baja Calif. (Los Coronados and San Martin). Isolated populations east of Sierra Nevada of Calif. at Grant Lake, Mono Co.; near Independence and at Walker Creek near Olancha, Inyo Co. Occurs in desert along Mojave R., Calif. Introduced at Las Vegas, Nev. **Map 119**
Subspecies: CALIFORNIA ALLIGATOR LIZARD, *G. m. multicarinatus.* Red blotches on back. Top of head often mottled. 1–3 rows of scales on upper arm; scales weakly keeled in adult. SAN DIEGO ALLIGATOR LIZARD, *G. m. webbi.* Larger size and more prominent keeling than in other subspecies. Temporal scales keeled, upper ones strongly so. OREGON ALLIGATOR LIZARD, *G. m. scincicauda.* Dorsal scales less heavily keeled than in San Diego Alligator Lizard. Temporals smooth or only upper ones weakly keeled. Scales of lateral fold cinnamon. Head usually not mottled.
Remarks: Individuals from the southern end of the range in Baja Calif. have a mixture of color and scale characteristics that suggest possible intergradation with the San Lucan Alligator Lizard (p. 241).

PANAMINT ALLIGATOR LIZARD Pl. 29

Gerrhonotus panamintinus

Identification: 3⅝–6 in. (9–15 cm). Light yellow or beige above, with *regular, broad brown crossbands; 7 or 8 bands between back of head (marked by ear openings) and front of thighs.* Similar bands on tail. Ventral markings may form lengthwise stripes down center of scale rows or they may be scattered. Eyes pale yellow. Dorsal scales in 14 rows, smooth or weakly keeled. Tail long — up to twice as long as body. ***Young:*** Dark crossbars contrast with pale ground color. ***Male:*** Head broader, more triangular than female's.

Ranges from scrub desert and the Joshua-tree zone into the lower edge of the piñon-juniper belt. Found beneath thickets of willow and wild grape near water or in drier habitats grown to

creosote bush and desert mint. A secretive species that spends much of its time in rockslides and dense plant growth. Sometimes nocturnal. Look for it under rocks in damp gullies and along streams. Presumably lays eggs. Eats insects and other arthropods.
Similar species: (1) Madrean Alligator Lizard (below) has orange or pink eyes and 8–11 crossbands between back of head and front of thighs. (2) Southern Alligator Lizard (p. 164) has 9–13 crossbands; young often have a broad middorsal stripe on body and tail.
Range: Desert Mts. of Inyo Co. and se. Mono Co., Calif.—Panamint Mts. (Surprise and Wildrose Canyons and Middle Fork of Hanaupah Canyon), Nelson Mts. (Grapevine Canyon), Inyo Mts. (Long John, Daisy, and other canyons), and White Mts. (Westgard Pass; Black, Marble, Silver Creek, and Cottonwood Canyons; Coldwater Creek). A sight record for Cosos Mts., Inyo Co. From around 2500 to 6800 ft. (760–2070 m). **Map 119**

MADREAN ALLIGATOR LIZARD **Pl. 29**

(Arizona Alligator Lizard) *Gerrhonotus kingii*

Identification: 3–5 in. (7.5–12.5 cm). Belly with scattered dusky spots and bars; usually no lengthwise stripes. Pale gray, beige, or brown above, with distinct wavy crossbars, 8–11 between back of head (marked by ear openings) and front of thighs. Eyes orange or pink. *Conspicuous black and white spots on upper jaw.* Scales smooth or weakly keeled. Dorsal scales usually in 14 rows. ***Young:*** Contrasting dark crossbars on back and tail.

Chiefly a mountain form that frequents chaparral, oak woodland, and pine-fir forests in rocky places near permanent or temporary streams. May also occur in broadleaf stream-border habitats along major drainageways in desert and grassland. Found under logs, rocks, and in woodrat nests and leaf litter in and near dense plant growth. Sometimes abroad at dusk or after dark. Chiefly ground-dwelling but occasionally climbs. Clutch of 9–15 eggs, laid June–July. Eats insects and scorpions.
Similar species: Panamint Alligator Lizard (p. 165).
Range: Southern edge of central plateau of Ariz. southward in Sierra Madre to Jalisco. Huachuca, Santa Rita, Pajarito, and Chiricahua Mts., Ariz.; sw. N.M., east to Florida Mts., Luna Co. From 2400 to around 9000 ft. (730–2770 m). **Map 119**

NORTHERN ALLIGATOR LIZARD **Pl. 29**

Gerrhonotus coeruleus

Identification: 2¾–5⅜ in. (6.9–13.5 cm). Dark *stripes on belly between the scale rows;* sometimes absent. Dorsal scales *usually in 16 rows.* At midbody, crossbands seldom regular enough to count. Eyes completely dark or dark around the pupils. Gray, olive, greenish, or bluish above, usually heavily blotched or barred with dusky. Some individuals unpatterned; others have a broad middorsal stripe. ***Young:*** Crossbanded or with a broad (lengthwise) dorsal stripe of brassy, beige, or gray. ***Male:*** Head broader and more triangular than female's.

Chiefly inhabits woodland and forest, but also grassland and sagebrush habitats. Occurs under bark, inside rotten logs, and under rocks and other objects. Generally found in cooler, damper places than the Southern Alligator Lizard. Live-bearing; 2–15 young, born June–Sept. Eats insects, ticks, spiders, millipedes, and snails.

Similar species: See Southern Alligator Lizard (p. 164).

Range: B.C. to central coast and Sierra Nevada of Calif.; Rocky Mts. of w. Mont. and n. Idaho. Isolated populations at Hart Mt. Antelope Refuge, Lake Co., Ore., in the Breckenridge and Piute Mts., Kern Co., and Warner Mts., Modoc Co., Calif. On islands in Puget Sound, Straits of Georgia and Juan de Fuca, in San Francisco Bay and on Año Nuevo I. off Calif. coast. Sea level to around 10,500 ft. (3200 m). **Map 121**

Subspecies: SAN FRANCISCO ALLIGATOR LIZARD, *G. c. coeruleus.* Usually large dark blotches or irregular crossbands on back. Scales of back and sides heavily keeled. Otherwise resembles Northwestern Alligator Lizard (below). SHASTA ALLIGATOR LIZARD, *G. c. shastensis.* Dorsal scales in 16 rows. Temporals smooth. In northern part of range, head may be slate gray and body yellowish green. Young crossbanded. NORTHWESTERN ALLIGATOR LIZARD, *G. c. principis.* Small — usually less than 4 in. (10 cm) long. Usually has a broad stripe of tan, olive, golden brown or grayish down the back, with or without spots. Sides dusky, contrasting with back color. Dorsal scales weakly keeled, in 14 rows. Temporals (behind eye) weakly keeled. SIERRA ALLIGATOR LIZARD, *G. c. palmeri.* Markings extend across back, are confined to sides, or are absent. Dorsal scales in 16 rows. Temporals all keeled.

California Legless Lizards: Family Anniellidae

Snakelike burrowing lizards, about the size of a lead pencil. Two species, confined to Calif. and Baja Calif. They are covered with small, smooth, cycloid scales, which make it easy for them to move through sand or loose soil. Eyes small, with movable lids. Snout shovel-shaped; lower jaw inset, forming a seal that keeps sand from getting in the mouth when burrowing. No ear openings. Blunt tail aids in occasional backward movements in soil. Although these lizards are limbless and snakelike, their movable eyelids distinguish them from snakes. When picked up, these lizards may probe your hand with their snout with surprising force.

Legless lizards inhabit washes, beaches, and loamy soil. They are susceptible to drying and must live where they can reach damp soil. Live-bearing.

CALIFORNIA LEGLESS LIZARD **Pl. 34**

Anniella pulchra

Identification: $4\frac{3}{8}$–7 in. (10.9–17.5 cm). Although the eyes are small, the lids can be seen. Watch an individual in good light to see it blink. Generally silver or beige above, yellow below. A black middorsal line runs the length of the body; other lines on sides where dorsal and ventral colors join. The skin looks polished. Dark brown or black individuals with contrasting yellow underparts are found in several areas along the Calif. coast. ***Young:*** Cream or silver above, light gray or pale yellow below.

Needs loose soil for burrowing (sand, loam, or humus), moisture, warmth, and plant cover. Frequents the sparse vegetation of beaches, chaparral, pine-oak woodland, and streamside growth of sycamores, cottonwoods, and oaks. Occasionally enters desert-scrub. Bush lupine often grows in habitats where conditions are suitable for this lizard. Burrows in washes, dune sand of beaches, and loose soil near the bases of slopes and near permanent or temporary streams. Forages in leaf litter by day. May emerge on the surface at dusk or at night. Look in leaf litter under the overhang of trees and bushes on sunny slopes and under rocks, driftwood, logs, and boards. To uncover buried individuals, drag a stick through soil exposed when objects are turned over. Sometimes enters the twig base of woodrat nests. Live-bearing; 1–4 young born Sept.–Nov. Eats insects and spiders.

Range: From near Antioch, Calif. south in Coast Ranges, Transverse Mts., and Peninsular Ranges into nw. Baja Calif. Scattered occurrences on floor of San Joaquin Valley, in southern Sierra, Walker Basin, and in the Piute, Scodie, and Tehachapi Mts. On e. and s. Los Coronados and Todos Santos Is. Desert-edge localities at eastern end of Walker Pass, Kern Co.; Morongo Valley, San Bernardino Co., in the Little San Bernardino Mts. at Whitewater, Riverside Co., Calif., and on eastern slope of Peninsular Ranges. Coexists with Baja California Legless Lizard (Pl. 47, p. 242) at mouth of Rio Santo Domingo near Colonia Guerrero and lives next to it at Arroyo Pabellon. Occurrence spotty. This lizard has been eliminated by agriculture in many parts of Great Valley, Calif. Old records from Redwood Canyon, Marin Co., San Francisco, and Palo Alto. Sea level to around 5100 ft. (1550 m).

Map 122

Subspecies: SILVERY LEGLESS LIZARD, *A. p. pulchra.* Silvery, gray, or beige above, with a dark middorsal line. Yellow below, with fine lengthwise lines between the scale rows. Animals from Porterville area, Tulare Co., have dark blotches on underparts. BLACK LEGLESS LIZARD, *A. p. nigra.* Black or dark brown above. Yellow below, without lengthwise lines or lines very faint or confined to tail. Young resemble Silvery Legless Lizard but darken with age. Most typical form on Monterey Peninsula and southern coast of Monterey Bay.

Venomous Lizards: Family Helodermatidae

The Gila Monster *(Heloderma suspectum)* of sw. U.S. and Sonora and the Mexican Beaded Lizard *(H. horridum),* the only members of the family, are the only known venomous lizards. They have a large, heavy body; a massive head; a sausage-shaped tail; and short limbs with strong curved claws. The dorsal surfaces are covered with small, round, closely set scales and patterned with contrasting markings of pink, orange, or yellow and black, suggesting colorful beadwork. The tail, a fat-storage organ, becomes slim in starved individuals.

These lizards live in deserts, wooded areas, and around farms, often near washes and intermittent streams where they have access to water or damp soil. In captivity they sometimes nearly completely immerse themselves. They are chiefly active at dusk and at night and crawl with an awkward, lumbering gait, but should be approached with care because they may lash out and bite quickly. Venom produced in glands in the lower jaw is expelled into the mouth along grooves in the teeth and injected by chewing. The venom is evidently used in subduing some prey and perhaps also as a defense against some predators.

Although formidable in appearance, these lizards are not dangerous unless molested or handled and should not be killed.

GILA MONSTER — Pl. 20

Heloderma suspectum

Identification: 9–14 in. (22–35 cm). A large, heavy-bodied lizard with a short *swollen tail* and a gaudy pattern of black and pink, orange, or yellow. *Dorsal surfaces with beadlike scales;* belly scales (ventrals) squarish. Loose folds of skin on neck. Well-developed gular fold. Unusual among lizards in having 4th toe nearly the same length as 3rd toe. Dark forked tongue flicks out in snakelike fashion.

Inhabits chiefly shrubby, grassy, and succulent desert; occasionally enters oak woodland. Frequents the lower slopes of mountains and nearby plains and beaches (Sonora). Found in canyon bottoms or arroyos with permanent or intermittent streams, where it digs burrows or uses those of other animals. Also seeks shelter in

mammal burrows, woodrat nests, dense thickets, and under rocks. Seems to prefer irrigated lands or rocky areas grown to scattered bushes. Often abroad at dusk or after dark following warm rains in summer. Diurnal, especially in spring (occasionally in winter). Chiefly ground-dwelling. The color pattern helps conceal this lizard in dim light. On dark backgrounds the black markings blend in and the light markings look like sticks and rocks, while on pale backgrounds the disruptive dark markings may delay recognition of the animal's shape. Clutch of 1–8 eggs (possibly to around a dozen), laid July–Aug. Eats small mammals; eggs, chiefly of ground-nesting birds (quail, mourning doves) and reptiles, lizards, insects, and carrion. **Caution:** The bite of these lizards is tenacious and extremely painful. Fortunately, it is rarely fatal to humans. **Range:** Extreme sw. Utah to n. Sinaloa; sw. N.M. to Colorado R. In Calif. in the Piute, Clark, and Kingston Mts., San Bernardino Co. Old records for the Providence Mts. and Imperial Dam. May occur as far east in N.M. as the Kilbourne Hole-Aden Crater area. Sea level to around 5000 ft. (1520 m). **Map 120**
Subspecies: RETICULATE GILA MONSTER, *H. s. suspectum.* Adults mottled and blotched with black and pink, with black predominating on back of most individuals; a reticulate pattern with crossbands nearly or completely obscure. Dark tail bands mottled, and mottling in light interspaces. BANDED GILA MONSTER, *H. s. cinctum.* Adults retain juvenile pattern. Four black saddles or irregular double crossbands on body. Tail with 5 dark bands, little or not at all mottled; mottling slight or absent in the interspaces. **Remarks:** It is illegal to collect the Gila Monster without a permit.

10

Snakes

Slender Blind Snakes: Family Leptotyphlopidae

These snakes are sometimes called "worm snakes" because of their resemblance to earthworms. They are usually under 1½ ft. (45 cm) in length; brown, gray, or pink above, lighter below. The body is slender and cylindrical and there is no neck constriction. Scales are uniform in size, cycloid, smooth, and shiny and appear moist. There are *no enlarged ventrals.* Our species have a spine at the tip of the tail. The eyes are vestigial, appearing as dark spots beneath the oculars. Teeth are scarce and confined to the lower jaw. The slender form, uniform scalation, and degenerate eyes distinguish them from all our other snakes.

Blind snakes are crevice dwellers and burrowers. They live in loose soil — sand, loam, or humus — and emerge on the surface at night or on overcast days. In our species the track is distinctive. It consists of regular lateral undulations that show signs of skidding and in the latter respect differ from tracks of the ground snakes. The tail spine leaves a fine wavy line on the ground. Blind snakes are susceptible to drying, and generally live where there is damp subsoil. They feed on ants; ant eggs, larvae and pupae; and on termites. They find ant nests by following the scented trails of their prey. The solidly constructed skull; smooth, tough scales; and slender form permit them to enter ant nests and to resist the attacks of their prey. Our species are oviparous (lay eggs).

The genus *Leptotyphlops,* with some 75 species, ranging from sw. and s.-cen. U.S. to Argentina, the West Indies, tropical Africa, and sw. Asia, contains all species in the family except a single w. African form.

WESTERN BLIND SNAKE *Leptotyphlops humilis* **Pl. 36**
Identification: 7–16 in. (18–41 cm). A slim snake with no neck constriction and a *blunt head and tail.* Eyes vestigial, appearing as dark spots under the head scales. A tiny spine at tip of tail. Scales shiny and cycloid, not enlarged on the belly. *A single scale between the oculars* (Fig. 22, opp. Pl. 36). Purplish, brown, or pink above, with a silvery sheen. Somewhat lighter below — cream, pink, purplish, or light gray.

Ranges from the desert to brush-covered mountain slopes where

there is soil suitable for burrowing. Often frequents rocky hillsides with patches of loose soil, and canyon bottoms or washes near permanent or intermittent streams. Found in beach sand above the high-tide mark. Burrows among the roots of shrubs, beneath rocks, and enters ant nests in search of prey. Eats small insects and their larvae, spiders, millipedes, and centipedes. Occasionally crawls exposed on the surface at night, and sometimes can be found by night driving. By day, search crevices and the soil under rock flakes that lie flat on the ground or against boulders, especially where the soil is slightly damp. Clutch of 2–6 eggs, laid July–Aug.
Similar species: The Texas Blind Snake (below) usually has 3 scales between the oculars (Fig. 22), and 2 labials rather than 1 between the ocular and lower nasal.
Range: S. Nev. and sw. Utah south to Colima and tip of Baja Calif.; w. Tex. to coast of s. Calif. Perhaps isolated in Cottonwood-Sedona area, Yavapai Co., Ariz. Below sea level in desert sinks to around 5000 ft. (1520 m). **Map 123**

TEXAS BLIND SNAKE **Fig. 22, opp. Pl. 36**
Leptotyphlops dulcis
Identification: 5–10¾ in. (13–27 cm). A close relative of the Western Blind Snake (above). Brown, pink, to reddish brown above, often with a silvery sheen. Pale gray or pink below. *Usually more than 1 scale between the oculars* (Fig. 22, opp. Pl. 36) and usually 2 labial scales between the ocular and lower nasal.

Habits similar to the Western Blind Snake's. Lives in prairies, canyon bottoms, and rocky or sandy deserts; ranges into the juniper-live oak plant community. Found in crevices, among roots of trees and shrubs, under stones and other objects, and on roadways at night. Most commonly seen after spring and summer rains. Diet similar to that of the Western Blind Snake. Clutch of 2–7 eggs, laid June–July. Females tend eggs and may share underground nesting sites.
Similar species: See Western Blind Snake (above).
Range: Southern Kans. to n. Hidalgo; cen. Tex. to se. Ariz. Sea level to around 5800 ft. (1830 m). **Map 125**

Boas and Pythons: Family Boidae

A large family (around 80 species) containing the world's largest snakes as well as many smaller forms. Found throughout the tropics and subtropics of both hemispheres and extending well into temperate western N. America. Generally heavy-bodied snakes with smooth, glossy scales and vertical pupils. Vestiges of the hind limbs are present and usually show externally, in male snakes especially, as a small spur on each side of the vent. Some species have temperature-sensitive pits on the labial scales that help them find and capture warm-blooded prey. Prey is killed by constriction. Pythons and their relatives are found chiefly in the Old World and are oviparous. Boas occur in both New and Old Worlds and are live-bearing. Two species of boas occur in the West, the only members of the family native to the U.S. They are thick-bodied snakes, seldom more than 3 ft. (1 m) long, with a small head, small eyes, a blunt tail, and small, smooth scales. Ventrals (see rear endpapers) are reduced. When alarmed these snakes may roll themselves into a ball, concealing the head among the coils.

RUBBER BOA *Charina bottae* **Pl. 36**
Identification: 14–33 in. (35–83 cm). A stout-bodied snake that looks and feels like rubber. Sometimes called the "two-headed snake" because the *tail is shaped somewhat like the head.* Skin smooth and shiny, thrown into folds when the body is bent sharply. Tail short and blunt. Dorsal scales small and smooth. *Top of head covered with large symmetrical plates.* Pupil vertically oval. No enlarged chin shields. Plain brown to olive green above, yellow to cream below, usually with no pattern or with a few dusky flecks on the lower sides. Ventrals with dark flecks or mottling of brown, orange, or black at some northern localities. ***Young:*** Pinkish to tan above, belly light yellow to pink. ***Male:*** Anal spurs usually present; small or absent in female.

Frequents grassland, broken chaparral, woodland, and forest, in and beneath rotting logs, under rocks, and under the bark of fallen and standing dead trees. A good swimmer, burrower, and climber. Eats small mammals (especially young mice and shrews), birds, salamanders, and snakes. When feeding on nestling mice, it may fend off parental attacks with "strikes" of its blunt, elevated tail. Live-bearing; 2–8 young born Aug.–Nov.

Range: Southern B.C. (Quesnel area) to s. Utah (to Panguitch Lake), cen. Nev., and s. Calif.; Pacific Coast to n.-cen. Wyo. (Bighorn Mts.). Found on the following mountains in s. Calif.: Mt. Pinos, Mt. Abel, and the Tehachapi, San Bernardino, and San Jacinto Mts. Sight record for Echo Park, Moffat Co., Colo. Vancouver I., B.C. report not yet confirmed. Distribution spotty. Near sea level to around 10,000 ft. (3050 m). **Map 127**

Subspecies: PACIFIC RUBBER BOA, *C. b. bottae.* 45 or more lengthwise scale rows at midbody (not counting ventrals). Parietal usually divided. ROCKY MOUNTAIN RUBBER BOA, *C. b. utahensis.* Usually 44 or fewer scale rows. Parietal usually not divided. More than 191 ventrals. SOUTHERN RUBBER BOA, *C. b. umbratica.* Scale rows as in Rocky Mountain Boa but fewer than 192 ventrals. S. Calif., Mt. Pinos south.

ROSY BOA *Lichanura trivirgata* **Pl. 36**
Identification: 24–44 in. (60–110 cm). A heavy-bodied snake; the head only a little wider than the neck. Scales smooth and shiny. Eyes small, pupils vertical. *No chin shields or large head plates,* except on snout. Slaty, beige, or rosy above; with 3 broad, brown or gray lengthwise stripes or irregular brown patches. Markings sometimes absent. Cream below, spotted or blotched with gray.

Young: Generally lighter than adult and pattern more distinct. ***Male:*** Anal spurs usually well developed.

Inhabits rocky shrublands and desert. Attracted to oases and permanent or intermittent streams, but does not require permanent water. Chiefly nocturnal but may be active at dusk and (rarely) in the daytime. A good climber. Search blacktop roads in rocky canyons or along rocky buttes or lower mountain slopes. Eats small mammals and birds. Live-bearing; 3–12 young, born Oct.–Nov.

Range: Death Valley region (Hanaupah Canyon), Calif. to tip of Baja Calif. and Guaymas, Sonora; coastal s. Calif. to s.-cen. Ariz. Absent from Coachella Valley southward, in extreme low desert. Distribution spotty. Sea level to around 4500 ft. (1370 m). Sight record for San Gabriel Mts. in s. Calif. at 6790 ft. (2070 m).

Map 126

Subspecies: COASTAL ROSY BOA, *L. t. roseofusca.* Stripes of pink, reddish brown, or dull brown, with irregular borders; on a bluish gray ground color. Stripe color may be present on scattered scales between the stripes or, occasionally, over all dorsal surfaces. DESERT ROSY BOA, *L. t. gracia.* Prominent stripes of rose, reddish brown or tan; even-edged and contrasting with the gray or beige of the ground color. Stripes more distinct than in Coastal Rosy Boa. Spotting of stripe color seldom present between the stripes. Brown flecking below. Isolated populations in Cerbat, Harquahala, Harcuvar, Kofa, Castle Dome, Gila and other mountains in w. and sw. Ariz. MEXICAN ROSY BOA, *L. t. trivirgata.* Contrasting lengthwise stripes of chocolate brown on a light drab background. Creamy white below with only occasional black flecks. S. Ariz. (Organ Pipe Cactus National Monument) to Guaymas, Sonora; s. half of Baja Calif.

Colubrids: Family Colubridae

As treated in this guide, this family includes most snakes in all continents except Antarctica and Australia, where elapids — relatives of the coral snakes and cobras — are more numerous. The structure of colubrids varies greatly in relation to their highly diverse habits, which include terrestrial, burrowing, arboreal, and aquatic modes of life. The family is therefore difficult to characterize and probably does not represent a natural group. Head plates are usually large and symmetrical and the teeth may be solid or grooved toward the back of the jaw. No hollow fangs. Some species are venomous, but none in our area is dangerous to humans. About $\frac{3}{4}$ of the snakes in the West belong to this family. Over 1500 species worldwide.

RINGNECK SNAKE *Diadophis punctatus* **Pl. 37**

Identification: 8–30 in. (20–75 cm). Typically a slender olive, brownish, blue-gray, or nearly black snake with a dark head and usually a conspicuous yellow, orange, or cream neck band. The neck band is absent in some populations in southern N.M., Utah, and elsewhere. Yellow-orange to red below, the red intensifying on underside of tail. Belly usually spotted with black. Rarely, melanistic individuals are found that lack both the neck band and orange ventral color, and have dark crossbars on the belly. In the West and cen. U.S., when alarmed, this snake coils its tail and turns up the underside of the tail, revealing the bright red color. Scales smooth, usually in 15 or 17 rows at midbody. Loreal scale present. ***Young:*** Often dark above, sometimes nearly black. ***Male:*** Tubercles on scales above the vent (sometimes also present, but less prominent, in female).

A snake of moist habitats — woodland, forest, grassland, chaparral, farms, and gardens. In the arid parts of the West, it is restricted to mountains and water courses where it may descend, in desert areas, to around 2400 ft. (730 m). Seldom seen in the open. Usually found on the ground under bark, beneath and inside rotting logs, and under stones and boards. One, perhaps 2 clutches of 1–10 eggs, laid June–July, often in a communal nest. Eats slender and other salamanders, small frogs, lizards, small snakes, slugs, and worms. May be venomous to small animal prey. Rear upper jaw teeth enlarged but not grooved.

Similar species: (1) Black-headed snakes (*Tantilla* species, pp. 216–220) usually have a whitish or beige neck band, and lack black spots on belly; the reddish color on the belly is bordered on each side by pale gray, and there is no loreal scale. (2) See also Sharp-tailed Snake (p. 176).

Range: S. Wash. and Idaho to n. Baja Calif. and San Luis Potosí. Atlantic to Pacific Coasts. Sight record near Troy, ne. Ore. Distribution spotty. Sea level to around 7000 ft. (2150 m). **Map 128**

Subspecies: PACIFIC RINGNECK SNAKE, *D. p. amabilis.* Scale rows usually 15, 15 or 15, 13 (counted on neck and at midbody). Neck band 1–1½ scale lengths wide. Ventral color extends onto ½–1½ rows of lowermost dorsal scales. Numerous black spots on belly. SAN BERNARDINO RINGNECK SNAKE, *D. p. modestus.* Scale rows usually 17, 15. Ventral color confined to 1st row of dorsal scales. Conspicuous black spots on belly. NORTHWESTERN RINGNECK SNAKE, *D. p. occidentalis.* Ventral color on 1½–2 or more rows of dorsal scales. Neck band 1½–3 scales wide. A few small black dots on belly. CORAL-BELLIED RINGNECK SNAKE, *D. p. pulchellus.* Like Northwestern Ringneck but 1st 2 rows of dorsal scales not flecked with black. Belly lightly or not at all spotted. SAN DIEGO RINGNECK SNAKE, *D. p. similis.* Scale rows usually 15, 15 or 15, 13. Ventral color on ½ to ⅔ of each scale of 1st row of dorsals. MONTEREY RINGNECK SNAKE, *D. p. vandenburghi.* Scale rows usually 17, 15. Ventral color on 1½–2 rows of dorsal scales. Black spots on belly few and small. PRAIRIE RINGNECK SNAKE, *D. p. arnyi.*

Belly color confined to ventrals except occasionally at extreme front end. Low ventral scale count. REGAL RINGNECK SNAKE, *D. p. regalis*. Usually larger and paler than preceding subspecies — gray with bluish, greenish, or slaty cast. Neck band sometimes faint or absent. Ranges into the aspen-fir belt. Intergrades with Prairie Ringneck in cen. and w. Tex., but the two forms tend to retain their identities in the Guadalupe Mts. on the Tex.-N.M. border.

SHARP-TAILED SNAKE *Contia tenuis* **Pl. 39**

Identification: 8–18 in. (20–45 cm). Reddish brown or gray above, tending toward reddish on the tail. Often with an indistinct yellowish or reddish line on each upper side. Distinctively marked with *regular, alternating crossbars of black and cream below.* Scales smooth. Single preocular. Tail with sharp spine at tip. ***Young:*** Red above, fine dark lines on sides.

Frequents woodland, grassland, broken chaparral, and forest, usually near streams. Often found in pastures or open meadows on the edge of coniferous forests or among oaks in the lower foothills. Occasionally lives in groups. A secretive snake of moist environments, abroad when the ground is damp but keeping out of sight under logs, bark of standing and fallen trees, rocks, and other objects. Most likely to be found following rains; retreats underground when the surface dries. Clutch of 2–9 eggs, probably laid June–July. Apparently feeds almost entirely on slugs, for which its long teeth are especially suited.

Similar species: Melanistic Ringneck Snakes (p. 174) resemble the Sharptail, including the dark and light crossbars on the belly, but are much darker above and lack the tail spine.

Range: B.C. to s. Sierra Nevada and cen. coast (Pine Mt., San Luis Obispo Co.), Calif. Isolated populations on N. and S. Pender Is. and at Metchosin on Vancouver I.; in Wash. along Yakima Canyon from Cle Elum to south of Ellensburg, at northern end of Gravelly Lake, Pierce Co., at 4.2 mi. (6.7 km) northeast of Carson, Skamania Co., and at Lyle, Klickitat Co. and in Ore. at Rock Creek Reservoir, Wasco Co. Distribution spotty. Sea level to around 6600 ft. (2010 m). **Map 129**

WESTERN HOGNOSE SNAKE **Pl. 40**
Heterodon nasicus

Identification: 16–36 in. (40–90 cm). A heavy-bodied, blotched snake with a broad neck and an upturned snout. Dark blotches extend from back of head onto tail. *Rostral much enlarged, spadelike and keeled above.* Prefrontals separated by small scales. Dorsal scales keeled. Anal divided. Enlarged teeth toward rear of upper jaw. Much black pigment on underside of body and tail.

This snake frequents sandy or gravelly prairies, open woodland, farmlands, and floodplains of rivers. In the extreme western part of its range it occurs in semidesert habitats and occasionally in mountain canyon bottoms or on the floodplains of streams where there is loose soil suitable for burrowing. Stream courses may be canopied by deciduous broadleaf trees. The Hognose uses its shovel-shaped snout in digging and its enlarged teeth in holding and perhaps deflating toads, a staple food. In addition it eats frogs, salamanders, lizards, snakes, turtles, and reptile eggs. Clutch of 4–23 eggs, laid June–Aug.

When disturbed this snake often spreads its head and neck and strikes with open mouth, hissing but seldom biting. This behavior has earned it the names "puff adder" or "blow snake." It may "play possum," suddenly turning belly up, writhing violently for a few moments, then lying still with its mouth open and tongue lolling. The tail, in a tight coil suggesting a head, is often held near the head and excrement is discharged.

Similar species: (1) Hook-nosed snakes (*Gyalopion* species, pp. 215–216) have smooth dorsal scales, and the rostral is concave rather than keeled above. (2) Leaf-nosed (*Phyllorhynchus* species, below) and (3) patch-nosed snakes (*Salvadora* species, pp. 184–185) have the tip of the rostral turned back between the internasals instead of extending forward and free. (4) The Eastern Hognose Snake *(H. platyrhinos),* expected in e. Colo., lacks black on the underside of the tail, and the prefrontals meet.

Range: S. Canada to San Luis Potosí; se. Ariz. to cen. Ill. From near sea level to around 8000 ft. (2440 m). **Map 124**

Subspecies: PLAINS HOGNOSE SNAKE, *H. n. nasicus.* Dark middorsal blotches extend from head to area of back above vent; over 35 blotches in males, over 40 in females. DUSTY HOGNOSE SNAKE, *H. n. gloydi.* Dark middorsal blotches, fewer than 32 in males, fewer than 37 in females. MEXICAN HOGNOSE SNAKE, *H. n. kennerlyi.* Similar in color and pattern to Dusty Hognose, but 2–6 small scales (azygous scales) in a group on top of snout behind rostral, rather than 9 or more as in the Dusty Hognose Snake.

Remarks: A specimen of the Eastern Hognose Snake *(Heterodon platyrhinos)* was collected in 1943 9 mi. (14.5 km) west of Lamar, Bent Co., Colo. None has been found since, so the species has not been included here. Specimens from extreme w. Kans. suggest the snake may extend up the Arkansas R. Valley into Colo. It differs from the Western Hognose Snake in having the underside of the tail lighter than the belly, rather than with masses of black color.

SPOTTED LEAF-NOSED SNAKE **Pl. 40**

Phyllorhynchus decurtatus

Identification: 12–20 in. (30–50 cm). A pale, blotched snake with a blunt snout formed by a *much enlarged rostral scale with free edges.* Pink, tan, yellowish, or pale gray above, with more than 17 middorsal brown blotches between the back of the head and the region above the vent. Blotches also extend onto the tail. White below, unmarked. *Pupils vertical.* Dorsal scales smooth, except occasionally in males. Suboculars present. Rostral completely separates internasals. Anal single.

A secretive, nocturnal snake of sandy or gravelly desert. Most of its range in the U.S. corresponds closely with the distribution of the creosote bush. Found on open desert plains. The modified rostral is used in burrowing. Clutch of 2–4 eggs, presumably laid June–July. Eats small lizards, including banded geckos and their eggs. Search roads at night; otherwise it is rarely encountered.

Similar species: (1) Saddled Leaf-nosed Snake (below) has fewer than 17 blotches on back (excluding the tail). (2) In patch-nosed snakes (*Salvadora* species, pp. 184–185), the internasals are usually only partly separated by the rostral. (3) In the Western Hognose Snake (p. 176), the front end of the rostral extends forward and is free.

Range: S. Nev. to tip of Baja Calif. and s. Sonora; sw. Ariz. to desert base of mountains in s. Calif. Known from a single locality in s. Sinaloa. Below sea level (in desert sinks) to around 3000 ft. (910 m). **Map 131**

Subspecies: CLOUDED LEAF-NOSED SNAKE, *P. d. nubilis.* 42–60 blotches down middle of back (excluding tail); blotches same width or wider (along dorsal midline) than interspaces between them. Male has conspicuous keels on dorsal scales. WESTERN LEAF-NOSED SNAKE, *P. d. perkinsi.* 24–48 blotches down middle of back (excluding tail); blotches narrower than interspaces. BAJA CALIFORNIA LEAF-NOSED SNAKE, *P. d. decurtatus.* Blotches on back wider than interspaces. Male lacks conspicuous keels on dorsal scales.

Remarks: Occasionally coexists in rocky, gravelly desert foothills with the Saddled Leaf-nosed Snake (below).

SADDLED LEAF-NOSED SNAKE **Pl. 40**

Phyllorhynchus browni

Identification: 12–20 in. (30–51 cm). Resembles the Spotted Leaf-nosed Snake (above) in form and scalation, including the enlarged rostral scale, but differs greatly in color. *Fewer than 17* large, brown, dark-edged blotches (saddles) on back, excluding the tail. Light color on the head and between the blotches, pink or cream. White below, without markings.

In northern part of range, this snake inhabits desertscrub grown to mesquite, saltbush, creosote bush, paloverde and saguaro cactus. In southern areas it frequents thornscrub and the lower edge of thornforest. A burrower in relatively coarse, rocky soils as well as in sand. Nocturnal. Usually found only by patrolling highways at night. Most active after the summer rains begin, especially on humid nights. Clutch of 2–5 eggs, probably laid in summer. Apparently eats chiefly lizards and their eggs.

Similar species: See Spotted Leaf-nosed Snake (above).

Range: Vicinity of Tucson west to Organ Pipe Cactus National Monument, Ariz.; southern base of Ariz. plateau (Phoenix-Supe-

rior region) to s.-cen. Sinaloa. From about 1000–3000 ft. (300–910 m). **Map 130**
Subspecies: PIMA LEAF-NOSED SNAKE, *P. b. browni.* Dark blotches considerably wider than light interspaces. 166 or fewer ventrals in males, 179 or fewer in females. MARICOPA LEAF-NOSED SNAKE, *P. b. lucidus.* Blotches only slightly wider (if at all) than interspaces. 167 or more ventrals in males, 180 or more in females.
Remarks: The Pima Leaf-nosed Snake may actually represent an intermediate form between the Maricopa Leaf-nosed Snake and a Mexican subspecies to the south.

SMOOTH GREEN SNAKE *Opheodrys vernalis* **Pl. 39**
Identification: 12–26 in. (30–65 cm). A slender snake, *plain green above* and white or yellowish below, often becoming bright yellow on underside of tail. The dorsal color changes to dull blue or gray upon death. *Dorsal scales smooth,* in 15 rows at midbody. A single anterior temporal scale. Each nostril centered in a single scale. Anal divided. ***Young:*** Dark olive gray above. Hatchlings slate gray to brown above.

Ranges from prairies to open damp grassy areas in forests. In the West it inhabits meadows, stream borders, and rocky habitats interspersed with grass. Secretive and chiefly ground-dwelling, but occasionally climbs bushes. Well-camouflaged in green plant growth. Several females may share a favorable nest site. Clutch of 3–18 eggs, laid June–Sept., sometimes hatching within a few days after laying. Eats insects and spiders.
Similar species: (1) Greenish examples of the Racer (p. 180) have 2 anterior temporals, the lower preocular is wedged between the upper labials, and each nostril is located between 2 scales. (2) Green Rat Snake (p. 186) has 25 or more rows of dorsal scales; the middorsal rows are weakly keeled along the middle of the back.
Range: S. Canada to s. Tex.; Nova Scotia and N.J. to Utah. Isolated populations mostly in mountains in southern and western parts of range from Wyo. and se. Idaho (Bear Lake Co.) to s. N.M. and Chihuahua. Sight record in Guadalupe Mts. Sea level to around 9500 ft. (2900 m). **Map 137**
Subspecies: The WESTERN SMOOTH GREEN SNAKE, *O. v. blanchardi,* occurs in our area. The Black Hills population (e. Wyo. and w. S.D.) may belong to the eastern subspecies, the EASTERN SMOOTH GREEN SNAKE, *O. v. vernalis.*

Racers and Whipsnakes: Genera *Coluber* and *Masticophis*

Slender, fast-moving, diurnal snakes with a broad head, large eyes, and slender neck. *Lower preocular wedged between the upper labials* (Fig. 7, No. 7, p. 31). Adult racers (genus *Coluber*) are usually plain-colored above and the young are blotched. They range from s. Canada to Guatemala. Related species occur in Asia, Europe, and n. Africa. Whipsnakes (genus *Masticophis*) are striped or more or less crossbarred and the young generally resemble the adults. Some 7 species range from the U.S. to northern S. America; 4 species occur in the West.

When hunting, these snakes commonly crawl with the head held high and occasionally moved from side to side, perhaps to aid depth perception. Prey is seized with great speed, pinioned under loops of the body, and engulfed without constriction. Some individuals are aggressive, striking vigorously when cornered and biting when handled. When held by the neck, with body dangling, they may thrash with such force as to nearly jerk free. Most are good climbers and when pursued may escape by climbing shrubs or trees.

RACER *Coluber constrictor* **Pl. 36**

Identification: 20–73 in. (50–182 cm); in our area usually under 36 in. (90 cm). A slim snake with large eyes and smooth scales, in 15–17 rows at midbody (15 rows just in front of vent). Lower preocular wedged between upper labials. Anal divided. In the West this snake is *plain brown, olive, or bluish above,* and unmarked whitish or pale yellow below. Bluish dorsal coloration predominates in the region south of the Great Lakes, black (including the belly) in the East and Southeast, and light-colored speckling in e. Tex. and La. ***Young:*** Brown saddles on back, smaller blotches on sides, fading on tail. Faint blotching sometimes evident in individuals 1½–2 ft. (45–60 cm) long.

In the West, this snake favors open habitats — meadows, prairies, sagebrush flats, open chaparral, piñon-juniper woodland, and forest glades. It is found in both semiarid and moist environments but is absent from extremely dry areas and usually from high mountains. Often found in grassy places near rocks, logs, and other basking sites sought by lizards, upon which it feeds, or in the grass of streambanks. Chiefly ground-dwelling, but may climb shrubs and trees. Clutch of 2–31 eggs, laid June–Aug. (Western Yellow-bellied Racer, below, lays 3–7 eggs.) Eats small mammals, reptiles, frogs, and insects.

Similar species: (1) Young resemble the young of the Gopher Snake (p. 189), but have smooth scales and wedged preocular (Fig. 7, No. 7, p. 31). (2) Night Snake (p. 221) has vertical pupils. (3) See also Smooth Green Snake (p. 179).

Range: From s. B.C. (interior dry belt) and s. Sask. to Guatemala; Pacific to Atlantic Coasts. Isolated populations in mountains and river valleys in arid Southwest — at St. George, Utah; Boulder Dam, Nev.; and Eagar, Apache Co., Ariz. Sea level to around 8300 ft. (2550 m). **Map 136**

Subspecies: WESTERN YELLOW-BELLIED RACER, *C. c. mormon.* Usually 8 upper labials. 85 or more caudals. Young have 70–85 dorsal blotches. EASTERN YELLOW-BELLIED RACER,

C. c. flaviventris. Usually 7 upper labials. Usually fewer than 85 caudals. In some parts of range, belly is bright lemon yellow. Young have 65–80 dorsal blotches. Intergrade zone in cen. Wyo. shown on map with uncertainty.

COACHWHIP *Masticophis flagellum* **Pl. 36**
Identification: 36–102 in. (90–255 cm). The *wedged lower preocular* (Fig. 7, No. 7, p. 31), *smooth scales in 17 rows at midbody* (13 or fewer just before vent), and *lack of well-defined lengthwise stripes* are diagnostic. Coloration highly variable (see Subspecies). Throughout most of our area the general tone above is tan, gray, or pink with black crossbars on the neck. Occasional individuals are black. The slender body and tail, and scalation suggesting a braided whip, have earned it its common name. Usually 2 or 3 anterior temporals. Anal divided. ***Young:*** Blotched or crossbanded with dark brown or black on a light brown background. Black neck markings often faint or absent.

Frequents a variety of habitats — desert, prairie, scrubland, juniper-grassland, woodland, thornforest and farmland. Generally avoids dense vegetation. The ground surface may be flat or hilly, sandy or rocky. More tolerant than most snakes of dry, warm environments, hence abroad by day in hot weather even in deserts. Crawls with great speed, often taking refuge in a rodent burrow, among rocks, or the branches of a bush where it may defend itself with spirit, hissing and striking repeatedly, and sometimes approaching aggressively. When caught it usually attempts to bite; large individuals can lacerate the skin. Clutch of 4–20 eggs, laid June–July. Eats small mammals, birds and their eggs, lizards, snakes, insects, and carrion.
Range: Southern half of U.S. from coast to coast, south to tip of Baja Calif. and Querétaro, Mexico. Below sea level (in desert sinks) to around 7700 ft. (2350 m). **Map 133**
Subspecies: Among the following subspecies, the Red, Sonoran, and Baja California Coachwhips have a dark phase. Some of the localities where this phase has been found are shown with black squares on Map 133. RED COACHWHIP (Red Racer), *M. f. piceus.* Reddish or pinkish above, often grading to tan toward the tail. Wide black, dark brown or pink crossbands on neck, sometimes more or less united, and sometimes faint or absent. *Dark phase* (called Western Black Coachwhip): Black above. Pale below, or more or less blackened, becoming salmon pink to red toward tail. Found in s-cen. Ariz.; outnumbers red phase around Tucson. Young with dark crossbands about 3 scales wide. LINED COACHWHIP, *M. f. lineatulus.* Tan or light gray above, sometimes pinkish toward rear, each dorsal scale toward front of body with a lengthwise streak. Salmon pink below, toward tail. Often a yellowish to tan collar mark. Young with dark crossbands about 1 scale wide and a pale collar mark. Intergrades with Central Coachwhip (next subspecies) are usually grayish or brown above,

have fainter scale markings, and yellowish ventral color. CENTRAL COACHWHIP, *M. f. testaceus.* Tan, brown, pinkish to red above with dark, narrow crossbands on neck (sometimes absent) and sometimes continuing far toward rear. Some individuals are light-colored and lack pattern, others have a few broad (10–15 scales wide) crossbands. Cream below, with a double row of dark spots. The red phase is most common in e. Colo., n. and e. N.M., and w. Tex. SAN JOAQUIN COACHWHIP, *M. f. ruddocki.* Light yellow, olive brown, or occasionally reddish above with a few faint or no neck bands. May be light tan below. Range includes Sutter Buttes, Calif. SONORAN COACHWHIP, *M. f. cingulum.* Coloration highly variable — wide dark red or reddish brown crossbands above, separated by narrower light pink interspaces (common color phase in our area); also plain pink, reddish brown, tan, or black; rarely only a pale collar band is present. Some individuals are black above toward the front and reddish toward the rear. Dark individuals are pink to salmon below, toward the rear. BAJA CALIFORNIA COACHWHIP, *M. f. fulginosus.* Two color phases. *Dark phase:* Dark grayish brown above with light lines on sides, especially toward front. *Light phase:* Pale to dark yellow, tan, or light gray above with dark zigzag crossbands on body and wider dark bands on neck. Light phase common in Cape region.

CALIFORNIA WHIPSNAKE (Striped Racer) Pl. 36

Masticophis lateralis

Identification: 30–60 in. (75–152 cm). Plain black or dark brown above; lighter on the tail. *A conspicuous pale yellow or whitish stripe on each side* (often orange in San Francisco Bay area), extending from back of head to or beyond vent. Whitish, cream, pale yellow, or orange below, becoming coral pink on underside of tail. Dorsal scales smooth, in 17 rows at midbody. Wedged lower preocular. Anal divided.

The "chaparral snake" of Calif. Its favorite haunts are scrublands broken by scattered grassy patches, and rocky hillsides, gullies, canyons, or stream courses. Chiefly a snake of the foothills, but ranges in the mountains into mixed deciduous and pine forests. Ranges onto open flatland desert in cen. Baja Calif. An active diurnal species that may be seen foraging with its head held high. Sometimes climbs or seeks shelter among rocks or in a burrow. Clutch of 6–11 eggs, laid May–July. Eats frogs, lizards, snakes, small mammals, birds, and insects. Lizards (particularly spiny lizards — *Sceloporus*) are especially important in the diet.

Similar species: (1) Striped Whipsnake (below) has 15 scale rows at midbody and each light lateral stripe is bisected by a black line. (2) Sonoran Whipsnake (p. 183) has 2 or 3 light stripes on each side that fade out before reaching the tail, and the venter (underside) is pale yellow toward the tail.

Range: From n. Calif., west of Sierran crest and desert, to cen. Baja Calif. (San Jose de Comondú and about 9 mi. (14 km) east of

San Ignacio). Apparently absent from floor of Great Valley except in northern part. In s. Calif. ranges to desert foothills. From near sea level to around 7400 ft. (2250 m). Its distribution in Calif. coincides closely with that of chaparral. **Map 132**
Subspecies: CHAPARRAL WHIPSNAKE, *M. l. lateralis.* Stripes cream or yellow, 2 half-scale rows wide. ALAMEDA WHIPSNAKE, *M. l. euryxanthus.* Stripes and anterior ventral surface orange. Stripes broad, 1 and 2 half-scale rows wide. The Cape Whipsnake (p. 243) may prove to be a subspecies of the California Whipsnake.

STRIPED WHIPSNAKE *Masticophis taeniatus* **Pl. 36**
Identification: 36–72 in. (90–183 cm). A close relative of the California Whipsnake (above). In our area black, dark brown, or gray above, often with an olive or bluish cast. *A cream or white stripe on each side, bisected by a black line.* Additional black lines on the lower sides. Yellowish below, grading to white toward the head and coral pink toward tail. Dorsal scales smooth, *in 15 rows at midbody.* Wedged lower preocular. Anal divided.

Frequents shrublands, grasslands, sagebrush flats, and canyons, piñon-juniper woodland, and open pine-oak forests. Often attracted to rocky stream courses, permanent and intermittent. Frequents both flatlands and mountains. An alert, fast-moving, diurnal snake that seeks shelter in rock outcrops, rodent burrows, and in trees and shrubs. Clutch of 3–12 eggs, laid June–July. Eats lizards, snakes, small mammals, young birds and insects.
Similar species: See (1) California Whipsnake (above) and (2) Sonoran Whipsnake (below).
Range: S.-cen. Wash. south in Great Basin between Cascade-Sierran crest and Continental Divide, thence southeast across the Divide in N.M. into w. and cen. Tex.; south to se. Michoacán. Occurs west of Cascade Mts. in n. Calif. (to near Mugginsville, Siskiyou Co.) and sw. Ore. in Rogue R. Valley. An apparently isolated population exists near Cave Junction, Josephine Co., Ore. Sea level to around 9400 ft. (2860 m, in Panamint Mts., Calif.). **Map 134**
Subspecies: The DESERT STRIPED WHIPSNAKE, *M. t. taeniatus,* occurs in our area.

SONORAN WHIPSNAKE *Masticophis bilineatus* **Pl. 36**
Identification: 24–67 in. (60–170 cm). Olive, bluish gray, or light gray-brown above; lighter on rear $^2/_3$ of body. *Usually 2 or 3 light-colored stripes on each side, fading rapidly toward the tail.* Cream below, becoming *pale yellow toward tail.* Dorsal scales smooth, usually in 17 rows at midbody. Wedged lower preocular. Anal divided.

Ranges from semiarid lower mountain slopes, with growth of grass, saguaro cactus, paloverde, and ocotillo, through chaparral and juniper into the pine-oak belt in the mountains. Attracted to rocky stream courses. Both terrestrial and arboreal, climbing

gracefully in bushes and trees. Clutch of 6–13 eggs, laid June–July. Eats young birds, lizards, and frogs.
Similar species: Striped Whipsnake (above) is darker above and usually has 15 scale rows at midbody and 4 conspicuous lengthwise dark lines on each side.
Range: Cen. Ariz. and extreme sw. N.M., south to Oaxaca. From near sea level to 6100 ft. (610–1860 m). **Map 135**
Subspecies: SONORAN MOUNTAIN WHIPSNAKE, *M. b. bilineatus.* Olive to light bluish gray above. Uppermost light stripe covers adjacent halves of 2 scale rows, beginning usually on 4th scale behind the last upper labial. Chin usually unmarked. AJO MOUNTAIN WHIPSNAKE, *M. b. lineolatus.* Back darker than in Sonoran Mountain Whipsnake. Uppermost light stripe narrow — only one-half scale row wide, covering inner portion of 2 adjacent scale rows, beginning usually on 8th scale behind last upper labial. Chin spotted. Ajo Mts., Pima Co., Ariz.

WESTERN PATCH-NOSED SNAKE **Fig. 24, opp. Pl. 40**
Salvadora hexalepis
Identification: 20–46 in. (55–115 cm). A slender snake, with a broad yellow or beige, dark-bordered middorsal stripe and a large, patchlike rostral. Middorsal stripe usually 3 scales wide (or nearly so); occasionally faint or obscured by crossbands. Dark stripe on side usually on 3rd scale row, but sometimes on 4th row (Fig. 24) or on 3rd and 4th scale rows, counting upward from ends of ventrals. Plain white below, sometimes washed with dull orange, especially toward the tail. *2–3 small scales between rear pair of chin shields. 9 upper labials, none or 1 or 2 of which sometimes reach eye.* Dorsal scales smooth. Anal divided. ***Male:*** Keeled scales above vent and at base of tail. Keeling weak or absent in female.

An active diurnal resident of grasslands, chaparral, sagebrush plains, piñon-juniper woodland, and desertscrub. Found in both sandy and rocky areas on the lower slopes of mountains and on low, dry creosote bush plains in the most extreme parts of the desert. Crawls rapidly, like a whipsnake. Chiefly ground-dwelling, but occasionally climbs into vegetation. Clutch of 4–10 eggs, probably laid May–Aug. Eats small mammals, lizards, and reptile eggs.
Similar species: (1) Graham Patch-nosed Snake (below) usually has 8 upper labials, and the rear pair of chin shields either touch or are separated by a single small scale. (2) The rostral in the leaf-nosed snakes (pp. 177–178) more often completely separates the internasals; the back is blotched or crossbanded, rather than usually striped; and the anal is single.
Range: W.-cen. Nev. south to tip of Baja Calif. and nw. Sonora. Coastal s. Calif. to sw. Utah and cen. Ariz. In Calif. ranges to northern end of Carrizo Plain, extreme southern end of San Joaquin Valley, and Wendel area, Lassen Co. From below sea level (in desert sinks) to around 7000 ft. (2130 m). **Map 138**
Subspecies: DESERT PATCH-NOSED SNAKE, *S. h. hexalepis.*

1 upper labial reaches the eye. Loreal divided. Top of head gray. Median stripe 3 scale rows wide. COAST PATCH-NOSED SNAKE, *S. h. virgultea.* Like previous subspecies, but top of head brown, and dorsal stripe narrower — 1 and 2 half scale rows wide. Sides may be dark, including all but lowermost 1 or 2 scale rows. Usually 1 upper labial reaches the eye. Loreal usually divided into 2–4 scales. MOJAVE PATCH-NOSED SNAKE, *S. h. mojavensis.* Upper labials usually fail to reach the eye. Dorsal pattern of stripes sometimes vague or broken up and, around edges of range and especially in the eastern part, crossbars obscure the stripes. BAJA CALIFORNIA PATCH-NOSED SNAKE, *S. h. klauberi.* 2 upper labials usually reach eye. Loreal often divided. Light middorsal stripe 3 scales wide; stripe extends onto top of head. Lower lateral stripe well defined, on 3rd and 4th scale rows. BIG BEND PATCH-NOSED SNAKE, *S. h. deserticola.* 2 upper labials usually reach eye. Loreal usually single. Narrow dark stripe on 4th scale row (and sometimes including part of 3rd scale row) may shift to 3rd scale row toward front and rear.

Similar species: See Western Patch-nosed Snake (above).

Range: Se. Ariz., s. N.M., extreme w. Tex., south to Chihuahua and s. Sinaloa. From near sea level to 5000 ft. (1520 m). Coexists with Graham Patch-nosed Snake (below) in some areas.

Map 138

Remarks: The Big Bend Patch-nosed Snake may well be a distinct species, but there is as yet lack of adequate documentation in the scientific literature.

GRAHAM PATCH-NOSED SNAKE **Fig. 24; Pl. 40**

(Mountain Patch-nosed Snake) *Salvadora grahamiae*

Identification: 22–47 in. (56–119 cm). A white, gray, yellowish, or pale orange middorsal stripe that in our area is 3 (or nearly so) scale rows wide; stripe lighter than the sides and bordered on each side by a brown to nearly black stripe that is 2 or more scale rows wide. Our subspecies lacks or may have only a faint narrow dark line on the 3rd scale row; elsewhere the line may be distinct. Plain white or yellowish below, sometimes with a pinkish cast toward the tail. *Rear pair of chin shields touch or are separated by a single small scale. 8 upper labials.* Dorsal scales smooth. Anal divided.

A snake of rough terrain — rocky canyons, plateaus, and mountain slopes. In the West, it lives chiefly in open woodland and forests in the mountains, within the general range of the Western Patch-nosed Snake, but usually at higher elevations, above 4000 ft. (1220 m). In the more humid eastern part of its range, the Graham Patch-nosed Snake inhabits prairies, arid shrublands, and lowlands to sea level (s. Tex. and Mexico). Clutch of around 6–10 eggs, laid in spring and early summer. Eats lizards, lizard eggs, and probably small mammals.

Similar species: See Western Patch-nosed Snake (above).

Range: Se. Ariz., n.-cen. N.M., and cen. Tex. to n. Zacatecas. An isolated population at Oak Creek Canyon, Ariz. Sea level to over 6500 ft. (1980 m) but in West seldom below 4500 ft. (1370 m). Distribution spotty. **Map 140**

Remarks: Coexists with the Western Patch-nosed Snake at a number of localities, perhaps including the Santa Catalina and Baboquivari Mts., Ariz.

Subspecies: The PLATEAU PATCH-NOSED SNAKE, *S. g. grahamiae,* occurs in our area.

CORN SNAKE *Elaphe guttata* **Pl. 38**

Identification: 24–72 in. (60–183 cm). A long, slender snake that varies greatly in color over its wide range. In the West it is usually light gray with dark-edged brown or dark gray blotches on its back, and a pair of dark, lengthwise neck blotches that usually unite to form a *spear point between the eyes.* Usually a distinct eyestripe. In the north the blotches are especially numerous and narrow. Back occasionally unblotched, with 4 dark stripes. Belly with squarish black markings that usually merge to form stripes on the underside of the tail. *Dorsal scales in 25–31 rows at midbody,* mostly smooth but weakly keeled on the back. Ventral surface flat, forming an angle with the sides, which helps the snake climb. *Anal divided.*

Occurs in a variety of habitats — along stream courses and river bottoms, on rocky wooded hillsides, in canyons and arroyos, and in coniferous forests. May be found on farms. Although it climbs well it is usually found on the ground. It is a secretive snake that spends much time in rodent burrows. Nocturnal during warm weather. Look for it beneath logs, rocks, and other objects and on highways at night. When caught it often voids feces and the contents of its anal scent glands. Clutch of 3–21 eggs, laid May–July. Eats small mammals (including rodents and bats), birds, lizards, and frogs, which it kills by constriction.

Similar species: (1) Trans-Pecos Rat Snake (p. 187) has suboculars and H-shaped dorsal blotches. (2) Green Rat Snake (below) in our area is greenish above, with or without a faint pattern, and plain whitish below. Spotted young lack spear point on head. See also (3) Glossy Snake (p. 187), (4) Gopher Snake (p. 189), and (5) Common Water Snake (p. 197).

Range: E. Utah and cen. N.M. to Atlantic and Gulf Coasts; s. Neb. to s. Coahuila and San Luis Potosí. In w. Colo. and e. Utah, found in major valleys of the Colorado R., including Green R. near Colo. border, Uintah Co., Utah. Sea level to around 6000 ft. (1830 m). **Map 143**

Subspecies: THE GREAT PLAINS RAT SNAKE, *E. g. emoryi,* occurs in our area.

GREEN RAT SNAKE *Elaphe triaspis* **Pl. 38**

Identification: 24–50 in. (60–125 cm). In our area and over much of its range, this is a *slim, plain green, greenish gray, or olive* snake with *unmarked, whitish or cream underparts* that are tinged with yellow. (Adults blotched on Yucatan Peninsula, Mex.). *25 or more dorsal scale rows,* weakly keeled along the middle of the back. Anal divided. ***Young:*** Blotched, much as in Corn Snake (above). In our area hatchlings are tan above, with brown blotches.

In our area this species is primarily a mountain snake that frequents wooded, rocky canyon bottoms near streams. It occurs in woodland, thornscrub, and chaparral. Plants may include pine, oak, sycamore, walnut, cottonwood, wild grape, and willow. Its habits are little known; it appears to spend much time during the day in trees or shrubs, retiring at night into rock crevices and other underground retreats. Its slender form and color help conceal it among plants. Eats rodents (woodrats), other small mammals, lizards, and birds.

Similar species: (1) Smooth Green Snake (p. 179) has smooth dorsal scales, in 15–17 rows at midbody. See also (2) Corn Snake (above) and (3) Lyre Snake (p. 221).

Range: Se. Ariz. and s. Tamaulipas, southward along slopes of Mexican highlands to Costa Rica. In Ariz. in Baboquivari, Pajarito, Santa Rita, Empire, Whetstone, and Chiricahua Mts.; in N.M. in the Peloncillo Mts. (Guadalupe Canyon). Near sea level to around 7000 ft. (2130 m). **Map 144**

Subspecies: The WESTERN GREEN RAT SNAKE, *E. t. intermedia,* occurs in our area.

TRANS-PECOS RAT SNAKE *Elaphe subocularis* **Pl. 38**

Identification: 34–66 in. (86–168 cm). The "H-snake," named for its *dorsal pattern of black or dark brown, H-shaped blotches* with pale centers on a yellowish olive or yellowish tan background. The sides of the H's may join to form lengthwise stripes down each side, especially toward the head. Olive-buff below, becoming white on the neck and throat. Dorsal scales in 31–35 rows at midbody, weakly keeled along middle of back. Head broad, body slender, eyes large. *A row of small scales (suboculars) below the eye and preocular.* Anal divided.

A primarily nocturnal snake of arid and semiarid habitats, found in the following plant associations — agave, creosote bush, acacia, and ocotillo; persimmon, shin oak, and cedar; yucca, mesquite, and cactus. Seems to prefer rocky areas. Chiefly an inhabitant of the Chihuahuan Desert. Clutch of 3–7 eggs, laid in summer. Eats small mammals (rodents, bats), birds, and lizards, killed by constriction.

Similar species: See (1) Corn Snake (p. 186), and (2) Lyre Snake (p. 221).

Range: Southern N.M. to s. Coahuila. In w. Tex. in Apache, Guadalupe, Davis, and Chisos Mts. and sw. edge of Edwards Plateau. From around 1500 to 5000 ft. (460–1520 m). **Map 145**

GLOSSY SNAKE *Arizona elegans* **Pl. 39**

Identification: 26–70 in. (66–178 cm). Looks like a faded Gopher Snake. Light brown, cream, pinkish, or yellowish gray above, with tan, brown, or gray blotches that are edged with blackish. Sometimes called the "faded snake" because of its bleached appearance in the more arid parts of its range. White or pale buff below, with *no markings* (outer edges of ventrals sometimes have dark markings). *Dorsal scales smooth and glossy,* in 25–35 rows at midbody. 2 prefrontals. *Lower jaw inset (countersunk).* Pupils slightly vertical. *Anal single.*

Occurs in a variety of habitats — light shrubby to barren desert, sagebrush flats, grassland, chaparral-covered slopes, and woodland. Generally prefers open areas. The ground is often sandy or loamy but some rocks may be present. This snake is an excellent burrower. In the West, it remains underground by day and is rarely encountered beneath objects on the surface. Active mostly at night except in the eastern part of its range, where it is often diurnal. Clutch of 3–23 eggs, laid in summer. Eats lizards (especially), snakes, and small mammals, which may be killed by constriction.

Similar species: (1) Gopher Snake (below) has keeled scales. (2) Rat snakes (*Elaphe* species, pp. 186–187) have keeled scales and a divided anal. (3) Night Snake (p. 221) has a flattened head, distinctly vertical pupils, and a divided anal. (4) Corn Snake (p. 186) lacks inset lower jaw and has a divided anal. (5) See also Lyre Snake (p. 221).

Range: Southwest U.S. from sw. Neb. and e. Tex. to cen. Calif.; s. Utah to s. Baja Calif., s. Sinaloa, and San Luis Potosí. Reported from Egan Canyon, Ely, Nev. Below sea level (in desert sinks) to around 6000 ft. (1830 m). **Map 142**

Subspecies: KANSAS GLOSSY SNAKE, *A. e. elegans.* 29–31 dorsal scale rows at midbody. Usually 197–219 (avg. 206) ventrals in males, 208–227 (avg. 216) in females. 39–69 (avg. 53) large, dark blotches on body. A large-blotched, dark-colored, long-tailed form. PAINTED DESERT GLOSSY SNAKE, *A. e. philipi.* Dorsal scales at midbody usually in 27 or fewer rows (not over 29 rows). 183–202 (avg. 195) ventrals in males, 192–211 (avg. 204) in females. 53–80 (avg. 64) body blotches. Also a long-tailed form. CALIFORNIA GLOSSY SNAKE, *A. e. occidentalis.* Usually 27 rows of dorsal scales. 51–75 (avg. 63) body blotches. Marks on edges of ventrals. Lower labials often spotted. The darkest western subspecies, with dark ground color and chocolate-colored body blotches on a dark background. This and the remaining subspecies are short-tailed forms. ARIZONA GLOSSY SNAKE, *A. e. noctivaga.* 25–29 dorsal scale rows. No marks on ventrals or spots on labials, except occasionally on last lower labial. Body blotches slightly wider or equal to spaces between them. DESERT GLOSSY SNAKE, *A. e. eburnata.* Usually 1 preocular. 27 or fewer dorsal scale rows. 208–238 (avg. 219) ventrals in males, 220–241 (avg. 231) in females. A pale subspecies with 53–85 (avg. 68) small narrow dorsal blotches, narrower than the spaces between them, rarely more than 7 scale rows wide at dorsal midline. MOJAVE

GLOSSY SNAKE, *A. e. candida.* Usually 2 preoculars. 27 or fewer dorsal scale rows. 203–220 (avg. 214) ventrals in males, 220–232 (avg. 223) in females. 53–73 (avg. 63) narrow blotches on body, about 9 scale rows wide at dorsal midline. Blotches narrower than the spaces between them. A light-colored form. PENINSULA GLOSSY SNAKE, *A. e. pacata.* Differs from other subspecies in having fewer blotches on the body (36–41, avg. 39) and 27 middorsal scale rows.

GOPHER SNAKE *Pituophis melanoleucus* **Pl. 39**

Identification: 36–110 in. (90–275 cm). In our area, a large yellow or cream-colored snake with black, brown, or reddish brown dorsal blotches, usually more widely spaced on the tail than on the body. Some populations have reddish orange in the dorsal interspaces between the blotches. Smaller secondary blotches on the sides. Usually a dark line across the head in front of the eyes and from behind the eye to the angle of the jaw. White to yellowish below, often spotted with black. Striped-unblotched and striped-blotched individuals are found occasionally, chiefly in cen. and w.-cen. Calif. *Dorsal scales keeled, in 27–37 rows* at midbody. *Usually 4 prefrontals.* Anal single.

Lives in a variety of habitats, from the lowlands high into the mountains and from coast to coast. Frequents desert, prairie, brushland, woodland, open coniferous forest, and farmland. In the West it is especially common in grassland and open brushland. Soil conditions vary — sand, loam, rock, or hardpan. This snake is a good climber and burrower, active chiefly by day except in hot weather. When aroused it hisses loudly and sometimes flattens its head and vibrates its tail. This behavior, along with its markings, which are sometimes diamond-shaped, causes these snakes to be mistaken for rattlesnakes and killed. 1–2 clutches of 2–24 eggs, laid June–August. Eats rodents, rabbits, birds and their eggs, and occasionally lizards and insects. Kills by constriction.

Similar species: (1) The blotched young of the Racer (p. 180) resemble the Gopher Snake, but they have smooth scales and large eyes. (2) Glossy Snake (p. 187) has smooth scales. (3) Rat snakes (*Elaphe* species, pp. 186–187) have a divided anal. See also (4) Corn Snake (p. 186) and (5) Lyre Snake (p. 221).

Range: From Pacific to Atlantic Coast; sw. Canada, cen. Minn., Mich., N.J. to near tip of Fla., Gulf Coast, Veracruz, s. Sinaloa, and tip of Baja Calif. Sight record at McBride, B.C. Below sea level (in desert sinks) to around 9000 ft. (2740 m). **Map 141**

Subspecies: BULLSNAKE, *P. m. sayi.* Rostral narrow, much higher than wide, raised well above nearby scales. 41 or more blotches down back. SONORAN GOPHER SNAKE, *P. m. affinis.* Rostral broad, raised only slightly (if at all) above nearby scales. Ground color of sides with no gray wash, as in Central Baja California Gopher Snake (below). Dorsal blotches toward front of body brown, unconnected to other blotches. Blotches darken toward rear. GREAT BASIN GOPHER SNAKE, *P. m. deserticola*. Resembles the Sonoran Gopher Snake, but dorsal blotches toward front of body usually black (blotches gray with black edges in young) and connected to one another and the secondary blotches on sides of neck to form a lateral dark band, leaving interspaces as isolated pale dorsal blotches. PACIFIC GOPHER SNAKE, *P. m. catenifer*. Suffusion of grayish dots on sides of body and on underside of the tail. Dorsal blotches toward front of body brown or black, separated from one another and the secondary blotches. SAN DIEGO GOPHER SNAKE, *P. m. annectens*. Resembles the Pacific Gopher Snake but dorsal blotches toward front black, more or less joined to each other and the secondary blotches. SANTA CRUZ GOPHER SNAKE, *P. m. pumilis*. A dwarf race resembling the San Diego Gopher Snake. Usually 29 or fewer dorsal scale rows at midbody (other subspecies usually have over 29). No black-streaked scales toward front of body in the light spaces between the dorsal blotches. Santa Cruz, Santa Rosa, and San Miguel Is. off s. Calif. coast. CENTRAL BAJA CALIFORNIA GOPHER SNAKE, *P. m. bimaris*. Ground color of sides not suffused with gray. Dorsal blotches on front of body usually black or, in immatures, composed of gray scales with black edges. Fewer than 50 blotches on body. Light dorsal interspaces toward front of body clear or faintly streaked. CAPE GOPHER SNAKE, *P. m. vertebralis*. Ground color as mentioned above. Dorsal blotches toward front of body red or burnt orange and united at sides; rear blotches black (at base of tail). Head may completely lack dark markings. A dark stripe usually present under tail.

Kingsnakes and Milk Snakes: *Genus Lampropeltis*

The generic name means "shiny skin." Medium-sized snakes with smooth scales and a single anal. Head little wider than the neck. The dorsal pattern is highly variable but frequently consists of dark and light crossbands. Dark markings below.

Kingsnakes are found in a variety of habitats — woodland, coniferous forests, grassland, cultivated fields, tropical scrub, and desert, from se. Canada to Ecuador. Although some species are excitable when first encountered, and vibrate the tail, hiss, and strike, many quickly become tame and make good pets. Because of their snake-eating habits they should not be caged with other snakes. Prey is killed by constriction.

Four species occur in our area. A 5th is probable — the Gray-banded Kingsnake *(L. mexicana),* known from the southern end of the Guadalupe Mts. in w. Tex. Most of this mountain range extends into se. N.M. The snake is gray to dusky with well-spaced, light-edged, dark crossbands, usually variously split by red or orange.

COMMON KINGSNAKE *Lampropeltis getulus* **Pl. 37**
Identification: 30–82 in. (75–208 cm). Over most of this snake's range in the West, its pattern consists of alternating *bands of plain black or dark brown* and white or pale yellow, the pale bands broadening on the belly. Pattern alone will distinguish most individuals. In se. Ariz. and N.M., however, light bands give way to varying amounts of *light speckling on a dark background,* and some individuals are entirely speckled (Fig. 23, opp. Pl. 37). Other pattern types are found farther east. A black form without bands occurs in s. Ariz. and a striped phase with a more or less continuous pale yellow or whitish middorsal stripe occurs at scattered localities chiefly in s. Calif. and Baja Calif. (see Map 148, vertical black bars). Individuals with a banded pattern but dusky above and dark below occur in coastal Los Angeles Co., Calif. Black-bellied individuals with pale crossbands that broaden on the lower sides to form a lateral stripe are found in the northern part of the San Joaquin Valley, Calif. (see Map 148, open triangles). Scales smooth and polished-looking, in 19–25 rows at midbody. Caudals divided. Anal single. ***Young:*** Usually patterned like the adult but in s. Ariz. blotched at first, becoming spotted with age.

Frequents a great variety of habitats — coniferous forest, woodland, swampland, coastal marshes, river bottoms, farmland, prairie, chaparral, and desert. Often found in the vicinity of rocky outcrops and clumps of vegetation and under rotting logs, old lumber, and rocks. Chiefly terrestrial but sometimes climbs. Active mostly in the morning and late afternoon but in hot weather abroad at night. Usually gentle but occasionally strikes, hisses, and vibrates its tail. Sometimes rolls into a ball with its head often at the center and everts the lining of its vent. Clutch of 2–24 eggs, laid May–Aug. Eats snakes (including rattlers), lizards, small turtles, reptile eggs, frogs, birds and their eggs, and small mammals.
Similar species: (1) In the Sierra Nevada the California Mountain Kingsnake (p. 192) sometimes lacks red markings and resembles the Common Kingsnake, but the white rings usually are not broadened on the lowermost rows of dorsal scales. (2) In the Long-nosed Snake (p. 195) some or all of the caudals are undivided.
Range: Coast to coast, from s. N.J. to Fla. in the East, Neb. to the Gulf in cen. U.S., and sw. Ore. to tip of Baja Calif. in the West. On Mexican mainland to n. Sinaloa, San Luis Potosí, and n. Tamaulipas. Hovenweep National Monument area, San Juan Co., Utah, and McElmo Canyon area, Montezuma Co. and near La Junta, Otero Co., Colo. Sea level to around 7000 ft. (2130 m).
Map 148
Subspecies: CALIFORNIA KINGSNAKE, *L. g. californiae.* Two pattern types — (1) banded and (2) striped, with intermediate forms. (1) Dark brown or black above with 21–44 white to yellowish dorsal crossbands that extend to or onto the belly. In some areas brown or dusky pigment may be present on bases of the scales of the light crossbands — especially in s. Calif., sw. Ariz., and

s. Baja Calif. (2) Dark brown or black above, with a whitish to cream middorsal stripe and lateral stripes formed by a series of light-centered scales on rows 1–3 or 1–6 (lowermost scales may be almost completely light-colored). Usually uniformly dark or light below. The striped pattern is especially common in San Diego Co., Calif. (seen in about ⅓ of snakes encountered). See Map 148 for some localities where this phase has been found. Intermediate forms between (1) and (2) are variously striped or crossbanded. In occasional individuals in cen. and s. coastal Calif., light crossbands do not extend to belly but stop on 1st scale row, leaving belly uniformly black. Other individuals may have crossbands connected along 1st scale row to form light lateral stripes, and the belly is usually black. Sometimes a complete or partial middorsal stripe is present. This phase has been found in cen. Calif. at Gadwall, Firebaugh, Mendota, Los Banos, Friant, and Clovis. BLACK KINGSNAKE, *L. g. nigritus.* Uniformly dark brown or slaty black above, usually without traces of crossbands or stripes. Sometimes small light centers on lateral scales. Usually solid black below, except for light-colored anal scale. DESERT KINGSNAKE, *L. g. splendida.* Brown or black above, usually with 42–97 narrow (1–2 scales wide) whitish to yellowish crossbands formed by light-centered scales. Light crossbands sometimes absent. Occasionally scales between light bands have light centers, producing an entirely light-spotted back (see Fig. 23, opp. Pl. 37). Lateral scales with light centers, from rows 1–10. Usually dark below (except for light-colored anal scale) or sometimes blotched (in eastern part of range).

CALIFORNIA MOUNTAIN KINGSNAKE Pl. 37

Lampropeltis zonata

Identification: 20–40 in. (51–102 cm). A beautiful serpent with glistening scales and black, white, and red crossbands, the red bordered on each side with black. A harmless snake, sometimes called the Coral Kingsnake because of its resemblance to the venomous coral snakes. The red bands may be interrupted on the back, appearing as a wedge on each side within a broad black band; may be wider than either the black or white bands; and, on Todos Santos I. off Baja Calif. and occasionally in the cen. Sierra Nevada, the red bands may be completely absent. The combination of red and black markings (a black band more or less split by red) is called a *triad.* Head black in front of the 1st white band on back of head. *Snout generally black,* with or without red markings. Usually the *white bands do not broaden conspicuously on the lower scale rows.* Pattern on back imperfectly but variously carried onto the belly. Scales smooth, in 21 or 23 rows at midbody. Anal single.

An inhabitant of moist woods — coniferous forest, woodland, and chaparral, ranging from sea level high into the mountains. Search for this snake in the vicinity of well-lit rocky streams in wooded areas where there are rotting logs. Chiefly diurnal, but

nocturnal in warm weather. Clutch of 3–8 eggs, laid June–July. Eats lizards, snakes, bird eggs and nestlings, and small mammals.
Similar species: (1) In the Sonoran Mountain Kingsnake (below) the black bands become narrow or disappear on the sides, and the snout is white or pale yellow. (2) In the Milk Snake (p. 194) the white bands usually become wider on the lowermost scale rows. (3) Long-nosed Snake (p. 195) has single caudals. (4) In the Western Coral Snake (p. 222) the red markings are bordered with white or yellow rather than black.
Range: S. Wash. to n. Baja Calif.; mountains of coastal and interior Calif. except deserts. Distribution spotty: isolated populations in the vicinity of White Salmon, Wash. and near The Dalles, and in the Maupin-Tygh Valley area (sight records) in n. Ore. On South Todos Santos I., Baja Calif. Sea level to around 9000 ft. (2750 m). **Map 146**
Subspecies: SIERRA MOUNTAIN KINGSNAKE, *L. z. multicincta.* Rear edge of the 1st white band on the head located behind corner of mouth. 23–48 (avg. 35) body triads, usually fewer than 60% of triads split by red (red sometimes absent). SAINT HELENA MOUNTAIN KINGSNAKE, *L. z. zonata.* First white band as above but 24–30 (avg. 27) body triads, usually 60% or more completely split by red. Snout dark. Black pigment, bordering the red on the sides, usually more than 1 scale wide. COAST MOUNTAIN KINGSNAKE, *L. z. multifasciata.* Rear edge of the 1st white band on the head located behind or in front of the corner of the mouth. 26–45 (avg. 35) body triads, 60% or more completely split by red. Snout with red markings. SAN BERNARDINO MOUNTAIN KINGSNAKE, *L. z. parvirubra.* Rear edge of the 1st white band located on or in front of the last upper labial. 35–56 (avg. 41) body triads, usually fewer than 60% split by red. Snout dark. SAN DIEGO MOUNTAIN KINGSNAKE, *L. z. pulchra.* 1st white band as in San Bernardino Mountain Kingsnake. 26–39 (avg. 33) body triads, usually 60% or more of them split by red. Snout dark. BAJA CALIFORNIA MOUNTAIN KINGSNAKE, *L. z. agalma.* High triad count — over 40 on body. Considerable red on body and red on snout.

SONORAN MOUNTAIN KINGSNAKE **Pl. 37**

Lampropeltis pyromelana

Identification: 18–41 in. (45–104 cm). A red-, black-, and white-banded kingsnake with a rather wide, flat head. The amount of red in the black bands varies greatly, forming a wedge on each side or completely splitting the black bands. In some individuals the red forms broad bands that are narrowly bordered by black. *Black bands often become narrow or disappear on the sides.* Pattern on back imperfectly but variously carried onto the belly. *Snout white, pale yellow, or black flecked with white.* Scales smooth, in 23 or 25 rows at midbody. Over 210 ventrals in individuals from our area. Anal single.

A mountain-dweller, ranging from piñon-juniper woodland and chaparral to the pine-fir belt. Frequents both shrubland and coniferous forest, often near streams and springs. Usually found in places with rocks, logs, and dense clumps of vegetation — under objects or occasionally exposed. Clutch of 3–6 eggs, laid June–July. Eats lizards and probably snakes and small mammals.
Similar species: (1) The snout of the California Mountain Kingsnake (p. 192) is solid black or black with red markings, and the black bands usually do not become narrow on the sides of the body. (2) Milk Snake (below) in the West has fewer than 210 ventrals (fewer than 200 in areas of overlap with the Sonoran Mountain Kingsnake), and the pale bands become wider on the lower sides. (3) Venomous Western Coral Snake (p. 222) has broad red bands that are bordered with white or yellow rather than black.
Range: Distribution spotty: Cen. Utah and e. Nev. south in mountains of Ariz. and sw. N.M. into Sierra Madre Occidental to s. Chihuahua. Isolated populations in Egan (Water and Sawmill Canyons) and Shell Creek Ranges, Nev., the Wah Wah Mts., Utah, and in the Hualapi Mts., Ariz. Other scattered mountain populations farther south. From 2800–9100 ft. (850–2800 m). **Map 149**
Subspecies: UTAH MOUNTAIN KINGSNAKE, *L. p. infralabialis.* 9 lower labials. Half or more of the white body bands extend unbroken across the belly. ARIZONA MOUNTAIN KINGSNAKE, *L. p. pyromelana.* 10 lower labials. Usually half, or less than half of the white body bands are complete across the belly. Usually over 43 white bands.

MILK SNAKE *Lampropeltis triangulum* **Pl. 37**
Identification: 14–54 in. (35–135 cm). Broad bands or saddles of red, orange, or brown on back, bordered by black and separated by narrower white or yellow bands. The *white bands tend to widen on the lowermost scales.* Width of dark and light bands varies widely over this snake's range, which includes most of the U.S. The bands are very wide and red in parts of se. and s. U.S. within the range of the venomous Eastern Coral Snake (which also has wide red bands), a condition regarded as mimicry that helps protect the Milk Snake from predators. Dorsal pattern usually imperfectly but variously carried onto the belly. Scales smooth. Anal single.

Frequents a variety of habitats — coniferous and tropical hardwood forests, broadleaf woodland, river bottoms, rocky hillsides, prairies, sand dunes, farmland, and suburban areas, from the lowlands well up into the mountains. Secretive — found inside rotten logs and stumps and under rocks, logs, bark, and boards. Occasionally encountered in the open. Often nocturnal, especially in warm weather. Clutch of 2–17 eggs, laid June–July in the U.S. Eats snakes, lizards, reptile eggs, small mammals, birds and their eggs, and occasionally insects and earthworms. Because in the East these snakes are often found in barnyards where they hunt mice, they have been erroneously accused of milking cows, hence the common name.

Similar species: See (1) California Mountain (p. 192) and (2) Sonoran Mountain Kingsnakes (above). (3) Long-nosed Snake (p. 193) has single caudals. (4) Arizona Coral Snake (p. 223) has the red bands bordered with white or pale yellow instead of black.

Range: Se. Canada to Ecuador, Atlantic Coast to cen. Mont. and cen. Utah. Black dot (on map) in N.M. is Roadrunner Ranch, 33 mi. (53 km) east of Corona, Lincoln Co. Old records for Ft. Benton, Chouteau Co., Mont., and Ft. (Camp) Apache, Navajo Co., Ariz. In Ariz., known from the drainage of the Little Colorado R. at Wupatki National Monument and near St. Johns; reported from Petrified Forest National Park. The subspecies relationship of these snakes is uncertain. A far northern locality in the West is near Sun Prairie, Phillips Co., Mont. Sea level to around 9000 ft. (2740 m). **Map 147**

Subspecies: CENTRAL PLAINS MILK SNAKE, *L. t. gentilis*. Snout usually mottled black and white. Triads (see p. 192) united across the belly, with the black bands often constricting or completely separating the red color at dorsal midline and usually interrupting it at ventral midline. PALE MILK SNAKE, *L. t. multistrata*. Snout light orange or whitish flecked with black. Triads not completely united across the belly. Red tends to be replaced by orange. Belly light with a few black spots, frequently unmarked. NEW MEXICO MILK SNAKE, *L. t. celaenops*. Snout mottled black and white or occasionally black. Black borders expand middorsally but usually do not interrupt red bands. Red bands separated by black border on edge of ventrals with midventral light area between. In some individuals the ventral dark markings are shaped like the Roman numeral II, the top and bottom bars representing the black triad borders and the vertical "posts" black margins that enclose the ventral portion of the red band, which sometimes is replaced by black. White bands expanded at the dorsal midline. Front pairs of chin shields frequently flecked with black. UTAH MILK SNAKE, *L. t. taylori*. Snout entirely black or light with black along lengthwise furrow between prefrontals and internasals. Red bands separated by black on 1st scale row or edge of ventrals. Black pigment frequently interrupts red bands at dorsal midline.

LONG-NOSED SNAKE *Rhinocheilus lecontei* Pl. 37

Identification: 20–41 in. (50–104 cm). Typically a slim, speckled snake with black saddles that are flecked with whitish on the sides. Spaces between saddles are cream, yellow, pink, or red, except for a whitish border next to the saddles. Spaces between saddles usually marked with dark flecks on the sides. Belly whitish or yellow, with a few dark spots toward sides. Snout long and pointed, and head only slightly wider than neck. Lower jaw countersunk (inset). Most *scales under tail in a single row*. Scales smooth, in 23 rows. Anal single. ***Young:*** Speckling on sides faint or absent.

An inhabitant of deserts, prairies, shrubland, and tropical habitats in Mexico. In the Southwest it is crepuscular and nocturnal and likely to be found on roadways at night. When alarmed it may vibrate its tail, writhe the hind part of its body, and evert its vent lining, releasing blood and feces. A good burrower. 1, perhaps 2, clutches of 4–11 eggs, laid June–Aug. Eats lizards and their eggs, small snakes, small mammals, and occasionally birds. Large prey is killed by constriction.

Similar species: (1) Differs from the kingsnakes (pp. 190–193) in having most of the caudal scales in a single rather than double row. (2) See also Thornscrub Hook-nosed Snake (p. 216).

Range: Sw. Idaho and se. Colo. to cen. Baja Calif. (Mission San Borja), San Luis Potosí and s. Tamaulipas; cen. Tex. to cen. and s. coastal Calif. Populations apparently isolated in the South Range, Idaho, and the Dragerton area, Carbon Co., Utah. On Cerralvo I., Gulf of Calif. Below sea level (in desert sinks) to around 5400 ft. (1650 m). **Map 150**

Subspecies: TEXAS LONG-NOSED SNAKE, *R. l. tessellatus.* Snout sharp; rostral raised above nearby scales, giving snout an upward tilt. WESTERN LONG-NOSED SNAKE, *R. l. lecontei.* Snout blunter than in Texas Long-nosed Snake; rostral only slightly raised and snout without an upward tilt. In the more arid parts of its range a contrastingly banded color phase occurs (formerly regarded as a distinct species, *R. clarus*) that usually lacks red in the interspaces and has scant black spotting on the sides. The black saddles are longer and fewer than in the typical form.

PLAIN-BELLIED WATER SNAKE Pl. 43

Nerodia erythrogaster

Identification: 30–62 in. (76–157 cm). In our area known only from extreme se. N.M. A moderately heavy bodied, plain-colored or blotched snake that has *strongly keeled scales with apical pits.* Olive, gray, brown or reddish brown above, often with dark brown blotches edged with black down the back. In our western subspecies, adults tend to retain juvenile blotching. Smaller blotches on the sides often alternate with the dorsal ones. Sometimes the dorsal pattern is represented only by pale crossbars edged with black. *Belly plain yellow* (in our area), orange, or red, but occasionally with dark color on edges of ventrals. In our subspecies, underside of tail usually plain orange or reddish. In central and eastern part of its range, adults usually plain-colored above, the belly red or orange-red, hence the names "redbelly" and "copperbelly." Anal usually divided. ***Young:*** Strongly blotched. ***Male:*** Knobs on scale keels above the anal region.

Highly aquatic, usually found in or near water, but may move away from it in wet weather. Frequents river bottoms, springs, swamps, wooded borders of streams, rivers, lakes, and ponds. In the West it follows river courses into arid country, seeking the permanent or semipermanent water of streams, ditches, and cattle tanks. When first caught it often bites and discharges foul-smelling musk from its anal scent glands. Live-bearing. One, perhaps 2, litters of 5–32 young, born Aug.–Oct. Eats crayfish, fish, frogs, tadpoles, and salamander larvae.

Similar species: (1) Garter snakes (*Thamnophis* species, pp. 198–210) have a single anal. (2) Rat snakes (*Elaphe* species, pp. 186–187) have weakly keeled scales, confined to the upper part of the back. (3) See also Common Water Snake (below).

Range: S. Mich. to Gulf Coast and cen. Nuevo León with isolated populations in e.-cen. Durango and Zacatecas; Atlantic Coast to extreme w. Okla. and se. N.M. (Lower Pecos R. drainage). Sea level to around 6700 ft. (2040 m, in Mexico). **Map 151**

Subspecies: The BLOTCHED WATER SNAKE, *N. e. transversa,* occurs in our area.

COMMON WATER SNAKE *Nerodia sipedon* **Pl. 43**

Identification: 22–53 in. (56–135 cm). In our area, known only from e. Colo. A moderately heavy-bodied serpent with *prominently keeled scales that have apical pits* (see rear endpapers). The pits are sometimes represented by oval discolored spots that are not actually indented. Dark crossbands on the front part of the body give way near midbody to large dorsal blotches that continue onto the tail and alternate with smaller blotches on the sides. Ground color varies from pale gray to dark brown or black, and markings from bright reddish brown to black. Some individuals and populations have little or no dorsal pattern. Old individuals may be black. *Black or reddish half-moons on the belly, in regular or irregular arrangement;* or belly with yellow, orange, or pinkish stripe down middle and stippled with gray at the sides. Anal divided. ***Young:*** More contrastingly marked than adult. Pattern black or dark brown on a pale gray or light brown background. ***Male:*** Knobbed keels on dorsal scales in anal region.

Found in or near swamps, marshes, ponds, streams, rivers, lakes, reservoirs, and coastal areas of brackish or salt water. Individuals may be seen basking on shore, or on logs or piles of rotting vegetation in the water, and when alarmed swim to the bottom or to the cover of emergent vegetation. A highly aquatic snake that seldom ventures far from water. When caught it often bites and may expel a foul-smelling secretion from its anal glands. Live-bearing, 8–46 (rarely to around 100) young, born Aug.–Oct. Eats crayfish, insects, fish, salamanders, frogs, toads, tadpoles, young turtles, and small mammals.

Similar species: (1) Plain-bellied Water Snake (above) usually has an unmarked belly, and the crossbands are largely confined to the neck. (2) Garter snakes (*Thamnophis* species, pp. 198–210) lack apical pits on the dorsal scales and have a single anal. (3) Corn Snake (p. 186) has smooth scales on the sides and a spear-shaped mark on the head.

Range: E. Colo. to Atlantic Coast; se. Canada to Gulf Coast from e. La. to w. Fla. Sea level to around 5500 ft. (1680 m).
Map 152
Subspecies: The NORTHERN WATER SNAKE, *N. s. sipedon,* occurs in our area.

RED-BELLIED SNAKE *Storeria occipitomaculata* **Pl. 41**
Identification: 8–16 in. (20–41 cm). Typically a red-bellied snake with dorsal stripes and usually 3 *light-colored blotches at the back of the head.* Top of head blackish. Blotches may be small or absent in Black Hills population in our area (see below). *Usually 4 narrow, dark dorsal stripes* or a broad, light-colored middorsal stripe, or both. Plain brown or gray above; occasionally black. The belly, usually bright red, varies through orange to pale yellow, or may be dark in generally darkened individuals. Dorsal scales keeled, in 15 rows. Anal divided. ***Young:*** Resemble adult but darker, sometimes blackish.

Over much of its range, this snake primarily lives in wooded hilly and mountainous regions. It occurs under stones, logs, and boards, and inside rotten stumps, often at the edge of clearings and in or near sphagnum bogs. Found near houses and other buildings. Live-bearing; 1–21 young, born June–Sept. Eats slugs, earthworms, and soft-bodied insects.
Range: Widespread over e. U.S. but distribution spotty. Extreme s. Canada to Gulf Coast. Atlantic Coast to e. N.D. in north, and e. Tex. in south. Isolated population in Black Hills of sw. S.D. and ne. Wyo. Sea level to around 5600 ft. (1710 m). **Map 153**
Subspecies: The BLACK HILLS RED-BELLIED SNAKE, *S. o. pahasapae,* occurs in our area. Two color phases — (1) gray and (2) reddish brown with the pair of black dorsolateral stripes bordering a paler brown middorsal stripe.
Remarks: A Brown Snake *(Storeria dekayi)* is reported to have been collected in Las Animas Co., Colo. in 1883. Since the snake occurs in sw. Kans., it should continue to be sought in Colo. It differs from the Red-bellied Snake in having 17 dorsal scale rows and lacking a red belly.

Garter Snakes: Genus *Thamnophis*

Moderately slender serpents with head slightly wider than the neck. Dorsal scales keeled and without apical pits. Anal usually single. The scales of water snakes (genus *Nerodia*) have apical pits (see rear endpapers) and the anal is divided. Dorsal scale counts are important in identification. A count of 17, 17, 15 means 17 rows at the neck, 17 at midbody, and 15 in front of the vent. Most species have a conspicuous pale yellow or orange middorsal stripe and a pale stripe set low on each side. The fancied resemblance of this pattern to an old-fashioned garter has earned these snakes their common name. The position of the side stripe varies; it may be on scale rows 2 and 3, 3 and 4, or confined to row 3. Count upward from the ends of the ventrals about 1/4 the body length behind the head. Some species are unstriped or have only the lateral stripes and a spotted or checkered pattern.

Garter snakes occupy a great variety of habitats from sea level to high in the mountains. Many are aquatic or semiaquatic but some are almost completely terrestrial. Like the water snakes, when caught they often void feces and expel musk from their anal glands. Live-bearing. Some 22 species occur in the region from Canada to Costa Rica and the Pacific to the Atlantic Coasts. The Common Garter Snake ranges farther north than any other reptile in the Western Hemisphere.

NARROW-HEADED GARTER SNAKE **Pl. 43**
Thamnophis rufipunctatus

Identification: 18–34 in. (46–86 cm). Olive, tan, gray-brown, or brown above, marked with *conspicuous dark brown, blackish or reddish brown spots* that fade on the tail. No well-developed stripes or pale crescent behind the corner of the mouth as in some species of garter snakes. Traces of dorsal and side stripes sometimes present on neck. Brownish gray below, paling on throat. Often a row of black wedge-shaped marks on each side of belly. Head long; snout blunt. Eyes high on head. *8 upper labials.* Scales keeled, in 21 rows at midbody. Anal usually single. ***Young:*** Throat often cream-colored and belly dull yellowish. In both structure and habits, this snake appears to be close to the water snakes (*Nerodia* species, pp. 196–197).

Ranges from the piñon-juniper and oak-pine belts into forests of ponderosa pine along clear, permanent, or semipermanent rocky streams, where it seems to prefer the quieter, well-lit sections. Highly aquatic; seldom seen more than a yard (meter) from the water's edge. When frightened, it usually dives to the bottom for refuge, often hiding under a stone. Live-bearing; young born in summer. Eats fish, frogs, tadpoles, and salamanders.

Range: Upland drainages of cen. and e. Ariz. and sw. N.M., south in Sierra Madre Occidental to cen. Durango. In Ariz., it originally ranged north to Fort Valley Creek, Coconino Co. **Map 158**

COMMON GARTER SNAKE *Thamnophis sirtalis* **Pl. 43**

Identification: 18–52 in. (46–130 cm). Coloration highly variable but the back and side stripes are usually well defined. Dorsal stripe yellow or white. Frequently there are red spots or blotches and a double row of alternating black spots on the sides between stripes. Light-colored side stripe usually on 2nd and 3rd scale rows. Top of head brown, olive, gray, red, or black. Bluish gray, bluish, or blue-green below, sometimes becoming dusky or black toward the tail. Throat pale. Eyes relatively large. *Usually 7 upper and 10 lower labials.* Rear pair of chin shields usually longer than front pair. Scales keeled, in 19 rows at midbody. Anal single. ***Male:*** Knobbed keels on scales above vent.

Found in many environments — in grassland, woodland, scrub, chaparral, and forest. Lives in or near ponds, marshes, prairie swales, roadside ditches, streams, sloughs, damp meadows, woods, farms, and city lots. Tends to stay near water, entering it freely and retreating to it when alarmed. A spirited snake that often defends itself energetically when cornered. When caught, it often bites and smears its captor with excrement and the odorous contents of its anal glands. Live-bearing; 3–85 (often 12–18) young, born May–Oct., earlier in southern part of range. Eats fish, toads, frogs, tadpoles, salamanders and their larvae, birds, small mammals, reptiles, earthworms, slugs, leeches, and perhaps insects. One of the few predators that can eat Pacific newts (*Taricha* species, pp. 40–43) without being poisoned.

Similar species: The usual presence of red markings between the stripes, the 7 (occasionally 8) upper labials, and the relatively large eyes (see Pl. 43) generally distinguish this species from other garter snakes within its range. See also (1) Northwestern Garter Snake (p. 208), (2) Western Terrestrial Garter Snake (below) and (3) Western Aquatic Garter Snake (p. 204).

Range: From Pacific to Atlantic Coasts; se. Alaska (Stikine R. area) and Canada to Gulf Coast and nw. Chihuahua. Now rare south of Santa Barbara Co. and Ventura Co. in s. Calif. Formerly to Temecula R., Riverside Co., Calif. Absent from most of arid Southwest. Sea level to around 8000 ft. (2540 m). **Map 157**

Subspecies: RED-SPOTTED GARTER SNAKE. *T. s. concinnus*. Ground color of back black, extending onto the belly. Pale dorsal stripe well defined, covering the middorsal row of scales and half of each adjacent scale row. Side stripes sometimes hidden by black pigment. Top and sides of head usually red. PUGET SOUND GARTER SNAKE, *T. s. pickeringi.* Dark-colored like the Red-spotted Garter Snake but top of head dark and dorsal stripe largely confined to the middorsal scale row. VALLEY GARTER SNAKE, *T. s. fitchi.* Ground color slaty, black, or brownish. Dorsal stripe broad, with regular, well-defined borders. Top of head black or dark gray. Black on belly usually confined to tips of ventrals. Slate-gray individuals that match their rock background occur within the caldera of Crater Lake, Ore. (along the lakeshore and on Wizard I.). SAN FRANCISCO GARTER SNAKE, *T. s. tetrataenia* (Pl. 43) **Endangered.** One of the most beautiful serpents in N. America. Wide dorsal stripe of greenish yellow edged with black, bordered on each side by a broad red stripe followed by a black one. Belly greenish blue. Top of head red. Most typical form found in western part of San Francisco Peninsula from about San Francisco Co. line south along crest of hills at least to Crystal **Lake and along coast to Point** Año **Nuevo, San Mateo Co., Calif.** RED-SIDED GARTER SNAKE, *T. s. parietalis.* Ground color dark olive to nearly black. Dark spots on back. Usually red or orange bars on sides varying in size and intensity. Top of head mostly olive. Stripes may be yellow, orange, greenish, or bluish.

Melanistic populations in cen. Mont. CALIFORNIA RED-SIDED GARTER SNAKE, *T. s. infernalis* (Pl. 43). Resembles the Red-sided Garter Snake, but ground color generally darker. Dark spots on back less distinct. Stripes usually narrower and bright greenish yellow, those on sides often merging with ground color on belly. NEW MEXICO GARTER SNAKE, *T. s. dorsalis*. Resembles Red-sided Garter Snake but looks duller — dusky or muddy with a more diffuse pattern, or generally greenish with prominent white or yellowish white stripes. Olive on upper sides, with red flecks and alternating rows of black spots. Upper black blotches tend to fuse with each other along their upper edges to form a black border along the dorsal stripe. Young occasionally rust-colored. An isolated population along Río Casas Grandes, Chihuahua.

WESTERN TERRESTRIAL GARTER SNAKE *Thamnophis elegans* **Pl. 43; Fig. 28**

Identification: 18–43 in. (45–107 cm). Usually a well-defined middorsal stripe extends the length of the body, and a stripe is present on each side, on the 2nd and 3rd scale rows. The pale ground color between the stripes is checkered with dark spots, or is generally dark with scattered white flecks (Fig. 28). Gray, brownish, or bluish below, flecked or blotched with reddish or salmon. *Internasals usually broader than long and not pointed at front end.* Usually 8 upper labials; the *6th and 7th enlarged, often higher than wide.* Usually 10 lower labials. *Both pairs of chin shields about equal in length.* Dorsal scales keeled, in 19 or 21 rows at midbody. Anal single.

Occurs in a great variety of habitats — grassland, brushland, woodland, and open forest, from sea level to high in the mountains. Often found in damp environments near water; occasionally far from water. *Habits chiefly terrestrial but also aquatic,* depending upon the subspecies. When frightened, terrestrial forms tend to seek shelter in dense plant growth or other cover on land, and aquatic forms usually enter water. Live-bearing; 4–19 young, born July–Sept. Eats slugs, snails, leeches, earthworms, fish, salamanders, frogs, toads, tadpoles, lizards, snakes, small mammals, and occasionally birds, insects and carrion.

Similar species: (1) The distinct dorsal stripe will usually distinguish members of this group in areas of overlap with the Oregon and Sierra Garter Snakes, subspecies of the Western Aquatic Garter Snake (p. 204). East of the crest of the Calif. Sierra Nevada, however, some difficulty may be encountered in distinguishing the Wandering Garter Snake (see Subspecies, below) from the Western Aquatic subspecies, the Sierra Garter Snake (p. 206). The latter has a narrow, dull dorsal stripe, ordinarily confined to the front third of the body and a checkered pattern of large squarish spots. The Wandering Garter Snake usually has a wider stripe that extends the full length of the body, and pattern of more rounded,

well-separated spots. Along the Calif. coast where striped members of the Western Aquatic Garter Snake (Santa Cruz and Aquatic Garter Snakes) overlap in range the Coast Garter Snake (below) the former differ in lacking red markings, in usually having an orange (rather than yellow) dorsal stripe, a yellow (rather than cream) chin and throat, and generally a golden to orange suffusion or blotches on the ventrals. In addition to the foregoing differences, the Western Aquatic subspecies usually have narrow, pointed internasals and the 6th and 7th upper labials are no higher than wide. (2) Northwestern Garter Snake (p. 208) has 17, 17, 15 scale rows; 7 upper labials; 8 or 9 lower labials; and a bright yellow, red, or orange dorsal stripe; whereas in the area of overlap with the Western Terrestrial Garter Snake the latter has 19, 19, 17 or more scale rows; 8 upper labials; 10 lower labials; and usually a dull yellow, brown, or gray dorsal stripe. (3) The Common Garter Snake (p. 199) has relatively larger eyes, generally 7 upper labials, and usually a plain bluish gray belly. Where it coexists with the Coast Garter Snake, it usually has a greenish yellow dorsal stripe.
Range: B.C. (Peace R. district) to n. Baja Calif. and s. Durango; w. S.D. and extreme w. Olka. to Pacific Coast. Isolated populations in nw. Ore.; San Bernardino Mts., s. Calif.; San Pedro Mártir Mts., Baja Calif.; Ash Meadows, Nye Co., Nev.; Capitan-Sacramento Mts. area, N.M.; and elsewhere. Sea level to 13,100 ft. (3990 m) in San Miguel Co., Colo. **Map 161**
Subspecies: MOUNTAIN GARTER SNAKE, *T. e. elegans* (Fig. 28). Well-defined stripes on sides and back are separated by velvety black to dark gray-brown (San Bernardino Mts.) ground color. Dorsal stripe yellow, orange-yellow, or whitish, and in occasional dark individuals reduced to a trace on neck. No red markings. Belly pale, with no markings except light dusky spots or some black down middle of belly. Terrestrial. COAST GARTER SNAKE, *T. e. terrestris* (Pl. 43, Fig. 28). Dorsal stripe typically bright yellow. Bright red or orange flecks or blotches usually present on belly and sides, including side stripes. Usually seeks shelter on land. Considerable color variation occurs in the s. Bay area and to the south. On the San Francisco Peninsula 3 yellowish stripes are evident and a checkerboard of dark spots occurs between the stripes on a reddish ground color. The dark spots give way to alternating dark and reddish bars on the sides in areas along the outer coast from cen. San Mateo Co. to near Moss Landing, Monterey Co. This color type also occurs in the East Bay Hills. Increase in dark color, giving almost solid dark fields between the dorsal and side stripes, occurs in the Santa Cruz Mts. The middorsal stripe is pale yellow and the side stripes are reddish or salmon. WANDERING GARTER SNAKE, *T. e. vagrans* (Fig. 28). Mostly brown, greenish, or gray, with a dull yellow or brown dorsal stripe, fading on tail and edged with dark markings that make its borders irregular and which may break the stripe into dots and dashes. Dark

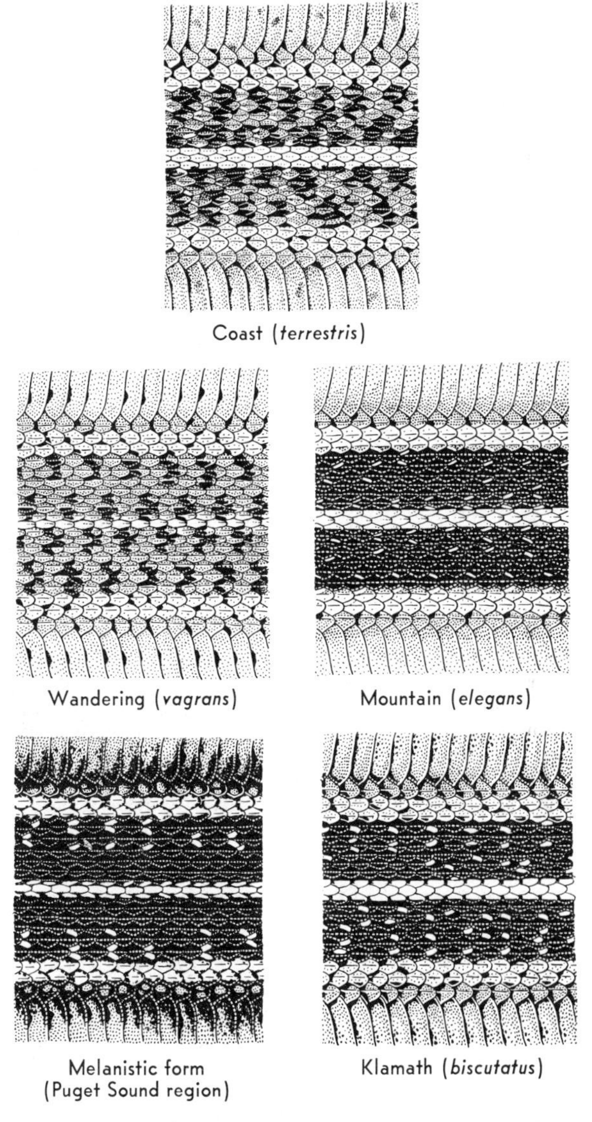

Fig. 28. Pattern variation in Western Terrestrial Garter Snake

spots on body usually small and well separated, but sometimes absent or variously enlarged, occasionally forming a completely black area between the stripes. Melanistic individuals (Fig. 28) occur in w. Wash. (Puget Sound region) and e. Ore. Aquatic and terrestrial. KLAMATH GARTER SNAKE, *T. e. biscutatus* (Fig. 28). Dorsal and side stripes separated by ground color of brown, black or gray with obscure spotting. Dorsal stripe uneven, yellow to brown. Light gray below, often suffused with black or slate, especially on rear half of body. Head rather long and narrow. Prefers rocky streams. SAN PEDRO MÁRTIR GARTER SNAKE, *T. e. hueyi.* Dark olive or grayish brown above with dark spots that are sometimes distinct. Stripes well defined, dorsal one yellow. Little or no spotting below.

WESTERN AQUATIC GARTER SNAKE *Thamnophis couchii* **Pl. 43; Fig 29**

Identification: 18–64 in. (46–160 cm). Coloration varies greatly depending upon the subspecies (see Fig. 29). Over much of its range, this snake has dark spots or blotches and has only a weak dorsal stripe, if any. The stripe is well defined, however, in cen. coastal Calif. Side stripe, when present, located on 2nd and 3rd scale rows. *Internasals tend to be longer than wide and pointed at front end.* Usually 8 upper labials, 6th and 7th not enlarged, ordinarily not higher than wide. *Rear pair of chin shields usually longer than front pair.* Dorsal scales keeled, usually in 19 or 21 rows at midbody. Anal single.

Primarily a snake of rivers and streams, but occurs in a great variety of aquatic environments, from brackish marshes at sea level to high mountain streams, the habitat varying with the subspecies. Usually retreats to water when frightened. Primarily diurnal. Live-bearing; 7–25 young, born in late summer and probably fall. Eats fish, fish eggs, frogs, toads, tadpoles, salamanders and their larvae, earthworms, and leeches.

Similar species: (1) Lack of well-defined dorsal stripe in the blotched subspecies will distinguish them from the Western Terrestrial Garter Snake (p. 201). The striped subspecies (Santa Cruz and Aquatic Garter Snakes), however, must be distinguished by other pattern characteristics (see below) and by their pointed internasals, unenlarged rear pair of upper labials, and more elongate rear chin shields. Adult males have tubercles on internasals and prefrontals, lacking in males of Western Terrestrial Garter Snake. (2) Common Garter Snake (p. 199) usually has 7 upper labials, larger eyes, a well-defined dorsal stripe, and distinct red blotches on the sides.

Range: Sw. Ore. to cen. Calif.; extreme w. Nev. to Pacific Coast. Sea level to around 8000 ft. (2440 m). **Map 162**

Subspecies: OREGON GARTER SNAKE, *T. c. hydrophilus* (Fig. 29). Conspicuous dark markings in an irregular checkered

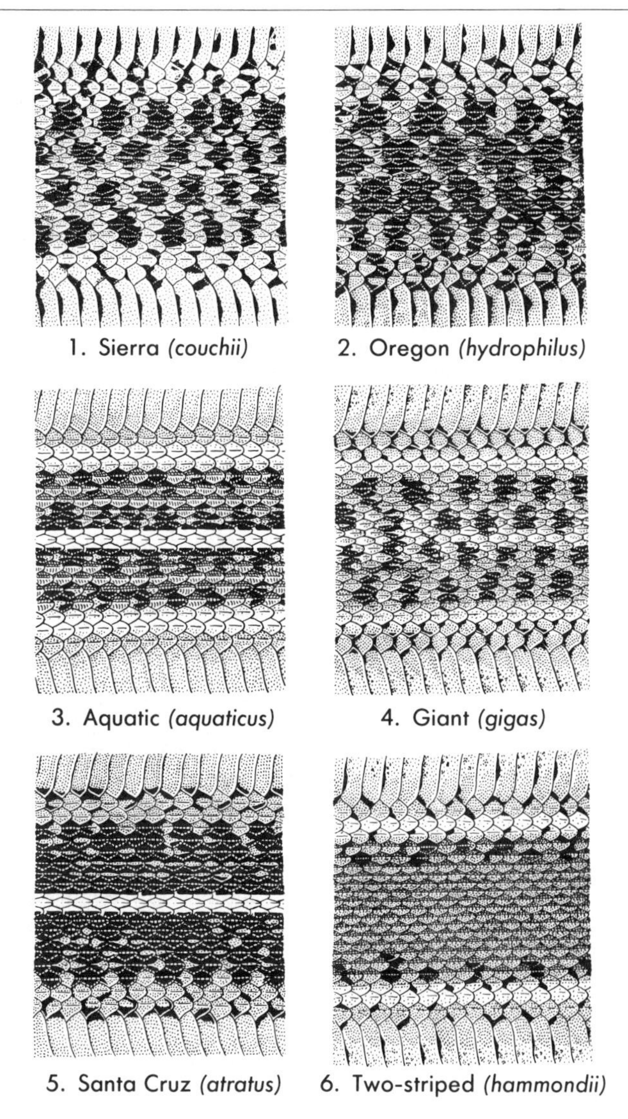

Fig. 29. Pattern variation in subspecies of Western Aquatic Garter Snake (1–5) and pattern of Two-striped Garter Snake (6)

arrangement (sometimes blurred by joining of spots, as shown) on a pale gray ground color. Dorsal stripe narrow and dull. Lateral stripe, when present, on 2nd and 3rd scale rows. Light-colored and unmarked below, with a flesh-colored or purplish tinge toward tail. Usually 10 lower labials. Permanent streams with rocky beds and swift, clear water. SIERRA GARTER SNAKE, *T. c. couchii* (Fig. 29). Similar to Oregon Garter Snake but usually has 11 lower labials. Dorsal stripe narrow and faint, usually confined to the front of the body. Yellowish or greenish gray below, often heavily marked with black. Rocky streams with protected pools near shore. GIANT GARTER SNAKE, *T. c. gigas* (Fig. 29). To over 48 in. (120 cm). Well-separated spots on the back, in a checkered arrangement. Dorsal stripe dull yellow, often with irregular edges. Brown below. Streams and sloughs, usually with mud bottoms. Floor of Central Valley of California from Delevan National Wildlife Refuge, Colusa Co., to Los Banos Creek and Mud Slough in San Joaquin Valley. Apparently extinct farther south; originally to Buena Vista Lake, Kern Co. AQUATIC GARTER SNAKE, *T. c. aquaticus* (Fig. 29). Yellow to orange dorsal stripe. Ground color between the dorsal and lateral stripes dark olive to black. Throat often lemon yellow. Belly blotched with golden or pale salmon on light blue to green ground color. Eye with gray iris. Ponds, small lakes, and sluggish streams. SANTA CRUZ GARTER SNAKE, *T. c. atratus* (Pl. 43, Fig. 29). Resembles Aquatic Garter Snake in appearance and habitat, but dorsal stripe usually slightly narrower, throat more often bright lemon yellow, and iris nearly black. Color pattern varies. These snakes have 3 stripes (a middorsal orange or orange-yellow stripe and a paler yellowish stripe low on each side) throughout most of range, but in w. Santa Clara, Santa Cruz, San Mateo, and San Francisco Counties, dark pigment obscures the side stripes and the middorsal stripe is yellowish. South of Monterey Bay, this subspecies and the Coast Garter Snake *(T. e. terrestris)* are similar in color, but the Santa Cruz Garter Snake has a deeper yellow stripe that is broader in the neck region, a belly that darkens toward the tail, is often distinctly darker beginning at the throat (rather than having a gradual color change from chin toward rear), has some yellow or orange below (instead of no yellow on belly), and a yellowish (rather than whitish) throat and chin.

Remarks: The Santa Cruz Garter Snake coexists and occasionally apparently hybridizes with the Two-striped Garter Snake (below). The Oregon Garter Snake *(T. c. hydrophilus)* and Sierra Garter Snake *(T. c. couchii)* occur along the Pit R., Shasta Co., Calif., yet few intergrades or hybrids have been found. The Sierra Garter Snake may prove to be a distinct species. Should this happen, the other forms of the Western Aquatic Garter Snake would then be treated as subspecies of the species *Thamnophis atratus*. In the Pit R. area, the Sierra Garter Snake has much black pigment on both the head (especially the upper labials) and the venter.

TWO-STRIPED GARTER SNAKE **Pl. 48; Fig. 29**
Thamnophis hammondii

Identification: 24–36 in. (60–90 cm). A *two-striped* garter snake — middorsal stripe absent or represented by a trace (nuchal spot) on the neck. Formerly regarded as a subspecies of the Western Aquatic Garter Snake (see Fig. 29, No. 6, p. 205). Olive, brown, or brownish gray above, with 4 lengthwise rows of small, well-separated dark spots between the lateral stripes, or dark spots confined to lower sides. No red flecks on sides. Dull yellowish to orange-red or salmon below, either unmarked or slightly marked with dusky. Throat may be pale. Black individuals, sometimes with obscure lateral stripes, have been found along the coast from Oceano, Monterey Co. to Montaña de Oro State Park, San Luis Obispo Co., Calif.

Found in or near permanent fresh water, often along streams with rocky beds bordered by willows or other streamside growth. Often active at dusk or at night but may be encountered in the daytime. Highly aquatic. A captive gave birth to 25 young on Oct. 30. Adults eat tadpoles, toads, frogs, fish, fish eggs, and earthworms.

Similar species: The following garter snakes have middorsal stripes: (1) Common (p. 199), (2) Western Terrestrial (p. 201), and (3) Western Aquatic, p. 204 (in area of overlap with the Two-striped Garter Snake).

Range: Coastal Calif. from vicinity of Salinas, Monterey Co., to nw. Baja Calif., at least as far south as the mouth of Rio Rosario. Isolated populations at San Ignacio (*T. digueti* here regarded as of this species), Mulege, Cadeje, Comondú, and at San Pedro la Presa, Baja California Sur. The latter population closely resembles the subspecies *T. h. hammondii* (below). Sea level to around 7000 ft. (2130 m). **Map 162**

Subspecies: HAMMOND TWO-STRIPED GARTER SNAKE, *T. h. hammondii.* Striped with dark spots, usually low on sides. A population at San Pedro la Presa appears to be of this subspecies (on Map 162, toward southern end of Baja Calif.). DIGUET TWO-STRIPED GARTER SNAKE, *T. h. digueti* (Pl. 48). Unstriped, or vaguely so. Nearly uniform olive to dusky above. Frequents permanent streams of the Sierra de la Giganta, Baja Calif. (localities are San Ignacio, Mulege, and Comondú). This snake may prove to be a distinct species.

Remarks: The Two-striped Garter Snake coexists with the Common, Western Terrestrial, and Western Aquatic Garter Snakes along the cen. Calif. coast. Housing and urban developments have greatly reduced its range in s. Calif. It occurs adjacent to (and perhaps overlaps) the range of the Sierra Garter Snake *(T. c. couchii)* in the Mt. Pinos-Frazer Mt. area.

NORTHWESTERN GARTER SNAKE Pl. 42

Thamnophis ordinoides

Identification: 13–38 in. (32–95 cm). Coloration varies greatly: Usually a well-defined dorsal stripe of yellow, orange, red, blue, or white, but the stripe may be faint, a trace on the neck, or absent. Side stripes distinct or faint; located on 3rd or 4th scale rows. Dorsal ground color varies — black, various shades of brown, olive, greenish, gray, or bluish; usually spotted or speckled with black. Belly yellowish, olive, brown, bluish, slaty, or black; *often with reddish blotches or tinge and sometimes marked with black,* especially in northern part of range. Dorsal scales keeled, in 17 rows at midbody. *Usually 7 upper labials and 8 or 9 lower labials.* Anal single. Some populations in coastal Ore. have individuals with 1, 2, or 3 stripes that vary from brown, black, or bluish to almost all red. Occasional melanistic individuals may be all black above with a faint stripe on neck.

Chiefly terrestrial, frequenting meadows and clearings in forested areas where there is abundant low vegetation. Active on warm sunny days. When frightened, usually seeks dense vegetation rather than water. Live-bearing; 3–15 young born June–Aug. Eats slugs, earthworms, salamanders, and frogs.

Similar species: (1) Western Terrestrial Garter Snake (p. 201) usually has 8 upper labials and a higher dorsal scale row count. (2) Oregon Garter Snake, a subspecies of the Western Aquatic Garter Snake (p. 204), with which it overlaps in range, generally has a narrow, dull yellow, brown, or gray dorsal stripe and 8 upper labials. (3) Common Garter Snake (p. 199) lacks red markings on the belly; has a longer, more triangular head; larger eyes; and usually 19 scale rows at midbody.

Range: From Bella Coola area and Vancouver I. in sw. B.C. to extreme nw. Calif.; chiefly west of crest of Cascade Mts., but extends east of crest in s. Wash. and n. Ore. Sea level to around 4500 ft. (1370 m). **Map 164**

BLACK-NECKED GARTER SNAKE Pl. 42

Thamnophis cyrtopsis

Identification: 16–43 in. (40–107 cm). A whitish or pale yellow middorsal stripe separates 2 *large black blotches at the back of the head.* Stripe may be orange and wavy in neck region. A white crescent occurs between each blotch and corner of mouth. Top of head gray. *Side stripe on the 2nd and 3rd scale rows,* often wavy because of intrusion of bordering black spots. Olive-brown or olive-gray above, with 2 alternating rows of black spots between the stripes; the spots often fade out at about midbody. Belly light greenish white, bluish white, or brownish. Scales keeled, *usually in 19 rows at midbody.* 7 or 8 upper labials. Anal single.

Chiefly a stream snake of foothills and mountains. Habitats vary — desert, grassland, mesquite flats, chaparral-covered hill-

sides, oak woodland, and forests of pine and fir. Extends into tropical habitats in southern part of range. Frequents permanent and intermittent streams, spring seepages, and irrigation canals, but in wet weather may wander far from water. Live-bearing; about 7–25 young, born June–Aug. Eats frogs, toads, tadpoles, and crustaceans *(Triops).*
Similar species: (1) Checkered Garter Snake (p. 210) usually has 21 scale rows at midbody and the side stripe is confined on front of body to 3rd scale row. The checkered pattern extends well out onto the tail. (2) Mexican Garter Snake (below) has 19 or 21 scale rows at midbody and the side stripe is on 3rd and 4th scale rows. (3) Common Garter Snake (p. 199) lacks dark neck blotches and has red markings on its sides.
Range: Se. Utah to Guatemala; cen. Tex. to cen. and s. Ariz. Isolated populations in Hualapai Mts., Burro Creek area, and Ajo Mts. in w. Ariz. Distribution spotty. Sea level to around 8700 ft. (2700 m). **Map 156**
Subspecies: The WESTERN BLACK-NECKED GARTER SNAKE, *T. c. cyrtopsis,* occurs in our area.

MEXICAN GARTER SNAKE *Thamnophis eques* **Pl. 42**
Identification: 18–40 in. (45–100 cm). A 3-striped garter snake with a whitish to greenish crescent behind each corner of mouth, *paired black blotches at back of head,* yellow to cream middorsal stripe, and *side stripe on 3rd and 4th scale rows at front of body.* Sides checkered with dark spots on an olive or brown ground color. Dorsal scales keeled, in 19 or 21 rows at midbody. 8–9 upper labials. Anal single.

Primarily a highland canyon snake of pine-oak forest and piñon-juniper woodland, but also enters mesquite grassland and desert, especially along valleys and stream courses. In se. Ariz., it occurs in lowland areas such as San Pedro Valley and vicinity of Douglas. Formerly at Rillito Wash near Tucson. Usually found in or near water, where it apparently feeds chiefly on frogs. Live-bearing, young born June–July or perhaps Aug.
Similar species: (1)In the Checkered Garter Snake (p. 210), the side stripe is usually confined to the 3rd scale row on front of body and more prominent paired dark blotches at the back of the head. See also (2) Black-necked (above) and (3) Plains Garter Snakes (p. 210).
Range: Se. Ariz. and extreme sw. N.M., south in highlands of w. and s. Mexico, to Oaxaca. Now nearly gone from lowland habitats in Ariz. and nearby Sonora. Black dot (on map) in N.M. is 5 mi. (8 km) east of Virden, Hidalgo Co. An isolated population at Mule Creek, Grant Co., N.M., but condition unknown. From around 2000–8500 ft. (610–2590 m). **Map 155**
Subspecies: The NORTHERN MEXICAN GARTER SNAKE, *T. e. megalops,* occurs in our area.

CHECKERED GARTER SNAKE **Pl. 42**
Thamnophis marcianus
Identification: 18–42 in. (45–105 cm). A rather pale snake with a *checkered pattern of large squarish black blotches on a brownish yellow, brown, or olive ground color.* A cream or white middorsal stripe becomes yellowish toward head. Paired black blotches at back of head. A whitish or yellowish crescent between the dark blotches and corner of mouth. *Side stripe usually confined to 3rd scale row* on front of body (may include 4th row in lower Colorado R. area) and on 2nd and 3rd scale rows on rear of body. Top of head usually olive. White below, sometimes with a tinge of yellowish, greenish, or a clouding of slaty gray. Scales keeled, usually in 21 rows at midbody. Anal single.

Chiefly a lowland river system snake that frequents ponds, springs, streams, rivers, and irrigation ditches in arid and semiarid regions. It also ranges sparingly into the pine-oak belt in the mountains. A grassland species that is able to exist along streams in the desert, and which has entered irrigated areas in some parts of the desert. Live-bearing, 6–18 young, born June–Aug. Eats fish, toads, frogs, tadpoles, lizards, and invertebrates. In the warmer, more arid parts of its range, this snake feeds chiefly at night.
Similar species: (1) Black-necked Garter Snake (p. 208) usually has 19 scale rows at midbody and side stripe on 2nd and 3rd scale rows on front of body. (2) In Plains (below) and (3) Mexican Garter Snakes (p. 209), the side stripe is on 3rd and 4th scale rows. (4) Wandering Garter Snake (a subspecies of the Western Terrestrial Garter Snake, p. 201) has side stripe on 2nd and 3rd scale rows and lacks dark neck blotches.
Range: Sw. Kans. and s. Ariz. to Zacatecas and n. Veracruz; se. Calif. to e.-cen. Tex. Reported from 3 mi. (4.8 km) south of Show Low, Navajo Co., Ariz. but substantiation needed. An isolated population in vicinity of Tehuantepec, Oaxaca. Sea level to around 5400 ft. (1640 m). **Map 154**
Remarks: This snake is rapidly disappearing on major river systems of s. Ariz., N.M., and adjacent Mexico.

PLAINS GARTER SNAKE *Thamnophis radix* **Pl. 42**
Identification: 20–42 in. (51–105 cm). Well-defined dorsal stripe, orange or yellow on front of body, becoming paler toward rear. *Side stripe on 3rd and 4th scale rows toward front.* Double row of dark blotches, often in a checkered arrangement, between the stripes on a greenish gray, olive, reddish, or brownish ground color. Occasional dark individuals with obscure blotches. Prominent black bars on whitish or yellow upper labials. Whitish, yellow, bluish green, or gray below, with a row of dark, sometimes vague spots down each side of belly. *Usually 7 upper labials. Dorsal scales keeled, usually in 21 rows at midbody.* Anal single.

Chiefly inhabits prairies and farmland, but ranges into the

piñon-juniper belt. Found near ponds, sloughs, marshes, lakes, streams, and rivers. Live-bearing, 5–60 (occasionally 90 or more) young, born July–Sept. Eats salamanders, frogs, toads, tadpoles, fish, small mammals, earthworms, insects, and carrion.
Similar species: (1) In the Common (p. 199), (2) Western Terrestrial (p. 201), (3) Western Aquatic (p. 204), and (4) Black-necked (p. 208) Garter Snakes, the side stripe is on the 3rd and 4th scale rows on front part of body. (5) Checkered Garter Snake (above) usually has side stripe on 3rd scale row only. (6) Mexican Garter Snake (p. 209) has 8–9 upper labials. (7) See also Western Ribbon Snake (below).
Range: S. Canada through the Great Plains to the Rockies and ne. N.M. and nw. Ark.; cen. Mont. to cen. Ohio. From around 400–7500 ft. (120–2290 m). **Map 160**
Subspecies: The WESTERN PLAINS GARTER SNAKE, *T. r. haydeni,* occurs in our area.

WESTERN RIBBON SNAKE Pl. 42

Thamnophis proximus

Identification: 18–48½ in. (45–123 cm). A slender snake with *pale, unmarked upper labials that contrast with the darker color on top of the head.* Dorsal stripe usually orange or tan in our area but yellow, orange, reddish, brown, or greenish elsewhere. *Lateral stripe on 3rd and 4th scale rows* at front. A narrow, dark ventrolateral stripe is sometimes present. Ground color between the stripes olive-brown, brown, gray, or black. A pair of large, light-colored parietal spots usually touch each other on head. Belly unmarked. *A very long tail, ¼–⅓ total length of snake.* 7 or 8 upper labials. Dorsal scales keeled, in 19 rows. Anal single.

A highly adaptable species that occurs in a great variety of habitats from temperate woodland and grassland to the tropics. Agile and alert, frequenting the vegetation bordering streams, lakes, ponds, sloughs, and marshes. When frightened this snake often retreats to water and swims with speed and grace, usually staying among emergent plant growth near shore. It is an efficient climber and may first be seen as it drops from a basking site in overhanging vegetation into the water. Live-bearing; 4–27 young, born July–Sept. Eats frogs, toads, tadpoles, fish, insects, and earthworms; sometimes scavenges.
Similar species: The long tail and contrasting, pale, unmarked upper labials distinguish this snake from those species with which it coexists.
Range: S. Wisc. to Gulf Coast, through ne. Mexico to Costa Rica; eastern N.M. to Miss. Valley. Old records for Rio Grande Valley, N.M. Sea level to around 8000 ft. (2440 m, in Sierra Madre Oriental). **Map 159**
Subspecies: The ARID LAND RIBBON SNAKE, *T. p. diabolicus,* occurs in our area.

LINED SNAKE *Tropidoclonion lineatum* **Pl. 41**
Identification: 7½–21 in. (19–53 cm). A close relative of the garter snakes. Middorsal and side stripes well-defined and bordered by dark spots set in a dark or light olive-gray or light brown ground color. Middorsal stripe whitish, pale gray, yellow, or orange. Side stripe on 2nd and 3rd scale rows. Belly whitish or yellow, marked with *2 rows of black spots along the midline.* Head about the same width as neck. *Five or 6 upper labials.* Scales keeled, in 19 rows. Anal single.

A locally abundant but secretive snake of prairies, open woods, floodplains, city dumps, grassy vacant lots, and parks. This snake hides under objects in the daytime, venturing forth at dusk and at night in search of the earthworms upon which it feeds. Activity is stimulated by wet weather. When first caught, it often voids the contents of its anal glands. Live-bearing; 2–12 young, born in Aug.
Range: Se. S.D. to s. Tex.; ne. N.M. and e. Colo. (Boulder-Denver region and southeastern part) to cen. Ill. Isolated populations near Sandia Park, Bernalillo Co. and in Capitan Mts., Lincoln Co., N.M. Near sea level to around 6000 ft. (1830 m). **Map 163**
Subspecies: The NORTHERN LINED SNAKE, *T. l. lineatum,* occurs in our area.

GROUND SNAKE *Sonora semiannulata* **Pl. 38**
Identification: 8–18 in. (20–46 cm). A small crossbanded, striped, or plain-colored snake with a head that is only slightly wider than the neck. Brown, reddish, orange or gray above, lighter on sides. Dorsal pattern varies greatly — (1) dark crossbands may encircle the body, form saddles on back, or be reduced to a single neck band; (2) dark crossbands may be entirely absent; (3) some populations (along lower Colorado R.) have a broad beige, red, or orange middorsal stripe and greenish gray or bluish gray sides. Plain, crossbanded, and striped individuals sometimes all occur at the same locality. *Usually all types of coloration have a dark blotch or bar (sometimes faint) at the front of each scale,* particularly evident on sides. Whitish or yellowish below, unmarked or with dark crossbands. Scales smooth and glossy, usually in 15 rows toward front. Anal divided.

A secretive nocturnal snake of arid and semiarid regions, where the soil may be rocky, gravelly, or sandy and has some subsurface moisture. Frequents river bottoms, desert flats, sand hummocks, and rocky hillsides where there are pockets of loose soil. Vegetation may be scant, as on the sagebrush plains of the Great Basin and in creosote bush desert, but along the lower Colorado R. this snake occurs among thickets of mesquite, arrowweed, and willows. Ranges from prairies through desert plant communities, thornscrub, piñon-juniper to the oak-pine zone. Clutch of 4–6 eggs, laid June–Aug. Eats spiders, scorpions, centipedes, crickets, grasshoppers, and insect larvae. Shallow grooves on outer sides of the

rear teeth suggest that these snakes may be venomous, but they are not dangerous to humans.
Similar species: (1) Shovel-nosed snakes (*Chionactis* species, below) and (2) Banded Sand Snakes (p. 214) regularly have dark crossbands, a flatter snout, and a deeply inset lower jaw. (3) Black-headed snakes (*Tantilla* species, pp. 216–220) have black heads, no loreal, and lack crossbands on body.
Range: Snake R. region of sw. Idaho south to tip of Baja Calif., cen. Chihuahua, and Tamaulipas; se. Calif. to s. Mo. and e.-cen. Tex. Sea level to around 6000 ft. (1830 m). **Map 165**

WESTERN SHOVEL-NOSED SNAKE **Pl. 38**

Chionactis occipitalis

Identification: 10–17 in. (25–42 cm). *A dark- and light-banded snake* with a shovel-shaped snout, flatter than in most other snakes; *lower jaw deeply inset.* Head little wider than the neck. The *dark brown or black crossbands, usually 21 or more on the body,* are saddle-like or encircle the body. The ground color is whitish or yellow. Orange or red saddles are sometimes present between the black ones. *Dorsal scales smooth, usually in 15 rows at midbody. Internasals not separated by rostral.* Anal divided.

Restricted to the desert, occurring even in its driest parts. Frequents washes, dunes, sandy flats, loose soil, and rocky hillsides where there are sandy gullies or pockets of sand among rocks. Vegetation usually scant — creosote bush, desert grasses, cactus, or mesquite. A burrowing nocturnal species that can move rapidly through loose sand. The smooth scales, inset lower jaw, nasal valves, and angular abdomen are adaptations for "sand swimming," which consists of wriggling through sand rather than tunneling in it. Usually stays underground in the daytime but roams on the surface at night, leaving smoothly undulating tracks on the bare sand between bushes. When hunting these snakes on foot, move quickly from bush to bush with light in hand in order to catch them on the surface before they have time to submerge or climb into the lower branches of bushes. Clutch of 2–4 (perhaps as many as 9) eggs, laid in summer. Eats insects (including larval stages), spiders, scorpions, centipedes, and buried chrysalids (pupae) of moths.
Similar species: (1) Banded Sand Snake (p. 214) has 13 scale rows at midbody and the rostral separates the internasals. (2) Ground Snake (p. 212) has dark pigment at the base of most dorsal scales and less extreme flattening of snout. (3) See also Sonoran Shovel-nosed Snake (p. 214).
Range: Sw. Nev. to upper end of Gulf of California; s. Ariz. to desert base of mountains of s. Calif. Below sea level to around 4700 ft. (1430 m). **Map 167**
Subspecies: MOJAVE SHOVEL-NOSED SNAKE, *C. o. occipitalis.* Bands brown, no black or brown secondary bands between

the primary ones. Usually 45 or more bands on body plus the unmarked front band positions on the lower surface (indicated by ends of dorsal bands). Narrow red crossbands absent. COLORADO DESERT SHOVEL-NOSED SNAKE, *C. o. annulata.* Bands usually black. Usually fewer than 45 bands on body plus the unmarked front band positions on the lower surface. Narrow red crossbands present. TUCSON SHOVEL-NOSED SNAKE, *C. o. klauberi.* Black or brown secondary bands between the primary bands. Usually fewer than 152 ventrals in males and fewer than 160 in females. NEVADA SHOVEL-NOSED SNAKE, *C. o. talpina.* Dark scales in interspaces between broad bands may form secondary bands. Usually 152 or more ventrals in males and 160 or more in females.

SONORAN SHOVEL-NOSED SNAKE **Pl. 38**

Chionactis palarostris

Identification: 10–17 in. (25–40 cm). Resembles the Western Coral Snake but is harmless. Crossbanded with black, yellow (or whitish), and red, most of the black bands encircling the body. The red saddles vary in width: in individuals from s. Ariz., they are about the same width as the black bands, but in Sonora they may be 2 or nearly 3 times wider. *Usually fewer than 21 black bands on body,* bordered in front and back by a narrow or wide (Sonora) yellow band. Snout yellow, slightly convex in profile; back of head black. Scales smooth, usually in 15 rows. Anal divided.

A snake of arid lands. Vegetation includes cactus, creosote bush, and mesquite. In Ariz. it occurs in upland desert in the paloverde-saguaro association. The ground surface may be rocky or sandy, but generally is coarser (rockier) and more irregular than that occupied by the Western Shovel-nosed Snake. Eats invertebrates. 4 eggs found in female of the Organ Pipe subspecies (see below).

Similar species: (1) Western Shovel-nosed Snake (p. 213) lacks broad red saddles, usually has more than 21 body bands, and has a flatter, more pointed snout. (2) Western Coral Snake (p. 222) has a black snout, broader black bands, and the red bands encircle the body.

Range: In our area, known only from extreme s. Ariz., mainly in Organ Pipe Cactus National Monument, and along the Sonoyta-Ajo road to about 25 mi. (40 km) north of the Mexican line; in nw. Sonora to south of Hermosillo. Sea level to around 2500 ft. (760 m). **Map 166**

Subspecies: The ORGAN PIPE SHOVEL-NOSED SNAKE, *C. p. organica,* occurs in our area.

BANDED SAND SNAKE *Chilomeniscus cinctus* **Pl. 38**

Identification: 7–10 in. (17–25 cm). A highly efficient "sand-swimmer." Adaptations for burrowing life even more extreme than those of the Western Shovel-nosed Snake (p. 213). Head no wider than neck, lower jaw deeply inset, snout flat, nasal valves present, eyes small and upturned, and belly angular on each side. The skin appears varnished. The total number of black or dark brown dorsal crossbands varies from 19 to 49; bands on tail usually completely encircle it. Ground color whitish, pale yellow, or reddish orange, sometimes with orange saddles or a continuous area of orange on the back, between the black bands. Belly whitish to dull yellow. *Rostral separates the internasals. Scales smooth, in 13 rows at midbody.* Anal divided.

An arid lands species that lives in fine to coarse sand or loamy soil, in which it "swims." It seldom emerges on the surface except at night. It frequents both open desert (mesquite-creosote bush association), sandy-gravelly washes and arroyos in rocky uplands (paloverde-saguaro association), and thornscrub habitats in Mexico. When sand snakes burrow near the surface, the soil collapses behind them to form serpentine furrows that are usually found in sandy areas among bushes. Use a stick, hoe, or rake to uncover buried individuals. A female from cen. Baja Calif. contained 3 large eggs (ova) in late July. Eats centipedes, sand-burrowing cockroaches, and probably ant pupae and other insects.

Similar species: See (1) Western Shovel-nosed Snake (p. 213) and (2) Bandless Sand Snake (p. 244).

Range: Cen. and sw. Ariz. from about 12 mi. (20 km) east-northeast of Wickenburg to extreme s. Sonora; throughout Baja Calif. except northern and northeastern part and s. Cape. In the s. Cape region, this species appears to be replaced by the Bandless Sand Snake. On the Pacific Coast of Baja Calif., ranges north to vicinity of Santo Tomas. Sea level to 3000 ft. (910 m). **Map 168**

CHIHUAHUAN HOOK-NOSED SNAKE Pl. 40

(Western Hook-nosed Snake) *Gyalopion canum*

Identification: 7–14 in. (17–36 cm). A smooth-scaled, crossbanded snake with a rather stout, cylindrical body and an upturned snout. The *rostral scale is flat or concave above and widely separates the internasals.* 30 or more brown or yellowish brown, dark-edged crossbands on body, 8–12 on tail; bands on head may be particularly prominent. Grayish brown or yellowish gray above. Whitish below with salmon down middle of belly. Usually 17 scale rows at midbody. Anal divided.

Seldom encountered in our area, perhaps because of its burrowing and nocturnal habits. Most individuals have been found roaming on the surface on warm nights following rains. Primarily a snake of the Chihuahuan desert. In the U.S., it inhabits semiarid environments of grass, piñon-juniper woodland, and other scrubby plant growth. It has been found in rocky areas, deposits of loose soil, and on grassy desert flats. When first disturbed, it often writhes and contorts its body, swings its tail forward, and everts the lining of its vent with a bubbling, popping sound. Record of a female laying 1 egg in July. Eats spiders, centipedes, scorpions, and snakes.

Similar species: Western Hognose Snake (p. 176) has keeled scales and the rostral has a ridge down the middle.
Range: Se. Ariz., cen. and s. N.M. to cen. Tex., south to ne. Sonora, Nayarit, Zacatecas, and San Luis Potosí. From around 1000 to 6500 ft. (330–1980 m). **Map 169**

THORNSCRUB HOOK-NOSED SNAKE **Pl. 40**
(Desert Hook-nosed Snake) *Gyalopion quadrangularis*

Identification: 6–12 in. (15–30 cm). The *upturned* snout and the *black saddles on the back* distinguish this rarely found snake. A *red or rust-colored band,* broken by the black saddles, runs the length of the body on each side. Ground color between saddles and red bands is ash-white, and from above forms pale rectangular patches along middle of back. Belly pale greenish yellow without pattern. Scales smooth, usually in 17 scale rows at midbody. Anal usually single. ***Young:*** Red bands usually darker than in adult.

A secretive burrowing snake, found in loose soil of canyon bottoms and outwash plains on the western slope of the Sierra Madre Occidental of Mexico and southern headwaters of the Gila R. drainage in Ariz. In Ariz. it occurs in rolling foothills of mesquite grassland, including partly cultivated sections. Ranges into dry tropical forest in w. Mexico. It is evidently strictly nocturnal and is seen abroad on the surface chiefly during and after rains in summer and fall. Eats spiders, centipedes, and scorpions.
Similar species: (1) Long-nosed Snake (p. 195) lacks the upturned snout. (2) See also Western Hognose Snake (p. 176).
Range: Extreme s. Ariz. in the Patagonia-Pajarito Mts. area, Santa Cruz Co., south to Nayarit. From near sea level to around 4400 ft. (1340 m). **Map 170**
Subspecies: The SONORAN HOOK-NOSED SNAKE, *G. q. desertorum,* occurs in our area.

Black-headed Snakes: Genus *Tantilla*

Small, slender, smooth-scaled, flat-headed snakes. Top of head black or dark brown; back plain (unpatterned) brown. Most species have a white collar, usually followed by a black band or row of black dots. Belly salmon or coral red, without dark spotting, the red not extending to ends of ventrals. Slightly enlarged and grooved teeth at rear of upper jaw are thought to inject venom (not dangerous to humans) into prey. Scales in 15 rows. No loreal. Anal divided. Absence of the loreal and lack of red color on ends of ventrals distinguish these snakes from the Ringneck Snake (p. 174). Differences in the copulatory organs (hemipenes) of these snakes are sometimes useful in species recognition, so, although difficult to examine in the field, they are mentioned in the accounts (see Fig. 30).

Secretive and ground-dwelling, spending much time under

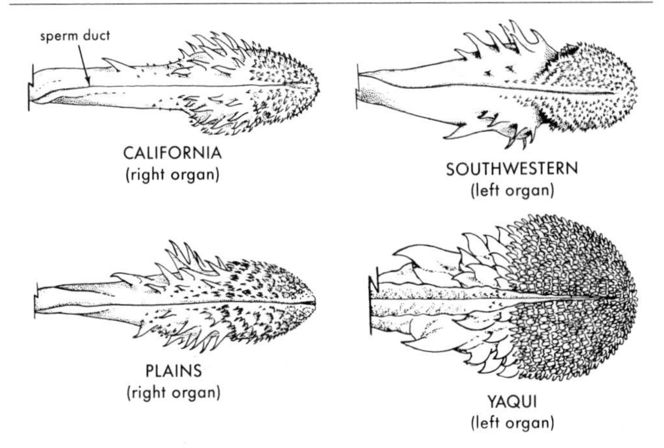

Fig. 30. Hemipenes of Black-headed Snakes

stones and in crevices. Food includes millipedes, centipedes, spiders, and insects. About 50 species. Cen. U.S. to n. Argentina.

CALIFORNIA BLACK-HEADED SNAKE Pls. 37, 41

Tantilla planiceps

Identification: 5–15½ in. (13–39 cm). The blackish cap usually extends 2–3 scale lengths beyond posterior (hindmost) end of furrow between parietal scales, and downward ½–2 scales below corner of mouth. Rear border of cap convex or straight, followed by a narrow white or cream collar, ½–1 scale row wide, which may or may not be bordered by dark dots. Plain brown to olive-gray above, sometimes faintly *marked with a narrow dark middorsal stripe.* Broad orange or reddish stripe down middle of belly, not extending to tips of ventrals; rest of belly whitish, unmarked. *Hemipenes nearly cylindrical, without enlarged globular tip, lacking small spines near enlarged basal spine* (Fig. 30). Scales smooth, in 15 rows. Anal divided.

In the more arid parts of its range (desert side of the mountains in s. Calif.), the upper surface is pale brown and the dark cap usually does not extend below corner of mouth. The white collar may be faint or absent and seldom has a dark border.

Little is known of the habits of this snake. It has been found in grassland, chaparral, oak and oak-pine woodland, desert-edge and thornscrub habitats, under stones on both level ground and hillsides. In arid lands it occurs along rocky edges of washes, arroyos, and streams and on rocky hillsides. It apparently spends most of its time underground in crevices and in burrows of other animals. Seldom encountered abroad on the surface except on warm nights, when it may be found on roadways. Look under flat rocks, logs, boards, dead agaves, yuccas, and other plant debris. Clutch of 1–3 eggs, laid May–June. Eats insects (especially beetle larvae) and centipedes.

Similar species: (1) In the Southwestern Black-headed Snake (below) the black cap usually does not extend below corner of mouth, and there are no dark spots bordering pale collar. Hemipenes have enlarged globular tip and 2 enlarged spines at base. (2) Plains Black-headed Snake (p. 219) is usually larger, and the black cap is usually somewhat pointed toward rear and extends 3–5 scales behind parietal furrow; no light collar.

Range: Distribution very spotty. Coastal mountains of Calif. from vicinity of San Francisco Bay (south of San Jose and southeast of Livermore) to tip of Baja Calif. In s. Calif. it ranges to the desert side of the mountains. Questioned locality in Calif. is Fresno, where a specimen was reportedly collected in 1879. Near sea level to around 4000 ft. (1220 m). **Map 172**

Remarks: The distribution of this species and the Southwestern Black-headed Snake in cen. Calif. needs further study. The structure of the hemipenes has been the chief basis for species recognition in determining present ranges.

SOUTHWESTERN BLACK-HEADED SNAKE **Pl. 41**

Tantilla hobartsmithi

Identification: 5⅕–15 in. (13–37 cm). Similar to California Black-headed Snake. Head cap dark brown or black, extending ½–3 scales beyond posterior (hindmost) end of furrow between parietal scales, but usually *not below corner of mouth.* Rear border of cap usually convex or straight, followed by a white to cream collar ½–2 scales wide. *Usually no dark band or dark spots bordering rear edge of collar.* Plain brown or beige above. Broad coral red or rufous stripe below, not extending to outer edges of ventrals. *Hemipenes club-shaped with enlarged globular tip and 2 medium to large spines at base* (Fig. 30, p. 217). Mental scale usually touches front pair of chin shields. Scales smooth, in 15 rows. Anal divided.

Frequents habitats of brushland, grassland, sagebrush-greasewood, mesquite-yucca and creosote bush, open chaparral, thornscrub, piñon-juniper woodland, and open coniferous forests. In the eastern part of its range, it enters persimmon-shin oak, mesquite-creosote bush, and cedar-savannah habitats. Attracted to canyon bottoms and stream courses. Found beneath rocks, logs, boards, dead yuccas, agave, sotols, and other plant debris. Clutch of presumably 1–3 eggs, laid June–July or perhaps Aug. Eats centipedes, millipedes, and insects (beetle larvae, caterpillars, etc.).

Similar species: See California Black-headed Snake (p. 217).

Range: Distribution very spotty. From s. Sierran foothills and Great Basin Desert, Calif., east through s. Nev. and s. Utah to w.-cen. Colo. Farther south it ranges through Ariz. across s. N.M. to w. Tex.; south in Mexico to s. Chihuahua and w. Coahuila. A single specimen known from southern side of Tulare Lake, Kings Co., Calif. Sight record, Stansbury Mts., Tooele Co., Utah. Sea level to around 5000 ft. (1520 m). **Map 172**

PLAINS BLACK-HEADED SNAKE **Pl. 41**

Tantilla nigriceps

Identification: 7–14¾ in. (18–37 cm). *Black or gray-brown cap, convex or pointed behind, extending 2–5 scale lengths behind posterior end of furrow separating parietals.* Usually *no white collar.* Back brown with a yellowish or grayish cast. Whitish below with pink or orange stripe on belly. Mental scale usually separated from chin shields by 1st lower labials. Hemipenes lack globular tip; 1 large spine at base near sperm groove and a moderate-sized one on opposite side (Fig. 30, p. 217). Scales smooth, in 15 rows. Anal divided. ***Young:*** Hatchlings grayish silver with black head cap and salmon midventral stripe.

A secretive snake of plains and desert grassland, shrubland, and woodland, where it is found under rocks, boards, and other objects by day and occasionally in the open at night. Look under flat rocks on hillsides, especially when the soil is damp. Clutches of 1–3 eggs, laid in spring and summer. Eats centipedes, millipedes, spiders, and insect larvae, pupae, and adults.

Similar species: See Southwestern Black-headed Snake (above).

Range: Sw. Neb. south into Mexico; se. Ariz. to cen. Tex. Sea level to around 7000 ft. (2130 m). **Map 173**

Subspecies: The WESTERN PLAINS BLACK-HEADED SNAKE, *T. n. nigriceps,* occurs in our area.

CHIHUAHUAN BLACK-HEADED SNAKE **Pl. 41**

Tantilla wilcoxi

Identification: 7–14 in. (18–36 cm). The black cap is bordered by a contrasting *broad white collar that crosses tips of parietals.* Collar bordered with black. Cap extends on side of head to corner of mouth. Brown above, with dark spots on sides. Scales smooth, in 15 rows. Anal divided.

Found under rocks, logs, and dead plants (agave, yucca, and sotol) in shaded rocky canyons and on relatively open, sunny, rocky slopes in desert-grassland and evergreen woodland. Extremely rare in our area.

Similar species: The broad white collar crossing the tips of the parietals will distinguish this species from all our other black-headed snakes (*Tantilla* species).

Range: Huachuca (Ramsey Canyon), Santa Rita, and Patagonia Mts., Ariz. south to San Luis Potosí. From around 3000 to around 8000 ft. (910–2440 m). **Map 171**

Subspecies: The HUACHUCA BLACK-HEADED SNAKE, *T. w. wilcoxi,* occurs in our area.

YAQUI BLACK-HEADED SNAKE **Pl. 41**

Tantilla yaquia

Identification: 7–12¾ in. (18–32 cm). Dark brown or black cap, usually strikingly darker than the back, which is light brown or beige. Cap extends 2–4 scales beyond posterior end of furrow that separates the parietals, and downward ½–3 scales below corner of mouth. Rear border of cap usually straight, followed by a white or cream collar ½–1½ scales wide, which may be bordered by several distinct brown to black spots. *White or cream-colored area on side of head contrasts strongly with dark cap.* Hemipenes with somewhat globular tip and 2 very large spines at base (Fig. 30, p. 217). Mental scale usually separated from anterior (front) pair of chin shields by anterior lower labials. Scales smooth, in 15 rows. Anal divided.

Chiefly inhabits deciduous short-tree forests (thornforests) of the Sierra Madre Occidental of Mexico, but reaches the coastal plain to the south where it occurs in tropical and semiarid woodland. Found in evergreen and streamside woodlands in se. Arizona, where it generally occurs above around 3300 ft. (1010 m). The Southwestern Black-headed Snake tends to occur at lower elevations, chiefly in desert grassland and scrub. Clutch of 1–4 eggs, probably laid late spring and summer. Apparently eats mainly soft-bodied invertebrates.

Similar species: The whitish spot on the side of the head will distinguish this species from our other black-headed snakes (above).

Range: Se. Ariz. in the Pajarito, Mule, and Chiricahua Mts., south through Sonora and Sinaloa to the Rio Santiago Valley in Nayarit. Near sea level to around 5500 ft. (1680 m). **Map 174**

BROWN VINE SNAKE **Pl. 40**

Oxybelis aeneus

Identification: 36–60 in. (90–152 cm). An extremely slender snake, *vinelike in shape and color.* Head long, snout elongate and pointed. In our area, ash gray to grayish brown above, grading to bronze or yellowish brown on front of body. Gray below, grading through whitish to yellow on underside of head. Lips cream to yellowish, unmarked. A dark eyestripe. Scales smooth, in 17 rows. Anal divided.

Rare in our area. Lives chiefly on brush-covered hillsides and stream bottoms grown to sycamore, oak, walnut, and wild grape. To the south in both arid and moist tropical forest. A well-camouflaged climber that feeds on lizards, which it catches among vegetation and on the ground and subdues by injecting venom with its enlarged grooved teeth toward the back of its upper jaw. A person bitten on the hand experienced numbness of the hand for about 12 hrs. Look closely at vinelike objects in brush tangles and treetops. Hunt for this snake in the morning or late afternoon when lizards are basking, or at night when it may be found sleeping in a loose,

exposed coil on top of low bushes. Clutch of 3–5 eggs, laid in spring and summer.
Range: Pajarito and Patagonia Mts. of extreme s. Ariz. south through w. and e. Mexico to se. Brazil. Sea level to around 8200 ft. (2500 m). **Map 139**

LYRE SNAKE *Trimorphodon biscutatus* **Pl. 39**
Identification: 18–47¾ in. (45–121 cm). A "cat-eyed" snake; *pupils vertical.* Head broad; neck slender. Named for the lyre- or V-shaped mark on top of the head. Light brown to pale gray above, with brown blotches on back; each blotch roughly hexagonal in shape and split by a pale crossbar. Cream or pale yellow below, often with brown dots scattered on belly. Dark individuals that tend to have a middorsal stripe of light brown have been found at the Pisgah lava flow in the Mojave Desert, Calif. Scales smooth, in 21–27 rows. Anal single or divided.

Chiefly a rock-dwelling snake of lowlands, mesas, and lower mountain slopes but may occur in rockless areas. Often frequents massive rocks, hiding by day in deep crevices and emerging at night. Found in desert grassland, creosote-bush desertscrub, chaparral, piñon-juniper and oak woodland, open coniferous forest, thornscrub, and thornforest. Eats lizards, especially crevice dwellers, birds, and small mammals, including bats, which are caught at their roosts and immobilized with venom injected by enlarged grooved teeth toward back of upper jaw. Prey may be constricted. Little is known about the effect of the venom on humans. To find this snake, search roads in rocky areas at night. Clutches of 7 and 20 eggs have been reported.
Similar species: (1) Gopher Snake (p. 189) and (2) Glossy Snake (p. 187) have round pupils and a broad neck. (3) See also Night Snake (below).
Range: S. Calif., sw. Utah, s. N.M., south to tip of Baja Calif. and Costa Rica; s. Calif. coast to w. Tex. Sea level to around 7400 ft. (2260 m). **Map 177**
Subspecies: CALIFORNIA LYRE SNAKE, *T. b. vandenburghi.* Distinct lyre- or V-shaped head marking. 28–43 (avg. 35) dorsal blotches. Anal usually single. SOUTHERN BAJA CALIFORNIA LYRE SNAKE, *T. b. lyrophanes.* Resembles California Lyre Snake, but anal divided. 21–28 dorsal blotches. SONORAN LYRE SNAKE, *T. b. lambda.* Distinct lyre- or V-shaped head marking. 34 or fewer (avg. about 28) dorsal blotches. Anal divided. TEXAS LYRE SNAKE, *T. b. vilkinsonii.* Head pattern usually obscure or absent. 17–24 dorsal blotches. Anal divided.

NIGHT SNAKE *Hypsiglena torquata* **Pl. 39**
Identification: 12–26 in. (30–65 cm). A pale gray, light brown, or beige snake with dark gray or brown blotches on the back and sides, and usually a pair of *large dark brown blotches on the neck.* Neck markings vary considerably. The blotches may be connected, sometimes in a group of 3, or occasionally absent. A black or dark

brown bar behind the eye contrasts with whitish upper labials. Belly yellowish or white. Head usually flat. *Pupils vertical.* Scales smooth, in 19–21 rows. Anal divided.

Frequents a variety of habitats — grassland, chaparral, sagebrush flats, deserts, woodland, moist mountain meadows, thornscrub, and thornforest. Occurs in both rocky and sandy areas. A nocturnal and crepuscular prowler that eats lizards, small snakes (blind snakes), frogs, and salamanders, which it subdues by injecting venom with enlarged teeth toward back of upper jaw. Look in crevices and under rocks, boards, dead branches of Joshua-trees, mesquite, saguaro, and other surface litter. Sometimes found on highways at night. Clutch of 2–9 eggs, laid April–Aug.

Similar species: (1) Lyre Snake (above) has pale crossbars within hexagonal blotches on the body and usually a V- or lyre-shaped mark on the head. (2) Glossy Snake (p. 187) has a single anal and rounded pupils. (3) Young Racers (p. 180), which are blotched, have round pupils and wedged lower preocular. (4) Young Gopher Snakes (p. 189) have round pupils and usually 4 prefrontals. (5) Young rattlers (pp. 225–234) have a horny button or rattle on tail.

Range: N. Calif., cen Wash., n. Utah, sw. Kans. south to tip of Baja Calif. and through mainland Mexico; coastal mountains of Calif. east to e. Tex. Record for Kaleden, extreme s. B.C. Populations in n. Calif., perhaps isolated, southwest of Tulelake, at Lava Beds National Monument, and south of Hornbrook, Siskiyou Co. Sea level to around 8700 ft. (2650 m). **Map 175**

Coral Snakes: Family Elapidae

Venomous serpents with immovable, hollow fangs in the front of the mouth. Around 200 species. Old World representatives of the family occur in Africa, Asia, Malay Archipelago, and Australia and include the cobras, kraits, mambas, and most of the snakes of Australia, notably the deadly Taipan and Tiger Snake. New World representatives, the coral snakes, are usually gaudily ringed with red, black, and yellow, and are particularly abundant in Cen. and S. America. Only 2 coral snakes reach the U.S. Although they seldom bite, their venom is highly dangerous, and they should not be handled. Among our harmless snakes the red-banded kingsnakes, shovel-nosed snakes, and banded sand snakes have a color pattern resembling that of the coral snakes. Differences between these snakes and the Western Coral Snake are pointed out in the accounts of these species.

WESTERN CORAL SNAKE **Pl. 37**
(Arizona Coral Snake) *Micruroides euryxanthus*
Identification: 13–21 in. (33–53 cm). A strikingly colored snake

with broad, *alternating rings of red and black separated by narrower rings of white or yellow.* The markings encircle the body, becoming paler on the belly. Head black to behind the eyes. A broad white or yellow band at the back of the head extends across the tips of the parietals. Snout blunt; head and body somewhat flattened. Scales smooth and glossy, in 15 rows at midbody. No loreal. Anal divided.

An inhabitant of arid and semiarid regions in a variety of habitats, including thornscrub, brushland, woodland, grassland, and farmland. Occurs both on the plains and lower mountain slopes, often among rocks. In Ariz. it is most abundant in rocky upland desert, especially along arroyos and river bottoms. A secretive species, abroad chiefly at night but sometimes encountered in the daytime on overcast days or after rains. Spends much time underground. The flattened shape suggests crevice-dwelling habits. When disturbed the head may be hidden under coils, the tail elevated and waved with the tip in a tight coil, and the vent lining everted with a popping sound. Presumably lays clutch of 2–3 eggs in summer. Eats lizards and snakes, especially blind and ground snakes.

Similar species: (1) In red-banded kingsnakes (*Lampropeltis* species, pp. 190–193) the red bands are bordered by black. (2) Shovel-nosed (pp. 213–214) and (3) Banded Sand Snakes (p. 214) have pale snouts.

Range: Cen. Ariz. and sw. N.M. to s. Sinaloa. Sea level to 5800 ft. (1770 m). **Map 176**

Subspecies: The ARIZONA CORAL SNAKE, *M. e. euryxanthus,* occurs in our area.

Remarks: Venom neurotoxic (affects the central nervous system) and highly dangerous.

Sea Snakes: Hydrophiidae

Sea-dwelling snakes that primarily eat fish. All sea snakes are venomous and have a fang structure like that of their close relatives, the coral snakes (previous family, Elapidae). Fangs located in the front of the mouth — erect, immovable, and hollow. Most species reach 3 or 4 ft. (1–1½ m) in length, but some grow to around 9 ft. (2¾ m). Highly adapted for marine life, these snakes can swim and dive gracefully, propelled by side-to-side undulations of the body and tail. The tail is a flattened sculling organ in many species. Most sea snakes, including the single species that reaches our area, bear live young that are born at sea or in rocky tidal areas near shore. Other sea snakes, however, come on shore to lay eggs. Sea snakes are widespread in tropical and subtropical seas, but absent from the Atlantic Ocean. Some 50 species in the family.

YELLOW-BELLIED SEA SNAKE **Pl. 48**
Pelamis platurus
Identification: 20–45 in. (50–113 cm). An ocean-dwelling snake, highly adapted for marine life. In our area and over much of its range, it is dark brown or black above and bright yellow below, the two colors meeting in a sharp line along the sides. Tail contrastingly marked with black spots or bars on a bright yellow background. Dark spotting or barring may extend forward on body in some individuals. Head elongate, narrow, and flattened. Body, and especially tail, flattened from side to side, which facilitates the snake's eel-like swimming. *Tail oarlike* and used as a scull. Eyes and valvular nostrils set high on head. No straplike scutes across belly, as in most other snakes. Short fangs in front of upper jaw. ***Male:*** Usually smaller than female, with a slightly longer tail.

The bright colors and contrasting pattern are considered to be warning coloration. This snake appears to have few predators.

Completely aquatic. Attracted to offshore waters of continental and insular coasts, but also found far out in the open sea. Eats small fish, including eels, which it immobilizes with its quick-acting venom. Forages, often in large numbers, along slicks (where sea currents converge) and where flotsam of seaweed, wood, and other debris accumulates. The small fishes that comprise the diet are attracted to such floating material. The Yellow-bellied Sea Snake is an excellent diver and swimmer, but is completely helpless when stranded on land. Bears 1–8 young, perhaps throughout the year. Venom potent, but there have been few human fatalities. The snakes are generally not aggressive and are reluctant to strike except at the small fish upon which they feed. When humans are bitten, venom appears to be seldom injected.
Range: The most widely distributed snake. Indian and Pacific Oceans from the coasts of Africa, Asia, and Australia to s. Siberia and the Pacific Coast, including Central America and Mexico, where it ranges north to the n. Gulf of Calif. and along the west coast of Baja Calif. Occasionally reaches the San Diego area of s. Calif. and has been reported off the coast as far north as San Clemente, Orange Co.

Vipers: Family Viperidae

Pit Vipers: Subfamily Crotalinae

Rattlesnakes, cottonmouths, and the Copperhead — all venomous serpents — are members of this subfamily, but only the rattlesnakes reach our area. The family has the most highly developed venom-injection mechanism among snakes. Large, hollow, movable fangs are located at the front of the upper jaw. In biting, the fangs are swung forward from their folded position of rest and the victim is stabbed and poisoned in a rapid thrust. Pit vipers have a distinctive loreal pit — a temperature-sensitive structure on each side of the face between the eye and nostril, which helps them locate their prey.

Pit vipers range from s. Canada to Argentina and in the Old World in e. Europe and Asia. They are closely related to the Old World "true vipers" (subfamily Viperinae) and probably were derived from them; hence their inclusion in the same family. True vipers occur in Europe, Asia, and Africa. About 200 species in the family (Viperidae); about 123 species in the subfamily (Crotalinae).

Rattlesnakes: Genera *Sistrurus* and *Crotalus*

Thirty-four species from s. Canada to n. Argentina, the greatest number in sw. U.S. and n. Mexico. Thirteen species in our area, one of which is a Ground Rattlesnake *(Sistrurus),* readily distinguished by its enlarged head scales. Rattlesnakes frequent a great variety of habitats from sea level to around 11,000 ft. (3350 m).

These are heavy-bodied, dangerously venomous snakes with a slender neck, broad triangular head, elliptical pupils, keeled scales, and usually single caudals, especially toward base of tail. The rattle, a series of loosely interlocking horny segments at the end of the tail, is found in no other serpents. A segment is added at the base each time the snake sheds. A young snake may add 3 or 4 segments a year, but an old one will add only 1 or none. Recently born young have a blunt horny button at the tip of the tail that persists until broken off. All other western snakes except the boas have a slender tapered tail. Boas have no button and the neck is nearly as broad as the head. The rattle is not included in measurements of rattlesnakes.

Rattlers are often heard before they are seen. When alarmed, they may make a sound resembling a sudden burst of steam, but when only slightly disturbed, they may merely click the rattle. Volume and quality of the sound vary with age, size, and species. The rattling of the little Twin-spotted Rattler (p. 233) resembles the sound made by some kinds of cicadas. Occasionally a harmless snake such as a Gopher Snake vibrates its tail among dry leaves, making a sound resembling that of a rattler, and may broaden its head, hiss, and strike in a threatening manner. If you hear a rattlesnake, stand still until you have located it; avoid jumping and running blindly. Treat a dead rattler with care. People have been bitten by reflex action of the jaws, even of badly mangled specimens.

Small mammals and birds are the chief foods, but lizards and frogs are also eaten. Live-bearing.

MASSASAUGA *Sistrurus catenatus* **Pl. 45**

Identification: 16–40½ in. (40–100 cm). A row of large rounded dark brown, gray, or black blotches down middle of back; 3 rows of smaller, usually fainter, alternating spots on the sides. *Elongate dark brown markings on the head extend onto the neck,* sometimes forming a lyre-shaped mark. Broad dark eyestripe. Ground color of back gray or grayish brown. Belly pale, largely unmarked in the West. Some individuals nearly or completely black, especially in northeast part of range. *Large plates on top of head.* Dorsal scales keeled, in 23–25 rows. ***Young:*** Ground color paler and pattern more conspicuous than in adult. Tail yellowish white.

The "swamp rattler" of e. U.S. It frequents river bottoms, wet prairies, swamps, and bogs, but also enters dry plains grassland and dry woodland. In the West it occurs in desert grassland, particularly in low areas of rank growth — in the Rio Grande Valley in low plains of mesquite, juniper, and grassland and in se. Ariz. in yucca grassland. Live-bearing; 2–19 young, born July–Sept. Eats lizards, snakes, small mammals, and frogs.

Similar species: The enlarged head scales and elongate head markings of this snake will distinguish it from our other rattlers.

Range: Cen. N.Y. and s. Ont. diagonally across U.S. to extreme se. Ariz. and Gulf Coast of Tex. The population in se. Colo. is apparently now isolated and intermediate in characteristics between the Desert Massasauga and the subspecies to the east (the Western Massasauga). Sea level to around 5500 ft. (1680 m). **Map 178**

Subspecies: The DESERT MASSASAUGA, *S. c. edwardsii,* occurs in our area, but is not often encountered.

WESTERN DIAMONDBACK RATTLESNAKE Pl. 44

Crotalus atrox

Identification: 30–84 in. (76–213 cm). The largest western rattlesnake. Gray, brown, pink, or yellowish above, with light brown to blackish, light-edged, diamond-shaped or hexagonal blotches on the back and fainter smaller blotches on the sides. Melanistic populations on dark lava flows in cen. N.M. *Markings often indefinite and peppered with small dark spots,* giving the snake a speckled or dusty appearance overall. *Tail with broad black and white or light gray rings,* about equal in width; thus sometimes called the "coontail" rattler. A light diagonal stripe behind each eye intersects the upper lip well in front of the corner of the mouth. Dorsal scales keeled, in 25–27 rows. ***Young:*** Markings more distinct than in adult.

Frequents a variety of habitats in arid and semiarid regions from the plains into the mountains — desert, grassland, shrubland, woodland, open pine forests, and rank growth of river bottoms. Ranges from sandy flats to rocky upland areas. Crepuscular and nocturnal, but also abroad in daytime. Perhaps the most dangerous N. American serpent, often holding its ground and boldly defending itself when disturbed. Live-bearing; 4–23 young, born in summer and fall. Eats mammals (rabbits, squirrels, mice, rats), lizards, and birds.

Similar species: (1) Red Diamond Rattlesnake (below) is pink to

reddish brown, lacks conspicuous dark dots in body blotches, and the first pair of lower labials is usually divided transversely. (2) Mojave Rattlesnake (p. 232) has enlarged scales between the supraoculars (Fig. 25, opp. Pl. 44), narrow black tail rings, and the white stripe behind the eye extends behind the corner of the mouth. (3) Speckled Rattlesnake (p. 228) usually has salt-and-pepper markings; the prenasals are usually separated from the rostral by small scales; or the supraoculars are pitted, deeply furrowed, or appear to have broken outer edges.
Range: Se. Calif. to Ark. and e. Tex.; Ariz., N.M., and Okla. south to n. Sinaloa and San Luis Potosí. Isolated populations in s. Mexico. Sea level to around 7000 ft. (2130 m). **Map 185**

RED DIAMOND RATTLESNAKE *Crotalus ruber* **Pl. 44**
Identification: 30–65 in. (75–162 cm). A tan, pink, or reddish relative of the Western Diamondback (above). Diamonds on back usually light-edged, sometimes indistinct; diamonds usually have only faint pepper marks, if any. A conspicuous "coontail" — the broad black and white rings contrast with the rest of the body color. *1st pair of lower labials usually divided transversely.* Scales keeled, in 29 rows. ***Young:*** Dark gray at first, but in northern part of range changing to reddish brown.

Frequents desertscrub, thornscrub, open chaparral, and woodland; occasionally also found in grassland and cultivated areas. On the desert slope in s. Calif., it often occurs in areas of mesquite and cactus on the rocky alluvial fans near the base of the mountains, but it also ranges well out onto the desert floor. Usually less aggressive than the Western Diamondback — less prone to stand its ground. Live-bearing; 3–20 young, born in summer. Eats ground squirrels, rabbits, and birds.
Similar species: See Western Diamondback Rattlesnake (above).
Range: Sw. Calif. from near Pioneertown and Morongo Valley, San Bernardino Co., Desert Hot Springs, Riverside Co. (northeast of San Gorgonio Pass), and Riverside area to the west; southward through Baja Calif. to the Cape. Found on both sides of the Peninsular Ranges in southern Calif., but mostly below 4000 ft. (1200 m). Sea level to 5000 ft. (1520 m). **Map 187**
Subspecies: NORTHERN RED RATTLESNAKE, *C. r. ruber.* Brick red to pinkish tan diamonds, usually uniformly colored, with no light areas. Ground color light pinkish gray or tan. Little or no pattern on head. CAPE RED RATTLESNAKE, *C. r. lucansensis.* Brown diamonds usually contain light areas. Ground color light yellowish brown. Top of head with dark spots. Baja California Sur from Loreto south to the Cape. **Map 187**

ROCK RATTLESNAKE *Crotalus lepidus* **Pl. 45**
Identification: 15–33 in. (38–83 cm). *Back marked with widely and regularly spaced, narrow, black, dark brown, or gray crossbands,* which sometimes become faint toward front of body. The

bands are bordered with light color and are irregular in outline. The general tone of the back varies greatly and usually matches background colors — pale gray, bluish gray, greenish gray, tan, or pinkish, sometimes heavily speckled with dusky. Tail yellowish brown or salmon, with narrow, dark, often widely spaced rings. Upper preocular split vertically. Scales keeled, in 23 rows. ***Young:*** In Banded Rock Rattlesnake (see Subspecies), tail is bright yellow at tip.

Chiefly a mountain rock dweller that frequents rocky ridges, hillsides, streambeds, and gorges in arid and semiarid habitats, but may occur in the lowlands. Ranges from desert grassland through brushland to the lower edge of ponderosa pine forest. Often found in the vicinity of permanent or intermittent streams. Basks among rocks on rather barren ridges or in open areas in woods. Live-bearing; 2–8 young, born July–Aug. Eats lizards, snakes, frogs, and small rodents.

Range: Se. Ariz., southern N.M., and w. Tex., south to Jalisco. From around 1000 (outside our area) to 9600 ft. (300–2930 m).

Map 182

Subspecies: MOTTLED ROCK RATTLESNAKE, *C. l. lepidus.* Dusky overall, but sometimes quite pale in color, with fading of blotches, especially anteriorly (Stockton and Edwards Plateaus, Tex.). Considerable dark spotting between the dark body bands, sometimes forming additional bands between the primary ones. Dark stripe extends from eye to corner of mouth. In our area known only from Guadalupe Mts. of s. N.M. BANDED ROCK RATTLESNAKE, *C. l. klauberi.* Dark body bands distinct and widely spaced, contrasting with bluish green or greenish (males), or bluish gray (females) ground color. Spaces between bands moderately dark-spotted. No dark stripe from eye to corner of mouth. Mts. of sw. N.M. (Black Range, Magdalena and Big Hatchet Mts.) and se. Ariz. (Santa Rita, Dragoon, Huachuca, and Chiricahua Mts.).

SPECKLED RATTLESNAKE **Pl. 44**

Crotalus mitchellii

Identification: 23–52 in. (57–132 cm). Color of back varies greatly — cream, gray, yellowish, tan, pink, brown, or black — and usually harmonizes with background. Dark individuals on Pisgah lava flow, San Bernardino Co., Calif. The rough scales and salt-and-pepper speckling, in specimens from some areas, suggest decomposed granite. The markings, which are sometimes vague, usually consist of bands, but may be hexagonal, hourglass- or diamond-shaped. Dark rings on the tail. *Prenasals usually separated from rostral by small scales; or supraoculars pitted, creased, or with rough outer edges* (Fig. 25, opp. Pl. 44). Scales keeled, in 23–27 rows.

Over much of its range, this rattler is a rock-dweller but it also occurs occasionally on loose soil or in sandy areas. Found in sagebrush, creosote bush, and succulent desert, thornscrub, chaparral, and piñon-juniper woodland. Usually an alert, nervous snake that

often holds its ground when cornered. Live-bearing; 2–11 young, born July–Aug. Eats small mammals, lizards, and birds.
Similar species: (1) Western Diamondback Rattlesnake (p. 226) has "coontail" markings, lacks pitted and creased supraoculars and small scales between the prenasals and rostral. (2) Mojave Rattlesnake (p. 232) has enlarged scales between the supraoculars and usually a better-defined dorsal pattern. (3) See also Tiger Rattlesnake (p. 230).
Range: S. Nev. to tip of Baja Calif.; s. Calif. to nw. and w.-cen. Ariz. Sea level to around 8000 ft. (2440 m). **Map 188**
Subspecies: SAN LUCAN SPECKLED RATTLESNAKE, *C. m. mitchelli.* Ground color yellowish gray. Blotches heavily speckled with dark spots. Head small. Rattle large. SOUTHWESTERN SPECKLED RATTLESNAKE, *C. m. pyrrhus.* (Fig. 25, opp. Pl. 44). Small scales usually separate the prenasals from the rostral. Supraoculars unmodified (see below). Ground color highly variable — white to dark gray or varying shades of pink or orange. Dark bands on back, often split by a lighter color. PANAMINT RATTLESNAKE, *C. m. stephensi* (Fig. 25). No small scales between the prenasals and rostral. Supraoculars often pitted, furrowed, or the outer edges irregular. Tan or gray, with light brown blotches or bands that are more regular in outline and more distinctly edged with light color than in previous subspecies.

SIDEWINDER *Crotalus cerastes* **Pl. 44**
Identification: 17–33 in. (42–82 cm). The sidewise locomotion, with the body moving in an S-shaped curve, is characteristic. Back generally pale, harmonizing with background — cream, tan, pink, or gray, patterned with grayish, yellowish brown, or tan blotches down back. A dark eyestripe. *Supraoculars hornlike,* pointed, and upturned — this snake is sometimes called the "horned rattler." Scales keeled, in 21–23 rows.

A desert species, usually found in areas of fine windblown sand in the vicinity of rodent burrows (kangaroo rats, etc.). Most common where there are sand hummocks topped with creosote bushes, mesquite, or other desert plants, but it may also occur on windswept flats, barren dunes, hardpan, and rocky hillsides. Sidewinding is a rapid form of locomotion and appears to be best suited to open terrain where the broadside movements of sidewinding are unobstructed by rocks and vegetation. Sidewinding also minimizes slippage on loose soil and heat uptake from hot surfaces because of the greatly reduced contact between the snake's body and the ground. Most easily found by tracking or night driving in sandy areas. The track often shows impressions of the belly scutes and consists of a series of parallel J-shaped marks with the hook of the J pointing in the direction of travel. Chiefly nocturnal, usually hiding by day in animal burrows or coiled, camouflaged, in a shallow self-made pit at the base of a shrub. Eats pocket mice, kangaroo rats, lizards, and occasionally birds. The "horns" seem to act as sunshades and, by reducing glare, may help this snake ambush its prey in daytime from its location beneath a shrub. Live-bearing; 5–18 young, born chiefly in fall.

Range: S. Nev. and extreme sw. Utah into ne. Baja Calif. (to Llano de San Pedro) and nw. Sonora; desert base of mountains of s. Calif. to s.-cen. Ariz. Below sea level (in desert sinks) to around 6000 ft. (1830 m). **Map 186**

Subspecies: MOJAVE DESERT SIDEWINDER, *C. c. cerastes.* Basal segment of rattle brown in adult. Usually 21 dorsal scale rows at midbody. SONORAN SIDEWINDER, *C. c. cercobombus.* Basal segment of rattle black in adult. Dorsal scales usually in 21 rows. COLORADO DESERT SIDEWINDER, *C. c. laterorepens.* Basal segment of rattle black in adult. Usually 23 dorsal scale rows.

BLACK-TAILED RATTLESNAKE **Pl. 45**

Crotalus molossus

Identification: 28–49½ in. (70–126 cm). *Tail and sometimes the snout black,* contrasting with rest of body. Tail sometimes gray with vague rings. Back with black or brown blotches or crossbands of irregular outline, each edged with whitish and having a single or double patch of light scales at the center. Dark markings toward front and middle of back sometimes diamond-shaped. Scales in pattern areas usually one color, not partly dark and light. Ground color cream, yellow, grayish, olive, greenish, or dark rust. Dark individuals occur on dark lava flows. Enlarged scales on the upper surface of snout. Scales keeled, in 27 rows. ***Young:*** Dark rings visible on tail.

Over much of its range, this rattler is a mountain snake that inhabits rockslides, outcrops, areas near cliffs, and stream courses. It avoids barren desert. Ranges from arid tropical scrub and paloverde-cactus-thornbush association through chaparral, into the pine-oak belt. It is abroad both day and night, and is especially active after warm rains. Usually nonaggressive. Live-bearing; 3–6 young, born in summer. Probably eats small mammals.

Range: N. Ariz. to southern edge of Mexican plateau; w. Ariz. to Edwards Plateau of cen. Tex. In w. Ariz. in the Ajo, Kofa, Castle Dome, and Hualapai Mts. Sea level to around 9600 ft. (2930 m). **Map 180**

Subspecies: The NORTHERN BLACK-TAILED RATTLESNAKE, *C. m. molossus,* occurs in our area.

TIGER RATTLESNAKE *Crotalus tigris* **Pl. 45**

Identification: 18–36 in. (45–90 cm). Back with irregular crossbands ("tiger" markings) of gray or brown; composed of dark dots and often with vague borders. Generally *more extensively crossbanded* than other western rattlesnakes. Head small, rattle large. Ground color gray, bluish gray, pink, lavender, or buff, becoming pale orange or cream on the sides. Tail rings usually indistinct because of darkened light rings. Scales keeled, in 23 rows.

Largely restricted to rocky canyons and foothills of desert mountain ranges, where it occurs in arid environments of cactus, mesquite, creosote bush, ocotillo, saguaro, and paloverde on the lower slopes up into the oak belt. Active both day and night; often abroad after warm rains. Live-bearing. Eats small mammals (kangaroo rats, pocket mice, deer mice, and often woodrats).

Similar species: (1) Speckled Rattlesnake (p. 228) has small scales between the rostral and prenasals. (2) Western Rattlesnake (below) has dark dorsal blotches on front part of body rather than crossbands.

Range: Cen. and s. Ariz. to s. Sonora. Sea level to around 4800 ft. (1460 m). **Map 181**

WESTERN RATTLESNAKE *Crotalus viridis* **Pl. 44**

Identification: 15–65 in. (37–162 cm). A blotched rattlesnake, usually with a light stripe extending from behind the eye to corner of mouth. Blotches various shades of brown to black, usually edged with darker color and often with light-colored borders. Blotches often give way at rear to crossbands. The ground color of this snake varies greatly over its wide range, often harmonizing with soil color — may be cream, yellowish, gray, pink, greenish, brown, or black. Tail with dark and light rings but usually not sharply contrasting with body color. Our only rattlesnake that usually has *more than 2 internasals touching the rostral* (Fig. 25, opp. Pl. 44). Scales keeled, in 25–27 rows.

Frequents a great variety of habitats, from shrub-covered coastal sand dunes to timberline and from prairies and desert-edge habitats to mountain forests. Rocky outcrops, talus slopes, rocky stream courses, and ledges are favorite haunts of this snake; in cooler areas (more northerly parts of range and at high altitudes) it may den in mammal burrows, rock crevices, or caves, sometimes in large numbers. Live-bearing; 1–25 (often 4–12) young, born Aug.–Oct. Eats mammals (mice, ground squirrels, rabbits), nestling birds, lizards, snakes, and amphibians.

Similar species: The presence of more than 2 internasals touching the rostral generally will distinguish this rattler from all other species.

Range: Extreme sw. Canada to cen. Baja Calif. and n. Coahuila; Pacific Coast to w. Iowa and cen. Kans. Absent from lowland desert. On Santa Catalina I. and s. Coronado I. Sea level to around 11,000 ft. (3350 m). **Map 184**

Subspecies: PRAIRIE RATTLESNAKE, *C. v. viridis*. Usually has a greenish cast above, but also may be brown or grayish. Blotches brown, usually well defined and edged with a thin, light line (Fig. 26 opp. Pl. 44). GRAND CANYON RATTLESNAKE, *C. v. abyssus*. Red or salmon above. Body blotches slightly darker, fading with age; oval-shaped on back. Found in Grand Canyon, Ariz. ARIZONA BLACK RATTLESNAKE, *C. v. cerberus*. Dark gray, olive, brown, or black above, with large dark brown or black blotches that are often separated by light lines. Blotches on sides conspicuous except in dark individuals. Some individuals nearly solid black. Usually 2 loreal scales on each side. Mts. of Ariz. and extreme w. N.M. MIDGET FADED RATTLESNAKE, *C. v. concolor.* Cream, yellowish, or tan above. In adults, blotches are oval and slightly darker than ground color (often faint or absent). Rarely more than 24 in. (60 cm). Venom potent. SOUTHERN PACIFIC RATTLESNAKE, *C. v. helleri.* Resembles the Arizona Black Rattler but ground color usually lighter; a single loreal scale. Blotches dark, angular, and light-edged. Terminal dark tail ring poorly defined and about twice as wide as the others. Young with bright yellow tail. This subspecies hybridizes with the Mojave Rattlesnake in w. Antelope Valley, Calif. NORTHERN PACIFIC RATTLESNAKE, *C. v. oreganus.* Resembles the Southern Pacific Rattler, but dark tail rings well defined and of quite uniform width. Young with bright yellow tail. GREAT BASIN RATTLESNAKE, *C. v. lutosus.* Usually buff, pale yellowish, light gray, or tan above, with contrasting brown to blackish blotches that are about as wide as the spaces between them. HOPI RATTLESNAKE, *C. v. nuntius.* Pink, red, or reddish brown above, with well-defined reddish brown blotches that have light edges. Rarely over 24 in. (60 cm). The rattler commonly used in the Hopi Indian snake dance.

MOJAVE RATTLESNAKE *Crotalus scutulatus* **Pl. 44**

Identification: 24–51 in. (60–129 cm). Well-defined, light-edged dark gray to brown diamonds, ovals, or hexagons down middle of back; light scales of pattern usually entirely light-colored. (Dorsal blotches usually lack light borders at extreme southern end of range.) Ground color greenish gray, olive green, brownish, or yellowish. A white to yellowish stripe extends from behind the eye to a point behind the corner of the mouth (except at extreme southern end of range). Tail with contrasting light and dark rings; *dark rings narrower than light rings. Enlarged scales on snout and between the supraoculars* (Fig. 25, opp. Pl. 44). Scales keeled, in 25 rows.

Chiefly inhabits upland desert and lower mountain slopes, but ranges to about sea level near the mouth of the Colorado R. and to high elevations in the Sierra Madre Occidental. Habitats vary — barren desert, grassland, open juniper woodland, and scrubland. This rattler seems to be most common in areas of scattered scrubby growth such as creosote bush and mesquite. Not common in broken rocky terrain or where vegetation is dense. Live-bearing; 2–11 young, born July–Aug. Eats kangaroo rats and other rodents, and probably other reptiles. An extremely dangerous snake — excitable and with highly potent venom.

Similar species: See (1) Western Diamondback (p. 226), (2)

Western Rattlesnake (p. 231), and (3) Speckled Rattlesnake (p. 228).

Range: S. Nev. to Puebla, near southern edge of Mexican plateau; western edge of Mojave Desert, Calif., to extreme w. Tex. From near sea level to around 8300 ft. (2530 m). **Map 189**

Subspecies: The MOJAVE GREEN RATTLESNAKE, *C. s. scutulatus,* occurs in our area.

TWIN-SPOTTED RATTLESNAKE *Crotalus pricei* **Pl. 45**

Identification: 12–26 in. (30–65 cm). A small, slender, light brown to bluish gray rattlesnake with *2 rows of brown or blackish spots on its back;* spots alternate or are arranged in pairs and sometimes joined across the back to form transverse blotches. Smaller spots on sides. Fine brown speckling over upper surfaces. Dark stripe behind the eye with light border. Tail often with distinct brown bands. Throat sometimes salmon-pink. Scales keeled, in 21 rows. ***Young:*** Dark, often with obscure spotting.

A mountain rock dweller of pine-oak woodland, grassy and brushy areas, and open coniferous forest. Its activity is restricted by cool night temperatures and thundershowers, but it may be abroad during warm rains. Search well-lit rocky slopes on sunny mornings when the snakes are basking or hunting. Well camouflaged. Hidden individuals can sometimes be made to rattle by tossing rocks into talus. The sound is weak, resembling a locust or beetle buzzing among leaves. Usually a mild-tempered snake. Live-bearing; 3–8 young, born July–Aug. Eats small rodents and lizards.

Range: Se. Ariz. (Pinaleño, Graham, Dos Cabezas, Santa Rita, Huachuca, and Chiricahua Mts.) south in Sierra Madre Occidental to s. Durango and possibly Aguacalientes. Isolated populations in ne. Mexico. From around 4000 to 10,500 ft. (1220–3200 m). **Map 179**

Subspecies: The WESTERN TWIN-SPOTTED RATTLESNAKE, *C. p. pricei,* occurs in our area.

RIDGE-NOSED RATTLESNAKE *Crotalus willardi* **Pl. 45**

Identification: 15–25½ in. (37–64 cm). Reddish brown or gray above, with *whitish crossbars that are edged with dark brown or black; crossbars merge with color on sides.* A ridge contours the snout, which may have a single vertical white line at its tip. Often with contrasting light and dark marks on each side of face. Tail rings usually confined to anterior part of tail, near base. Scales keeled, in 29 rows. ***Young:*** Sometimes with bright yellow tail.

A mountain snake chiefly found in the pine-oak and pine-fir belts, but ranges into foothill canyons in piñon-juniper habitat. May be found basking on sunny rocky slopes in moist woodland and forest, or crawling over the forest floor. Frequents canyon bottoms grown to alder, box elder, maple, oak, and other broadleaf

deciduous trees. Live-bearing; 2–9 young, born Aug.–Sept. Eats small mammals, birds, lizards, scorpions, and centipedes.
Range: Se. Ariz. and extreme sw. N.M. south in Sierra Madre Occidental to Zacatecas. From around 5000–9000 ft. (1520–2750 m). **Map 183**
Subspecies: ARIZONA RIDGE-NOSED RATTLESNAKE, *C. w. willardi.* A white vertical line on the rostral and mental scales. Back brown. Little dark spotting on head. Huachuca Mts. (Ramsey and Carr Canyons), Santa Rita Mts., and Empire Mts., Ariz. ANIMAS RIDGE-NOSED RATTLESNAKE, *C. w. obscurus.* **Threatened.** No vertical white line on rostral or mental scales; white markings on sides of face often obscure. Back gray or brown above, with abundant dark spotting on head. In the U.S., known only from several canyons in the Animas Mts., N.M., in pine, oak, and juniper forest.

11

Baja California "Endemics"

(See Maps 84, 119, 132, 190–200.)

Seventy-five species of reptiles and amphibians that were covered in my 1966 *Field Guide* range into Baja California. This represents most of the amphibian and reptile fauna of the area. To provide complete coverage of mainland species in Baja California has required the addition of 17 species, most of which are confined to the area, and several species new to both the U.S. and Baja California. Most of the additions are endemic to Baja California and are described below. (See Maps 190–200.) Some, however, range onto the Mexican mainland and/or have populations on the offshore islands of Baja California, and thus are not strictly endemic to the region. For this reason, the word "endemic" appears in quotes. Island occurrences are shown by black dots on the maps. Unfortunately, because of space limitations in this guide, it has not been possible to list the islands occupied in the species accounts, nor to describe island subspecies. A few endemics appear elsewhere in the book (see Maps 84, 119, and 132).

Poor road access made it difficult to study the plants and animals of Baja California until 1974, when Mexican Highway 1 (which runs the length of the peninsula) was paved, and other roads were improved. Intensive exploration and study of the peninsula's reptiles and amphibians is now underway and much new distributional information and some taxonomic changes can be expected in the years ahead. The results of recent studies already challenge the previous taxonomy of some groups. Since I do not feel that a *Field Guide* is the place for presenting new taxonomic arrangements, and because I believe it is desirable to allow the scientific community a period of time to evaluate new taxonomic proposals, especially somewhat controversial ones, I have been conservative in my taxonomic approach. For example, although there is considerable biochemical evidence that previously recognized Baja California subspecies of the Desert Spiny Lizard are full species, I treat them as subspecies pending more intensive field study of distribution, variation, and habits, especially in areas where one form gives way to another. Under the Remarks heading in the accounts, I have noted species for which an alternative taxonomic treatment is being considered or has already been proposed.

The following accounts are deficient in a number of ways — size ranges of adults are often unknown, information on food habits and reproduction is frequently scanty, and elevational and geographic ranges are often poorly known. These gaps should be a challenge to field observers to improve our knowledge of Baja California reptiles and amphibians.

SAN LUCAN GECKO *Phyllodactylus unctus* **Pl. 47**
Identification: $1\frac{1}{2}$–$2\frac{1}{8}$ in. (3.7–5.3 cm). Similar to the Leaf-toed Gecko (Pl. 35). Purplish sooty above, blotched with yellowish brown. Yellowish brown eyestripe may extend onto neck. Tail with brown crossbars. Pale pinkish purple to whitish below, sometimes slightly tinged with brown. Underside of toe pads white. In pale phase becomes pale gray or creamy white. Minute rounded dorsal scales *not interspersed with larger tubercles.* No enlarged tubercles on tail. *Each toe has 2 large plates at tip.*

Nocturnal. By day found in rock crevices and beneath bark, rocks, and other objects on the ground. Abroad on rock and bark surfaces at night.

Similar species: The Leaf-toed Gecko (p. 112) has numerous projecting keeled tubercles on its back.

Range: Known only from the Cape Region of Baja Calif. and Partida and Ballena Is. (off western side of Espiritu Santo I.) in the Gulf. Ranges to the vicinity of La Paz. Coexists with the Leaf-toed Gecko in some areas. **Map 190**

SPINY-TAILED IGUANA *Ctenosaura hemilopha* **Pl. 47**
Identification: 8–10 in. (20–25 cm). The largest lizard in Baja Calif. Adults are easily recognized by their *large size and spiny tails.* Back and sides covered with small smooth scales. Grayish or olive gray above, mottled with black. Dark crossbands across upper back. Ground color varies from pale gray or yellowish gray to dark slaty brown. May undergo marked color change from pale gray to sooty. Limbs dark, spotted and mottled with gray. Throat, chest, and sometimes front part of belly dusky or black. Belly pale dull yellowish. ***Male:*** Spiny crest on neck and shoulders well developed. Throat, chest, and sometimes upper abdomen black. ***Female:*** Crest absent or reduced; less dark color on throat and chest. ***Young:*** Middorsal row of slightly enlarged keeled scales from neck to midback. Dark crossbands or saddles extend length of back.

Found on rocks and in trees; seldom descends to the ground. Seeks shelter in crevices where, like the Chuckwalla, it may resist extraction by puffing up its body and lashing out with its tail. Handle with care — large individuals can inflict a severe bite. Feeds chiefly on plants, but may also occasionally eat invertebrates, including crabs in coastal areas.

Range: Southern part of Baja Calif. from just south of Santa Rosalia through Sierra Gigantea to the Cape. Cerralvo, San Pedro

Nolasco, and San Esteban Is. in the Gulf; w.-cen. Sonora. Sea level to 4000 ft. (1220 m). **Map 191**

Subspecies: The PENINSULAR SPINY-TAILED IGUANA, *C. h. hemilopha,* occurs in our area.

Remarks: Evidently introduced in Baja Calif. as a source of human food, but it may also have been present naturally. It is known locally as the "Iguana."

CAPE SPINY LIZARD *Sceloporus licki* **Pl. 46**

Identification: 2½–3⅛ in. (6.2–7.8 cm). Olive brown or gray-brown above, with a *light dorsolateral stripe* on upper side; stripe pale beige or yellowish on front of body, fading at midbody or near hind limbs. Top of head light brown to coppery brown. Dusky or black blotch toward lower side of neck, with or without a light spot at center or lower edge. *Throat pale with diagonal gray streaks, the 2 streaks at center often parallel.* ***Male:*** Broad blue to metallic purple dorsal stripe extends from area above forelimbs to tail base. Blue-green patches on belly become dull, light brownish yellow toward sides. Central part of belly, underside and front of thighs, and groin blackish. Sometimes a blue throat patch. Tail with dusky-edged, light yellowish green or greenish scales that become yellowish tan toward tip. Scales on neck and sides edged with brown, with light areas of scales yellowish or with a pinkish copper cast. ***Female:*** Lacks blue or purple dorsal stripe, has duller markings on belly and lower sides, lacks black color on thighs and groin, and tail lacks greenish markings. Dusky flecks on body and limbs.

Generally found on large rocky outcrops like those occupied by the Hunsaker Spiny Lizard (below), but also in trees. Particularly common in the more sheltered gullies and canyon bottoms, and often found on rocks in the mottled light and shade of strangler figs. Seems to be less wary than the Hunsaker Spiny Lizard.

Similar species: The Hunsaker Spiny Lizard (below) lacks the dorsolateral stripe on neck and shoulders.

Range: Found at intermediate to high elevations in Cape region of Baja Calif. **Map 194**

HUNSAKER SPINY LIZARD **Pl. 46**
Sceloporus hunsakeri

Identification: 2½–3½ in. (5–8.6 cm). Closely resembles the Granite Spiny Lizard (Pl. 27). Blue throat in male mostly or entirely suffused with black. Blue belly patches usually fused with throat patches. Sides with steeply diagonal crossbars. ***Male:*** Blue belly and throat markings brighter than in female; markings sometimes quite faint in female.

Chiefly a rock dweller, frequenting arid tropical scrub and forest. Eats insects.

Similar species: (1) The Granite Spiny Lizard (p. 129) is usually larger and has lower combined dorsal scale-total femoral pore count (59 or fewer, not 61 or more). Count dorsal scales along midline, from interparietal scale to rear of thighs. (2) See also Cape Spiny Lizard (above).

Range: Cape region of Baja Calif., and Espiritu Santo and Balena Is. in the Gulf. **Map 84**

Remarks: This lizard coexists with the Cape Spiny Lizard.

BLACK-TAILED BRUSH LIZARD **Pl. 47**

Urosaurus nigricaudus

Identification: $1\frac{3}{4}$–2 in. (4.4–5 cm). A close relative of the Small-scaled Lizard (p. 137). Gray, yellow-brown, brownish olive to black or sooty brown above, usually with a *sooty to blackish tail;* dark tail contrasts with paler body when lizard is in light phase. A row of gray or dusky to black blotches or crossbars on each side of back, separated by an irregular, pale gray or brownish stripe with scalloped borders down middle of back. Crossbars edged with whitish, especially those toward front of body. Neck bar(s) darker than other bars, especially in males. Tinges of rust or yellowish brown often present on neck, tail base, and upper sides. Whitish to yellowish gray below, sometimes spotted and mottled with dusky on underside of tail. *Broad area of enlarged keeled scales down center of back,* giving way at sides to small granular scales. Scales on tail keeled and pointed (mucronate — see rear endpapers). ***Male:*** Throat orange to yellow; *no blue.* Blue to blue-green belly patches, sometimes joining at midline. Enlarged postanal scales. ***Female:*** Usually smaller. Throat yellow-orange, lemon yellow, to whitish. Lacks belly patches and enlarged postanal scales. Scalloped pale gray or gray-brown middorsal stripe, usually more definite than in male, and tail less often dark.

In the dark phase, these lizards are highly conspicuous when on light-colored rocks. In excited males, tail and crossbars on body darken, setting them off from the bordering white spots and bars and enhancing the overall contrast in pattern. The conspicuous black tail may divert a predator's attention to an expendable part that can be regenerated. In dark-phase females, the scalloped middorsal stripe may remain pale, contrasting strongly with the darkened sides. In both sexes in the light phase, the dark neck bars tend to remain conspicuous when rest of body pales.

Found in a variety of habitats from coastal plains to mountains. Common in thornscrub. Especially abundant near streams and oases. A quick, agile species that climbs readily and frequents rocky areas, trees, and old buildings. Seldom found on level ground except when moving between elevated sites. Eats insects and other small arthropods.

Similar species: (1) In spiny lizards (*Sceloporus* species; pp. 125–129, 237), the gular fold is incomplete and the scales down the middle of back are not enlarged. (2) Side-blotched Lizard (p. 135) is more of a ground-dweller, has a dark blotch behind forelimb, back scales of nearly uniform size, and lacks distinct blue belly

patches. (3) Small-scaled Lizard (p. 137) less often has a dark tail; large males usually have blue on throat.
Range: Cape region of Baja Calif., north along the west coast to San Jorge. **Map 193**
Remarks: This lizard and the Small-scaled Lizard, *U. microscutatus,* may prove to be the same species. They are difficult to distinguish.

BAJA CALIFORNIA BRUSH LIZARD Pl. 47

Urosaurus lahtelai

Identification: $1\frac{1}{2}$–$2\frac{1}{8}$ in. (4–5.3 cm). Resembles the Long-tailed Brush Lizard (Pl. 25). Sooty to pale gray above, depending on color phase, with crossbars on sides. Broad gray area down center of back, sometimes with scalloped borders. *Tail of same general color as body, not notably darkened.* Ground color dusky to dull white below, variously streaked and flecked with gray. *Strip of enlarged keeled scales down middle of back.* Granular scales on sides. Scales on tail and large scales on limbs keeled, those on tail also mucronate. A *single frontal scale.* ***Male:*** Buff speckling on body and limbs. Orange-yellow or orange throat. Blue-green belly patches. Enlarged postanal scales. ***Female:*** Lacks buffy spotting, has yellowish to orange throat patch, no belly patches, and postanal scales not enlarged.

Frequents an area of rounded granite boulders in an upland region of s.-cen. Baja California Norte. Tends to occur on the smaller boulders about the larger outcrops, often where the rocks are shaded by shrubs. Rock surfaces and the decomposing granite soil are beige with rust tints. Plants in the area include cardons, boojum, creosote bush, mesquite, agave, salt bush, ocotillo, goatnut, cholla, buckwheat, encelia, and mulefat along seeps.
Similar species: (1) Spiny lizards (*Sceloporus* species, pp. 125–129, 237), have an incomplete gular fold and lack the strip of enlarged scales down middle of back. (2) Side-blotched Lizard (p. 135) has a dark blotch on each side behind the forelimb, back scales of nearly uniform size, and lacks distinct bluish belly patches. (3) Small-scaled Lizard (p. 137) lacks strip of enlarged dorsal scales down the back and has a shorter tail. (4) Black-tailed Brush Lizard (above) has a shorter and dark tail, fewer enlarged dorsal-scale rows, and a less distinct dorsal pattern. (5) Long-tailed Brush Lizard (p. 135) has a divided frontal scale and more supraoculars (5–7, not 3–5).
Range: Baja Calif., from vicinity of Catavina to about 10 mi. (16 km) north. **Map 193**

BAJA CALIFORNIA ROCK LIZARD Pl. 46

Petrosaurus thalassinus

Identification: $3\frac{1}{2}$–7 in. (8.7–17.5 cm). *Body somewhat flattened.* Scales on back smooth and granular; those on tail may be weakly keeled. *Three or 4 dark crossbars on upper back, each edged at* *rear with lighter color.* Individuals in Cape region are very brightly colored — head bluish with red or orange in eye region. Blue spots and streaks on neck. Lower back dull yellowish to salmon, with broad crossbands of yellowish brown, slaty, to bluish. Numerous dusky vermiculations (wormlike markings) often present on back. Rump rust to tan. Tail with bluish crossbands separated by narrower paler bands. Throat yellowish to orange with diffuse sooty to black patch at center. Chest yellow to orange with sooty to brownish blotches; rest of underparts dull whitish to pale beige with dusky blotches. In northern part of range animals are duller and lack orange head and bluish colors. Back of head and base of tail often tan. ***Young:*** Stripes on rear part of back more pronounced than in adult. ***Male:*** Usually considerably larger than female. Crossbands on upper back edged at rear with yellow. Enlarged postanal scales. Femoral pores larger than in female. ***Female:*** In breeding season, black crossbands on upper back are edged at rear with bright orange or red. Sides of neck suffused with red or orange. Orange or red on throat and chest; color sometimes extends to midbelly. No enlarged postanal scales. Femoral pores minute. Although these lizards are readily seen at close range, beyond about 30 yds. (27 m) they usually blend well with rock surfaces.

Primarily a rock dweller, found especially in areas of massive outcrops, but occasionally found on the ground when foraging and when traveling between rocky areas. An excellent climber that moves over rock with its legs spraddled and leaps nimbly from rock to rock. Eats leaves, blossoms, berries, and probably insects.

Similar species: The Banded Rock Lizard (p. 137) has only a single black marking (collar) on the neck.

Range: From northern end of Sierra de Calamajue y San Jose, in Baja California Norte, south in rocky habitats to the Cape. Absent from Viscaiño Desert and lowlands of Magdalena Plain. Near sea level to around 5400 ft. (1650 m). **Map 192**

Subspecies: SHORT-NOSED ROCK LIZARD, *P. t. repens.* Usually 1 row of scales between subocular and labials. Snout shorter and blunter. Hind limbs shorter. Four distinct dark crossbands toward front of body. Throat brownish, becoming blackish toward center. Lacks bright orange head and blue color. SAN LUCAN ROCK LIZARD, *P. t. thalassinus.* Usually 2 rows of scales between subocular and labials. Snout longer, less blunt at tip. Three distinct dark crossbands toward front of body. Head orange. Body tinged with blue. Throat yellow, orange, or pale blue at center.

BAJA CALIFORNIA WHIPTAIL **Pl. 46**

Cnemidophorus labialis

Identification: 2–2⅓ in. (5–5.8 cm). A striped whiptail that has no light spots in the dark fields. Dark fields on sides tan or *reddish* *brown* to black. *At least 6, usually 7, and sometimes 8 pale stripes;* a total of 8 results when middorsal stripe is divided. Upper stripes beige to yellowish; lowermost stripes whitish. Top of head greenish olive to gray-brown. Tail grades from greenish blue through blue to purplish blue at tip, with a *black stripe on each side, almost to tip.* Whitish below. ***Male:*** Bluish wash on sides of face, limbs, and belly. ***Female:*** Lacks or has reduced blue color.

This lizard frequents areas of fine sand and scattered low shrubs and grass along the coast, mostly within about ½ mi. (1 km) from the high-tide mark. Search for this lizard after the coastal fog has lifted, which may be near midday.

Similar species: The Orange-throated Whiptail (p. 152) has an undivided frontoparietal and, at midbody, has 5 light dorsal stripes where it coexists with the Baja California Whiptail. Its middorsal stripe, however, is sometimes partly forked at both ends.

Range: West coast of Baja California Norte from Rio San Rafael at Colonet to Guerrero Negro and west to Punta Eugenia in n. Baja California Sur. **Map 194**

SAN LUCAN ALLIGATOR LIZARD **not shown**

Gerrhonotus paucicarinatus

Identification: 3–5 in. (7.5–12.5 cm). In general appearance, resembles the Southern Alligator Lizard (Pl. 29), but dark crossbars on back are usually narrower; also usually has conspicuous *alternating black and white marks on labials.* A broad dorsal stripe of olive, brown, orange, reddish, or grayish olive. Pale to dusky on sides, sometimes blackish. Some 11–14 irregular, narrow dark brown or black crossbands on body (not counting the tail). Similar but less clearly defined markings on tail. Some adults have a broad, bronze-colored stripe above, with faint or indefinite crossbars. Soft skin of lateral fold (see p. 164) cream-colored, pale beige, or orange, crossed by dusky to black bands and/or a network that often sets off pale spots of ground color. Yellowish or grayish white below, with a dark line or series of dots along middle of each lengthwise scale row. Temporal scales smooth. Usually 14–16 dorsal-scale rows; each scale moderately keeled on back but only faintly so on sides. ***Young:*** A broad, bronze-colored or brownish dorsal stripe.

At higher elevations this lizard frequents grassy meadows in mixed forests of pine, oaks, madrone, and shrubs. At lower elevations it ranges into habitats with agaves, cactus, mesquite, and acacias, often near springs or in other cool, moist localities. Usually found under dead yuccas, logs, and other plant debris or crawling among grass and leaves.

Similar species: Southern Alligator Lizard (p. 164) lacks black and white markings on labials.

Range: Cape region of Baja Calif., chiefly in foothills and uplands of Sierra de la Laguna. Has also been found at Rancho Los

Dolores (on coast opposite Isla San Jose) and at San Ignacio. Expected at scattered localities throughout the Sierra de la Giganta. From sea level to around 6200 ft. (1890 m). **Map 119**
Remarks: The Cedros Island Alligator Lizard (*G. cedrosensis,* not shown) appears to be closely related.

BAJA CALIFORNIA LEGLESS LIZARD **Pl. 47**

Anniella geronimensis

Identification: 4–6 in. (10–15 cm). Resembles the California Legless Lizard (Pl. 34), but snout flatter in profile, less pointed from above. Silvery to light beige above, with a dark, narrow middorsal line. Dull white stripes on sides between *numerous narrow lengthwise blackish lines.* Tail more pointed than in California Legless Lizard.

Frequents coastal dunes and sand flats in areas stabilized by low-growing bushes and mats of ice plant *(Mesembryanthemum),* and sand verbenas. Can be found by raking surface layers of sand beneath bushes where invertebrates are abundant and the sand just below the surface is damp. Seems to prefer the southern, sunny side of bushes and hummocks in cool weather. 1–2 young born in summer. Eats small arthropods.
Similar species: In the California Legless Lizard (p. 168), the snout is more pointed from above but more rounded in profile; body has fewer thin, lengthwise dark lines. Orange-yellow below.
Range: Narrow zone along western coast of Baja California Norte, from Rio Santo Domingo at Colonia Guerrero to El Rosario. San Geronimo I. **Map 195**
Remarks: Coexists with the California Legless Lizard in the northern part of its range (see p. 168).

MOLE LIZARD (Ajolote) *Bipes biporus* **Pl. 47**

Identification: 7–9½ in. (17.4–23.8 cm). A subterranean, burrowing, earthworm-like reptile with a short, broad, *molelike pair of sharply clawed forelimbs and no hind limbs.* This reptile is a member of the family Amphisbaenidae and is not a true lizard. Tail short and blunt, not regenerated when lost. Head short, snout rounded, no neck constriction. Eyes vestigial. Body and tail ringed with numerous, regularly spaced, closely set furrows. Usually pinkish to pinkish white above; occasionally whitish with a bluish cast. Deeper pink below, especially beneath forelimbs. ***Young:*** Generally more pinkish than adults.

This animal burrows in fine, loose alluvial soils of the Baja Calif. lowlands. Search for it by digging around the bases of shrubs, trees, and termite-infested stumps and abandoned fenceposts until you find a network of tunnels, each about ¼–⅜ in. (6–9 mm) in diameter. Best results are usually obtained where damp soil is available within a spade depth or so of the surface. Look for patches of shade and a leaf-litter mat that slows the loss of soil moisture, provides warm and cool areas near the surface, and attracts small arthropods, upon which this animal feeds. Mole lizards rarely expose themselves on the surface, but when surface moisture is suitable they may emerge to forage just beneath the leaf litter. They dig by ramming their blunt, solidly constructed head into the soil and moving it from side to side as they scrape away soil with one forelimb, then another.

When this animal crawls on the surface, the walking movements of the forelimbs are aided by a "caterpillar" action of the body, resembling that of some snakes. The short, forked tongue is frequently protruded. Clutch of 1–4 eggs, laid in July.

Range: Slopes and plains of western side of the Baja Calif. Peninsula, from Bahia de Sebastian Viscaiño and the vicinity of Guerrero Negro to the Cape. Includes the Viscaiño Desert and Magdalena Plain. **Map 195**

Remarks: Rumors of a *Bipes*-like animal in the Huachuca and Santa Rita Mts. of s. Ariz. have recently been given further support. In the early 1970s, Kenneth Swartz found a "worm lizard" in Paradise Valley near Phoenix. It was about 6 in. (15 cm) long; a bit thicker than a pencil; had pearly, slightly translucent scales; legs about $^{3}/_{16}$ in. (5 mm) long and $^{1}/_{16}$ in. (2 mm) wide, tipped with tiny claws; and no trace of hind limbs. It crawled in clumsy, snakelike fashion and seemed to use its nose in digging when it was returned to its burrow. Termite tubes were present in the mud around the burrows.

Mole lizards can easily be overlooked. They rarely emerge on the surface, are spotty in occurrence (requiring fine-grained, moist soils and associated insect prey), and can easily be mistaken for earthworms by the casual observer. A renewed effort should be made to find these animals in Ariz. Perhaps a new species awaits discovery.

CAPE WHIPSNAKE *Masticophis aurigulus* Pl. 48

Identification: 30–42 in. (75–105 cm). Similar to the California Whipsnake (Pl. 36), and probably a member of that species. Head long, with a flattened top and a narrow, rounded snout. Body very slender. Dark brown above, becoming black toward the head. Head light brown, shaded with yellow. Narrow yellowish stripe from eye to snout. Yellowish stripe on side is broken toward the front. *A dark stripe along lower edge of light side stripe covers 2nd and 3rd scale rows, and is interrupted by light-colored areas.* Labials, chin, and anterior part of belly yellow, unspotted. Belly dull yellowish. Scales smooth, in 17 rows. Anal divided (see rear endpapers).

Found near springs and stream bottoms. At San Bartolo, it has been found along wash bottom in sandy soil bordered by bush lupines, clumps of willow, and palms, with strangler figs on nearby rocky slopes. Eats lizards.

Similar species: In the California Whipsnake (p. 182), the dark side stripe is solid, not interrupted by a series of lighter areas.
Range: Cape region of Baja Calif. **Map 132**
Remarks: The Espiritu Santo Island Whipsnake, *M. barbouri* (see locality shown with a black dot on the map), may be of this species. The Cape Whipsnake is expected at localities throughout the Sierra de la Giganta. It may prove to be a subspecies of the California Whipsnake, p. 182.

BAJA CALIFORNIA RAT SNAKE *Elaphe rosaliae* **Pl. 48**
Identification: 34–58 in. (85–145 cm). Head moderately long, distinct from neck. Body rather slender. *Uniform olive or reddish brown above,* with no dark markings; becoming yellowish or greenish on lower sides. Grayish or greenish yellow below. *Scales smooth, each with 2 apical pits* (see rear endpapers); *in 33 or 34 rows.* Anal divided. ***Young:*** Paler than adult and with cream or light yellow streaks across back.

Frequents hill slopes and arroyos, especially near springs, seeps, and streams, but also occurs in dry areas. Primarily nocturnal. Presumed to feed mainly on rats and other small mammals.
Range: San Ignacio south through Sierra de la Giganta to the Cape. Single records from southern end of Sierra de los Cocopah (Guadalupe Canyon), Baja California Norte, and about 1½ mi. (2.5 km) east of Mt. Spring, Imperial Co., Calif., suggest that this snake ranges on the eastern slope of Baja Calif. in the intervening area. **Map 198**

PACIFIC WATER SNAKE *Nerodia valida* **Pl. 48**
Identification: 23–38 in. (58–94 cm). Head distinct from neck. Snout rounded. *Eyes large and dark, set high on head. Uniformly light grayish, yellowish, or brownish above;* with more or less distinct *blackish markings on sides.* Pale grayish yellow to sooty below; tips of ventrals tinged with the back color. (Melanistic individuals are grayish black above and below.) A light-colored lateral stripe, set low on the side, extends from neck to tail, often becoming indistinct toward rear. Toward the front, it is located on the 3rd, 2nd, and part of the 1st scale rows. Some individuals have a number of alternating light and dark stripes. Scales keeled, in 19–23 rows. Anal divided.

Highly aquatic. Found in and near oases, ponds, seeps, streams, and rivers. Eats amphibians, including tadpoles, and fish.
Range: Cape region of Baja Calif. and on Pacific slopes of w. Mexico, from Durango to Guerrero. **Map 199**

BANDLESS SAND SNAKE **Pl. 48**
Chilomeniscus stramineus
Identification: 9–11 in. (22–27 cm). Similar in structure and habits to the Banded Sand Snake (p. 214), but different in coloration.

Head not much wider than neck. Snout round from above, flattened and pointed in profile. *Lower jaw inset* (countersunk). Ground color brownish to bright yellowish cinnamon above, with a variable dorsal pattern: (1) in Cape region, dorsal scales are brownish, especially toward their bases, and a *small dark brown dot* is usually present *near tip of each dorsal scale,* except those of the 1st and sometimes 2nd rows; (2) north of the Cape, dark dots absent and scale bases dark brown; (3) in Sonora, dark dots absent on dorsal scales, and scale bases not notably darkened. Top of head pale gray in adults, set off in some individuals by dark area on each side of head behind the eye. Ground color on lower sides yellowish white. Straw-colored below, unmarked. Scales smooth, in 13 rows. Anal divided. ***Young:*** Ground color cream-buff.

Most commonly found in deposits of fine, chiefly wind-sorted sand of coastal and inland dunes, flats, hummocks, and wash borders. Search under dead cardons and other surface debris in washes and sandy areas in thornscrub and desert-edge habitats. An excellent burrower. This snake has been observed at dusk with just its head exposed, the pale cap blending with the sandy background. It eats grasshoppers and other insects.

Similar species: Banded Sand Snake (p. 214) has dark saddles down the back.

Range: From Loreto and probably the northern end of Magdalena Plain to tip of Baja Calif.; cen. coast of Sonora. Coexists with Banded Sand Snake at La Paz and elsewhere.

Map 197

Remarks: This snake may prove to be a color variant of the Banded Sand Snake; the matter is under study.

BAJA CALIFORNIA NIGHT SNAKE Pl. 48

Eridiphas slevini

Identification: 12–22½ in. (30–56 cm). Resembles the Night Snake (Pl. 39), but *parietal scale usually touches lower postocular scale.* A slender, dark-blotched snake with a somewhat elongate, rather flattened head that is only slightly wider than its neck. Eyes large, *pupils vertical.* Rear maxillary teeth enlarged but not grooved. Numerous dark brown or gray-brown blotches on back and tail, largest along back where some may join to form irregular, sometimes dumbbell-shaped crossbars. Scales in areas of ground color have light-colored edges. Occasionally dark spots on neck form large blotches similar to those of the Night Snake. Unmarked yellow-gray color may be present along ventral midline. Dorsal scales smooth, in 21–23 rows at midbody. Anal divided. This snake is venomous, but not considered dangerous to humans; however, handle large ones with care.

Frequents rocky areas chiefly on the warm humid eastern slope of Baja Calif. Chiefly nocturnal. Individuals have been found on roadways after dark and along rock-strewn washes and arroyos.

One specimen was taken from a small crack at the base of a boulder and another from the moist wood inside the decaying trunk of a palm tree. A captive laid 2 elongate, kidney-shaped eggs that were found in a terrarium on Oct. 9. Captives have eaten lizards, snakes, frogs, toads, and salamanders. This snake sometimes holds its prey toward the back of its mouth for several minutes before swallowing it, perhaps to give the venom time to be absorbed.
Similar species: In the Night Snake (p. 221), the parietal scale does not touch the lower postocular scale; it usually has large nuchal blotches on the neck, not just spots.
Range: Distribution spotty; from the vicinity of Bahia de los Angeles to the Cape. Nearly all localities north of the Cape are from east of the crest of the Sierra Giganta and other mountain ranges that border the eastern side of the peninsula. The snake is expected to occur farther north, probably to the eastern side of the San Pedro Mártir Mts. On Cerralvo, Danzante, and San Marcos Is. in the Gulf of Calif. **Map 200**
Subspecies: The SLEVIN NIGHT SNAKE, *E. s. slevini,* occurs in our area.

BAJA CALIFORNIA RATTLESNAKE **Pl. 48**
Crotalus enyo
Identification: 20–35½ in. (50–89 cm). Head relatively narrow for a rattler. Eyes large; supraoculars slant notably upward. Ground color brown to silvery gray above, with reddish or yellowish brown, dark-edged blotches down the back. *Each blotch often has a black or dusky spot close to or attached to the lower border on each side,* especially in blotches from midbody toward the tail. Blotches tend to fade and become more like bands toward rear part of body and on tail. Tail lacks contrasting light and dark rings. A light stripe extends across head over eyes. 2 internasal scales. Dorsal scales keeled, in 25–27 rows. Anal single.

Frequents arid thornscrub, mainly in rocky canyons and mesas. Eats small mammals. Live-bearing; 2–9 young, presumably born in summer and fall.
Similar species: (1) Western Rattlesnake (p. 231) has more than 2 internasals and, in Baja Calif., usually blackish to dark brown dorsal blotches with contrasting light edges. (2) Red Diamond Rattlesnake (p. 227) has contrasting black and white bands on tail and dark speckling in diffusely bordered blotches on back. (3) Speckled Rattlesnake (p. 228) has contrasting black and white marks on tail.
Range: Throughout most of the peninsula, from the vicinity of San Telmo in Baja California Norte to the Cape. On San Francisco, Carmen, Partida, and Cerralvo Is. in the Gulf of Calif. and on Margarita I. on the Pacific side. **Map 196**

12

Amphibian Eggs and Larvae

The eggs and larvae of most western amphibians are illustrated here in Figs. 31–40. Species omitted are mostly those that have not been described or are poorly known. Descriptions of some species are brief and not fully diagnostic because of inadequate information. Refer to information on distribution (see maps), habitat, and breeding sites under the species accounts, in Chapters 6 and 7. See p. 24 for help in using the keys, which differ only in minor details from those in Chapter 5.

Counts of eggs laid are obviously subject to change as more information becomes available. In some cases, clutch size is inferred from counts of enlarged ova in ovaries or eggs in oviducts of gravid females.

In making identifications, examine the mouthparts of tadpoles and the gelatinous envelopes of eggs under magnification. Tooth rows are expressed as a fraction — $\frac{2}{3}$, $\frac{3}{4}$, etc. The numerator is the number of rows in the upper lip; the denominator, the number of rows in the lower lip. Hyphenated numbers (2-3/3-4) indicate variation in the number of rows. To examine specimens, immerse them in shallow water to eliminate distracting highlights. Color patterns may also be enhanced in this way. A dissecting microscope will usually be needed to study egg capsules; view eggs with transmitted light. To count gill rakers in salamander larvae (Fig. 34, p. 259), enlarge the gill openings of preserved specimens by snipping the tissues between the gill arches. All measurements of salamander larvae and tadpoles are of total length. The keys to eggs and larvae apply only to western species.

Caution: Amphibian eggs and larvae may quickly succumb if overheated. Keep them cool if to be studied fresh; otherwise, preserve in 1 part commercial Formalin to 14 parts of water.

KEY TO AMPHIBIAN EGGS

(See Fig. 31 for explanation of terms, and Figs. 32 and 33 (pp. 250–251) for illustrations of eggs.

1A. Ovum uniformly white or cream, unpigmented — see 2
1B. Upper surface or entire ovum pigmented olive, brown, or black — see 5

2A. Eggs arranged like a string of beads, connected by slender strands of jelly; found in cold streams **Tailed Frog**
2B. Eggs not connected like a string of beads, or, if so, found on land — see 3

3A. Each egg suspended by a single slender strand of jelly (Fig. 33, 13–15) or in a rosary-like string (Fig. 33, 12); eggs may become separated and bear a slender jelly strand at one or both ends (Fig. 33, 12) — see 4
3B. Eggs attached by very short jelly strands, or broadly clinging to each other or attachment surface (Fig. 33, 7–11) **Olympic, Pacific Giant, Woodland Salamanders, and Ensatina**

4A. Eggs suspended by their jelly strands; strands elongated, often intertwined (Fig. 33, 13–15) **Climbing Salamanders**
4B. Eggs more or less connected by their strands, arranged like a string of beads (Fig. 33, 12) **Slender Salamanders**

5A. Gelatinous envelope firm, rubberlike; ovum (when fertilized) moves freely in large capsular chamber (Fig. 33, 1–4); eggs usually in globular clusters (laid singly in Rough-skinned Newt) **Newts and Northwestern Salamander**
5B. Jelly less firm; ovum not in large capsular chamber (Fig. 32); eggs in rounded clumps, strings, floating rafts, or single — see 6

6A. Eggs in cylindrical strings (Fig. 32; 7, 8, 10–12) or more or less connected like string of beads (Fig. 32; 9, 13, 14) **True Toads**
6B. Eggs not in strings but in grapelike cluster or single — see 7

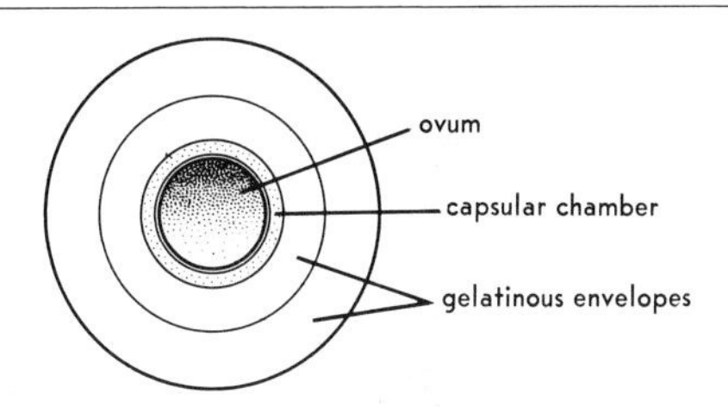

Fig. 31. Amphibian egg

7A. Gelatinous envelope flattened on 1 side (Fig. 32; 3)
Great Plains Narrow-mouthed Toad

7B. Gelatinous envelope not flattened see 8

8A. Eggs in floating raft, 1 to few eggs thick (Fig. 32)
Bullfrog and Green Frog

8B. Eggs single, or in globular or irregular clusters
Tiger and Long-toed Salamanders, Frogs and Hylids

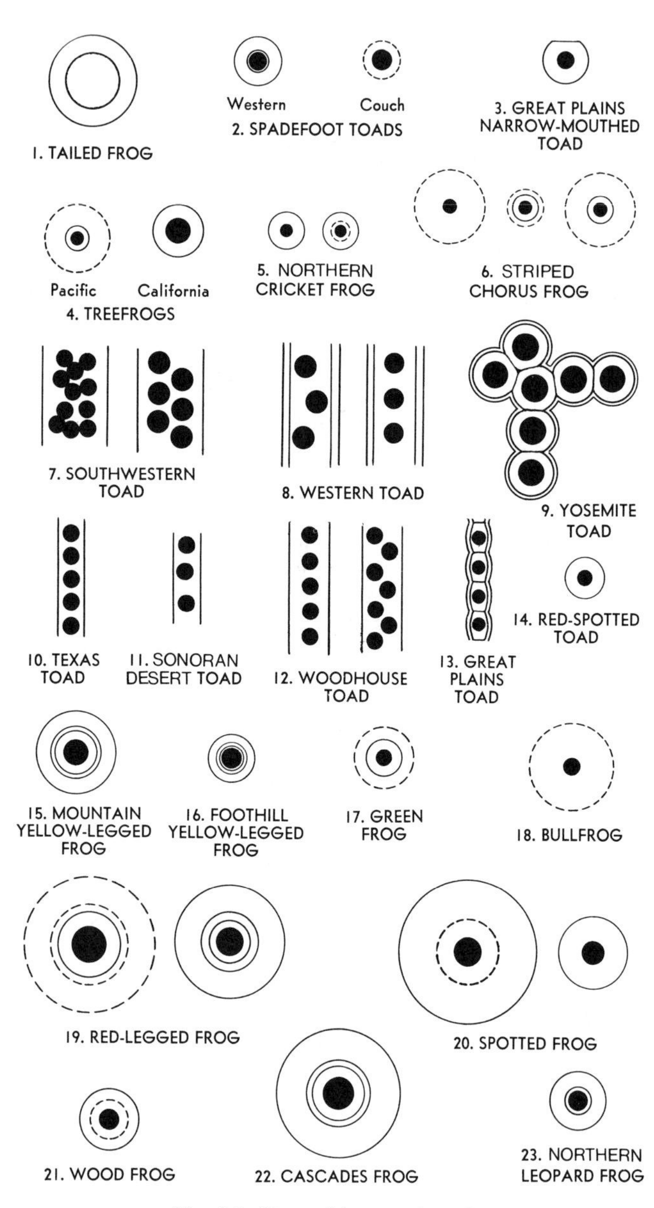

Fig. 32. Eggs of frogs and toads

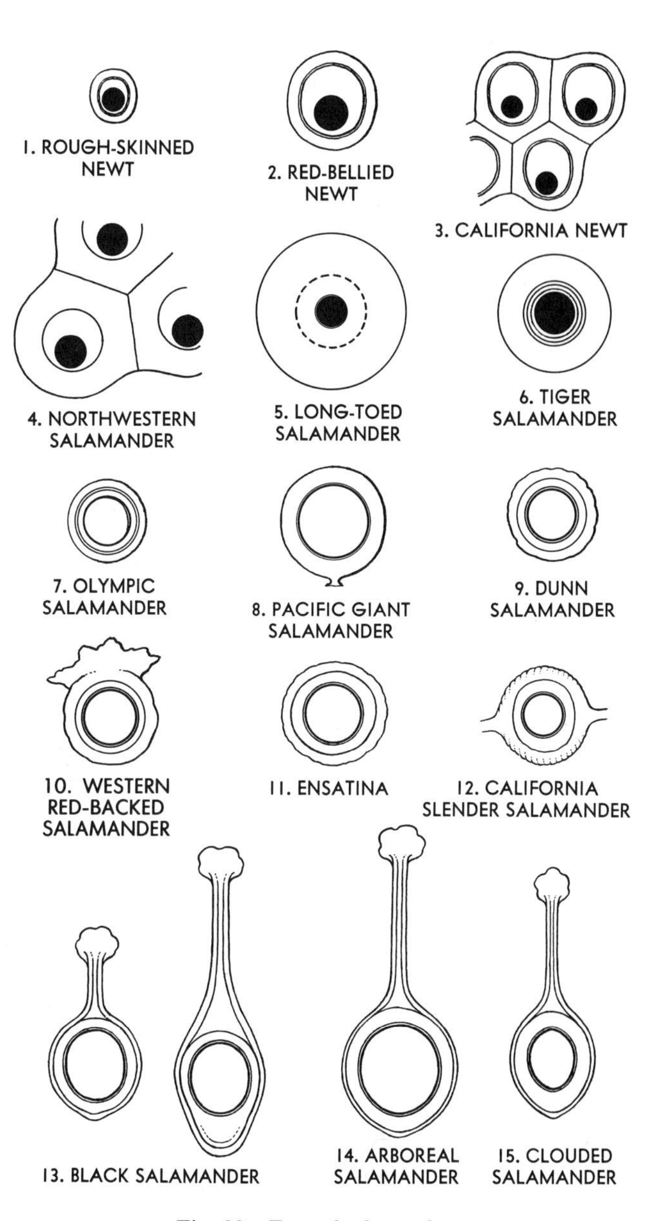

Fig. 33. Eggs of salamanders

Eggs of Salamanders

See Fig. 33, p. 251 × $1\frac{3}{4}$

In Fig. 33, eggs shown in black have pigment on the upper surface of the ovum and are usually exposed to daylight. Those shown in white are unpigmented and are laid under stones or in crevices in logs or the ground. Numbers in parentheses are averages.

Eggs Pigmented

Rough-skinned Newt, *Taricha granulosa.* In this and other newts, the eggs are in firm gelatinous capsules. Fertilized egg moves freely in large capsular chamber. Usually laid singly, attached to vegetation and other objects in quiet or slowly flowing water. Map 6

Red-bellied Newt, *Taricha rivularis.* Laid in flattened, firm clusters of 5–16 (10) eggs. Clusters about 1 in. (2.5 cm) in greatest diameter, often only 1 egg thick, and usually attached to the undersides of stones in streams. Map 9

California Newt, *Taricha torosa.* Laid in rounded, firm clusters of 7–39 (often 16–22) eggs. Clusters about ½–1 in. (1.2–2.5 cm) in diameter, attached to sticks, the undersides of stones, and vegetation in quiet or flowing water. Map 8

Northwestern Salamander, *Ambystoma gracile.* Laid in rounded, firm clusters of 30–270 (often 60–140) eggs. Clusters 2–6 in. in diameter; attached to submerged branches and other firm supports in ponds, lakes, and slowly flowing streams. Individual eggs in large capsular chambers. Map 2

Long-toed Salamander, *Ambystoma macrodactylum.* Laid singly or in clusters of 5–100 eggs, attached to vegetation or free on bottom of shallow pools, ponds, lakes, and quiet parts of streams. A single female may contain from around 85 to over 400 eggs. Map 3

Tiger Salamander, *Ambystoma tigrinum.* In the West, usually laid singly or in small rows or clusters ranging in size from a few to around 120 eggs; attached to twigs, weeds, and other objects in ponds, lakes, and quiet parts of streams. Large females may contain 7000–8000 eggs. California Tiger Salamander lays eggs singly or in small clusters attached to grass or dead weeds, often in temporary pools. Map 5

Eggs Unpigmented

Olympic Salamander, *Rhyacotriton olympicus.* Laid singly, apparently without special organs of attachment, clustered in crevices of seepage areas. Clusters of 2–16 (8 or 9) eggs, but larger groupings may be found because of communal laying. Map 4

Pacific Giant Salamander, *Dicamptodon ensatus.* Laid singly, close together, attached by short peduncles to rocks and other objects, usually on the roof of the nest chamber. In concealed locations in springs and streams. Clutches of around 70 to over 200 eggs. Map 1

Cope Giant Salamander, *Dicamptodon copei* (not shown). Laid in hidden nest sites (under stones, logs, cutbanks) in streams. Clutches of 25–115 (50) eggs. Map 1

Dunn Salamander, *Plethodon dunni.* Laid in grapelike clusters attached by a slender stalk in damp crevices or other underground sites. Clutches of 4–15 (9) eggs. Drawing based on eggs laid in the laboratory. Map 12

Western Red-backed Salamander, *Plethodon vehiculum.* Laid in clusters, the individual eggs broadly attached by their capsules; in talus or deep crevices. Clutch size (based on enlarged ova) 4–19 (10). Map 11

Del Norte Salamander, *Plethodon elongatus* (not shown). Laid in grapelike clusters suspended by a common strand; in damp, concealed locations. Females with 2–18 (9) enlarged ova. A clutch of 10 eggs has been found. Map 13

Jemez Mountains Salamander, *Plethodon neomexicanus* (not shown). Eggs on stalks, 5–17 (8) per clutch, laid in concealed sites, probably usually underground. (Count based on enlarged ova.) Map 15

Larch Mountain Salamander, *Plethodon larselli* (not shown). Laid in damp concealed locations, in clutches of 3–11 (7). (Count based on enlarged ova.) Map 14

Van Dyke Salamander, *Plethodon vandykei* (not shown). Information fragmentary; only a single nest is known. The eggs were in a grapelike mass attached by a slender strand. Ovarian counts 4–12 (7), in females from n. Idaho. Map 16

Ensatina, *Ensatina eschscholtzii.* Laid in grapelike clusters; outer envelopes more or less adherent. Deposited in mammal burrows, ground crevices, beneath the bark and in hollows of decayed logs. Clutches of 3–25 (13) eggs. Map 10

Sacramento Mountain Salamander, *Aneides hardii* (not shown). Laid in grapelike clusters suspended by intertwined strands that are usually united at a common base; attached to chambers in decomposing Douglas fir logs, and probably elsewhere in concealed sites. Clutches of 3–10 (5) eggs. Map 21

Black Salamander, *Aneides flavipunctatus.* Clusters as in Sacramento Mountain Salamander. 5–18, perhaps to 25, eggs based on counts of enlarged ova. Laid in cavities in the soil, under rocks, and in other concealed locations. Map 22

Clouded Salamander, *Aneides ferreus.* Attached separately, but close together, on stalks twisted around one another and attached at a common point to roof or wall of cavity, usually in a Douglas fir log. Clusters of 8–18 eggs. Map 19

Arboreal Salamander, *Aneides lugubris.* Eggs resemble those of Clouded Salamander, and are deposited in tree hollows (chiefly live oaks), decaying logs, or in cavities in the ground. Clusters of 12–23 eggs. Map 20

Oregon Slender Salamander, *Batrachoseps wrighti* (not shown). In clusters; eggs joined by a single strand, like a string of beads, laid in hollows under bark and in rotten logs. Clutches of 3–11 (6 or 7) eggs, based on ovarian counts (enlarged ova). Map 18

California Slender Salamander, *Batrachoseps attenuatus.* Laid in clusters; individual eggs connected by slender jelly strand like a string of beads, but strands may break and eggs become separated. Under logs, rocks, and other objects on the surface and in hollows in logs or the ground. Clutches of 2–12 (commonly 4–7) eggs, but far higher counts at communal laying sites. Map 17

Pacific Slender Salamander, *Batrachoseps pacificus* (not shown). Clusters and egg-laying sites as in California Slender Salamander. Information fragmentary. 15–20 enlarged ova in females and a group of 18 eggs have been found. Communal laying probably occurs. Map 17

Mount Lyell Salamander, *Hydromantes platycephalus* (not shown). Information fragmentary; presumably lays in damp crevices and soil cavities. 6–14 enlarged ova found in females. Map 7

Shasta Salamander, *Hydromantes shastae* (not shown). Most eggs have a slender stalk at each end, the stalks intertwined at the center of the cluster. Clutches of 9–12 eggs, laid in recesses of limestone caves. Map 7

Eggs of Frogs and Toads

See Fig. 32, p. 250 × 1⁴⁄₅

In Fig. 32, eggs shown in black have pigment on the upper surface and are usually exposed to daylight. Those shown in white are unpigmented and laid in concealed locations. Broken lines indicate indistinct boundaries between gelatinous envelopes. Numbers in parentheses are averages. Maximum counts of eggs laid are approximate.

Eggs Pigmented

Western Spadefoot, *Scaphiopus hammondii.* In irregular cylindrical clusters of about 10–42 (24) eggs, attached to plant stems and other objects in temporary or permanent ponds and quiet parts of streams. Map 25

Southern Spadefoot, *Scaphiopus multiplicatus* (not shown). Clusters of 10–42 eggs, attached to plants or rocks. A single female may lay 300–500 eggs. Map 25

Plains Spadefoot, *Scaphiopus bombifrons* (not shown). In loose cylindrical or elliptical masses, usually less than 1 in. (2.5 cm) in diameter, of about 10–250 eggs; attached to vegetation or other support in permanent and temporary waters. Map 24

Great Basin Spadefoot, *Scaphiopus intermontanus* (not shown). In small packets, 3⁄5–4⁄5 in. (1.5-2 cm) in diameter, of around 20–40 eggs; attached to vegetation, pebbles, or lying on the bottom of pools. Female's total complement may be 300–500 eggs. Map 23

Couch Spadefoot, *Scaphiopus couchii.* Eggs resemble Western Spadefoot's, but smaller. Laid in cylindrical masses of 6–145 eggs. A single female may lay 350–500 eggs. Map 26

Great Plains Narrow-mouthed Toad, *Gastrophryne olivacea.* Laid singly, but often close together in groups in shallow temporary pools or quiet parts of streams. Capsules flattened on one side. One envelope. A single female may lay around 500 to over 2000 eggs. Map 29

Pacific Treefrog, *Hyla regilla.* Laid in loose, irregular clusters of 9–80 (often 20–25) eggs; attached to plant stems, sticks, or other objects in shallow, quiet water of ponds, lake borders, and streams. 2 envelopes. A single female may lay over 600 eggs. Map 43

Mountain Treefrog, *Hyla eximia* (not shown). Laid in loose masses, about the size of a teacup; loosely attached to grass or weed stems just below the surface. Map 44

California Treefrog, *Hyla cadaverina.* Laid singly; attached to leaves, sticks, rocks, or free on the bottom in quiet water of rocky, clear streams. One envelope. Map 45

Northern Cricket Frog, *Acris crepitans.* Laid singly or in small clusters; attached to leaves, twigs, grass stems or on the bottom in shallow, quiet water of springs, ponds, and streams. 2 envelopes. A single female may lay around 225–350 eggs. Map 42

Striped Chorus Frog, *Pseudacris triseriata.* In small, loose, irregular clusters — diameter often less than 1 in. (2.5 cm) — of around 7–300 (often 30–75) eggs; attached to vegetation in clear, quiet water of ponds, lakes, and marshy fields. One indistinct envelope. A single female may contain up to 1500 eggs. Colo. females laid 137–793 eggs (450). Map 40

Southwestern Toad, *Bufo microscaphus.* Laid in tangled strings of up to 4000 eggs. Eggs in 1–3 irregular rows, usually deposited on the bottom in quiet parts of clear streams. 1 envelope. Map 32

Western Toad, *Bufo boreas.* Laid in tangled strings of up to 16,500 (often around 12,000) eggs, in 1–3 rows; often greatly entwined in vegetation along edges of ponds, reservoirs, and streams. 2 envelopes. Eggs often in a zigzag double row. Map 30

Black Toad, *Bufo exsul* (not shown). Eggs resemble Western Toad's, but less often in a zigzag double row; single row common. Map 30

Yosemite Toad, *Bufo canorus.* In beadlike strings and clusters, often covered with silt, in the shallows of meadow pools in the Sierra Nevada. 2 envelopes. Map 31

Texas Toad, *Bufo speciosus.* In strings coiled about in rain pools, irrigation and cattle tanks, and other quiet water. One envelope, sometimes slightly scalloped. Map 36

Sonoran Desert Toad, *Bufo alvarius* (not shown). Laid in long strings of 7500–8000 eggs, in temporary pools or shallow streams. Look for them after the first heavy summer showers. One envelope. Map 38

Woodhouse Toad, *Bufo woodhousei.* Laid in strings of up to 25,000 eggs, in 1 or 2 rows; intertwined about vegetation or debris in almost any type of pool or stream. One envelope. Map 33

Canadian Toad, *Bufo hemiophrys* (not shown). Laid in long strings, like closely strung beads; entwined among vegetation or not. One envelope. Map 34

Great Plains Toad, *Bufo cognatus.* Laid in strings of up to 20,000 eggs; attached to vegetation and debris on the bottom of temporary pools, reservoirs, springs, and small streams. 2 envelopes, decidedly scalloped. Map 35

Red-spotted Toad, *Bufo punctatus.* Laid singly, in short strings, or as a loose flat cluster, on the bottom of small, shallow, often rocky pools. One envelope. Map 39

Green Toad, *Bufo debilis* (not shown). Laid in small clumps or strings, or perhaps occasionally laid singly; attached to grass and weed stems. Ova faintly pigmented. Two envelopes. Map 37

Sonoran Green Toad, *Bufo retiformis* (not shown). Eggs resemble those of the Green Toad. Map 37

Mountain Yellow-legged Frog, *Rana muscosa.* Laid in globular but often somewhat flattened clumps, around 1–2 in. (2.5–5 cm) across; attached to stems of sedge or other vegetation or to the bank itself in ponds, lakes, and streams mostly above 7000 ft. (2130 m) in Sierra Nevada, and in streams at lower elevations in mountains of s. Calif. Map 52

Foothill Yellow-legged Frog, *Rana boylii.* Laid in a compact, grapelike cluster — 2–4 in. (5–10 cm) in diameter — of around 100 to over 1000 eggs; in shallow water near edges of clear streams and attached to stones (often on downstream side). May become coated with silt. Three firm envelopes. Map 49

Green Frog, *Rana clamitans.* In a floating cluster usually 1 egg thick and less than 1 sq. ft. (30 sq. cm) in area, of around 1000–7000 eggs. Attached to vegetation or free, usually deposited near the edges of permanent quiet water. Two envelopes. Map 49

Bullfrog, *Rana catesbeiana.* Eggs resemble Green Frog's, but clusters large, 1–5 ft. (0.3–1.5 m) across and containing up to 20,000 eggs. One envelope. Map 47

Red-legged Frog, *Rana aurora.* In loose to compact, round to oval clusters — 3–10 in. (7.5–25 cm) in diameter — of around 1000–4000 (often 500–1000) eggs. Jelly loose and viscid. Eggs attached to vegetation at or up to 3 ft. (1 m) below surface of lake margins and permanent pools. Three envelopes. Map 48

Spotted Frog, *Rana pretiosa.* Laid in globular clusters — 3–8 in. (7.5–20 cm) in diameter — of around 150–2000 (often 500–600) eggs; in shallow water, often unattached among grasses at edges of ponds, the top layer of eggs exposed at surface. One or 2 envelopes. A single female may contain about 3000 eggs. Map 50

Wood Frog, *Rana sylvatica.* Laid in firm spherical masses — $2\frac{1}{2}$ to sometimes 6 in. (6.2–15 cm) in diameter — of around 100–3000 eggs (42–1570, avg. about 780, in an Alaskan study). Often many clusters in a small area, and in contact. Usually in shallow ponds, lakes, and streams near the surface, occasionally to depths of 2 or 3 ft. (60–90 cm) attached to vegetation or floating free. Two envelopes. Map 46

Cascades Frog, *Rana cascadae.* Eggs resemble Red-legged Frog's but clusters usually smaller — 300–500 eggs, deposited in shallow water of pools and lake margins. Map 51

Northern Leopard Frog, *Rana pipiens.* In firm globular clusters — 2–6 in. (5–15 cm) in diameter — of up to 6500 eggs; usually attached to vegetation in quiet water of ponds, lake margins, reservoirs, canals, and streams. Two or 3 envelopes. Map 54

Plains Leopard Frog, *Rana blairi* (not shown). Eggs resemble Northern Leopard Frog's but clusters smaller, containing around 200–600 eggs; deposited in temporary or permanent pools, usually attached to plants in shallow water. Map 54

Rio Grande Leopard Frog, *Rana berlandieri* (not shown). Eggs resemble Northern Leopard Frog's. Clutches of around 500–1200 eggs. Map 54

African Clawed Frog, *Xenopus laevis* (not shown). Attached singly or sometimes in pairs to grass, reeds, and submerged stems. Three envelopes. Eggs of a single female number in the thousands. Map 56

Eggs Unpigmented

Tailed Frog, *Ascaphus truei.* In rosarylike strings of around 33–98 (44–75) eggs, arranged in globular clumps and attached to the undersides of stones in cold running water. Map 27

Barking Frog, *Hylactophryne augusti* (not shown). Laid on land in rain-soaked hollows, seepage areas, or damp places under rocks or in caves. Clutches of 50–76 eggs (based on enlarged ova) reported. Map 28

KEY TO SALAMANDER LARVAE

(See Fig. 34 for explanation of terms, and Fig. 35, p. 261, for illustrations of larvae.)

Both front and hind limbs present; external gills.

1A. Pond type, usually found in ponds, lakes, or quiet parts of streams — see 3
1B. Stream type, usually found in streams or trickles — see 2

2A. Prominent light and dark mottling on tail fin; gills short but bushy and well developed; eyes small; to over 11 in. (27.5 cm)
Pacific Giant Salamander
2B. Tail fin not colored as in 2A; gills reduced to nubbins; eyes large; under 3 in. (7.5 cm)
Olympic Salamander

3A. Head broad and rather flat; eyes set well in from outline of head as seen from above; 9–22 gill rakers on front side of 3rd gill arch — see 6
3B. Head narrower and less flattened; eyes on or near outline of head as seen from above; 5–7 gill rakers on front side of 3rd gill arch — see 4

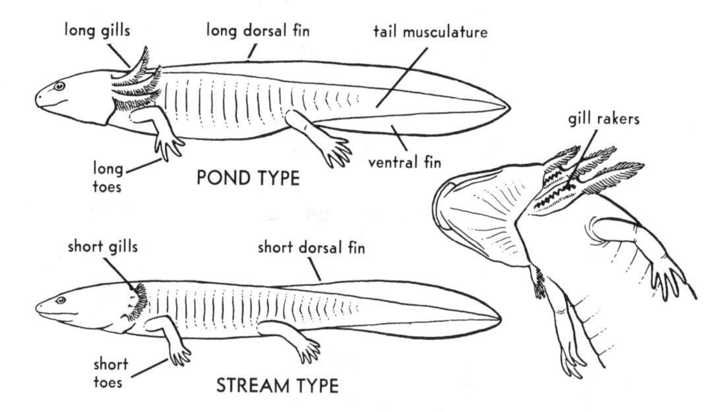

Fig. 34. Salamander larvae

4A. Dorsal fin does not reach shoulders; dark color rather evenly distributed over back and sides; streams of Sonoma, Medocino, and s. Humboldt Counties, Calif.; usually under 2½ in. (6.2 cm). **Red-bellied Newt**

4B. Dorsal fin usually reaches shoulders; dark color not evenly distributed; usually under 2½ in. (6.2 cm). see 5

5A. 2 irregular black stripes on back, 1 on each side of dorsal fin **California Newt**

5B. No black stripes; light spots on sides often arranged in lengthwise rows that may join to form light stripes **Rough-skinned Newt**

6A. Rough strip of skin (formed by openings of poison glands) along upper side of tail musculature, near base of upper fin; similar rough patch behind eyes on each side of head; glandular patches in preserved specimens often with adherent whitish secretion; to approximately 6 in. (15 cm) **Northwestern Salamander**

6B. No roughened glandular areas see 7

7A. 9–13 gill rakers on front side of 3rd gill arch; usually under 3 in. (7.5 cm) **Long-toed Salamander**

7B. 15–24 gill rakers on front side of 3rd gill arch; to 10 in. (25 cm) **Tiger Salamander**

Salamander Larvae

See Fig. 35, p. 261; relative size not shown.

California Newt, *Taricha torosa.* Pond type. Dark dorsolateral stripes. Transformation at usually under 2½ in. (6.2 cm). Map 8

Rough-skinned Newt, *Taricha granulosa.* Pond type. Trunk usually with 2 lengthwise rows of light spots, which may more or less unite to form a single light stripe. Sometimes reaches 3 in. (7.5 cm) at transformation. Map 6

Red-bellied Newt, *Taricha rivularis.* Tends toward stream type (Fig. 34); dorsal fin usually fails to reach shoulders. Back and sides of nearly uniform pigmentation. Transformation at around 2 in. (5 cm). Map 9

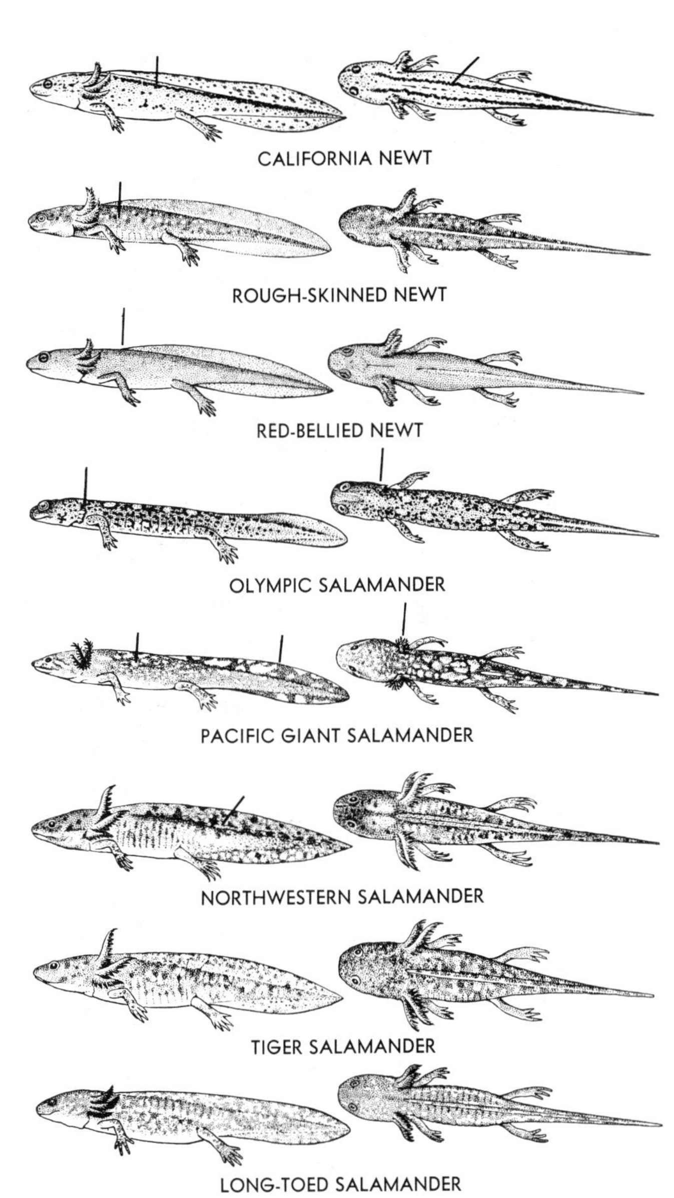

Fig. 35. Salamander larvae

Olympic Salamander, *Rhyacotriton olympicus.* Stream type. Gills and gill rakers (0–3 per gill arch) reduced to nubbins. Olive or brown above, speckled with black. May transform at nearly adult size, around 2½ in. (6.2 cm). Map 4

Pacific Giant Salamander, *Dicamptodon ensatus.* Stream type. Smoky dark and light mottling on back and fins; light stripe behind eye. Pattern obscure and upper surfaces dark in streams with dark-colored rocks. Short, bushy, dark red gills. Toes of adpressed limbs usually overlap 1–4 costal folds. Transformation usually at 6–8 in. (15–20 cm), but as axolotl may reach 11 in. (27.5 cm). Map 1

Cope Giant Salamander, *Dicamptodon copei* (not shown). Resembles Pacific Giant Salamander larva, but slimmer and does not grow as large. Costal folds between toes of adpressed limbs 2½ to none. Belly much darker at sizes above 2 in. (5 cm) in snout-vent length. Apparently rarely transforms. Map 1

Northwestern Salamander, *Ambystoma gracile.* Pond type (Fig. 34). Deep brown, olive-green, or light yellow above, blotched with sooty and spotted with yellow on sides. Glandular strip runs length of base of tail fin, and may produce a whitish poisonous secretion. 7–10 gill rakers on front border of 3rd arch. Transformation at 3–6 in. (7.5–15 cm). Map 2

Tiger Salamander, *Ambystoma tigrinum.* Pond type. Usually olive or greenish above, mottled with dark brown or black. 17–22 gill rakers on front border of 3rd arch. Transformation at 3–5 in. (7.5–12.5 cm), but as axolotl may reach over 10 in. (25 cm). Map 5

Long-toed Salamander, *Ambystoma macrodactylum.* Pond type. Light olive gray to brownish gray above, mottled with brownish and black. 9–13 gill rakers on 3rd arch. Transformation at 2½–4 in. (6.2–10 cm). Map 3

KEY TO TADPOLES

(See Fig. 36 for explanation of terms, and Figs. 37–40, pp. 265–271, for illustrations of tadpoles.)

1A. No horny jaws or rows of labial teeth — see 2
1B. Horny jaws and labial teeth present — see 3

2A. Tentacle at each side of mouth
African Clawed Frog
2B. Tentacles absent
Great Plains Narrow-mouthed Toad

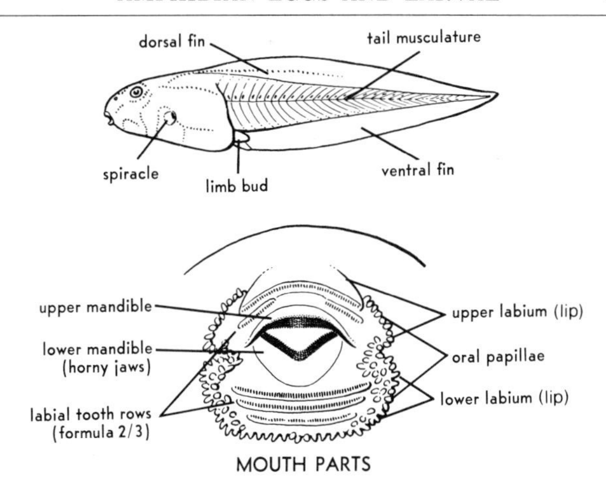

Fig. 36. Tadpole

3A. Large, round, suckerlike mouth occupying $\frac{1}{3}$ to $\frac{1}{2}$ underside of body **Tailed Frog**
3B. Mouth not greatly enlarged see 4

4A. Oral papillae encircle mouth or are interrupted by a very small gap in middle of upper labium (lip) **Spadefoot Toads**
4B. Upper labium (lip) without oral papillae except at sides; middle part of lower labium with or without papillae see 5

5A. Oral papillae on lower labium confined to sides **True Toads**
5B. Oral papillae present along entire edge of lower labium see 6

6A. Lip margin indented at sides **True Frogs**
6B. Lip margin not indented **Treefrogs and Relatives**

Tailed Frog, Narrow-mouthed and Spadefoot Toads

See Fig. 37, p. 265 $\times \frac{5}{6}$

Most tadpoles are dark-colored when young. Descriptions of color here and in subsequent accounts are of older tadpoles. A useful reference is Altig, R., "A Key to the Tadpoles of the Continental United States and Canada," *Herpetologica,* 26 (2), 1970, Lawrence, Kansas.

Tailed Frog, *Ascaphus truei.* Large round mouth occupying nearly $\frac{1}{2}$ lower surface of body. Labial tooth rows 2–3/7–10. Tip of tail often white or rose-colored, set off by dark band. To $2\frac{1}{3}$ in. (5.8 cm). Cold streams. Map 27

Great Plains Narrow-mouthed Toad, *Gastrophryne olivacea.* Distinctive mouth parts — upper lip fleshy, notched at midline, overlying beaklike lower lip. No horny jaws or labial teeth. Eyes widely separated, on outer edges of head as viewed from above. Under $1\frac{1}{2}$ in. (3.7 cm). Extreme s. Ariz. Map 29

Spadefoot Toads *(Scaphiopus)*

Oral papillae encircle mouth (occasionally a small gap in middle of upper labium). Labial tooth rows usually 4–5/4–5. Eyes set close together, and situated well inside outline of head as viewed from above. Some populations of Plains, Western, and Southern Spadefoot Toads tend to develop predaceous and cannibalistic tadpoles that have a beak on upper jaw, a notch in lower jaw, and enlarged jaw muscles.

Plains Spadefoot, *Scaphiopus bombifrons.* Body broadest just behind eyes, giving a "muttonchop" contour. Light to medium gray or brown above. In predaceous and cannibalistic tadpoles, upper mandible beaked, lower mandible notched. Labial tooth rows often 4/4. To $2\frac{3}{4}$ in. (6.8 cm). Often in muddy temporary pools. Map 24

Western Spadefoot, *Scaphiopus hammondii.* Resembles Plains Spadefoot tadpole, but jaws of predaceous and cannibalistic tadpoles have a less-developed beak and notch. Labial tooth rows usually 5/5. To around $2\frac{4}{5}$ in. (7 cm). Map 25

Great Basin Spadefoot, *Scaphiopus intermontanus* (not shown). Resembles Western Spadefoot. Brown to blackish above. Golden highlights may be present on abdomen. To around $2\frac{4}{5}$ in. (7 cm). Map 23

Couch Spadefoot, *Scaphiopus couchii.* Smaller and darker than Great Basin Spadefoot larva — dark gray, bronze, to nearly black above. To $1\frac{1}{4}$ in. (3.1 cm). Map 26

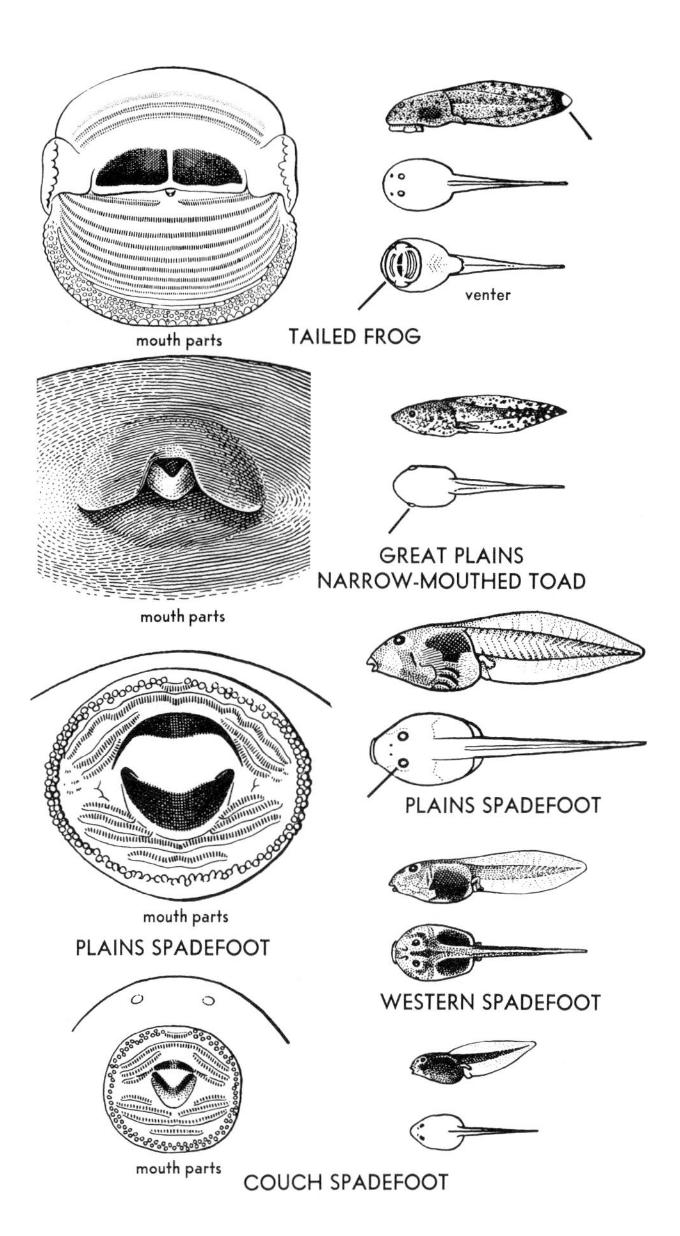

Fig. 37. Tailed Frog, Great Plains Narrow-mouthed Toad, and Spadefoot Toads

True Toads *(Bufo)*

See Fig. 38, p. 267 × 5/6

Tadpoles often small and dark. Oral papillae confined to sides of mouth and indented. Labial tooth rows usually 2/3. Anus usually on ventral midline.

Western Toad, *Bufo boreas.* Body uniformly black, dark brown, or dark gray, including tail musculature. To around 2 in. (5 cm), but often much smaller. Map 30

Black Toad, *Bufo exsul* (not shown). Resembles Western Toad tadpole, but tip of tail more rounded. Labial tooth rows sometimes 1/3. Body nearly solid black above. Map 30

Yosemite Toad, *Bufo canorus.* Resembles Western Toad tadpole, but body and tail musculature darker, snout blunter, and tip of tail more rounded. To around 1½ in. (3.7 cm). Sierra Nevada, Calif., usually above 6500 ft. (1980 m). Map 31

Sonoran Desert Toad, *Bufo alvarius* (not shown). Body somewhat flattened, gray to light golden brown. Tail tip rounded. Throat and chest with a few or no dark specks. To around 2¼ in. (5.6 cm). Map 38

Red-spotted Toad, *Bufo punctatus.* Black or deep brown above. Rather coarse spotting on dorsal fin. Upper labium (lip) and its tooth rows extend downward on each side of mouth. To around 1⅖ in. (3.5 cm). Map 39

Green Toad, *Bufo debilis* (not shown). Patches of gold on back. Labial tooth rows usually 2/2. Anus on right side of ventral midline. Map 37

Sonoran Green Toad, *Bufo retiformis* (not shown). Resembles Green Toad tadpole. Tail musculature tends to be bicolored, and larger individuals lack melanophores (black spots) in ventral fin. Map 37

Canadian Toad, *Bufo hemiophrys.* Black or nearly so above, slightly lighter below. Clear area on throat and chest. Tail musculature dark except for narrow light ventral area. Map 34

Woodhouse Toad, *Bufo woodhousei.* Gray to slate above, commonly with light mottlings. Lower part of tail musculature lacks melanic (dark) pigment. To around 1 in. (2.5 cm). Map 33

Southwestern Toad, *Bufo microscaphus.* Olive, gray, or tan above, commonly spotted or mottled with blackish to brown. Tail musculature colored like body. White below in life. To around 1½ in. (3.7 cm). Map 32

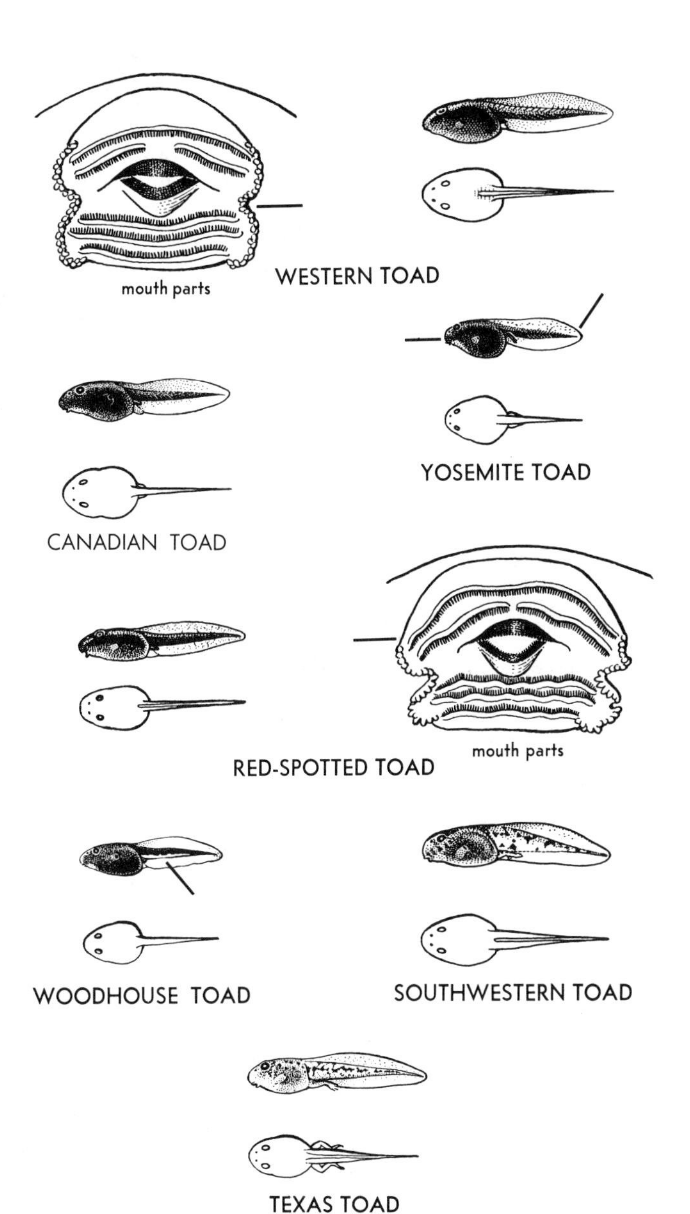

Fig. 38. True toads

Texas Toad, *Bufo speciosus.* Drab or grayish olive above. Tail musculature with irregular, dark-colored lateral stripe, or blotches tending to form a stripe. Light tan to pinkish below. Extreme se. N.M. Map 36

Great Plains Toad, *Bufo cognatus* (not shown). Mottled brown and gray, dark gray, or blackish above, but becomes paler and may develop adult pattern at around 1 in. (2.5 cm). Light greenish below with yellow and reddish iridescence. Dorsal fin highly arched. To around 1 in. (2.5 cm). Map 35

Treefrogs and Relatives

See Fig. 39, p. 269 × $^5/_6$

Mouth round, not indented at the sides. Middle part of upper lip lacks oral papillae. Labial tooth rows usually 2/3. Large dark areas on bodies of treefrog and chorus frog tadpoles shown in Fig. 39 result from loss of overlying pigment in preserved specimens.

Pacific Treefrog, *Hyla regilla.* Eyes on outline of head as viewed from above. Blackish, dark brown, to olive brown above, often heavily spotted with blackish. Whitish below with a bronze or coppery sheen. Intestines not visible. To around 1$^3/_4$ in. (4.4 cm). Map 43

Mountain Treefrog, *Hyla eximia.* Eyes as in Pacific Treefrog. Brown above with minute silvery gold flecks. Dark below with overlying tinge of pale gold. Map 44

California Treefrog, *Hyla cadaverina.* Eyes set inside outline of head, as viewed from above. Light to dark brown above. Dorsal surface of tail musculature marked with alternating dark cross-bars. Intestines visible. Third lower row of labial teeth about $^1/_2$ length of 2nd row. To 1$^3/_4$ in. (4.4 cm). Map 45

Canyon Treefrog, *Hyla arenicolor.* Eyes as in California Treefrog. Golden brown above. No dark bars on tail musculature. Third lower row of labial teeth usually shorter than second. To around 1$^1/_4$ in. (3.1 cm). Map 45

Striped Chorus Frog, *Pseudacris triseriata.* Black, gray, to olive above. Silver with a coppery sheen below. Dorsal fin highly arched. To around 1$^1/_2$ in. (3.7 cm). Map 40

Northern Cricket Frog, *Acris crepitans.* Fins with bold dark markings. Tip of tail usually black. Labial tooth rows 2/2 or 2/3. To around 1$^3/_4$ in. (4.4 cm). Map 42

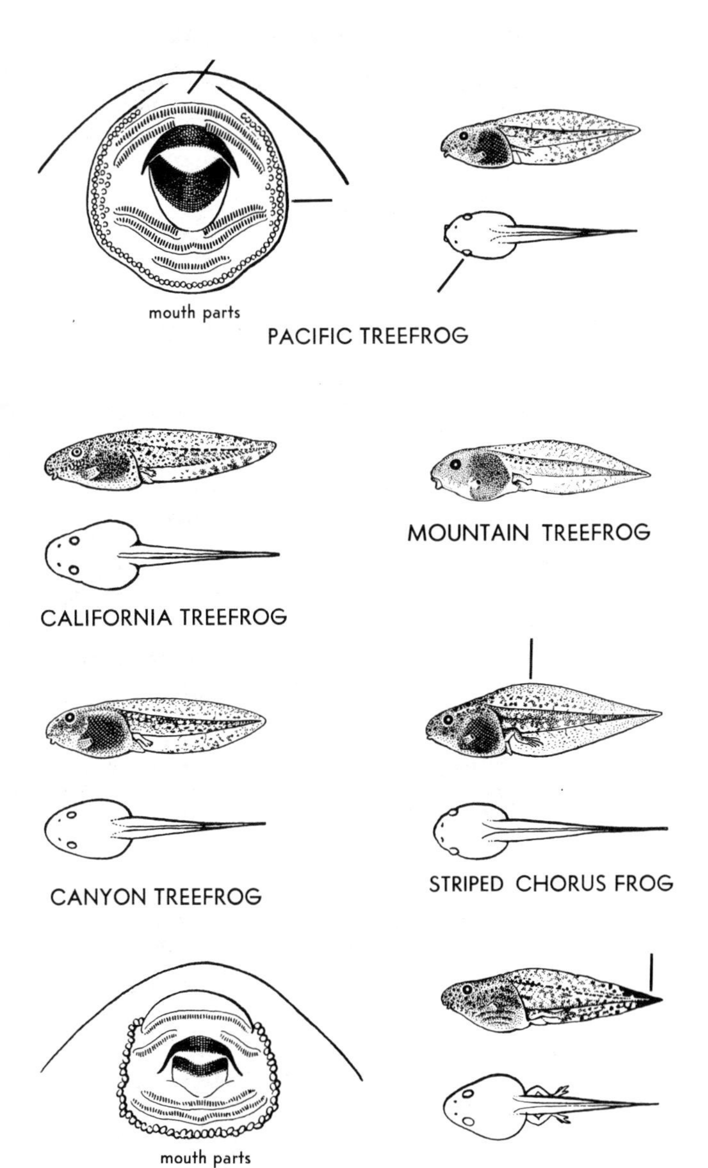

Fig. 39. Treefrogs and relatives

Northern Casque-headed Frog, *Pternohyla fodiens* (not shown). Body globular, tail little longer than body. Dull tan with olive brown mottling above. A whitish stripe behind eye. Whitish below. To around $1\frac{3}{4}$ in. (4.2 cm). Map 41

True Frogs *(Rana)*

See Fig. 40, p. 271 × $\frac{5}{6}$

Oral papillae absent from middle part of upper lip. Mouth indented at sides. Eyes situated well inside outline of head as viewed from above.

Red-legged Frog, *Rana aurora.* Dark brown or yellowish above; pinkish iridescence below. Labial tooth rows 2/3 or 3/4. To around 3 in. (7.5 cm). Ponds, lakes, or slowly flowing streams. Map 48

Spotted Frog, *Rana pretiosa* (not shown). Uniformly dark above, flecked with gold; iridescent bronze below. Labial tooth rows usually 2/3 but also 1–3/3. To around 3 in. (7.5 cm), occasionally to 4 in. (10 cm). Map 50

Cascades Frog, *Rana cascadae* (not shown). Dark brown or occasionally greenish above. Silvery to brassy below. Tail tip blunt. Labial tooth rows 3/4. To around 2 in. (5 cm). Map 51

Foothill Yellow-legged Frog, *Rana boylii.* Body and tail musculature olive gray with rather coarse brown mottling, usually matching stream bottom. Labial tooth rows often 6–7/6. To around 2 in. (5 cm). Rivers and streams. Map 49

Mountain Yellow-legged Frog, *Rana muscosa* (not shown). Brown with golden tint above. Faintly yellow below, intestines vaguely evident. Dark spots often present on massive tail musculature and fins. Labial tooth rows usually 2–4/4. To over 2 in. (5 cm). Map 52

Tarahumara Frog, *Rana tarahumarae.* Greenish gray to dark brown above. Body and tail with numerous dark spots. Labial tooth rows usually 4–5/3. To around 4 in. (10 cm). Streams. In our area known only from extreme s. Ariz. Map 53

Wood Frog, *Rana sylvatica.* Body and tail musculature rather uniformly colored, dusky or brownish with a greenish sheen. Cream below, with pinkish iridescence. Cream line along edge of mouth. Tail tip pointed and fins high. Labial tooth rows usually 2–4/3–4. To around 2 in. (5 cm). Map 46

Northern Leopard Frog, *Rana pipiens.* Dark brown or olive to gray above, often with fine gold spots. Cream to whitish below, often weakly pigmented, intestines showing through. Labial tooth rows usually 2/3. To around $3\frac{1}{2}$ in. (8.7 cm). Map 54

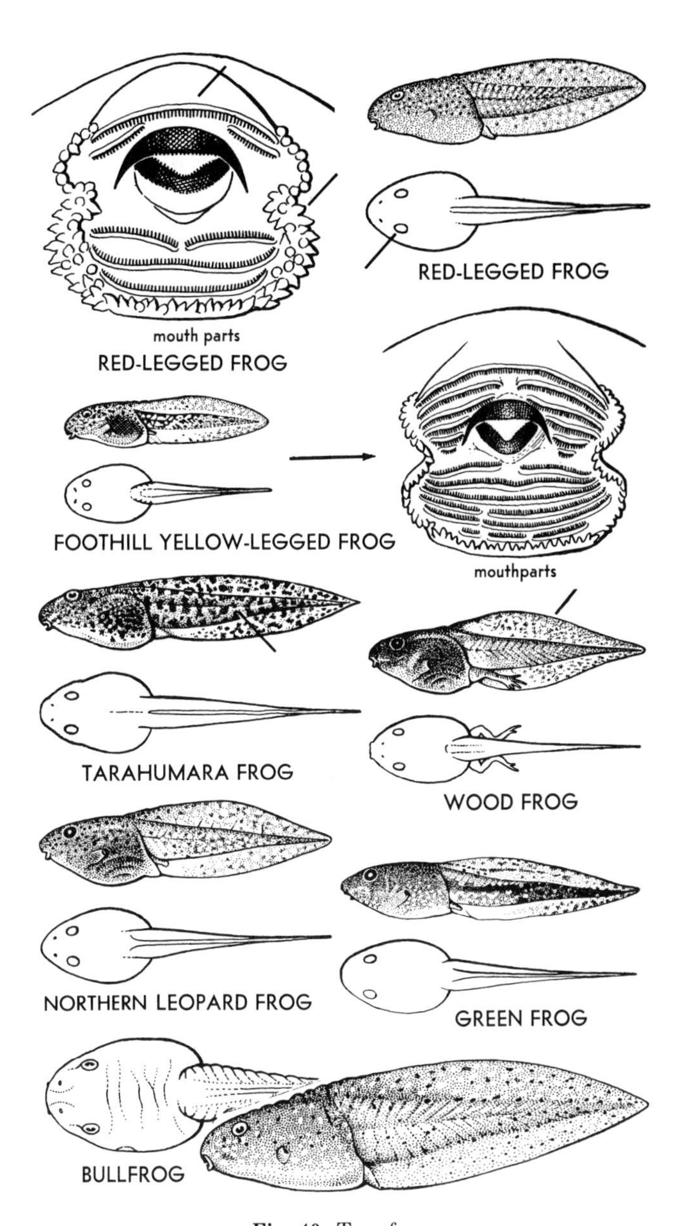

Fig. 40. True frogs

Plains Leopard Frog, *Rana blairi* (not shown). Resembles Northern Leopard Frog tadpole, but body more cylindrical — less full-bodied toward rear, and snout more rounded from above. Mouth set further back from tip of snout. Map 54

Rio Grande Leopard Frog, *Rana berlandieri* (not shown). Tail may average longer than in Northern and Plains Leopard Frogs; tail musculature well developed, fins relatively low and mottled or blotched. Map 54

Relict Leopard Frog, *Rana onca* (not shown). Greenish olive above. Tail pale greenish yellow with heavily mottled fins. Intestines visible. To around 3¼ in. (8.1 cm). (Based on animals from Vegas Valley, Nev., now apparently extinct.)

Green Frog, *Rana clamitans.* Olive green to brown above, with numerous distinct dark spots. Cream below, with a coppery sheen. Tail spotted. Labial tooth rows usually 2/3 or 1/3. To around 4 in. (10 cm). In our area, known only from Toad Lake, Whatcom Co., Wash.; lower Weber R., Ogden, Utah; and extreme sw. B.C. Map 49

Bullfrog, *Rana catesbeiana.* Resembles Red-legged Frog tadpole, but snout more rounded from above and eyes more widely separated. Olive-green above. Whitish to pale yellow below, without pinkish iridescence. Labial tooth rows usually 2/3 or 3/3. To around 6½ in. (16.2 cm). Map 47

Clawed Frogs *(Xenopus)*

African Clawed Frog, *Xenopus laevis* (not shown). Body transparent, internal organs evident. Tentacle on each side of mouth. Mouth parts soft, no labial teeth. To 1½ in. (3.7 cm). Introduced in s. Calif., Ariz., and n. Baja Calif. Map 56

Glossary

Adpress. To press close to or against; to lay flat against. As a measure of relative limb length in salamanders, the fore- and hind limbs on one side are laid straight along the side of the body and the amount of overlap of the extended toes, or the distance separating them (measured in number of folds), is noted. In frogs the hind limb is extended forward, while the body is held straight, and the position of the heel in relation to the nostril is noted. Species accounts refer to condition in adults only.

Alluvial fan. The alluvial deposit (silt, etc.) of a stream where it issues from a gorge onto an open plain.

Amplexus. An embrace; the sexual embrace of a male amphibian. *Pectoral amplexus:* position of amplexus in which the forelimbs of the male clasp the female from behind in the chest or axillary region. *Pelvic amplexus:* position of amplexus in which the male clasps the female from behind about her waist.

Anal scent glands. Scent glands that open on each side of the vent in certain snakes and lizards.

Anal spur. A horny, pointed, sometimes hooked, spur (a hind limb vestige), one on each side, just in front of vent in boid snakes (boas and pythons).

Anterior. Before, or toward the front.

Apical pits. *See* **Scale pits.**

Arboreal. Dwelling in shrubs or trees.

Axilla. The "armpit."

Axolotl. Any of several larval salamanders of the genus *Ambystoma.* Such larvae may live and breed in the larval condition but are capable of absorbing their gills and fins, while beginning to breathe air at the surface, and of eventually being able to live on land as terrestrial adults.

Boss. A protuberance or rounded swelling between the eyes in some spadefoot toads and true toads. It may be glandular or bony.

Capsular cavity. In amphibians, the chamber occupied by the egg and enclosed by the jelly envelope(s). It is typically filled with a viscous jelly in which the egg moves freely, after fertilization.

Carapace. In turtles, the upper part of the shell, including its bony plates and horny shields.

Casque-headed. Having an armored head; an area of thickened skin and/or bone on the heads of certain amphibians.
Coast Ranges. Mountains along the coast of California. South of San Francisco Bay, these consist of the inner (toward the Great Valley) and outer (toward the coast) Coast Ranges.
Costal folds. In salamanders, the vertical folds of skin on the sides of the body set off by the costal grooves.
Costal grooves. In salamanders, the vertical furrows on the sides of the body that set off the costal folds.
Countersunk. Sunk beneath the margins of — as in the jaws of burrowing snakes, in which the lower jaw fits snugly within the margins of the upper jaw.
Cranial crests. The ridges that frame the inner rim of the upper eyelids in toads.
Cusp. A toothlike projection, as on the jaw of a turtle.
Cycloid scales. Scales whose free rear borders are smoothly rounded.
Diurnal. Active in the daytime.
Dorsal. Pertaining to the upper surface of the body.
Dorsolateral. Pertaining to the upper sides of the body.
Dorsolateral fold. A lengthwise glandular ridge between the side of the body and the middle of the back in certain frogs.
Dorsum. The upper, or dorsal, surface of the body, including (when present) the tail.
Egg capsule. In amphibians, the covering of the egg, consisting of the jelly envelope(s).
Egg envelope. In amphibians, a jellylike membrane that surrounds the egg. There may be 1–3 envelopes, depending on the species.
Femur. The part of the leg between the knee and hip.
Femoral pores. Pores containing a waxlike material, found on the underside of the thighs in certain lizards.
Gill arch. One of the bony or cartilaginous arches or curved bars located one behind the other on each side of the pharynx, supporting the gills of fishes and amphibians.
Gill raker. One of the bony or cartilaginous filaments on the inside of the gill arches of fishes and certain amphibians (larvae, etc.), which help prevent solid substances from being carried out through the gill slits.
Gravid. Laden with eggs; pregnant.
Gular fold. Fold of skin across the rear or lower part of the throat; well developed in salamanders and some lizards.
Hemipenis (pl., **hemipenes**). One of the paired copulatory organs of lizards and snakes.
Hybrid. The offspring of the union of a male of one race, variety, species, genus, etc., with the female of another; a crossbred animal or plant.
Inset lower jaw. *See* **countersunk.**

Intergrade. With reference to subspecies, to gradually merge one subspecies with another through a series of forms that are intermediate in color and/or structure.

Interorbital. The region between the eyes. In reptiles, interorbital scales may occupy the area between the supraoculars (see rear endpapers).

Interspace. The patch of color between two markings (such as bands or blotches) on the back of lizards and snakes.

Juvenile. A young or immature individual, often displaying proportions and coloration differing from that of the adult.

Keel. A lengthwise ridge on the scales of certain lizards and snakes, or down the carapace or plastron of a turtle.

Labial teeth. Small horny teeth arranged like the teeth of a comb and attached in crosswise rows to the lips (labia) of tadpoles. The number of rows in the upper and lower lips is expressed by a fraction. The upper digit indicates the number of rows (a row divided at the midline is counted as one) on the upper lip, while the lower digit is the number of rows on the lower lip. A common formula is $^2/_3$.

Labium (pl., **labia**). Lip.

Lamellae. The transverse plates or straplike scales that extend across the underside of the toes in lizards.

Larva (pl., **larvae**). The early form of an animal that, while immature, is unlike its parent and must pass through more or less of a metamorphosis before assuming the adult characters. The tadpole of a frog is an example among amphibians.

Lateral stripe. A lengthwise stripe on the side of the body.

Melanistic. The condition in which black pigment is accentuated, sometimes to the point of obscuring all other color.

Melanophore. Pigment cell containing black or brown pigment (melanin).

Mental gland. A gland on the chin of certain male salamanders. Its secretion appears to make the female receptive to mating.

Nasolabial groove. A hairline groove extending from the nostril to the edge of the upper lip in all salamanders of the family Plethodontidae. A hand lens will usually be needed to see it.

Neotenic (neoteny). Having the period of immaturity indefinitely prolonged. Some salamanders may remain in the larval condition well beyond the usual time of metamorphosis, and may even breed as larvae.

Nuptial pad. In amphibians, a patch of roughened, usually darkly pigmented skin that appears in males during the breeding period. Such pads generally develop on certain of the digits and help the male hold the female during amplexus.

Ocellus (pl., **ocelli**). A small eyelike spot.

Ocular scale. In blind snakes, the scale overlying the vestigial eyes.

Oral papillae. In tadpoles, the small nipplelike projections that commonly form a fringe encircling the mouth. They are sensory in function, perhaps picking up tastes and scents as well as sensing surface textures.

Oviparous. Producing eggs that hatch after laying.

Ovoviviparous. Producing eggs that have a well-developed shell or membranous covering, but which hatch before or at the time of laying, as in certain reptiles.

Ovum (pl., **ova**). A female germ cell; an egg cell or egg apart from any enclosing membrane or shell.

Paravertebral stripe. A stripe (usually one of a pair) located to one side and parallel to the dorsal midline.

Parotoid gland. One of a pair of large, wartlike glands at the back of the head in toads, and rarely in some salamanders.

Parthenogenesis. Reproduction by the development of an unfertilized egg.

Pectoral. Pertaining to the chest.

Peninsular Ranges. The mountains of s. California and n. Baja California, extending from Mt. San Jacinto to the San Pedro Mártir.

Plastron. The underside of the shell of a turtle, consisting typically of 9 symmetrically placed bones overlain by horny shields.

Playa. The flat-floored bottom of an undrained desert basin, which may lack water much of the time.

Plethodons. Lungless salamanders of the genus *Plethodon.*

Postanal scale. A scale situated behind the vent or anus. In the males of most iguanid lizards, 2 or more of these scales are enlarged.

Postantebrachials. Scales on the back of the forearm of lizards.

Posterior. Behind or to the rear; at or toward the hind end of the body.

Postrostral scales. Scales between the rostral and internasals, as in certain rattlesnakes.

Preanal scale. A scale situated in the pelvic region, in front of the vent or anus. In certain lizards, several of these scales may have pores that secrete a waxlike substance.

Prehensile. Adapted for seizing or grasping, especially by wrapping around; in this guide, used in reference to tails.

Premaxillary teeth. Teeth attached to the premaxillary bones, which are located at the front of the upper jaw.

Prenasal. In rattlesnakes, the scale located immediately in front of the nostril.

Relict. A survivor, especially of a vanishing race, type, or species; belonging to a nearly extinct class.

Scale pits. Small paired pits or oval-shaped modifications near the free (apical) end of the scales of certain snakes.

Shield. In turtles, any one of the horny plates that cover the shell.

Subspecies. A subdivision of a species; a variety or race; a category (usually the lowest category recognized in classification) ranking next below a species. The differences separating subspecies are usually slight and are commonly bridged in zones of intergradation (intermixture of characters). Some researchers insist that intergradation should be the criterion in deciding whether two adjacent, slightly different animal populations should be considered as subspecies or species; if intergradation does not exist, they are regarded as distinct species.

Supraorbital ridges. Ridges above the eyes.

Sympatric populations. Two or more distinct populations (species or subspecies) that overlap geographically, yet maintain their distinctness.

Temporal horns. In horned lizards, the horns toward the sides of the crown.

Tibia. The part of the leg between the knee and heel.

Transformation. A marked and more or less abrupt change in the form and structure (and usually also in the habits, food, etc.) of an animal during postembryonic development, as when the larva of an insect becomes a pupa, or a tadpole changes to a frog.

Transverse Ranges. The mountains of s. California, extending west to east from the Sierra Madre to, and including, the San Bernardino Mts.

Tubercle. Any of various small, knoblike projections or bumps; a tubercle is generally considered to be smaller than a wart.

Vent. The opening on the surface of the body of the cloaca, which in reptiles and amphibians is the common chamber into which the intestinal, urinary, and reproductive canals discharge.

Vent lobes. Fleshy lobes located on each side and usually to the rear of the vent. Found in certain male salamanders.

Venter. The underside of an animal, including the tail when present.

Ventral. Pertaining to the underside, or lower surface, of the body.

Vertical pupil. An elliptical pupil with its long axis vertical.

Vocal sac. A sac of loose skin on the throat of frogs and toads that becomes distended and acts as a resonating chamber when they vocalize.

References

Listed below are journals and selected general references that provide further information on species covered by this book and general information on the biology of reptiles and amphibians. Many additional references are cited in the bibliographies of most of these publications. Some of the older works are out of print, but are available in libraries.

General References

Behler, J.L. and F.W. King. 1979. *The Audubon Society Field Guide to North American Reptiles and Amphibians.* New York: Alfred A. Knopf.

Bellairs, A. 1970. *The Life of Reptiles.* New York: Universe Books. 2 vols.

Cochran, D.M. 1961. *Living Amphibians of the World.* Garden City, N.Y.: Doubleday.

Conant, R. 1975. *A Field Guide to Reptiles and Amphibians of Eastern and Central North America.* 2nd ed. Boston: Houghton Mifflin Co.

Ernst, C.H. and R.W. Barbour. 1972. *Turtles of the United States.* Lexington: University Press of Kentucky.

Fitch, H.S. 1970. *Reproductive Cycles in Lizards and Snakes.* University of Kansas Museum of Natural History, Misc. Publication no. 52.

Gans, C., *et al.* (eds.). 1969–82. *Biology of the Reptilia.* New York: Academic Press. 13 vols. Vols. 14 and 15, in press, John Wiley and Sons, Inc.; expected to appear in 1985.

Goin, C.J., O.B. Goin, and G.R. Zug. 1978. *Introduction to Herpetology.* 3rd ed. San Francisco: Freeman.

Klauber, L.M. 1972. *Rattlesnakes: Their Habits, Life Histories, and Influence on Mankind.* 2nd ed. Berkeley and Los Angeles: University of California Press. 2 vols. Abridged version by K.H. McClung, 1982.

Leviton, A.E. 1972. *Reptiles and Amphibians of North America.* New York: Doubleday.

Noble, G. 1931. *The Biology of the Amphibia.* New York: McGraw-Hill Book Co., Inc. Reprinted by Dover Publications, Inc., 1955.

Pritchard, P.C.H. 1967. *Living Turtles of the World.* Neptune, N.J.: T.F.H. Publications.
———. 1979. *Encyclopedia of Turtles.* Neptune, N.J.: T.F.H. Publications.
Schmidt, K.P. and R.F. Inger. 1957. *Living Reptiles of the World.* Garden City, N.Y.: Hanover House.
Shaw, C.E. and S. Campbell. 1974. *Snakes of the American West.* New York: Alfred A. Knopf.
Smith, H.M. 1978. *Amphibians of North America.* New York: Golden Press.
——— and E.D. Brodie, Jr. 1982. *Reptiles of North America.* New York: Golden Press.
Vial, J.L. 1973. *Evolutionary Biology of the Anurans.* Columbia: University of Missouri Press.
Wright, A.H. and A.A. Wright. 1949. *Handbook of Frogs and Toads of the United States and Canada.* Ithaca, N.Y.: Comstock.
———. 1957, 1962. *Handbook of Snakes of the United States and Canada.* 3 vols., including bibliography. Ithaca, N.Y.: Cornell University Press.

Regional References

Pacific Northwest

Campbell, R.W., M.G. Shepard, B.M. Van Der Raay, and P.T. Gregory. 1982. *A Bibliography of Pacific Northwest Herpetology.* Victoria, B.C.: British Columbia Provincial Museum, Heritage Record no. 14.
Nussbaum, R.A., E.D. Brodie, Jr., and R.M. Storm. 1983. *Amphibians and Reptiles of the Pacific Northwest.* University Press of Idaho, A Division of the Idaho Research Foundation, Inc.

United States

Alaska

Hodge, R.P. 1976. *Amphibians and Reptiles of Alaska, the Yukon and Northwest Territories.* Anchorage: Alaska Northwest Publishing Co.

Arizona

Lowe, C.H., Jr. 1964. *The Vertebrates of Arizona. Annotated Check Lists of the Vertebrates of the State: the Species and Where They Live.* Tucson: University of Arizona Press.

Colorado

Hammerson, G.A. 1982. *Amphibians and Reptiles in Colorado.* Colorado Division of Wildlife, Department of Natural Resources.

Idaho

Linder, A.D., and E. Fichter. 1977. *The Amphibians and Reptiles of Idaho.* Pocatello: The Idaho State University Press.

Montana

Black, J.H. 1970. *Amphibians of Montana.* Montana Wildlife Publication of the Montana Fish and Game Department.

Nevada

Banta, B.H. 1965. An Annotated Chronological Bibliography of the Herpetology of Nevada. *The Wasmann Journal of Biology.* Vol. 23, nos. 1 and 2.

Lindsdale, J.M. 1940. Amphibians and Reptiles in Nevada. *Proceedings of the American Academy of Arts and Sciences.* Vol. 73, no. 8.

New Mexico

Campbell, H. 1979. Section on Reptiles and Amphibians, in Handbook of Species Endangered in New Mexico. Santa Fe, N.M.: New Mexico Dept. of Game and Fish.

Degenhardt, W.G. and J.L. Christiansen. 1974. Distribution and Habits of Turtles in New Mexico. *The Southwestern Naturalist.* Vol. 19, no. 1.

Oregon

St. John, A.D. 1980. *Knowing Oregon Reptiles.* Salem, Oregon: Salem Audubon Society.

Utah

Tanner, W.W. 1975. Checklist of Utah Amphibians and Reptiles. *Proceedings of the Utah Academy of Sciences, Arts and Letters.* Vol. 52, Part 1.

Wyoming

Baxter, G.T. and M.D. Stone. 1980. *Amphibians and Reptiles of Wyoming.* Wyoming Game and Fish Department, Bull. 16.

Baja California

Murphy, R.W. 1983. Paleobiogeography and Genetic Differentiation of the Baja California Herpetofauna. Occasional Papers of the California Academy of Science, no. 137.

Canada

Cook, F.R. 1984. *Introduction to Canadian Amphibians and Reptiles.* Ottawa: National Museum of Natural Sciences. National Museums of Canada.

British Columbia

Green, D.M. and R.W. Campbell. 1984. *The Amphibians of British Columbia.* Victoria, B.C.: British Columbia Provincial Museum, Handbook no. 45.

Gregory, P.T. and R.W. Campbell. 1984. *The Reptiles of British Columbia.* Victoria, B.C.: British Columbia Provincial Museum, Handbook no. 44.

Saskatchewan

Cook, F.R. 1966. *A Guide to the Amphibians and Reptiles of Saskatchewan.* Regina: Saskatchewan Museum of Natural History, Popular Series, no. 13.

Journals

Copeia. Published quarterly by The American Society of Ichthyologists and Herpetologists, Florida State Museum, University of Florida, Gainesville, Fla. 32611.

Herpetologica. Published quarterly by the Herpetologists League, Inc., 1041 New Hampshire St., Lawrence, Kans. 66044.

Journal of Herpetology. Published quarterly by the Society for the Study of Amphibians and Reptiles, Dept. of Zoology, Ohio University, Athens, Ohio 45701. The Society also publishes the *Catalogue of American Amphibians and Reptiles,* a series of loose-leaf accounts of species, each prepared by a specialist, and *Herpetological Review,* which often includes a comprehensive list of current herpetological titles.

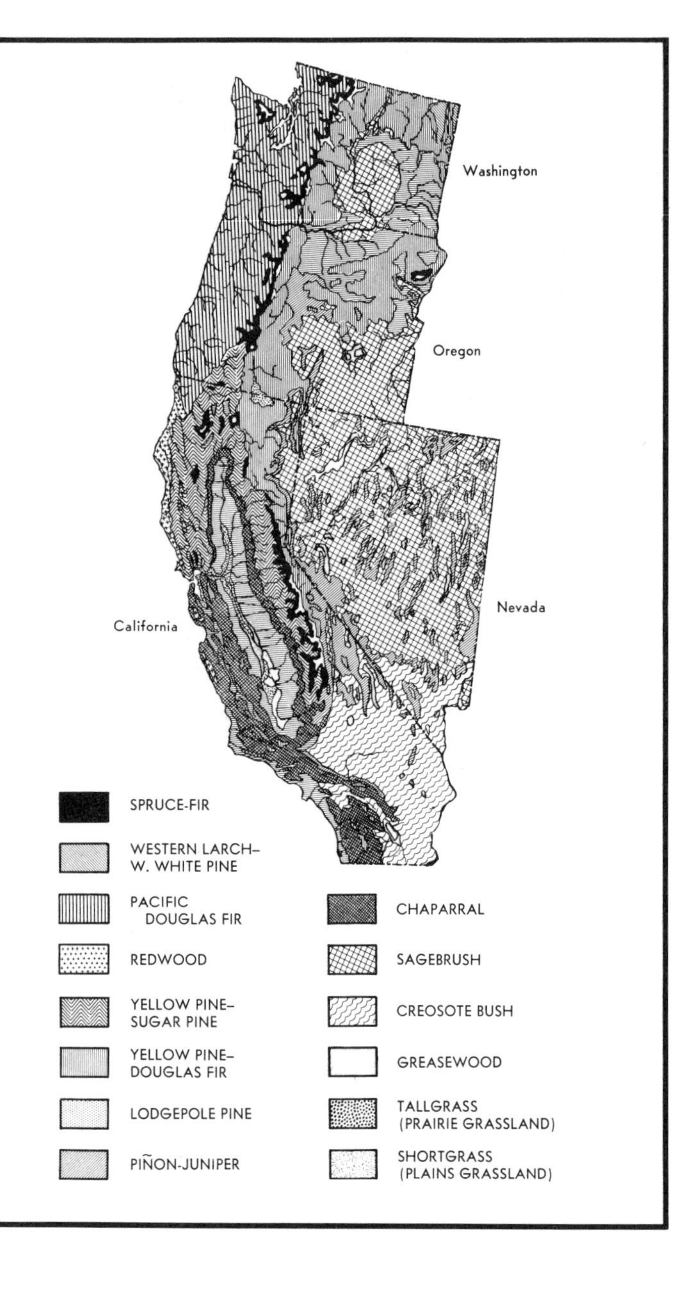
Washington
Oregon
Nevada
California
SPRUCE-FIR
WESTERN LARCH–
W. WHITE PINE
PACIFIC
DOUGLAS FIR
REDWOOD
YELLOW PINE–
SUGAR PINE
YELLOW PINE–
DOUGLAS FIR
LODGEPOLE PINE
PIÑON-JUNIPER
CHAPARRAL
SAGEBRUSH
CREOSOTE BUSH
GREASEWOOD
TALLGRASS
(PRAIRIE GRASSLAND)
SHORTGRASS
(PLAINS GRASSLAND)

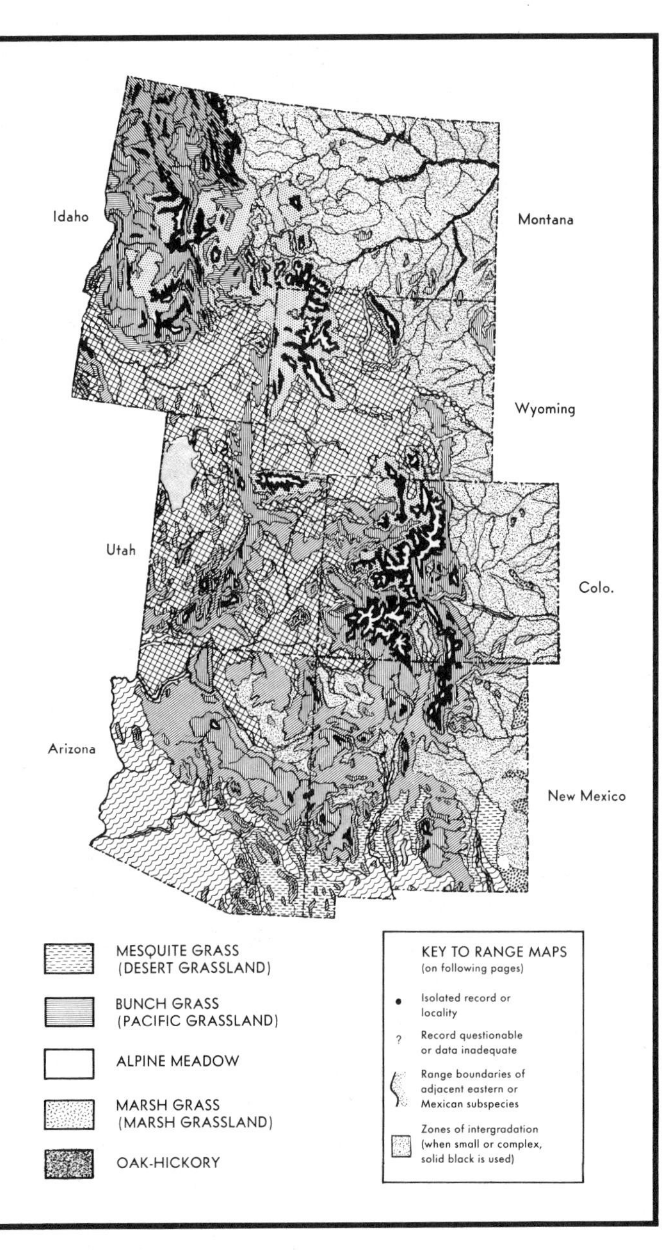
Idaho
Montana
Wyoming
Utah
Colo.
Arizona
New Mexico
MESQUITE GRASS
(DESERT GRASSLAND)
BUNCH GRASS
(PACIFIC GRASSLAND)
ALPINE MEADOW
MARSH GRASS
(MARSH GRASSLAND)
OAK-HICKORY
KEY TO RANGE MAPS
(on following pages)
Isolated record or locality
Record questionable or data inadequate
Range boundaries of adjacent eastern or Mexican subspecies
Zones of intergradation (when small or complex, solid black is used)

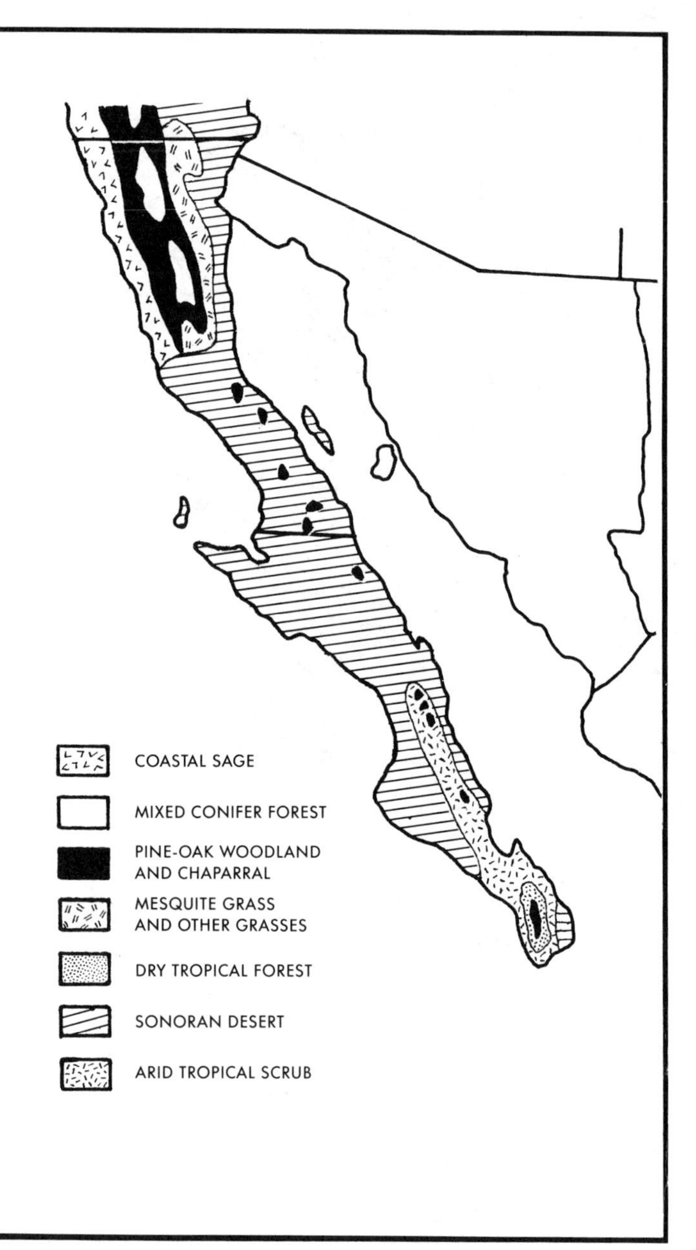
COASTAL SAGE
MIXED CONIFER FOREST
PINE-OAK WOODLAND
AND CHAPARRAL
MESQUITE GRASS
AND OTHER GRASSES
DRY TROPICAL FOREST
SONORAN DESERT
ARID TROPICAL SCRUB

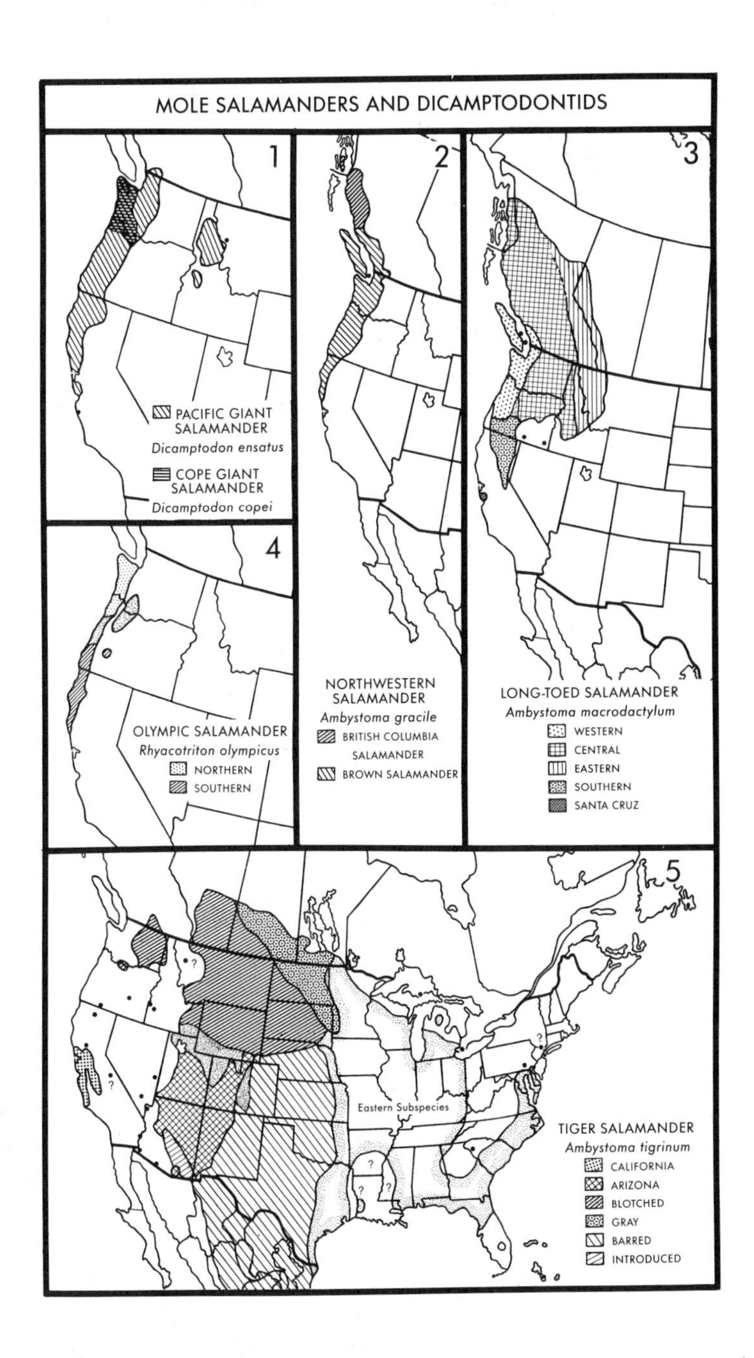
MOLE SALAMANDERS AND DICAMPTODONTIDS
1
PACIFIC GIANT SALAMANDER
Dicamptodon ensatus
COPE GIANT SALAMANDER
Dicamptodon copei
2
NORTHWESTERN SALAMANDER
Ambystoma gracile
BRITISH COLUMBIA SALAMANDER
BROWN SALAMANDER
3
LONG-TOED SALAMANDER
Ambystoma macrodactylum
WESTERN
CENTRAL
EASTERN
SOUTHERN
SANTA CRUZ
4
OLYMPIC SALAMANDER
Rhyacotriton olympicus
NORTHERN
SOUTHERN
5
Eastern Subspecies
TIGER SALAMANDER
Ambystoma tigrinum
CALIFORNIA
ARIZONA
BLOTCHED
GRAY
BARRED
INTRODUCED

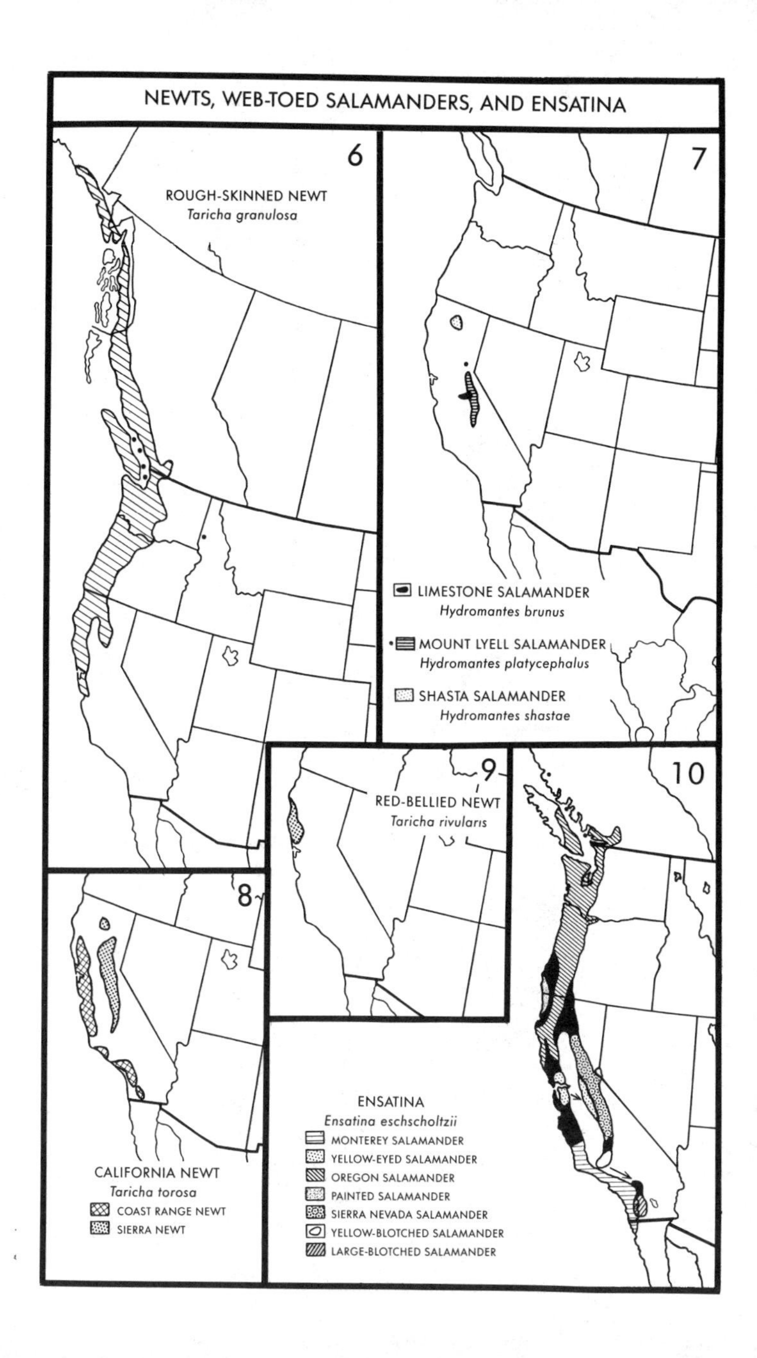
NEWTS, WEB-TOED SALAMANDERS, AND ENSATINA
6
ROUGH-SKINNED NEWT
Taricha granulosa
7
LIMESTONE SALAMANDER
Hydromantes brunus
MOUNT LYELL SALAMANDER
Hydromantes platycephalus
SHASTA SALAMANDER
Hydromantes shastae
8
CALIFORNIA NEWT
Taricha torosa
COAST RANGE NEWT
SIERRA NEWT
9
RED-BELLIED NEWT
Taricha rivularis
10
ENSATINA
Ensatina eschscholtzii
MONTEREY SALAMANDER
YELLOW-EYED SALAMANDER
OREGON SALAMANDER
PAINTED SALAMANDER
SIERRA NEVADA SALAMANDER
YELLOW-BLOTCHED SALAMANDER
LARGE-BLOTCHED SALAMANDER

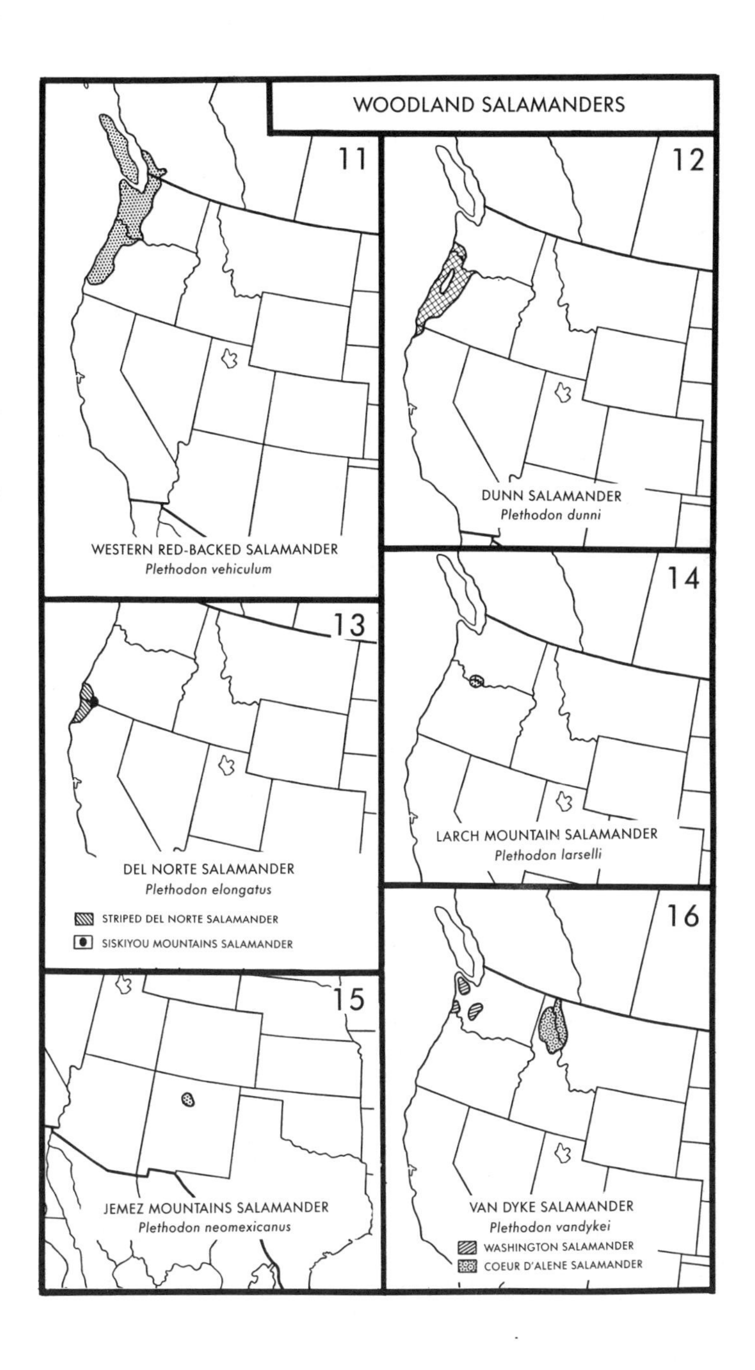
WOODLAND SALAMANDERS
11
WESTERN RED-BACKED SALAMANDER
Plethodon vehiculum
12
DUNN SALAMANDER
Plethodon dunni
13
DEL NORTE SALAMANDER
Plethodon elongatus
STRIPED DEL NORTE SALAMANDER
SISKIYOU MOUNTAINS SALAMANDER
14
LARCH MOUNTAIN SALAMANDER
Plethodon larselli
15
JEMEZ MOUNTAINS SALAMANDER
Plethodon neomexicanus
16
VAN DYKE SALAMANDER
Plethodon vandykei
WASHINGTON SALAMANDER
COEUR D'ALENE SALAMANDER

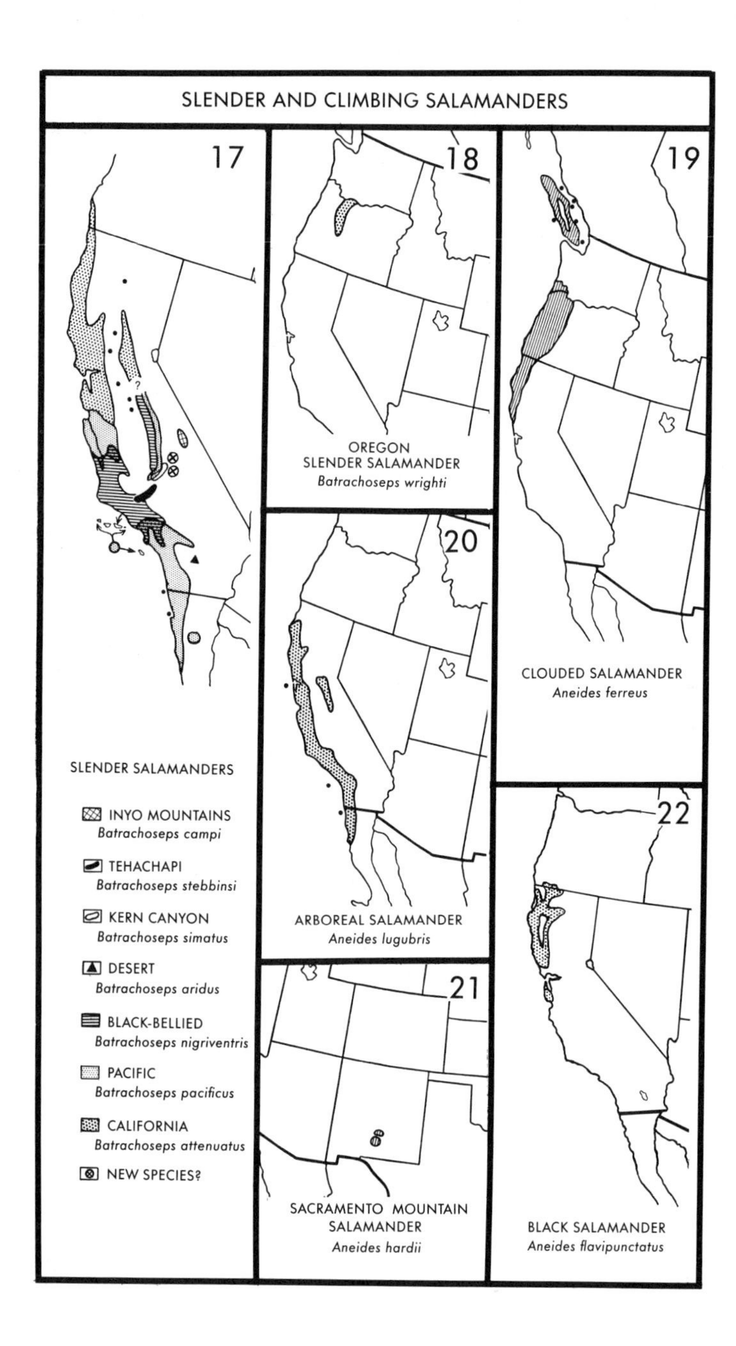
SLENDER AND CLIMBING SALAMANDERS
17
18
19
?
OREGON
SLENDER SALAMANDER
Batrachoseps wrighti
20
CLOUDED SALAMANDER
Aneides ferreus
SLENDER SALAMANDERS
INYO MOUNTAINS
Batrachoseps campi
TEHACHAPI
Batrachoseps stebbinsi
KERN CANYON
Batrachoseps simatus
DESERT
Batrachoseps aridus
BLACK-BELLIED
Batrachoseps nigriventris
PACIFIC
Batrachoseps pacificus
CALIFORNIA
Batrachoseps attenuatus
NEW SPECIES?
22
ARBOREAL SALAMANDER
Aneides lugubris
21
SACRAMENTO MOUNTAIN
SALAMANDER
Aneides hardii
BLACK SALAMANDER
Aneides flavipunctatus

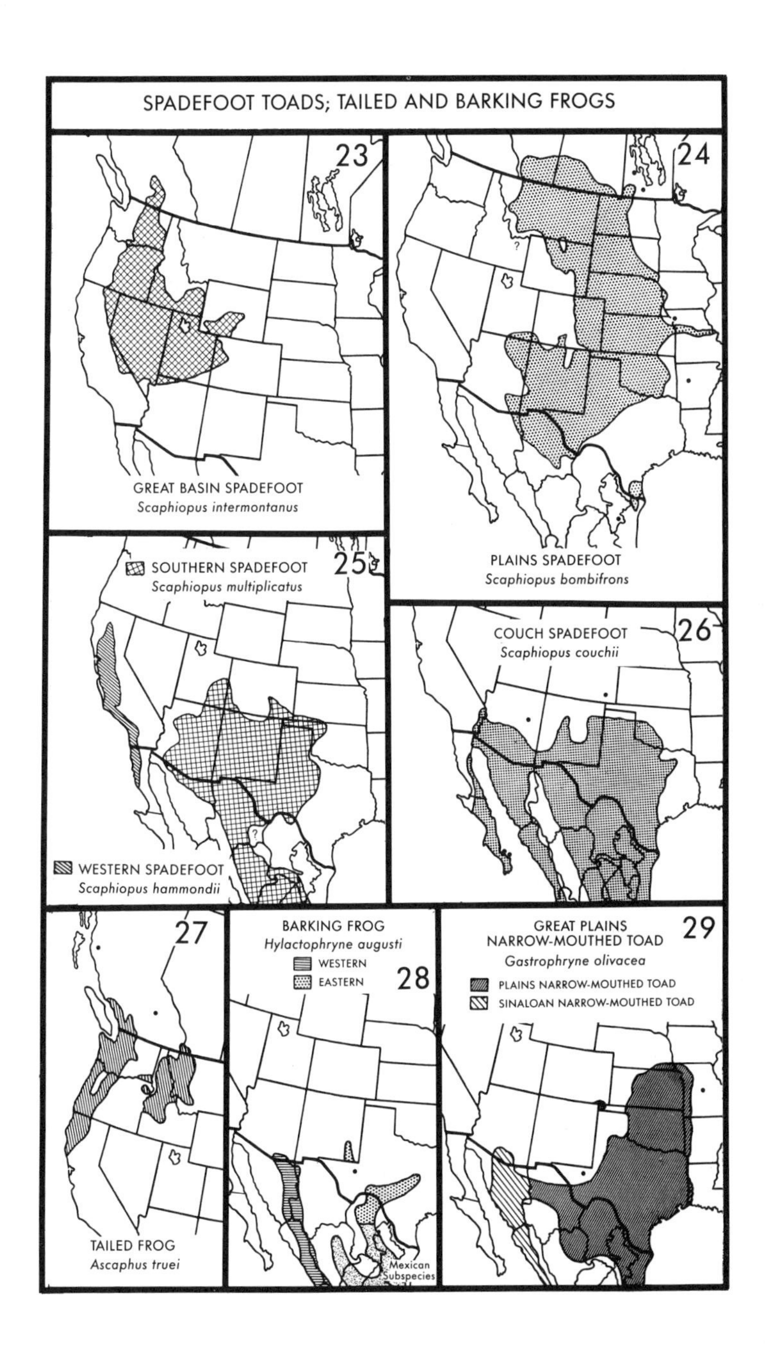
SPADEFOOT TOADS; TAILED AND BARKING FROGS
23
GREAT BASIN SPADEFOOT
Scaphiopus intermontanus
24
?
PLAINS SPADEFOOT
Scaphiopus bombifrons
25
SOUTHERN SPADEFOOT
Scaphiopus multiplicatus
?
WESTERN SPADEFOOT
Scaphiopus hammondii
26
COUCH SPADEFOOT
Scaphiopus couchii
27
TAILED FROG
Ascaphus truei
BARKING FROG
Hylactophryne augusti
WESTERN
EASTERN
28
Mexican Subspecies
GREAT PLAINS NARROW-MOUTHED TOAD
29
Gastrophryne olivacea
PLAINS NARROW-MOUTHED TOAD
SINALOAN NARROW-MOUTHED TOAD

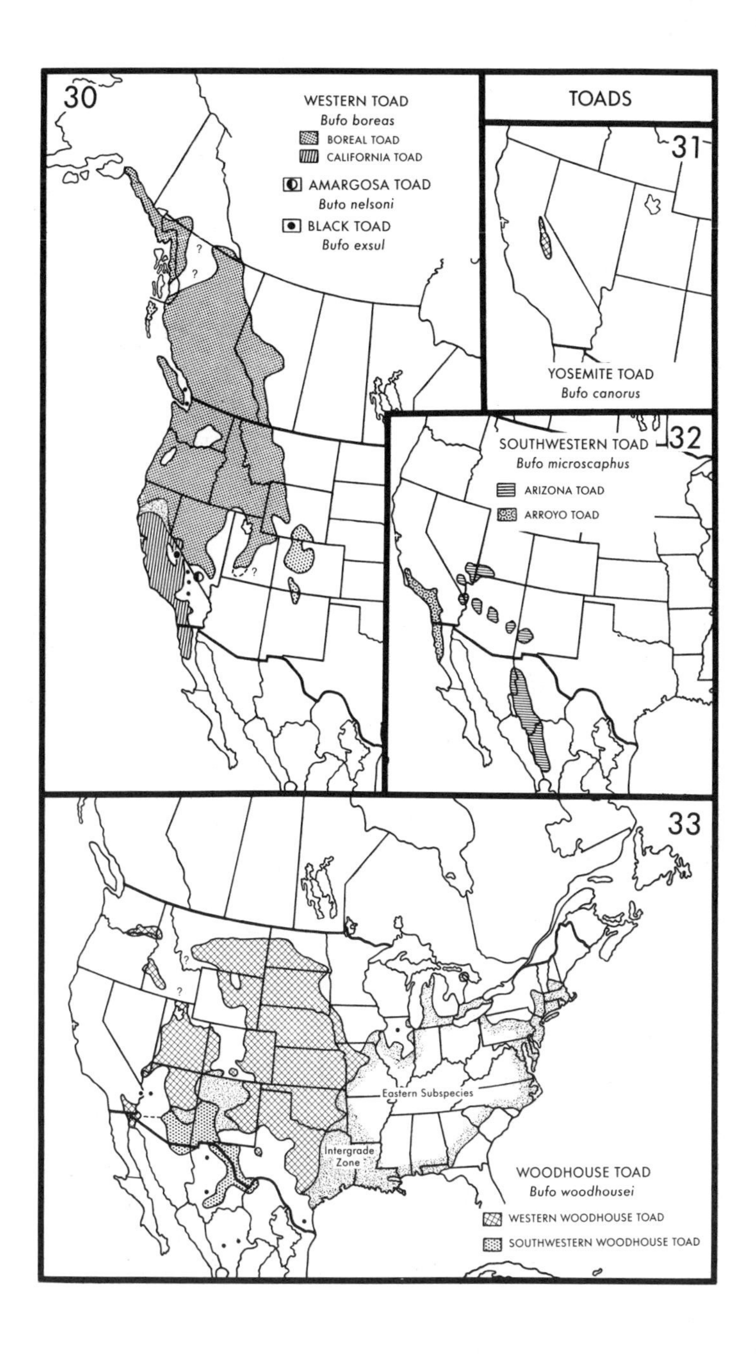
TOADS
30
WESTERN TOAD
Bufo boreas
BOREAL TOAD
CALIFORNIA TOAD
AMARGOSA TOAD
Buto nelsoni
BLACK TOAD
Bufo exsul
31
YOSEMITE TOAD
Bufo canorus
32
SOUTHWESTERN TOAD
Bufo microscaphus
ARIZONA TOAD
ARROYO TOAD
33
Eastern Subspecies
Intergrade Zone
WOODHOUSE TOAD
Bufo woodhousei
WESTERN WOODHOUSE TOAD
SOUTHWESTERN WOODHOUSE TOAD

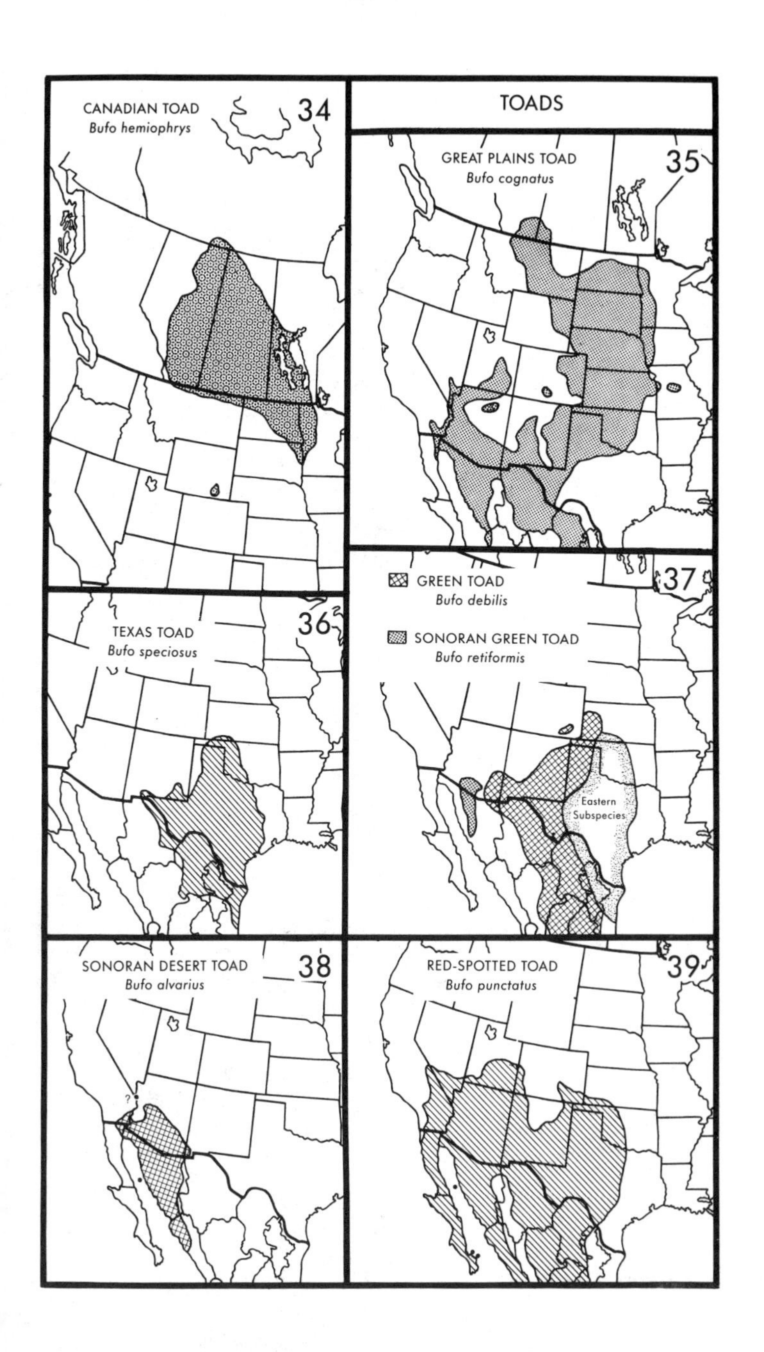
TOADS
CANADIAN TOAD
Bufo hemiophrys
34
GREAT PLAINS TOAD
Bufo cognatus
35
TEXAS TOAD
Bufo speciosus
36
GREEN TOAD
Bufo debilis
SONORAN GREEN TOAD
Bufo retiformis
Eastern
Subspecies
37
SONORAN DESERT TOAD
Bufo alvarius
?
38
RED-SPOTTED TOAD
Bufo punctatus
39

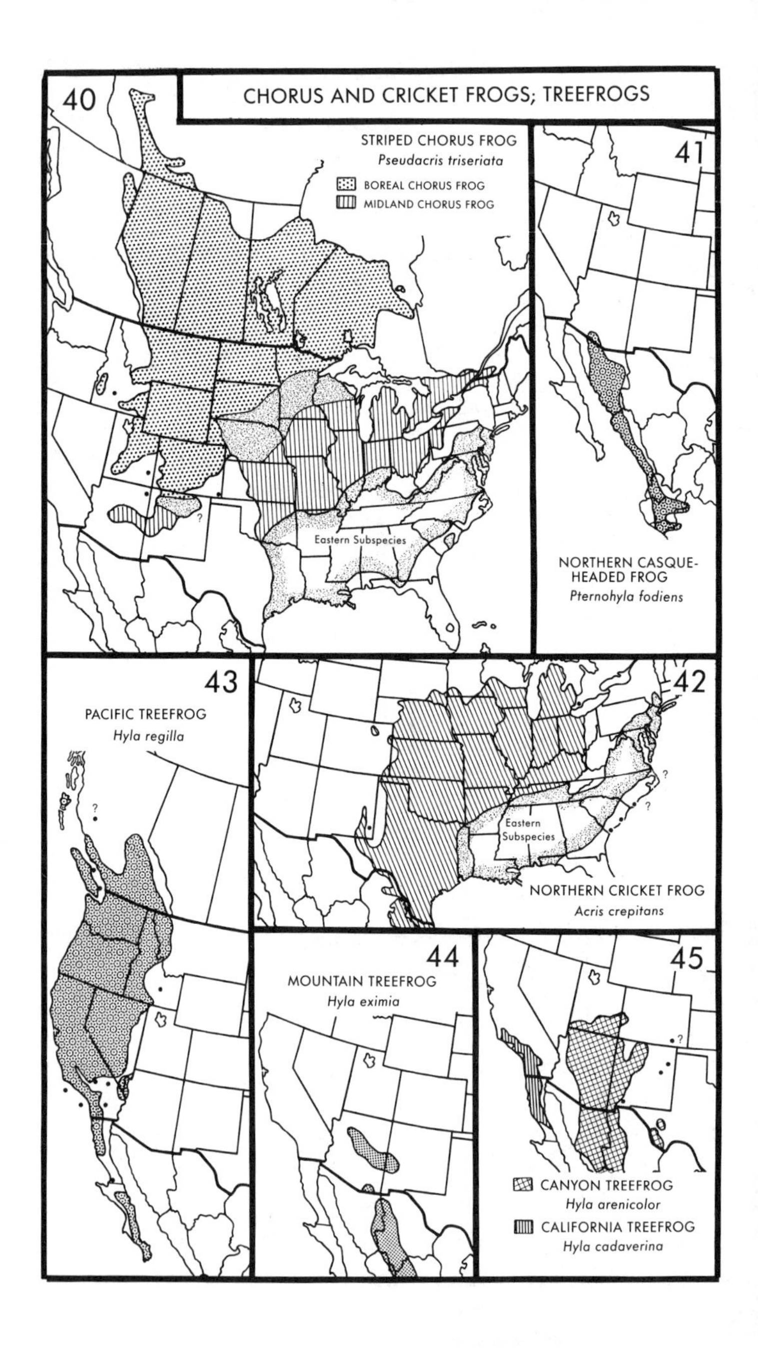
40
CHORUS AND CRICKET FROGS; TREEFROGS
STRIPED CHORUS FROG
Pseudacris triseriata
BOREAL CHORUS FROG
MIDLAND CHORUS FROG
Eastern Subspecies
41
NORTHERN CASQUE-HEADED FROG
Pternohyla fodiens
43
PACIFIC TREEFROG
Hyla regilla
42
Eastern Subspecies
NORTHERN CRICKET FROG
Acris crepitans
44
MOUNTAIN TREEFROG
Hyla eximia
45
CANYON TREEFROG
Hyla arenicolor
CALIFORNIA TREEFROG
Hyla cadaverina

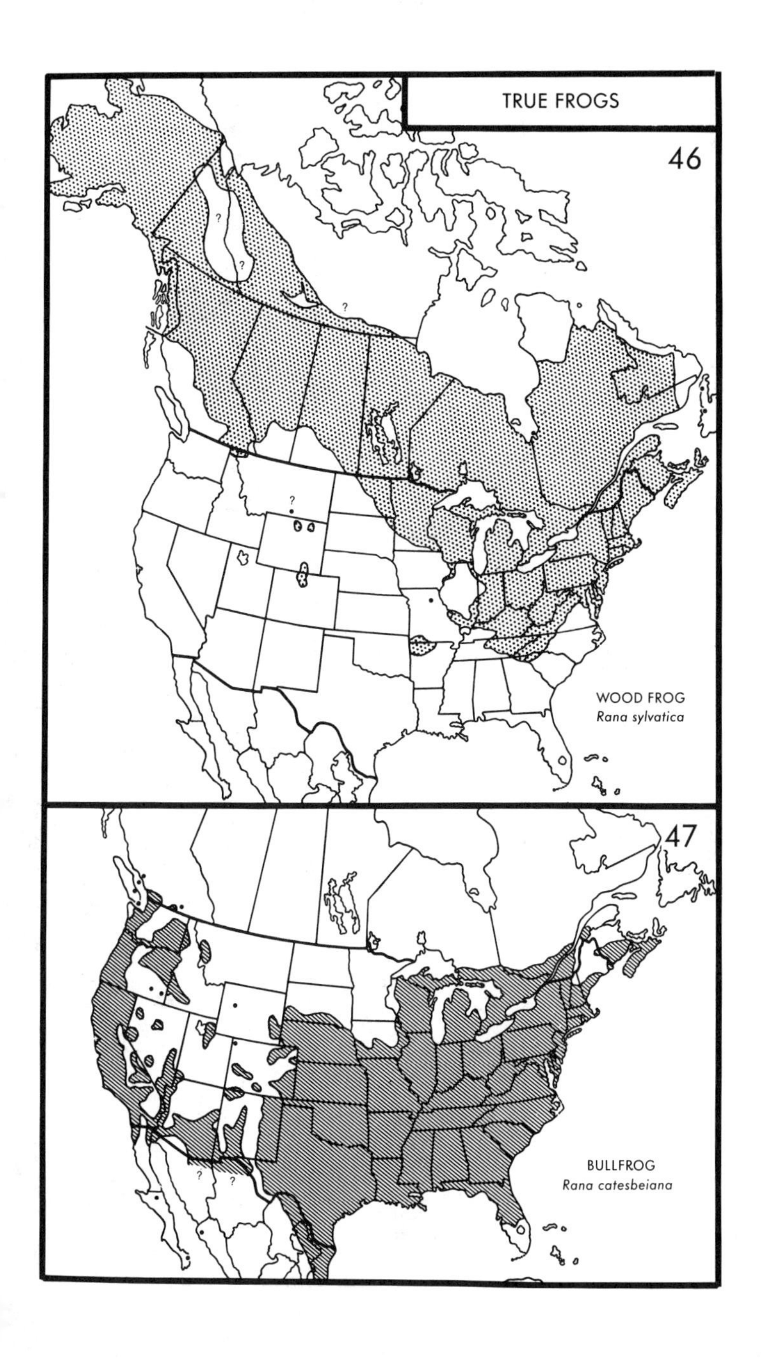
TRUE FROGS
46
WOOD FROG
Rana sylvatica
47
BULLFROG
Rana catesbeiana

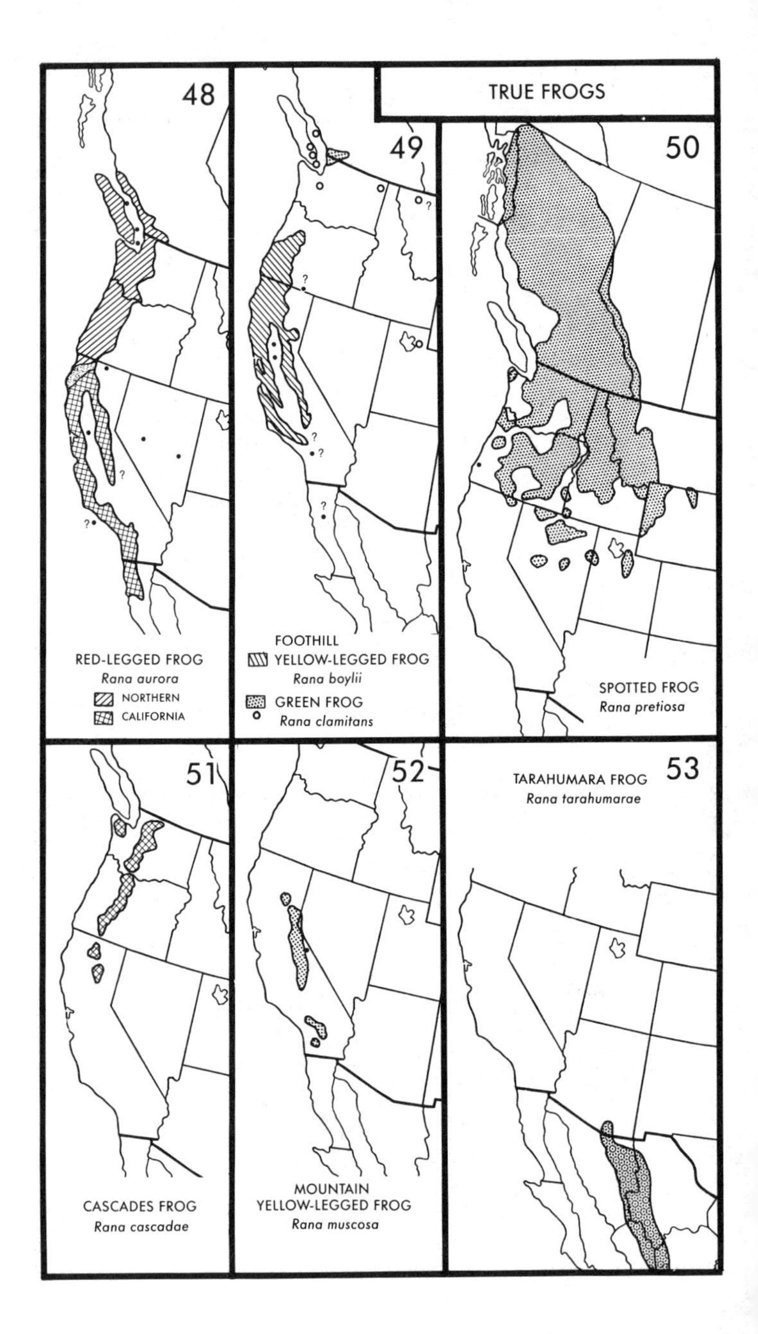

TRUE FROGS
48
RED-LEGGED FROG
Rana aurora
NORTHERN
CALIFORNIA
49
FOOTHILL
YELLOW-LEGGED FROG
Rana boylii
GREEN FROG
Rana clamitans
50
SPOTTED FROG
Rana pretiosa
51
CASCADES FROG
Rana cascadae
52
MOUNTAIN
YELLOW-LEGGED FROG
Rana muscosa
53
TARAHUMARA FROG
Rana tarahumarae

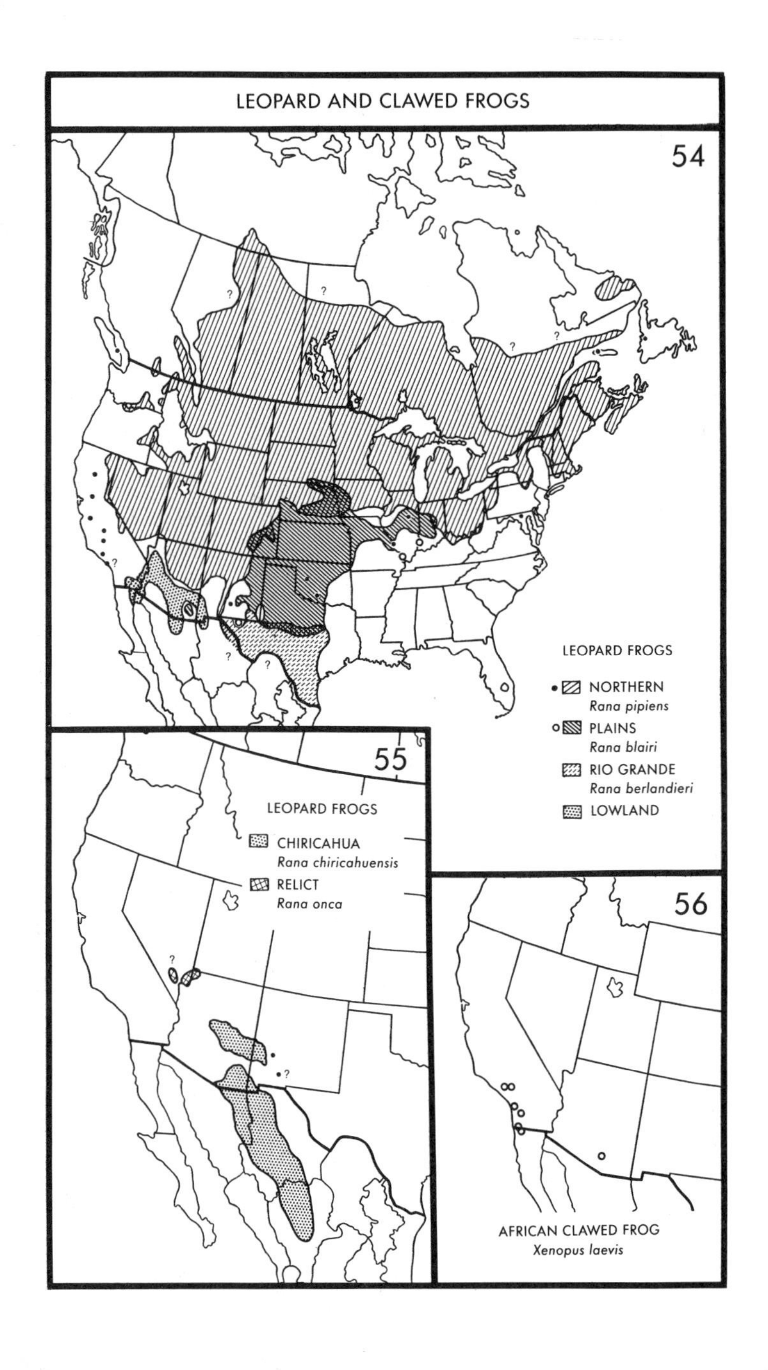
LEOPARD AND CLAWED FROGS
54
LEOPARD FROGS
NORTHERN
Rana pipiens
PLAINS
Rana blairi
RIO GRANDE
Rana berlandieri
LOWLAND
55
LEOPARD FROGS
CHIRICAHUA
Rana chiricahuensis
RELICT
Rana onca
56
AFRICAN CLAWED FROG
Xenopus laevis

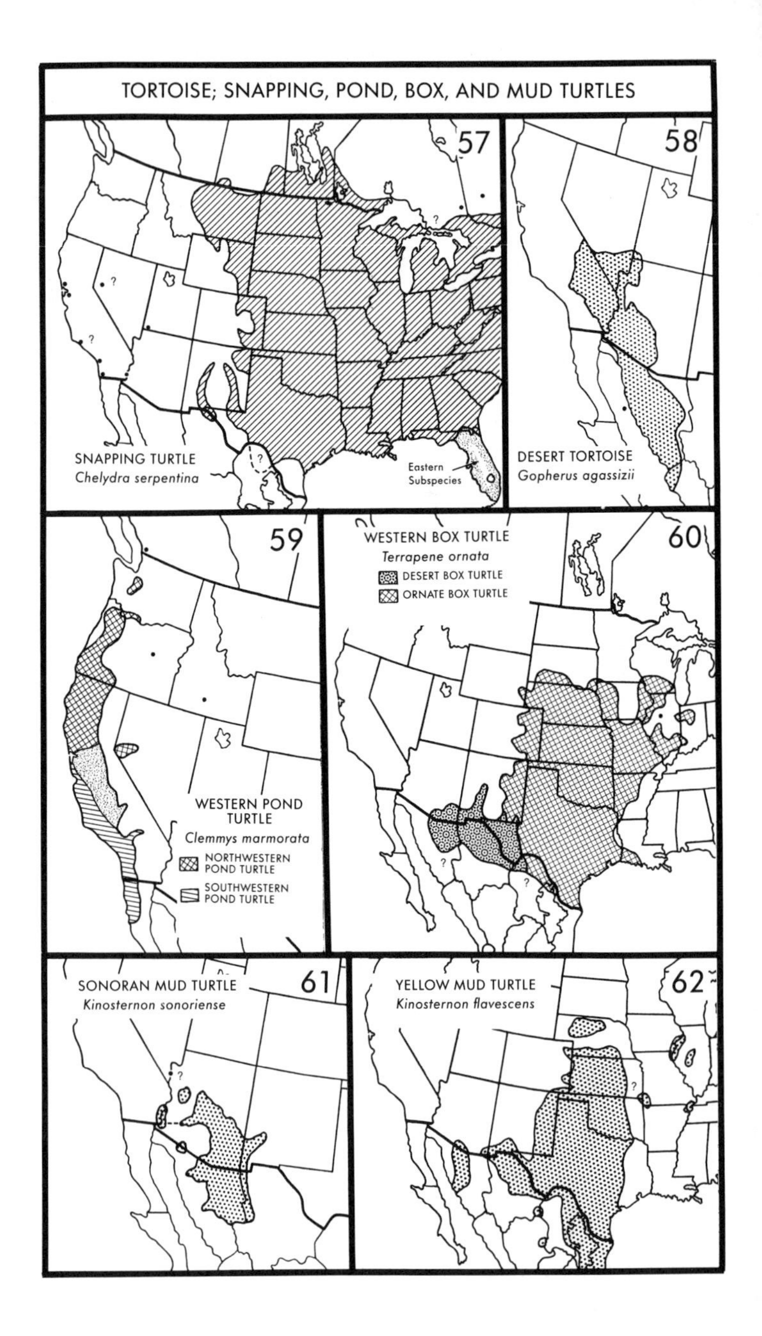
TORTOISE; SNAPPING, POND, BOX, AND MUD TURTLES
57
SNAPPING TURTLE
Chelydra serpentina
Eastern
Subspecies
58
DESERT TORTOISE
Gopherus agassizii
59
WESTERN POND
TURTLE
Clemmys marmorata
NORTHWESTERN
POND TURTLE
SOUTHWESTERN
POND TURTLE
60
WESTERN BOX TURTLE
Terrapene ornata
DESERT BOX TURTLE
ORNATE BOX TURTLE
61
SONORAN MUD TURTLE
Kinosternon sonoriense
62
YELLOW MUD TURTLE
Kinosternon flavescens

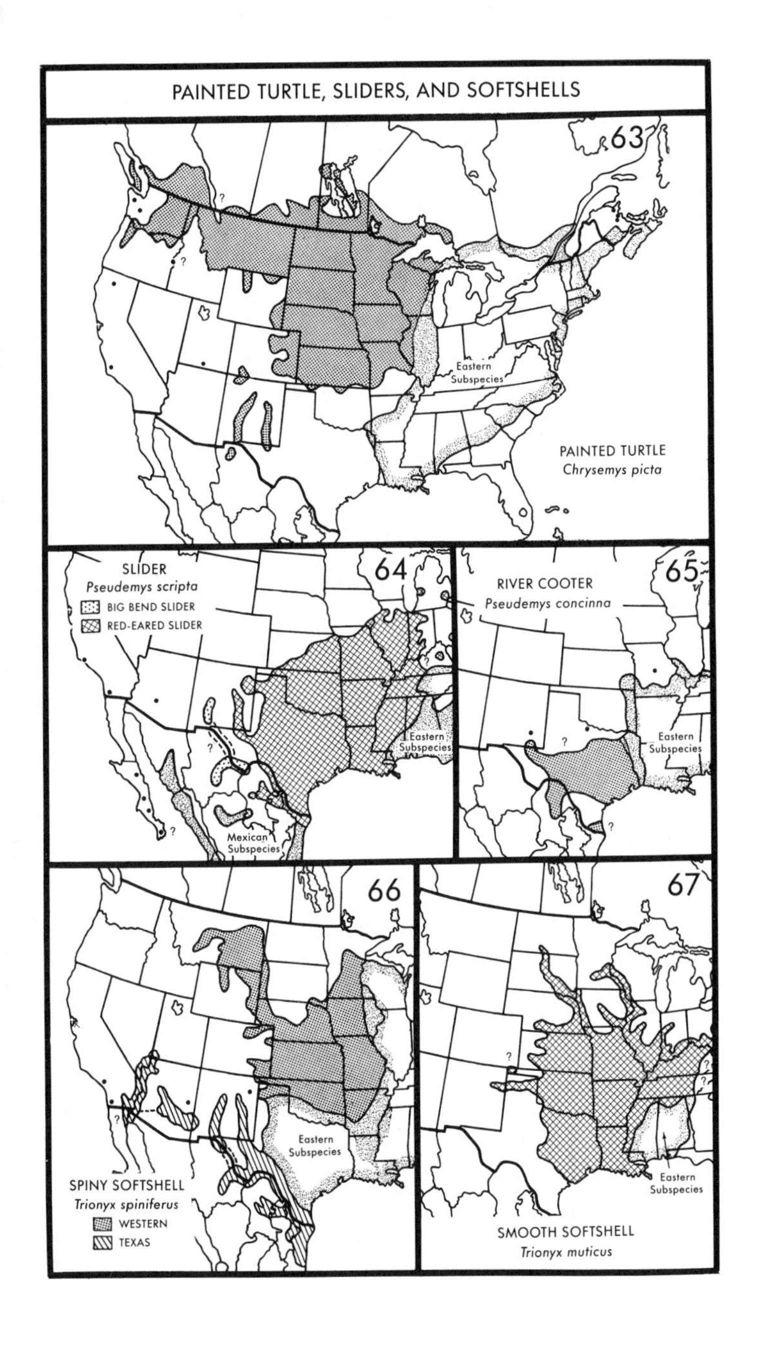
PAINTED TURTLE, SLIDERS, AND SOFTSHELLS
63
Eastern Subspecies
PAINTED TURTLE
Chrysemys picta
SLIDER
Pseudemys scripta
BIG BEND SLIDER
RED-EARED SLIDER
64
Eastern Subspecies
Mexican Subspecies
RIVER COOTER
Pseudemys concinna
65
Eastern Subspecies
66
Eastern Subspecies
SPINY SOFTSHELL
Trionyx spiniferus
WESTERN
TEXAS
67
Eastern Subspecies
SMOOTH SOFTSHELL
Trionyx muticus

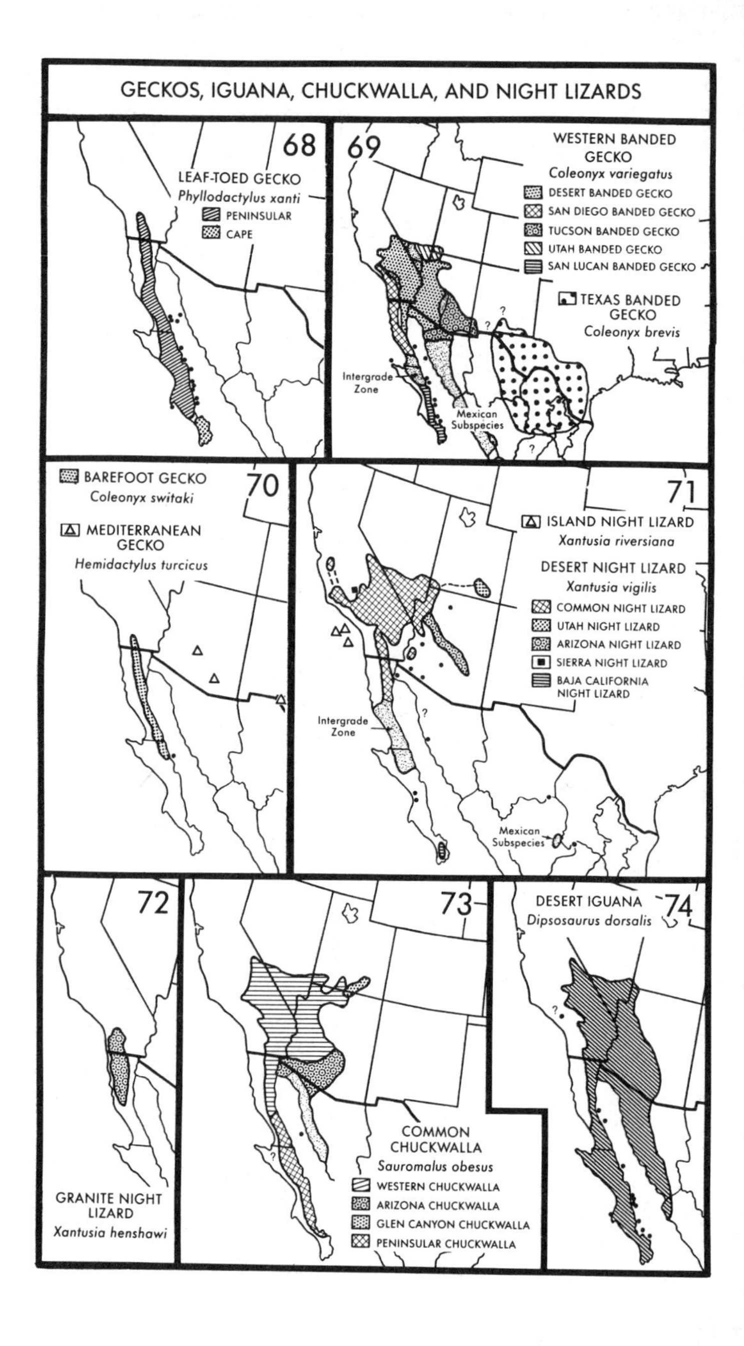
GECKOS, IGUANA, CHUCKWALLA, AND NIGHT LIZARDS
68
LEAF-TOED GECKO
Phyllodactylus xanti
PENINSULAR
CAPE
69
WESTERN BANDED GECKO
Coleonyx variegatus
DESERT BANDED GECKO
SAN DIEGO BANDED GECKO
TUCSON BANDED GECKO
UTAH BANDED GECKO
SAN LUCAN BANDED GECKO
TEXAS BANDED GECKO
Coleonyx brevis
Intergrade Zone
Mexican Subspecies
70
BAREFOOT GECKO
Coleonyx switaki
MEDITERRANEAN GECKO
Hemidactylus turcicus
71
ISLAND NIGHT LIZARD
Xantusia riversiana
DESERT NIGHT LIZARD
Xantusia vigilis
COMMON NIGHT LIZARD
UTAH NIGHT LIZARD
ARIZONA NIGHT LIZARD
SIERRA NIGHT LIZARD
BAJA CALIFORNIA NIGHT LIZARD
Intergrade Zone
Mexican Subspecies
72
GRANITE NIGHT LIZARD
Xantusia henshawi
73
COMMON CHUCKWALLA
Sauromalus obesus
WESTERN CHUCKWALLA
ARIZONA CHUCKWALLA
GLEN CANYON CHUCKWALLA
PENINSULAR CHUCKWALLA
74
DESERT IGUANA
Dipsosaurus dorsalis

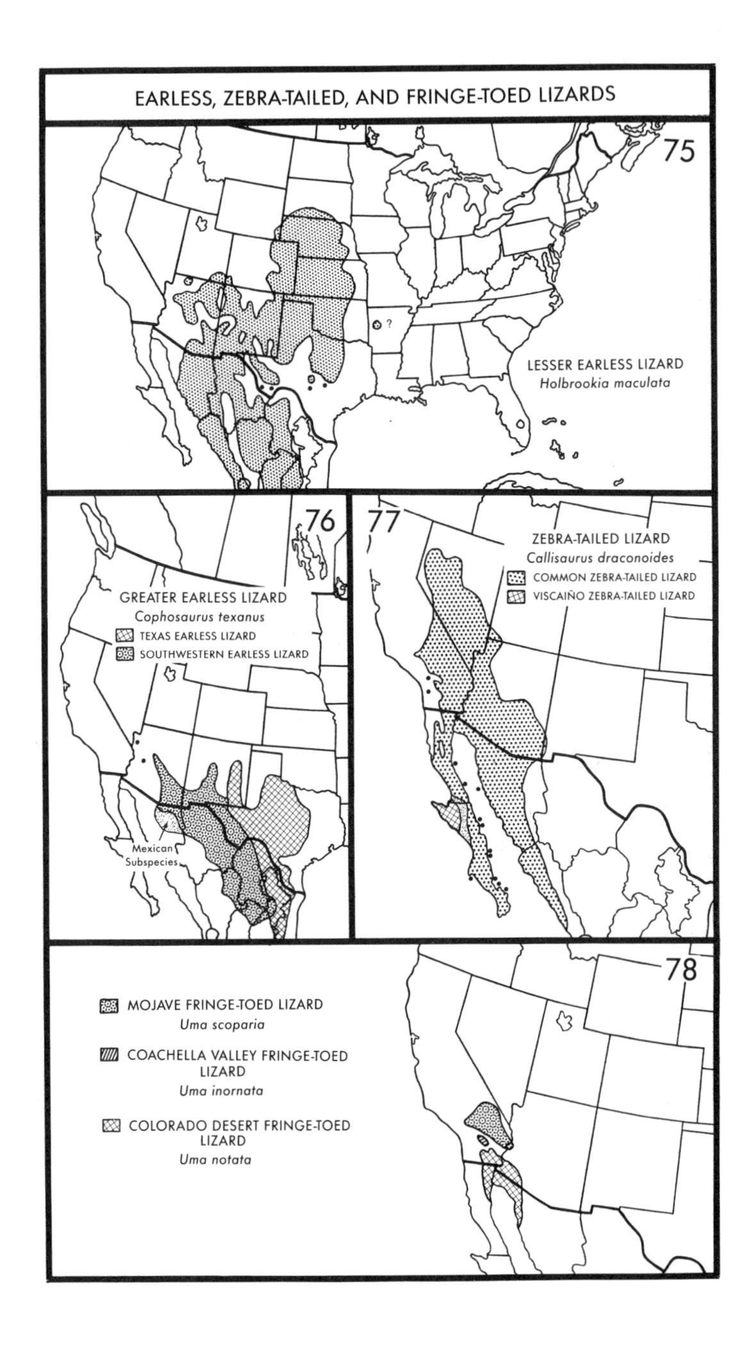

EARLESS, ZEBRA-TAILED, AND FRINGE-TOED LIZARDS
75
?
LESSER EARLESS LIZARD
Holbrookia maculata
76
GREATER EARLESS LIZARD
Cophosaurus texanus
TEXAS EARLESS LIZARD
SOUTHWESTERN EARLESS LIZARD
Mexican Subspecies
77
ZEBRA-TAILED LIZARD
Callisaurus draconoides
COMMON ZEBRA-TAILED LIZARD
VISCAIÑO ZEBRA-TAILED LIZARD
78
MOJAVE FRINGE-TOED LIZARD
Uma scoparia
COACHELLA VALLEY FRINGE-TOED LIZARD
Uma inornata
COLORADO DESERT FRINGE-TOED LIZARD
Uma notata

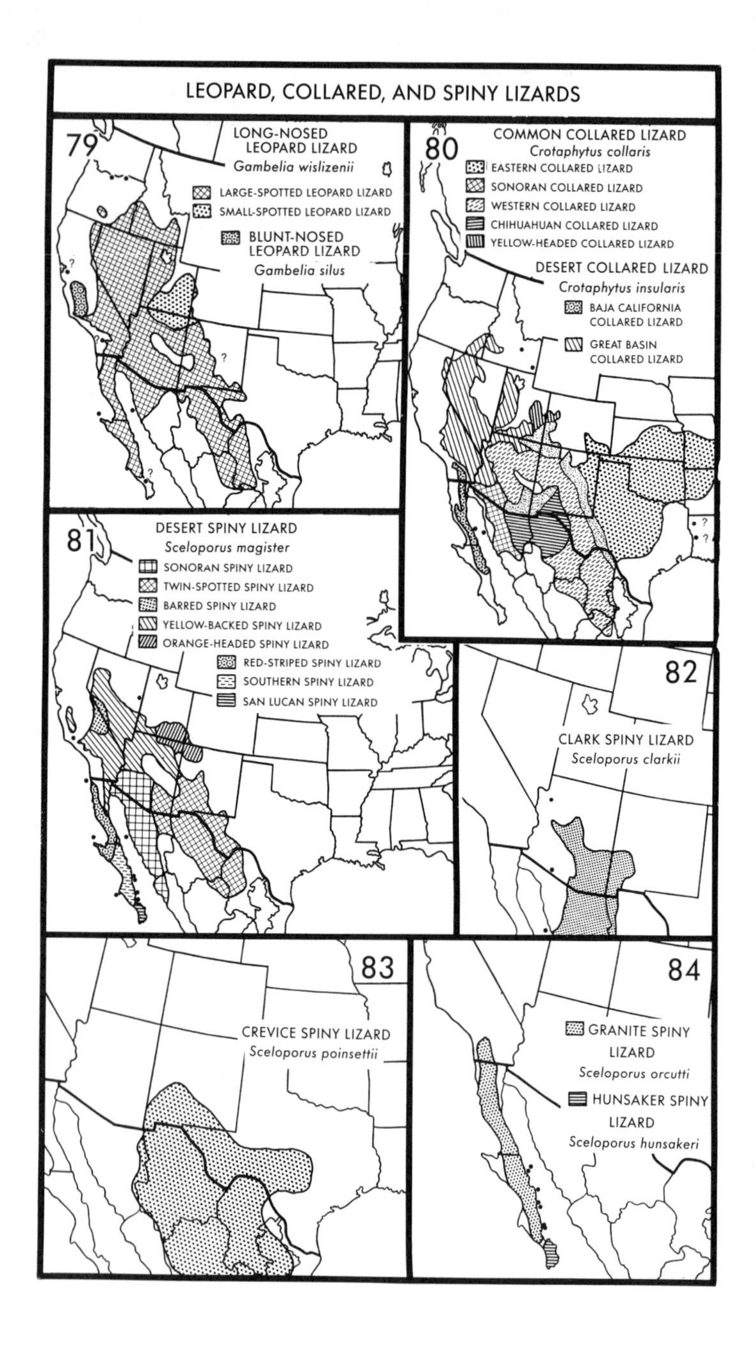
LEOPARD, COLLARED, AND SPINY LIZARDS
79
LONG-NOSED LEOPARD LIZARD
Gambelia wislizenii
LARGE-SPOTTED LEOPARD LIZARD
SMALL-SPOTTED LEOPARD LIZARD
BLUNT-NOSED LEOPARD LIZARD
Gambelia silus
80
COMMON COLLARED LIZARD
Crotaphytus collaris
EASTERN COLLARED LIZARD
SONORAN COLLARED LIZARD
WESTERN COLLARED LIZARD
CHIHUAHUAN COLLARED LIZARD
YELLOW-HEADED COLLARED LIZARD
DESERT COLLARED LIZARD
Crotaphytus insularis
BAJA CALIFORNIA COLLARED LIZARD
GREAT BASIN COLLARED LIZARD
81
DESERT SPINY LIZARD
Sceloporus magister
SONORAN SPINY LIZARD
TWIN-SPOTTED SPINY LIZARD
BARRED SPINY LIZARD
YELLOW-BACKED SPINY LIZARD
ORANGE-HEADED SPINY LIZARD
RED-STRIPED SPINY LIZARD
SOUTHERN SPINY LIZARD
SAN LUCAN SPINY LIZARD
82
CLARK SPINY LIZARD
Sceloporus clarkii
83
CREVICE SPINY LIZARD
Sceloporus poinsettii
84
GRANITE SPINY LIZARD
Sceloporus orcutti
HUNSAKER SPINY LIZARD
Sceloporus hunsakeri

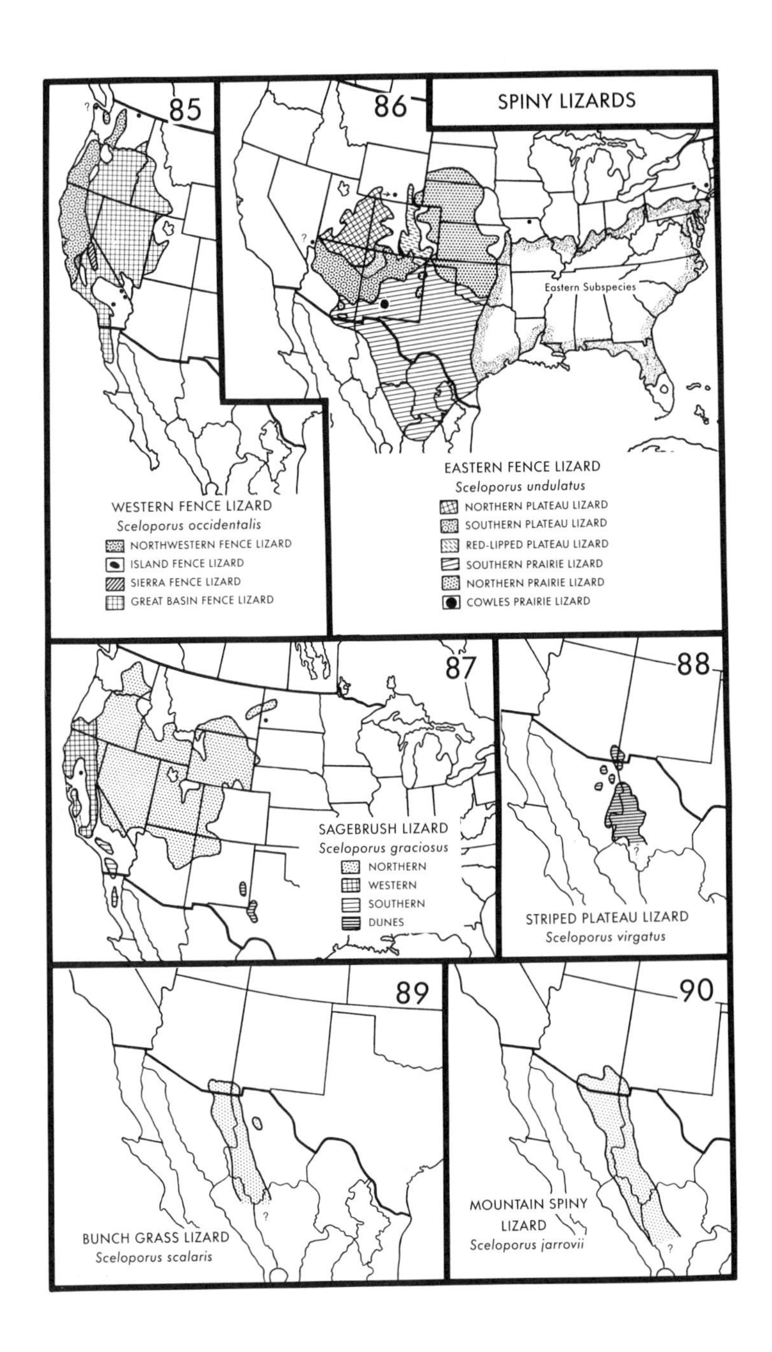
SPINY LIZARDS
85
86
Eastern Subspecies
WESTERN FENCE LIZARD
Sceloporus occidentalis
NORTHWESTERN FENCE LIZARD
ISLAND FENCE LIZARD
SIERRA FENCE LIZARD
GREAT BASIN FENCE LIZARD
EASTERN FENCE LIZARD
Sceloporus undulatus
NORTHERN PLATEAU LIZARD
SOUTHERN PLATEAU LIZARD
RED-LIPPED PLATEAU LIZARD
SOUTHERN PRAIRIE LIZARD
NORTHERN PRAIRIE LIZARD
COWLES PRAIRIE LIZARD
87
SAGEBRUSH LIZARD
Sceloporus graciosus
NORTHERN
WESTERN
SOUTHERN
DUNES
88
STRIPED PLATEAU LIZARD
Sceloporus virgatus
89
BUNCH GRASS LIZARD
Sceloporus scalaris
90
MOUNTAIN SPINY LIZARD
Sceloporus jarrovii

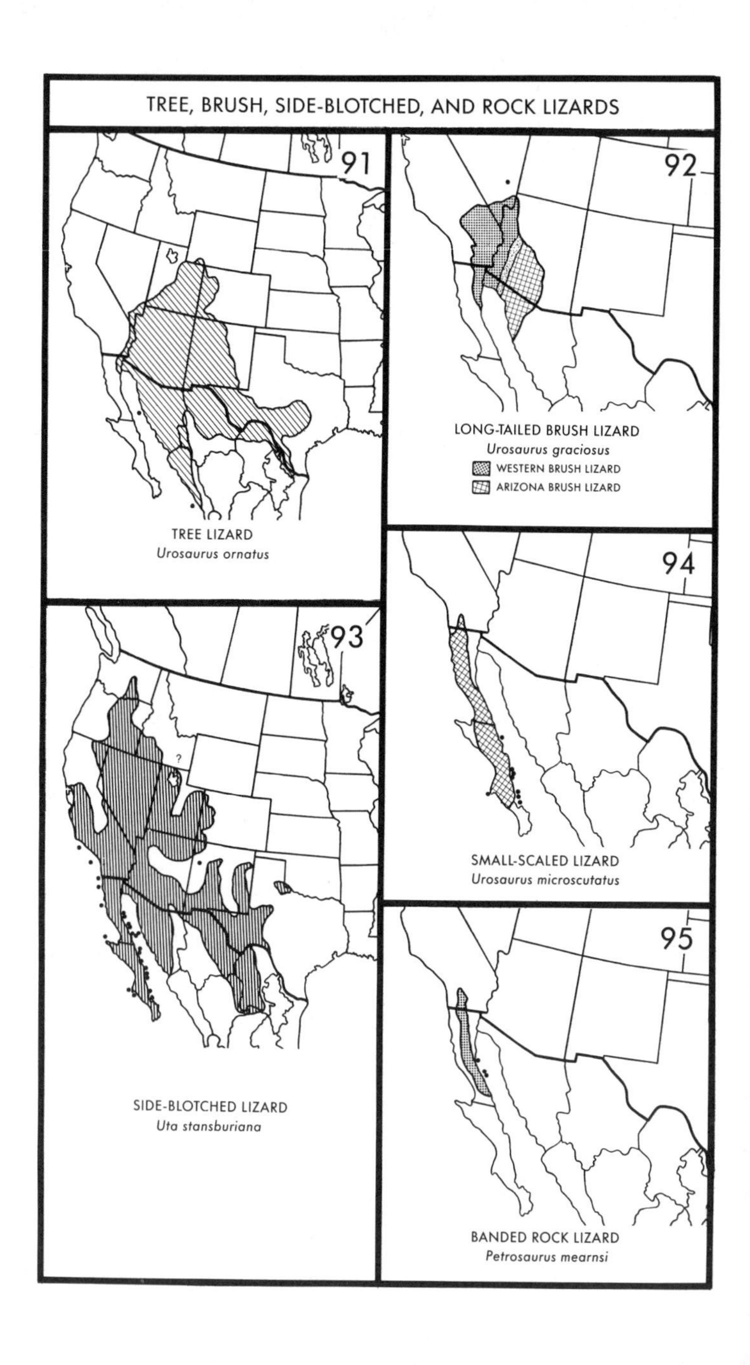

TREE, BRUSH, SIDE-BLOTCHED, AND ROCK LIZARDS
91
TREE LIZARD
Urosaurus ornatus
92
LONG-TAILED BRUSH LIZARD
Urosaurus graciosus
WESTERN BRUSH LIZARD
ARIZONA BRUSH LIZARD
93
?
SIDE-BLOTCHED LIZARD
Uta stansburiana
94
SMALL-SCALED LIZARD
Urosaurus microscutatus
95
BANDED ROCK LIZARD
Petrosaurus mearnsi

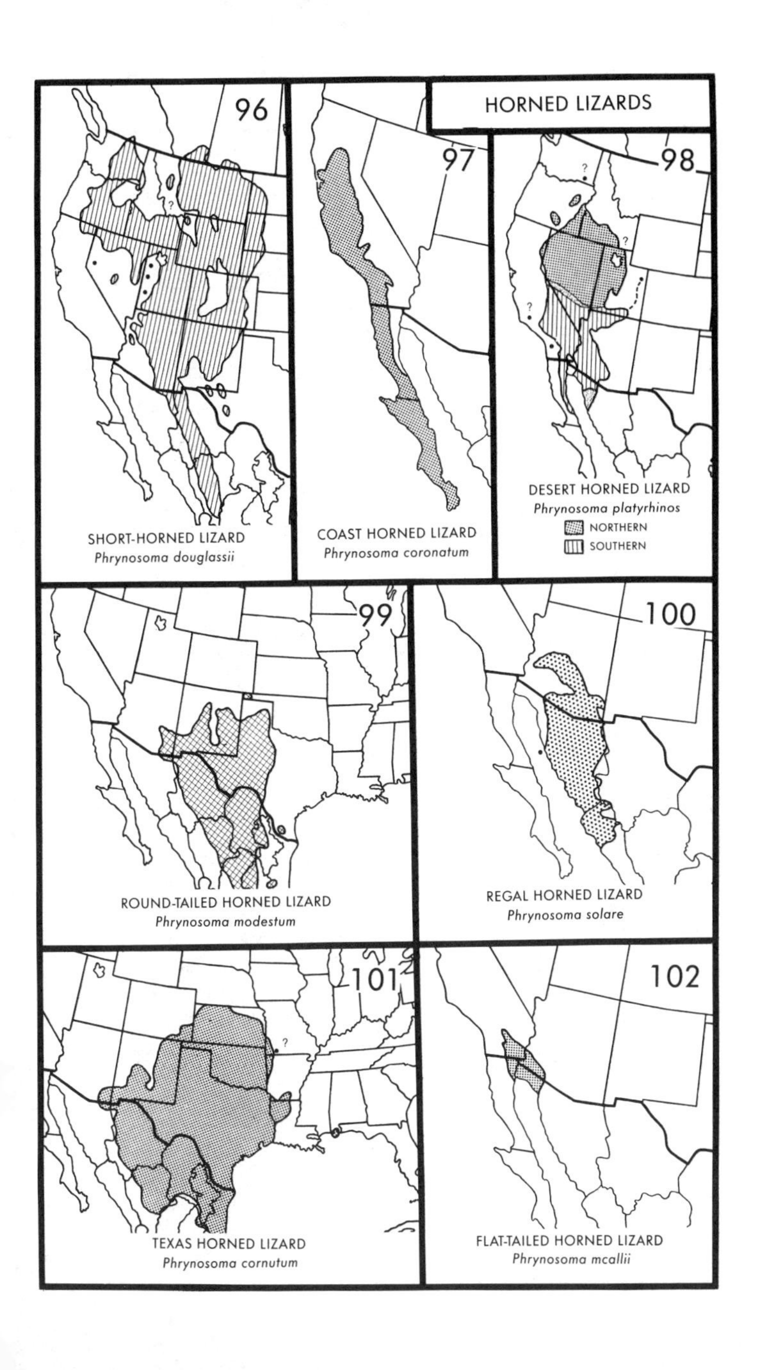
HORNED LIZARDS
96
SHORT-HORNED LIZARD
Phrynosoma douglassii
97
COAST HORNED LIZARD
Phrynosoma coronatum
98
DESERT HORNED LIZARD
Phrynosoma platyrhinos
NORTHERN
SOUTHERN
99
ROUND-TAILED HORNED LIZARD
Phrynosoma modestum
100
REGAL HORNED LIZARD
Phrynosoma solare
101
TEXAS HORNED LIZARD
Phrynosoma cornutum
102
FLAT-TAILED HORNED LIZARD
Phrynosoma mcallii

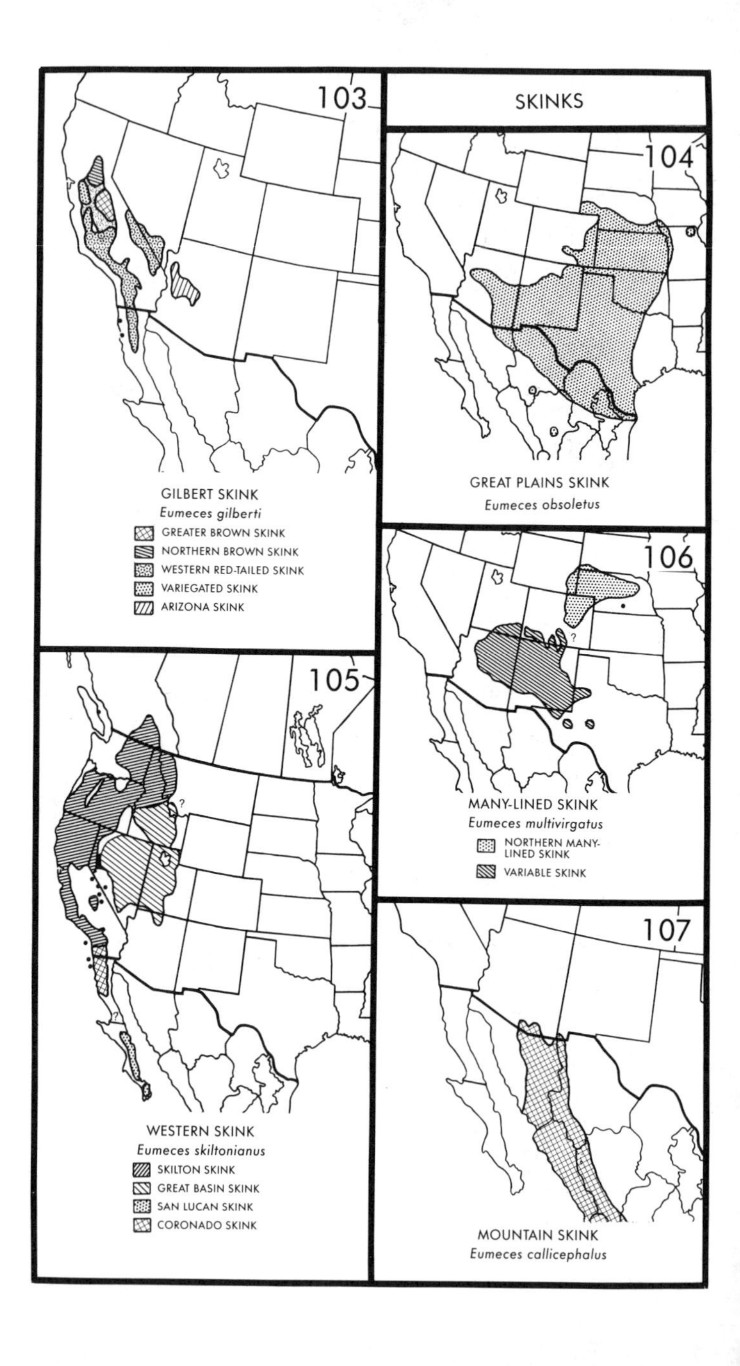

SKINKS
103
GILBERT SKINK
Eumeces gilberti
GREATER BROWN SKINK
NORTHERN BROWN SKINK
WESTERN RED-TAILED SKINK
VARIEGATED SKINK
ARIZONA SKINK
104
GREAT PLAINS SKINK
Eumeces obsoletus
105
WESTERN SKINK
Eumeces skiltonianus
SKILTON SKINK
GREAT BASIN SKINK
SAN LUCAN SKINK
CORONADO SKINK
106
MANY-LINED SKINK
Eumeces multivirgatus
NORTHERN MANY-LINED SKINK
VARIABLE SKINK
107
MOUNTAIN SKINK
Eumeces callicephalus

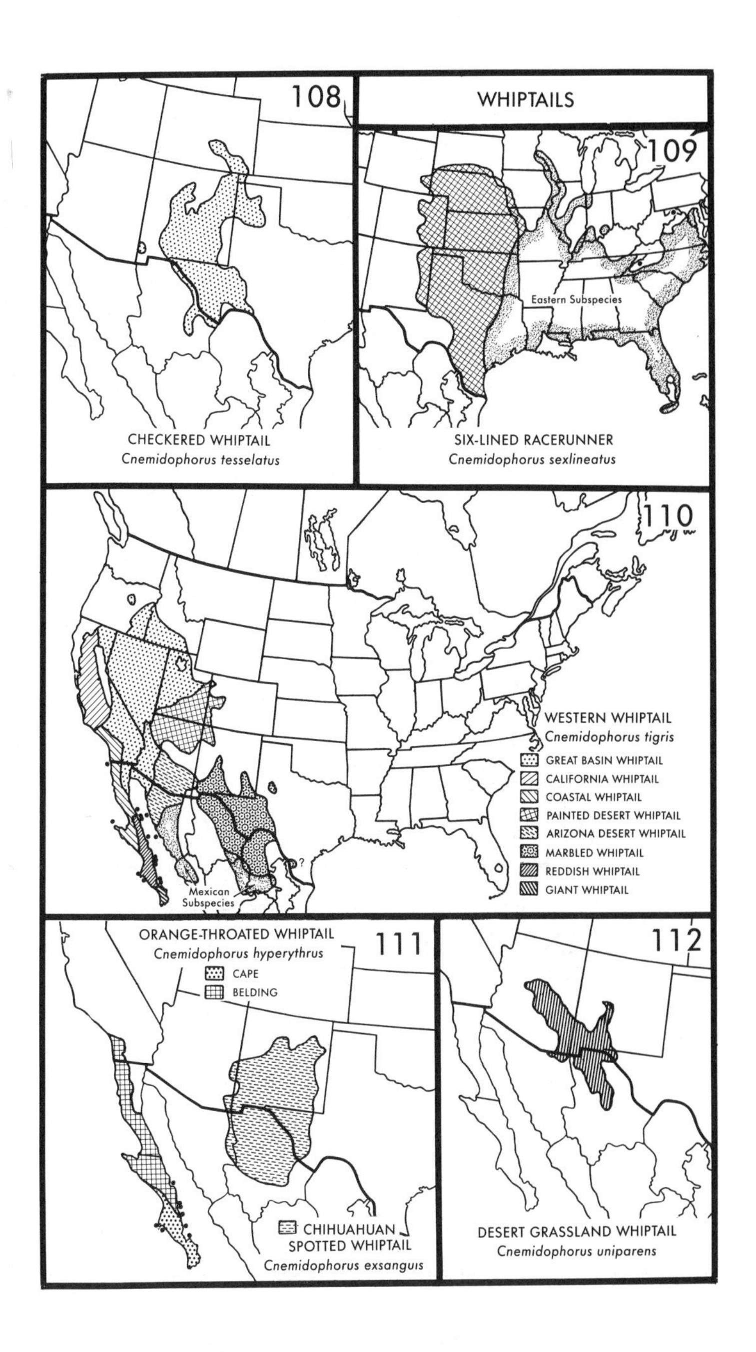
108
WHIPTAILS
109
Eastern Subspecies
CHECKERED WHIPTAIL
Cnemidophorus tesselatus
SIX-LINED RACERUNNER
Cnemidophorus sexlineatus
110
WESTERN WHIPTAIL
Cnemidophorus tigris
GREAT BASIN WHIPTAIL
CALIFORNIA WHIPTAIL
COASTAL WHIPTAIL
PAINTED DESERT WHIPTAIL
ARIZONA DESERT WHIPTAIL
MARBLED WHIPTAIL
REDDISH WHIPTAIL
GIANT WHIPTAIL
Mexican Subspecies
?
ORANGE-THROATED WHIPTAIL
Cnemidophorus hyperythrus
CAPE
BELDING
111
CHIHUAHUAN SPOTTED WHIPTAIL
Cnemidophorus exsanguis
112
DESERT GRASSLAND WHIPTAIL
Cnemidophorus uniparens

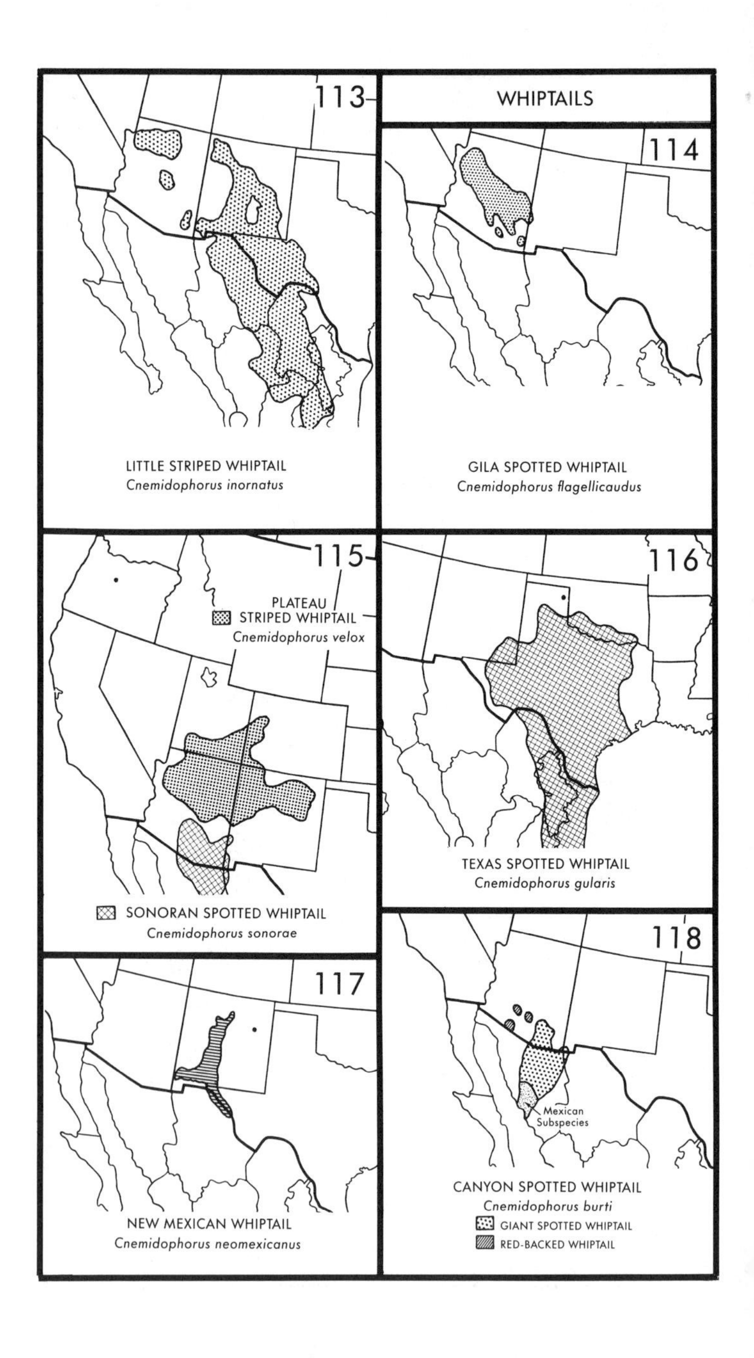
113
WHIPTAILS
114
LITTLE STRIPED WHIPTAIL
Cnemidophorus inornatus
GILA SPOTTED WHIPTAIL
Cnemidophorus flagellicaudus
115
PLATEAU
STRIPED WHIPTAIL
Cnemidophorus velox
116
TEXAS SPOTTED WHIPTAIL
Cnemidophorus gularis
SONORAN SPOTTED WHIPTAIL
Cnemidophorus sonorae
117
118
Mexican
Subspecies
CANYON SPOTTED WHIPTAIL
Cnemidophorus burti
GIANT SPOTTED WHIPTAIL
RED-BACKED WHIPTAIL
NEW MEXICAN WHIPTAIL
Cnemidophorus neomexicanus

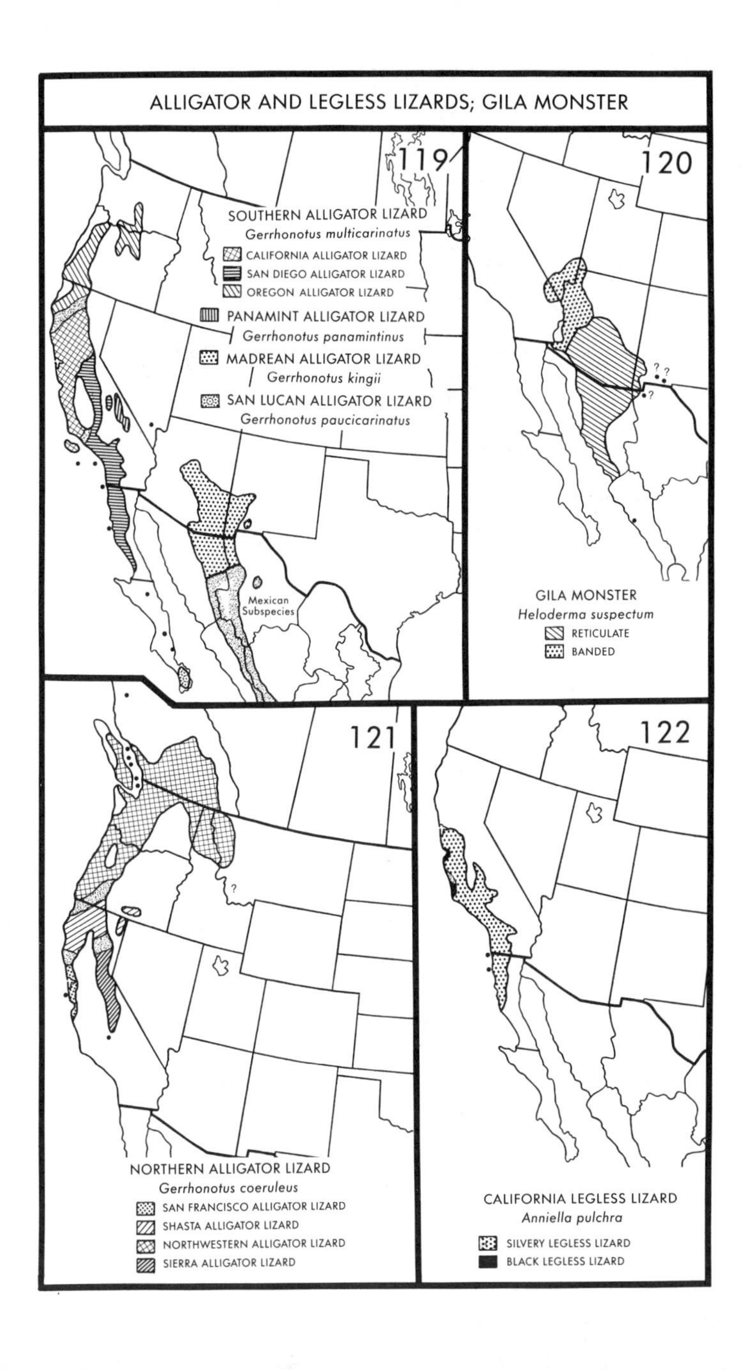

ALLIGATOR AND LEGLESS LIZARDS; GILA MONSTER
119
SOUTHERN ALLIGATOR LIZARD
Gerrhonotus multicarinatus
CALIFORNIA ALLIGATOR LIZARD
SAN DIEGO ALLIGATOR LIZARD
OREGON ALLIGATOR LIZARD
PANAMINT ALLIGATOR LIZARD
Gerrhonotus panamintinus
MADREAN ALLIGATOR LIZARD
Gerrhonotus kingii
SAN LUCAN ALLIGATOR LIZARD
Gerrhonotus paucicarinatus
Mexican Subspecies
120
GILA MONSTER
Heloderma suspectum
RETICULATE
BANDED
121
NORTHERN ALLIGATOR LIZARD
Gerrhonotus coeruleus
SAN FRANCISCO ALLIGATOR LIZARD
SHASTA ALLIGATOR LIZARD
NORTHWESTERN ALLIGATOR LIZARD
SIERRA ALLIGATOR LIZARD
122
CALIFORNIA LEGLESS LIZARD
Anniella pulchra
SILVERY LEGLESS LIZARD
BLACK LEGLESS LIZARD

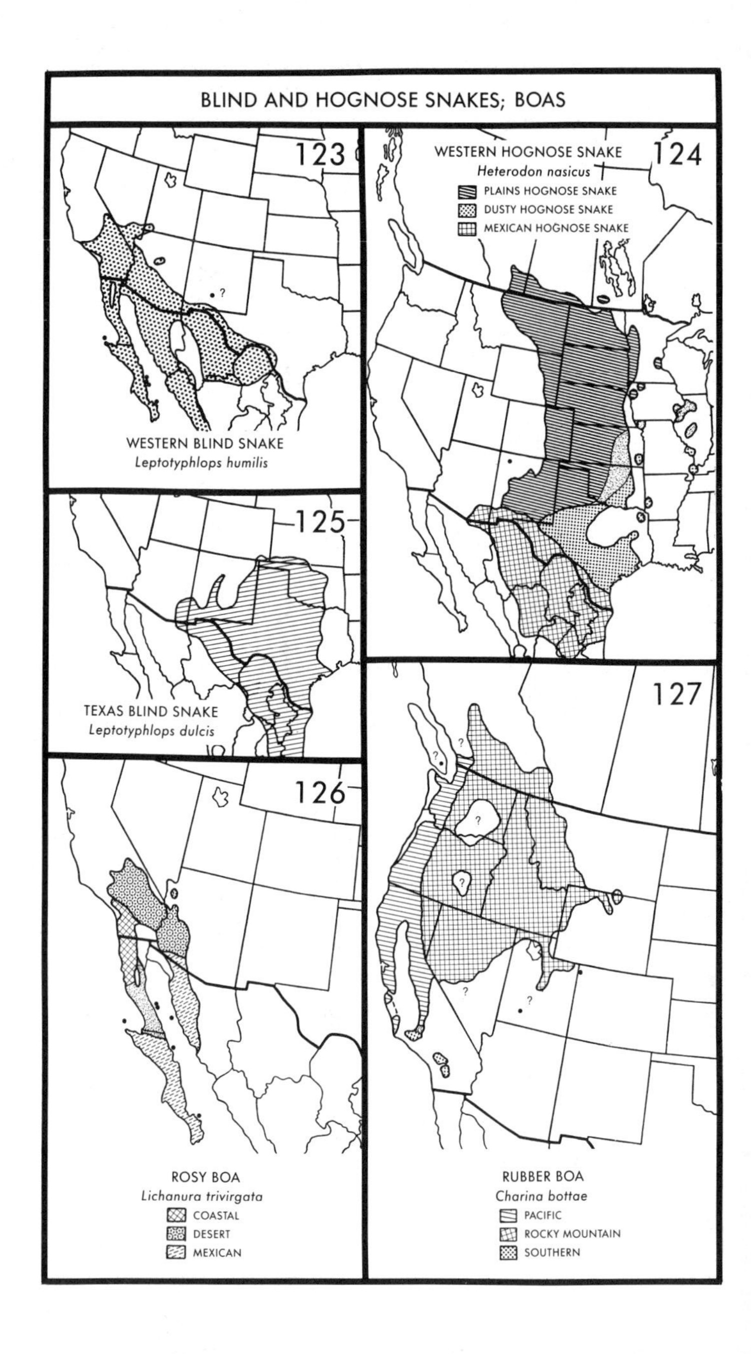
BLIND AND HOGNOSE SNAKES; BOAS
123
WESTERN BLIND SNAKE
Leptotyphlops humilis
124
WESTERN HOGNOSE SNAKE
Heterodon nasicus
PLAINS HOGNOSE SNAKE
DUSTY HOGNOSE SNAKE
MEXICAN HOGNOSE SNAKE
125
TEXAS BLIND SNAKE
Leptotyphlops dulcis
126
ROSY BOA
Lichanura trivirgata
COASTAL
DESERT
MEXICAN
127
RUBBER BOA
Charina bottae
PACIFIC
ROCKY MOUNTAIN
SOUTHERN

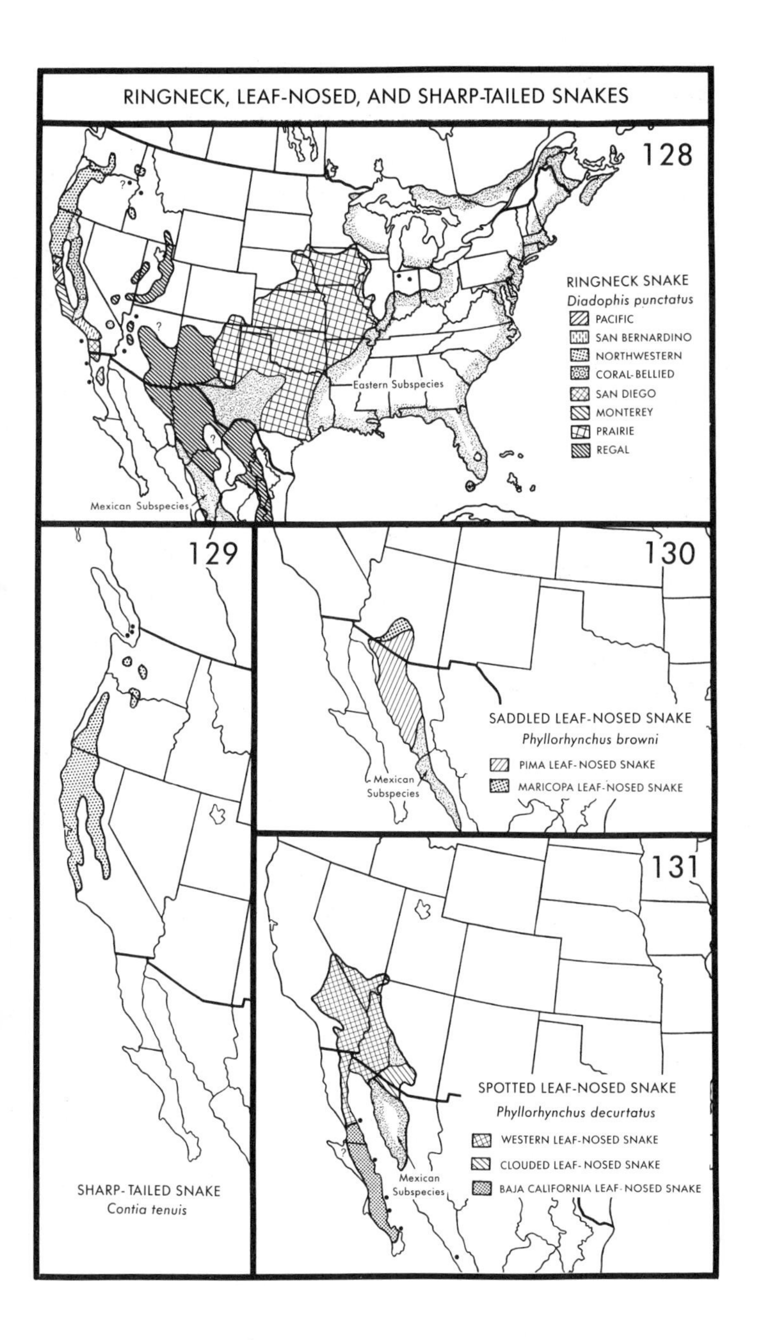
RINGNECK, LEAF-NOSED, AND SHARP-TAILED SNAKES
128
RINGNECK SNAKE
Diadophis punctatus
PACIFIC
SAN BERNARDINO
NORTHWESTERN
CORAL-BELLIED
SAN DIEGO
MONTEREY
PRAIRIE
REGAL
Eastern Subspecies
Mexican Subspecies
129
SHARP-TAILED SNAKE
Contia tenuis
130
SADDLED LEAF-NOSED SNAKE
Phyllorhynchus browni
PIMA LEAF-NOSED SNAKE
MARICOPA LEAF-NOSED SNAKE
Mexican Subspecies
131
SPOTTED LEAF-NOSED SNAKE
Phyllorhynchus decurtatus
WESTERN LEAF-NOSED SNAKE
CLOUDED LEAF-NOSED SNAKE
BAJA CALIFORNIA LEAF-NOSED SNAKE
Mexican Subspecies

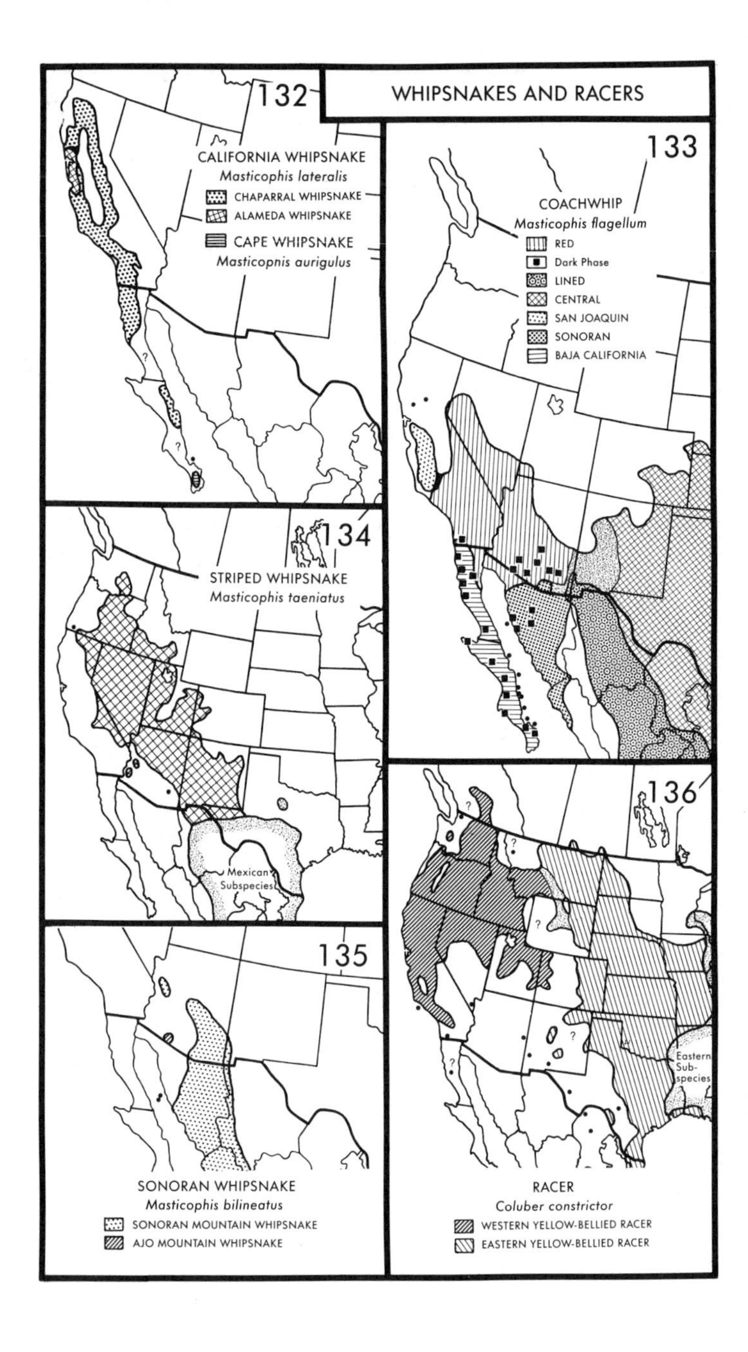
WHIPSNAKES AND RACERS
132
CALIFORNIA WHIPSNAKE
Masticophis lateralis
CHAPARRAL WHIPSNAKE
ALAMEDA WHIPSNAKE
CAPE WHIPSNAKE
Masticopnis aurigulus
133
COACHWHIP
Masticophis flagellum
RED
Dark Phase
LINED
CENTRAL
SAN JOAQUIN
SONORAN
BAJA CALIFORNIA
134
STRIPED WHIPSNAKE
Masticophis taeniatus
Mexican
Subspecies
135
SONORAN WHIPSNAKE
Masticophis bilineatus
SONORAN MOUNTAIN WHIPSNAKE
AJO MOUNTAIN WHIPSNAKE
136
Eastern
Sub-
species
RACER
Coluber constrictor
WESTERN YELLOW-BELLIED RACER
EASTERN YELLOW-BELLIED RACER

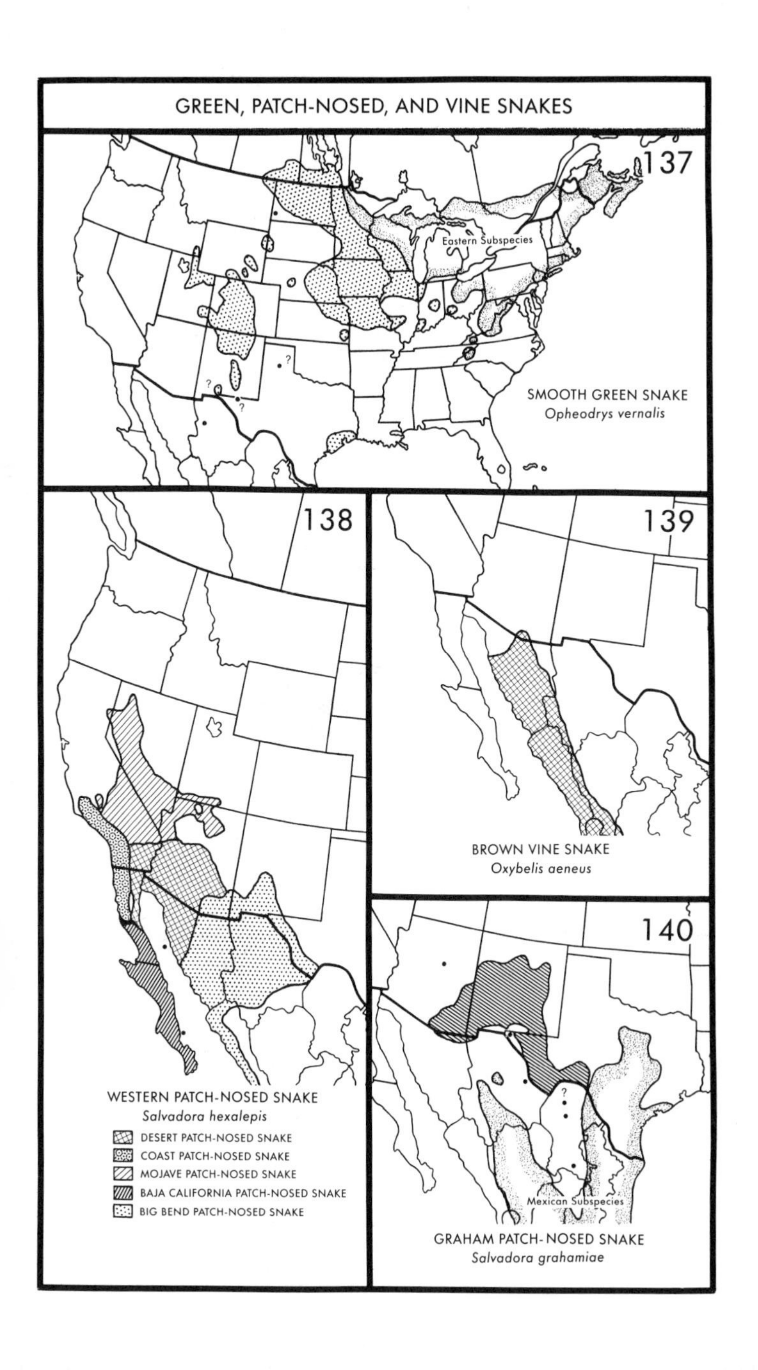
GREEN, PATCH-NOSED, AND VINE SNAKES
137
Eastern Subspecies
?
?
?
SMOOTH GREEN SNAKE
Opheodrys vernalis
138
WESTERN PATCH-NOSED SNAKE
Salvadora hexalepis
DESERT PATCH-NOSED SNAKE
COAST PATCH-NOSED SNAKE
MOJAVE PATCH-NOSED SNAKE
BAJA CALIFORNIA PATCH-NOSED SNAKE
BIG BEND PATCH-NOSED SNAKE
139
BROWN VINE SNAKE
Oxybelis aeneus
140
?
Mexican Subspecies
GRAHAM PATCH-NOSED SNAKE
Salvadora grahamiae

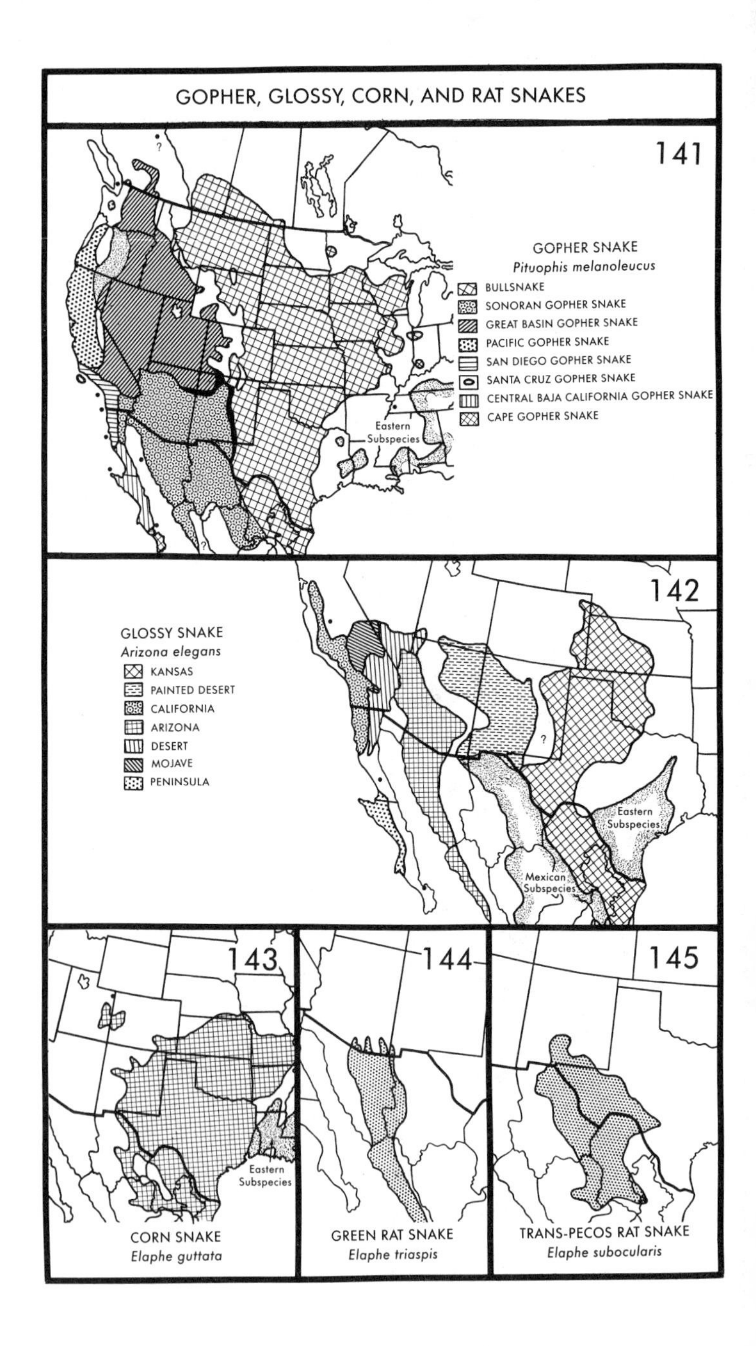
GOPHER, GLOSSY, CORN, AND RAT SNAKES
141
GOPHER SNAKE
Pituophis melanoleucus
BULLSNAKE
SONORAN GOPHER SNAKE
GREAT BASIN GOPHER SNAKE
PACIFIC GOPHER SNAKE
SAN DIEGO GOPHER SNAKE
SANTA CRUZ GOPHER SNAKE
CENTRAL BAJA CALIFORNIA GOPHER SNAKE
CAPE GOPHER SNAKE
Eastern Subspecies
142
GLOSSY SNAKE
Arizona elegans
KANSAS
PAINTED DESERT
CALIFORNIA
ARIZONA
DESERT
MOJAVE
PENINSULA
Eastern Subspecies
Mexican Subspecies
143
Eastern Subspecies
CORN SNAKE
Elaphe guttata
144
GREEN RAT SNAKE
Elaphe triaspis
145
TRANS-PECOS RAT SNAKE
Elaphe subocularis

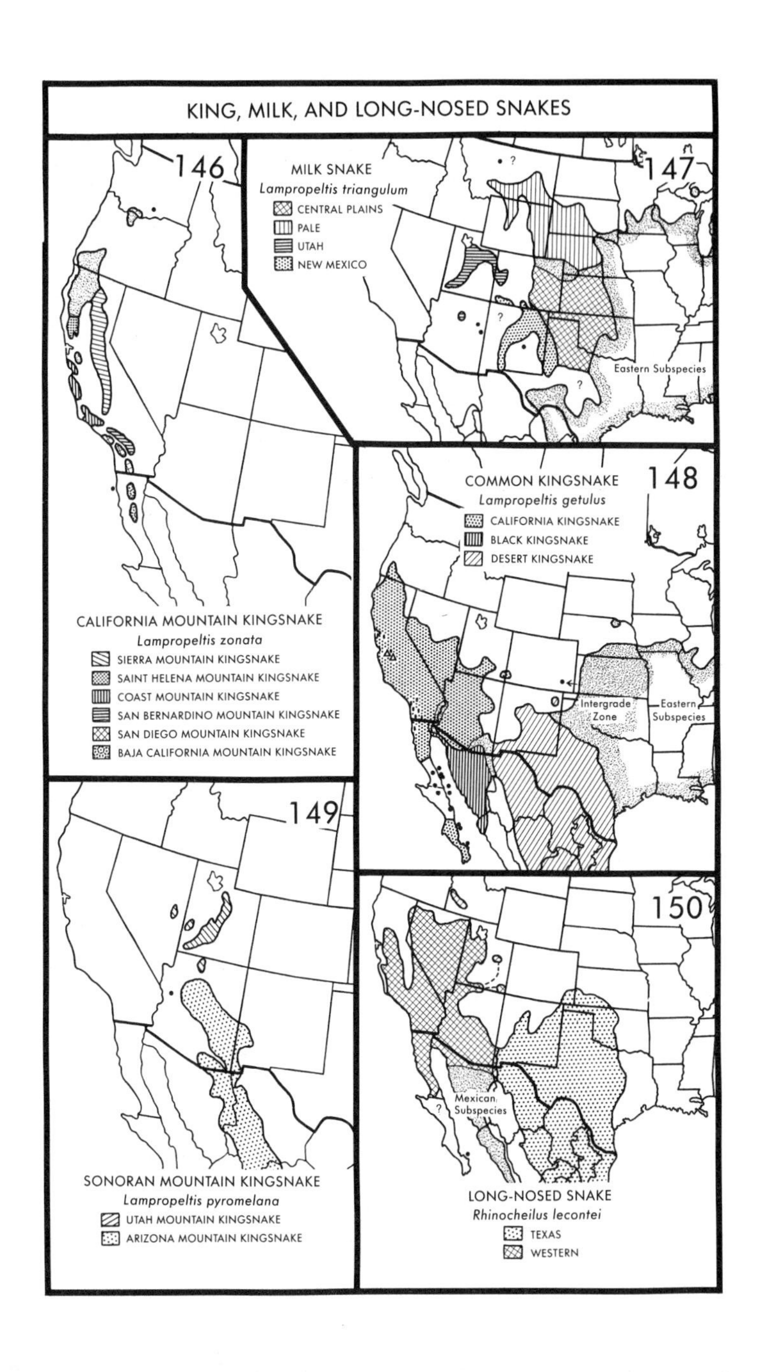
KING, MILK, AND LONG-NOSED SNAKES
146
CALIFORNIA MOUNTAIN KINGSNAKE
Lampropeltis zonata
SIERRA MOUNTAIN KINGSNAKE
SAINT HELENA MOUNTAIN KINGSNAKE
COAST MOUNTAIN KINGSNAKE
SAN BERNARDINO MOUNTAIN KINGSNAKE
SAN DIEGO MOUNTAIN KINGSNAKE
BAJA CALIFORNIA MOUNTAIN KINGSNAKE
147
MILK SNAKE
Lampropeltis triangulum
CENTRAL PLAINS
PALE
UTAH
NEW MEXICO
Eastern Subspecies
148
COMMON KINGSNAKE
Lampropeltis getulus
CALIFORNIA KINGSNAKE
BLACK KINGSNAKE
DESERT KINGSNAKE
Intergrade Zone
Eastern Subspecies
149
SONORAN MOUNTAIN KINGSNAKE
Lampropeltis pyromelana
UTAH MOUNTAIN KINGSNAKE
ARIZONA MOUNTAIN KINGSNAKE
150
Mexican Subspecies
LONG-NOSED SNAKE
Rhinocheilus lecontei
TEXAS
WESTERN

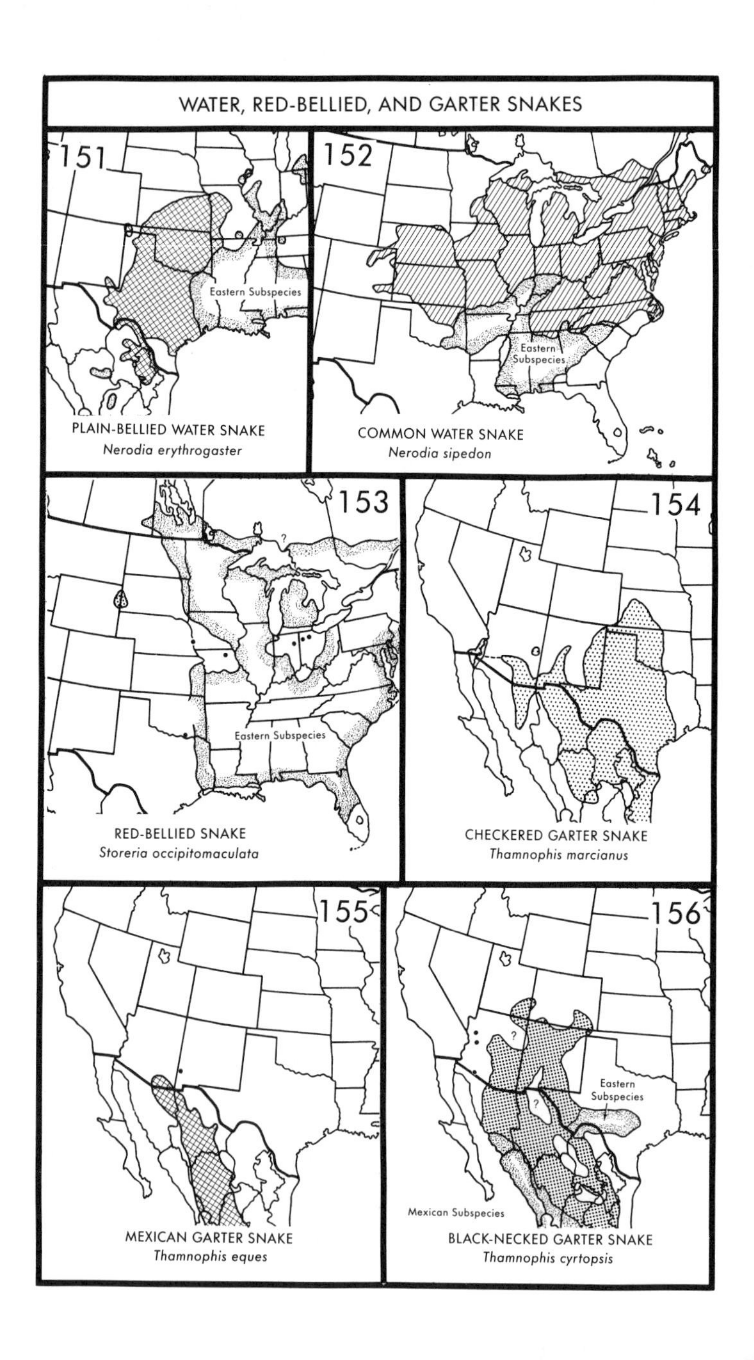

WATER, RED-BELLIED, AND GARTER SNAKES
151
Eastern Subspecies
PLAIN-BELLIED WATER SNAKE
Nerodia erythrogaster
152
Eastern Subspecies
COMMON WATER SNAKE
Nerodia sipedon
153
?
Eastern Subspecies
RED-BELLIED SNAKE
Storeria occipitomaculata
154
CHECKERED GARTER SNAKE
Thamnophis marcianus
155
MEXICAN GARTER SNAKE
Thamnophis eques
156
?
?
Eastern Subspecies
Mexican Subspecies
BLACK-NECKED GARTER SNAKE
Thamnophis cyrtopsis

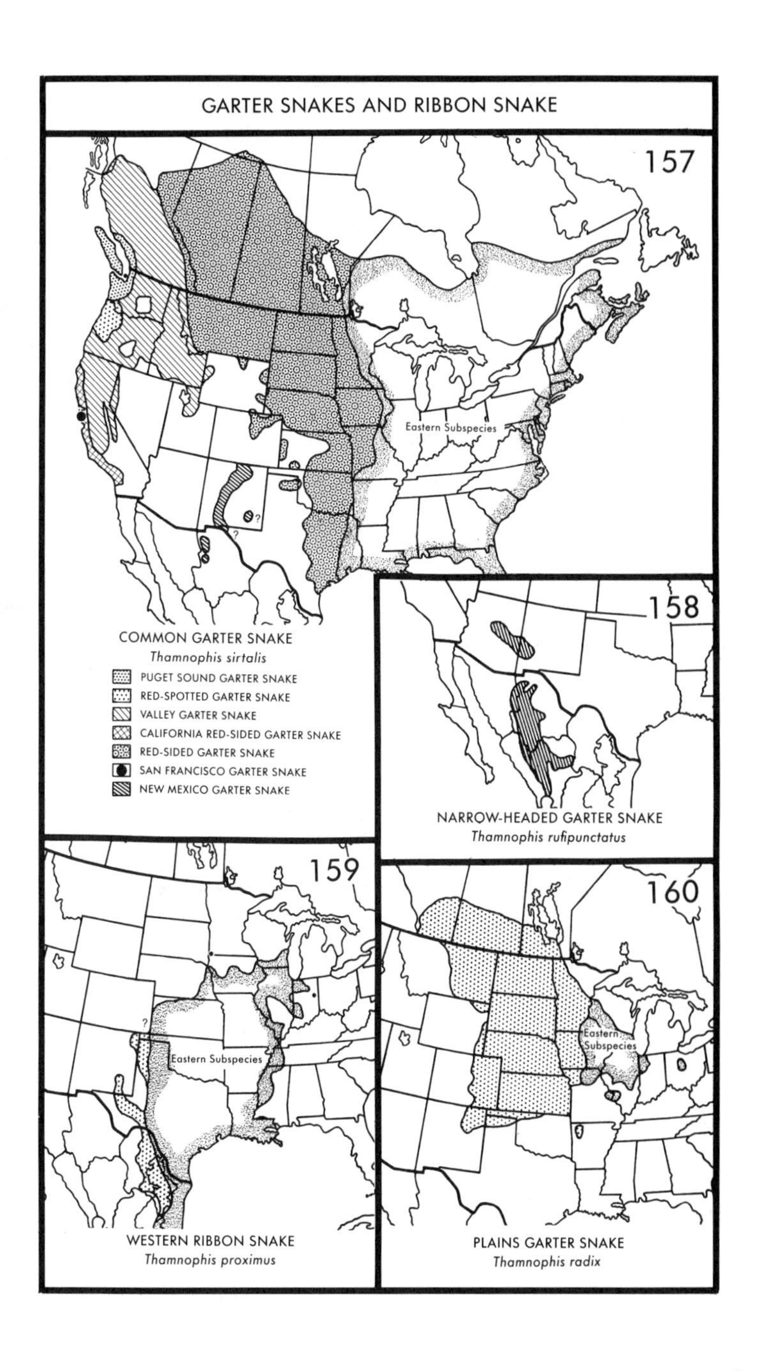

GARTER SNAKES AND RIBBON SNAKE
157
Eastern Subspecies
?
COMMON GARTER SNAKE
Thamnophis sirtalis
PUGET SOUND GARTER SNAKE
RED-SPOTTED GARTER SNAKE
VALLEY GARTER SNAKE
CALIFORNIA RED-SIDED GARTER SNAKE
RED-SIDED GARTER SNAKE
SAN FRANCISCO GARTER SNAKE
NEW MEXICO GARTER SNAKE
158
NARROW-HEADED GARTER SNAKE
Thamnophis rufipunctatus
159
Eastern Subspecies
?
WESTERN RIBBON SNAKE
Thamnophis proximus
160
Eastern Subspecies
PLAINS GARTER SNAKE
Thamnophis radix

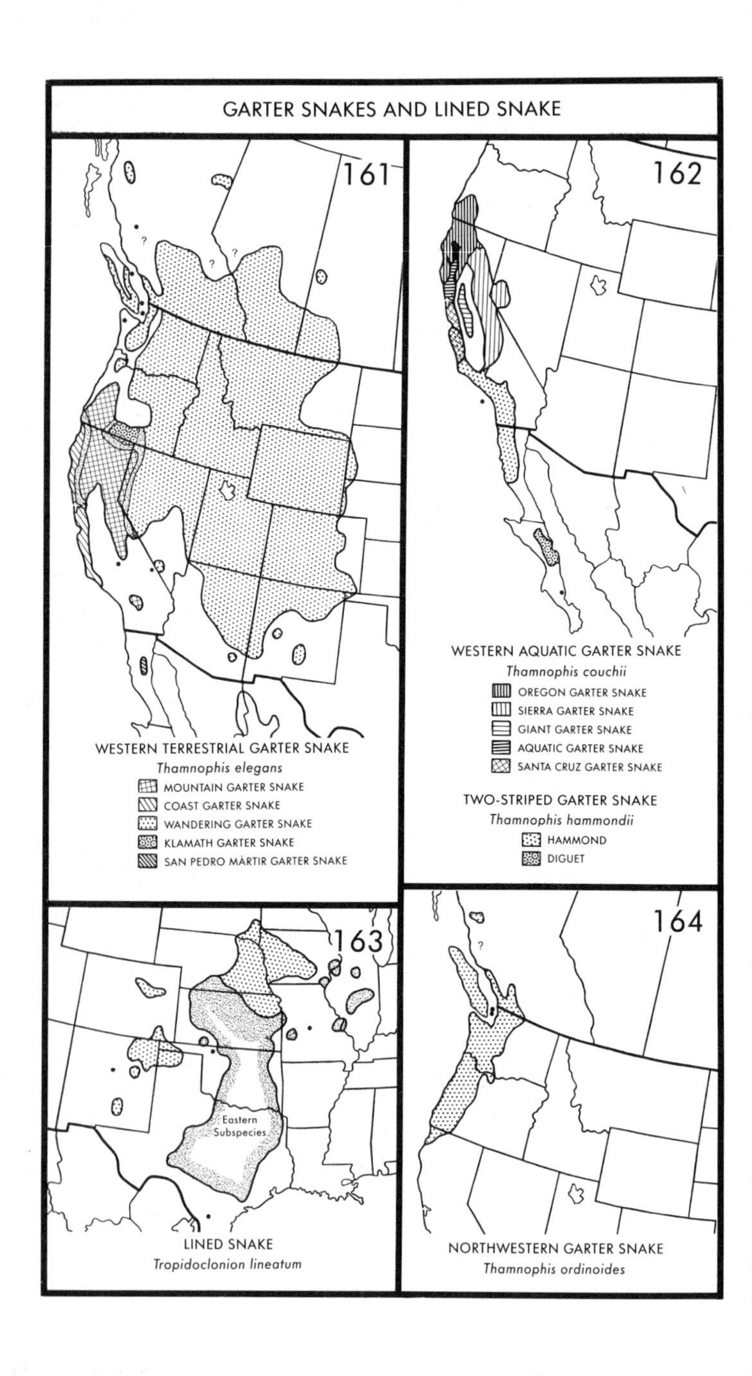
GARTER SNAKES AND LINED SNAKE
161
WESTERN TERRESTRIAL GARTER SNAKE
Thamnophis elegans
MOUNTAIN GARTER SNAKE
COAST GARTER SNAKE
WANDERING GARTER SNAKE
KLAMATH GARTER SNAKE
SAN PEDRO MÁRTIR GARTER SNAKE
162
WESTERN AQUATIC GARTER SNAKE
Thamnophis couchii
OREGON GARTER SNAKE
SIERRA GARTER SNAKE
GIANT GARTER SNAKE
AQUATIC GARTER SNAKE
SANTA CRUZ GARTER SNAKE
TWO-STRIPED GARTER SNAKE
Thamnophis hammondii
HAMMOND
DIGUET
163
Eastern Subspecies
LINED SNAKE
Tropidoclonion lineatum
164
NORTHWESTERN GARTER SNAKE
Thamnophis ordinoides

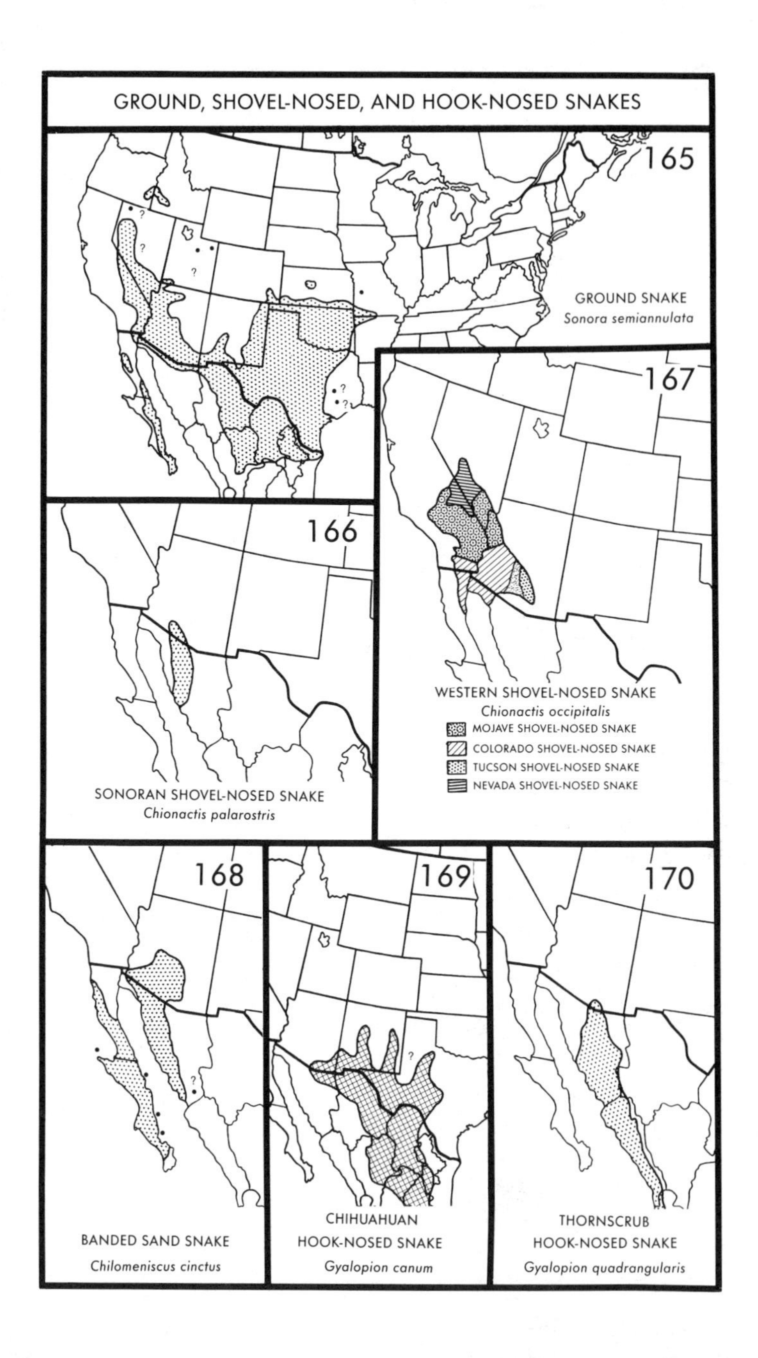

GROUND, SHOVEL-NOSED, AND HOOK-NOSED SNAKES
165
GROUND SNAKE
Sonora semiannulata
166
SONORAN SHOVEL-NOSED SNAKE
Chionactis palarostris
167
WESTERN SHOVEL-NOSED SNAKE
Chionactis occipitalis
MOJAVE SHOVEL-NOSED SNAKE
COLORADO SHOVEL-NOSED SNAKE
TUCSON SHOVEL-NOSED SNAKE
NEVADA SHOVEL-NOSED SNAKE
168
BANDED SAND SNAKE
Chilomeniscus cinctus
169
CHIHUAHUAN
HOOK-NOSED SNAKE
Gyalopion canum
170
THORNSCRUB
HOOK-NOSED SNAKE
Gyalopion quadrangularis

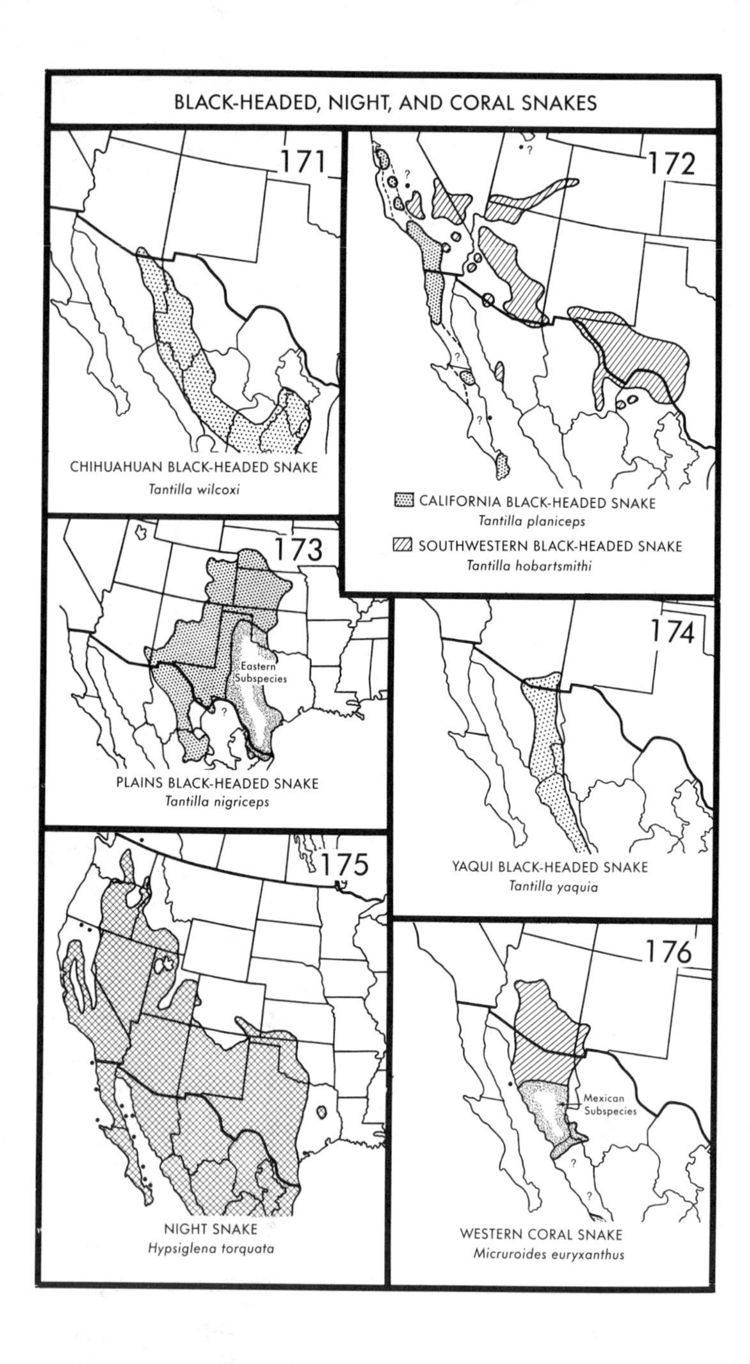
BLACK-HEADED, NIGHT, AND CORAL SNAKES
171
CHIHUAHUAN BLACK-HEADED SNAKE
Tantilla wilcoxi
172
CALIFORNIA BLACK-HEADED SNAKE
Tantilla planiceps
SOUTHWESTERN BLACK-HEADED SNAKE
Tantilla hobartsmithi
173
Eastern Subspecies
PLAINS BLACK-HEADED SNAKE
Tantilla nigriceps
174
YAQUI BLACK-HEADED SNAKE
Tantilla yaquia
175
NIGHT SNAKE
Hypsiglena torquata
176
Mexican Subspecies
WESTERN CORAL SNAKE
Micruroides euryxanthus

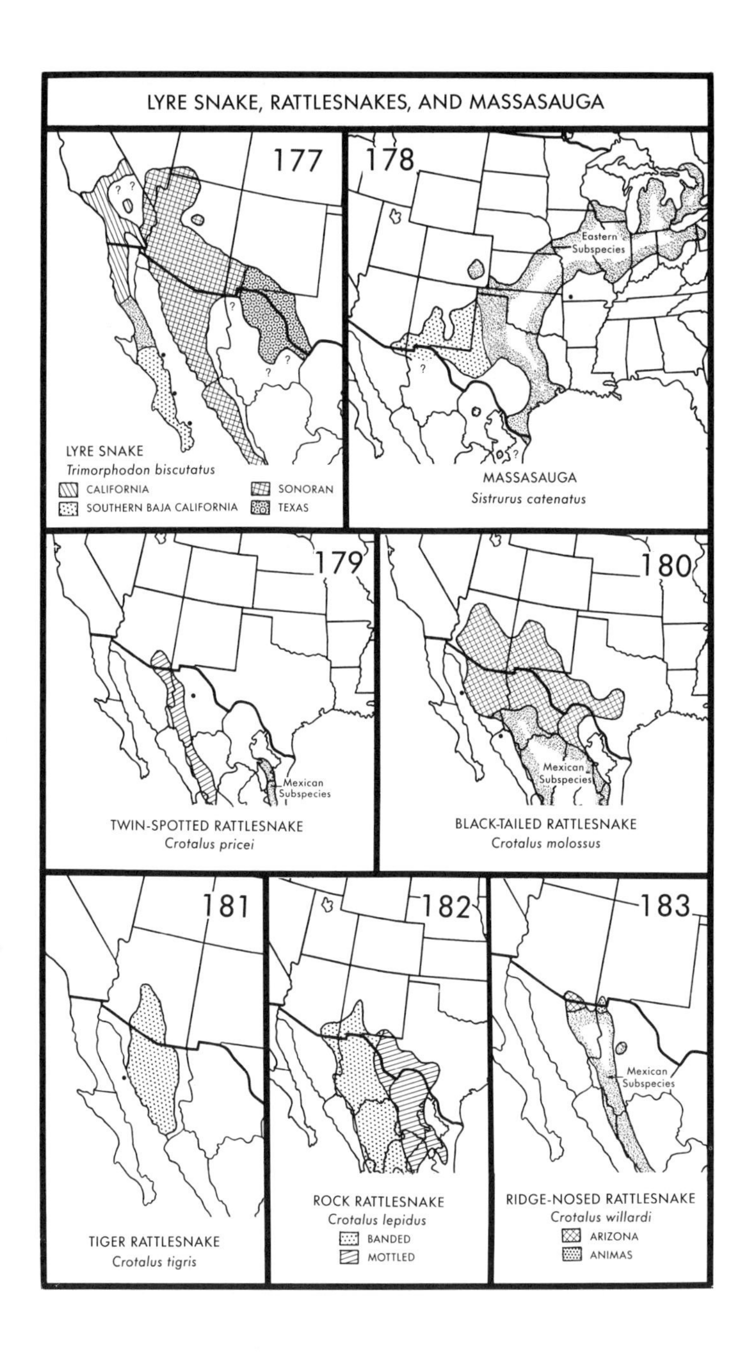
LYRE SNAKE, RATTLESNAKES, AND MASSASAUGA
177
LYRE SNAKE
Trimorphodon biscutatus
CALIFORNIA
SOUTHERN BAJA CALIFORNIA
SONORAN
TEXAS
178
Eastern Subspecies
MASSASAUGA
Sistrurus catenatus
179
Mexican Subspecies
TWIN-SPOTTED RATTLESNAKE
Crotalus pricei
180
Mexican Subspecies
BLACK-TAILED RATTLESNAKE
Crotalus molossus
181
TIGER RATTLESNAKE
Crotalus tigris
182
ROCK RATTLESNAKE
Crotalus lepidus
BANDED
MOTTLED
183
Mexican Subspecies
RIDGE-NOSED RATTLESNAKE
Crotalus willardi
ARIZONA
ANIMAS

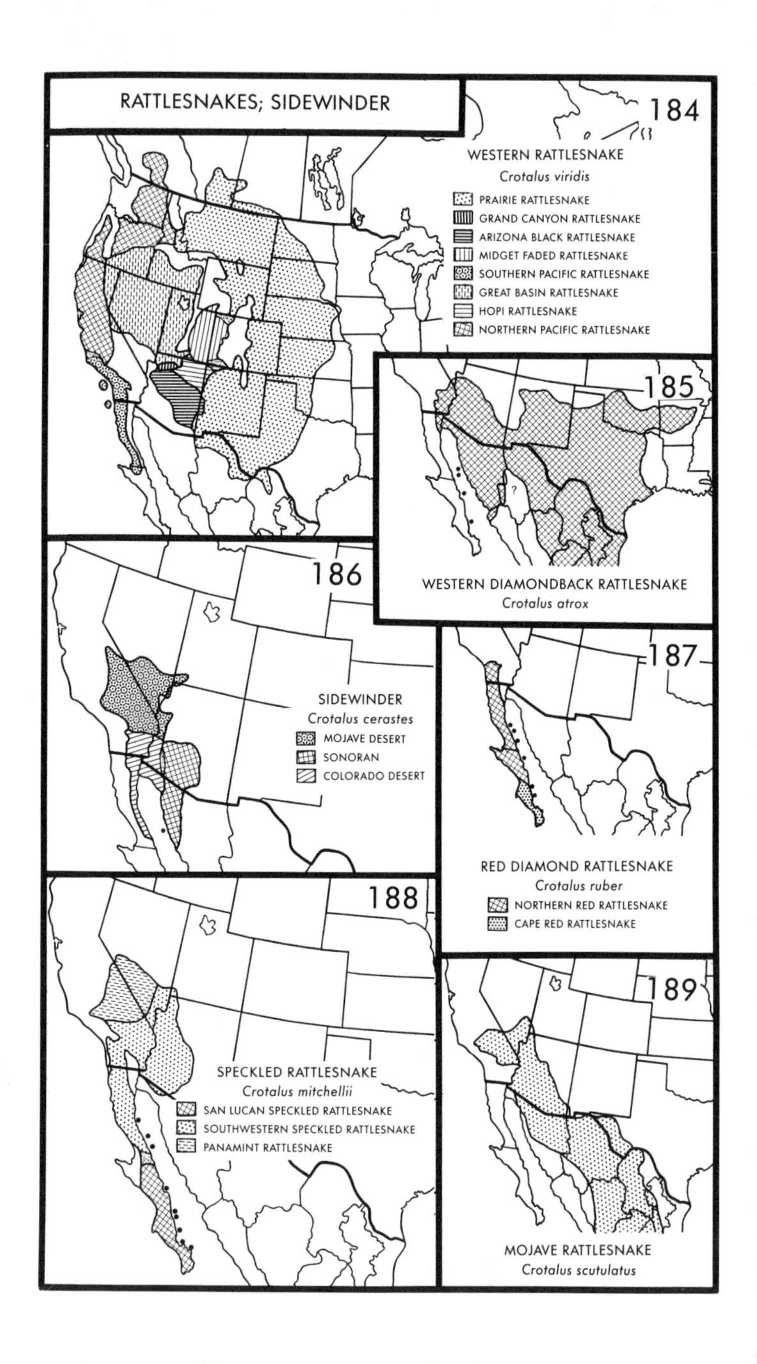
RATTLESNAKES; SIDEWINDER
184
WESTERN RATTLESNAKE
Crotalus viridis
PRAIRIE RATTLESNAKE
GRAND CANYON RATTLESNAKE
ARIZONA BLACK RATTLESNAKE
MIDGET FADED RATTLESNAKE
SOUTHERN PACIFIC RATTLESNAKE
GREAT BASIN RATTLESNAKE
HOPI RATTLESNAKE
NORTHERN PACIFIC RATTLESNAKE
185
?
WESTERN DIAMONDBACK RATTLESNAKE
Crotalus atrox
186
SIDEWINDER
Crotalus cerastes
MOJAVE DESERT
SONORAN
COLORADO DESERT
187
RED DIAMOND RATTLESNAKE
Crotalus ruber
NORTHERN RED RATTLESNAKE
CAPE RED RATTLESNAKE
188
SPECKLED RATTLESNAKE
Crotalus mitchellii
SAN LUCAN SPECKLED RATTLESNAKE
SOUTHWESTERN SPECKLED RATTLESNAKE
PANAMINT RATTLESNAKE
189
MOJAVE RATTLESNAKE
Crotalus scutulatus

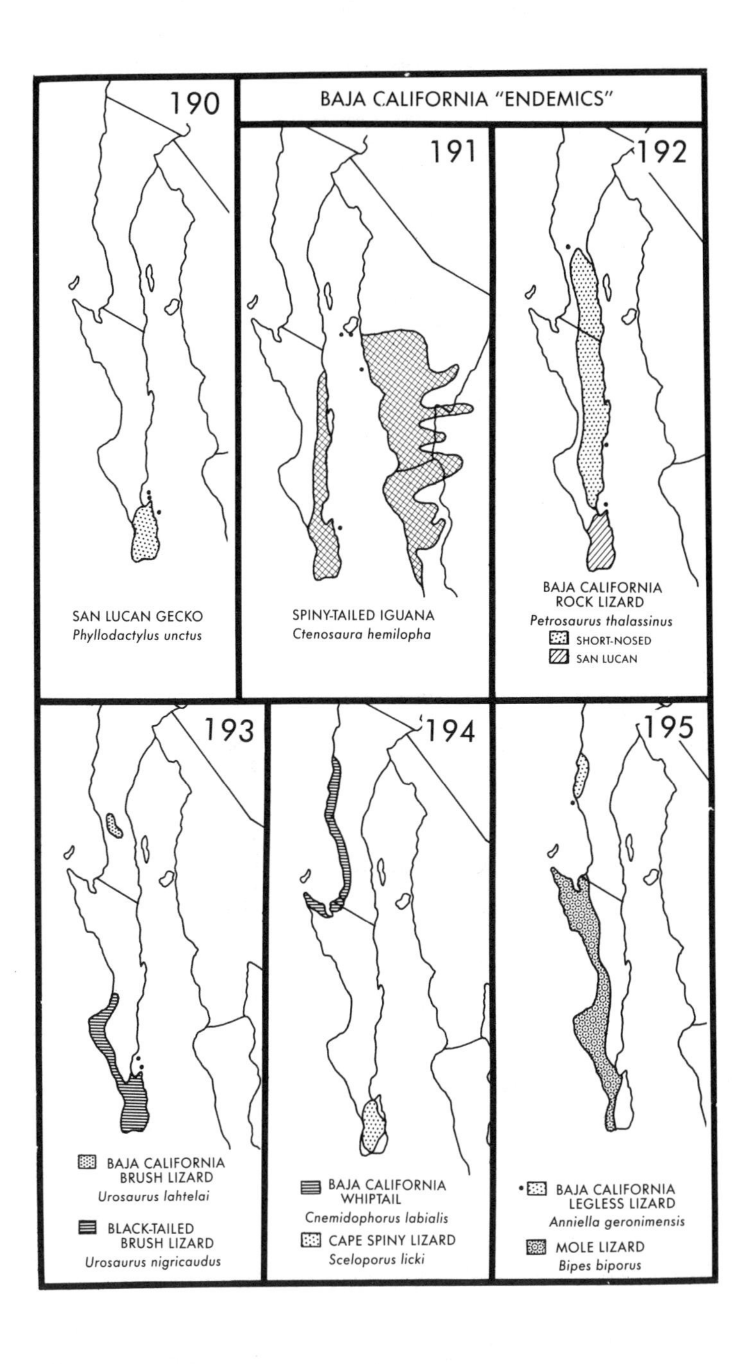

BAJA CALIFORNIA "ENDEMICS"
190
SAN LUCAN GECKO
Phyllodactylus unctus
191
SPINY-TAILED IGUANA
Ctenosaura hemilopha
192
BAJA CALIFORNIA
ROCK LIZARD
Petrosaurus thalassinus
SHORT-NOSED
SAN LUCAN
193
BAJA CALIFORNIA
BRUSH LIZARD
Urosaurus lahtelai
BLACK-TAILED
BRUSH LIZARD
Urosaurus nigricaudus
194
BAJA CALIFORNIA
WHIPTAIL
Cnemidophorus labialis
CAPE SPINY LIZARD
Sceloporus licki
195
BAJA CALIFORNIA
LEGLESS LIZARD
Anniella geronimensis
MOLE LIZARD
Bipes biporus

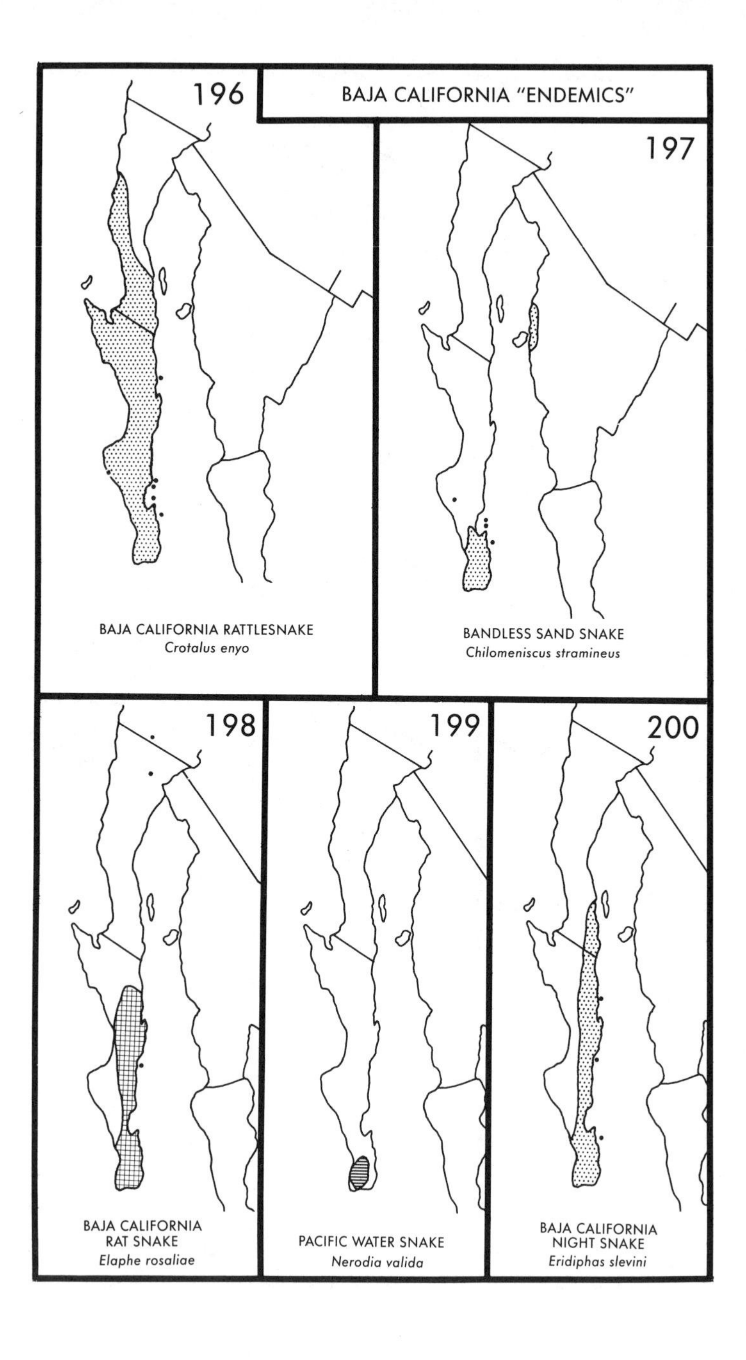
196
BAJA CALIFORNIA "ENDEMICS"
197
BAJA CALIFORNIA RATTLESNAKE
Crotalus enyo
BANDLESS SAND SNAKE
Chilomeniscus stramineus
198
199
200
BAJA CALIFORNIA
RAT SNAKE
Elaphe rosaliae
PACIFIC WATER SNAKE
Nerodia valida
BAJA CALIFORNIA
NIGHT SNAKE
Eridiphas slevini

Index

LIZARDS

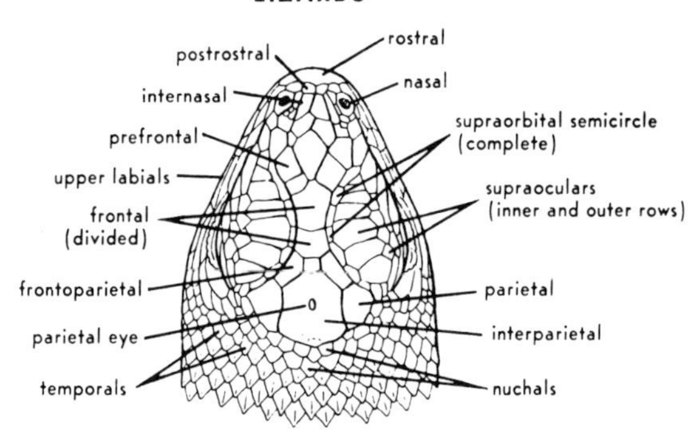

rostral
postrostral
nasal
internasal
supraorbital semicircle
(complete)
prefrontal
upper labials
supraoculars
(inner and outer rows)
frontal
(divided)
frontoparietal
parietal
parietal eye
interparietal
temporals
nuchals

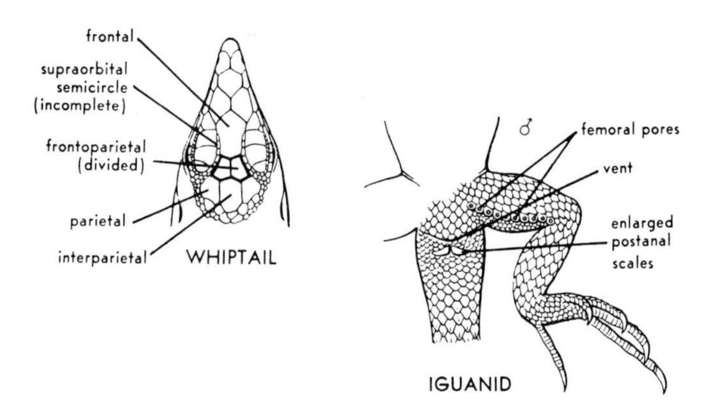

frontal
supraorbital
semicircle
(incomplete)
frontoparietal
(divided)
parietal
interparietal
WHIPTAIL
♂
femoral pores
vent
enlarged
postanal
scales
IGUANID

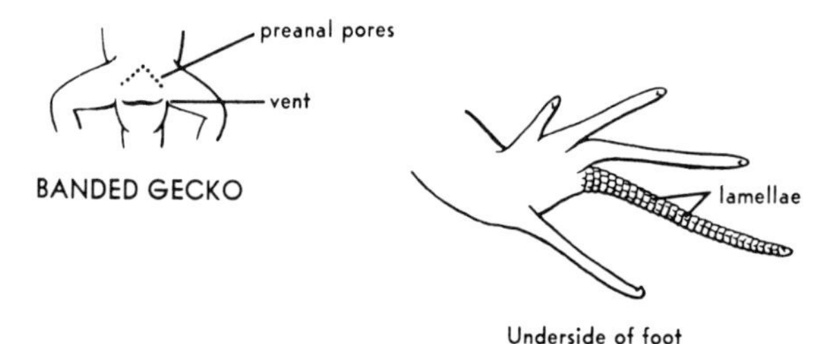

preanal pores
vent
BANDED GECKO
lamellae
Underside of foot

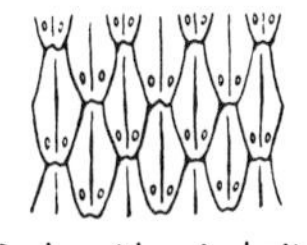
Scales with apical pits
(Nerodia)

Cycloid

Keeled mucronate

Granular

SCALE TYPES

(Lizards and Snakes)

SNAKES

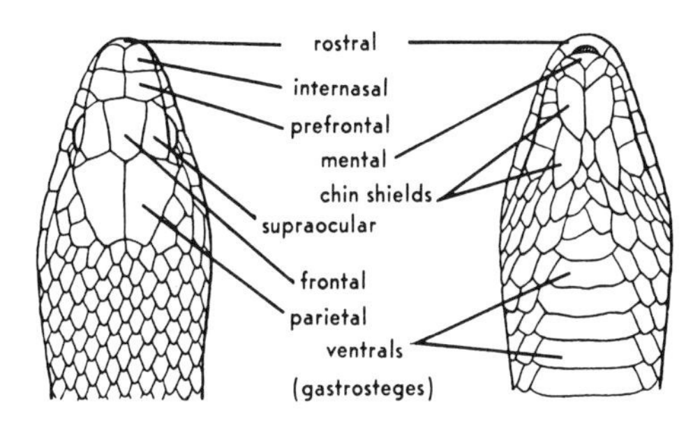

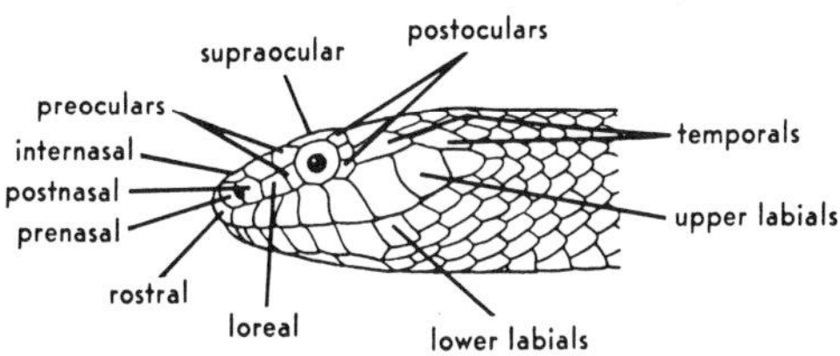

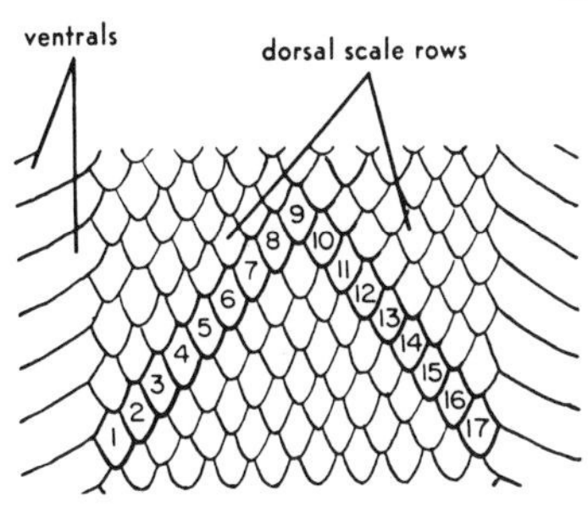

Method of counting dorsal scale rows

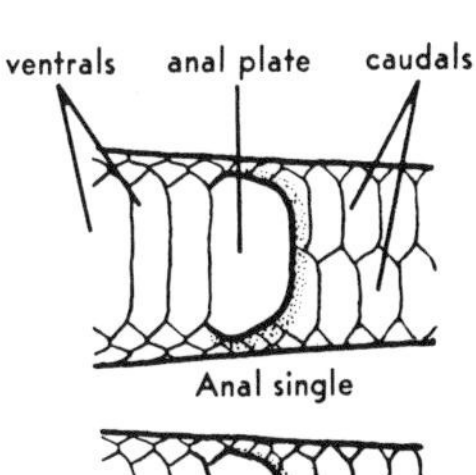

Anal single

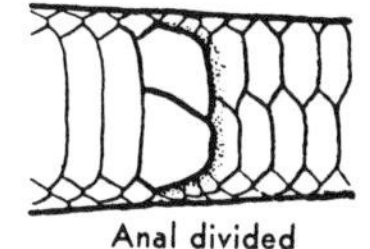
Anal divided